THE
MFECANE
AFTERMATH

THE

MFECANE

AFTERMATH

Reconstructive Debates in Southern African History

EDITED BY

CAROLYN HAMILTON

 WITWATERSRAND UNIVERSITY PRESS

UNIVERSITY OF NATAL PRESS

The Mfecane Aftermath
is a joint publication of

Witwatersrand University Press
1 Jan Smuts Avenue
2001 Johannesburg, South Africa

and

University of Natal Press
Private Bag X01
3209 Scottsville
Pietermaritzburg, South Africa

© Witwatersrand University Press 1995

ISBN 1 86814 252 3

Cover design Thea Soggot
Typesetting by University of Natal Press
Printed and bound by Creda Press

The front cover picture depicts the historic
remains of the underground settlement
at Lepalong, dated by oral records to the
1820s and 1830s.
Photograph courtesy of the Department of Archaeology,
University of the Witwatersrand

Contents

Maps

The financial assistance of the Centre for Science Development (HSRC, South Africa) towards the publication of this work is hereby acknowledged. Opinions expressed in this publication and the conclusions arrived at, are those of the authors and are not necessarily to be attributed to the Centre for Science Development.

Preface

This book comprises a revised selection of the papers delivered at the colloquium 'The Mfecane Aftermath: Towards a New Paradigm', held at the University of the Witwatersrand in September 1991. A full list of the papers presented at the colloquium is reproduced at the end of the volume.

The book has been divided into three sections. Each of the sections is preceded by a specially commissioned contextualising essay which offers an overview of the section, together with discussion of the main areas of debate among the contributors to the section. The contextualising essays are designed to serve as introductions to the dense arguments which follow, while their review of debated evidence gives non-specialists the benefit of the evaluation of a scholar well versed in that particular area.

Part One takes stock of the major historiographical and methodological issues. Part Two is concerned largely with the history of the eastern coastal region in the late eighteenth and early nineteenth centuries, and deals with some of the major debates over sources and their interpretation. Part Three examines events in the interior of southern Africa in the same period. Readers will detect greater methodological refinement in the use of sources in the essays in Part Two than in Part Three, as well as more detail and a better established chronology of political events. This unevenness is a consequence of the 'Zulu aftermath'. Interest in the Zulu kingdom resulted in a long-standing concern with the history of the KwaZulu-Natal region, whereas the myth of the depopulated interior underlay the neglect, until recently, of the precolonial history of the highveld. Scholars like John Wright and Jeff Peires, working on the coastal areas, are able to draw on substantial bodies of recorded oral traditions, about which considerable background material exists, whereas the oral history of the interior has been relatively little attended to. The essays in Part Three prepare the ground for studies of events and close analysis of the pertinent texts of the kind already begun for the coastal regions.

Together, the various contributions to the book provide one of the first detailed overviews of the major developments of the later precolonial period in southern Africa. While the volume offers the beginnings of a synthesis, there has been little attempt to impose editorial consistencies of historical detail, usage of concepts and vocabulary among the various essays, for these differences frequently signal the debates that are the very stuff of the book.

The collected essays do not represent a definitive account of the later precolonial history of southern Africa. Rather, they point up issues of contention among scholars working in this field, reveal lacunae in our knowledge of the period and suggest areas for further research.

One noticeable gap in this collection is the lack of contributions from black South African historians. Some scholars, like the Zulu nationalist historian, Simon Maphalala, have, since the colloquium, begun to engage in these debates. It is to be hoped that the publication of this volume, at a time when the study of the precolonial past is at last freed from association with the construction of apartheid's ethnicities, will stimulate a new generation of young historians to work on these topics and to make good that omission.

Another gap is the absence of a contribution from the initiator of the debate, Julian Cobbing. Although he presented two papers at the colloquium, and initially agreed to prepare an essay for this volume, Cobbing subsequently declined to submit his contribution. When the book was in proof it was sent to Cobbing together with an invitation to contribute an Afterword. Clarification and qualification of his arguments in the light of the discussions generated in this volume, as well as his view of how the debate has developed, would have been an invaluable addition to the corpus of material presented here. These Cobbing provided in response to the invitation, but declined to have them published without engaging in further debate with the contributors to this volume. To permit one of the protagonists in these debates such a privileged position would have been at the expense of the others. Regretfully, the editor and publishers abide by Cobbing's desire to have all or nothing in the book. Cobbing's single, but seminal and controversial, publication on the topic is readily available in the *Journal of African History* and his ideas are extensively discussed and debated in the following pages.

The text is augmented by detailed maps. In addition, there is an extensive consolidated bibliography to which extra items of interest – in particular, recent publications concerning the precolonial history of the region – have been added. It will be a useful guide to students starting out in this field, as well as a valuable resource for established scholars seeking their way through the textual intricacies of varied editions and secondary texts that have become the primary sources for the historiographical and methodological debates that are a feature of this volume.

CAROLYN HAMILTON

Acknowledgements

The production of a book which is focused on a set of debates poses many problems. The original dialogue on the conference floor was frequently heated and tense. The contributors to this book fail to agree on, indeed, they passionately contest, the orthography of the subject of the book (is it 'The *Mfecane*', mfecane or 'mfekaan'), not to mention their disagreements over the meaning of the term. Under such conditions, an editor treads a potentially treacherous path. The contributors to this book have, however, given me an easy passage, graciously agreeing to the compromises which I have proposed. They have also demonstrated enormous patience with the delays and rearrangements which were a consequence of the restructuring of the book to accommodate the absence of a contribution from Julian Cobbing.

The book's content covers a number of specialist areas, and the various contributors represent a range of perspectives. Alone I could not have hoped to contextualise the varied offerings adequately and fairly. In this task I have been skilfully assisted by Norman Etherington, John Wright and Neil Parsons who each undertook to provide a contextualising essay on an area of the debates in which each is expert. Readers of the book will doubtless be as grateful as I am for their efforts.

It has been a great pleasure to work with the highly experienced Africana librarian, Yvonne Garson, who is responsible for the consolidated bibliography. Yvonne began the work of creating the bibliography from the footnotes to the various essays, and rapidly exposed the deficiencies of even the most meticulous citations. As many of the debates which arise in this book are located in the way sources are read and cited, a definitive bibliography of the kind compiled by Yvonne is invaluable.

There are many more debts of gratitude. I am grateful to Professors Patrick MacAllister and David Hammond-Tooke for encouraging me to go ahead with the colloquium. Professor Hammond-Tooke gave his permission for the Department of Social Anthropology at the University of the Witwatersrand to host the event and the Research Office of the same university provided the initial funds which made the colloquium possible. Permission from the *Journal of African History* to reproduce articles by E. Eldredge and C. Hamilton is gratefully acknowledged. Lastly I would like to thank the co-publishers, Wits University Press and the University of Natal Press for all that they have done to bring this complex work to completion. In particular I am grateful to Margery Moberly of the University of Natal Press who rescued this book from the nightmare of its own internal controversies, and provided crucial support and guidance, both practical and moral.

CAROLYN HAMILTON

Notes on Orthography and Names

A degree of orthographic standardisation has been imposed on the various contributions to the book to facilitate its consultation by readers not fully familiar with the field.

- Though many contributors regard it as desirable to use prefixes for Sotho and Zulu people, as in baSotho/Basotho and amaZulu/Amazulu, and for the languages, as in seSotho/Sesotho and isiZulu/Isizulu, the English equivalents have been used in preference to the many linguistic and orthographic variants.

- Except for the names of people, such as Moshoeshoe, Sotho names have generally been given in the South African spelling, rather than in the form used in Lesotho.

Place names present a particular set of problems.

- Many names were corrupted in colonial writings and on early maps. Wherever possible modern spellings have been used in this book even where these differ from those which are in common usage. Thus Thukela and Mzimvubu have been used, not Tugela and Umzimvubu.

- In some instances an appropriate usage is not easily established. A case in point is Karechuenya which is better known as Kaditshweni. Our use of Karechuenya is based on the following argument provided by Neil Parsons:

  > David Livingstone, writing to his mother on 27 April 1844, in a letter not published until 1959, used the name Karechuenya. Livingstone explained that the town was next to a conical peak called Chuenyane ('little baboon'). 'Karechuenya' meant 'By it we are vexed' or 'A vexation by or near us', a reflexion of people's complaints about the depradations of baboons on their gardens, putting the blame jocularly on the 'little baboon'.[1] The name 'Kaditshwene', on the other hand, is a neologism which was first suggested to the archaeologist P. W. Laidler in the 1930s by a white farmer at Zeerust called Hattingh. As Desmond Cole points out, 'People with no knowledge of linguistics or of the Tswana language have confused *tshwenyana* or

---

1. Schapera, I. (ed.), *David Livingstone, Family Letters 1841–1856. Volume One 1841–1848*, London: Chatto & Windus, 1959, pp. 96–97; *Botswana Notes and Records*, Vol. 6 (1984), p. 38.

tshwenyane, meaning "young or small baboon" and *go tshwenyana* meaning "to bother or trouble one another".'[2]

- Wherever possible, the use of anachronistic place names is avoided. While the forms trans-Kei, trans-Vaal and trans-Orange introduce the problem of a Cape-based perspective and in some instances refer to later river names, they are used in preference to their later counterparts (Transkei, Transvaal and Orange Free State), so as to signal a sensitivity to the problems of naming which are a feature of the study of this period of history.

- Where the reference is to modern archaeological sites rather than precolonial settlements, the contemporary form is used, thus the 'Iron Age archaeology of the Transvaal', but the 'Iron Age in the trans-Vaal region'.

- Since these essays were written new structures have replaced the former provinces and homelands. It was decided not to adopt the new names as the book was already at an advanced stage of production. In some of the regions new names are still under discussion.

2. Desmond Cole *Botswana Notes and Records,* vol. 23 (1991). Jan Boeyens's contributions to this discussion are also gratefully acknowledged.

Contributors

Thomas Dowson

Formerly a Researcher in the Rock Art Research Unit, Department of Archaeology, University of the Witwatersrand. He is currently Rock Art Research Fellow in the Department of Archaeology at the University of Southampton.

Elizabeth Eldredge

Associate Professor of History at Michigan State University. She has recently published *A South African Kingdom: The Pursuit of Security in Nineteenth-century Lesotho* and *Slavery in South Africa: Captive Labor on the Dutch Frontier* (with Fred Morton).

Norman Etherington

Professor of History at the University of Western Australia and a Fellow of the Academy of the Social Sciences in Australia. His books include: *Preachers, Peasants and Politics in Southeast Africa; Theories of Imperialism: War, Conquest and Capital; Rider Haggard; The Annotated* She, and *Peace, Politics and Violence in the New South Africa.*

Jan-Bart Gewald

An historian who studied at Rhodes University. He is currently completing a Ph.D. at Leiden University in the Netherlands on the socio-economic history of the Herero between 1890 and 1920.

Simon Hall

Lectures in the Department of Archaeology at the University of the Witwatersrand. His general research interests are the nature of interactions between farmers and hunter-gatherers, and the history of Sotho/Tswana speakers.

Carolyn Hamilton

Senior lecturer in the Department of Anthropology, University of the Witwatersrand. Her research interests include the precolonial history of the KwaZulu-Natal region, and the production of the images that dominate that history.

Guy Hartley

A Ph.D. candidate in the Department of History at the University of Cape Town.

Margaret Kinsman

An educationalist working in Cape Town. Her research interest is in the southern Tswana 1780–1880, with a particular focus on the social history of the period and the changing position of women.

Andrew Manson

Associate Professor of History at the University of Bophuthatswana. He has published in the field of Zulu and Tswana history. He holds a Ph.D. from the University of Cape Town.

John Omer-Cooper

Professor of History at the University of Otago and author of *The Zulu Aftermath: A Nineteenth-century Revolution in Bantu Africa*.

Neil Parsons

A freelance writer. He has held research fellowships in Gaborone, London and Cape Town. His publications include general textbooks on southern Africa and articles on the history of Botswana, and he is a former co-editor of the *Journal of Southern African Studies*. His most recent book is *Seretse Khama, 1921–80*.

Jeff Peires

The author of two books on Xhosa history, *The House of Phalo* and *The Dead Will Arise*. Formerly Professor of History at the University of Transkei, he is now an ANC Member of Parliament representing the Eastern Cape in the National Assembly.

Christopher Saunders

Associate Professor in the History Department at the University of Cape Town. He is the author of *The Making of the South African Past* and other books.

Alan Webster

Teaches at Stirling High School in East London and at Rhodes University.

John Wright

Associate Professor in the Department of Historical Studies, University of Natal, Pietermaritzburg. He is co-editor of *The James Stuart Archive of Recorded Oral Evidence Relating to the History of the Zulu and Neighbouring Peoples* (4 vols. Further volumes in preparation.)

Dan Wylie

Teaches in the Academic Development Programme at Rhodes University, Grahamstown. His doctoral research examines the European literary mythologies of Shaka.

Introduction
History and Historiography
in the Aftermath

CAROLYN HAMILTON

In 1991 a colloquium was held at the University of the Witwatersrand, Johannesburg, South Africa, entitled 'The Mfecane Aftermath: Towards a New Paradigm'.
The title was a play on the name of John Omer-Cooper's 1966 publication, *The Zulu
Aftermath: A Nineteenth-Century Revolution in Bantu Africa.*[1] Omer-Cooper,
following George McCall Theal's writings some seventy years earlier, argued that
the emergence of the powerful Zulu kingdom in the early decades of the nineteenth
century caused massive upheaval among neighbouring chiefdoms. This, in turn, set
in motion a ripple effect of dislocation and disruption that extended through much of
southern Africa, namely, the 'Mfecane'.[2] Omer-Cooper's study celebrated both the
revolutionary changes within the Zulu kingdom which lay at the root of the tumult,
as well as African responses to it – the innovations and achievements which
underlay the period of migrancy and increased state-building throughout the
sub-continent. This, then, was what Omer-Cooper focused on as the 'aftermath' of
the Zulu.

In a series of papers presented at seminars starting in 1983, Rhodes historian
Julian Cobbing mounted a campaign for the 'jettisoning' of the concept of the
mfecane. Cobbing argued that the idea of a 'Zulu explosion' which set in motion the
mfecane was a settler myth which conveniently obscured the disruptions of local
societies caused by the labour needs of the Cape colonists and the demands of the
Delagoa Bay-based slave trade. Despite their preparation for prestigious forums
such as the seminar of the Centre for African Studies, University of Cape Town, and
the African Studies Institute seminar at the University of the Witwatersrand,

---

1. J.D. Omer-Cooper, *The Zulu Aftermath: A Nineteenth-century Revolution in Bantu Africa*, London,
   1966.
2. 'Mfecane' is the form of the word conventionally used in association with the Nguni-speaking peoples of
   the coastal areas of southern Africa. 'Lifaqane' is the equivalent term written in the Southern Sotho
   orthography that is used in Lesotho, while 'difaqane' is the same word rendered in Southern Sotho
   orthography as used in South Africa. The origins of the word are a matter of debate. Scholars who view
   the term as a word with African origins place it in italics, as they do any other non-English terms that
   occur in an English text. Likewise some scholars who view the mfecane as a major phenomenon in the
   history of the period elect to capitalise the first letter. Those scholars who see the term as a European
   invention without any foundation in African lexicons use the term without either italics or an initial
   capital letter, as do writers who seek simply to indicate a down-scaling (itself of different orders for
   different authors) of the term. These choices are maintained in the book as a clear signal of one of the
   lines of debate around the topic of the mfecane.

1

Cobbing's early papers elicited little response from historians. Then, in 1987, Cobbing presented yet another version of his case at the University of Durban-Westville, 'The myth of the mfecane'.[3] Shortly after that, in 1988 and 1989, an eminent historian of Natal and the Zulu kingdom, John Wright, collaborated with Cobbing in joint presentations to seminars at the University of the Witwatersrand and the University of Cape Town, entitled 'The Mfecane: Beginning the Inquest'.[4] Attention to the debate shown by Natal-based interests and historians of the Zulu kingdom was stimulated in the later 1980s both by an efflorescence of new scholarship on the early Zulu kingdom and by contemporary political developments within Natal and KwaZulu. This period saw a number of academic historians enter into public debate over the history of the Zulu kingdom, and the beginnings of a challenge to the near monopoly over the public presentation of Zulu history which Inkatha had enjoyed since the early 1980s.[5] In 1988 the influential *Journal of African History* published a version of Cobbing's critique of the mfecane.[6]

From the mid-1980s a cohort of graduate students working under Cobbing at Rhodes University began to research topics which extended his critique of the mfecane. Although unpublished, this work stimulated further interest in the debate.[7] The 1988 Reader's Digest *Illustrated History of South Africa* included comment on the emerging debate concerning the notion of the mfecane.[8] At the 1990 'Workshop on Natal and Zululand in the Colonial and Precolonial Periods', held at the University of Natal, Pietermaritzburg, Cobbing presented yet another paper, 'Grasping the Nettle: The Slave Trade and the Early Zulu', while three of his students also gave papers.[9] In April 1991 a panel discussion on the debate was held at

---

3. Cobbing delivered a spoken presentation at Durban-Westville. The revised notes of his talk subsequently circulated as a 'paper'.
4. The two papers delivered at the combined seminars were J. Cobbing, 'Jettisoning the Mfecane (with *Perestroika*)', and J. Wright, 'Political Mythology and the Making of Natal's Mfecane'.
5. For a discussion of Inkatha's presentation of Zulu history see D. Golan, 'Inkatha and its Use of the Zulu Past', *History in Africa*, 18 (1991), 113–26; P. Forsyth, 'The Past in Service of the Present: The Political Use of History by Chief A. N. M. Buthelezi, 1951–1991', *South African Historical Journal*, 26 (1992), 74–92. For a discussion of the engagement of academics in debate over the public presentation of Zulu history see C. A. Hamilton, 'Authoring Shaka: Models, Metaphors and Historiography', Ph.D. thesis, The Johns Hopkins University, Baltimore, 1993, 14–26.
6. J. Cobbing, 'The Mfecane as Alibi: Thoughts on Dithakong and Mbolompo', *Journal of African History*, 29 (1988), 487–519.
7. See, most notably, J. Richner, 'The Withering Away of the "Lifaqane": Or a Change of Paradigm', B.A. Hons. essay, Rhodes University, 1988; A. C. Webster, 'Ayliff, Whiteside, and the Fingo "Emancipation" of 1835: A Reappraisal', B.A. Hons. essay, Rhodes University, Grahamstown, 1988.
8. Reader's Digest *Illustrated History of South Africa: The Real Story,* (Consultant Editor C. Saunders, Historical Advisor C. Bundy), Cape Town, The Reader's Digest, 1988, 2nd ed. with amendments, 1989.
9. A selection of the papers from this conference was produced in a bound form, edited by D. R. Edgecombe, J.P.C. Laband and P.S. Thompson, and entitled *The Debate on Zulu Origins: A Selection of Papers on the Zulu Kingdom and Early Colonial Natal*, Pietermaritzburg, 1992. The papers reproduced were those which focused on the Cobbing intervention and associated issues concerning the production of the history of the Zulu kingdom. Note also that in May 1990, the Wits History Workshop held a History Teachers' Conference on 'Perspectives on Pre-industrial South Africa in the Late Eighteenth and Early Nineteenth Centuries' at which John Wright gave an invited paper entitled 'Beyond the Mfecane: What do we put in its place?'

the University of Natal, Durban.[10] Cobbing's 'case against the mfecane' was finally beginning to elicit sustained attention from the academy.

By July 1991 the *Journal of African History* had accepted for publication two responses to Cobbing's published article. (These articles by Eldredge and Hamilton were also presented at the Wits colloquium and are reproduced in this volume.) Two months later, a total of twenty-four papers was presented at the Wits colloquium which all, one way or another, addressed aspects of Cobbing's work. Participants at the colloquium were mostly historians, but a number of anthropologists, archaeologists, literary specialists, teachers and journalists also attended.

The colloquium attracted widespread attention. A large contingent of secondary school teachers attended a workshop[11] held immediately afterwards which focused directly on the debates at the colloquium, as well as on the problems of teaching the mfecane in the South Africa of the 1990s. The *South African Historical Journal* carried a substantial report on the colloquium, with comments by five participants,[12] as did another South African journal, *Social Dynamics*.[13] The colloquium was widely reported in the press,[14] and merited a full-page report in *The Times Higher Education Supplement*.[15] By the end of 1991, the debate commanded the attention of both the academy and the general public. While it was the eventual publication of an article by Cobbing that precipitated the debate into the public domain, the timing of the efflorescence of interest in the topic was tied at least as much to the changing context within South Africa. As Cobbing himself put it at the colloquium, '[E]ven as we deliberate, Zulu impis are on their murderous march with the myth of Shaka ringing in their ears and a new mfecane is being threatened, a desperate last throw of the dice to forestall the united, ethnicless South Africa that has to be born.'[16] Cobbing's quest for 'a new paradigm' for the history of southern Africa in the immediately precolonial period was motivated both by a re-examination of sources and by pressing political concerns.

10. Organised by the History Department, University of Natal, Durban, the panel included Julian Cobbing, John Wright, John Omer-Cooper, Shula Marks and Jeff Guy.
11. Immediately following the colloquium the Wits History Workshop hosted as part of their series of Teachers' Conferences, a special one-day workshop on 'Teaching the Mfecane'. In November 1993, a four-day colloquium on 'School History Textbooks for a Democratic South Africa' was held at Sparkling Waters, Magaliesberg, the organising theme of which was the mfecane debate.
12. N. Etherington, 'The Aftermath of the Aftermath', *South African Historical Journal*, 25 (1991), 154–62; P. Maylam, 'The Death of the Mfecane?', *South African Historical Journal*, 25 (1991) 163–6; J. du Bruyn, 'Ousting Both the Mfecane and the Anti-Mfecane', *South African Historical Journal*, 25 (1991) 166–70; A. Webster, 'The Mfecane Paradigm Overthrown', *South African Historical Journal*, 25 (1991) 170–2; S. Meintjes, 'The Mfecane Colloquium: Impressions', *South African Historical Journal*, 25 (1991) 173–6.
13. C. Saunders, 'Conference Report: Mfecane Afterthoughts', *Social Dynamics*, 17 (2), 1991, 171–7.
14. See for example, Iden Wetherall's article, 'The Mfecane: Fact or Fantasy?' in *Vrye Weekblad*, 25–31 Oct. 1991; report by Portia Maurice, *Weekly Mail*, 13–19 Sept. 1993; also see the letters pages, *Guardian Weekly*, 21 June 1992 and 19 July 1992; N. Etherington, 'Shrinking the Zulu', *Southern African Review of Books*, Sept.–Oct.1992; see more recently, Joe Louw, 'Hills Hide Secrets of Unhappy Past', *Saturday Star*, 30 July 1993.
15. Stephen Taylor, 'Zulu History Rewritten and Rerun', *The Times Higher Education Supplement*, 1 Nov. 1991.
16. Cited in Taylor, 'Zulu History Rewritten and Rerun'.

A further perspective on the timing of the eruption of the controversy around the mfecane is provided by contextualizing the debate within the development of precolonial[17] southern African studies since the time of Omer-Cooper's publication. In his essay in this volume, Christopher Saunders traces in detail the use of the concept of the mfecane in southern African historiography. It is not my purpose to rehearse here his arguments about the mfecane, but rather to examine briefly broader developments within the field of precolonial history so as to help situate the current debate.

In the late sixties and early seventies Africanist trends elsewhere on the continent, backed by the path-breaking work of Jan Vansina[18] on the usefulness of oral traditions as historical sources, prompted a new interest in precolonial southern Africa. As Saunders shows, the work of Omer-Cooper and Leonard Thompson initiated this development. Their endeavours were soon overtaken by a new generation of students working within a materialist paradigm, and trained mostly, though not exclusively, at two institutions, the University of California, Los Angeles, and the School of Oriental and African Studies, University of London. The work of these scholars featured in forums such as Shula Marks' interdisciplinary seminar on the societies of southern Africa, at the Institute of Commonwealth Studies.

In July 1976, this interest led to the holding of a workshop on 'Pre-capitalist Social Formations and Colonial Penetration in Southern Africa' at the National University of Lesotho, Roma.[19] As the workshop title makes clear, the participants

---

17. The term 'precolonial' remains an unsatisfactory label for a period which ends with the establishment of a colonial presence in southern Africa (the date of which varies from region to region, ranging from the establishment of the Cape colony in the late 1600s to the destruction of the Zulu kingdom after 1879, the latter being not strictly the establishment of a colony). The beginning point of this period is even less precise, varying in common – but seldom explicit – usage anywhere between 1400 and 1750, again with regional variation. The term is not only imprecise, it is also intrinsically colonially-centered in terms of the perspective which it induces. Alternatives are not readily available. Terms such as 'pre-industrial or 'precapitalist' suffer similar problems. As research in the period conventionally designated 'precolonial' develops, regional and temporal disaggregation and specification will, hopefully, reduce the need for such a catch-all label.

18. J. Vansina, *Oral Tradition: A Study in Historical Methodology*, London, 1965.

19. Papers listed on the programme: W. Beinart, 'Labour and Technology: Penetration into Pondoland, 1830–1930'; P. Bonner, 'The Swazi Kingdom'; W.G. Clarence-Smith, 'Capitalist Penetration among the Nyaneka of Southern Angola, 1840–1918'; P. Delius, 'The Structure of the Pedi State'; A. Erwin, 'The Concept of the Mode of Production'; M. Evers and M. Taylor, 'The Archaeologist and the Investigation of the Economic Base'; J.J. Guy, 'Production and Exchange in the Zulu Kingdom'; M. Hall, 'Dendroclimatology, Rainfall and Human Adaptation in the Later Iron Age of Natal and Zululand'; J. Keenan, 'On the Concept of the Mode of Production in Precapitalist Social Formations: (An Anthropological View)'; J. Kimble, 'The Economic History of Lesotho in the Nineteenth Century'; N. Parsons, 'The Economic History of Khama's Country in Southern Africa'; J. Peires, 'Economic History of the Xhosa up to 1835'; I. Phimister, 'Pre-colonial Goldmining in Southern Zambesia: A Reassessment'; with summing up and discussion led by Shula Marks. (Details taken from the organisers' letter dated 13 June 1976.) A different programme (undated, but probably subsequent as I have never seen any of the following papers) does not mention papers by Evers and Taylor, Phimister, and Delius. I am grateful to Philip Bonner for giving me access to his set of conference papers, correspondence, and notes.

were concerned to investigate the nature of pre-capitalist economies, and were particularly interested in questions of social stratification and forms of exploitation, as well as how these aspects of precolonial societies were transformed by the penetration of mercantile, and later industrial, capitalism. The publication in 1975 of Barry Hindess and Paul Hirst's *Pre-capitalist Modes of Production*[20] powerfully influenced the papers and discussion at the conference. The Lesotho conference set in place many of the major theoretical ideas which informed a crop of doctoral theses which were completed in the middle and late 1970s dealing with the economies and histories of a range of precolonial polities such as the Zulu and Swazi kingdoms, the Pedi paramountcy, and so on.[21]

A follow-up conference was held in Lesotho in 1977, and, in the same year the University of Natal, Pietermaritzburg, hosted a regionally specific conference. The prime purpose of this latter meeting was 'to provide a forum for students of Zulu history working in southern Africa to discuss the nature of the Zulu political economy before 1879'.[22] The Pietermaritzburg workshop also drew inspiration from the latest developments within Marxist thinking. Earlier that year, Claude Meillassoux had given a seminar in Pietermaritzburg, and the workshop title, 'Production and Reproduction in the Zulu Kingdom', drew attention to the central concepts of the French Marxist anthropologists. The tight regional focus of the Pietermaritzburg conference, and the conscious effort by the organizers to solicit papers from outside the discipline of history, reflected an awareness of a need for new sources of evidence within the field.

A further conference, also concerned with themes of differentiation, production and exchange, focused on the precolonial history of Nguni-speakers more broadly. It was held at Rhodes University, Grahamstown in 1979, and the conference proceedings were edited by Jeff Peires and published under the title *Before and After Shaka*.[23] These papers reflected a growing concern about the inability of the available evidence to show contradictions, conflict and social cleavages, the

20. B. Hindess and P.Q. Hirst, *Pre-capitalist Modes of Production*, London, 1975.
21. G. Liesegang, 'Beitrage zur Geschichte des Reiches der Gaza Nguni im Sudlichen Mocambique, 1820–1895', Ph.D. thesis, Köln, 1967; M. Legassick, 'The Griqua, the Sotho-Tswana and the Missionaries, 1780–1840', Ph.D. thesis, University of California, Los Angeles, 1969; A. Smith, 'The Struggle for Control of Southern Mocambique, 1720–1835', Ph.D. thesis, University of California, Los Angeles, 1970; R. Mael, 'The Problems of Political Integration in the Zulu Empire', Ph.D. thesis, University of California, Los Angeles, 1974; H. Slater, 'Transitions in the Political Economy of South-East Africa', D.Phil. thesis, University of Sussex, Brighton, 1976; J. Cobbing, 'The Ndebele under the Khumalos, 1820–1896', Ph.D. thesis, University of Lancaster, 1976; P. Bonner, 'The Rise, Consolidation and Disintegration of Dhlamini Power in Swaziland between 1820–1899', Ph.D. thesis, University of London, 1977; D. Hedges, 'Trade and Politics in Southern Mozambique and Zululand in the Eighteenth and Early Nineteenth Centuries', Ph.D. thesis, University of London, 1978; W. Beinart, 'Production, Labour Migrancy and the Chieftaincy: Aspects of the Political Economy of Pondoland, 1860–1930', Ph.D. thesis, University of London, 1979; P. Delius, 'The Pedi Polity under Sekwati and Sekhukhune, 1828–1880', Ph.D. thesis, University of London, 1980.
22. M. Hall and J. Wright, eds., *Production and Reproduction in the Zulu Kingdom*, workshop papers, Pietermaritzburg, 1977, Introduction, 1.
23. J.B. Peires, ed., *Before and After Shaka: Papers in Nguni History*, Grahamstown, 1981.

dominant themes of a Marxist conception of history. Evidence difficulties, coupled with an increasing sense of the irrelevance of precolonial history in apartheid South Africa, led a number of the scholars hitherto involved in the study of pre-capitalist societies to turn their attention to the history of twentieth-century southern Africa. The emergence of the Wits History Workshop – with its focus on industrialisation and the impact of capitalism – as the pre-eminent historical forum of the period, was an important marker of this trend.

As a result, little new research into the precolonial past was undertaken in the early 1980s. The major publications of the period drew on the seminars and doctoral theses of the previous decade. Marks and Atmore reproduced as *Economy and Society in Pre-industrial South Africa* a selection of the seminar papers delivered in the 1970s, and a number of the doctoral theses appeared as published monographs.[24] It was to be seven years before the next meeting of scholars working on the precolonial past and the presentation of fresh perspectives and research.

This happened at the 1986 'Workshop on Precolonial History' organised by the Centre for African Studies at the University of Cape Town, which was attended by historians, anthropologists, linguists and archaeologists.[25] The papers and the conference debates revealed a shift away from the strong political economy approach of the materialist scholars of the 1970s to an examination of questions of ideology, and a concern with methodology. Increasingly influenced by literary theory, a new approach was emerging at the conference and in other work produced at this time, which raised fundamental questions about historians' reading of their evidence, and about the genealogies of their sources.[26] In addition a number of papers took up questions of the public presentation of the precolonial past in textbooks and popular histories.

This brief review of the development of precolonial studies in the 1970s and 1980s reveals that Cobbing's early papers were presented in a hiatus between the Rhodes and Cape Town conferences, at a time when interest among historians had swung away from the precolonial past to a concern with the making of the apartheid state. However, the new directions which emerged at the Cape Town conference

---

24. S. Marks and A. Atmore, eds., *Economy and Society in Pre-industrial South Africa*, London, 1980. The publication in 1982 of *A History of South Africa to 1870*, edited by M. Wilson and L. Thompson was a reprint of *The Oxford History of Southern Africa* of 1969 (minus chapter one on the archaeological background by Ray Inskeep).

25. Among others, papers were given by M. Hall, W.D. Hammond-Tooke and T. Evers, C. Hamilton, H. Webster, J. Wright, M. Kinsman, P. Harries, and A. Mazel.

26. J.B. Wright, 'Politics, Ideology and the Invention of the Nguni', in T. Lodge, ed., *Resistance and Ideology in Settler Societies*, 4, Johannesburg, 1986, 96–118; C. Hamilton, 'Ideology, Oral Traditions and the Struggle for Power in the Early Zulu Kingdom', M.A. thesis, University of the Witwatersrand, 1986; J. Wright and C. Hamilton, 'Traditions and Transformations: The Phongolo-Mzimkhulu Region in the Late Eighteenth and Early Nineteenth Centuries', in A. Duminy and B. Guest, eds., *Natal and Zululand From Earliest Times to 1910: A New History*, Pietermaritzburg, 1989; also see J.B. Wright, 'A.T. Bryant and the "Wars of Shaka"', *History in Africa*, 18 (1991), 409–25, first presented as a seminar paper in 1988; J.B. Wright, 'The Dynamics of Power and Conflict in the Thukela-Mzimkhulu Region in the Late Eighteenth and Early Nineteenth Centuries: A Critical Reconstruction', Ph.D. thesis, University of the Witwatersrand, 1990.

interlocked with certain of the concerns of the Cobbing critique, notably an interest in how received versions of the past came into place. This congruence of interests underlay the subsequent attention paid to Cobbing's arguments and ultimately, the holding of the Wits colloquium in 1991.

The colloquium itself was preceded by an upsurge of public interest in Zulu history and invocations of the mfecane (widely reported in the South African press) in terms of which contemporary political transformations and upheavals were likened to a modern mfecane.[27] The methodological concerns of the academy were thus further complemented by the pressing question in the public domain of how the role of the history of southern Africa before European domination, and narratives of first contact, are drawn on as metaphors for current political developments. Interest in the debate over the mfecane in 1991 reflected the intersection of the Cobbing critique with, on the one hand, specific developments within precolonial historiography, and, on the other hand, contemporary political developments.

This convergence allowed the set of debates which characterised the colloquium to take place when they did, and in the form that they did, even though Cobbing's critique had first been made much earlier, and even though he had sought a different form for his intervention. I use the phrase 'set of debates' for not all the contributors would necessarily agree what those debates are, nor is there any consensus on their ranking in terms of importance.

Generally, it is assumed that in order to have an historical debate, the participants and adversaries must agree on what is at issue. They have to agree broadly on how arguments are properly made, on how sources should be read, on what constitutes evidence or proof, and on what might be persuasive. Usually, in a debate about events in temporally distant times, the participants must agree to share the same imagined idea of what societies were like in remote times, before an argument can be made about the causes of changes in such societies, or about the reconstruction of those causes later in time.[28]

Readers of the various essays in the book are likely to find such agreements elusive, and occasionally even absent. For this reason, it is not possible to see the book as centred on a single debate, or to regard essays that say different things about particular events as necessarily opposed. This Introduction, and the contextualising essays which precede each of the three sections into which the book is divided, point

27. See for example Bra Mzala in *Natal Mercury*, 11 Apr. 1991 and Piet 'Skiet' Rudolph quoted in *Weekly Mail*, 10–16 May, 1991; see also speech by G. Buthelezi, Ulundi, 20 Aug. 1983.

28. My discusssion of the nature of historical debate draws heavily on D. W. Cohen, *The Combing of History*, Chicago, 1994. Significantly, Cohen uses the example of the debates around the mfecane to stress the temporality and temporicity of historiographical debate. He notes that the mfecane debates are also arguments about the 'fate of implicit social theory concerning the role of ethnicity in the formation of African communities; the value of core and periphery models in the historicization of early capitalism in southern Africa; and the relationship between past, as constituted in historical texts, and the present' (p. 74). Cohen suggests that the mfecane debates, amongst others, are beginning to prompt historiographers to pay greater attention to the ethnography and economy of any particular historical debate.

up some of the areas of debate and difference. Doubtless, readers will find others, and will be able to explore for themselves the significance of points of abrasion between the various studies.

Julian Cobbing argues that *the* debate is whether the notion of the mfecane should be retained within, or 'jettisoned' from, southern African historiography. Other scholars argue about whether the concept of the mfecane carries the meanings within the historiography which Cobbing ascribes to it. There are debates amongst the essays in this volume about the very issues which are usually agreed upon in the setting of the parameters of an historical debate. The 'rules' of historical reconstruction are themselves contested. Where, for one contributor, a dissembling colonial official is an unreliable or 'bad' source who cannot be used, for another scholar, the same source – indeed, the official's very act of cloaking a motive or misrepresenting an event – becomes the meat of rigorous historical reconstruction.

One debate which percolates through the various essays is the question of African and European agency. Was the period of exceptional violence which most contributors agree occurred in the early decades of the nineteenth century a consequence of African activities (the eruption of the Zulu, and refugees from Zulu imperialism, on to the highveld as proposed by Omer-Cooper, among others) or was it the result of European activities (labour-raiding and slaving from the Cape in the south and from Delagoa Bay in the north, as argued by Cobbing)? In this debate, the contributors have agreed that it is fruitful to pose the question in terms of African and European agency. But there are clear indications in a number of the essays that this argument itself may impose a structure on the study of the period that limits, rather than opens up, historical enquiry. In this form, the disagreements over the relative weighting of European and African agency repeat the conventional bifurcation of the southern African past into black histories and white histories, meeting only in conflict. This division continues despite the wealth of evidence which reveals a more fluid situation, in which European and African actions (and, indeed, the activities of hunter-gatherers – as Thomas Dowson shows in his contribution) are but different ingredients in a well-shaken cocktail. It may be necessary to entertain the idea that the discussions of African and European agency, while facilitating a debate in these pages, may be responsible for the exclusion from these essays of evidence and material which does not fit the bipolar form taken by the debate. There is a further danger that this division of the history of later precolonial times will tempt post-apartheid authors of a revised history of this period – especially the writers of new South African history textbooks – into replacing unproblematically black villains with white villains, instead of encouraging them to come to grips with the full complexity of relations of domination, subordination, resistance and interaction within and between the various societies of precolonial southern Africa.

The collection of these varied essays and their publication in a single volume will help students of the debates to ask crucial questions about what has been occluded from the debates, what has been elided in their presentation in this form, what has been left silent, and what might be absent. The presentation in the book of ongoing debates prompts not only the identification of such silences and absences, but a questioning as to why the agreements about these silences come about. In so far as this volume facilitates the posing of these questions, it seeks to go beyond the presentation of the particular set of positions currently debated to pose further questions about this historiography and this period, and to begin the work of setting the agenda for new research directions.

The title of the book is a reminder that while the ongoing debates are important, the attacking of the mfecane by Cobbing creates a time of aftermath. In this aftermath, for some, the mfecane is, as it was put at the colloquium, dead and buried; for others it is about to have new life breathed into it. For still others, aftermath connotes a mown field with new horizons created by the cropping of the grass. Some scatterings may remain to be raked in and a range of species in the fallow growth – some new, others residual – begin the struggle to assert themselves. In the aftermath, however, the mfecane is, at least, a concept that cannot be taken for granted. However it is used, whether it is treated as a massive historical myth, or a real historical phenomenon, or neither, a new precision, care and explicitness is demanded of its usage.

Acknowledgements

An abridged version of this Introduction was presented to the Sparkling Waters Colloquium on School History Textbooks for a Democratic South Africa (November 1993). I am grateful to John Wright, Thomas Dowson, Rob Morrell, Jeff Peires and Jeff Guy for their comments on that version. I would like to thank David William Cohen for inviting me to host a seminar at the Institute for the Advanced Study in the African Humanities, Northwestern University, where my ideas for this Introduction first crystallised.

PART ONE

Historiography and Methodology

Putting the Mfecane Controversy into Historiographical Context

NORMAN ETHERINGTON

Julian Cobbing presents not one, but three arguments in his challenge to accepted versions of the mfecane:

> Troubled times in southern Africa were not a consequence of the rise of the Zulu kingdom;

> A continuous series of writers seeking to justify white settlement blamed the Zulu for devastating and depopulating vast territories;

> The root causes of commotions in the first few decades of the nineteenth century were labour raiding and slaving expeditions mounted to feed demand generated in the Cape colony and Portuguese Mozambique.

The first argument has been widely accepted. The other two have provoked spirited controversy. Essays in Part One of this book take up some of the issues raised by the second and third of Cobbing's propositions.

Settler History and the Mfecane

Cobbing regards the mfecane as the masterpiece of settler history, and in so doing aligns himself with a long-standing tendency of South African scholarship to emphasise the political uses of history. Afrikaner nationalists have at various times advertised their intention to find a past that serves their cause. English-speaking historians such as the influential amateurs George McCall Theal and George Cory made clear their own intentions to write the sort of history that would 'heal' divisions between Boer and Briton. In various ways 'liberal' historians of the 1940s, 1950s and 1960s consciously wrote history 'against apartheid'. Those scholars were in turn attacked by radicals for deliberately concealing the functional relationship between segregation and capitalism.

Against this background, Cobbing's assumption of a linkage between what he regards as mfecane theorists and settler interests amounts to a normal reflex action for a South African historian. That does not mean, however, that it deserves to be accepted without examination. It is a proposition that can be tested according to normal canons of historical proof.

Christopher Saunders sets out to do precisely that, and finds no evidence that a continuous chain of settler apologists stretches from Theal to John Omer-Cooper. Without at all denying that historians write in an ideological context, he points to marked contrasts in interpretations of the mfecane. He draws a sharp contrast between Theal and Cory, who traced all violence to Shaka, and William Macmillan, who strongly suspected that the slave trade to Mozambique had much to do with disruptions in what became the Zululand region, the highveld and even the eastern Cape frontier. Moving into the 1960s, Saunders argues that the correct context for Omer-Cooper's influential *Zulu Aftermath* was not bantustan policies in the Republic of South Africa but movements of nation-building in independent black Africa north of the Limpopo. Floors van Jaarsveld and other apologists for apartheid misused data provided by Leonard Thompson and Omer-Cooper, but that was neither the fault nor the intention of the liberal historians.

One of the most interesting passages in Saunders's article ponders the reasons why Macmillan's speculations on the disruptive influence of invading colonial capitalism should have been forgotten by the liberal historians who followed. Could it, he asks, have been a result of the fire which destroyed the John Philip papers on which Macmillan relied? Or was it that scholars found more important questions to be asked in other parts of the historical record?

I take up the same question at the outset of my essay on the Great Trek and suggest yet another answer: that the narrative structures which give form to historical discourse have a shaping power of their own, quite apart from the ideological agendas of self-serving interested parties. Nationalism favours myths of origins rooted in primordial landscapes in which peoples grow independently from the soil itself and then go into battle against threatening alien forces. Settlers needed their land cleared by the mfecane so that they could take root there through the formative process of 'pioneering'. Black nationalists responded to the idea that nations like the Zulu grew up from mother earth fully formed according to their own organic genius. Neither settler nationalism nor African nationalism could be expected to welcome Cobbing's version of history in which communities congeal into nations through a series of complex interactions with external forces.

Thomas Dowson's contribution makes a related point, which is that the construction of one group's national consciousness can suppress or even obliterate knowledge about other groups. Dowson cites the Bushmen peoples as a prime example. Standard accounts of the mfecane either ignore their presence or shuffle them off the stage at the earliest possible opportunity. Nevertheless, evidence from several different sources shows that the Bushmen were there and adapted in interesting, dynamic ways to the changes engulfing south-east Africa in the eighteenth and nineteenth centuries.

Whereas Dowson tries to fill silences in the written records by looking to other evidence, Dan Wylie dismantles the language used by white writers on Shaka and the Zulu. He discovers deep countercurrents and contradictions which continually subvert protestations of sympathy for African ways of life. When language itself is so loaded a weapon for conveying knowledge, what hope can there be of ever knowing 'what actually happened'? Once this question is asked, we have moved far beyond Cobbing's proposition that the true causes of turmoil in the early nineteenth century have been suppressed by 'settler history'. The past looks far more problematical than Cobbing will allow. It is easier to falsify old stories about the mfecane than to put new knowledge in its place. We see the historical landscape of two centuries' past through a very dark glass indeed.

Truth in History

The predominant intellectual currents of our time are sceptical of claims to Truth. 'Truth claims,' writes Pauline Rosenau 'are a form of terrorism.'[1] Jacques Derrida's notorious claim that 'there is nothing beyond the text' has pushed some scholars into extreme suspensions of belief. Jane Caplan succinctly expresses the tendencies of this trend:

> There remains a basic anxiety for historians in the face of deconstruction: namely that, in making the text ultimately undecidable, it abolishes the grounds for privileging any one interpretation, and therefore makes the writing of conventional history impossible. If all of history is also seen as a text, this only compounds the problem. It may be that here we have to concede deconstruction's ability to discern the paralogies or guilty secrets on which our own practices depend. A deconstructive critique of the historian's practice would point out that it represses what it has in common with its ostensible object, in order to create the illusion of its difference both from literary writing, and from the real. Critical history has shifted from arguing that every 'fact' is an interpretation to arguing that every historical account is a language-act; in other words, from the denial that facts are transparent, to the denial that language is transparent. This is true of language whether used by historians' sources or by historians themselves.[2]

The revival of language as a central concern for scholars presents no problems for some historical enterprises. Historians who delight in showing how vested interests generate self-serving knowledge about the past can readily decant their old wine into newly labelled bottles. Where once they exposed ruling ideologies and pinpointed mystifications, they can now subvert dominant discourses by attending to gaps and silences.

Other kinds of history look distinctly old fashioned when viewed through the postmodern lens. Up-to-date scholars keep jars of quotation marks handy on their writing tables, and use them constantly to distance themselves from 'what really happened', 'the facts', 'the historical record' and 'the truth' about just about anything. Historical narratives become 'stories'.

1. P.M. Rosenau, *Postmodernism and the Social Sciences: Insights, Inroads and Intrusions*, Princeton, 1992, 78.
2. J. Caplan, 'Postmodernism, Poststructuralism, and Deconstruction: Notes for Historians', *Central European History*, 22 (1989), 272–3.

These contemporary trends in historical interpretation impact on the mfecane debate in different ways, as can be seen by looking closely at the three parts of Cobbing's case against the mfecane. The first of Cobbing's three theses sets out to correct a mistake. It does not aim to say what is true, but to falsify the statement that social turbulence in southern Africa flowed from the rise of the Zulu state. Even those who are most hostile to 'truth claims' are likely to admit the validity of this part of Cobbing's case. It is always easier to confute false statements about the past than to propound true ones. As it turns out, the most convincing falsifications of the Zulucentric mfecane ultimately come not from Cobbing himself but from others who have been drawn into the discussion. Neil Parsons's essay in another section of this book virtually nails down the coffin.

The second of Cobbing's propositions is an argument of an altogether different order. It asserts that the notion of the Zulu-generated mfecane was invented and perpetuated to serve the interests of white settlers. The proposition could have been put in a form that would be difficult to deny. Cobbing might simply have contended:

> That the story of the mfecane told in the 1830s and 1840s provided a justification for incoming settlers to claim the highveld as waste and unoccupied land;

> That the repetition of the story by later historians could be used to justify the distribution of land ownership in the twentieth century.

As evidence he might have adduced settler statements about depopulated lands and Van Jaarsveld's statements about the consequences of the mfecane.[3] Such a case could only be logically refuted by showing that the evidence was forged or misinterpreted. Instead, Cobbing imposes on himself the argument that everyone who ever told the story of the mfecane was writing settler history. Unless he wishes to resort to the old Marxian doctrine that every social act has an 'objective' character quite distinct from the consciousness of the actor, the task of proving such a case is sisyphean. The way is open for dozens of MA dissertation writers to show that particular historians questioned the mfecane or despised settler history. Christopher Saunders's chapter in this section shows how the job is done. Cobbing himself does not even begin to verify his propositions about settler history.[4] Substantiating the case would be the work of a lifetime. Even then it would be open to question from those who treat works of history as literary texts open to a multiplicity of readings. Should Cobbing wish to persevere in a labour which is totally superfluous to his central argument, he would be well advised to join the postmodernists and do some deconstructive readings of major historians' texts on the mfecane.

Judging from the arguments he employs in support of his third proposition,

---

3. See N. Etherington, 'The Great Trek in Relation to the Mfecane: A Reassessment', *South African Historical Journal*, 25 (1991), 12–13.

4. The closest he comes is implying that Eric Walker invented the word in 1928. More thesis writers can follow in the footsteps of Jeff Peires and Neil Parsons by spotting earlier uses of the word or its Sotho equivalent, *difaqane*.

Cobbing is no post-modern. His contention that labour-raiding to serve the Cape and Mozambican economies was the root cause of commotions on the highveld and in Natal is accompanied by a plethora of categorical statements. 'There is no doubt' that missionaries at Dithakong 'were fully and consciously engrossed in what they were doing, i.e. collecting slaves.'[5] 'Everyone knew what Somerset meant.'[6] 'The conclusion is inescapable' . . . 'there is a single, unavoidable, explanation' . . . 'it is clear, then, that slaving was having a dramatic impact'.[7] When he writes in these terms Cobbing does indeed rush upon his readers like a 'terrorist of truth'. Historians of all tendencies are likely to react with scepticism, if not hostility, when assaulted in this way. The vehemence of the counter-attack could have been expected. The pity is that it appears to many scholars to have cast doubt on all three of Cobbing's central propositions.

In order to see why this is not the case, it is necessary to recognise the difference between the method of argumentation used to discredit the Zulucentric mfecane and the quite different method employed to assert the vital importance of slaving as a cause of turmoil among southern African societies. The first argument proceeds, as we have seen, by falsification. It shows that certain state formations and events which had previously been attributed to the impact of Zulu raiding following the rise of the Shakan kingdom could not have been the result of Zulu activity. The second argument proceeds by inference: if the Zulu could not have produced the turmoil attributed to them, what did? Documents indicate that Griquas, Bergenaar and others were engaged in labour raiding on the highveld. Documents also say that slaves were sold in Mozambique. Raiding and slaving are known to have produced great turmoil in other parts of Africa. Therefore we may infer that the turmoil of the early nineteenth century was caused by slaving. Only Cobbing does not say he is making an inference. He says he is revealing the truth.

The argument is scantily clad. Having attacked the notion of a Zulu-generated mfecane because researchers thus far have failed to show the mechanism by which the rise of the Zulu state was linked to trade, drought, population pressure or any of the other phenomena cited by previous scholars,[8] Cobbing should acknowledge the same problem with his own argument based on slaving. What amount of raiding is required to produce reactive militarised state formations? Why do the most formidable states not appear closer to the centres of raiding? Why is people-raiding more disruptive than raiding for cattle or some other item? He can only respond to these queries by putting forward hypotheses as untestable as those he has attacked. Worse still, he lets himself be drawn on to terrain where he should not be fighting. If the Zulu were not responsible for the round of state formation and population

5. J. Cobbing, 'The Mfecane as Alibi: Thoughts on Dithakong and Mbolompo', *Journal of African History*, 29 (1988), 493.
6. Cobbing, 'The Mfecane as Alibi', 503.
7. Cobbing, 'The Mfecane as Alibi', 509; 'Rethinking the Roots of Violence in Southern Africa 1740–1840', paper presented to the colloquium on the Mfecane Aftermath, University of the Witwatersrand, Johannesburg, 1991, 21, 15.
8. Cobbing, 'The Mfecane as Alibi', 488.

movement that occurred in the first half of the nineteenth century, the Zulu kingdom ceases to be an object of special interest. The reasons for its appearance are no more nor less interesting than the reasons for the appearance of any other African state in the region. Scholars can give up the elusive search for a first cause which set the process of Zulu state formation into motion. While the study of rival hypotheses will continue to be a useful way of introducing undergraduate students to the study of African history, it ceases to be *the* 'revolution in Bantu Africa'.

However, by putting so much emphasis on slave trading at Delagoa Bay, Cobbing gives the appearance of offering yet another explanation for the rise of the Zulu kingdom.[9] He should be able to share Elizabeth Eldredge's doubts about the extent of the Delagoa Bay trade. After all, Delagoa Bay is only important if one accepts the key role of the Zulu state. Similarly Cobbing should not be greatly worried by Carolyn Hamilton's view that 'Shaka the monster' was as much a creation of the Zulus' black neighbours as of Port Natal freebooters. Reviving the psychopathic image cannot restore Shaka's status as 'the black Napoleon'. The available texts on both the slave trade and the character of Shaka are capable of enough different readings to keep critical theorists happy for years to come. Cobbing need not have tied his colours to specific interpretations. The work brought together in Parsons's essay, 'Prelude to *Difaqane* in the Interior of Southern Africa' pushes the onset of conflict, population mobility and state formation so far back that the Shakan state begins to look like a relative late-comer.

Conclusion

This introduction to Part One has attempted to combine a setting for the historiographical essays with an assessment of argumentation and 'truth' in the mfecane debate. In an era more than usually suspicious of truth, the historian's task is especially burdensome. We must be more than usually careful to bear in mind that most of our knowledge about the past is provisional. The kinds of evidence available to us carry most weight when they are used to falsify propositions about the past. When, on the other hand, we argue inductively, our inferences are uncertain and always subject to correction. That is why the case against the Zulu-generated mfecane reads more convincingly than the arguments that the mfecane was the creation of 'settler history' and that slaving was the ultimate source of terror and turmoil in the South African interior.

Leonard Thompson can thus be seen to be only partly right when he writes in his new *History of South Africa*, that Cobbing's argument 'cannot be substantiated'. Those parts based on inference cannot be substantiated, but the parts based on falsification can be. To judge how far this is so, the reader needs to do no more than appraise how much revision is now required in Thompson's own text on the mfecane:

---

9. Or, more precisely, to be reviving an explanation which attracted W.M. Macmillan.

Until the late eighteenth century the Bantu-speaking mixed farmers south of the Limpopo River lived in small chiefdoms . . . The nucleus of change lay in northern Nguni country . . . This transformation was in essence an internal process within the mixed farming society in southeastern Africa. By the last quarter of the eighteenth century the relation between the population level and the environment was changing . . . Previously, the society had been expansive and the scale of political organization had remained small . . . Gradually, however, the population of the region had been increasing to a level where that expansive process was no longer possible . . . Zulu impis (regiments) and bands composed of people who had been driven from their homes by the Zulu . . . had created the widespread havoc throughout southeastern Africa that became known as the *Mfecane*.[10]

Should there be another edition of Thompson's book, virtually the whole of that section would require rewriting. To that extent, at least, we can revise 'historical truth'.

10. L. M. Thompson, *A History of South Africa*, New Haven, 1990, 80–5.

1 Pre-Cobbing Mfecane Historiography

CHRISTOPHER SAUNDERS

The title of Julian Cobbing's article, 'The Mfecane as Alibi', suggested a key part of his argument: that the view of the Mfecane held by previous historians was not only a false one, but had diverted attention from something else of greater importance. What Cobbing called in his article 'mfecane theory' – the idea of a great upheaval caused by the Zulu – was, he claimed, 'integral to a white settler, "Liberal" history', and had been refined and elaborated in the 1960s. For Cobbing, settler historians, liberal historians and apartheid apologists were essentially all of one mind in believing that the Mfecane began with, or was caused by (if they confined that term to the consequences of the rise of the Zulu state), 'a self-generated internal revolution' in what became known as Zululand. That these 'mfecane theorists' all treated the Mfecane as something separate from the colonial history of South Africa was, he argued, no accident. There was, he claimed, an ideological purpose at work, in particular a concern to justify the racially unequal division of the land.[1] What these historians had failed to point to, as the major process at work in the early nineteenth century, as later, was the violence of colonialism.

In what follows I discuss some of the earlier historical writing on the Mfecane to demonstrate that Cobbing has presented too stereotypical a view of what previous historians – hardly 'theorists' in any usual definition of that word – said about the Mfecane. He did not allow for the way in which views had changed over time, nor did he discuss previous work in its historical context.[2] Historians from Theal to the liberal Africanists of the 1960s all to a greater or lesser extent saw the Zulu as playing a major role in the Mfecane, but they by no means all agreed either on its causes or its consequences. Nor did they all treat the Mfecane as something entirely separate from the history of colonisation, or ignore the violence associated with colonialism. That the liberal historians failed to give more weight to colonial violence was not because,

---

1. J. Cobbing, 'The Mfecane as Alibi: Thoughts on Dithakong and Mbolompo', *Journal of African History*, 29 (1988), 487 and 519.
2. In his unpublished papers 'The Case against the Mfecane', seminar paper presented to the Centre for African Studies, University of Cape Town, 1983; and 'Jettisoning the Mfecane (with *Perestroika*)', seminar paper presented to the African Studies Institute, University of the Witwatersrand, Johannesburg, 1988, Cobbing did devote more attention to the historiography than in 'The Mfecane as Alibi'; I here concentrate on his published paper.

as Cobbing suggested, they supported or were linked to segregation and apartheid,[3] but for other reasons. And it is pointed out that the main ideas in Cobbing's anti-Mfecane critique are also to be found elsewhere.

Theal and Walker

Cobbing rightly recognised the crucial importance of George McCall Theal in advancing what was for long an extremely influential view of what happened in the Natal/Zulu kingdom area and the interior in the early nineteenth century. Theal's *History*, written towards the end of that century, told of a time of vast destruction, from the Natal/Zulu kingdom area to the far interior, begun by Shaka. Theal did not use 'Mfecane' – nor 'Great Trek', for that matter – but in essence his view of 'the Zulu wars' – or, as he sometimes called them, 'the wars of Tshaka'[4] – was the same as that of Eric Walker and later historians who did write of the 'Mfecane'. Theal was not the first to describe great wars in the Natal/Zulu kingdom area in the 1810s and 1820s; earlier writers had also ascribed them to the career of one frequently compared to Napoleon Bonaparte, Shaka's European counterpart, and had gone on to describe Mzilikazi as responsible for much of the death and destruction carried far into the interior.[5] Nor was Theal the first to link violence in the Natal/Zulu kingdom area and the interior,[6] but he systematised and carried further earlier views, and his *History* was long considered by many as a basic text and near-'definitive'.

After describing the rise of Shaka, his reorganisation of the Zulu army – 'The world has probably never seen men trained to more perfect obedience' – and his military innovations, Theal wrote of Shaka's aggression and cruelty – 'such cruelty as is hardly comprehensible by Europeans' – and of the sequence of warfare from the Zulu kingdom westwards, what Omer-Cooper was to call 'the great chain of wars and migrations'[7] and Cobbing a 'chain reaction or "shunting sequence"'.[8] No writer before Theal had presented a picture of quite such destruction and devastation flowing from Shaka's conquests; his narrative, which was dull and lifeless on most

---

3. E.g. Cobbing, 'The Mfecane as Alibi', 519. Similarly, he is too ready to accept that James Stuart shared the racist views of his fellow magistrates: cf. J. Cobbing, 'A Tainted Well: The Objectives, Historical Fantasies and Working Methods of James Stuart, with Counter Argument', *Journal of Natal and Zulu History*, 11 (1988) and C. A. Hamilton, '"The Character and Objects of Chaka" A Reconsideration of the Making of Shaka as "Mfecane" Motor', in this volume, pp. 183–211.

4. E.g. G.M. Theal, *The Republic of Natal. The Origin of the Present Pondo Tribe, Imperial Treaties with Panda and Establishment of the Colony of Natal . . .*, Cape Town, 1886, 1.

5. E.g. W.C. Holden, *The Past and Future of the Kaffir Races*, London, 1866, ch. 2. This book, by a Wesleyan missionary, was written in the early 1850s and published in 1866. The comparison between Shaka and Napoleon Bonaparte continues down to the present day; for one recent example, see B. Magubane, *The Politics of History in South Africa*, New York, 1982, 17.

6. As suggested in e.g. J.B. Wright, 'Political Mythology and the Making of Natal's Mfecane', *Canadian Journal of African Studies*, 23, 2 (1989), 278–9.

7. J.D. Omer-Cooper, *The Zulu Aftermath: A Nineteenth-century Revolution in Bantu Africa*, London, 1966, 5.

8. Cobbing, 'The Mfecane as Alibi', 517.

topics, came alive at this point. Clearly he wished to leave his readers with an image of black barbarism at its most extreme. After writing of 'a torrent of invasion', and a land 'covered with skeletons', Theal concluded that 'The number of individuals that perished in the whole of the ravaged country from war and its effects can only be roughly estimated, but it must have been nearer two millions than one.'[9] Theal also wished to give his readers the impression that, compared to precolonial savagery and violence, colonial rule was peaceful and beneficial.[10] The 'Zulu wars,' said Theal, 'rendered insignificant the total loss of human life occasioned by all the wars in South Africa in which Europeans have engaged since first they set foot in the country.'[11]

But even for Theal the events occurring in the interior were not altogether unconnected with the Cape colony. Had the Griqua not intervened at the battle of Dithakong in 1823, he believed, the Cape would have been invaded from the north.[12] And his picture of what happened in the interior at this time was not entirely negative. His reference to nearly two million deaths concludes a chapter entitled 'Terrible Destruction of Bantu Tribes during the Early Years of the Nineteenth Century'. One turns the page to find the following chapter called 'Formation of New Bantu Communities . . .' There Theal writes in positive terms of the early history of Moshoeshoe's Sotho state and of the survival of some Tswana polities through the period of upheaval.[13] In his chapter on 'The Wars and Devastations of Shaka' in *South Africa* (1894), Theal describes a 'process of reconstruction' which had taken place under Moshoeshoe, 'in one corner of the vast waste that had been created'.[14]

Yet the map which he included in the 1891 edition of his *History* showed a large part of South Africa 'nearly depopulated by the Zulu wars before 1834'.[15] And he did not alter his text to take account of new evidence uncovered in his own work, while even for his original version the evidence available to him should have led him to a more nuanced interpretation of events. Only in one footnote in his *History*, and in a mention in passing there drawing upon African traditions, does he provide clues to his sources on 'the Zulu wars'. We know that he not only read what was available in the Cape archives, but also collected oral evidence from Africans in the eastern Cape

9. G.M. Theal, *History of South Africa from 1795 to 1828*, London, 1903, 389.
10. Heinrich Vedder had the same purpose in his history of precolonial Namibia, published in German in 1934 and in English in 1938 as *South West Africa in Early Times*; see B. Lau, '"Thank God the Germans Came": Vedder and Namibian Historiography', in University of Cape Town, Centre for African Studies, African Seminar, *Collected Papers*, vol.2, ed. by K. Gottschalk and C. Saunders, Cape Town, 1981.
11. G.M. Theal, *History of South Africa*, 1891 ed., quoted in Cobbing, 'The Case Against the Mfecane', 7.
12. G.M. Theal, *Compendium of South African History and Geography*, Lovedale, 3rd ed., 1877, 198.
13. G.M. Theal, *History of South Africa from 1795–1872*, vol.1, 4th ed., London, [1916], chs.19 and 20.
14. G.M. Theal, *South Africa*, London, 1894, 170–1.
15. This map is reproduced in T.R.H. Davenport, *South Africa: A Modern History*, Johannesburg, 3rd ed., 1987, 14. It was omitted from later editions of Theal's *History*.

and trans-Kei in the 1870s, and consulted a number of published accounts, such as those by P. Mhlanga ('An Aged Fingo') and Moloja.[16] Instead of analysing this evidence critically, he seized upon what would serve his purpose. Thus he took over as fact a statement recorded from an unnamed missionary in a book by J.C. Chase (1843) that 'twenty-eight distinct tribes' had disappeared in this time of upheaval, 'leaving not so much as a trace of their former existence'. Theal should have realised that the list of these twenty-eight 'tribes' in Chase's book included the names of many Tswana chiefdoms which continued to exist after the Mfecane.[17] And he ignored the evidence he came across when he edited the archival records which he included in the many volumes of *Records of South-East Africa* and *Records of the Cape Colony*. In the latter, for example, he printed a report which Thomas Pringle sent to Cape Governor Somerset in 1825 concerning 'Fetcani' who had been driven from their land by 'a people of yellow complexion with black beards and long hair and who were armed with swords. This long-haired people must certainly be the Portuguese,' Pringle added, 'tho' it is odd they are not described as being armed with firearms rather than swords'.[18]

Alas, many later historians merely repeated, or embroidered, what Theal had written in his *History*. George Cory, another extremely influential amateur historian, told his readers that 'twenty-eight tribes' were 'completely wiped out' and that 'the loss of human life . . . has been roughly estimated at two millions', adding: 'Probably never in the history of the world has there been such an upheaval and such carnage caused by one man as took place during this enormous disturbance.'[19] Eric Walker, Professor of History at the University of Cape Town, drew upon Theal's 1891 map for his *Historical Atlas* (1922), and in the first edition of his *History of South Africa* (1928), wrote of the 'pandemonium' that 'raged' east and west of the Drakensberg in the 1820s and early 1830s.[20] Walker, who now introduced 'Mfecane', a word of Xhosa origin[21] – he added in a note: '= the crushing' – pointed out that those defeated at the battle of Dithakong were possibly not the

16. P. Mhlanga, 'A Story of Native Wars', *Cape Monthly Magazine*, New Series, 14, 84 (1877) 248–52; Moloja, of Jozani's Village, 'The Story of the "Fetcani Horde" by One of Themselves', *Cape Quarterly Review*, 1, 2 (1882), 267–75.
17. J.C. Chase, *The Cape of Good Hope and the Eastern Province of Algoa Bay*, London, 1843, 1. Cf. W. Lye, 'The Distribution of the Sotho Peoples after the Difaqane' in L.M. Thompson, ed., *African Societies in Southern Africa*, London, 1969, 192 and n.1. If Theal did use Theophilus Shepstone's 1875 paper on early Natal, 'The Early History of the Zulu-Kafir Race' reprinted in J. Bird, ed., *Annals of Natal*, vol.1, Pietermaritzburg, 1885, as suggested by J. Raum in 'Historical Concepts and the Evolutionary Interpretation of the Emergence of States: The Case of the Zulu Reconsidered Yet Again', *Zeitschrift für Ethnologie*, 114 (1989), 127 and n.2, one wonders why he did not repeat the story of Dingiswayo going to the Cape.
18. G. Theal, comp., *Records of the Cape Colony*, vol.22, London, 1904, 433.
19. G. Cory, *The Rise of South Africa*, vol.2, London, 1913, 231.
20. E.A. Walker, *A History of South Africa*, London, 1928, 210 n.2, 182–3. Though he does not use 'Mfecane' in his discussion on pp.182–3, it is clear that he viewed 'Mfecane' as a general term for this upheaval: cf. the sub-head on p.164. 'Fetcani' was much used in the 1820s and 1830s, and after, for refugees who entered the trans-Keian region: see e.g. Cory, *Rise of South Africa*, vol.2, 236.
21. Not Zulu, as claimed e.g. in D. Denoon and B. Nyeko, *Southern Africa since 1800*, London, 1984, 25.

Tlokwa of 'MaNthatisi, but Fokeng.[22] In the second edition of his *History* (1\
read 'The Bantu still call those the days of the Mfecane . . .',[23] while in the third
(1957) Walker expressed no doubt that it was the Fokeng who were defeated at
Dithakong, and he used 'Mfecane' more often, as in a new paragraph in which he
was, for the first time, openly sceptical of Theal's account. 'It is . . . easy', he wrote,
'to exaggerate the numbers of the slain and to forget that there was much
displacement . . . Theal estimated the number of dead at "nearer two millions than⇁
one" but gave no authority for the estimate.'[24] It had taken Walker almost three
decades to get that far in challenging Theal. This despite the fact that at the very time
Walker published the first edition of his *History*, his far more imaginative colleague
at the University of the Witwatersrand, William Macmillan, had discarded much of
the interpretation put forward by Theal.

Before turning to Macmillan, let us consider Cobbing's claim that what Walker
and later professional historians said about the Mfecane was integral to their view of
South African history. Like Theal, Walker showed himself interested enough in the
history of Africans to include a brief passage on 'the Mfecane' in a general history of
the country – more Eurocentric historians omitted the topic – but as with other
historians of his time, and many of his successors, he had little interest in precolonial
history, where the sources were so problematic and it was so difficult even to provide
a chronology. For Walker and other early liberal historians, the dominant theme of
South African history was the advancing frontier and the white racism that emerged
there and dominated the political life of the country after the frontier closed. The
Mfecane received relatively little attention in their work, and was hardly central to
it.

This is also true for later liberal historians. The first chapter of the most detailed
recent history of the country, the successor to Walker's *History*, begins with a
chapter which takes us 'From the Dawn of History to the Time of Troubles', but the
balanced interpretation of the Mfecane which T.R.H. Davenport offers there is
relatively brief and hardly integral to his vision of South African history as a whole.
The same applies to Leonard Thompson's interpretation – very different from
Walker's, as we shall see – in his shorter *History*.[25] In all these general histories, the
Mfecane receives relatively minor attention, and in the collection of essays on 'The
Shaping of South African Society' edited by two leading specialists on early South
African history, no significant reference is made to the Mfecane at all.[26]

22. Walker, *History of South Africa*, 182, n.1.
23. Walker, *History of South Africa*, 2nd ed., London, 1940, 18. Cobbing is, I think, wrong to suggest that
    Walker is here using Mfecane in a broader sense than he had in 1928, and therefore wrong to link a
    broader usage to the rise of Nazism in Europe: Cobbing 'The Case Against the Mfecane', 8–9.
24. Walker, *History of Southern Africa*, 3rd ed., London, 1957, 175–6.
25. Davenport, *South Africa: A Modern History*, 4th ed., Johannesburg, 1991, ch.1; L.M. Thompson, *A
    History of South Africa*, New Haven, 1990, 80–7.
26. R. Elphick and H.B. Giliomee, eds., *The Shaping of South African Society, 1652–1820*, Cape Town,
    1979. In reviews of both editions I was critical of the title of the book for this reason. In the second
    edition, *The Shaping of South African Society, 1652–1840*, Cape Town, 1989, J.B. Peires 'The British
    and the Cape', refers to the Mfecane as 'a series of wars set in motion by the Zulu king Shaka', 486.

Macmillan and De Kiewiet

Though Macmillan in his classic *Bantu, Boer, and Briton: The Making of the South African Native Problem* (1929) followed Theal in writing of 'the Chaka wars' and their effect 'even on tribes far away in the interior', he went on to anticipate, in outline, central features of Cobbing's argument in 'The Mfecane as Alibi'. For Macmillan the 'great upheaval among the Bantu' in the Natal/Zulu kingdom area and the interior was not unrelated to the process of colonisation. In fact, he linked it specifically to the slave trade, while at the same time making clear that the lack of source material posed a serious problem to any analysis of what had happened. Macmillan wrote as follows:

> How far this great upheaval among the Bantu must be attributed, in Bishop Stubbs' words, to the 'generally unsettled state of all tribes bordering' on European conquests,[27] can never be fully known. While from the nature of the case the effects of the frontier wars on the remoter tribes are not directly evident, the suggestion that there was a connexion is not wholly to be dismissed. It is significant that the rise of Chaka came at the very moment when things were moving towards a climax on the Cape frontier . . .
>
> Further, to meet the demands of European planters, slave-traders had not only raided on their own account for a hundred years past, but set tribe against tribe in such ruthless fashion that if the consequences were often bloody it is not for Europeans to cast a stone. There is no reason to believe that the slave trade left the southern part of Africa unaffected.[28]

Macmillan then cited various pieces of evidence in support of the idea that slave-raiding was important: that Lord Charles Somerset had in 1823 considered annexing Delagoa Bay as a check on the slave trade; that John Philip of the London Missionary Society had reported that the Tswana-speaking people in the interior feared the ravages of the slave trade; and that Mzilikazi was said to have met slave-raiders from Portuguese ports before he headed west, and that explains why he did not go north. Macmillan went on to quote Philip as saying both that Mzilikazi's people had to 'maintain an incessant struggle against the Portuguese slave-traders', and that 'To Farewell's establishment at Port Natal we are to trace the devastations of Chaka.'[29] Writing in the *Cambridge History of the British Empire* a few years later, Macmillan cited references in Theal's *Records of South East Africa* to Delagoa Bay being used by slavers, before adding: 'the effects of the slave trade upon the natives in what is now called Zululand have never been considered. Nor is it possible to gauge the

---

27. Macmillan referred to William Stubbs's *Select Charters and Other Illustrations of English Constitutional History from the Earliest Times to the Reign of Edward the First*, one of the setworks he had studied as an undergraduate at Oxford.
28. W.M. Macmillan, *Bantu, Boer, and Briton*, London, 1929, 19.
29. Macmillan, *Bantu, Boer, and Briton*, 18–20.

repercussions of the check administered on the Fish River to the coast tribes lying to the west of Chaka's sphere of action.'[30]

Macmillan's brilliant student C.W. de Kiewiet also rejected Theal's version of the Mfecane. Under Macmillan's guidance, De Kiewiet had written a thesis at the University of the Witwatersrand – no copy survives – on the Cape northern frontier in the period just after the Mfecane. When he came to write about the upheaval itself in the 1930s, first in a chapter in the *Cambridge History of the British Empire* and then in his *History of South Africa Social and Economic*, De Kiewiet, though aware that 'the causes of these events can never be adequately investigated', advanced an ecological interpretation. Conflict had occurred because of 'an intense competition amongst the tribes for sowing and grazing land'. There was 'much reason', he asserted, to think that what had been written about 'the devastation of the Zulu, Matabele and Mantati "hordes" was very greatly exaggerated'. What had happened in the 'confusion of the eighteen-twenties' was 'much displacement', after which people 'poured back into their lands'. And in his *History* he added: 'Amongst the causes of this singular crisis that smashed tribes, scattered others, and dashed the fragments into new combinations, the halting of the Bantu vanguard on the Eastern Frontier probably had much influence.'[31]

For John Philip in the 1830s, then, as for Macmillan and De Kiewiet a century later, the upheavals in Natal and the interior were by no means divorced from the process of colonisation. Only in a paragraph concerning the Ndebele in 'The Mfecane as Alibi' does Cobbing, in passing, acknowledge that Macmillan, 'slightly deviant here as in some other respects', linked the ejection of Mzilikazi to the slave trade and that 'this hypothesis is better than anything we have'.[32] Elsewhere in his article Cobbing suggests a line of interpretation running from Theal through Macmillan to Omer-Cooper and beyond. As these historians in fact advanced vastly different interpretations, we must ask why the suggestive insights which Macmillan and De Kiewiet made in the 1920s and 1930s were not followed up. The loss of the Philip papers in the fire at Wits in 1931, and Macmillan's departure from the country – De Kiewiet had already left – is part of the explanation. Macmillan and, to a lesser extent, De Kiewiet were regarded as radicals, and their work was marginalised within the country because it was viewed in ruling circles as politically dangerous. But there are also other reasons. The very few leading South African professional historians of the 1940s and 1950s believed precolonial history was appropriately the terrain of anthropology, and devoted their attention to more traditional themes for historians, such as the imperial connection and constitutional issues.[33] Such

30. W.M. Macmillan, 'The Frontier and the Kaffir Wars, 1792–1836', in A.P. Newton and E. Benians, eds, *The Cambridge History of the British Empire*, vol. 8, Cambridge, 1936, 301.
31. C.W. de Kiewiet, 'Social and Economic Developments in Native Tribal Life', in *Cambridge History*, vol. 8, 808–9; *A History of South Africa: Social and Economic*, Oxford, 1941, 50.
32. Cobbing, 'The Mfecane as Alibi', 489.
33. For elaboration see C. Saunders, *The Making of the South African Past*, Cape Town, 1988.

graduate students as there were in those decades were directed to similar topics. No one did significant work on the Mfecane.

What of Cobbing's claim that the idea of 'cataclysmic black-on-black destruction' was an 'alibi'? He speaks of historians attributing 'the land distribution of 1913 . . . to a black-on-black holocaust in the period 1815–35', and continues: 'Since the Second World war, the stress of the alibi has been on the natural "pluralism" of black societies and how they self-sequestered themselves into proto-Bantustans in the era of Shaka, leaving the whites merely the task of surveying and recognition.' The Mfecane was 'a characteristic product of liberal history used by the *apartheid* state to legitimate South Africa's racially unequal land division'.[34] This is a serious charge against the liberal historians.

Macmillan was in fact a leading critic of the unequal distribution of land, and of racial segregation in general. His first public statement on African affairs, made to a Dutch Reformed Church conference in 1923, started with a critique of the 1913 Land Act and its effects.[35] Macmillan was also firm in his rejection of any idea of a separate African history. De Kiewiet did not return to South Africa in large part because of his opposition to racial segregation, and Walker actively campaigned against Hertzog's franchise and land policies before he left the country in 1936. In their writings, Macmillan and De Kiewiet wrote much about the hardships brought by colonial penetration. Indeed, few since have written more eloquently than De Kiewiet about the consequences of conquest and dispossession.[36] While what the early liberals wrote had numerous shortcomings, and must be seen in the context of the time, their work did not defend segregation. And the liberal Africanists of the 1960s, whom we will now consider, were fundamentally opposed to the apartheid state and what it stood for.

Omer-Cooper and Others

In 'The Mfecane as Alibi' Cobbing fails to bring out the great change in attitude among historians that became evident about 1960 and flowed from the revolution in African historiography that occurred as the countries of tropical Africa moved to independence.[37] For those who identified with that 'Africanist revolution', the Mfecane was now reinterpreted as primarily constructive and creative. These writers wanted to show that Africans had acted with initiative, and positively. The destructive aspects of the Mfecane and European influences were both downplayed, though neither was ignored altogether. Omer-Cooper's eastern Cape roots, which Cobbing regards as significant to his view of the Mfecane,[38] were a much less important influence on his work than the fact that he taught at the University of

---

34. Cobbing, 'The Mfecane as Alibi', 518–9.
35. Cf. W.M. Macmillan, *My South African Years: An Autobiography*, Cape Town, 1975, 181.
36. Especially De Kiewiet, 'Social and Economic Developments'; cf. C. Saunders, *C.W. de Kiewiet: Historian of South Africa*, Cape Town, 1986.
37. In his earlier, unpublished papers, Cobbing did take note of this change. Cf. n. 2 above.
38. Cobbing, 'The Mfecane as Alibi', 487 n. 3.

Ibadan in Nigeria while he was writing his seminal book, *The Zulu Aftermath: A Nineteenth-century Revolution in Bantu Africa* (1966). It was at Ibadan that he was exposed to the new thinking on African history, which in the West African case argued convincingly that the European role had been grossly exaggerated in previous histories.

The Zulu Aftermath was a pioneering work of synthesis and interpretation which told the history of a 'socio-political revolution' beginning in South Africa and reaching to 'the southern shores of Lake Victoria'. Omer-Cooper saw this revolution as 'independent of European influence in origin', but though he wished to stress that the Mfecane was the result of internal rather than external forces, he did add that as it developed, it 'interlocked with expanding European activity affecting and being affected by it'.[39] His main theme was state building, with the movement of people over vast distances a secondary positive development. Besides the Zulu, the other states whose history he summarises were seen as reactive states, created in response to the raiding to which they were subject. In his relatively brief chapter on the Zulu kingdom, Omer-Cooper accepted the importance of Shaka, but also recognised that the process of change had begun before, and therefore independently of, Shaka. The argument for a lengthy process of change, which at least implicitly plays down the importance of the 1820s in the state-building process east of the Drakensberg, has a long pedigree.[40]

Omer-Cooper's general synthesis was soon followed by the completion of more detailed research, especially on the area west of the Drakensberg. This was because Leonard Thompson, who began teaching African history at the University of California, Los Angeles (UCLA), in the early 1960s, at a time when there was a great expansion in doctoral programmes in African studies, started to direct doctoral students to the topic. Thompson had decided to write a major biography of Moshoeshoe, and wished the highveld background explored. He himself wrote about the Mfecane, in similar vein to Omer-Cooper, in his chapters for the first volume of *The Oxford History of South Africa* (1969), and then in his Moshoeshoe book (1975).[41] The students of his who worked on aspects of the topic included William Lye, Martin Legassick and Alan Smith.

For Lye, a Mormon, the many migrations of the 1820s and 1830s, white and black, could be compared to the Morman trek, as Eric Walker had suggested in his history of the Great Trek.[42] Lye could build on some revisionist work done by non-historians

---

39. Omer-Cooper, *The Zulu Aftermath*, 2 and 7.
40. Cobbing does not provide evidence for his statement ('Jettisoning the Mfecane', 16) that 'the tea room at UCT' was important in the development of the overpopulation hypothesis; in discussions on this subject in the African Studies tea room there, Monica Wilson stressed the Delagoa Bay trade hypothesis. The case for a long process of change has been advanced recently for the Phongolo-Mzimkhulu region by John Wright and Carolyn Hamilton, 'Traditions and Transformations: The Phongolo–Mzimkhulu Region in the Late Eighteenth and Early Nineteenth Centuries', in A.H. Duminy and B. Guest, eds, *Natal and Zululand from Earliest Times to 1910: A New History*, Pietermaritzburg, 1989, ch.3.
41. L.M. Thompson, *Moshoeshoe of Lesotho 1786–1870*, Oxford, 1975.
42. E.A. Walker, *The Great Trek*, London, 1934, 7–8.

on one part of his topic: in his edition of the journals and letters of the London Missionary Society missionary Robert Moffat (1951),[43] the anthropologist Isaac Schapera had shown that 'MaNthatisi's Tlokwa had never been anywhere near Dithakong, and a fuller discussion followed from Marion How, who, like Cobbing later, found an alibi, though of a very different kind: hers was for the Tlokwa ruler 'MaNthatisi.[44] In a paper presented at the conference on 'African Societies in Southern Africa' which Thompson organised at the University of Zambia in 1968, Lye offered 'a corrective' to the view of massive social destruction on the highveld: in place of devastation and depopulation, he showed – this time through a detailed examination of the evidence – that there had only been displacement.[45] And in his thesis, Legassick pointed to the importance of Griqua raiding in the history of this period,[46] a theme Cobbing was to take up almost two decades later, with the new hypothesis that their raiding had been for slaves. In another dissertation completed at UCLA after Thompson left, R. Kent Rasmussen explored the history of the Ndebele state south of the Limpopo River, a central aspect of the Mfecane,[47] showing that the Ndebele had not been forced out of the trans-Vaal by the Zulu, but by Griqua and later Boer attacks, and in the process uncovering many errors in previous work, such as Lye's uncritical use of the account of Ndebele raids in Alfred Bryant's *Olden Times in Zululand and Natal* (1929).[48]

No work of comparable depth was completed in the 1960s or early 1970s on the Zulu in the Shakan period. Alan Smith investigated trade at Delagoa Bay, concluding that the slaves exported from there did not come from the south and were not significant in number before the 1820s.[49] Shula Marks wrote a short survey of 'The Rise of the Zulu Kingdom' and presented a critique of Bryant's work to the Lusaka conference, but did no further work on the topic.[50] Among her doctoral

43. Robert Moffat and Mary Moffat, *Apprenticeship at Kuruman: Being the Journals and Letters of Robert and Mary Moffat 1820–1828*, ed. by I. Schapera, London, 1951.
44. M. How, 'An Alibi for Mantatisi', *African Studies*, 13 (1954), 65–76; and see the discussion in W.F. Lye, 'The Difaqane: The Mfecane in the Southern Sotho Area, 1822–24', *Journal of African History*, 8 (1967), 109 and n.5.
45. Lye, 'The Distribution of the Sotho Peoples' and Thompson's summary of Lye's chapter in *African Societies*, 15.
46. M. Legassick, 'The Missionaries, the Griqua and the Sotho-Tswana: The Politics of a Frontier Zone', Ph.D. thesis, University of California, Los Angeles, 1969.
47. R.K. Rasmussen's thesis was published as *Migrant Kingdom: Mzilikazi's Ndebele in South Africa*, Cape Town, 1978. The history of the Ndebele north of the Limpopo was written by J. Cobbing, then in Zimbabwe, for a Lancaster University doctorate entitled 'The Ndebele under the Khumalos, 1820–1896', 1976. Thompson's post at the University of California, Los Angeles had gone to Terence Ranger, whose main interest was Zimbabwe history.
48. Rasmussen, *Migrant Kingdom*, esp. 202 and n.96. Cf. J. Wright, 'A.T. Bryant and "the Wars of Shaka"', *History in Africa*, 18 (1991), 409–25.
49. A. Smith, 'The Trade of Delagoa Bay as a Factor in Nguni Politics, 1750–1835', in L.M. Thompson, ed., *African Societies*. Smith's thesis, completed in 1970, was, like Lye's, never published.
50. S. Marks, 'The Rise of the Zulu Kingdom' in R. Oliver, ed., *The Middle Age of African History*, London, 1967; 'The Traditions of the Natal "Nguni"', in Thompson, ed., *African Societies in Southern Africa*. Marks was at the time completing what became *Reluctant Rebellion: The 1906–8 Disturbances in Natal*, Oxford, 1971, a history of the early twentieth-century Bambatha rebellion.

students at the University of London, Jeff Guy and Philip Bonner both moved in their work from the Mfecane period to later ones, and neither David Hedges's highly speculative thesis, completed in 1978, on 'Trade and Politics in Southern Mozambique and Zululand in the Eighteenth and Early Nineteenth Century', nor Henry Slater's at Sussex, tackled the overall concept of the Mfecane.[51]

Meanwhile, Floors van Jaarsveld, the eminent Afrikaner historian, and other apartheid-apologists writing in the 1970s drew upon the new liberal Africanist work by Omer-Cooper and Thompson in the *Oxford History* to suggest that the Mfecane had created a pattern of settlement which formed the basis for the Bantustans of grand apartheid policy. Such writers also now used the Mfecane to justify the white seizure of land.[52] Omer-Cooper and Thompson were appalled when they found their work so used by apartheid apologists, for *The Zulu Aftermath* and the *Oxford History* were written to begin the task of restoring Africans to history as active agents and not just victims, and so to help undermine apartheid.[53]

From the mid-1970s Africanist work began to flourish in South Africa, with workshops being held at the National University of Lesotho in July 1976 and August 1977, at the University of Natal, Pietermaritzburg in October 1977,[54] and at Rhodes University in mid-1979. But in none of this work, much of it heavily rooted in materialist theory, was there a general critique of the concept of Mfecane.[55] In his introduction to the published collection of papers presented at the Rhodes Nguni workshop, J.B. Peires began by saying that Omer-Cooper's *Zulu Aftermath* 'firmly established the Mfecane as a central event in the history of Africa, a revolutionary process of change spreading from a single centre'. He went on to say that the

51. The theses by Guy and Bonner were published as J.J. Guy, *The Destruction of the Zulu Kingdom: The Civil War in Zululand, 1879–1884*, London, 1979; and P. Bonner, *Kings, Commoners and Concessionaires: The Evolution and Dissolution of the Nineteenth-Century Swazi State*, Cambridge, 1983. D. Hedges, 'Trade and Politics in Southern Mozambique and Zululand in the Eighteenth and Early Nineteenth Centuries', Ph.D. thesis, University of London, 1978; and H. Slater, 'Transitions in the Political Economy of South-East Africa Before 1840', D.Phil. thesis, University of Sussex, 1976, were not published.

52. Cf. e.g. F. van Jaarsveld, *Van Van Riebeeck tot Vorster*, Johannesburg, 1975. Such ideas were taken up and further elaborated in such publications as the official *South Africa 1977*, which M. Cornevin criticised in *Apartheid, Power and Historical Falsification*, Paris, 1980, and in school textbooks.

53. Thompson's response appeared eventually in *The Political Mythology of Apartheid*, New Haven, 1985; Omer-Cooper's, in a paper presented to the Australian African Studies Association in 1981, was never published.

54. E.g. J.J. Guy, 'Production and Exchange in the Zulu Kingdom', *Mohlomi*, 2 (1978), 96–106 (and in J.B. Peires, ed., *Before and After Shaka: Papers in Nguni History*. Grahamstown, 1981); 'Ecological Factors in the Rise of Shaka and the Zulu Kingdom', in S. Marks and A. Atmore, eds, *Economy and Society in Pre-Industrial South Africa*, London, 1980; J.B. Wright, 'Pre-Shakan Age-Group Formation among the Northern Nguni', *Natalia* 8 (1978) 23–9. Cf. a paper which has appeared since this essay was written: J. Peires, 'Paradigm Deleted: The Materialist Interpretation of the Mfecane', *Journal of Southern African Studies*, 19, 2 (1993), 295–313.

55. James O. Gump's doctoral thesis at the University of Nebraska on 'Revitalisation through Expansion in South Africa *c.*1750–1840: A Reappraisal of the "Open" Mfecane', 1980, was centrally on the Mfecane. Its first chapter offered a critique of the materialism of, for example, John Wright's article on 'Pre-Shakan Age-Group Formation', and instead proposed a cultural explanation, suggesting parallels between Shaka and Hiawatha.

Mfecane had, as a result of recent work, to be seen 'as a social and economic revolution rather than as a military upheaval', but he did not question the idea of the Mfecane.[56] Nor did Cobbing at that time; his contribution to the Nguni workshop volume accepted that Mzilikazi 'was one of the greatest figures thrown up by the *mfecane*'.[57]

In 'The Mfecane as Alibi', Cobbing said that the earliest criticism of the Mfecane he had traced was that in Marianne Cornevin's *Apartheid, Power and Historical Falsification* (1980).[58] Her discussion of the topic in that book on apartheid historical myths was brief and not entirely accurate;[59] many South African historians probably shared Peires's view that she had said nothing new.[60] The first general and detailed critique of the prevailing view of the Mfecane came in fact from the pen of Hosea Jaffe, amateur historian and Unity Movement activist. In *Three Hundred Years: A History of South Africa*, published as early as 1952, he had very briefly introduced the idea of a colonial vice to explain what happened to African societies in the early nineteenth century, referring to 'the southward influence of the Portuguese and the northward influence of the British', and relating the Portuguese role to the Delagoa Bay slave trade.[61] In the early 1980s Jaffe prepared a *History of Africa* in which he wrote of 'a legend of a "Mfiqane" or "destruction of the people" by Tshaka's Zulus, to cover up the colonial Mfiqane . . . of Boers, British and Portuguese between whom the Zulus were trapped'.[62] Not knowing that in Grahamstown Cobbing was beginning to elaborate his own critique of the Mfecane, Jaffe, who was based in London and Italy, sent to the Cape Town-based *Educational Journal* an article entitled 'The Difaqane: Fact vs Fiction' specifically challenging what historians, especially Thompson in *The Oxford History*, had written about the Mfecane. In this article, published in September 1983 under the pseudonym V. E. Satir, an anagram of 'Veritas',[63] Jaffe discussed the process of colonial dispossession, and concluded as follows:

> the Liberal-manufactured accounts in their histories would have us believe that the Mfecane took place in a vacuum; that the sole agency for these events, the only actor on the stage, was the Zulu Tshaka, who chased the tribes into the

56. Peires, *Before and After Shaka*, 1 and back cover.
57. J. Cobbing, 'The Ndebele State', in Peires, *Before and After Shaka*, 160.
58. Cobbing, 'The Mfecane as Alibi', 487, n. 5.
59. E.g. she lumped together Cory, Walker and Macmillan, and said that all Theal's works are characterised by a profound contempt for blacks: Cornevin, *Apartheid, Power and Historical Falsification*, 103.
60. See his review in *Social Dynamics*, 6 (1980), 89–90.
61. 'Mnguni' [H. Jaffe], *Three Hundred Years. A History of South Africa*, Cape Town, 1952, 90–1. While Jaffe stressed colonial dispossession above black self-destruction, his colleague Dora Taylor [N. Majeke] wrote of the 'chaos of tribal warfare', *The Role of the Missionaries in Conquest*, Johannesburg, 1952.
62. H. Jaffe, *A History of Africa*, London, 1985, 67, n. 36.
63. H. Jaffe to C. Saunders, 9 October 1991; interview with H. Jaffe, Cape Town, 16 January 1992.

wilderness. The Boers, the British colonists and the Portuguese were innocent, disinterested onlookers, playing no part at all.

The myth of the Mfecane or Difaqane was fabricated by the Boers and the British to disguise and justify their land-robbery and to whitewash their own genocidal Mfecane . . . [their] crushing of peoples by slave-running . . . [and] chasing out of the peoples whose land they wanted to grab.[64]

Some months before the appearance of Jaffe's article Cobbing presented his first version of his critique – 'The Case Against the Mfecane' – at a seminar at the University of Cape Town.

Conclusion

Until relatively recently, historians who wrote about the Mfecane either merely repeated what others had said or offered speculations without having done detailed research. Though, as we have seen, all historians by no means presented the same views, they were too ready to link an explanation for the process they described to the Zulu, and Shaka in particular. When detailed work was undertaken, from the 1960s, it was narrowly focused; Jaffe and Cobbing were the first, in 1983, to begin to present detailed critiques, in which the 'Mfecane' was both disaggregated and presented as a myth, distracting attention from the main cause of the upheaval, slaving and colonialism.

Fundamental problems relating to the evidence for this interpretation remain. On many aspects it is unlikely that we shall ever be able to say for certain what happened. We can see now that Rasmussen went too far when he asserted that there are 'simply not sufficient data to support intelligent discussion of most issues'.[65] But what Macmillan wrote with reference to this topic is still relevant: 'History, for want of serious and sufficient documentary evidence, must walk warily.'[66] His caution will have to be borne in mind by anyone bold enough to attempt the 'new and integrated conceptual framework for analysis of the period' which Wright and Hamilton have recently called for.[67] Any such framework will have to rest on detailed, careful checking of the available evidence, the kind of analysis which Cobbing himself employed when in the 1970s he subjected the arguments in Terence Ranger's *Revolt in South Rhodesia* to criticism.[68]

---

64. V. E. Satir [H. Jaffe], 'The Difaqane: Fact vs Fiction', *The Education Journal* (September 1983), 10.
65. Rasmussen, *Migrant Kingdom*, 3; W. F. Lye, 'The Difaqane: The Sotho Wars in the Interior of South Africa, 1822–1837', Ph.D. thesis, University of California, Los Angeles, 1969; 'The Ndebele Kingdom South of the Limpopo River', *Journal of African History*, 10 (1969), 87–104.
66. Macmillan, 'The Frontier and the Kaffir Wars', 301.
67. Wright and Hamilton, 'Traditions and Transformations', 69.
68. J. Cobbing, 'The Absent Priesthood: Another Look at the Rhodesian Risings of 1896–1897', *Journal of African History*, 18 (1977), 61–84. I thank Nigel Penn for this point.

Cobbing's presentation of his case against the Mfecane since 1983 has not only been marred by inaccurate references to the historiography – as shown above – but also by overstatements, exaggerated claims and a selective use of evidence, examples of which are cited elsewhere in this book. Nevertheless, his achievement remains: to have challenged old ideas, destroyed the concept of an upheaval that was solely Zulu-inspired, and generally to have stimulated new interest in, and research on, central themes in early nineteenth-century South African history.

Acknowledgement

I wish to thank Pam Scully for her comments on a draft of this paper.

2

Old Wine in New Bottles
The Persistence of Narrative Structures in the Historiography of the Mfecane and the Great Trek

NORMAN ETHERINGTON

If Julian Cobbing is right in his contention that the root causes of the mfecane lie not in the Zulu kingdom but in disruptive forces emanating from Mozambique and the Cape, then rethinking the mfecane means rethinking the Great Trek. One of the oddest circumstances in historical writing about South Africa is that those contemporaneous phenomena, each of which has been called 'the central event in South African history', have been treated as isolated occurrences. According to the dictates of a peculiar historiographical apartheid, the only recognised linkage is the supposition that the mfecane cleared the highveld of people at the very moment the Voortrekkers decided to go and live there. This essay offers some revisionist propositions about the 1830s developed from a bird's-eye view of the historio-graphical landscape. The word 'revision' is used in its original sense. No new archival research findings which change our picture of the past are reported here. Instead, some familiar and obvious sources are re-examined with a view to changing standard versions of history. In particular, an attempt is made to explain the remarkable persistence of certain narrative structures in accounts of the Great Trek and mfecane written by historians working in different periods and informed by dramatically different ideologies.

When Cobbing finds the same story repeated in different eras, he suspects historians of complicity in a lie which serves the interests of dominant groups in South African society.[1] Such explanations, whether cast in terms of interest group theory or structuralist theory, have much to be said for them but are less than totally satisfying because they have flourished not just at home but also abroad. Why should foreign scholarship dance to the favourite tunes of South African politicians, miners and farmers? What could move John Omer-Cooper in Nigeria or Kent Rasmussen in California to serve among the legions of 'settler history'?[2] Are there not other possible reasons for the persistence of certain story-lines?

1. J. Cobbing, 'The Mfecane as Alibi: Thoughts on Dithakong and Mbolompo', *Journal of African History*, 29 (1988), 487–519.
2. J. Omer-Cooper, *The Zulu Aftermath: A Nineteenth-century Revolution in Bantu Africa*, London, 1966; R.K. Rasmussen, *Migrant Kingdom: Mzilikazi's Ndebele in South Africa*, London, 1978.

Narrative Structures that have Shaped the Trek and the Mfecane

In many ways the Great Trek and mfecane are twins beneath the skin. Each was retrospectively discovered by nationalists and historians. (Decades passed before the 'movement of the emigrant farmers' was inscribed as the Great Trek; the word mfecane first appears in history books in the twentieth century.) Each has been touted as the 'central event' or 'centrepiece' of the history of a people.[3] Each, indeed, has been held to express the peculiar genius of a people. Each has been characterised as a movement of people out of touch and out of tune with the surging tides of nineteenth-century capitalist development. With a few exceptions, historians have accepted each as a unique event in human history.[4]

Both the Zulu kingdom and the Trekker republics are conventionally treated as states which desired more than anything else to be left alone once they had achieved their initial objectives. The similarities do not end there. Each phenomenon has been reified in both academic and non-academic publications. Their historicity is no more doubted than that of the Hebrew Exodus or the French Revolution. Although only a tiny number of historians have tackled either movement as a whole, swarms of industrious researchers have beavered away within the paradigms specifying precisely who was who, who did what, where and how.

Rising above the detailed unfolding of events, it is possible to discern three different templates governing narrative structure in standard accounts of the Trek and mfecane:

> The onward march of civilisation;
>
> The growth of a nation;
>
> The advance of the capitalist mode of production.

Naturally, the content of these narrative structures differs according to local circumstances. Here are some examples.

The March of Civilisation

The Trek as the march of civilisation (or, in the words of Albert Grundlingh, 'resilient Afrikanerdom marching inexorably to its predetermined destination as the legitimate rulers over non-Afrikaners in South Africa'[5]) is pictured, not just in the works of historians such as J. A. Wiid, A. J. H. van der Walt and D. W. Kruger, but in the very bricks and stones of the Voortrekker Monument.[6]

---

3. J. B. Peires, ed., *Before and After Shaka: Papers in Nguni History*, Grahamstown, 1981, 1; E. A. Walker, *The Great Trek*, London, 1938, 2nd ed., ix.
4. C. W. de Kiewiet is the most notable exception.
5. A. M. Grundlingh, 'Politics, Principles and Problems of a Profession: Afrikaner Historians and their Discipline, *c.* 1920–1965', *Perspectives in Education*, 12 (1990), 1–19.
6. See K. Smith's discussion in *The Changing Past: Trends in South African Historical Writing*, Athens, Ohio, 1988, 73. See also A. Grundlingh on the influence of H. B. Thom on Stellenbosch, in 'Politics, Principles and Problems'

The official guide still in use today explains:

> [At the gate] assegaais [*sic*] represent the power of Dingane, who sought to
> block the path of civilisation . . . [The statue of mother and child] symbolises
> the civilisation and Christianity that were maintained and developed by the
> women during the Great Trek. Black wildebeest: symbolise Dingane's
> warriors, but also the barbarism that yielded to civilisation. Triangular
> Cornice: Around the top of the Monument is a cornice in a zig-zag pattern. This
> symbolises fertility. The civilisation brought by the Voortrekkers must grow
> . . . The floor of the Hall of Heroes is lined with ever-widening rings of
> marble . . . which represents ripples after a stone has been cast into the water,
> become progressively wider until it [*sic*] fills the entire building. It symbolises
> the diffusion of the spirit of sacrifice that was generated by the Voortrekkers,
> and that eventually spread throughout the entire country . . . Flame: sym-
> bolises the flame of civilisation in South Africa.[7]

The theme is continued on the panels of the historical frieze that lines the interior.
The Voortrekkers, immaculately groomed and dressed, leave the Cape colony with
herds and fancy bibles. The land they enter is anything but empty. To possess it they
must go into battle (the men wearing coats and ties, the women, their best frocks)
against countless savage and deceitful enemies.

The classic stories of the Trek written in English propagate a very different
version of the march of civilisation. According to their accounts, the torch of
enlightenment carried ashore by Van Riebeeck glowed but dimly in the camps of
rude frontiersmen. Out on the veld the volk lost touch with progress, took on the
colours of their wild environment and passed on from generation to generation the
stunted mentality of Calvinist slaveholders. When British rule stoked up the bonfires
of civilisation the trekboers shrank back from the unaccustomed light. With their
flocks, bibles ands bondsmen they fled to the wilderness.

Beatrice Webb had this version of history in mind when, in 1899, she called the
South African War a clash between the nineteenth century and a 'remnant of
seventeenth-century puritanism'.[8] So did Edgar Brookes 60 years later when he
called the Great Trek a reaction 'of the eighteenth century against the nineteenth'.[9]

More than a hint of patronising hauteur creeps into most of the accounts. It
resembles in many particulars nineteenth-century stereotypes of the Irish.
W.M. Macmillan was not immune:

> Under these easy-going and yet arduous conditions, Dutch and Huguenots . . .
> were welded into South Africans with a predominantly Calvinistic religious
> tradition, and, for the rest, a love of sun and open spaces, hardy self-reliance,
> consummate skill in handling a gun, . . . love of independence [which] tended

7. D. Heymans, *The Voortrekker Monument*, Pretoria, 1986.
8. B. Webb, writing in *Fabian News*, (10 October 1899), 188.
9. E. Brookes, *Apartheid: A Documentary Study of Modern South Africa*, London, 1968, xx.

to harden not only into an impatience of Government control, but into an incapacity for co-operation even with his own fellows.[10]

Macmillan's student, C. W. de Kiewiet, because he painted with a broader brush, conveyed an even stronger picture of a white tribe in Africa competing with black farmers for the same ecological niche in the environment.[11]

The opening pages of Eric Walker's *The Great Trek* read more like anthropology than history. The frontier farmers of the 'thirties were necessarily limited and ignorant of many things. It could not have been otherwise . . . Their knowledge of the older parts of their Colony was apt to be sketchy and, in times of excitement, highly erroneous, while their conception of the outer world was sometimes 100 years out of date . . . Perhaps imagination was deadened by the sameness of the Karoo scenery . . . That attitude pointed to a *hereditary* preoccupation with concrete, matter of fact, personal things and with not much else.'[12]

It comes as no surprise to the reader to discover later that the root cause of the Trek was 'the steady advance of the forces of regular government' which made life more difficult for 'a stubborn folk who found it far more difficult than it had been to escape from unfamiliar influences by edging away a little farther into the wilds'.[13]

Oliver Ransford's 1972 version of *The Great Trek* is more extreme. By the end of the eighteenth century, he asserts, 'a new breed of men had evolved in South Africa – the trekboers. No people quite like them had ever existed before'.[14]

The state-imposed task of demarcating recognized plots of 6 000 acres is transmuted by Ransford into an animalistic marking of territory:

> Their farms usually approximated to the conveniently-managed size (for Africa) of 6 000 acres, and they generally marked out this area in a rough and ready manner by trotting a horse from the wagon along all four points of the compass for half an hour.[15]

Ransford explains Afrikaner behaviour partly by genes – 'Trekking was in the blood of these land Vikings' – and partly by the environment – ' these new comers had become as much a part of Africa as its indigenous people *and as the Bantu*'.[16] These folk, operating not by reason, but by 'instinct', eventually 'reached the happy

10. W. M. Macmillan, *Bantu, Boer and Briton: The Making of the South African Native Problem*, London, 1929, 25.
11. C. W. de Kiewiet, *A History of South Africa: Social and Economic*, London, 1941, 58: 'In one sense the Great Trek was the eighteenth century fleeing before its more material, more active, and better organized successor'.
12. E. A. Walker, *The Great Trek*, London, 1934, 48–9 (my italics).
13. Walker, *The Great Trek*, 67; Walker's invocation of 'the forces of regular government' is quite close to Jeff Peires's much more recent emphasis on 'the revolution in government' which British rule brought to the Cape. See Peires 'The British and the Cape' in R. Elphick and H. B. Giliomee, eds, *The Shaping of South African Society, 1652–1840*, Cape Town, 1989.
14. O. Ransford, *The Great Trek*, London, 1974, 13.
15. Ransford, *The Great Trek*, 16.
16. Ransford, *The Great Trek*, 16, 17, (my italics).

state of living in balance with nature'.[17] 'Life for them had taken on a special rhythm of its own.'[18] Horse, man, and gun fused into a latter-day centaur:

> The men depended on a single weapon the flintlock . . . and a singular style of fighting, charging their perfectly trained horses right up to an enemy group, firing from them without dismounting, retiring to reload, and then returning to repeat the attack. These tactical movements came to them *almost naturally* . . .[19]

The last act in the Anglo version of the march of civilisation is, of course, what Martin Legassick called the frontier tradition in South African history. By a series of flukes – the first Anglo-Boer War, the discovery of gold in the wrong place and Lord Milner's 'magnanimous' peace – the anachronistic ethos of the trekboer and Voortrekker is enshrined in the constitution of the Union, thus delaying for decades the inevitable triumph of modernity.

The Growth of a Nation

Afrikaner nationalists have shown a surprising tolerance for this patronising, virtually racist history. The revisionist enterprise of André du Toit and Hermann Giliomee has made only sluggish headway against the prevailing mythologies.[20]

The Voortrekker Monument's alternative version enjoys much less visible public support. Why should this be so, when so much ill-concealed ethnic denigration lurks in the Anglo alternative? The answer may lie in the conventions which govern narratives of nationalism. The nation is conceived as the happy, innocent child of the land who is denied his patrimony by sinister forces which must be overcome before the adult can come into his rightful inheritance. An essentialist premise underlying the master narrative is that the nation is a fact of nature on its own soil. This has always been easier to establish in Europe, where the mists of time conveniently obscure historical vision, than in settler colonies whose migratory origins are fulsomely documented.

The myth of the trekboer as child of the South African wilderness overcomes the problem far more elegantly than its counterparts in other settler societies.[21] It

17. Ransford, *The Great Trek*, 18, 19.
18. Ransford, *The Great Trek*, 20.
19. Ransford, *The Great Trek*, 21, (my italics).
20. A. du Toit, 'No Chosen People: The Myth of the Calvinist Origins of Afrikaner Nationalism and Racial Ideology', *American Historical Review*, 88 (1983), 920–52; A. du Toit and H. B. Giliomee, *Afrikaner Political Thought: Analysis and Documents*, 2 vols, Berkeley, 1983. See also Smith, *The Changing Past*, 96–8.
21. Similar problems were faced and solved by equally suspect devices. The *Quebecois* are mythologized as woodsmen in a fashion similar to the Afrikaners. Alternative methods naturalised the *pieds noirs* settlers of Algeria and the Australian colonists. Daniel Boorstin and others have pointed to the way in which a fictive 'true American', supposedly in existence by the time of the Revolution, challenged later 'unnatural' European migrants in the nineteenth and twentieth centuries. I would also like to emphasise that I accept that people who make homes for themselves on and beyond the frontier had to adapt to local realities. In one sense the trekboers were indeed 'Africanized'. The point I am making is that nationalist narratives ascribe a single set of characteristics to the founding sons of the soil which are then attributed to their 'descendants'.

substitutes a shroud of distance for the European shroud of time and answers the challenge of black African nationalism with a white nationalism which claims to be equally African. It lays the foundation for subsequent acts in the drama:

- Persecution by British invaders leading to loss of patrimony and withdrawal into the wilderness (the Great Trek);
- Struggle to reclaim the patrimony marked by incredible suffering (concentration camps in the South African War);
- Triumph of the mature nation (1948 election and proclamation of the Republic).

The only formidable problem remaining for the nationalist historian was to make these key experiences the common property of all who were defined as part of the nation.[22] Since an overwhelming majority of Afrikaans-speaking people did not go on the Trek and many of them put their 'hends op' at the time of Anglo-Boer conflict, this was by no means an easy task.[23] It could only be done, as Albert Grundlingh and Hilary Sapire observe – borrowing a phrase from Benedict Anderson – through the construction of an 'imagined community'.[24]

I do not intend to add to what is already a substantial literature on how the Trek was mythologised, promoted and internalised by twentieth-century Afrikaners. I merely note that the nationalist historiography needed a particular kind of Great Trek and was not interested in exploring alternative versions. The racial slur barely concealed in Anglo versions of the Trek could be forgiven because the idea of a stubborn folk, rooted in the land and unamenable to reform, had an evident political utility.

Advance of the Capitalist Mode of Production

It is worth remarking that the great historiographical revisions of the last two decades, which have demystified and deracialised large chunks of previously standard historiography, have left the Great Trek and mfecane largely untouched. Why? One reason may be that, after the paradigms were set, the dense accumulation of empirical scholarship discouraged newcomers from entering the fray. Every possible piece of evidence appeared already to have been subjected to the most intense scrutiny possible. In addition, some scholars seem to have made a deliberate point of ignoring or downplaying the Trek, implying by their neglect that the really significant forces which shaped modern South Africa are to be found elsewhere.[25]

22. Peter Novick, in the unpublished paper 'Why Dan Quayle was Right', presented to the Humanities Research Centre of the Australian National University, July 1991, has traced the way American Jews managed to assimilate the experience of the holocaust even though their nation had fought against Hitler.
23. On the Afrikaner collaborators see A.M. Grundlingh, *Die 'Hensoppers' en 'Joiners': Die Rasionaal en Verskynsel van Verraad*, Cape Town and Pretoria, 1979.
24. A.M. Grundlingh and H. Sapire, 'From Feverish Festival to Repetitive Ritual? The Changing Fortunes of Great Trek Mythology in an Industrializing South Africa, 1938–1988', *South African Historical Journal*, 21 (1989), 19–37.
25. As an example, Dan O'Meara managed to write *Volkskapitalisme*, a book with the subtitle, *Class, Capital and Ideology in the Development of Afrikaner Nationalism, 1934–1948*, Johannesburg, 1983, with only a couple of small references to the Great Trek (see 71, 76). In John Pampallis's *Foundations of the New South Africa*, London, 1991, the Great Trek gets two sentences on page 38.

It is ironic that Martin Legassick, whose doctoral thesis shed so much new light on the far interior of early nineteenth-century South Africa, announced soon after receiving his degree that it was pointless to look further for the origins of twentieth-century segregation on the frontier.[26]

Those who heeded his message pulled up their stakes and retreated to the developed regions of the Cape. Those who stayed in the field long enough to contribute to the important collections published in the late 1970s (in Britain by Marks and Atmore, in America by Elphick and Giliomee) did not much disturb established versions of the mfecane or the Great Trek. While David Hedges's new work on trade into the area that became Zululand remained unpublished, Jeff Guy dominated the study of the precolonial Zulu kingdom. Working within the paradigm of a Zulucentric mfecane, he maintained that the kingdom showed remarkable resistance to the penetration of capitalism right up to the time of the Anglo-Zulu War.

Revisionist scholarship concerned with the Cape frontier (which also accepted the Zulucentric mfecane) did not revise liberal and conservative explanations of the Trek; it restated them in new language. Although not every revisionist who touched on the Trek wrote from the theoretical perspective of neo-Marxist scholarship, almost everyone accepted a new working vocabulary focused on relations of production. The result was that the old Anglo version of the Great Trek as a flight from the advancing forces of civilisation was not discarded. It was just dressed up in the latest language. Without too much thought about what it might mean to exclude the Voortrekkers from the realm of capitalist production, they were consigned to a vague precapitalist limbo.

Thus Jeff Peires could assert in the 1989 revised version of *The Shaping of South African Society*, that 'the central causes of this emigration are commonly agreed on by most historians'. In Peires's restatement, the advancing forces of 'a fully capitalist free market' brought a 'revolution in government' to the Cape after the British annexation. 'The territories north of the Orange and the Vaal Rivers were settled by Cape Afrikaners determined to perpetuate their threatened precapitalist social order.' The British, he writes, brought with them the new conception, 'foreign to both African and Afrikaner farmers, that land was a commodity that could be acquired and sold without ever necessarily being possessed and worked first'.[27]

Giliomee, rejecting S.D. Neumark's unique attempt of the 1950s to link trekboer expansion to the growth of commodity production, sees Afrikaner frontier rebels as 'poor, landless and desperate colonists' who could not reach the accommodation

---

26. M. Legassick, 'The Frontier Tradition in South African Historiography', *Collected Seminar Papers on the Societies of Southern Africa in the 19th and 20th Centuries*, 2, London, Institute of Commonwealth Studies, 1971, 1–33. In 1985 John D. Omer-Cooper protested against the abandonment of frontier studies as aids to the understanding of twentieth-century segregation in 'The South African Frontier Revisited', paper presented at a conference of the African Studies Association of Australasia and the Pacific, Melbourne, 1985.
27. Peires, 'The British and the Cape', esp. 472, 480, 499, 511.

with British rule achieved by 'wealthier farmers [who] had come to agree that their interests lay in supporting the government'.[28]

Elphick and Giliomee, summing up what they see to be the dominant view of frontier history among historians at the end of the 1980s, declare that:

> In the mid-1830s emigrant Afrikaner farmers, the Voortrekkers, left the eastern regions of the Cape Colony to plant new societies in the interior of southern Africa. In large part they wished to restore the traditional social order of the Cape as they knew it . . . Their successful secession . . . greatly expanded the area of extensive, low-capitalized agriculture . . . [Their] conviction and social realities formed the fateful legacy of the preindustrial Cape to the modern people of South Africa.[29]

Thus, what the old version of the march of civilisation depicted as a flight of 'seventeenth-century' or 'eighteenth-century' trekboers from the advancing forces of nineteenth-century progress becomes a flight of 'precapitalist' and/or 'pre-industrial' producers from the onrush of a more mature capitalist mode of production. While the denigrating anthropological stereotype of the trekboer is dumped, the underlying narrative structure survives intact in the transition from liberal-humanist to Marxist discourse.

Applying Cobbing's Revisionist Thinking to the Great Trek

All three of the narrative structures I have identified in standard views of the Great Trek are also evident in classic accounts of the mfecane.

> *The advance of civilisation, again cast in two versions*
> One version pictures barbarous, virtually self-exterminating peoples pushed on by Zulu *izimpi* into clearing a place for expanding settlers. The other sees the genius of black invention and statecraft working in isolation to open another dynamic chapter in the constantly changing pageant of African history.

> *Growth of nations, cast in a form practically identical to the Afrikaner version.*
> A new nation springs up in secluded valleys north of the Thukela, grows to manhood in the wars of Shaka and Dingane, suffers under the oppression of High Commissioner Bartle Frere and Natal colonists, and struggles towards a rebirth of freedom in a time yet to come. Similar narratives are, with appropriate variations, applied to the new states raised up in the turbulence that followed the rise of the Zulu.

28. 'The Eastern Frontier, 1770–1812' in Elphick and Giliomee, eds, *The Shaping of South African Society*, 450. S.D. Neumark's ideas appear in *Economic Influences on the South African Frontier,* Stanford, 1957.
29. Concluding paragraph of Elphick and Giliomee, eds, *The Shaping of South African Society*, 560–1.

Advance of the capitalist mode of production
The self-sufficient, pre-capitalist political economies of the Zulu state and its Nguni-speaking offshoots seek to resist incorporation into the capitalist system of production but eventually succumb to (or are 'articulated' into) that system as mining and capitalist agriculture demand the 'freeing' of their labour.

The revisionist enterprise begun by Cobbing, and lately joined by John Wright, identifies the same fatal flaw in all three master narratives: the wrong assumption that the Zulu state arose in isolation. Cobbing and Wright hypothesise the previous penetration of both the highveld and the Natal/Zulu kingdom area by trading and raiding enterprises linked to disturbing economic activity at the Cape and Mozambique, which were in turn linked to the developing world economy. This denies neither the dynamism nor the originality of Zulu or other state-builders, but it does reject the idea of primordial nations developing purely in response to their local environments. Neither is there a denial of the importance of relations of production, only a denial that the enterprises of individuals, groups and states were determined in the final instance by the predominant *local* mode of production. There are also, from at least as early as the second half of the eighteenth century, dynamic, disturbing forces emanating from nearby colonies.

Cobbing and Wright, who see 'mfecane theory' functioning in the interests of definable economic and political interests in the modern South African state, are perfectly aware that their own project reverberates with significance for contemporary political struggles. It challenges long-standing concepts of land rights and the legitimacy of all sorts of claims about the origins and meaning of various ethnic nationalisms. In particular, they notice how Omer-Cooper's formulation of the mfecane was spectacularly misused by F.A. van Jaarsveld in 1971 in an attempt to show that land distribution in contemporary South Africa was historically generated by the black devastations of the early nineteenth century.[30] In a single amazing map Van Jaarsveld manages to link imaginary Bantu-speaking migrations from Central Africa in the eighteenth century to both the Great Trek and the Bantustans of the 1960s.

Applying to the Great Trek the kind of thinking Cobbing used to attack the mfecane also has contemporary implications, though of a different sort. Ken Smith has called attention to the way in which the Afrikaner nationalist interpretation of history began to decline from the very moment of its supreme triumph in 1961.[31] Faced with the growing force of black nationalism at home and anti-apartheid movements abroad, National Party governments sought support from voters of British descent. The anti-British elements in the saga of national achievement were muted. The fiasco of the sesquicentennial celebrations, described by Grundlingh and

30. F.A. van Jaarsveld, *Van Van Riebeeck tot Verwoerd, 1652–1966*, Johannesburg, 1971, 114–5. A similar use of the mfecane is made by C.F.J. Muller in *Die Oorsprong van die Groot Trek*, Cape Town, 1974, in which the mfecane becomes one more factor disturbing the 'security' of white frontier farmers on the Cape eastern frontier: see especially 94–104.
31. Smith, *The Changing Past*, 90–2.

Sapire, demonstrated that meaning is fast ebbing from the Great Trek. When I visited the Blood River monument in mid-February 1993, my name became the 62nd on the register for the month. Except for the woman serving tea I had the battlefield to myself. Plummeting enrolments in the history departments of the Afrikaans-medium universities suggest that a whole generation is fleeing the past.

One of the most interesting passages in E.H. Carr's eternally youthful *What is History?* is his analysis of the process by which a 'fact about the past' becomes an 'historical fact'. His illustration of the gingerbread vendor kicked to death by an angry mob in 1850 is meant to show that what one historian seizes upon as a 'fact' of great significance becomes an 'historical fact' only when other professionals accept the claim and write it into their own books.[32]

Because Carr, for all his relativism, believed in the project of cumulative historical knowledge, he did not contemplate the possibility that an historical fact might slip back into the primeval ooze of facts about the past. Something of the sort had been foreseen by F.F.J. Muller when he predicted in 1963 that if white South Africa disappeared as a political factor 'the Great Trek would be seen as merely a brief era of white imperialism that moved up from the Cape as far as the Limpopo or Zambezi Rivers'.[33]

The remainder of this essay speculates on what the meaning of the Trek may be for historians if we forsake old narratives and reshape the Great Trek to mesh with the new understanding Cobbing and Wright have brought to the mfecane.

Cobbing, like many other historians writing in the last decade, abandons the idea that analysis of a particular economy should be keyed completely to the locally dominant mode of production.[34] By cutting loose from the notion that the starting point for the study of any society is a scrutiny of the predominant internal forces and relations of production, he can see a variety of factors at work. It seems to me unnecessary to ask whether slaving or trade was *the* external force that provoked the ingenious creation of the Zulu state. Trading and slaving, hunting, climatic change and labour-raiding can all be incorporated into a larger picture of defensive reactions and novel opportunities stirring the African people of the southern African interior toward the end of the eighteenth century.

Applying a similar breadth of vision to the Trek requires in the first instance little more than picking up where Legassick left off in 1970, on a frontier where a range of economic activities overlapped, and where no clear delineation of a person's role in production could be made on the basis of colour alone. The change in perspective which is needed can be illustrated quite simply by considering two of the maps that appear in the 1989 edition of *The Shaping of South African Society*.[35]

32. E.H. Carr, *What is History?*, London, 1961, 12.

33. Quoted in Smith, *The Changing Past*, 71.

34. He is not alone in this; African historians have been dumping mode of production analysis in increasing numbers since the early 1980s. See the special issue devoted to the question by the *Canadian Journal of African Studies*, 19, 1 (1985). See also my discussion of Peires, ed., *Before and After Shaka* in the *Journal of Southern African Studies*, 3 (1984), 157–61.

35. Figures 8.4 and 8.2 in Elphick and Giliomee, eds, *The Shaping of South African Society*.

Several threatening black arrows thrust east and north from the Zulu kingdom. Others, even more menacing, which push south-west from the highveld are countered by a single grey counterthrust of Voortrekker movement. Cobbing and Wright ask us to reverse the direction of most of the arrows. A new map drawn to their specifications would show the Great Trek as only the latest in a series of invasive forces.

A second obvious step is to challenge the enduring view of the trekkers as pre-capitalist, eighteenth-century white nomads in flight from modernising British rule. Five decades have passed since the work of P.J. van der Merwe exposed the fallacy of identifying the trekboer with the Voortrekker, but still the stereotype lives on.[36]

Building on Van der Merwe's work, Timothy Keegan has, in a few short but suggestive paragraphs at the beginning of a recent article, taken an important step toward resituating the Voortrekkers in the capitalist economy of the eastern Cape.[37]

Neumark may have been wrong to single out wool production as the contribution of the Voortrekker in carrying commodity production into the interior. But why should the opposite therefore be assumed to be true – that the trekkers had no intentions other than to establish themselves as self-sufficient, precapitalist agriculturists?

More needs to be done to relate the Voortrekkers to the frontiersmen who went ahead of them – not just pioneers in trans-Orangia, but also the Griqua. Legassick and Robert Ross, in complementary studies, have shown how the Griqua shifted among different kinds of economic activities and how their willingness to consider land as a commodity gradually undermined their position in Griqualand West.[38]

In Cobbing's version of the mfecane, the Griqua are just one of several fearsome advance guards of the world economy. We should perhaps take Hendrik Potgieter precisely at his word when he tells Adam Kok, 'We are emigrants together with you . . . who together with you dwell in the same strange land and we desire to be regarded as neither more nor less than your fellow-emigrants, inhabitants of the country, enjoying the same privileges with you.'[39]

Taken literally, this envisaged a life in which hunting for game, cattle and people would be regular events.

To what extent slaving as well as slave-holding were on the agenda of individual

36. P.J. van der Merwe, *Die Noordwaartse Beweging van die Boere voor die Groot Trek 1770–1842*, The Hague, 1937. See the discussion of this point in Smith, *The Changing Past*, 76–7.

37. T. Keegan, 'The Making of the Orange Free State, 1846–54: Sub-Imperialism, Primitive Accumulation and State Formation', *Journal of Imperial and Commonwealth History*, 17, 1 (1988), 26–8.

38. R. Ross, *Adam Kok's Griqua*, Cambridge, 1976, 134.

39. Quoted by Peires in Elphick and Giliomee, eds, *The Shaping of South African Society*, 508. See also Macmillan, *Bantu, Boer and Briton*, 172: 'The presence of the Griquas helps in part to explain why it was that from the very beginning the mass of the trekkers moved so far away, instead of planting their secession states on the reputedly "empty" land immediately adjoining the parent Colony.'

Voortrekkers is hard to tell. We have the testimony of J.N. Boshof in 1838 that 'it was the intention at first to proceed far into the interior, with the view to settle in the vicinity of Delagoa Bay, for the purpose of carrying on a trade with the inhabitants of that settlement'.[40]

The harrowing journey of the Tregardt party revealed the hazards of that enterprise, but why were the allegedly pre-capitalist Voortrekkers making for a Portuguese port? The project sometimes attributed to them of securing access to the sea for Paul Kruger's future republic is ridiculously anachronistic and contradicts the idea that they only wanted to be alone in their wilderness. If participation in the east African slave and slaving economy was on their agenda, they had, of course, to shut up about it. Nothing would be more likely to send the furies of Exeter Hall chasing after them. Naturally all such intentions are denied in Piet Retief's celebrated manifesto which has so often been scoured for meaning. However, scholars who have recently looked at what was done in the Zoutpansberg after the Trek have had little trouble in confirming that hunting for game and children went hand in hand.[41]

Retief's apologia has been too often taken at face value. As Du Toit and Giliomee point out, it needs to be read against the grain.[42] Retief notoriously led the trekkers from behind, joining up in 1837. He had the benefit of judging the reaction of public opinion in Britain and at the Cape when he took up his pen to write to the *Graham's Town Journal*. The text was taken with more than a grain of salt by the *Commercial Advertiser*, who smiled at the idea that the 'Farmers have been induced to withdraw from under a settled Christian Government, to seek a "quiet life" among the gentle kings of central Africa.'[43]

In view of Retief's own background, however, activities other than slaving were likely to have been foremost in his mind. Like Louis Tregardt and other Voortrekker leaders, he was anything but a self-sufficient trekboer. He was a businessman, a government contractor of dubious integrity and a land speculator.[44]

His experience with the 1820 settlers had shown him all the myriad ways in which money could be made out of pioneering. From the time Graham cleared the Zuurveld, the acquisition and transfer of land in marketable parcels had been a regular feature of frontier life – a fact obscured by the legend of trekboers living on vaguely defined tracts out of sight of their neighbours' chimneys. No account of the Trek has ever ignored land hunger as a cause of the emigration, but the kind of emphasis Giliomee puts on the 'poor, landless and desperate' rebels who followed behind a few well-off leaders has, no doubt, discouraged historians from considering that the Trek had anything to do with land speculation. In the settlement of

40. Quoted in Ransford, *The Great Trek*, 99.
41. See, for example, J. Boeyens, '"Zwart Ivoor": Inboekelinge in Zoutpansberg, 1848–1869', *Suid-Afrikaanse Historiese Joernaal*, 24 (1991), 31–66.
42. Du Toit and Giliomee, *Afrikaner Political Thought*, vol. 1, 213.
43. M. Streak, *The Afrikaner as Viewed by the English 1795–1854*, Cape Town, 1974, 158.
44. Peires, eager to make his point about the 'revolution in government' brought by the British de-emphasizes Retief's land speculations in order to point up the way he carried on into the nineteenth century manipulations of government characteristic of the Dutch East India Company (VOC) past. See Elphick and Giliomee, *The Shaping of South African Society*, 508–10.

nineteenth-century colonies in 'new lands' around the globe, the speculative hopes of a few were more often than not grounded on the prospects they could hold out to landless migrants. Before the Homestead Act in the United States and selection acts in Canada and Australia regularised the process of land grants to poor farmers, the work of laying out new settlements was generally carried on by private contractors who hoped to profit from resales, particularly of town acres. Could Retief have so left his past behind him as to be blind to such prospects in 1837?

The best evidence about the trekkers' intentions is to be found in the way they handled land in the republics which they founded. The fact that a man found among the trekkers with surveying tools was almost killed as a government spy is not an indication that they were against surveying.[45] It shows not only their objection to the British land regulations, but also their intention that nothing should interfere in any way with their reaping the full benefit of whatever annexations they should succeed in making. Retief in a sense dies for the cause of land speculation, leaving behind him in his knapsack the deed of cession from Dingane that would protect Voortrekkers in Natal from other claimants, especially the British traders at Port Natal. (Retief had already assured the latter of special consideration in the matter of land grants.[46])

Much of the work of the Natal Volksraad was taken up with land business. Boshof supplied the expertise in law-making that was lost through the death of Retief, and the new state speedily demonstrated its intention of raising most of its revenue through the sale of land. As Walker noticed, Boshof 'worked hard to regularise the land laws and to push on with systematic and genuine settlement, the closer the better'.[47]

There was nothing like a vague marking out of vast tracts by riding horses to the four points of the compass. Town acres in Pietermaritzburg were dispensed on the same system that applied in Adelaide (contemporary capital of the thoroughly modern, 'systematic colony' of South Australia), through the drawing of lots.[48] At Port Natal, town plots were sold outright.

Land claimants showed far more sophistication than legend ascribes to them. Far from being satisfied with one 6 000-acre farm per family, 'men went on staking claims right down to the Umzimvubu and far beyond the Tugela, in the lands claimed by Panda and Faku. Soon 1 800 farms had been staked out, two or three for each family and the rest by unattached men . . .'.[49] Similar scenes were enacted on the highveld. Potchefstroom had for a time not one registrar of land titles, but two, competing against one another.[50]

The keeping of records may have been haphazard, the resources of administration inadequate, and the officials inept, but, in all the new republics, dealing in land as a

45. Elphick and Giliomee, *The Shaping of South African Society*, 504.
46. Walker, *The Great Trek*, 154.
47. Walker, *The Great Trek*, 248.
48. Walker, *The Great Trek*, 220.
49. Walker, *The Great Trek*, 249.
50. Walker, *The Great Trek*, 247.

commodity was fundamental to the enterprise of settlement. It would, of course, be decades before speculative profits were reaped in most parts of the interior. It would also be some time before the staples of production were identified through experiment and market-place demands. But to deny that commodity production was prominent on the agenda of the trekkers – especially the leaders – misunderstands the way new lands were brought into production by Europeans and North Americans in the nineteenth century. Prohibitions against black ownership of land in the new republics were certainly grounded in concepts of inequality, but, like restrictions on the rights of white newcomers to acquire land on the same basis as the founding burghers, they were also a device to maximise speculative gains for the pioneers. Through all the crises of the Transvaal up to the annexation of 1877, control of land dealing was crucial to the shaky operations of the state.[51]

The colonising of the new territory by the Great Trek shared many features in common with contemporaneous outward movements in other parts of the world. Following the Napoleonic Wars, population growth, booming demand for agricultural commodities, and improvements in transportation and storage led to the seizure of land from old indigenous owners. In every case these movements marked out land for sale or lease. This was so in the Louisiana territory, Texas, Oregon, Algeria, New Zealand and Australia. The Trek began in the same year that Wakefield's South Australia Company surveyed its capital and the Texas Republic seized its independence from Mexico. Historians have ignored this conjuncture and clung to concepts of South African exceptionalism embodied in the master narratives analysed earlier in this essay. From Macmillan and Walker to Du Toit, Peires and Giliomee, historians have tenaciously insisted that the Trek was a reactive and conservative movement.[52]

This deserves to be questioned.

From the 1820s the annexation of Natal had been contemplated by speculative commercial minds at the Cape.[53] The trekkers made a pre-emptive strike. No doubt the business would have been more neatly managed by the British Empire, but after their own fashion the trekkers did the job. They had some peculiar reasons for wanting to escape from British rule, but so had the Mormon founders of Utah some peculiar reasons to escape from Yankee rule. So had Silesian migrants who took up land in South Australia. Those peculiarities should not blind us to the fact that Utah, South Australia and the Orange Free State shared ideas about the owning, farming and selling of land.

---

51. The work of Peter Delius on the relationship of the Pedi polity to the Transvaal government is especially revealing. See *The Land Belongs to Us: The Pedi Polity, the Boers and the British in the Nineteenth-century Transvaal*, Johannesburg, 1983.
52. This is true even of De Kiewiet, who noticed in *A History of South Africa*, 57, that 'between the exodus of the Boers and other colonizing movements in the nineteenth century similarities are easily discerned'. None the less, he too insisted that the 'Boers moved inland not to found a new society and to win new wealth . . . theirs was not the aggressive movement of a people braving the wilderness for the profit that it would bring their purses, or the education that it would give their children', 58–9.
53. J.B. Wright, 'Political Mythology and the Making of Natal's Mfecane', *Canadian Journal of African Studies*, 23, 2 (1989), 272–91.

Andries Stockenstrom, the archetypal progressive Afrikaner, is remembered by liberals (and excoriated by nationalists) as the opponent of the Trek, but it should be remembered that his preferred policy was not a closed frontier. It was systematic 'colonization of all depopulated territories'.[54] That is to say, he would have preferred a thorough job done by British rule to the half-botched job done by the trekkers.

Daniel Lindley, the American missionary eye-witness to the Trek, regretted the ignorance of the pioneers, but did not doubt that they represented the same outward movement of invasive migration that had taken place in Indian territories in the land of his birth.[55]

Neither did the Voortrekkers. Piet Uys affirmed in 1838 that he and his fellows proposed 'to establish our settlement on the same principles of liberty as those adopted by the United States of America'. The Lydenburg Republic's executive in 1860 cited in defence of their record of colonisation not only the ancient Israelites but also the European colonisers of Asia, America and Australia.[56]

Cobbing argues that we should shift our conception of the mfecane from an aggressive movement sparked off by the Zulu to a period of turbulence resulting from a stepping up of intrusive forces stemming from the advance agents of the world economy. A corollary shift is required in thinking about the Great Trek. The trekkers were part of the intrusive process, not weird anachronisms in flight from it. The mfecane had not depopulated Natal and the highveld. It had rendered certain sections free of obvious owners and therefore available for partition in a typical early nineteenth-century scheme of settlement. The trekkers were not merely reacting to British restrictions. Advance guards speaking their language had gone ahead of them. They did not walk backwards into an empty land.

---

54. Macmillan, *Bantu, Boer and Briton*, 235n.
55. Houghton Library, Harvard University, Archives of the American Board of Commissioners for Foreign Missions, folio 15.4, vol. 2, D. Lindley to Rufus Anderson, 27 March 1838.
56. Du Toit and Giliomee, *Afrikaner Political Thought*, vol. 1, 228, 284.

3 Hunter-Gatherers, Traders and Slaves

The 'Mfecane' Impact on Bushmen, their Ritual and their Art

THOMAS A. DOWSON

Julian Cobbing's critique of the notion of the 'mfecane' has, despite some criticism, provided a framework for the integration of what have been many different sectional histories of South Africa.[1] But, because early accounts of South Africa's past have not yet been totally unloaded of prejudice and of the colonists' legitimising ideologies, other myths and cultural stereotypes continue to act as alibis for present-day cultural divisionist policies. One such myth is the part played by various Bushman groups[2] in the colonial history of southern Africa. If we are to abandon the 'mfecane' myth because of its role in legitimising the apartheid state, the new historical constructions of the period conventionally designated the 'mfecane' should take cognisance of all peoples present on the landscape at the time.

Here I challenge the once explicit, now implicit, view that 'of the unlucky Bushman there is little for history to say'.[3] Perhaps one of the reasons for this view having become implicit is that although some historians have already confronted the issue,[4] they have not been able to develop an approach that reincorporates the Bushmen fully into southern African history. As a result many historians have ignored archaeological discourse and have tended to rely on cultural stereotypes. Nigel Penn, however, presents us with a notable exception in this regard for the western Cape.[5] In this essay I advance a methodology that will allow us to restore the

1. J.B. Wright, 'Political Mythology and the Making of Natal's Mfecane', *Canadian Journal of African Studies*, 23, 2 (1989), 273.
2. Many writers prefer 'San' to 'Bushman' because of the latter's pejorative associations for some, but by no means all, people in southern Africa. Unfortunately, 'San', a Nama word, also has negative connotations: it could be translated 'vagabond', and its use by historians, archaeologists and anthropologists ascribes to the Nama antagonistic attitudes towards Bushmen. Because there are so many Bushman languages, there is no generic word to cover all groups. Along with writers such as Lorna Marshall and Megan Biesele, I retain 'Bushman' but reject all possible pejorative associations.
3. W.M. Macmillan, *The Cape Colour Question*, London, 1927, 26.
4. S. Marks, 'Khoisan Resistance to the Dutch in the Seventeenth and Eighteenth Centuries', *Journal of African History*, 13 (1972), 55–80.
5. N. Penn, 'The Frontier in the Western Cape, 1700–1740', in J. Parkington and M. Hall, eds, *Papers on the Prehistory of the Western Cape*, Oxford, 1987; N. Penn, 'Labour, Land and Livestock in the Western Cape During the Eighteenth Century', in W.G. James and M. Simons, eds, *The Angry Divide*, Cape Town, 1989.

Bushman peoples to their rightful place not only in the events commonly known up until now as the 'mfecane' but also in the history of southern Africa.

The Bushmen in History

The Bushmen have been politically marginalised since the arrival of European colonists. The white settlers brought with them a specific set of European morals and standards, and it was against these that the Bushmen were seen and judged. Early writers forcefully convey these essentially conservative and racist attitudes. Missionaries in particular were scathing of the Bushmen: Robert Moffat and H. Tindall, for instance, were among many who emphasised what they considered to be a lacuna in Bushman life:

> Hard is the Bushman's lot, friendless, forsaken, an outcast from the world, greatly preferring the company of beasts of prey to that of civilized man. His *gorah* soothes some solitary hours, although its sounds are often responded to by the lion's roar or the hyeana's howl. He knows no God, knows nothing of eternity, yet dreads death; and has no shrine at which he leaves his cares or sorrows. We can scarcely conceive of human beings descending lower in the scale of ignorance and vice; while yet there can be no question that they are children of one common parent with ourselves. If, during a period of four thousand years, they have sunk thus low, what would have the world become if left without Divine revelation to grope in the mazes of heathen darkness?[6]

> He has no religion, no laws, no government, no recognised authority, no patrimony, no fixed abode . . . a soul debased, it is true, and completely bound down and clogged by his animal nature.[7]

These views still permeate much of southern Africa's history as it is being written by many historians, as opposed to archaeologists.[8] (Although I join others in questioning the validity of this distinction between archaeology and history, it clearly exists in the southern African context.) For decades the Bushmen have been portrayed as simple nomads, wandering aimlessly across a landscape they did not own or manipulate. Living as if in a garden of Eden, 'hunter-gatherers had time and energy for subtle and complex aesthetic expression in rock art and in music'.[9] But when some writers consider the leisure time the Bushmen, but not the herding or

---

6. R. Moffat, *Missionary Labour and Scenes in Southern Africa*, London, 1842, 15.
7. H. Tindall, *Two Lectures on Great Namaqualand and its Inhabitants*, delivered before the Mechanics' Institute, Cape Town, 1856, 26.
8. Marks, 'Khoisan Resistance to the Dutch'; J. Richner, 'Eastern Frontier Slaving and its Extension into the Transorangia and Natal', paper presented at the Colloquium on the Mfecane Aftermath, University of the Witwatersrand, Johannesburg, 1991.
9. L.M. Thompson, *A History of South Africa*, New Haven, 1990, 9.

farming groups, are supposed to have had, the difference is explicable: 'The herding way of life, moreover, required more work than hunting and gathering, so that pastoralists had less time and energy to devote to aesthetic pursuits.'[10]

Early colonial reaction to the delicate and complex rock art of southern Africa was also one of great surprise, given the low intellectual status then ascribed to the Bushmen. Sir John Barrow, for example, wrote: 'The force and spirit of drawings, given to them by bold touches judiciously applied, and by the effect of light and shadow, could not be expected from savages.'[11] Although they allowed aesthetic merit, the early writers denied any intellectual accomplishment. Despite research over the last two decades demonstrating that Bushman art was not the product of idle hours, these early racist attitudes linger in histories produced today. Thus conceived, the Bushmen's stature as human beings capable of creative thought and the control of their own destiny was and still is being obscured.

Attitudes like Moffat's and Tindall's that held the Bushmen in low regard informed early explorers' and missionaries' perceptions of the Bushman peoples' political role in southern Africa, a perception that persists today in both public and academic discourse. Because of their 'animal nature' it was inconceivable that the Bushmen could have had any impact on the colonial history of southern Africa. This perception has given rise to what have become the two most widely held stereotypic images of the Bushmen in history and literature today: the Bushmen as stock raiders and the Bushmen as a vanishing race.

Bushman Raiders

The early written records of events in southern Africa abound with references to Bushmen as raiders – some writers mention little else. For example, Thomas Arbousset makes repeated reference to this, describing how even the Sotho would not use some of the good pastures for their cattle because they were 'exposed to the depredations' of the Bushmen. In one incident during Arbousset's expedition with King Moshoeshoe, for example, their horses disappeared during the night; they immediately assumed it was the Bushmen:

> The previous winter, these vagrants had stolen all of Masopo's horses, and they had eaten them in the bush in the heart of the Maloti. We reckoned that the same thing must be happening to us. But we were wrong. Our horses had simply gone round a mountain, and we found them grazing quietly at the bottom of a valley.[12]

10. Thompson, *A History of South Africa*, 14.
11. J. Barrow, *An Account of Travels into the Interior of Southern Africa, in the Years 1797 and 1798 . . .*, London, 1801–04, vol. 1, 239.
12. D. Ambrose and A. Brutsch, eds, *Missionary Excursion: Thomas Arbousset*, Morija, 1991, 104.

This kind of incident must have happened more than once. It was supposedly because of these raids that the Boers mounted extensive commandos against the Bushmen, but the hatred ran deeper than this.[13] While I would not argue that Bushmen were not involved in raids throughout the subcontinent, I do argue against the importance this activity is given in both popular and academic discourse. These raids have to be placed within a wider, more enquiring social context.[14]

This outlawed existence, so the reconstruction goes, could not go on for much longer; there could only be one end to it. The 'Bushman as raider' stereotype leads directly to the next.

The Vanishing Bushmen
As a result of contact with Bantu-speaking farmers and white colonists, the Bushmen, supposedly the weakest of the various cultural groups, were said to have disappeared into the more mountainous and less hospitable parts of the country. A view still widely held and promoted in popular local histories is that some Bushman groups were forced to move into the drier areas of the Kalahari, where they still exist today:

> The struggle between the [whites and the Bushmen] went on for years, but there could only be one end to it. The Bushmen retreated into the mountains at first, but eventually moved into the desert areas of the Kalahari, Botswana and South West Africa, where they adapted themselves to conditions in which very few other people could have survived – a remarkable achievement in view of their limited equipment.[15]

Liberal histories, on the other hand, mention some form of economic relationship between Bushmen and the pastoralists or farmers in the different regions.[16] But these are scant and very generalised. Maps drawn to accompany such texts tend to present various Bantu-speaking groups as having displaced Bushman groups.[17] Leonard Thompson's map shows 'Khoisan' groups occupying more arid, less hospitable regions to the west of the subcontinent. Again, I do not want to argue that the

---

13. For details see 'Ergates', 'Bushmen's Stock Raids in Natal', *Natal Agricultural Journal*, 8 (1905); British Parliamentary Papers, (hereafter *BPP*), 'Reports and Papers on the Affairs of Cape Colony, the Condition of Native Tribes and the Sixth Kaffir War 1826–36'; and J. B. Wright, *Bushman Raiders of the Drakensberg 1840–1870*, Pietermaritzburg, 1971.
14. Wright, *Bushman Raiders of the Drakensberg*.
15. E. B. Hawkins, *The Story of Harrismith: 1849–1920*, Ladysmith, 1982, 10.
16. See papers in L. M. Thompson, ed., *African Societies in Southern Africa*, London, 1969, notably D. W. Phillipson, 'Early Iron-using Peoples of Southern Africa', 24–49; G. Harinck, 'Interaction between Xhosa and Khoi: Emphasis on the Period 1620–1750', 145–69; and S. Marks, 'The Traditions of the Natal "Nguni": A Second Look at the Work of A. T. Bryant', 126–44. See also M. Wilson and L. M. Thompson, eds, *A History of South Africa to 1870*, Cape Town, 1982 and Thompson, *A History of South Africa*.
17. See, for example, Thompson, *A History of South Africa*, Fig. 1.

Bushmen did not occupy these less favourable regions. What I am concerned with is the apparent ease with which Bushman populations are moved about on a map.

Maps like these, besides being demographically incorrect, construct a very simplified picture of the demography of the subcontinent; this in turn influences perceptions of the social dynamics of cultural interaction in the region. No idea of the complexity of the economic and social relations between hunter-gatherers and farmers is given. The impression is created that the Bushmen gave in to these stronger, less 'primitive' farmers and herders or were entirely assimilated, even though we know that some Bushman people developed strong ties with farming and herding communities. Although a different picture is beginning to emerge,[18] partly as a result of writers incorporating archaeological research, the principle of the so-called 'weaker' necessarily giving way to the 'stronger' is still firmly entrenched in the academic mind.

This view of the Bushmen vanishing into the mountains where they lived out their last days, carrying out raids from time to time, is produced by the same ideology that led to the notion that Natal was devastated during the 1810s and 1820s and that its population was either exterminated or driven out by the Zulu.[19] This idea of a 'devastated Natal' was then appropriated to justify British colonisation of the area and domination over African populations. The whites are thus presented as having put an end to Zulu ravages and having brought peace and stability to the area.

Where groups of Bushmen did remain, in the Drakensberg mountains of Natal and the eastern Cape, they are portrayed as a social nuisance, thus justifying the commandos sent out against them. 'The Bushmen became such a pest that it was necessary to hunt them down.'[20] The reinforcement of the idea of Bushmen as bandits in modern popular literature continues to excuse the early settlers for exterminating vast numbers of them.[21]

The persistence of these two stereotypes results in part from continuing to look at the Bushmen through the prejudices of early writers. Despite recent extensive research on historical and modern Bushmen challenging them, these stereotypes are not easily dislodged from histories of southern Africa. When one reads writers who, though still influenced by European values, were more sympathetic towards the

18. See, for example, T. R. H. Davenport, *South Africa: A Modern History*, London, 1991, 4th ed.
19. Wright, 'Political Mythology'.
20. A. A. Anderson, *Twenty-five Years in a Waggon*, London, 1888, 5–6.
21. In some interesting and illuminating papers, A. E. Voss, 'Thomas Pringle and the Image of the "Bushmen"', *English in Africa*, 9, 1 (1982); A. E. Voss, 'The Image of the Bushman in South African English Writing of the Nineteenth and Twentieth Centuries', *English in Africa*, 19, 1 (1987); A. E. Voss, 'Die Bushie is Dood: Long Live the Bushie. Black South African Writers on the San', *African Studies*, 49 (1990); and D. Haarhoff, *The Wild South-West: Frontier Myths and Metaphors in Literature in Namibia, 1760–1988*, Johannesburg, 1991, have shown how these images of the Bushmen have been used in South African English writing of the nineteenth and twentieth centuries as well as by black South African writers. Interestingly, this ideology finds a parallel in the United States with the notion of the 'vanishing American Indian', which also permeates all aspects of white culture, including art and literature; see B. W. Dippie, *The Vanishing American: White Attitudes and U.S. Indian Policy*, Middletown, 1982.

Bushmen, a different image of the Bushmen and their political role in southern Africa begins to emerge.[22]

Of course, an even more dramatically different image would have emerged if a history had been written by a Bushman and from a Bushman's perspective. In the absence of such a history, we do nevertheless have a record of another kind that can be used together with other historical sources to recover, at least in part, this Bushman perspective.[23] This record consists of archaeological remains.

The Archaeological Record

Although the written archaeological record is not seen from a Bushman perspective, some of it certainly contributes towards a more balanced view. The better-known part of the archaeological record comprises excavated remains such as lithic, ceramic, botanical, skeletal and faunal evidence, and it is with these that archaeologists have been primarily concerned. The other component of the archaeological record is rock art. I discuss each component in turn.

Excavated Remains

During the last decade in particular a number of studies have demonstrated that contact between Bushmen and Bantu-speaking farmers was much more complex than previously thought.[24] In the Thukela Basin, for example, excavations have provided empirical evidence for interaction between Stone Age and Iron Age groups.[25] Pieces of talc schist and soapstone, often used to make bowls and other vessels, have been found at hunter-gatherer sites in deposits post-dating 2000 BP; this material has not been recovered from deposits prior to this date, that is, before contact with the Iron Age farmers.[26] These sites are in the upper reaches of the Thukela River and some distance from the sources of these rock types. Similar stone

22. W.H.I. Bleek, 'Remarks on Orpen's "Mythology of the Maluti Bushman"', *Cape Monthly Magazine*, New Series, 9, 49 (1874), 10–13; W.H.I. Bleek, *Brief Account of Bushman Folklore and Other Texts*, Cape Town, 1875; T.L. Hodgson, *The Journals of the Reverend T.L. Hodgson, Missionary to the Seleke-Rolong and the Griquas 1821–1831*, ed. by R.L. Cope, Johannesburg, 1977; J.M. Orpen, 'A Glimpse into the Mythology of the Maluti Bushmen', *Cape Monthly Magazine*, New Series, 9, 49 (1874), 1–10; G.W. Stow, *The Native Races of South Africa*, London, 1905.
23. As in Wright, *Bushman Raiders of the Drakensberg*; Penn, 'The Frontier in the Western Cape'; and Penn, 'Labour, Land and Livestock in the Western Cape'.
24. See for example J. Parkington, 'Changing Views of the Late Stone Age of South Africa', in F. Wendorf and A.E. Close, eds, *Advances in World Archaeology*, 3, New York, 1984; J.R. Denbow, 'A New Look at the Later Prehistory of the Kalahari', *Journal of African History*, 27 (1986); A.B. Smith, 'Competition, Conflict and Clientship: Khoi and San Relationships in the Western Cape', *South African Archaeological Society, Goodwin Series*, 5 (1986); J. Kinahan, *Pastoral Nomads of the Central Namib Desert: The People History Forgot*, Windhoek, 1991; A.D. Mazel, 'People Making History: The Last Ten Thousand Years of Hunter-Gatherer Communities in the Thukela Basin', *Natal Museum Journal of Humanities*, 1 (1989); S.L. Hall, 'Hunter-gatherer-fishers of the Fish River Basin: A Contribution to the Holocene Prehistory of the Eastern Cape', Ph.D. thesis, University of Stellenbosch, 1990.
25. See Mazel 'People Making History' for the most recent syntheses and discussion.
26. Mazel 'People Making History', 141.

was recovered from sites occupied by farming communities, one of which also produced an assemblage of Stone Age or hunter-gatherer tools that archaeologist Tim Maggs believes are contemporary with the farming occupation of the site.[27]

Maggs and Aaron Mazel argue that the patterning of material culture in the Natal area shows that interaction between Bushmen and farmers, which must have started as soon as the farmers came into contact with Bushmen, was initially extensive and amicable. Mazel has demonstrated that these relationships, certainly at the outset, were on a relatively equal footing, unlike the kind of clientship the Bushmen entered into with the farmers as reported in the nineteenth-century records.[28] The possibility that clientship became more substantial as a result of decimation of the Bushman people by European colonists should be investigated; I touch on it again below. Further, there is every indication that new complex social relations accompanied and formed the basis of the new economic relations.[29]

Bushman reactions to Bantu-speaking farmers and European colonists can no longer be seen in terms of weaker people meekly submitting to more sophisticated people with more advanced modes of subsistence. Maggs and Gavin Whitelaw believe that further studies in this field need to deal with understanding the more complex 'intermeshing processes' between the various economies.[30] The key to these processes is, I argue, to be found in social and cognitive enquiries.[31] Turning to cognitive issues is a recent and important trend in archaeology.[32] In contrast, by relying heavily on early historical documents and emphasising economic concerns at the expense of cognitive issues, Kalahari revisionists have been able to argue that the Bushmen were merely an oppressed class within the overall farming society rather than a cultural group with its own values, religion and sense of identity.[33]

An examination of Bushman ritual and religion, however, shows that relations between the Bushmen and the farmers or pastoralists clearly did develop in some respects. Nevertheless, despite changes that took place within their society, the Bushman people did not lose their identity as a separate group. A social enquiry into

27. T.M.O'C. Maggs, 'Msuluzi Confluence: A Seventh-century Early Iron Age Site on the Tugela River', *Annals of the Natal Museum*, 24 (1980).
28. Mazel, 'People Making History', 142.
29. Mazel, 'People Making History', 132–52.
30. T.M.O'C. Maggs and G. Whitelaw, 'A Review of Recent Archaeological Research on Food-producing Communities in Southern Africa', *Journal of African History*, 32 (1991), 11.
31. J.D. Lewis-Williams, 'The Economic and Social Content of Southern San Rock Art', *Current Anthropology*, 23 (1982); J.D. Lewis-Williams, 'Ideological Continuities in Prehistoric Southern Africa: The Evidence of Rock Art', in C. Schrire, ed., *Past and Present in Hunter-gatherer Studies*, Orlando, 1984; Mazel, 'People Making History'; Hall, 'Hunter-gatherer-fishers'.
32. For a southern African perspective see J.D. Lewis-Williams, 'Social Theory in Southern African Archaeology', paper presented at the South African Association of Archaeologists Conference, Grahamstown, 1985; J.D. Lewis-Williams, 'Southern Africa's Place in the Archaeology of Human Understanding', *South African Journal of Science*, 85 (1989); T.N. Huffman, 'Cognitive Studies of the Iron Age in Southern Africa', *World Archaeology*, 18 (1986).
33. C. Schrire, 'An Enquiry into the Evolutionary Status and Apparent Identity of San Hunter-gatherers', *Human Ecology*, 8 (1980); C. Schrire, *Past and Present in Hunter-gatherer Studies*; E.N. Wilmsen, *Land Filled with Flies*, Chicago, 1989; E.N. Wilmson and J.R. Denbow, 'Paradigmatic History of San-speaking Peoples and Current Attempts at Revision', *Current Anthropology*, 31 (1990).

the nature of change both between Bushmen and other groups and within Bushman society itself leads to the second part of the twofold 'Bushman record': rock art.

Rock Art

For decades Eurocentric attitudes towards Bushman art prevailed. It was not until researchers began to use authentic Bushman beliefs[34] that a much deeper appreciation of the art began to emerge. The current trend began by recognising that much of the art in southern Africa reflected shamans' experiences during the trance ritual and beliefs about it.[35]

This research led to the investigation of the role of the shaman and rock art in Bushman society, before and after contact with farmers.[36] David Lewis-Williams, examining what was then thought to be 'traditional Bushman art', proposed that it

34. In the 1870s the linguist Wilhelm Bleek and his co-worker Lucy Lloyd took down, by dictation, some 12 000 pages of Bushman texts comprising transcriptions in phonetic script and literal English translations; see J. D. Lewis-Williams, *Believing and Seeing: Symbolic Meanings in Southern San Rock Paintings*, London, 1981, 25–37. Their informants came from the north-western Cape Province and, later, from the northern Kalahari Desert; see J. Deacon, '"My Place is the Bitterpits"; The Home Territory of Bleek and Lloyd's /Xam San Informants', *African Studies*, 45 (1986). More recent research has been carried out on the religious beliefs of the Kalahari Bushman groups. Although the relevance of this material was once held in question, a cautious use of this material is now generally accepted; see J. D. Lewis-Williams and M. Biesele, 'Eland Hunting Rituals among Northern and Southern San Groups: Striking Similarities', *Africa*, 48 (1978); and J. D. Lewis-Williams, 'Ethnographic Evidence Relating to "Trancing" and "Shamans" among Northern Bushmen', *South African Archaeological Bulletin*, 47 (1992).
35. For more on the essentially shamanistic nature of Bushman rock art throughout southern Africa see, for example, Lewis-Williams 'The Economic and Social Context'; J. D. Lewis-Williams, 'Introductory Essay: Science and Rock Art, *South African Archaeological Society, Goodwin Series*, 4 (1983); Lewis-Williams, 'Ideological Continuities in Prehistoric Southern Africa'; J. D. Lewis-Williams, 'Paintings of Power: Ethnography and Rock Art in Southern Africa', in M. Biesele, R. Gordon and R. Lee, eds, *Past and Future of !Kung Ethnography*, Hamburg, 1986; J. D. Lewis-Williams, *Discovering Southern African Rock Art*, Cape Town, 1990; Lewis-Williams, 'Ethnographic Evidence Relating to "Trancing" and "Shamans"'; T. N. Huffman 'The Trance Hypothesis and the Rock Art of Zimbabwe', *South African Archaeological Society, Goodwin Series*, 4 (1983); T. M.O'C. Maggs and J. Sealy, 'Elephants in Boxes', *South African Archaeological Society, Goodwin Series*, 4 (1983); R. Yates, J. Golson and M. Hall, 'Trance Performance: The Rock Art of Boointjieskloof and Sevilla', *South African Archaeological Bulletin*, 40 (1985); R. Yates, J. Parkington and T. Manhire, *Pictures From the Past: A History of the Interpretation of Rock Paintings and Engravings of Southern Africa*, Pietermaritzburg, 1990; S. L. Hall, 'Pastoral Adaptations and Forager Reactions in the Eastern Cape', *South African Archaeological Society, Goodwin Series*, 5 (1986); Hall, 'Hunter-gatherer-fishers'; A. H. Manhire *et al*, 'Cattle, Sheep and Horses: A Review of Domestic Animals in the Rock Art of Southern Africa', *South African Archaeological Society, Goodwin Series*, 5 (1986); P. S. Garlake, *The Painted Caves: An Introduction to the Prehistoric Rock Art of Zimbabwe*, Harare, 1987; P. S. Garlake, 'Themes in Prehistoric Art of Zimbabwe', *World Archaeology*, 19 (1987); P. S. Garlake 'Symbols of Potency in the Paintings of Zimbabwe', *South African Archaeological Bulletin*, 45 (1990); J. Deacon, 'The Power of a Place in Understanding Southern San Rock Engravings', *World Archaeology*, 20 (1988); T. A. Dowson, 'Revelations of Religious Reality: The Individual in San Art', *World Archaeology*, 20 (1988); T. A. Dowson, *Rock Engravings of Southern Africa*, Johannesburg, 1992; Kinahan, 'Pastoral Nomads', J. D. Lewis-Williams and T. A. Dowson, *Images of Power: Understanding Bushman Rock Art*, Johannesburg, 1989; Mazel, 'People Making History'; J. Parkington, 'Interpreting Paintings without a Commentary', *Antiquity*, 63 (1989).
36. Lewis-Williams, 'The Economic and Social Context'; C. Campbell, 'Contact Period Rock Art of the South-eastern Mountains', M.A. dissertation, University of the Witwatersrand, Johannesburg, 1987.

provided a permanent backdrop to the daily social relations that shamans maintained during their trance rituals. Colin Campbell, on the other hand, examined 'contact art', art that had elements such as cattle, shields, horses and wagons, and so clearly resulted from Bushman interaction with other cultural groups. Campbell argues that these new images were incorporated into the art to provide an appropriate backdrop to a new set of social relations that were, like the 'traditional' relations, still maintained by shamans. Both Lewis-Williams's and Campbell's analyses were, however, carried out with a misconception of what is and what is not 'contact art'; the division cannot be made on subject matter alone. Hence a new examination is required.

To begin with, I argue that the rock art is not just a reflection or depiction of beliefs and experiences associated with the trance ritual. The art is a material item that was always, both before and during the so-called contact period, actively implicated in the reproduction and transformation of social relations, specifically those relations involving shamans. Because of the detailed and abundant trance imagery in the paintings, it is highly likely that shamans were the principal if not only producers of the art. Most panels, if not all, have some depictions that can be unequivocally associated with trance belief and experience. The historical documents and Bushman art are thus strikingly similar. Both create, transform and reinforce dominant ideologies: the historical documents continue to negotiate white settler ideologies, whereas Bushman rock art negotiated shaman ideologies.

To be able to discern exactly how the art played this role we need to understand, first, how the depictions were produced. The cognitive structure of the art was socially produced in that meanings attached to specific combinations of formal attributes come out of day-to-day social practice. The art was thus intimately implicated in developing social relations and the reproduction and transformation of social forms. Generally, and very briefly, I demonstrate how these processes came together and how the art negotiated Bushman ideology, particularly shaman ideology.

The proximity of Bantu-speaking farmers generated a new set of social relations in which the Bushmen in general and the shamans in particular were implicated. Farmers recognised the Bushmen as the original inhabitants and custodians of the land, and it was natural for the farmers to turn to them. This relationship, posited essentially on land ownership, came to centre on rain-making. The farmers, more than the Bushmen themselves, were dependent on rain; even minor droughts and, perhaps more important, delayed rains, affected their crops and herds far more than they did the Bushmen's antelope and plant foods. The mediator thus turned out to be the shaman. Part of the shamans' symbolic work was rain-making.[37] Even though the farmers had occupied the land, they were unable to farm successfully without rain. The farmers requested Bushman rain-makers to perform rituals and gave them cattle

37. Lewis-Williams, *Believing and Seeing*, 103–16; Lewis-Williams, 'The Economic and Social Context'; Campbell, 'Contact Period Rock Art', 38–55.

in return. It was the shaman who had (ideological) control over the farmers' economy.

Because the shamans were paid for their rain-making services with cattle, presumably among other things, they acquired a new status as procurers of meat, and no doubt achieved power through a newly developed right to distribute the meat. With the depletion of antelope herds by white hunters and the extermination of the Bushmen by white commandos, Bushman shamans were forced to become more dependent on the farmers: the shamans had to tighten their grip on the farmers. This resulted in Bushman shaman families going to live with black farmers.[38] It could be that these Bushmen were acknowledging the farmers' control of the land, but, at the same time, trying to retain some power and status.

Within Bushman society, diminishing traditional resources and, at the same time, new sources of wealth resulting from new social and economic relations with the farmers engendered competition between shamans. People looked to them as their go-betweens with the farmers and, increasingly, as the most reliable procurers of food. Shamans thus began to compete with one another and with important non-shaman members of the group for positions of influence. These power struggles, as well as the stresses of cultural contact between farmers and hunter-gatherers, were manifested in the art. The art, produced by shamans, became active and instrumental in forging new social relations that developed out of these power struggles.

People negotiate personal and social identities by means of stylistic statements.[39] Social identities become important during situations of intergroup competition and the need for co-operation to attain social, political or economic goals. Competition among individuals and an increase in options for individual enterprise result in strong personal identities. Contact between Bushmen and Bantu-speaking farmers created situations where both social and personal identities were implicated in social relations, and both of these are negotiated in the art. I give two examples of how this happened.

First, the south-eastern mountains, the Drakensberg and the Malutis, contain the most variation in artistic 'styles', but at the same time, it is also in this region that diversity of animal depictions is not as marked as elsewhere. Eland and rhebuck are by far the most frequently painted animals. The limiting of animal diversity in the paintings of this region was one result of a new interest in projecting a social identity and a social unity during changing social conditions, that is, competition between hunter-gatherers and farmers. The Bushmen of the area spoke of themselves as being 'of the eland'.[40]

38. J.B. Peires, *The House of Phalo: A History of the Xhosa People in the Days of their Independence*, Johannesburg, 1981, 24.
39. P. Wiessner, 'Reconsidering the Behavioural Basis for Style: A Case Study Among the Kalahari San', *Journal of Anthropological Archaeology*, 3 (1984); P. Wiessner, 'Is there a Unity to Style?', in M. Conkey and C. Hastorf, eds, *The Uses of Style in Archaeology*, Cambridge, 1990.
40. P. Vinnicombe, *People of the Eland: Rock Paintings of the Drakensberg Bushmen as a Reflection of their Life and Thought*, Pietermaritzburg, 1976; J.D. Lewis-Williams, '"People of the Eland": An Archaeo-linguistic Crux', in T. Ingold, D. Riches and J. Woodburn, eds, *Hunters and Gatherers: Property, Power and Ideology*, Oxford, 1988.

Figure 1. Rock painting of a trance dance from the Ladybrand District, Free State. These human figures lack facial features, and are all treated in much the same way.

Another feature of the art in this south-eastern part of South Africa is that artists began painting human figures with details never, or very seldom, used before or in other regions. These details include facial features, a change from the stick-like figures to more fully rounded figures and more numerous body adornments. This trend towards greater detail in the paintings can be explained by style becoming personalised as individual identities were developing as a result of increasing competition between individual shamans and other influential members of the group. In one small area of the Drakensberg, paintings of human activities show the rise of personal identities in an unprecedented manner. In all other areas, paintings of individual human figures are very similarly executed (Figures 1 and 2). In this one small area, paintings of human activity scenes show a marked differentiation between one large human figure and the others (Figure 3). This prominent figure is unequivocally a shaman, always much bigger, painted in a different colour, and

Figure 2. Rock painting of a trance dance from the Mooi River District, KwaZulu-Natal. Like the human figures in Figure 1 the human figures here lack facial features and are painted in much the same way.

Figure 3. Rock painting of a trance dance with an apparent emphasis on rain-making — the large spotted animal is a rain animal. In this dance one man, a transformed shaman with antelope hooves instead of human feet, is painted in such a way as to stand out from the other figures (see Lewis Williams and Dowson, *Images of Power*, 68–70). He is a different colour, his 'infibulation' is more elaborate than others, and his head is more detailed. The shaman-artist thus manipulated these formal characteristics to make a statement about this shaman's position of power and influence in the band. Note, too, that the human figures have distinct facial features, unlike those in Figure 1 and Figure 2. As Bushman groups were becoming more stratified and power was becoming concentrated in individuals, human figures in the art were also becoming more personalised, and some figures — shamans — stand out from the rest.

often executed with more elaborate body adornments. Formal attributes were thus manipulated by shaman-artists to make social and political statements.[41]

These, then, were a few ways in which Bushmen used their art to negotiate changes brought about by contact with black farmers. It was, moreover, in comparable yet distinctive ways that the events towards the end of the eighteenth century and the early nineteenth century, commonly referred to as the 'mfecane', were negotiated in their art.

Bushmen in the 'Mfecane' Period

Cobbing's plausible construction of events at the end of the eighteenth and the start of the nineteenth century has many implications. It not only allows for a reintegration of black and white history, but, if we adopt the approach I have briefly outlined above, we can reintegrate Bushman history into southern African history. It is highly improbable that Bushman groups in the south-eastern mountains were not affected by the upheavals in other areas: the Cape, where Dutch and British settlers were seizing land and labour from neighbouring African groups; Delagoa Bay, where, at much the same time an export trade in ivory, cattle, and slaves was burgeoning; and the middle Orange River and lower Vaal River areas, where in the 1810s Griqua and other bands of armed horsemen were beginning to raid across the highveld.

Jürg Richner's evidence shows that the Bushmen were as affected by European slaving as other groups and that this is significant in considering events at the end of the eighteenth century and the start of the nineteenth century.[42] That the Bushmen were taken as slaves is not, however, a sufficient account of the Bushman people's role in the history of this period: we need to explore the social implications of slavery for the Bushmen. Not only were the Bushmen, mainly women and children, being used as slaves, but the men were being exterminated; Bushmen were also reported to be selling their children.[43] Survival of the Bushman social band with its own set of beliefs and values – albeit affected by contact – was thus placed under great threat.

Besides slaving, an important source of conflict was the export of ivory and cattle from Delagoa Bay. The role of the Bushmen in the ivory trade has been overlooked in recent discussions because the 'mfecane' is seen as an event brought about by and affecting only black South Africans. Moreover, the stereotypes outlined above have reduced the importance of the Bushmen in trade relations.

41. For a more fully developed discussion, see T. A. Dowson, 'Pictorial Pasts: Bushman Rock Art and Changing Perceptions of Southern Africa's History', Ph.D. thesis, University of the Witwatersrand, Johannesburg, in preparation.
42. Richner, 'Eastern Frontier Slaving'.
43. For numerous reports on Bushmen, their raids and raids against them, selling of their children, and slaving, see A. Smith, *Andrew Smith's Journal of his Expedition into the Interior of South Africa, 1834–1836*, intro. and notes by W. F. Lye, Cape Town, 1975, 44, 284; Richner, 'Eastern Frontier Slaving'; and *BPP*, 'Reports and Papers on the Affairs of Cape Colony', for numerous reports on Bushmen, their raids and raids against them, selling of their children, and slaving.

THOMAS A. DOWSON

Figure 4. Rock painting showing Bushmen herding cattle. Cattle not only became a source of food but keeping cattle for trade purposes had very important political implications.

One of the reasons for early traders tending to concentrate their efforts on the farmers could have been that the Bushmen lacked central political institutions. Settled farming communities were probably in a better position to organise the ivory trade. This does not mean, however, that Bushman groups were always passive observers of these events. For instance, in 1829 Andrew Bain was trading cattle for ivory directly with Bushmen in what became the Transkei, and he reports that he was not the first.[44] And later, in 1846, Jacobus Uys traded ammunition for 50 elephant tusks.[45] It is also likely that Bushman hunters were implicated in the trade networks with Nhlangwini groups acting as middlemen.[46] By the middle of the nineteenth century Bushmen were actively involved in the ivory trade, and this may, albeit indirectly, have started in the eighteenth century, or even earlier, when the Portuguese were collecting ivory from the south-east.[47]

The skill of the hunters in lifting livestock (Figure 4) also enabled them to forge

44. A.G. Bain, *Extracts from the Journals of Mr Andrew Geddes Bain: Trader, Explorer, Soldier, Road Engineer and Geologist*, ed. by M. Lister, Cape Town, 1949.
45. Wright, *Bushman Raiders of the Drakensberg*, 62.
46. Wright, *Bushman Raiders of the Drakensberg*, 34.
47. Vinnicombe, *People of the Eland*, 12, 14; see also Wright, *Bushman Raiders of the Drakensberg*, 33–4.

Figure 5. Rock painting of an elephant hunt with the hunters on horseback (near Taung). This is executed in the so-called finger tradition which is believed to be late. Elephants were last seen in the area in the 1850s, and horses were introduced in the area towards the end of the 18th century (T. A. Dowson, G. Blundell and S. Hall 'Finger Paintings in the Harts River Valley, Northern Cape Province, South Africa', *Southern African Field Archaeology*, 1 (1992) 27–32).

Figure 6. Rock painting of an elephant hunt, copied by G. W. Stow in the 1870s in the Wepener District, Free State (after G. W. Stow and D. F. Bleek, *Rock Paintings in South Africa*, London, 1930, plate 59).

political alliances with neighbouring farming communities. Silayi, a Thembu man who went to live with the Bushmen in the 1850s, told W.E. Stanford about the raids he participated in; he makes it plain that they were not simply raiding for food. Although Silayi's account is of a time towards the end of the period under discussion, his cannot have been the only such experience; other black people must have done similar things and earlier. Silayi does not say what happened to all the livestock taken, but on one occasion two horses were given to their Bushman chief.[48] Black chiefs like Mandela, Mchithwa and Moorosi offered the Bushmen protection in return for livestock and ivory.[49] Providing ivory and livestock, then, gave the Bushmen enormous political advantages during a time when their survival was being threatened more and more.

Impact of the 'Mfecane' on the Art

In this brief account of a fairly complex matter I refer to only two themes in the art, themes used by shaman-artists to establish and reinforce their power at this particular time: depictions of elephants, and conflict scenes.

In the south-eastern mountains paintings of elephants and scenes of elephant hunts are not infrequent. Given the shamans' control over other spheres of life, such as hunting,[50] it is likely that they would also have tried to appropriate the ivory trade to bolster their own status. This is not to say that all elephant hunters were necessarily shamans. As hunters engaged shamans for success in antelope and ostrich hunting, they probably also appealed to them to ensure success in the acquisition of ivory. Depictions of elephant were thus making statements about the power and the position of the shaman: they were statements about and evidence for the shaman's control over resources. They made paintings of elephant hunts (Figures 5 and 6) and elephants (Figure 7) to reinforce their control over Bushman involvement in the ivory trade. Depictions of elephants, included in panels with clear trance associations, seem to have become symbols of the shamans' political power. The paintings were thus actively involved in the reproduction and entrenchment of the shamans' power.

This leads me to depictions of conflict. Although reportedly numerous, in fact conflict scenes are not found in large numbers. Early rock art scholars concentrated on themes such as these because they seemed to match their stereotype of the Bushmen as hostile raiders. The biggest concentration of paintings of conflict scenes occurs in the lower Caledon River Valley. As Cobbing has shown, this is an important region for discussing the struggles of the 'mfecane' period.[51] Despite the

---

48. W.E. Stanford, 'Statement of Silayi, with Reference to his Life Among the Bushmen', *Transactions of the Royal Society of South Africa*, 1 (1910), 436.
49. Wright, *Bushman Raiders of the Drakensberg*, 189.
50. D.F. Bleek, 'Beliefs and Customs of the /Xam Bushmen', Part 7, entitled 'Sorcerers', *Bantu Studies*, 9 (1935).
51. J. Cobbing, 'The Mfecane as Alibi: Thoughts on Dithakong and Mbolompo', *Journal of African History*, 29 (1988), 487–519.

Figure 7. Rock painting of an elephant from the Giant's Castle area in the Natal Drakensberg. This depiction is part of a large and complex panel which is replete with trance imagery. This depiction is thus unequivocally linked to shaman ideology.

　　　　　　　　　　THOMAS A. DOWSON

Figure 8. Portion of a large panel of paintings depicting Bushmen/farmer conflict, Wepener District, Free State (after Stow and Bleek, *Rock Paintings*, plates 61, 62).

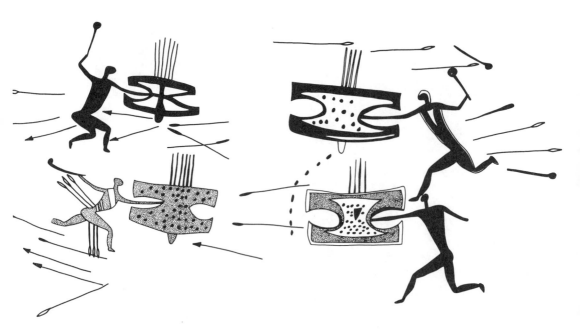

Figure 9. Portion of a large panel depicting farmer/farmer conflict, Rouxville District, Free State (after Stow and Bleek, *Rock Paintings*, plate 37).

problem of exact dates for each of the paintings, the concentration of fight scenes in this area can hardly be fortuitous.

The Caledon Valley paintings depict Bushman/Bushman, Bushman/farmer (Figure 8) as well as some farmer/farmer conflicts (Figure 9). An examination of these scenes in terms of Bushman beliefs shows they are not simple records of actual events. Many have elements that unequivocally relate to trance experience and thus place the paintings in the realm of shaman ideology.[52]

Traditionally, Bushman shamans in trance fought off marauding spirits and malevolent but nameless shamans. With the development of relations with the Bantu-speaking farmers and the colonists, this shamanistic activity was extended to include these new sources of conflict.[53] The shamans now used their powers to engage the intruders on their land. This is not, of course, a fully adequate explanation of the pictures. We need to enquire about the social relations issuing in the fights and also about the place of the shaman-artists themselves in these relations.

In the upheavals of the late eighteenth and early nineteenth centuries Bushman groups and individual shamans were drawn into conflicts between Bantu-speaking chieftainships. It may be that even as shamans had long made rain for specific leaders of farming communities, so those leaders called upon the Bushman shamans in times of strife with other farming groups. For instance, Moorosi, chief of the Phuti, was supposed to have been related to Bushmen.[54] He acted as a protector to some Bushman groups, but D.F. Ellenberger reports that during the 'mfecane' Moorosi's people were subservient to the Bushmen.[55] So too, I argue, were shamans' supernatural powers harnessed by participants in the 'mfecane' struggles. Shaman-artists then used their art to negotiate this new opportunity for developing their own political power. As they had painted elephant hunts so they came to paint conflict between Bantu-speaking groups and thereby enhanced their status. The power struggles of the 'mfecane' period were thus multidimensional.

Conclusion

Ironically, Moffat was right when he said, 'Hard is the Bushman's lot', a sentiment that has been picked up again and again. But Moffat could not have been aware of how his and other early commentators' attitudes were to underwrite the Bushmen's historical and political marginalisation; history said little for William Macmillan's 'unlucky Bushman' in 1927 and does not add much more today. In 1972 Shula Marks observed, 'History tends to be the history of the successful, and the Khoikhoi herders and San hunter-gatherers . . . have all but disappeared from twentieth-century South Africa, at least in their earlier guise. Most historians writing of South

52. C. Campbell, 'Images of War: A Problem in San Rock Art Research', *World Archaeology*, 18 (1986); Campbell, 'Contact Period Rock Art'.
53. Campbell, 'Contact Period Rock Art'.
54. Stow, *The Native Races of South Africa*, 229.
55. D.F. Ellenberger, *History of the Basuto: Ancient and Modern*, London, 1912.

Africa dismiss them in passing.'[56] Nothing has changed much. The role of Bushmen has merely changed from passing reference to a very generalised introductory chapter.[57] Historical constructions at a more general level have also ignored the Bushmen. For the eastern Cape, Gerrit Harinck accords greater significance to Khoi–Xhosa interaction; the Bushmen were simply 'eradicated and dispersed'.[58] Using both excavated material remains and rock art, Simon Hall has shown that 'this is a gross over-simplification'.[59] By taking seriously both parts of the twofold archaeological record, excavated material remains and rock art, we shall be able to start producing a history of southern Africa that includes all the people who were involved, in no matter what capacity. More specifically, and for the purposes of this volume, Bushman art, until recently a neglected part of the archaeological record, can play a major role in developing a new understanding of the 'mfecane' period, thus drawing the hunter-gatherers back into history. The 'invisible' Bushmen were active participants who should not be ignored. There is much that the Bushmen in their roles as hunter-gatherers, traders and slaves in a time of colonial oppression can contribute to the history of southern Africa through their art.

56. Marks, 'Khoisan Resistance to the Dutch', 55–80.
57. For example R. Hallett, *Africa to 1875*, Ann Arbor, 1970, 238, and Thompson, *A History of South Africa*, ch. 1.
58. Harinck, 'Interaction between Xhosa and Khoi', 146.
59. Hall, 'Hunter-gatherer-fishers', 243.

4 Language and Assassination
Cultural Negations in White Writers' Portrayal of Shaka and the Zulu

DAN WYLIE

The range of attitudes towards Shaka in 'colonial' writing is wide and tangled, but the strongest and most consistent has undoubtedly been one of 'character assassination'. This has varied from the openly vicious (Nathaniel Isaacs and Elizabeth Watt) through the jarringly ambivalent (A.T. Bryant and E.A. Ritter) to the concealed (J. Omer-Cooper and L. Thompson). It runs counter to, and often in confused company with, the tendency to lionise Shaka; it permeates even the most recent historiographical efforts to assess him 'objectively'.

This essay is concerned with recognisable patterns of language-use in the Shakan literature through which some common 'assassinatory' attitudes are expressed. Virtually all cross-cultural attempts to convey the Zulu 'reality', inevitably inscribe the individual and cultural identity of the writer as powerfully as they describe the subject. More accurately, what is inscribed is a certain *perception* of the subject, a mode of thinking about it, which is discernible in the manner in which words are chosen, juxtaposed or deployed in argument. I take it as axiomatic, then, that *style*, or *rhetoric*, is a seamlessly integral part of any portrayal of 'Shaka', and that any assessment of our primary or secondary sources depends in large part on an assessment of the heritage, resources and implications of their rhetorical choices.

There is no unmediated historical documentation of Shaka's reign. This is as true of the earliest eye-witness accounts[1] as of James Stuart's oral traditions or of the latest research. 'Shaka' is in every sense a 'verbal construct'. His 'history' consists very largely of legends, or anecdotes, or lies, or inventions, rather than what we conventionally think of as 'historical evidence' (i.e. statements which we can unproblematically assume to have a direct representational relationship with 'what happened'). His portrayal is conditioned by a plethora of Eurocentric prejudices, inherited concepts and narrative conventions; his is a 'literate' mythology, whose

---

1. For a more detailed examination of Nathaniel Isaacs's account, for example, see D. Wylie, 'Autobiography as Alibi: History and Projection in Nathaniel Isaacs's *Travels and Adventures in Eastern Africa* (1836)', *Current Writing*, 3 (1991), 71–90.

selection of words (and by extension, selection of allusion, metaphor, sentence structure, tense, narrative strategy, even genre) has so far hardly been examined.[2]

An example will sharpen the point. In almost all works on Shaka, the origin of his name is discussed, operating as a kind of synecdochal lens through which the question of Shaka's own origins – his birth, exile and accession to Zulu chieftainship – is refracted. A 'folk etymology' is used to support or crystallise the story. In each case the name 'Shaka' is translated, and into the gap between original word and interpretative translation the writer's predilections are inserted (this happens with many words, such as 'Zulu' and 'Bulawayo' and even, a more general case examined by Christopher L. Miller, 'Africa' itself).[3] This is, in effect, a microcosm of the process which occurs in all transcriptions of the reality of one culture into the discourse of another, or of the past into the present.

An ambivalence in the translation of Shaka's name is present from the beginning. Nathaniel Isaacs, without mediating comment, gives two versions. In one he derives it from 'Chekery or dysentery', which (the story goes) Shaka's mother, Nandi, was said to have contracted, in order to conceal her pregnancy. This crystallises the notion of Shaka's illegitimacy, which itself, as William Wörger wrote, 'forms, and becomes an emblem of, the man';[4] it is also echoed by Isaacs's allusions to disease and insanity in his descriptions of Shaka's 'symptoms'[5] and the repulsion informing his innumerable epithets of 'inhuman', 'insatiable', 'detestable' and so on. In the second, Isaacs connects the name with the word, 'in Sichuana at least', for 'battle-axe'.[6] This carries the obvious connotations of insatiable warfare; it also, incidentally, demonstrates the ease with which early travellers transferred information from one 'tribe' to another, tending to see them as essentially undifferentiated. Both etymologies are implicitly jettisoned, without comment, when Isaacs avers that the name was changed from Checker to Chaka.[7]

2. Unlike some other disciplines, South African historiography has been generally dilatory in coming to a full awareness of its rhetorical practice. See, for instance, J. Clifford and G.E. Marcus, eds, *Writing Culture: The Poetics and Politics of Ethnography*, Berkeley, 1986; and Paul Atkinson, *The Ethnographic Imagination*, London, 1990. For a rare South African foray, see C. Saunders, 'Our Past as Literature: Notes on Style in South African History in English', *Kleio*, 8 (1986) 46–55. For a methodology which could be fruitfully applied in this field, see A.J. Woodman, *Rhetoric in Classical Historiography: Four Studies*, Portland, 1988.

3. For example, the usual translation of 'Zulu' as 'sky' or 'heavens' can thus be negatively associated with overweening ambition (as in S. Kay, *Travels and Researches in Kaffraria*, London, 1833, 402), or positively read as 'a proud title, equalled only by the Chinese' (W. Holden, *The Past and Future of the Kaffir Races*, London, 1866, 8). Similarly, the place-name 'Bulawayo', negatively translated in most works as 'Place of Killing', alluding to Shaka's personal brutality, in a more approbatory account is rendered as '"The Place of the Ill-Treated Man", for Shaka considered himself to have been much afflicted in former years by ill-treatment and persecution' (T.V. Bulpin, *Shaka's Country: A Book of Zululand*, Cape Town, 1952, 15). C.L. Miller, *Blank Darkness: Africanist Discourse in French*, Chicago, 1985, 10–11.

4. W. Wörger, 'Clothing Dry Bones: The Myth of Shaka', *Journal of African Studies*, 6, 3 (1979), 147. A pioneering but, through neglect, not yet seminal essay.

5. N. Isaacs, *Travels and Adventures in Eastern Africa*, vol. 1, reprint ed. by L. Hermann, Cape Town, 1936, 264.

6. Isaccs, *Travels and Adventures*, vol. 1, 45.

7. Isaacs, *Travels and Adventures*, vol. 1, 269.

Except for the plagiarism by D.C.F. Moodie (1888), Isaacs's interpretations vanish from the literature. So does fellow eye-witness Henry Francis Fynn's more plausible derivation of 'looseness of the bowels' – with the exception of J.D. Omer-Cooper.[8] Both were overtaken by a more colourful· explanation: that of the 'intestinal beetle'. This only appears in the literature (as does so much else) with A.T. Bryant's *Olden Times in Zululand and Natal* (1929), a century after Shaka's death. In virtually every subsequent account,[9] and in conjunction with the 'stunted penis' story (also started by Bryant), it is utilised to support new, crudely Freudian explanations for Shaka's violence: his childhood of belittlement, implied in the 'beetle' appellation, fuels vengeance and ambition. Thus Huntly Stuart (nephew of James), in his play 'Shaka' (1981), has Dingane mock his predecessor with his 'royal BEETLE power . . . royal beetle authority'; and Lynn Bedford Hall's children's account (prudishly?) suppresses the illegitimacy-connection and has Shaka's young bullies use the term 'beetle' merely as insult.[10]

The importance, in this context, is not in the truth of the epithet but in how it is used. Thus Charles Ballard, in *The House of Shaka* (1988), wishing to lionise the man, evades the connotations of both the ludicrous and the Freudian in the 'beetle' story and gives the meaning of the name as 'break of day', 'fury', or possibly 'firebrand' (citing no source, but presumably resurrecting the obscurer derivation of the Revd J.L. Döhne and William Holden).[11] Accordingly, Ballard suppresses the illegitimacy issue, asserting that Senzangakhona 'officially' received Shaka as his 'legitimate son and heir designate by adoption', and has Shaka assume the Zulu chieftainship as 'his birthright', rather than by murder.[12] In effect, given the tenuousness of the evidence, this tells us more about Ballard than about Shaka; it is of a piece with Ballard's overriding concern to place himself on the right side of the

8. D.C.F. Moodie, *The History of the Battles and Adventures of the British, the Boers, and the Zulus* vol. 1, Cape Town, 1888, 395; H.F. Fynn, *The Diary of Henry Francis Fynn*, ed. by J. Stuart and D. McK. Malcolm, Pietermaritzburg, 1950, 12; J.D. Omer-Cooper, *The Zulu Aftermath: A Nineteenth-century Revolution in Bantu Africa*, London, 1966, adds, without explaining: 'This name which came to be attached to the boy is symbolic of much in his life and character', 29–30.

9. A.T. Bryant, *Olden Times in Zululand and Natal*, London, 1929, 48. See also V. Ridgway, *Stories from Zulu History: Izindaba zakwaZulu*, Pietermaritzburg, 1946, 40; S.G. Millin, *The King of the Bastards*, London, 1950, 125; E.A. Ritter, *Shaka Zulu*, London, 1955, 16; J. Michener, *The Covenant*, New York, 1980, 539; P.J. Schoeman, *Pamphata: The Beloved of King Shaka*, Cape Town, 1983, 17; W. Faure, director, *Shaka Zulu*, South African Broadcasting Corporation, Television Series, part. 1, 1986; L.B. Hall, *Shaka: Warrior King of the Zulu*, Cape Town, 1987, 2. To judge by the testimonies in C. de B. Webb and J.B. Wright, eds, *The James Stuart Archive*, 4 vols., Pietermaritzburg, 1976–86, the 'beetle' story did exist before Bryant's popularisation of it (vol. 1, 179); but cf. vol. 1, 5, 188; vol. 2, 230, 246; vol. 4, 198, 202, 213, 202. Cetshwayo asserted in 1880 that Shaka meant 'bastard', C. de B. Webb and J.B. Wright, *A Zulu King Speaks*, Pietermaritzburg 1987, 3 and 3n.

10. H. Stuart, unpubl. play 'Shaka', first performed at the Foundation Theatre, Durban, 7 July 1981, with Henry Cele as Shaka; ms. in Killie Campbell Africana Library, Durban, James Stuart Collection, 38. Hall, *Shaka: Warrior King of the Zulu*, 2.

11. C. Ballard, *The House of Shaka*, Durban, 1988, 15. Cf. J.L. Döhne, *A Zulu-Kafir Dictionary*, Cape Town, 1851, xiv (this etymology is supported by nothing in the body of the dictionary); Holden, *The Past and Future of the Kaffir Races*, 9.

12. Ballard, *The House of Shaka*, 16.

modern political fence, to align himself in a kind of 'affirmative action' with emerging Zulu power: 'I sincerely hope,' he writes in his Acknowledgements, 'that the interpretation rendered in the following pages lives up to Chief Buthelezi's expectations of a work that embraces a Zulu perspective of the Zulu monarchy.'

I have dwelt on this to highlight the manner in which a single lexical choice can be incorporated into the writer's ideological stance, personal affiliation and awareness of audience. This process of translating a single Zulu word into the icon of an essentially Eurocentric posture is a microcosm of the processes involved in most European inscriptions, whether fictionally empathetic or historiographically explicatory, of 'the other culture'. It is some broader patterns of these processes I want to deal with.

The aim here is to propose a tentative terminology for those textual expressions of attitude, perhaps best termed *gestures*, which are most often repeated in the Shakan literature. I isolate three such gestures, for which I have coined the terms *enterrment*, *layback* and *deadlighting*. Such a 'synchronic' terminology, which to some extent overrides 'diachronic' historical variation, is justified, I think, by the exceptionally high degree of incestuous plagiarism, paraphrasing and unquestioning repetition which characterises so much of the Shakan literature.[13]

Because I am viewing these works in a strong sense as *documents of a culture*, the gestures I delineate here recur in other colonial literatures, though I will not attempt a comparative perspective here. However, I do not offer my terms as being comprehensive, or conceptually omnipotent or normative; rather, they should be viewed as momentary crystallisations of cultural gestures which by nature are fluid, protean and subject to manifold qualification. Hence I will range freely over the genres of 'history', 'fiction', 'poetry', to focus on gestures common to all of them.

Enterrment

By the term enterrment – en-earth-ment – I denote very broadly a gesture of derogation, of dismissal or suppression, which is expressed by aligning Shaka and his Zulus with the earth, that is, positioning them on a 'lower' rung of an implicit or explicit hierarchy.

The manifestations are many-layered. Europe's intellectual heritage of the 'Great Chain of Being' and, later, popularised forms of Darwinism, polygenist anthropology and literate history, combined in various ways with the practical superiorities of numerate commerce, firepower and progressionist technology to rejustify the ancient imageries. Blacks were easily assimilated to ingrained symbolisms of darkness 'below' enlightenment; lack of 'enlightenment' is easily expressed in terms of the earth-bound – the static, the animal, the 'natural', the sensual; the sensual is

---

13. I have dealt in more detail with some of the 'diachronic' gestures in a revised 1990 Natal History Workshop paper, 'Textual Incest: Nathaniel Isaacs and the Development of the Shaka Myth', *History in Africa*, 19 (1992), 411–33.

readily subsumed by a puritanical evangelism in the Satanic, and hence the unrestrained, the insane and the simply unintelligible.

An extract from a clumsy 'epic poem' by D.J. Darlow (1937) exposes the coalition of these sub-gestures with startling clarity:

> What words are there to tell of deeds of blood?
> Like a great torrent after weeks of rain
> The Zulu army swept across the land,
> A ruthless desolation. Those who fled,
> In earnest of the flood worked their revenge
> On who withstood them; ruin everywhere;
> Behind the host the wolves devoured the slain,
> Dogs that trotted at their masters' heels,
> Hounds of Hell obedient to fiends,
> Ranging th'Inferno slavering with joy.[14]

The comparison with uncontrollable animals and attendant passions is the common stuff of racism everywhere, and need not detain us here. Worthy of more note is the identification of Zulus with natural forces: flood, fire, deluges and storms are the most common. Isaacs, for instance, states that 'After a form of government had been established [by Shaka] recognising all these barbarities, a calm ensued, not unlike that which intervenes between the first and last shocks of an earthquake . . .' .[15] Holden put it even more hyperbolically: 'As the raging volcano vomits forth from its fiery crater smoke, and ashes, and burning lava . . . entombing villages and cities at its feet, spreading dismay, destruction and death around; so, from the mouth of this despot a stream of fire was vomited forth . . .'.[16] This is not, at bottom, much different from Nickie McMenemy's characterisation of Shaka, hovering between dread and admiration, as 'a most magnificent product of nature', a 'personification of the darkness of earth, of the imperturbability of air in which silver lightning sets the sky ablaze, of the revivifying, malleable, fertile-making power of water, and the triumphant, unsubduable, all-changing potency of fire'.[17]

These are not isolated examples; and the metaphors persist into the mainstream histories. Thus Shaka unleashes a 'wave of bloodshed' (Cory),[18] or becomes the 'storm-centre' of the 'mfecane' (Eric Walker; Omer-Cooper);[19] the 'upheaval' and 'turbulence' caused by a 'galaxy of leaders' (Omer-Cooper)[20] is 'cataclysmic'

14. D.J. Darlow, *Tshaka: King of the Amazulu*, Lovedale, 1937, 40–1.
15. Isaacs, *Travels and Adventures*, vol. 1, 269.
16. Holden, *The Past and Future of the Kaffir Races*, 25.
17. N. McMenemy, *Assegai!*, London, 1973, 62, 66.
18. G. Cory, *The Rise of South Africa*, vol. 2, London, 1913, 230.
19. E. Walker, *A History of Southern Africa*, London, 1928, 182; Omer-Cooper, *The Zulu Aftermath*, 2.
20. Omer-Cooper, *The Zulu Aftermath*, 6.

(Davenport),[21] an 'eruption' (Ballard).[22] In this way the central idea of the revolutionary and irresistible power of the Shakan state is built into assessments otherwise quite different from each other. Similarly, even Omer-Cooper, despite his project of putting a positive gloss on Shaka's nation-building project, reveals a palpable repugnance in his diction of predation, rape and aberration: 'ravenous hordes of pillagers' throw 'peaceable tribes' into 'turmoil and confusion', 'accompanied by carnage and destruction on an appalling scale' in which 'whole tribes were massacred', and Shaka's armies 'ravished' others' territories and inflicted 'monstrous sufferings' on his own.[23]

More important is Darlow's assertion of linguistic inadequacy in the face of 'savagery'. It is the same kind of alleged inadequacy embodied in the language of the clichéd, formless, exaggeratedly violent popular literature to which Shaka has always been confined (in this sense, the choice of genre itself is a form of enterrment). Elizabeth Paris Watt's historical novel *Febana* (1962) is paradigmatic:

> All the torture and damnation of hell itself rent the shuddering night as human flesh and blood in searing anguish ran this fearful race of death . . . No words at the command of civilized man could describe the horror of all that followed . . . the awful bloodshed, the wild mingling of battle-cries, the screams of hate and fury, the groans of anguish, the massacre and revolting mutilation.[24]

This kind of dismissively unindividuated description still echoes through the histories: in Leonard Thompson's *A History of South Africa* women and children are 'massacred' with 'unprecedented ferocity' in a 'reign of terror', the landscape 'littered with human bones' in the Zulus' 'zeal for conquest'.[25] Thompson's 'despotic and capricious' Shaka is still the centrepiece of this 'internal' development. The characterisation is here also intimately related to the deepest possible enterrment, that of relegating the Zulus to the *under*world. In Watt, Shaka is 'Satan himself hearing the hiss of hell's flames and the dying agonies of the damned',[26] echoing Isaacs's duplicitous 'giant without reason'[27] and Bryant's 'Satanic majesty', 'devil', and 'arch-demon of iniquity'.[28]

Like Darlow, Watt explicitly states the incapacity of her 'civilized' language to accommodate the Zulu reality – hence the resort to cliché. As Russell Martin has noted, this syndrome begins with Isaacs's struggle 'to devise a suitable language that will convey his apprehension of an historical figure and a society, utterly outside his

21. T.R.H. Davenport, *South Africa: A Modern History*, 3rd ed., Johannesburg, 1987, 15.
22. Ballard, *The House of Shaka*, 16.
23. Omer-Cooper, *The Zulu Aftermath*, 3–4, 41.
24. E.P. Watt, *Febana*, London, 1962, 128.
25. L.M. Thompson, *A History of South Africa*, New Haven and Sandton, 1990, 83–86.
26. Watt, *Febana*, 130.
27. Isaacs, *Travels and Adventures*, vol. 1, 281.
28. A.T. Bryant, *A Zulu-English Dictionary*, Pinetown, 1905, 49; Bryant, *Olden Times*, 532; A.T. Bryant, *A History of the Zulu and Neighbouring Tribes*, Cape Town, 1964, 98.

own and his audience's experience and understanding'.[29] Hence, for instance, Isaacs's statement that Shaka 'finally succeeded in establishing a sort of *Zoolacratical* form of government (if I may so term it, for I do not know of anything resembling it in either ancient or modern history), a form that defies description or detail',[30] and his more ambivalent withdrawal from the effort to describe Shaka's atrocities 'too harrowing to be narrated'.[31] Similarly, Holden noted that 'those who have written about [Shaka] have laid the English language under contribution in order to find suitable epithets to describe his horrible and revolting conduct',[32] adding, 'No language can describe the frantic joy of the conquerors: their hideous yells, their vociferous songs, their savage delight, exceeded all bounds.'[33] George McCall Theal lamented Shaka's career of 'such cruelty as is hardly comprehensible by Europeans'.[34] This is echoed half a century later by Edgar Brookes and Colin Webb, for whom the suffering caused by Shaka is 'almost indescribable'.[35]

[In effect, language-use enacts those 'bounds', constitutes a 'pale' beyond which Shaka and the Zulu are linguistically banished, in its extreme form to a realm of utter incomprehensibility.]The Zulu are reduced to a 'blank darkness', to use Miller's title, the ultimate form of the negatives so commonly employed – unrestrained, irredeemable, insatiable, inhuman, and so on. This is one of the conceptual preconditions developed for white narratives of Africa, as Edgar Wallace wrote: 'There are many things that happen in the very heart of Africa that no man can explain . . . a story about Africa must be a mystery story.'[36] Thus, for Bryant, 'The Bantu character is one to us not easily analyzed. It is largely a study in contrasts; one may say, even in paradoxes.'[37] Shaka is the epitome of this indecipherability: 'But who shall fathom the devious ways of Shakan diplomacy?'[38] His 'caprice' and 'deviousness' is thus seen as iconic of a general incomprehensibility inherent in 'the Bantu character' (itself a reification which writers 'observe' and 'study' while simultaneously inscribing its impenetrability); this caprice serves as a cornerstone of historical explanation right up to, as already noted, Leonard Thompson. Brookes and Webb, again, attribute to Shaka 'complete unpredictability', then in order to circumnavigate the threat to a logical historical explanation that this poses, resort to a neat tautology: 'To reconcile these conflicting qualities is difficult except by the assumption that Shaka, like Napoleon, considered himself above morality, responsible to none, and free from ordinary restraints.'[39] This is the historiographical

29. S.R.J. Martin, 'British Images of the Zulu *c.*1820–1879', Ph.D. thesis, University of Cambridge, 1982, 51.
30. Isaacs, *Travels and Adventures*, vol. 1, 269.
31. Isaacs, *Travels and Adventures*, vol. 1, 266.
32. Holden, *The Past and Future of the Kaffir Races*, 9.
33. Holden, *The Past and Future of the Kaffir Races*, 23.
34. G.M. Theal, *History of South Africa from 1795 to 1872*, vol. 1, London, 1915, 438.
35. E.H. Brookes and C. de B. Webb, *A History of Natal*, Pietermaritzburg, 1965, 8.
36. Quoted in D. Hammond and A. Jablow, *The Africa that Never Was: Four Centuries of British Writing about Africa*, New York, 1970, 107.
37. Bryant, *Olden Times*, 156.
38. Bryant, *Olden Times*, 219.
39. Brookes and Webb, *A History of Natal*, 11–13.

version of McMenemy's fictional gesture of simultaneous repulsion, mystification and enterrment: Shaka is finally 'neither good not evil; more, he was a personification of that affliction which life produces now and again, an impersonal product of nature'.[40]

The impulse to associate the Zulu with raw nature is often entangled in another gesture of enterrment: the embedding of the people in the landscape. This usually occurs within the ethos of a kind of qualified 'Edenism' – qualified because it is not an Eden in which the white writer actually finds participation possible. J.M. Coetzee has argued that a pure Eden-myth failed to take hold of the South African literary imagination as it did the American: the white settlers in the former were rather 'apprehensive that Africa might turn out not to be a Garden but an anti-Garden, a garden ruled over by a serpent, where the wilderness takes root again in men's hearts'.[41] Shaka is the symbol of that fear.

A.T. Bryant puts it this way in *A History of the Zulu*:

> Out on the grassy plain, amidst the blue forget-me-nots and the pink gladioli, placidly moved the grazing herds, while groups of merry herdboys, clad only in the sheen of the setting sun, fluted plaintively on their panpipes hard by, as though to say, 'Sun! goodbye! goodbye!' Away in the distance, circles of grass brown huts, each with its attendant patch of waving millet, were scattered here and there where, had we approached, we should have found the elder folk peacefully assembled – busy women in their leathern kilts and swarthy damsels in their girdles of fringe, moving artlessly to and fro, while the men squatted leisurely about, plying their simple trades of wood-carving or basket-making, little knowing that the angel of death even then hovered above them.
>
> Such was the pleasing idyll that everywhere rejoiced the traveller's gaze as he passed through the breadth of Lalaland betwixt the Tukela and Mngeni in the year 1810. And with the dawn all this picture of living loveliness was to be blotted out. The reign of Appollyon [Shaka] would enter in the night and this happy spot would become the Armageddon on which the corpses of the wood carvers and basket makers would be strewn o'er the plains. Infants would be

---

40. McMenemy, *Assegai!*, 73.
41. J.M. Coetzee, *White Writing: On the Culture of Letters in South Africa*, New Haven, 1988, 3. Cf. Isaacs, *Travels and Adventures*, vol. 1, 8, 20, 58; also W.F.W. Owen, *Narrative of Voyages to Explore the Shores of Africa . . .*, London, 1833, 7. An unnamed officer of Owen's, writing as early as 1823, was perhaps the first to characterise Shaka as disruptor of a paradisal land, a 'tyrannical monster' whose 'bloody proceedings promised soon to leave the whole of this beautiful country . . . totally desolate'. But his practical experiences prompted him to scorn the Romantics' vision of beneficent primitivism:

> The state of these countries, which have scarcely had any intercourse with civilised nations, is a direct proof in refutation of the theories of poets and philosophers, who represent the ignorance of the savage as virtuous simplicity – his miserable poverty as frugality and temperance – and his stupid indolence as a laudable contempt for wealth. How different are the facts! We ever found uncultivated man a composition of cunning, treachery, drunkenness and gluttony.

pinned to the backs of their slaughtered mothers, tender trembling children would be struck down in their homes, cattle and panpipes would be swept furiously from the hillside – bloody devastation would stalk triumphant through the land and beautiful peace would die a violent death.[42]

Romantic language of sensual indolence and music in a Georgian landscape of levelled, floral luxuriance, in which nakedness is unabashedly paraded and labour is blissfully aimless, is reinforced by a sequence of gently tumbling relative clauses, present participles and archaisms, evoking a timeless idyll of humans in harmony with nature and each other.

Superficially, this is not a gesture of enterrment, appearing more positive than derogatory. But Bryant deliberately distances the scene: it is panoramic rather than insightful; some things we would observe only 'had we approached'; the traveller remains a hypothetical one, despite the spurious specificity of '1810'; the views of boys 'clad only in the sheen of the setting sun' and of 'swarthy damsels' are distinctly voyeuristic. The anachronisms ('panpipes'), clichés and stereotypes (the 'corpses . . . strewn o'er the plains' is a staple of Shakan literature from Fynn and Isaacs onwards) also serve to dislocate the scene from a reader's involvement; this is a world altogether whimsical and in any case destined to vanish. A taint of melancholy, as in the 'plaintive' music and 'Sun! goodbye! goodbye!', presages the drum-beat of 'would' verbs that enact the violence and, supported by the biblical millenialism of 'angel of death' and 'Armageddon', imply an inescapable fatedness.[43] The apparent approbation of the idyll, in short, is enclosed in a lexical and stylistic envelope which verbalises a dismissal, a burial and a vicarious nostalgia for a world which was not, in any case, the writer's own.

Similarly, in his *magnum opus*, *Olden Times in Zululand and Natal*, Bryant uses the stereotypical language of popular fiction to enliven an alleged incident of Shaka's reign, in which 'natural' sensuality is murderously punished:

> One hundred and seventy boys and girls caught in the height of their merriment, were hurdled like sheep for the slaughter within the cattle-fold, tremblingly awaiting their doom. Nor needed they wait long. His majesty, the personification of death, appeared at the gateway like an awful spectre, picked out several fine lads, 'the worst', ordered their necks to be wrenched by their own 'brothers', then be dragged away and beaten by sticks until life became extinct. After this fiendish prelude, a general and indiscriminate butchery followed . . . a happy spot on God's earth, a moment before sparkling with youthful vivacity, became at once transformed into a hell of moaning and pain; and with the golden sunshine as their pall, one hundred and seventy battered

---

42. Bryant, *A History of the Zulu*, 74.
43. This is strongly reminiscent of another missionary's view that Shaka was a 'scourge of God', an integral part of His plan to 'desolate nations, and pour out the vials of his wrath upon offending men', Holden, *The Past and Future of the Kaffir Races*, 42. This of course was part of Holden's justification for his own salvationist project, very like the kind of 'theodicy of occupation' which informed both the 'mfecane' concept and the pragmatics of apartheid.

children, like withered wild-flowers from the veld, were cast away on the green.[44]

Again, a paradisaical 'happy spot' is exploded by the implacable doom of an apocalyptic bearer of death, here even more explicitly associated with the fiendish and with Hell; again, the theme of an idyllic innocence of the young is ruptured by sibling-murder;[45] and again, the very language, the saccharine hyperbole of the closing metaphors, serve to insulate us from real sympathy.

Bryant's enterrment of the people, as opposed to the place, is more clearly revealed in another description of the rape of Paradise:

> The Bantu on the whole are tame and genial savages. But there are fighting-cocks amongst the hens, who now and again, here and there about the continent, grow fitfully gamy and make the feathers fly. Among such game-cocks our Nguni folk were numbered. Those halcyon days of the Golden Age ere Dingiswayo first disturbed the idyllic peace marked but an interval wherein the aggressive, plundering spirit of the race lay for the moment torpid. Once the ancient fire had been by Dingiswayo re-kindled, then fanned by Shaka to roaring conflagration, there was no longer any power to stay the natural impulse of the race. One after another wild spirits emerged among the clans, and led forth, north and west and south, fierce blood-thirsty hordes, revelling in slaughter and destruction . . .[46]

Here the people as a whole are animalised, their attackers simply more so; Shaka is seen merely as one form of animal life predating another, a 'wolf',[47] the 'king of beasts',[48] a 'wild animal',[49] a 'hyena'.[50] The derogation of these 'natural impulses', moreover, is delivered in a rhetoric of classical elevation, syntactic inversions and vocabulary of ponderous dignity, with an effect almost parodic; the prose itself enacts the elevation of reader above subject, and thus functions as a screen of formality.[51]

---

44. Bryant, *Olden Times*, 640. Doubtless Bryant is also indulging here in a kind of logographia – a term I take from Thucydides, meaning a compilation 'aimed at audience entertainment rather than truth' (Woodman, *Rhetoric*, 8) – which permeates all narrative history (see D. Wylie, 'Textual Incest').

45. This also originates with Isaacs, *Travels and Adventures*, 269; it is implicit in this description of the 'faulty Paradise' in C. Eden's 1871 novel, *An Inherited Task, or, Early Mission Life in Southern Africa*, Oxford, which functions as a prelude to Shaka's own predations:

   > The scene was indeed most attractive. The swallows skimmed the surface of the lake; flocks of guinea fowl . . . sought refuge from the heat of the plains . . .; the ravens croaked from the pliant boughs of the weeping-willows; hawks and vultures poised themselves in mid-air, swooping down with lightning rapidity on the young duckling incautious enough to stray from its mother . . .; the green serpent ascended the trees to suck the eggs and devour the young, while the parent birds, uttering piercing cries, fluttered round the enemy . . . (40–1).

46. Bryant, *Olden Times*, 446.
47. Bryant, *Olden Times*, 128.
48. Bryant, *Olden Times*, 477.
49. Bryant, *Olden Times*, 537.
50. Bryant, *Olden Times*, 637.
51. I am grateful to Malvern van Wyk Smith for this insight.

The 'pre-cataclysmic' 'Golden Age' evoked in the first two descriptions quoted above is, Bryant reveals in the third, seen merely as a temporary hiatus, a period of repression of innate ferocities which are capable of exploding anywhere on 'the continent' and in any direction. This is surely an expression of projected fears of a resurgence of African rebellion, such as that of 1906, through which Bryant himself had lived, and of which, again, Shaka is the most prominent and vivid icon. More accurately, Bryant invokes a myth of an Edenic state only opportunistically to reinforce a notion of revolutionary change, impelled by Shaka's personal violence.[52] Indeed, true paradise has no (indigenous) men in it at all: the many battles 'pollut[ed] the virgin sward with gore and putrid corpses . . . Such was the coming of man into this hallowed paradise where heretofore nature had luxuriated undefiled in unruffled bliss'.[53] Happily, the blacks' inveterate, autophagous violence, here expressed in the metaphors of disease, creates a 'No-Man's-Paradise'[54] into which the white man opportunely arrives:

> anon this most beautiful and fertile garden in all South Africa, this Black Man's arcady smiling, century long, in the joy of peace and plenty and perpetual sunshine, had become transformed into a sullen and desolate waste; and into this wilderness, in the nick of time, two streams of colonizing Whites, from east and from west, had as suddenly walked, and taken possession.[55]

Arguably, Bryant is here turning his characteristic sarcasm against the whites: the 'No-Man's-Paradise' is 'all a mirage, an illusion', the thousands of inhabitants were 'in being all the time, unseen, in hiding or in captivity', and soon making their unwelcome presence felt.[56] Bryant is not above pouring vitriol on his own party – within limits:[57]

> The history of modern European colonization among primitive peoples has proven beyond all gainsay that, where the White man wills he goes; that with him still might is right . . . this arrogant, greedy, lawless element struts over the face of the globe, disturbing all, molesting everybody, in its insatiable lust for further lands and further wealth.[58]

This sounds precociously 'liberal', but it is framed as a tentative hypothesis ('something of the Black man's criticism . . . might run somewhat on these lines'), and quickly slips into a revelation of Bryant's underpinning hierarchy:

---

52. Elsewhere, contradictorily, Bryant adulates Dingiswayo for bringing peace to a far-from-Edenic 'tumultuous and disintegrated mass of humanity' who are 'powerless and unproductive, because of continuously wasting their thought and energy on fighting each other', *Olden Times*, 96–7.
53. Bryant, *Olden Times*, 380–1.
54. Bryant, *Olden Times*, 237, 390.
55. Bryant, *Olden Times*, 236–7.
56. Bryant, *Olden Times*, 237.
57. For example, *Olden Times*, 78, 162, 297, 300, 563, 580.
58. Bryant, *Olden Times*, 235.

> To be sure, the Black man is not one whit better; but when the White man descends to do as the Black man does, he thereby lowers himself to the Black man's level and can claim no other justification for his deeds than that conferred by the Black man's sanctions. For, after all, that might is right *is* a law of nature; but of nature at its lowest, brutish stage, not of that higher and nobler nature which is enlightened by reason, guided by conscience, and ruled by a recognition of altruistic duties and responsibilities.[59]

This invokes the threat of 'going native' – the derogation of which is another gesture of enterrment – of becoming, like Shaka, 'arrogant, greedy, lawless'. Shaka *is* that man 'reverted not to the savage, but to the brutish stage',[60] the real propagator of imperialistic violence. So Bryant goes on ingenuously to exonerate the Natal whites altogether:

> The acquisition of Natal by Briton and Boer was not, we are happy to state, accomplished by such methods – in the last instance . . . The Natives of Natal lost their fatherland largely owing to a misunderstanding and a mischance [!].[61]

Bryant continues to place himself and his culture on the moral high ground, so enterring 'the Other' with a palpable defensiveness. In effect, he postulates a kind of 'reconstructed Eden', built by hard European work and suffused with Christian values.[62]

Bryant's propagation of those values, like Watt's, involves a withdrawal from insight and empathy, which in turn is the foundation of the language of clichéd, formless, exaggerated violence with which he describes the Zulu. In contradistinction, a certain *type of discourse* is being more or less explicitly privileged, one framed by a distinctively Western logical structure of cause and effect, classification, judgement.

This is inscribed, for example, in Isaacs's faintly ambivalent condemnation of Shaka as a 'giant without reason'[63] – a judgement consonant with and dependent on the views expressed in his Introduction. There, Africa is characterised as 'vast', 'trackless' and 'impenetrable', full of 'wild', 'noxious' and 'ignorant' people; Isaacs's ideal explorer's task is to achieve an Africa 'accurately described', 'delineated' and 'minutely investigated' by a 'general and comprehensive' mind, resulting in a 'stock of information' 'elaborately and clearly laid down':[64] the reconstructed Eden, again. This is the kind of late Enlightenment discourse privileged

59. Bryant, *Olden Times*, 235.
60. Bryant, *Olden Times*, 648.
61. Bryant, *Olden Times*, 236.
62. This was Isaacs's view, too, as evidenced by his repeated assessments of the landscape in terms of its agricultural potential, 'rich in verdure and lack[ing] only the art and industry of civilized man' (*Travels and Adventures*, vol. 1, 26; cf. 57, 111, 149 etc); the remedy 'prescribed against Africa's insidious corruptions was cheerful toil' (Coetzee, *White Writing*, 3).
63. Isaacs, *Travels and Adventures*, vol. 1, 269.
64. Isaacs, *Travels and Adventures*, vol. 1, xxiv–xxxii.

by Bryant, who repeatedly relates oral traditions in a wickedly sarcastic vein, only to revert triumphantly to his own conception of adequate historical explanation. The same is true of Watt's novel, in which a good deal of very precise documentary research into the whites' activities, expressed in the unvarnished style of the serious researcher, is dramatically juxtaposed with the virulence of the Zulu scenes.

Some implications of these interlocking and mutually reinforcing sub-species of enterrment may be drawn on two roughly congruent, superimposed planes. On one plane, a complex European mythology of an ambivalent 'Edenism' permits the use of a particular iconography of suppression which is essentially a psycho-cultural attitude towards the Zulu; it is the kind of iconography which has always been used by colonials in everyday life to justify and empower the practice of political control. The animal, the demonic, the lazy, the static, the irrational and the incomprehensible are categories everywhere used to establish the overlord identity of a people wishing to project themselves as humane, pious, vigorous, progressive, rational and knowledgeable.

A second plane is the *linguistic manner* in which that stance is described: the same broad division is re-enacted in the styles and structures of literary works. For instance, in virtually every historical work on Shaka's reign, the account begins with a more or less static description of 'Nguni society' as it 'stood' before the Shakan 'revolution'; then 'history' proper begins, coinciding, of course, with the advent of written records and the possibility of reconstructing a sequence of explicably linked events. This is the case even with recent works deliberately aimed at rehabilitating Shaka, such as Louis du Buisson's *The White Man Cometh* and Charles Ballard's *The House of Shaka*. Of course the lack of written records *is* in part responsible for this, given that explicable sequence is just what 'history' has come to comprise. But there is a dearth of written records for the 'state' of Shakan society, too, and I suggest that the stylistic and structural antinomies are equally the result of the received, centuries-ingrained 'iconographies of enterrment'.[65]

A final knot of examples will illustrate this. A structural partition between 'ethnographic observation' and 'historical narrative' begins with Isaacs, who, in the convention of the day, appended his notes on customs and practices to the end of his work. Notable is his intensive use of stative verbs and possessives:

---

65. Thus Louis du Buisson, *The White Man Cometh*, London, 1987, 17 writes:

> Zululand was a vast natural paradise, one of the most fertile on earth . . . a country with a gentle, generous climate devoid of extremes and with all the animals of creation intact, pursuing their own evolution. Including homo sapiens.
> . . . Unwarlike, fun-loving and hospitable, they lived in harmony with their neighbours and when conflicts arose they were settled in the gentlest possible way.

Cf. also P. Becker, *Path of Blood*, Harmondsworth, 1962, 22–7; D. Morris, *The Washing of the Spears*, London, 1967, 22–39 ('These, then, were the Kaffirs . . . an aimless people, happy and careless, with little sense of time and less of purpose'); Ballard, *The House of Shaka*, 13–14. For a survey of more recent blurrings and transcendences of these attitudinal rifts, see J. de Bruyn, 'The "Forgotten Factor" Sixteen Years Later: Some Trends in Historical Writing on Precolonial South Africa', *Kleio*, 16, (1984), 34–45.

> They *are*, doubtless, *the most* extraordinary people in existence, if we look into *their peculiarities of character*, and it is difficult to determine whether we should pity *their ignorance* or guard against *their duplicity*; for although *they are proverbially in a state of perfect simplicity*, yet *there is* a cunning about them, and an *irrevocable* desire for indulging in *all* their savage propensities . . .[66]

This is a good example of what Johannes Fabian has termed 'the ethnographic present'. As Fabian points out, this is another form of distancing, since the use of the present tense strongly implies a present speaker and hearer, a 'dialogic situation' from which the subject (here the Zulus) are in effect excluded; they are denied both 'personness' and an evolved and evolving position in time. Furthermore, the ethnographic present 'presupposes the givenness of the object of anthropology as something to be observed'.[67] 'Anthropological knowledge' is privileged; the Other is enterred.

Similar traces of this structurally differentiating gesture of enterrment can be found in the mainstream histories, even one like Omer-Cooper's *The Zulu Aftermath*, which explicitly states that the pre-Shakan world was 'far from idyllic'.[68] Times were still 'relatively peaceful', by contrast with the 'anarchy' which Shaka, working with 'forces which had been gathering strength over centuries', unleashed in the 1810s. While Omer-Cooper's historical explanations are certainly more sophisticated than most of his predecessors', he still demonstrates a tendency to attribute an essential stasis to pre-Shakan society: 'the southern sub-continent seems usually to have evolved at a slower pace than the rest'.[69] This more muted manifestation of the Edenic is inscribed in what might be termed an 'ethnographic past':

> Administrative authority in the tribe was distributed between the chief and a hierarchy of subordinates. Depending on its size, the tribal territory was divided into a number of sub-divisions, provinces and districts. Each of these was under the authority of a sub-chief and where the tribe was large there might be a two-tier system . . . All the important subordinate chieftaincies were normally held by close relatives of the chief.[70]

Phrases such as 'there might be' and 'normally' admit of the possibility that 'exceptions to this might arise', but essentially this is the language of Western categorisation and normative anthropology which would regard any deviation from it as aberrant. The use of the preterite, effectively distancing the subject, thus comes close to that 'narrative past' characterised by Roland Barthes as 'part of a security system . . . one of those numerous formal pacts made between the writer and society

---

66. Isaacs, *Travels and Adventures*, vol. 2, 243, my italics.
67. J. Fabian, *Time and the Other: How Anthropology Makes its Object*, New York, 1983, 80, 87.
68. Omer-Cooper, *The Zulu Aftermath*, 21.
69. Omer-Cooper, *The Zulu Aftermath*, 2.
70. Omer-Cooper, *The Zulu Aftermath*, 17.

for the justification of the former and the serenity of the latter'.[71] This same gesture, as Shula Marks has pointed out, commands the account in *The Oxford History of South Africa*, in which the 'pre-colonial history of the black man has been relegated to an anthropologist [Monica Wilson], and is handled in wholly static, a-historical terms':[72] Wilson states, for example, that 'the manners of 1686 are those of the same countryside nearly three centuries later'.[73]

Two final points can be made. Firstly, the whole concept of the 'mfecane' – as a kind of subcontinental, endemic autophagia[74] – is, in this perspective, as much the result of the myth of a destroyed paradise, constantly reinforced by the fear of renewed destruction of the reconstructed idyll, as it is the result of actual evidence. This is inscribed in numerous ways in the language of the overlord's judgementalism (enterrment). Secondly, of course, the concept itself (and whatever concept may arise to replace it, including any in the present study!) is the inscription of that logician's discourse of cause-and-effect, explication, categorisation and the representational word which, in the end, may conceal as much as it reveals.

Layback

When Nathaniel Isaacs, in a rare moment of self-reflection in his *Travels*, acknowledges his 'anomalous description of Zoolas – savage yet hospitable',[75] he is not merely balancing two irreconcilable facets and leaving the judgement to his narratee. Embedded in massive derogation and undisguised Eurocentrism, this momentary 'admission' is more likely to be just another reification of the incomprehensible. This is not to deny that there is a genuine inner tension here, but the actual manifestation of the tension, when placed in context, serves primarily to reinforce the Eurocentric foundation of the discourse itself.

The Shakan literature is riddled with ambivalences, contradictions and paradoxes: admiration vies with repulsion, derogation with lionisation, ethnographic insight with Eurocentric judgement, assiduous fascination with practical oppression. Doubtless much of this is unavoidable in any kind of cross-cultural discourse. Some of it, however, like this example from Isaacs, is more than simple equivocation; it actually functions, in a more backhanded way than enterrment, to promote the interests of the writer and his group. For this gesture I offer the term *layback*.

The word is derived from rock-climbing; it describes a technique used to climb a vertical crack in a chimney, in which the feet are placed against the rock and push

71. R. Barthes, *Writing Degree Zero*, New York, 1968, 32.
72. S. Marks, 'Towards a People's History of South Africa? Recent Developments in the Historiography of South Africa', in R. Samuel, ed., *People's History and Socialist Theory*, London, 1981, 300.
73. M. Wilson and L.M. Thompson, eds, *The Oxford History of South Africa*, vol.1, Oxford, 1969, 129.
74. I am reminded irresistibly here of Gillray's 1790s cartoon of cannibalistic French revolutionaries (echoing the many, probably apocryphal but widely-repeated stories of Zulu-induced cannibalism; see e.g. Thompson, *A History of South Africa*, 85). Such imagery cannot circulate without an ambience of extreme xenophobia and 'superiorist' revulsion.
75. Isaacs, *Travels and Adventures*, vol.2, 102.

outwards, while the hands, inserted in the crack, pull inwards; by the friction and tension thus achieved progress is made upwards. In the textual context to which I now transfer it, it denotes an inner tension or ambivalence, used within a single narrative gesture to reinscribe an aspect of Eurocentrism; for this reason I will isolate it largely among *stories* told of Shaka (stories of which even the 'history', or perhaps more accurately, the 'biography' of Shaka almost wholly consists).

The layback gesture is frequently made quite plain. For instance, when Viola Ridgway characterises Shaka in her novella as 'the cruel Brave', this is not merely the inscription of an unresolved paradox. It is already the distillation of numerous illustrative anecdotes; the adjective 'cruel' has already been laden with judgement. In its context, the epithet serves as the touchstone for the assertion of the writer's own values, which are kindness, even-handed justice, restraint. Much the same can be said of the antithetical motion of approbation contained by 'Brave'. Ridgway 'happens' to make this explicit in her very next lines:

> If these stories from the life of Shaka have softened the old ideas of this great leader, and brought the reader a deeper understanding of his faults and his greatness, they will not have been written in vain. Perhaps, some day, there will be another leader among the black men, with Shaka's genius for leadership and organization, tempered with the democratic ideas of the white man for trade, scientific cultivation of the soil and development of the wonderful inventions of the modern world, a leader who will believe in the doctrine of 'Live and let live,' with mercy and justice for all.[76]

The echoes of Isaacs's agricultural Eden and the missionary stance of the nineteenth century are clear here: 'leadership and organization' are primary virtues, structured by science, technology and the tolerance of a democratic judiciary. The 'deeper understanding' of Shaka, ostensibly Ridgway's objective, is not in fact a resolution or explanation of the antinomy of 'cruel Brave', but an exploitation of it in the inscription of a European world-view. Neither the Zulu chieftain nor his people are viewed as whole or are accorded their own voice; instead, approved aspects – 'the one who never allowed a worthy man to go unrewarded', the 'genius', and so on – are split off, while the condemned aspects are attributed to, say, an unexplained 'madness'.[77] This schizoid quality, it needs hardly be added, arises from an interpretation founded on a writer-centred adherence to values irrelevant to the Zulus themselves: the split attributed by Isaacs and his numerous clones to the Zulu character and thence epitomised by Shaka is inherent not in the Zulu but in the colonial mind, in what Abdul JanMohamed has termed a 'Manichean allegory'.[78]

76. Ridgway, *Stories From Zulu History*, Pietermaritzburg, 1946, 95. A Bryant clone.
77. Ridgway, *Stories From Zulu History*, 95, 87, 89.
78. A.R. JanMohamed, 'The Economy of Manichean Allegory: The Function of Racial Difference in Colonialist Literature' in H.L. Gates Jr, ed., *'Race', Writing and Difference*, Chicago, 1985 78–106. 'We can better understand colonialist discourse, it seems to me, through an analysis that maps its ideological function in relation to actual imperialist practices. Such an examination reveals that any evident 'ambivalence' is in fact a product of deliberate, if at times subconscious, imperialist duplicity . . .' (80).

Few writers, especially the more recent, are so blatant. But the tension of this kind of layback and its schizoid undercarriage is present in, for instance, Brookes and Webb's *History of Natal*: 'the qualities of the Zulu at his best are the qualities so fearfully taught in Shaka's blood-stained school – submission to authority, obedience to the law, respect for superiors, order and self-restraint, civic duty'.[79] Terror and blood as instruments of this education are condemned, but the values attributed to it are precisely those 'taught', by precisely this process of fear and bloodshed, to the subject black peoples by white authorities.

A particularly common species of anecdote which embodies the notion of layback involves the meeting of Shaka with items of European technology. There are numerous stories (many common to all colonial literatures), involving mirrors, medicines, Mr Petersen's music-box, the figurehead of the wrecked vessel *Mary*, firearms, writing, a knowledge of astronomical phenomena, and so on. In almost all cases, what is superficially told at the expense of the white man reveals an inner tension which, on examination, rebounds to promote the white over the black.

Almost all these gestures of layback are underpinned by the promotion of particular species of logic, of the 'scientific' thought-processes and modes of *expression* which are by definition opposed to irrationality, 'superstition' or unintelligibility. This attitude is unconcealed in the earlier texts. Isaacs, for instance, makes no effort to hide his derision even when apparently bettered in argument, as in this exchange between Isaacs, Shaka and a Portuguese man:

> [Shaka] then asked me to fight with the Portuguese, but I told him that, although our nation had conquered the Portuguese, we were now not only at peace with them, but were by treaties their protectors . . .
>
> 'Well,' said he, 'what need you care? You have once conquered, and may conquer again.' My Portuguese new acquaintance sat all this time and heard our conversation with concealed chagrin, and swelling with rage; but when we had left the presence of Chaka, we both laughed at the vanity of the savage.[80]

The implicit agreement between writer and narratee in this telling is that open derision is as acceptable to the narratee as it was to the white protagonists. The story is really designed to reassert the superiority of European morality over Shaka's unbridled violence. The same comfortable contempt informs Isaacs's other stories of Shaka's encounters with medicines, firearms and mirrors,[81] which became staples of the dramatisation of this particular culture-contact.

79. Brookes and Webb, *A History of Natal*, 14. This is plagiarised almost verbatim from Bryant, *Olden Times*, 641: 'Strange, but true, this Shaka was as sublime a moral teacher as martial genius. Submission to authority, obedience to the law, respect for superiors, order and self-restraint, fearlessness and self-sacrifice, constant work and civil duty, in a word, all the noblest disciplines of life were the very foundation-stones upon which he built his nation. So rigorously enforced was the life-long practice of all these excellencies, that he left them all a spontaneous habit, a second nature, amongst his people'.
80. Isaacs, *Travels and Adventures*, vol. 1, 60.
81. Isaacs, *Travels and Adventures*, vol. 1, 90, 93, 236.

Similar, though less arrogant, is Fynn's story, also frequently repeated, of Shaka's encounter with purgatives supplied by Petersen, one of the whites' financial backers:

> During my [Fynn's] absence Mbikwana informed Shaka that Mr Petersen also had medicine. Mr Petersen was requested to produce it and state its virtues. He produced a box of pills which he said were good for all diseases and strongly advised Shaka to take two. The King took four and giving one each to four chiefs, made them swallow them. Mr Petersen was also desired to take four. Mr Petersen after vainly endeavouring to convince the King that four were too much for one person was reluctantly compelled to swallow the four . . . The King now swallowed two and ordered Mr Petersen to keep him company. This Mr Petersen peremptorily refused to do, but the King insisting, and the chiefs adding the pressure of the argument that one who recommended medicines should not refuse to take them himself, Mr Petersen was compelled to swallow two more, that is, six in all. The consequences of this to a person of 63 does [sic] not require to be explained in detail.[82]

All the elements of subsequent stories of Zulu encounters with white technology are present here. Fynn laughs at his companion's predicament; the white man is apparently overcome by 'native logic'. But throughout there persists an awareness that it is Shaka who is misinterpreting the nature of the medicine, is being characteristically unrestrained; comment on the purgative's effects on Shaka himself is conspicuous by its absence; and Fynn suggests in an alternative version that it was 'fear', rather than logic, which forced Petersen's hand.[83]

Other stories, such as that of Shaka besting Francis Farewell's carpenter by forcing him to bend his house-building nails on a piece of ironwood, or demonstrating the impossibility of a round world by showing how pips fall off a turning pumpkin,[84] also momentarily demonstrate the efficacy of Shaka's 'native logic' within the confines of his own paradigms; but they inevitably carry the layback dimension of exposing limitations to those paradigms, so promoting the whites' wider ones.

The incident of Shaka's encounters with a meteor or eclipse (another perennial of colonial fictions),[85] has similarly been used to assert the expertise of the white man. It is presumably derived from a brief note in Fynn's Diary: 'On Shaka's preparing to attack the Ndwandwes, a meteor appeared which detained him some time from proceeding until perceiving it throwing its meteoric sparks in that direction announced a favourable issue, it being a sign that the enemy would be entirely defeated, which was verified [by the outcome of the battle]'.[86] Though Fynn is

82. Fynn, The Diary, 79n.
83. Fynn, The Diary, 79.
84. Fynn, The Diary, 90; Ritter, Shaka Zulu, 300.
85. See, for example, R. Haggard's, King Solomon's Mines, 1895; B. Mitford's, John Ames, 1900; C. Gilson's, In the Power of the Pygmies, Milford, 1919; P. White's Voss, 1957.
86. Fynn, The Diary, 317.

largely free of Eurocentric sneering here, there is no doubt that he disbelieves this explanation himself, and regards it as an ethnological curiosity symptomatic of 'the uninformed and unenlightened state of minds, the result of ages of the grossest ignorance' which make the Zulu, 'feeling conscious of existing superior powers, endeavour to supply that deficiency by invention from their own limited ideas'.[87]

It is worth touching on one retelling of this story which is *not* a layback, in order to sharpen my definition. In Elizabeth Paris Watt's account in *Febana*, Shaka is depicted as 'petrified, the victim of his own superstitious fears' and 'desperate that [the comet] might be subject to the influence of the white men'. The hero Francis Farewell, of course, is 'astronomer enough to know' when the comet will disappear, and turns this to advantage. The inevitable 'verification of [Farewell's] prophecy earned Frank a veneration which secretly amused him' – and which, by virtue of this privileged insight into Farewell's mind, less secretly amuses Watt and her narratee, at Shaka's expense.[88] The derogation of Shaka's fear and 'superstition' and promotion of 'science' is totally undisguised here: hence it does not qualify as layback. Where Fynn, or rather his editor, James Stuart, relegated the incident to the 'ethnographic' back pages, Watt transforms it into a turning-point of the plot, a hinge of 'historical' efficacy: such is the empowerment of logographic discourse.

A different, and subtler story of Shaka's reaction to a similar celestial phenomenon, an eclipse, is related by E. A. Ritter. There are no white characters involved here, and it is Shaka's stature which apparently is elevated, in accordance with Ritter's general lionising project. But there is a layback gesture involved nevertheless. Ritter portrays the Zulus as terrified, Shaka as calm but disturbed, 'mutter[ing]'; he is handed some medicine by one Mqalane, to spit at the sun, 'commanding it to return'. This Shaka does, the sun duly returns; Shaka's 'commanding figure seemed to be magnified to majestic proportions in that weird and unreal light'; and 'like Joshua of old, Shaka continued to exploit the dramatic possibilities of the situation', until, the eclipse over, 'there was one continuous roar of victory, which continued in triumphant waves of adulation for the all-powerful Warrior-King who had saved the nation'.[89]

This may or may not be tolerably close to how the Zulus might have seen it, but it is certainly not how Ritter sees it, or expects his readership to see it. It is, in Ritter's own, only partially concealed, view, no more than a 'dramatic' situation of which Shaka can shrewdly take advantage; he only 'seems' to be magnified; and the medicine is shown to be really beside the point, the 'saving of the nation' in some sense spurious. In the commandeering of a 'superstition' to a political stratagem, Shaka is seen to exploit the Zulu people's 'credulity'; but the credulity is also being exploited by Ritter. While there is a stated admiration for Shaka's self-control and shrewdness, the final flow of sympathy is in fact against Shaka, since Ritter (and, he assumes, his narratee) still knows better; were it not for the implicit gap between

87. Fynn, *The Diary*, 267.
88. Watt, *Febana*, 94.
89. Ritter, *Shaka Zulu*, 272–3.

species of knowledge, of which the European is clearly seen as the superior, this story would not have been told at all. Hence, Ritter manipulates narrative 'suspension of disbelief' up to a point at which, in this and numerous other cases in *Shaka Zulu*, he interrupts with an explicatory comment which reasserts the primacy of European paradigms of logic or historical perspicacity: 'It is appropriate at this point to note that Shaka was far too wary to engage in the very uncertain business of rain-making, which all other chiefs, and kings, dabbled in'.[90] Ritter's contempt is evident in the word 'dabbled', and here Shaka is commandeered to support him; Shaka's stature in the novel, in the end, depends upon his being crafted to conform with Ritter's own values. Like Viola Ridgway, Ritter cannot resist making these values plain:

> One outstanding fact, however, emerges and stands forth like a shining beacon above the haze of time and controversy, and that is that the White men had some dominant quality even when in rage which compelled the black men to regard them as their superior. Shaka not only recognised this but had it proclaimed to all his nation. It had nothing to do with sky-rockets or horses or firearms, for these had been met with in the hands of Portuguese half-castes, and of the White men's Hottentots who were regarded with contempt. No! the root of the European's superiority lay in his possession of *ubu-kosi* – the quality and air of chieftainship – for which only the Zulu language has a single word which fully defines that otherwise indefinable aristocratic ascendancy which radiates authority without any apparent effort.[91]

At least part of Shaka's stature in Ritter's eyes depends on Shaka's 'perception' in the whites of precisely the quality which Ritter has projected on to the Zulu chief in the first place; thus Shaka is, at best, admired for his 'white' traits, and at worst, positively overshadowed. Moreover, it is a *Zulu* word which is invoked as most adequately descriptive of this quality, a quality 'instantly and instinctively recognized by every Zulu'; a Zulu perspective is domesticated in order to justify the white assumption of superiority; the Zulus, in effect, are obliged (textually) to connive at their own subordination. In this textual acquisition of a 'Zulu point of view', layback overlaps with what I call *deadlighting*, which I will treat shortly.

One final example will serve. A crucial question which lurks behind a great deal of the writing on Shaka is the question of what light to judge his actions in. From the beginning the whites have with varying degrees of fervour condemned Shaka's alleged atrocities, even inventing increasingly dastardly deeds with which to 'assassinate' him. Isaacs almost certainly projected a great deal of his own violence on to Shaka. Some, like Holden, try to assimilate the atrocities into God's plan for the world. Some attempt in various ways to explain Shaka's violence in terms of practical politics: Lewis Grout, for instance: 'Cruel and bloody as this mighty African conqueror is reputed to have been, or as he really became in the progress

---

90. Ritter, *Shaka Zulu*, 274.
91. Ritter, *Shaka Zulu*, 268.

of his triumphs, his policy, especially at first, was not so much the utter destruction of the neighbouring tribes, as to subdue, and incorporate them with his own.'[92] However, Grout adds delicately, in Shaka's final years 'his own mind seems not to have been at rest';[93] there are hints here of the fast-developing idea, which would be carried by Bryant and Ritter in particular into the later histories, that after the death of his mother Nandi he went distinctly insane. Once again, Western logic seems determined either to dragoon Shaka into the realm of the perfectly logical, or utterly to banish him beyond it.

But a more subtle tack has been to compare Shaka's policies to those pertaining to the England of the time. This has been hinted at in numerous instances since Isaacs and Fynn related how horrified Shaka was at hearing of the practice of imprisonment. There appears to be a kind of irrefutable logic to the Zulu's argument in favour of the death sentence, and the white men are, again, momentarily bested in the exchange. But there is no question that Fynn believed, on moral grounds, that imprisonment was preferable to the atrocities which he and Isaacs repeatedly condemn in Shaka. Here again we see the gesture of layback.

Louis du Buisson's *The White Man Cometh* is a more recent representative. The opening paragraph of Du Buisson's Foreword is:

> It was a savage age. In England, the most 'civilised' nation in the world, boys were sent to sea at the age of six, children were made to labour for sixteen hours a day, seven days a week, in mines and cotton mills. In London, Mondays were still public hanging days.

Du Buisson then quotes A. K. Millar on the 'heartless' customs of the English, with 'no fewer than two hundred offences for which death by hanging was the prescribed punishment', and notes that in North America 'Europeans were systematically exterminating the natives and the animals and taking over their land', and doing the same in Africa with the pernicious addition of taking slaves.[94] This appears a useful reminder that, after all, Shaka's atrocities were not unusual. But Du Buisson fails to press the point, continuing:

> 1815. Jane Austen's *Pride and Prejudice* topped the bestseller list, Beethoven's *Fidelio* was first performed in Vienna, the waltz was all the rage in the ballrooms of Europe, Napoleon Bonaparte faced his Waterloo and President John Madison unveiled America's latest weapon, the *USS Fulton*, the world's first steam-powered warship. And in a grass-hutted village on the south-east coast of Africa a young Zulu invented the stabbing-spear. In the context of time and place he might as well have invented gunpowder. By the end of that year

92. L. Grout, *Zulu-land; or Life among the Zulu-Kafirs of Natal and Zulu-land, South Africa*, London, 1862, 72.
93. Grout, *Zulu-land*, 74.
94. Du Buisson, *The White Man Cometh*, 1.

with the great European star of Napoleon in its final eclipse, a new star was rising in Africa. *Shaka.*[95]

Du Buisson's purpose becomes immediately obscure. Is he merely setting the scene? But the juxtaposition of hanging-days and Austen is disconcertingly abrupt, even irrelevant, inviting awkward comparisons. The 'invention' of the stabbing spear is manifestly overstated, the tone of the passage melodramatic. This is a cinematic list of items designed for the Eurocentric reader, and whatever Du Buisson's stated purpose, 'grass-hutted' sounds either condescendingly 'natural', or slightly pathetic, against 'ballrooms', 'stabbing spear' frail against 'warship' and 'gunpowder'. It seems that something of Europe is meant to rub off on this Shaka, particularly something of Napoleon (I will have more to say on this gesture under 'Dead-lighting'). It is by no means clear whether we are to read this warship as iconic of laudable industry, or (rather indirectly) of the threat of the white man, or (perhaps unconsciously) of a belittlement of the Zulu. And it is by no means clear whether Du Buisson intends a defence of Zulu, alongside his condemnation of nineteenth-century English punishments, or to include Shaka in this 'savage age' and condemn both. In either case, the lens through which we are initially introduced to Shaka here is undeniably European; so, presumably, is the concept of justice which we are invited to bring to bear. Du Buisson goes on:

> Fynn and Isaacs ... professed themselves horrified that condemned criminals were dragged out of the [Zulu] capital and clubbed to death. But then king Shaka was equally horrified that Europeans should deprive people of their freedom for ever, something he considered more inhuman than the death penalty.
>
> . . . It is . . . true that the Zulu monarch's power was absolute and that life was cheap. Yet in the Cape, during king Shaka's lifetime, executions were still public affairs and accompanied by hair-raising brutality . . . Isaacs was aware of this.
>
> 'In such a rude state of society,' he wrote, 'the death penalty for crimes of a capital nature does not differ from more civilised nations, but the execution is exceedingly revolting and only to be found amongst barbarous hordes.'
>
> Yet, curiously, when 'king' Henry Fynn of Natal and his chief legislator Nathaniel Isaacs set up their own government and began meting out death sentences, their victims were executed in the traditional Zulu manner – by clubbing! Isaacs crowned his own duplicity with the following comment: 'These executions contributed not a little to enlighten them and prepare them for receiving those more important blessings which civilisation brings.'[96]

Several ambivalences are tangible here. Firstly, Du Buisson seems concerned to damage the credibility of Fynn and Isaacs: his insinuation is that they were not

---

95. Du Buisson, *The White Man Cometh*, 2.
96. Du Buisson, *The White Man Cometh*, 8–9, cf. 121.

actually horrified by Shaka's misdeeds – but Shaka was 'equally horrified' by theirs. Shaka is at least honest, it seems – or equally dishonest – even if, for him, 'life was cheap'. Not only does Du Buisson appear to accept the picture of Shaka as violent despot, he also implicitly agrees with Isaacs's judgement of 'exceedingly revolting', while simultaneously attacking Isaacs for his 'duplicity'. The final sentence here seems less an example of duplicity than of sheer, if defensive, Eurocentric arrogance; and one wonders why the contradiction between Isaacs's revulsion at Zulu executions and the meting out of his own should be merely 'curious'. 'Curiously' signals Du Buisson's hesitancy, evident throughout his book, adequately to press his conclusions; in this passage he fails to address the question of why, if Fynn and Isaacs really were not horrified, they 'professed' to be; or why, if everybody were living in a 'savage age', they thought their moral outrage should have had any effect. Behind these inner tensions, the layback gesture is visible: Du Buisson contextualises Shaka's world both against and within a European value-system which is equally distant; the nineteenth-century English being as 'other' to Du Buisson as the Zulu, he effectively inscribes his own, late twentieth-century morality over the heads of both.

In sum: once again, this is not a matter of mere fictions which may be discarded. The same impulses operate in historiographical texts, too: the crucial stories of Shaka's encounters with firearms and of his alleged land concessions are among those in the telling of which evidence is skewed or suppressed by deep-seated gestures of cultural negation.

Deadlighting

A third narrative gesture, closely related to layback, I term *deadlighting*, which I take from the nautical term for a stormshutter which is dropped over a cabin window or cannon-port. By it I denote a gesture by which the writer claims to 'shed light' on the Other, but inadvertently hides more than he or she reveals. There is often a certain defensiveness about this manoeuvre – a desire to conceal the writer's own predilections, or a lack of real knowledge, or a quiver of 'colonial guilt' – which the image of the deadlight also catches.

An extremely common gesture of deadlighting involves the comparison of the Other with something or someone European. This is a natural enough reaction for anyone trying to make sense of the culturally different; the Other is appropriated to, or domesticated by assimilation into, a familiar metaphor or figure. Essentially, this is a defence against the threat of the absolutely Other, an attempt to explain (and 'explanation' is the psychological cornerstone of a great deal of colonial discourse) what might otherwise be unassimilable, thus uncontrollable. The effect of this assimilation is to create a new, metaphorical 'reality' – here, a new, textual 'Shaka'.[97]

97. See G. Lakoff and M. Johnson, *Metaphors We Live By*, Chicago, 1980, 117, 156–8: 'metaphors allow us to understand one domain of experience in terms of another . . . [They] can . . . define reality . . . through a coherent network of entailments that highlight some features of reality and hide others . . . Such "truths" may be true, of course, only relative to the reality defined by the metaphor.'

A particular instance will demonstrate how this works. The comparison of Shaka to other 'tyrants' – Attila, Napoleon, Alexander and so on – has become almost a reflex, so ingrained a gesture that it earns a term of its own: *vindice*. This I have taken from the character in Cyril Tourneur's play *The Revenger's Tragedy*, in which Vindice induces the Duke to selfdestruct by kissing a poisoned skull disguised as his lover. This is, in effect, what happens to Shaka; he is poisoned (or at least violently misrepresented) by being juxtaposed with another autocrat or general with whom he is supposed to have affinities. This is frequently linked to a defensive admission that Europe has also had its tyrants and its injustices;[98] the term *vindice* thus appropriately carries the twinned connotations of vindictiveness and of vindication (either of Shaka, or of the writer's condemnation of him, or of the condemnation of his own society: the ambivalences here, as we have seen with Du Buisson, are multiple).

Once again, an example from Bryant will clarify these points. He writes: 'One judges the worth of an object by its contrast with the rest of its class. And one can gauge the true worth of Dingiswayo's character only by comparing him with other men of his position whose greatness is universally acknowledged.'[99] The first sentence here demands judgement by intra-cultural *contrast* (the epitome is Bryant's characterisation of Shaka as the 'active doer', utterly distinct from the rest of the Nguni). The second, which Bryant in fact proceeds to follow, proposes assessment by cross-cultural *similarity*. Bryant then gleans examples of 'the outstanding political geniuses of the ancient Mediterranean and Oriental world' to demonstrate 'how identical were the mental characteristics which drove these men to such glorious deeds'. Significantly, Bryant chooses models from '5,000 or more years ago', assuming that this is bound to be equivalent to the present African 'stage' of development. He also selects foreign (i.e. non-British) examples, even as he argues that these were 'the founders of our own civilization': a necessary defence to accommodate his own clear preference for enlightened European advancement. Thus he goes on to argue that Dingiswayo's talents 'were buried in a field whereon the light of knowledge had never shone, and whereto the fertilizing waters of foreign intercourse never penetrated', but these abilities were fortuitously liberated by his momentary contact with a white man or men (a legend if ever there was one). After several pages, in which Bryant provides more information on other leaders than he is able to provide on Dingiswayo himself (one of the primary impulses behind the *vindice* gesture is to compensate for the extreme paucity of concrete evidence), he concludes that 'If Shaka was the Timur and the Attila of his race, Dingiswayo was its Menes and its Alfred the Great.'[100]

At least part of this contrast derives from, and is designed to reinforce, the notion of Shaka's revolutionary violence and unnatural cruelty. Two further points need to be stressed. The first is the non-Britishness of the *vindice* comparison: in Bryant, it is Attila, Napoleon, Caesar, the Spartans, Timur. While the gesture is occasionally in

98. Bryant, *Olden Times*, 699.
99. Bryant, *Olden Times*, 168.
100. Bryant, *Olden Times*, 171.

praise (particularly with Napoleon), the figure is at best ambivalently heroic. The second point is to note the way in which the *vindice* gesture is constantly updated, warning us again that we are dealing with Eurocentric projections. Russell Martin detects a shift from the Attila comparison to Napoleon as Shaka becomes gradually less monstrous (though the Attila comparison persists sporadically right up to the 1986 South African Broadcasting Corporation (SABC) television series); Alexander the Great also becomes more common in the twentieth century, where Nero was more popular in the nineteenth. After the Second World War, Hitler and the Nazis are invoked; after the 1960s, Stalin. Leonard Thompson summons 'Robespierre, Stalin, Mao Zedong' to illuminate the process whereby the rule of 'revolutionary leaders' 'degenerated into a reign of terror' (this last phrase, like 'cohorts', 'legions', 'Golden Hordes', even 'regiments', is itself a kind of *vindice*).[101]

The effect of this is surreptitiously to associate Shaka with better-documented examples of genocide, the evidence for which in the Zulu case is extremely shaky, to reproduce the undocumented prejudice evident in the earliest comparisons with Nero and Tamurlaine, to obscure the individuality of Shaka's reign, and by proxy and proximity, rather than by evidence, to exaggerate the extent of Shaka's conquests and depredations. After all, Shaka could not possibly have conquered as much territory as Napoleon did, or murdered as many people as Hitler or Stalin.

Writers are sometimes aware of the potential absurdity; and so insert a counterbalancing (additional, not replacement) argument that Shaka had as dramatic an effect in his smaller, more primitive, less technological world as these other dictators had in theirs. This is to introduce a slightly different species of cross-cultural comparison, the difficulties of which Bryant almost inadvertently lays bare:

> In writing or reading of the rulers of simple, primitive tribes, we are wont to use the grandiloquent terms and to imagine the magnificent state appropriate to our modern European royalties. We assume that our reader possesses the ability to visualize things in their proper perspective and to realize that, though the events herein recorded occurred but one short century back, the conditions under which they occurred were those of many thousands of years ago. Yet it is not easy for everyone to place himself mentally two or three thousand years back in the days when our own 'kings' wore raiment and ate food and dwelt in habitations we would now not offer to a beggar, and ruled over 'peoples' too

---

101. Martin, 'British Images of the Zulu', 152–3. Cf. for example: H. Tracey, *Zulu Paradox*, Johannesburg, 1948, 21; Millin, *The King of the Bastards*, x; R. Niven, *Nine Great Africans*, London, 1964, 81; E.V. Walter, *Terror and Resistance*, New York, 1969, 127, and reprinted in F. Chalk and K. Jonassohn, eds, *The History and Sociology of Genocide: Analyses and Case Studies*, New Haven, 1990, 225. For Stalin, see M. de Villiers, *White Tribe Dreaming*, New York, 1987, 109; and Thompson, *A History of South Africa*, 85. J.M. Coetzee, *Age of Iron*, New York, 1990, 150 has his white heroine say to a black man: 'The Germans had comradeship, and the Japanese, and the Spartans. Shaka's impis, too, I am sure. Comradeship is nothing but a mystique of death, of killing and dying . . .'

few to run a modern factory. We call wretched and unsavoury grass hovels 'palaces,' and speak of 'great battles' and 'conquests' fought and won where the combatants were a couple of score a side . . . The general idea of presenting history in this fashion, is, of course, to create a proper atmosphere around the reader, to produce in his mind a relatively accurate impression by transporting him into the 'other people's' place and so enabling him to regard things as they appeared to, or were felt by them.[102]

Bryant shows himself keenly aware of the problem of the cross-cultural translation of terms, concepts and categories, and subsequent historians might have done well to take fuller heed of his initial warning. But Bryant himself continues the practice in the service of creating a 'proper atmosphere', that is, making the imaginative leap into the mind-space of the Other, producing a 'relatively accurate impression'. The word 'relatively' has an interesting *double entendre*: Bryant surely means it in the sense of 'more or less', allowing that the impression is bound to be no more than an approximation; but it also invokes the 'relativity' of the writer/reader's culture to that of the subject. Bryant seems to intend that when his narratee reads 'king' in *Olden Times* he is to imagine a man who, however undistinguished his accoutrements or 'relatively' mean his principality, commands a reverence from his subjects analogous to that accorded a European 'king'. But this importation of a European terminology functions as much to obscure the Zulu reality as to illuminate it. Instead of gaining insight into the individual particularity of the Zulu experience, the narratee in fact constructs a mental image relative to the *European* experience; instead of difference being inscribed, and the narratee carried over the cultural boundary into that difference, in this conceptual overlay (of 'kingship', say) the two cultures are effectively conflated. The use of Eurocentric terminology, in other words, embodies an implicit agreement between writer and narratee that the European concepts will finally dominate. The distortive effects of this are dramatically evident in the SABC TV series, in which costumes and 'palaces' are absurdly exaggerated, precisely to cater, not for the Zulu reality, but for the potential viewers' Eurocentric preconceptions.

Probably the commonest deadlighting gesture of this kind is the ostensible assumption of the 'Zulu point of view'. In this essentially fictional, cross-cultural foray of the white writers' imagination into the mindset of the world of the Other, an attempt is made to reproduce the Other's 'authentic' voice. I am far from arguing that such imaginative leaps and transcriptions should never be attempted; it is probable (following Schopenhauer) that no communication whatever can take place without some such empathetic effort, a temporary shedding of self-consciousness. However, these leaps – the diametric opposite of the logical imposition of more 'scientific' discourses noted earlier – are themselves fraught with the dangers of false

102. Bryant, *Olden Times*, 319.

transpositions or distortive translations, and in a number of cases they undoubtedly 'deadlight' more than they enlighten.

The most immediately accessible example of this is the 'quotation', more often invention, of the 'voices' of Zulu people themselves. This occurs from the so-called eyewitness accounts onwards. Fynn generally refrains from making direct quotations – with good reason, since he was writing in retrospect. His accounts of discussions with Shaka are almost wholly in reported speech; he simply summarises verbal exchanges, and there is no pretence to be giving the precise words. On three significant occasions, however, he departs from this practice. On the first occasion, he records one of his earliest conversations with Shaka in the form of a drama, with a touch of annotation stylistically more appropriate to the novel:

> 'I hear you have come from umGeorge, is it so? Is he as great a king as I am?'
>
> Fynn: 'Yes; King George is one of the greatest kings in the world.'
>
> Shaka: 'I am very angry with you,' said while putting on a severe countenance. 'I shall send a messenger to umGeorge and request him to kill you. He sent you to me not to give medicine to my dogs.' All present immediately applauded what Shaka had said. 'Why did you give my dogs medicine?' (in allusion to the woman I was said to have brought back to life after death).[103]

And so on. There are several difficulties with this. Its unembellished format signals an attempt to erase bias, to reduce the event to its essentials, to position the narratee himself, as it were, within earshot; the purely 'auditory' quality of the recording is aided with a minimum of interpolation. But this very paring down to 'pure' audition itself necessarily excludes a multiplicity of factors that may have coloured the situation. What, for instance, happened in the unsettling shift of subject from king George to Shaka's anger with Fynn's medical activities: did Shaka simply ignore Fynn's reply about George, show disbelief or embarrassment, unaccountably switch topics, displace unexpressed anger? And how did the process of translation progress, when by all accounts, 'Jacob' the interpreter was hardly a fluent speaker of English – nor perhaps of Zulu – and Fynn himself characterises him as untrustworthy? Furthermore, if James Stuart's annotation is correct,[104] this account was written up from memory in 1854, that is, thirty years later, and it is highly unlikely to have been recalled with the accuracy that its presentation is designed to suggest.[105]

Fynn's second deviation from the recorded-speech form is presented as the oration of Shaka's *induna* Ngomane:

---

103. Fynn, *The Diary*, 76.
104. Fynn, *The Diary*, 58n.
105. For the high degree of inaccuracy contained in even eyewitness accounts, see R. Buckhout, 'Eyewitness Testimony', *Scientific American*, 231, (1974), 31–2; and A.J. Woodman, *Rhetoric*, 12–23.

> The tribe had now lamented for a year the death of her [Nandi], who had now become a spirit, and who would continue to watch over Shaka's welfare. But there were nations of men, inhabiting distant countries, who, because they had not yet been conquered, supposed that they never should be . . .[106]

The implication of the textual presentation of this as direct speech is that Fynn is reiterating, presumably as closely as his translation will allow, Ngomane's actual words. But the displacement of the tenses from, for instance, 'have' to 'had', in fact inscribes Fynn's own distance from the original delivery of the speech; while we have no evidence to maintain it does not capture the gist of the original, it is certainly not the speech itself. That this hybrid of direct and indirect speech was conventional at the time − Isaacs also uses it[107] − only reinforces the point: what we are reading is a twice-, perhaps three-times, veiled shadow of an original, for the veracity, even the occurrence, of which we have no external evidence.

Historiographically, this is no trivial point, for Ngomane's reported speech concerns the 1828 Zulu attack on the Mpondo and its aftermath along the eastern frontier of the Cape colony − an attack in which Fynn himself was involved, may even have engineered, and which he has in this text therefore every reason to conceal. It is quite possible, if unprovable, that Ngomane's speech is a fictionalised attempt to authenticate with a 'genuine Zulu voice' a story which may well be an alibi.

The same reservations affect a reading of another 'quotation' of Fynn's: a song, said to have been composed by Shaka and sung on the return of the *izimpi* from the Mpondo raid, and Fynn's exegesis of it.[108] It is perhaps significant in this context that virtually the only instance in which Fynn 'quotes' Shaka's actual words − my third instance − is also during an argument about the Mpondo campaign. Fynn buttresses his personal defence by arguing that he attempted to dissuade Shaka from an attack too close to the colony; his account slips abruptly from a consideration of practical politics to a display of Shaka's innate violence: according to Shaka, 'Black people who had committed an offence should not be talked to but killed':

> 'How is it,' he observed, 'they attempt to play on your superiority of force and arms? You know they steal your cattle and kill your countrymen. By destroying a tribe entirely, killing the surviving chiefs, the people would be glad to join you on your own terms . . .'[109]

Apart from this sounding rather like a justification for what the *whites* did on the eastern frontier − and perhaps for what Fynn was trying to do himself − this bears all the hallmarks of a fictional invention.

The attribution to Shaka of such speeches, of course, tends to be substantial in the

106. Fynn, *The Diary*, 139.
107. For example, Isaacs, *Travels and Adventures*, vol. 1, 240.
108. Fynn, *The Diary*, 149–51.
109. Fynn, *The Diary*, 146.

novels and to be leached from the histories. A. T. Bryant hovers over the ill-defined ground between the two; thus, into his chapter 'Shaka's Home-life at Dukuza: Its Dreams and Realities', which wavers between the sensationalist and the ethnological, he inserts this anecdote:

> On one very rare occasion Shaka became – in a way suddenly humane: he abrogated the law prohibiting courting – for one night only. Towards evening, being in a playful mood, he popped his head above the *isiGodhlo* fence and bellowed out the general order, 'Proclaim to the *izimPohlo* boys that they dress and be off to *soma* (have intercourse with girls)'; then as suddenly vanished. This was indeed an equivocal pronunciamento. But none awaited further explanation; dressed or undressed, they were off in a jiffy. After a while Shaka affected great surprise. 'Dear me!' quoth he, 'things seem very still in the barracks tonight. Where are they gone?' 'Insooth, sire,' replied an attendant, 'there is not a soul in the kraal.' 'So, then, they heard that word of mine, and went? I have given them an evening out; but do they really then so like the girls?' – which, indeed, was what he wanted to discover. 'Most obviously, baba; not one of them not gone.' 'Well, call out the *emBelebele* brigade, and let them go and confiscate all *izimPohlo* cattle.' Thus was it that the *izimPohlo* boys got the girls for once, but lost their cattle for ever. They can't have their bread jammed on both sides, thought Shaka.[110]

Whether or not this is extrapolated from a genuine tradition, it is very clearly cast as a fiction, is a logographia; the tone of derision dismisses any idea that it might be intended as a genuine attempt to elucidate the Zulu mind or mores. The concentration is on Shaka's caprice; Bryant playfully colludes with his character (and with his narratee) in making the boys the butt of an obliquely lubricious jest: 'Of course, it was very wicked of Shaka to encourage vice in this wholesale fashion – if, indeed, vice there be in Nature's dictates.'[111] A strange statement for a priest to make, this verbal indulgence towards Africans' apparently liberated sexuality is characteristic of white writers' mingled envy and defensiveness towards a perceived threat to their own moralities. More important in the context of deadlighting is the way in which an absurd levity and contrived archaism ('quoth he', 'insooth', and so on) serve not to clarify the reality of Shaka, but to distance it. In the sentence in which Bryant pretends to 'quote' Shaka's actual thoughts (a technique possible only in a fictional, not an historiographical context), the 'light' is effectively extinguished by the trivialising anachronism.

Archaisms of language are frequent in the literature, particularly in direct speech. Probably Rider Haggard was the primary exponent of this 'imaginative, pregnant, compressedly aphoristic way [of speaking] which later writers have taught us to think typical' of 'natives', largely a legacy of Macpherson's *Ossian, Hereward the*

110. Bryant, *Olden Times*, 641.
111. Bryant, *Olden Times*, 641.

Wake, and the colonial literature of the Amerindians.[112] This combines with the hierarchic thought-patterns touched on earlier. Colonial writers' cross-cultural imaginative forays tended to be predicated on interwoven hierarchies of techno-logical, religious and societal or political development, at the pinnacle of which the European, and his current modes of expression, was perceived to stand. As with Bryant's injunction to step back '5,000 years', the perception of a temporal or evolutionary progression is transposed to the immediate spatial, social and racial differentiations of actual contact, and the difference expressed in a 'speech of temporality'; that is, 'primitives' were accorded the modes of expression thought appropriate to a much earlier stage of *European* development.

Archaic language is, ostensibly, intended to display with greater veracity the 'feel' of primitive society; in fact it banishes understanding in favour of logographic sensationalism. The Zulu world is portrayed as being as *different* as possible from that of the European writer. As Georg Lukacs writes of the historical novel: 'it is a present-day story-teller who speaks to present-day readers of [the past] . . . It follows therefore that archaism must be ruled out of the general linguistic tone of the historical novel as a superfluous artificiality. The point is to bring a past period *near* to a present-day reader.'[113] Lukacs is being prescriptive in terms of his Marxist framework, but his perception is accurate that the true ideological purpose of such popular novels and stories is often *not* to bring this particular past closer, but defensively to defuse it with varying admixtures of derision, improbability and voyeurism, to make it into a harmlessly bloodthirsty object of entertainment. This distancing, this spatialisation, is no different in its roots from that which impelled the pragmatics of apartheid.

Haggard's *Nada the Lily* was among the earliest of many stories ostensibly delivered by a Zulu narrator, among them W.C. Scully's poem 'Aceldama' (1892),[114] P.A. Stuart's *An African Attila* (1927), Geoffrey Bond's *Chaka the*

---

112. H.N. Fairchild, *The Noble Savage: A Study in Romantic Naturalism*, New York, 1961, 92. In Rider Haggard's, *Nada the Lily*, London, 1895, 63 the narrator Mopo confronts Shaka:

> Chaka drew near, and looked at the piled-up heaps of the slain and the cloud of dust that yet hung over them.
> 'There they lie, Mopo,' he said. 'There lie those who dared to prophesy falsely to the king! That was a good word of thine, Mopo, which taught me to set the snare for them; yet methought I saw thee start when Nobela, queen of the witch-doctresses, switched death on thee . . .'

Haggard weaves an envelope of occult spirituality, heroism, weapons with legendary names, and neo-lycanthropy which is more Nordic than Zulu in its mythic atmosphere, with an anti-mercantilism expressed as atavistic medieval chivalry. Within this, both the narrative and the direct speech are delivered in orotund archaisms, a simplified vocabulary and sentence structures, uncomplicated cause and effect, and stark contrast. Intellectualism, subtlety, and qualification are thereby excised.

113. G. Lukacs, *The Historical Novel*, London, 1962, 232.

114. Curiously, the only full works which pretend to be delivered in Shaka's voice are poems: Scully's successors are F.T. Prince, 'Chaka' in *Poems*, London, 1938, and S. Gray, *The Assassination of Shaka by Mhlangane, Dingane and Mbopa on 22 December 1828 at Dukuza by which Act the Zulu Nation First Lost its Empire*, Johannesburg, 1974.

Terrible (1960), and Cecil Cowley's *Kwa-Zulu: Queen Mkabi's Story* (1966). Even some third-person narratives claim to give 'a picture of Zulu life before the coming of the white man'. P.J. Schoeman considers it 'of vital importance that we as whites should have a deeper knowledge of "the man behind the black skin" and a thorough knowledge of his past, before he was influenced and perhaps contaminated by western civilisation', and his novel claims to deliver that knowledge.[115] This tendency is by no means confined to self-confessed fiction: several 'histories' also claim to be offering the Zulu point of view, including Bryant, Ritter and Ballard.

Probably the majority of Shakan works, from novels to theses, invoke the 'genuine' Zulu voice in another way: the appeal to 'oral tradition'. Again, it began with Fynn and Isaacs; subsequently William Holden claimed the authority of oral accounts to counter some of their assertions: 'I have been brought into contact with some of the oldest and most intelligent natives themselves, enabling me to look at what transpired from *their own stand-point*, and record events in the light in which *they beheld them*'.[116] Yet Holden's account alters little of substance, and even the appeal to the testimony of Shaka's nephew, 'Abantwana', is literally buried in Eurocentric comparisons and judgement. Shaka is appropriated to the Christian mythography, the Zulu said to be of 'Ishmaelitish descent',[117] and so on. Nowhere is 'Abantwana' quoted, even explicitly paraphrased. The essential defensive dead-lighting of this stance is finally made clear:

> We know 'how great a matter a little fire kindleth' sometimes among civilized nations; but among barbarians a single spark has been deposited in the heart, which lies smouldering for years, and then in some unexpected moment, without any apparent cause, has burst forth into a mighty flame, consuming all within its reach.[118]

This is the Shakan 'revolution' generalised; the fear of its resurgence – once again, capricious and mysterious – haunts almost all the white literature, often explicitly. Thus John Colenso wrote, with good reason: '[If the] tide of passion [remains p]ent up within the bosom of the [Zulu] race, they will either stagnate in sullen hatred, or burst forth again ere long in another terrible outbreak.'[119] The worry persists long after 1879, as the figure of John Laputa in Buchan's *Prester John* (1910) attests, and even longer after 1906. D.J. Darlow ended his epic poem:

115. E. Roberts, *The Black Spear*, London, 1950, 8; Schoeman, *Pamphatha: The Beloved of King Shaka*, Preface.
116. Holden, *The Past and Future of the Kaffir Races*, 7.
117. Holden, *The Past and Future of the Kaffir Races*, 2.
118. Holden, *The Past and Future of the Kaffir Races*, 33.
119. J.W. Colenso, *Ten Weeks in Natal*, Cambridge, 1855, xxxi.

> Where is the Thing
> That shook the hosts of men and made them cringe,
> The Thing that hurled them prostrate at his feet
> And bent their hearts to fervent loyalty?
> Perchance 'tis fleeing from the Hound of Heaven,
> Or else, maybe, it ever rests and broods
> Undaunted in the Amazulu hearts.[120]

The same formless fear shadows Viola Ridgway's pious hope, offering sentiments no different from those of Isaacs a century before: 'Perhaps some day the Zulu nation will rise again and, with the help of education, that fine spirit that existed under Shaka will find expression in usefulness and so tread the paths of peace and be a blessing on the world!'.[121] Even more recently, Sir Rex Niven, drawing closer to the ideological facets of the resurgence-fear, asked: 'Is it Chaka and his successors on the Zulu throne who are the real authors of Apartheid? Is it the unspoken fear of the great Chaka's spirit that forces the South African Government to take the line that has made them so unpopular abroad?'[122] More recently still (1986), the narrator of the SABC TV series asserts that the Zulu 'can and will rise again'. Perhaps here lies, in the ambiguously fearful and deeply guilt-ridden situation out of which colonial writers have attempted to write themselves, the root of the ambivalences perceptible in their rhetoric – the fascination and the revulsion, the liberalism and the derogation, and the inability to transcend the limitations of their own language.

Conclusion

Two deep, contrary problems run beneath this essay. One is the possibility that the logical structures of our historiography are a gesture of implicit enterrment, that they fail to capture the reality of Zulu dynamics (how many modern histories integrate Zulu spiritual beliefs as historical cause?); more, that history itself is a form of oppression, is part of the armature of what Edward Said calls a 'saturating hegemonic system' which is 'predicated upon exteriority'.[123] The second is the possibility that the opposite alternative, the 'nonethnocentric, nonprojective' imaginative leap into the Other's *weltanschauung*, is itself doomed to failure, an endeavour which 'will remain both indisputably desirable and ultimately unattainable'.[124] Both impulses are embedded and at war within our colonial narratives, producing the protean gestures of layback and deadlighting. It is simply a greater awareness of this war I have attempted.

120. Darlow, *Tshaka*, 48.
121. Ridgway, *Stories from Zulu History*, 90.
122. Niven, *Nine Great Africans*, 103.
123. E. Said, *Orientalism*, Harmondsworth, 1978, 14, 20.
124. C. L. Miller, 'Theories of Africans: The Question of Literary Anthropology', in Gates, *'Race', Writing and Difference*, 282.

At no point in this essay have I attempted to argue the historical, representational truth or untruth of any of these many texts' assertions. Without doubt my tentative terms will bear a great deal of refinement; a considerable amount of work remains to be done on distinguishing the numerous influences of mythologies and their attendant rhetorical tropes on the deployment of historical evidence. The two are certainly inseparable – mythologies suffuse evidence, the way the evidence was recorded and has been preserved, and even what we choose to stand as evidence; most of all the way we embed that evidence in narratives of our own.

It may be I am working here with nothing more exciting than a worn tautology: writers from one culture write about another culture; they are very different and we can see this difference in their writing. But in South Africa the inscription of difference has too often been turned to pernicious ends; we need to be intensely aware, I think, not only of what we write, but how.

PART TWO

The South - Eastern Coastal Region

Beyond the Concept of the 'Zulu Explosion'
Comments on the Current Debate

JOHN WRIGHT

Since the mid-nineteenth century, writers on the history of southern Africa in the early part of that century have seen the period as one in which an outburst of violent conflict swept through African communities across the central and eastern regions of the subcontinent. Few historians today, if any, would deny that the decades of the 1810s, 1820s and 1830s were a time of widespread upheaval in these regions, but in the last few years a number of commentators have begun to challenge the long-accepted explanation of its primary causes. They have stimulated a debate which has major implications for the way in which historians have so far portrayed the history of southern Africa before the mining revolution of the late nineteenth century. This essay seeks to contextualise a number of contributions to the debate in so far as they are concerned with the region which extends from the area which became Natal to the eastern Cape, and from the Indian Ocean to the basin of the Caledon River.

The north-eastern part of this region, i.e. the area which in the 1820s formed the core of the early Zulu kingdom, has almost universally been seen as the centre of the upheavals referred to. Until very recently these conflicts have generally been regarded in the literature as a consequence of the supposedly explosive expansion of the Zulu kingdom under the ambitious and ruthless leadership of Shaka. A full history of the development of this idea still needs to be written: all that can be said here is that it was the product of a complex interaction between white and black intellectuals, inside and outside southern Africa, that began in the mid-nineteenth century, if not earlier, and has continued to the present day.

The generally accepted view is that the upheavals of the early nineteenth century (which, since the publication of John Omer-Cooper's *The Zulu Aftermath* in 1966, have been known as the 'mfecane') began in the Thukela–Phongolo region in the 1810s with the rise of Shaka and the Zulu kingdom. Zulu depredations into the surrounding territories then set in train a number of separate sets of migrations, which in turn touched off further cycles of violence. In the region under study in Part Two, the Zulu supposedly devastated Natal south of the Thukela River, sending hordes of refugees fleeing southwards into the frontier regions of the eastern Cape, where they came to be known as *amamfengu* or Fingo. The Zulu are also widely held to have been responsible for driving the Ngwane across the Drakensberg into the

Caledon Valley, thus supposedly setting in train the series of conflicts and migrations which have commonly been called the 'difaqane'.

In the 1970s and 1980s, academic historians began opening up fruitful new lines of enquiry into the origins and early history of the Zulu kingdom, the supposed 'engine' of the mfecane. But virtually none of this work was concerned explicitly to confront the long-established notion that the upheavals of the 1820s and 1830s were primarily the product of a 'Zulu explosion'. It was not until the late 1980s, when the whole concept of the mfecane began to come publicly under fire, that historians began to reconsider the nature of these upheavals and the role played in them by the Zulu kingdom.

Slavers and Alibis

As is now well known, the first historian to mount a comprehensive critique of the concept of the mfecane was Julian Cobbing. In his controversial article of 1988, 'The Mfecane as Alibi: Thoughts on Dithakong and Mbolompo', he rejected the long-established idea that an internally generated process of political change, which had culminated in the so-called Shakan revolution, underlay the wars and migrations of the 1820s and 1830s.[1]

Instead, he argued that they had been caused primarily by an escalation in the demand for African slave labour on the part of European traders and settlers. From Delagoa Bay on the east coast, Portuguese slavers and their African allies were raiding further and further afield after 1810 in response to a rapidly rising demand for slaves in Brazil. To the south, in the frontier regions of the Cape colony, settler demands for locally acquired forced labour were increasing after Britain's abolition of the slave trade in 1807. Bands of white frontiersmen, Griqua, Kora and others were raiding deeper and deeper into the interior of the subcontinent to seize slaves and cattle to sell in the colony. Certain colonial officials, missionaries and army officers connived at their activities, and on occasion conspired in the organising of what were in effect semi-official slave raids.

By the late 1810s and early 1820s the expansion of raiding activities from these two centres of violence was subjecting the African societies of the interior to unprecedented pressures. Some, like the Zulu, consolidated into defensive states. Others fled or were driven out of their territories, carrying conflict across a wider and wider region. Contrary to the stereotyped view, Cobbing argues that the role played by the Zulu in these events was minimal. The emergence of the Zulu kingdom was not so much the *cause* as a *product* of the period of upheavals. In the 1820s and 1830s the kingdom was simply one of many political actors on the southern African scene. The notion that it was responsible for the upheavals was an 'alibi', the product of attempts made by settler writers to cover up the destructive impact of white slave-raiding by pinning the blame for its violent consequences on the Zulu. Later

1. *Journal of African History*, 29 (1988), 487–519.

historians continued to reproduce the myth of the 'Zulu wars' as a means of explaining the apparent depopulation of much of the interior of southern Africa which, from the 1830s on, had supposedly enabled advancing white settlers to occupy what were mainly empty lands. From Cobbing's perspective, then, the term 'mfecane' refers not so much to a set of events that took place in the 1820s as to a set of colonial-made *ideas* about the causes of those events.

From a broad critical perspective, Cobbing's arguments point decisively, in my view, towards the need for a fundamental re-examination of the history of the whole eastern half of the subcontinent from the mid-eighteenth to the mid-nineteenth century. Most importantly, they reassert the need to see the history of African societies in this period as having been increasingly influenced, from at least the mid-eighteenth century onwards, by the activities of European raiders, traders, and settlers. Other historians have pointed to this need often enough before, but nearly always in the context of relatively narrowly focused studies of particular societies or regions.[2]

Very few have attempted an integration of the history of precolonial African societies across southern Africa with that of intruding European communities. A basic conceptual obstacle to this exercise has been the notion of the mfecane, which has served largely to segregate the histories of Africans and Europeans in the late eighteenth and early nineteenth centuries. What Cobbing terms 'mfecane theory' rests on the assumption that, outside the Cape colony, the expansion of Europeans into southern Africa had little effect on African societies until the so-called Great Trek of the later 1830s. Cobbing's achievement has been to call this notion seriously into question, and to open the way towards rethinking the subcontinent's history in the period 1750–1850 in very different terms.

But if Cobbing succeeds in establishing the outlines of an alternative grand hypothesis, his attempt to put empirical flesh on its bones is in many respects badly flawed. Too often he seeks to make his case through a process of assertion rather than of argumentation; too often he makes sweeping judgements on the flimsiest of evidence; too often he overbalances in arriving at conclusions. For instance, in drawing attention to the development of the Delagoa Bay slave trade, he has made an original and important contribution to the debate on African 'state-formation' in the region. But in my opinion he puts too much weight on the trade as a factor for political change in the Delagoa Bay hinterland in the 1810s and early 1820s. Concomitantly, he does not give enough attention to the expansion of the ivory trade which had begun in the 1760s and 1770s, and which has long been seen by a number of historians as one of the causes of the intensified conflicts which were beginning in the region several decades before the 1810s. The size of the slave trade in the 1810s

---

2. For example, A. Smith, 'The Trade of Delagoa Bay as a Factor in Nguni Politics 1750–1835', in L. M. Thompson, ed., *African Societies in Southern Africa*, London, 1969, ch. 8; J. B. Peires, *The House of Phalo*, Johannesburg, 1981, 53ff.; P. Bonner, *Kings, Commoners and Concessionaires: The Evolution and Dissolution of the Nineteenth-century Swazi State*, Johannesburg, 1983, 12–14, 20–2.

is not the issue here: the point is that by presenting the impact of this trade as suddenly originating widespread and dramatic political change, rather than as feeding into ongoing processes of change, he distorts its probable historical role. Africans emerge as victims of the European presence rather than as actors capable of shaping their own responses to it.

Cobbing injects another important element into the debate by reviving and carrying further the arguments put forward by Martin Legassick more than twenty years ago about the role of Griqua, Kora and other raiders on the Cape northern and north-eastern frontiers in destabilising the highveld region in the early nineteenth century.[3] He also forces us to look in a new light at the historical significance of the European settler demand for African labour in the eastern Cape. But in arguing that missionaries like Robert Moffat and officials like Sir Richard Bourke were involved in conspiracies to raid slaves he is straining the evidence to the point where he risks undermining his whole thesis. The expeditions which led to the massacres at Dithakong (1823) and Mbholompo (1828) which feature in the title of his article may very well have provided the opportunity for some of the victorious parties to seize slaves from among the defeated. It is perfectly likely that this was all along the aim, if an unstated one, of some of the participating groups, Griqua in the one case, colonial settlers in the other. But to say this is very different from implying that the expeditions were from the start deliberately planned as slave-raids by government officials and missionaries. Conspiracy theories of this kind are usually bad history in that they are prone to lump together into a single, undifferentiated category of actors groups with widely differing aims and interests, and to see the outcome of events as preordained in their causes.

The same point can be made with regard to Cobbing's treatment of the way in which white writers since the 1820s and 1830s have presented the upheavals of the period as the product of Zulu rather than European expansionism. I would agree that, as used by historians, the concept of the 'Zulu wars', or mfecane, has over the years often *functioned* as an 'alibi' by serving to deflect attention away from the role played by Europeans in stimulating the conflicts of the early nineteenth century, and to justify European land-grabbing later in the century. But this is not the same thing as implying, as Cobbing does, that white historians deliberately *invented* the concept as an alibi in the mid-nineteenth century, and have continued consciously to use it as one ever since. As Carolyn Hamilton argues in detail in her essay in this volume, this kind of reductionist argument distorts the processes in which the history of the 'Zulu wars' has been constructed.

The Natal Region: Reconsiderations

Soon after the publication of Cobbing's seminal if lopsided article, my own research

---

3. M. Legassick, 'The Griqua, the Sotho–Tswana, and the Missionaries, 1780–1840: The Politics of a Frontier Zone', Ph.D. thesis, University of California, Los Angeles, 1969, 327ff.

into the precolonial history of the Natal region reached the point where I was able to enter the emerging debate on the mfecane with an article which in certain respects lent support to his critique.[4]

In reviewing the secondary literature on the subject, I argued that the entrenched view that Zulu armies had 'devastated' and 'depopulated' Natal south of the Thukela River in the 1820s was based not so much on empirical evidence as on the uncritical repetition by generations of historians of a stereotype whose origins date back to the writings of European traders and settlers in the 1820s and 1830s. Hamilton has rightly criticised this article for taking little account of the role played over time in the development of this view by African intellectuals, both literate and non-literate.[5] But this criticism does not alter my conclusion that there is little evidence to show that the Zulu played the exclusively destructive role usually ascribed to them in what I have called the 'prototype of all other regional mfecanes'.[6]

I followed up with an article in which I examined the presentation of the history of the region south of the Thukela in what has long been the standard source on the history of the Natal–Zulu kingdom region before the advent of Europeans, A.T. Bryant's well-known *Olden Times in Zululand and Natal*.[7] Most later writers have usually assumed that much of this work is based on oral traditions collected by the author. My investigation showed that his account of the upheavals of the early nineteenth century south of the Thukela was in fact based on an uncritical reading of the works of earlier writers, and could no longer be regarded as reliable.[8] The idea, which Bryant developed in some detail, that in the late 1810s and early 1820s Natal south of the Thukela had been devastated by four successive waves of refugees fleeing from the Zulu, and then by a series of Zulu invasions, was shown to have very little foundation in the sources which he had used.

In a third contribution, 'Political Transformations in the Thukela–Mzimkhulu Region of Natal in the Late Eighteenth and Early Nineteenth Centuries' (pp.163–81 in this volume), I present in outline a new interpretation of the existing evidence on the political history of Natal south of the Thukela during this period. My main findings can be summarised under four heads: first, that discernible political changes in the region began half a century before the emergence of the Zulu kingdom; second, that though the region as a whole experienced considerable political upheaval in the 1820s, it was not subject to wholesale devastation or depopulation by the Zulu or anyone else; third, that the Zulu kingdom under Shaka did not have the military or the political capacity to establish direct rule over the region south of the Thukela; fourth, that there were other important agents besides the Zulu in bringing about the complex series of changes that took place in the region in the 1820s.

4. J.B. Wright, 'Political Mythology and the Making of Natal's Mfecane', *Canadian Journal of African Studies*, 23 (1989), 272–91.
5. Personal communication.
6. Wright, 'Political Mythology', 287.
7. London, 1929.
8. J.B. Wright, 'A.T. Bryant and "The Wars of Shaka"', *History in Africa*, 18 (1991), 409–25.

The concept of the mfecane finds no empirical support in the evidence on the history of the territories south of the Thukela: in effect it dissolves away.

Cobbing's 1988 article has provided a departure point for three further contributions, in the form of the chapters in this book written respectively by Elizabeth Eldredge, Carolyn Hamilton and Jeff Peires, which bear directly on the concerns of the present essay.[9] For her part, Eldredge accepts the essence of Cobbing's argument that the Zulu were not responsible for most of the conflicts of the 1820s and 1830s. She concurs that the slave trade across the Cape frontier was an important cause of conflict on the highveld. But she rejects Cobbing's arguments about the involvement of missionaries in the slave trade in the interior. She regards as a retrograde step his depiction of African societies as simply 'reacting' to the European presence rather than as having aims and objects of their own: as she says, twenty years of Africanist historical scholarship in southern Africa is thereby disregarded. And, in a reappraisal of the evidence on slaving at Delagoa Bay, she argues that the trade there was of no significance before the early 1820s: Cobbing's thesis that intense conflict was set in motion by the expansion of the slave trade in the later 1810s is therefore without foundation.

As indicated above, my own opinion is that Cobbing puts too much explanatory weight on the slave trade as a factor in the conflicts of the pre-1820 period, and there seems little doubt that he has exaggerated its size in this period. But by the same token I think that some of the sources of evidence cited by Eldredge are more ambiguous than she allows in her argument on the timing and dimensions of this trade. Given that the slave trade from south-east Africa to Brazil was rising rapidly after 1810, and given that at the same time smuggling of slaves from south-east Africa to Mauritius and Réunion was taking place, it remains a possibility that the trade from Delagoa Bay was beginning to develop before the early 1820s. If this was so, it may help to explain the intensification of political conflict which took place, in the late 1810s it seems, in the region south of the bay.[10]

I say 'it seems': a feature of Eldredge's otherwise measured and carefully constructed argument that I would query is her retention without explicit justification of a number of conventional 'mfecane' datings. Do we have enough evidence to say that conflicts in the Phongolo–Thukela region broke out precisely in 1817, or that the Hlubi attacked the Tlokwa precisely in 1822, or that the Hlubi and Ngwane fought a decisive battle precisely in 1825? Much of the chronology of the conflicts of the 1810s and 1820s still needs to be properly researched: until this is done, and the results published, writers on the period should treat many accepted datings with circumspection.

9. Eldredge and Hamilton's chapters were originally published as articles in the *Journal of African History*, 33 (1992).
10. Debate on the impact of the Delagoa Bay slave trade needs to take into account the arguments put forth by Julian Cobbing in his conference paper, 'Grasping the Nettle: The Slave Trade and the Early Zulu', in D.R. Edgecombe, J.P.C. Laband and P.S. Thompson, comps, *The Debate on Zulu Origins: A Selection of Papers on the Zulu Kingdom and Early Colonial Natal*, Pietermaritzburg, 1992.

Eldredge's essay is not simply a reaction to Cobbing's article of 1988. She also has some important things to say about the connection between environmental and demographic forces and political conflict in the late eighteenth and early nineteenth centuries. Although it is not always clear from her argument whether she sees these forces as primary causes of 'the dramatic sociopolitical changes of the early nineteenth century' (p. 150), or simply as contributory to them, her points about the differences in the ways in which different social categories in African societies were affected by drought take current debates an important step forward. The useful references which she cites on the occurrence of drought in south-east Africa in the early nineteenth century remind us that a thoroughly researched study of this topic is still badly needed.

Like much of Eldredge's contribution, Hamilton's essay is also a 'reconsideration' of aspects of Cobbing's thesis. While expressly stating that she is not making a case for the mfecane, she takes Cobbing vigorously to task for the reductionism of his argument that the roots of modern mfecane theory are to be found in depictions of Shaka as a tyrant and monster produced by British traders at Port Natal in the 1820s. She puts forward two main sets of criticism. In the first place, she argues in detail that Cobbing has failed to look at the evidence which indicates that before 1829 the traders were not generally concerned to represent Shaka in pejorative terms. Different groups among them had different views of him which changed over time. In the second place, she argues that the unfavourable image of Shaka which was developed by European writers from the 1830s onward was in fact taken up from images originally produced by some of his own subjects. In the same way as Cobbing allows Africans no autonomous role as actors in the upheavals of the early nineteenth century, so he permits them no role in constructing the history of the period. The processes involved in the making of the historical images of Shaka, and of the concept of the mfecane itself, have been much more complex than Cobbing makes out.

Some elements of the empirical argument which Hamilton puts forward about the aims and activities of the British traders at Port Natal in the 1820s can be queried. It could be argued, for instance, that the traders were rather more concerned to engineer official British intervention in the Port Natal region than she allows for. And the nature of Shaka's policies towards the British in the Cape remains something of a puzzle. But her fine-grained article serves as a sharp reminder to historians who are seeking to move beyond the mfecane of the importance of grounding their arguments firmly in the available evidence. She also points to the need to develop a much more nuanced understanding of the relationship between history and ideology than is to be found in Cobbing's argument. This she directs particularly at students of the ways in which the concept of the mfecane has come to be so widely accepted.

The Career of Matiwane

Misuse of sources is also the main theme of the criticisms which Jeff Peires levels against Cobbing. He focuses specifically on Cobbing's handling of the career of

Matiwane kaMasumpa, chief of the Ngwane and, according to mfecane historiography, one of the central figures in the history of the southern highveld in the 1820s. The conventional view is that the Ngwane were driven out of the Natal region by Shaka in the early 1820s, and spent several years raiding and fighting on the highveld. After being attacked either by the Zulu or the Ndebele, they moved away south and south-east into the country of the Thembu. In 1828, in the battle of Mbholompo, they were defeated and broken up by a combined army of Thembu, Gcaleka and Mpondo assisted by a British force from the Cape frontier. This latter had been sent out to repel a threatened Zulu invasion, and ended up attacking the Ngwane in the belief that they were Zulu.

Cobbing argues by contrast that the Ngwane were driven out of the Natal region either directly or indirectly by slave raiders from Delagoa Bay. On the highveld they fell victim to attacks by Griqua raiding for slaves and cattle, and were driven across the Drakensberg into Thembu territory. The main aggressors at Mbholompo were the British, whose prime aim was to secure labour for the eastern Cape settlers.

In a detailed response, Peires maintains that there is little in Cobbing's interpretation of the history of Matiwane and the Ngwane which can stand up to close scrutiny. He accuses Cobbing of concealing the existence of five African accounts which depict a quite different scenario. These sources indicate clearly, in Peires's view, that the Ngwane left the highveld not because they were attacked by the Griqua but because, after defeats at the hands of the Zulu, the Sotho and the Hlubi, and after a rebellion by his followers against his authority, Matiwane felt that the only means of reasserting his leadership was to make 'a brand-new start in a brand-new country' (p.221). In his assessment of the events leading up to Mbholompo, Peires rejects Cobbing's argument that the British expedition was sent out specifically to acquire labourers. In his view the established explanation of the battle is correct. The capture of Ngwane refugees by the British was a by-product of the encounter, not its main purpose.

In sum, Peires concludes, Cobbing's account of Matiwane's history is based on misrepresentation of the evidence. He feels that the same is likely to be true of what he sees as the other two bases of Cobbing's hypothesis: that the Delagoa Bay slave trade was of central importance in stimulating intra-African conflict in the 1810s, and that the battle of Dithakong in 1823 was the culmination of a slaving expedition largely planned by officials and missionaries. The new paradigm which Cobbing is putting forward has no evidence to support it; the old paradigm of the mfecane should be retained until more convincing reasons for discarding it have been put forward.

I have indicated above my own opinion that Cobbing's portrayal of the British expedition which culminated in the battle at Mbholompo as an officially sanctioned labour-raid is intrinsically unlikely; on this score I agree with the thrust of Peires's argument. In fairness it should be pointed out that since the publication of his 1988 article Cobbing has modified his argument to take account of the differences of interest which existed in the 1820s between the colonial administration in Cape

Town and the eastern Cape settlers and military.[11] This is something that Peires needs to make more of: he is correct to insist that by this time British capitalism 'had long outgrown the smash-and-grab phase of primitive accumulation' (p. 227), but the same can hardly be said of embryonic settler capitalism on a remote African frontier. 'The capture of refugees by Colonel Somerset was a by-product of the battle rather than its cause,' Peires argues of Mbholompo. Yes, if Somerset is seen as representing the interests of the Cape administration, but a decided no if he is seen as representing the interests of the eastern Cape settlers. Peires himself states that it was Somerset's practice (as it was no doubt the practice of many other frontier officials) 'to entice Boer volunteers to military service with easy pickings in cattle and child servants' (p. 236). Mbholompo was not the product of an official labour-raid, but it certainly seems to have been the product of an officially sanctioned 'rescue' operation which, like many other official operations on colonial frontiers everywhere, was hijacked by ambitious soldiers and labour-raiding settlers.

As for the flight of the Ngwane from the highveld, we will not be in a position to understand this more clearly until we have a much more substantial account of highveld politics in the troubled times of the 1820s than either Cobbing or Peires has given us. I find Cobbing's hypothesis about the role played by the Griqua, Kora and other trans-frontier raiders highly suggestive: it is a factor which has been badly overlooked in conventional accounts. But, like Peires, I find it difficult to conceive of groups like the Ngwane simply as victims of slave-raiders: intra-African politics in the region need much closer attention than Cobbing is prepared to give them. Peires, for his part, makes a mistake, I think, in trying to argue away the role of the Griqua: the practice found in most mfecane historiography of treating the history of the southern highveld in the early nineteenth century in isolation from the history of the Cape colonial frontier to the south and the Griqua-Kora frontier to the west is an obstacle to a potentially fruitful line of historical enquiry.

I would fully support Peires's insistence that Cobbing – and other historians, for that matter – should give much more careful attention to records of African oral testimonies as sources on the history of the conflicts of the early nineteenth century.[12] But problems arise from the way in which Peires privileges the evidence from the five testimonies which he identifies as major sources on the history of Matiwane and the Ngwane. In my view he needs to interrogate them much more critically than he does in his essay. (What does it mean, for instance, to say of Msebenzi's *History of Matiwane* that it is 'probably the finest oral tradition ever recorded in the Zulu language'?) This is all the more important when some of the evidence in these sources is contradicted by evidence from other sources, as is the case, for example with the statements cited by Peires to the effect that the Ngwane were attacked on the highveld by the Zulu. Examining oral traditions for their 'authenticity', as Peires

11. J. Cobbing, 'Rethinking the Roots of Violence in Southern Africa *c.* 1790–1840', paper presented to the Colloquium on the Mfecane Aftermath, University of the Witwatersrand, Johannesburg, 1991, 19.
12. See also Hamilton's criticisms of Cobbing on this score on pp. 207–10 below.

does, does not take us very far in understanding their usefulness or otherwise as sources of historical evidence: more important, surely, is to examine them for the *meanings* which they contain. For example, what exactly did the verbal symbols 'Zulu' and 'Shaka' mean as used in the historical narratives constructed in the five texts which he cites? These narratives were made in the period from the late 1870s to the 1930s, a period in which the history of the early Zulu kingdom was becoming heavily contested, and when important elements of it were being reduced to formula-like statements by black and white intellectuals alike. We cannot go far in understanding the precise historical meanings of terms like these until we know much more about the circumstances of their production than Peires tells us.

Who were the Fingo?

Like Peires, Alan Webster focuses his attention on one particular strut of mfecane orthodoxy. But where Peires comes out in favour of holding on to the concept of the mfecane, Webster does the opposite. The subject of his case-study is the origins of the Fingo, or Mfengu as they have been called in the recent literature. The conventional view, which seems to have remained unchallenged by historians since it first emerged in the 1830s, is that the Fingo were originally migrants who had fled southwards from the Natal region during the wars of Shaka in the early 1820s. They had taken refuge with the Gcaleka, who had treated them harshly and reduced them virtually to the status of slaves. When the British made war on the Gcaleka in 1835, the Fingo, with missionary assistance, took the opportunity of fleeing from their oppressors, and placed themselves under British protection on the borders of the Cape colony.

Webster argues against this view at every turn. A sprinkling of the people who, after 1835, came to be called Fingo, both by themselves and by others, were from Natal, but the great majority were not. Most of them were people who had been displaced from the African societies of what is now the eastern Cape region. The prime cause of their dislocation was not the 'wars of Shaka' but the aggressions, particularly in 1835, of Cape officials and settlers hungry for African land, labour and cattle. The so-called frontier war of 1834–5 was not the product of a concerted African attack on white settlers as the great majority of white writers have portrayed it: it was the product of a calculated invasion of African territory by colonial forces. The argument that the Fingo were refugees who had been saved from the Gcaleka by the British was concocted by missionaries, particularly John Ayliff, with assistance from officials and settlers, to cover up the fact that large numbers of them were indigenes who had been seized as labourers by the British forces.

Webster brings a large body of evidence to bear in support of his contention that most of the Fingo of 1835 were of local origin. His line of argument is at times hard to follow, as when he writes, at several different points, of the circumstances in which Fingo were brought from the trans-Kei region by British troops. And he possibly needs to make more of the Natal origins of many of Matiwane's adherents, numbers of whom eventually ended up as Fingo. But his main thesis, that the Fingo were primarily of local origin, seems well substantiated by the evidence which he adduces. It ties in with my own findings that there is no evidence for the entrenched view that in the early 1820s there was a wholesale flight of refugees from Natal into the Cape frontier regions.[13]

But when it comes to the trickier business of explaining the origins of the conventional view of Fingo history, Webster's argument is unsatisfactory. One can commend him for the way in which he has revealed the role played by John Ayliff in the construction of this largely artificial history. And no doubt, as Webster argues, official and settler views were fed into it as well. But to leave the explanation at this point, as Webster does, is to fall back on the same kind of colonial conspiracy theory as Cobbing's, and which Hamilton forcefully inveighs against in her essay on the making of the imagery of Shaka. As important as white intellectuals in the creation of a Fingo history were surely the Fingo themselves. On the one hand were the intellectuals and political leaders, from widely differing backgrounds, who interacted with missionaries and officials in producing a homogenised history. On the other were the Fingo commoners who had to reconcile their existing traditions of origin with the new ones which were being presented to them. Given the heterogeneity of Fingo origins, and the struggles for domination which, Webster hints, took place within emerging Fingo society, the processes involved in making a generally accepted history would have been shot through with contradictions and conflicts, spread, one imagines, over a long period of time. If we want to understand how the history codified in writing by Ayliff took root, we need to know in detail about issues of this kind, but there is nothing in Webster's account which touches on them. Admittedly the story of the making of Fingo history belongs mostly to the period after 1835, where Webster's account stops. But the role played in its making by Fingo, and, for that matter, by later generations of white writers as well, needs to be put clearly on the agenda for future research.

The Mfecane Redefined

Finally, some comments on the essay by John Omer-Cooper, the person who, in 1966, first put the concept of the mfecane firmly into academic circulation. The essay is written as a response to the critiques which Julian Cobbing and I have made of the concept. Omer-Cooper first summarises the account of the mfecane which he presented in *The Zulu Aftermath* in 1966. He then goes on to identify what he sees as three key criticisms which Cobbing and I make of the notion, and to respond to them in some detail. In conclusion, he argues that, while our criticisms contain much that is valuable, they are directed against a caricature of the mfecane and not against its real substance. If anything, they serve to strengthen the case for retention of the mfecane.

---

13. See pp. 179–81 below.

First, some disclaimers. In general I find Omer-Cooper's summaries of Cobbing's and my arguments to be fair, and his comments on them generous. But I am concerned that he does not always sufficiently distinguish between our respective positions. In particular, I do not argue that the sharp increase in conflict which took place in the Delagoa Bay hinterland in the late 1810s resulted from 'a massive increase' in the slave trade through the bay (p. 282 below). This is Cobbing's argument, with which, as already stated, I disagree. My own argument focuses on the internal dynamics of the conflicts within and between local African chiefdoms, and on the likelihood that in the late 1810s a developing slave trade was beginning to affect, and to accelerate, processes of political change which were already under way (p. 168).

Nor would I support the argument that an external trade in ivory and cattle was the 'sole cause' of the conflicts (p. 283). My argument, which is based on the research of other academics, is that external trade of this sort seems to have provided the *initial dynamic* for political change after about 1760 (p. 165–6). As Carolyn Hamilton and I have argued elsewhere, numbers of other factors – intensified cattle-raiding, conflict over grazing lands, the impact of drought – may well have played a role in sustaining that dynamic.[14] I agree with Omer-Cooper (p. 283) that the 'trade' hypothesis does not destroy the 'Africanist thesis', if by this is meant the thesis that African initiatives were central in causing the upheavals of the early nineteenth century. The Africanist thesis is not the target of my criticisms: the target is the Zulucentricity of mfecane theory, which blocks our understanding of the extent to which the European presence in southern Africa was directly and indirectly affecting African societies all over the subcontinent several decades before the emergence of the Zulu kingdom.

To turn to the substance of Omer-Cooper's essay. It is significant that, while rightly taking Cobbing to task for his more unsubstantiated arguments, Omer-Cooper is willing to accept that some of Cobbing's basic propositions need to be seriously entertained. Thus he is prepared to debate the possible impact of the Delagoa Bay slave trade on African societies (pp. 280–83). He accepts that the role of the Griqua and other raiders on the highveld in and before the 1820s deserves attention (pp. 290–92). By the same token, he accepts much of my argument that the nature of the upheavals which took place south of the Thukela in the 1820s has been widely misrepresented in the literature, and that the role of the Zulu kingdom in causing these upheavals has been heavily exaggerated (pp. 284–5, 288).

Omer-Cooper refuses to accept, though, that these positions are incompatible with the notion of the mfecane, i.e. the 'Zulu explosion', and that if they are to be taken seriously, the notion has to be abandoned. If anything, he argues, Cobbing's critique

---

4. J. B. Wright and C. Hamilton, 'Traditions and Transformations: The Phongolo-Mzimkhulu Region in the Late Eighteenth and Early Nineteenth Centuries', in A. H. Duminy and B. Guest, eds, *Natal and Zululand from Earliest Times to 1910: A New History*, Pietermaritzburg, 1989, 59–62.

has served to reaffirm the validity and importance of the concept (p. 298). But he can say this only by shifting, though without admitting it, from one notion of the mfecane to another and rather different one. The concept of the mfecane which he seeks to defend is not the same one which he articulated in *The Zulu Aftermath* in 1966, and is not the one against which Cobbing, I and a number of other historians are levelling criticisms.

In 1966 Omer-Cooper succinctly defined the mfecane as 'the wars and disturbances which accompanied the rise of the Zulu'.[15] At the heart of the argument put forward in *The Zulu Aftermath* was the notion that the primary cause of the upheavals of the 1820s was the rise and expansion of the Zulu kingdom. The book's very title encapsulated this notion. This is the understanding of the mfecane which has become entrenched in the academic literature and popular historical conscious-ness alike.

In the first few pages of his essay in the present book, where he summarises the theme of *The Zulu Aftermath*, Omer-Cooper holds on to the old, established notion of the mfecane. The rise of the Zulu kingdom remains at the centre of the processes of political change which he outlines (pp. 277–9). But when he moves on to discuss the criticisms which Cobbing and I have mounted against this notion, Omer-Cooper significantly shifts his ground. It is no longer the *causes* of the upheavals which are important in giving meaning to the term 'mfecane', but their *character*, in particular the fact that the upheavals entailed a 'series of experiments in state building' undertaken on the initiative of African leaders (p. 283). This is what he seems to mean when he writes, 'It is not the cause of the insecurity which provoked the process of political change at the heart of the Mfecane, but the nature of the process itself which constitutes its Africanness' (p. 283).

In this conception of the mfecane, the role of the Zulu is largely written out. Omer-Cooper himself is quite explicit about this: '. . . the re-evaluation of the role of the Zulu in the Mfecane in no way implies that the concept itself must be abandoned', he writes (p. 287). The essence (his word) of the mfecane has to do with the processes of African state-building, 'not the extent to which it was, or was not, driven solely by Shaka's Zulu *izimpi*' (p. 287). Even if Cobbing's hypotheses were to be substantiated, Omer-Cooper argues, the essence of the mfecane, i.e. 'the state building achievements and migrations of the Zulu, Swazi, Gaza, Ngoni etc.', would remain (p. 295).

The notion of 'state-building' simply as an 'achievement' is something that I find problematic. But a more important criticism that needs to be made of Omer-Cooper's line of argument has to do with the way in which, without saying so, he seeks to redefine what he means by the term mfecane. Admittedly, as it has come to be used over the last twenty-five years, the term has acquired a range of slightly different meanings. But central to all of them I would argue is the notion that the

15. J. D. Omer-Cooper, *The Zulu Aftermath: A Nineteenth-century Revolution in Bantu Africa*, London, 1966, 5n.

upheavals of the 1820s and 1830s were set in train by the rise and expansion of the Zulu kingdom. From this perspective, attempts to redefine the mfecane cannot but have the effect of sowing more confusion in what is already a muddled debate. If we are to move on from the now patently inadequate Zulucentric explanations of the upheavals of the early nineteenth century, it is not going to help to tinker about with the concept of the mfecane: as Cobbing insists, we need to abandon it altogether.

The Way Forward

Historians now need to turn their attention to the question of what to put in place of mefecane-based accounts. For the region considered in this essay, urgently required now is a comprehensive history of the early Zulu kingdom and neighbouring regions which moves beyond stereotypes about the 'Zulu' explosion. Also required is a detailed study of relations on and across the north-eastern frontier of the Cape colony in the late eighteenth and early nineteenth centuries to enable the history of the southern highveld to be seen in a broader perspective. A third important topic which awaits its researcher is an examination of the impact of European expansion on the Xhosa-speaking communities of the eastern Cape region in the same period. More than two hundred years on, we still have little precise knowledge of what effect decades of warfare, cattle-raiding and land losses had on the internal workings of the various Xhosa chiefdoms. Without this kind of knowledge, it is clear from Alan Webster's essay, we shall not be able to fully understand the origins of the Fingo.

Abandoning the notion of the mfecane does not mean we have no option but to fall back uncritically on the 'grand hypothesis' put forward by Cobbing in his 1988 article. Cobbing would be the first to agree that he has done no more than set out, if in misleadingly categorical terms, an agenda for debate. Much of his empirical argumentation against the concept of the mfecane has come in for severe criticism, and is unlikely to be taken up by other historians. But at the same time the need which his article points to for an overall reorientation of thinking about the history of southern Africa in the late eighteenth and early nineenth centuries is not going to disappear. Shorn of its more distorted features, Cobbing's hypothesis, in my interpretation of it, is one with which it is difficult to argue: that the history of African societies across southern Africa even before the period of the so-called 'Great Trek' cannot be understood without taking into account the impact on them of forces rooted in the expansion of the frontiers of European trading, raiding and settlement. More than sixty years ago W.M. Macmillan, perhaps South Africa's greatest historian, was saying very much the same thing when he speculated that the 'great upheaval among the Bantu' in the early nineteenth century might have been due in some measure to 'the "generally unsettled state of all tribes bordering" on European conquests'.[16] For reasons that themselves require investigation, most

---

16. W.M. Macmillan, *Bantu, Boer and Briton: The Making of the South African Native Problem*, London, 1929, 18–19.

historians since have disregarded the import of his words. The demise of the mfecane makes it possible once again to understand their significance, and to proceed with the research needed to show that Macmillan's speculations were well founded.

Acknowledgments

This essay has benefited from comments made by Carolyn Hamilton, Elizabeth Eldredge and Julian Cobbing.

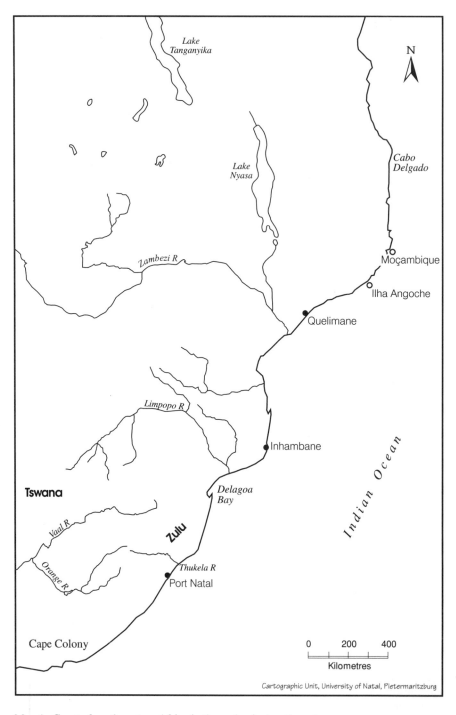

Map 1. Coast of south-eastern Africa in the early nineteenth century

5 Sources of Conflict in Southern Africa c.1800–1830
The 'Mfecane' Reconsidered

ELIZABETH A. ELDREDGE

During the 1820s the entire region of southern Africa was affected directly or indirectly by tremendous demographic upheaval and revolutionary social and political change. The period was marked by massive migrations, sporadic raids and battles, and frequent periods of privation and famine for many people in the region. This 'mfecane' has been explained in many ways by historians, but never adequately. The sociopolitical changes and associated demographic turmoil and violence of the early nineteenth century in southern Africa were the result of a complex interaction between factors governed by the physical environment and local patterns of economic and political organisation.

Increasing inequalities within and between societies coupled with a series of environmental crises at the beginning of the nineteenth century transformed long-standing competition over natural resources and trade in south-eastern Africa into violent struggles for dominance and survival. Trade at Delagoa Bay, involving primarily the export of ivory, had allowed some Africans to accumulate wealth and consolidate power, leading to political amalgamation at the expense of the weak. Increasing political inequality between chiefdoms and increasing socioeconomic inequality within societies made weaker people, with fewer entitlements to food, more vulnerable to famine in times of drought-induced food scarcity. When the area was struck by severe droughts and other ecological problems in the first two decades of the nineteenth century, competition became keen over fertile, well-watered land. Those who had already consolidated their power prevailed over weaker groups in the open contests that emerged. The weak found themselves incorporated into the lower echelons of stronger societies, either conquered involuntarily or submitting voluntarily for the sake of survival. The stage was set for the emergence of various strong leaders, some, like Shaka, who ruled with terror and others, like Moshoeshoe, who won the voluntary devotion of their followers.

The resulting period of state formation, often involving initial stages of conquest by force, was prolonged into two decades of violence because of the activities of Europeans encroaching from both east and west. In the east, slave traders found a new supply of ready victims in the area around Delagoa Bay and fostered continued violence to meet their demands for slaves. Similarly, across the northern border of the Cape colony, white frontiersmen supplied renegade Griqua and Kora with the

123

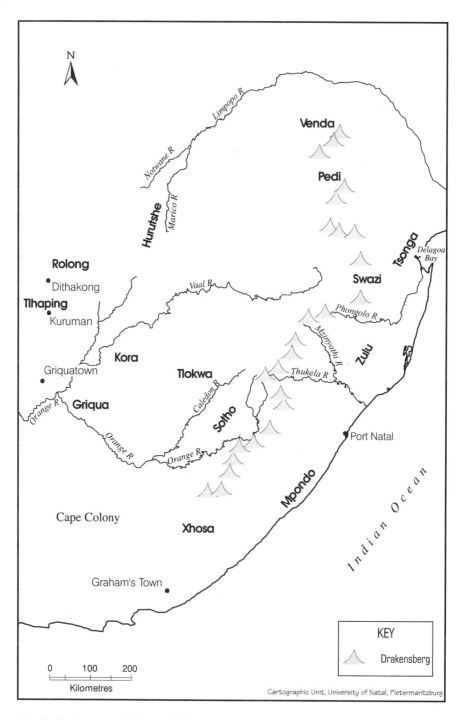

Map 2. South-eastern Africa, *c.*1830

guns and ammunition they needed to raid neighbouring Africans for cattle and slaves which they traded back to the farmers. With the massive migration of Dutch Boers into the interior to escape British rule in the 1830s and 1840s, white intrusion became overt and direct, and any African hope of political stability and peace was lost forever.

This essay uses a multidimensional approach to analyse these processes and events. There is no simple, monocausal explanation for these disruptions: neither great leaders, nor environment and ecology, nor overpopulation, nor trade (including the slave trade and raiding) alone set off the wars and migrations that plagued the area through these decades. The wide range of the one-dimensional interpretations which have been offered to date indicates the difficulties for historians posed by this problematic period. Each historian has furthered our understanding of the causes of these revolutionary disruptions, but all have provided only partial explanations for the events of early nineteenth-century southern Africa. Here I offer a critique and synthesis of earlier interpretations, and I reassess the controversial prominent role given European slavers in the interpretation of the 'mfecane' recently proposed by Julian Cobbing.[1] Recent syntheses, though useful, have failed to relate information about the environment to the economy and to sociopolitical change. In addition, most studies have focused on specific people, places or periods, whereas I attempt to present a more comprehensive picture by looking at the entire region, both east and west of the Drakensberg mountains, and by identifying changes over time in the dynamics of sociopolitical change and the generation of competition and conflict.

Determining the causes of the upheaval of the early nineteenth century is not merely an academic exercise, as the political ramifications of interpreting it are manifest in South Africa today. It has generally been assumed that the emergence of the Zulu kingdom under Shaka was the key event responsible for the ensuing devastation of southern African societies. It has been convenient for white South African defenders of apartheid to blame the Zulu for the chaos and destruction, because this interpretation falsely characterises Africans as inherently divisive and militaristic and thereby justifies the imposition and continuation of white rule in South Africa.

Rejection of the myth of Zulu culpability thus raises the question of why these conflicts arose in the first place. Recent work by Cobbing on the so-called 'mfecane' has appropriately refocused attention on the more fundamental causes of conflict in this period, especially in the role of slaving in the upheavals. Cobbing's reinterpretation is seriously flawed, however, by a distortion of chronology and misreadings of the evidence. I first demonstrate that an extensive slave trade at Delagoa Bay did not begin until after the regional conflicts broke out in 1817. Slaving there could not have initiated this violence. In the second part of this essay I

---

1. J. Cobbing, 'The Mfecane as Alibi: Thoughts on Dithakong and Mbolompo' *Journal of African History*, 29 (1988), 487–519.

challenge Cobbing's thesis that missionaries were engaging in systematic slave-raiding and slave-trading on the north-eastern Cape frontier. However, I support Cobbing's contention that Griqua and Kora allies of the white frontier farmers were themselves conducting an illicit slave trade and identify them, not Zulu or other Nguni-speakers, as the main sources of violence in the region throughout the 1820s and 1830s. In the third part I examine the conflicts of the 1810s and 1820s in terms of their environmental and sociopolitical contexts. However, initially I outline the economic and sociopolitical setting in which droughts resulted in famine and consequent competition for arable land and labour among Africans east of the Drakensberg. I then use the same approach to analyse disruptions among the Sotho- and Tswana-speaking peoples west of the Drakensberg and to reinterpret the early migrations and raids in light of the natural environment of the region.

The Delagoa Bay Slave Trade: A Reappraisal

So startling and compelling are Cobbing's arguments that readers who have no independent basis for judgement may wonder what to make of his evidence and conclusions. Cobbing has attributed the violent disruptions of the early nineteenth century to slave trades organised by Europeans, both at Delagoa Bay and on the northern frontier of the Cape colony, and has taken historians to task for failing to discuss this slave trade as the source of regional violence in this period.[2] However, the sources regarding Delagoa Bay indicate that the slave trade there was heavy only by 1824, several years *after* the early migrations and wars of the 'mfecane'. They show no extensive slave-trading out of Delagoa Bay before 1823, while disruptions associated with the regional violence of the period began in 1817.

Cobbing removes ultimate responsibility for the ensuing period of violence from Shaka and the Zulu by correctly pointing out that the earliest conflicts involved the Mthethwa, the Ngwane and the Ndwandwe prior to Shaka's rise to power. He draws on David Hedges's work to pinpoint the attack of Zwide's Ndwandwe on Matiwane's Ngwane in 1817 as 'initiating the Mfecane'.[3] The beginning of the 'mfecane' thus predated the emergence of the Zulu under Shaka, who were then still subordinate to the Mthethwa; this battle also moves the locus of violence northwards away from the site of the later Zulu state to the banks of the Mzinyathi River. Ndwandwe attacks on Sobhuza's Ngwane (later known as the Swazi) on the Phongolo River date from this period as well and also occurred further north.[4] Cobbing identifies slave-raiding as the cause of these early conflicts:

2. Cobbing, 'The Mfecane as Alibi', 489.
3. Cobbing, 'The Mfecane as Alibi', 503–4 ; cf. D. W. Hedges, 'Trade and Politics in Southern Mozambique and Zululand in the Eighteenth and Early Nineteenth Centuries', Ph.D. thesis, University of London, 1978.
4. This information also appeared in Omer-Cooper and has been repeated by both Hedges and P. Bonner; J.D. Omer-Cooper, *The Zulu Aftermath: A Nineteenth-century Revolution in Bantu Africa*, London, 1966, 29, 49, 86; Cobbing, 'The Mfecane as Alibi', 504, n.83.

the Ngwane flight from the Mzinyathi was a response either directly to slave raiders or to secondary raiders such as the Ndwandwe, Mthethwa and Zulu who were themselves turned against each other by the compressions of the slave trade and by the prospects of profitable business.[5]

In order to account for the slave trade and slave-raiding allegedly responsible for these initial conflicts, Cobbing relies heavily on an article by Patrick Harries.[6] However, neither the conclusions of this article nor the primary sources support Cobbing's assertion that there was an extensive slave trade from Delagoa Bay before 1817.

Harries generalises about the combined exports of slaves from Lourenço Marques, as Delagoa Bay was called by the Portuguese, and from Inhambane, over 300 kilometres further up the coast, without distinguishing the data from the two places. Harries notes that after treaties limited the Atlantic slave trade to the area south of the equator in 1815 and 1817, more Portuguese slavers began to buy slaves from south-east Africa. All the data provided by Harries to demonstrate the boom in slave exports from Delagoa Bay and Inhambane refer to the later 1820s and 1830s, however, and none to the period before 1823. In addition, much of his evidence derives not from Delagoa Bay, but from Inhambane, as can be ascertained by a careful reading of the notes or his original sources. Harries concludes only that

> At the height of the trade in the late 1820s and early 1830s, it seems likely that well over 1 000 slaves were exported every year from each port.[7]

Though Harries never suggests that the slave trade expanded before the 1820s, Cobbing nevertheless cites him to assert that 'The Portuguese trade had operated at a low level in the eighteenth century, but after 1815 it took off'.[8] Again, referring only to Harries's conclusions about the late 1820s, Cobbing arbitrarily projects the data backwards in time to state that

> Between about 1818 and the early 1830s at least a thousand, and probably twice if not three times that number of African males were exported from *both* Delagoa Bay and Inhambane *every year* [Cobbing's italics].[9]

Having claimed that slave exports amounted to thousands annually years earlier than is shown by the evidence, Cobbing links this alleged extensive slave trade to events in the interior. He concludes:

---

5. Cobbing, 'The Mfecane as Alibi', 507.
6. P. Harries, 'Slavery, Social Incorporation and Surplus Extraction: The Nature of Free and Unfree Labour in South-East Africa', *Journal of African History*, 22 (1981), 309–30.
7. Harries, 'Slavery', 316.
8. Cobbing, 'The Mfecane as Alibi', 504.
9. Cobbing, 'The Mfecane as Alibi', 504–5.

This slaving must after *c.* 1815 have dramatically heightened the previously critical, but continuing impact of the ivory and cattle trades.[10]

Moreover, although there is no evidence in Harries or elsewhere about the gender of the slaves, Cobbing assumes that every slave exported was male. He thus finally draws the unfounded conclusion that slave-trading resulted in 'a loss of between 25 per cent and 50 per cent of the entire male population, in precisely the years of the mfecane'.[11]

A survey of the primary and secondary literature on Delagoa Bay supports Alan Smith's assertion that the slave trade 'did not reach significant proportions until after the consolidation of the Zulu nation. . .'[12] The early trade out of Delagoa Bay did include slaves in small numbers, however, and it is therefore important to examine carefully the evidence about the numbers of slaves being exported from the bay in the eighteenth and early nineteenth centuries in order to assess Smith's judgement about what constitutes 'significant proportions'.

The earliest reference to slaves being exported from south-eastern Africa is a reference to Port Natal. In an appendix, Saxe Bannister quotes a mention of slaves being purchased there in 1719 by a slaver, Robert Drury:

> Here we traded for slaves, with large brass rings, or rather collars, and several other commodities. In a fortnight we purchased 74 boys and girls. These are better slaves for working than those of Madagascar, being not only blacker but stronger.[13]

From this single reference Bannister concludes, 'We find Natal about this time mentioned as a place of ordinary resort for slave-ships', but no other evidence suggests that this happened more than once.[14] On the contrary, Fynn wrote in the 1850s that:

> From the time the Dutch left Natal till the arrival of the 'Salisbury' [in 1822] there is no tradition amongst the natives that any vessel put into Port Natal.[15]

10. Cobbing, 'The Mfecane as Alibi', 506.
11. Cobbing, 'The Mfecane as Alibi', 506.
12. A. K. Smith, 'The Trade of Delagoa Bay as a Factor in Nguni Politics 1750–1835', in L. M. Thompson, ed., *African Societies in Southern Africa*, London, 1969, 177.
13. S. Bannister, *Humane Policy, or Justice to the Aborigines of New Settlements . . .*, London 1830; reprinted London, 1968, xxxii. Bannister mis-cites the title as 'The Adventures of Robert Drury'. The book has also appeared in several editions only under the title *Madagascar; or, Robert Drury's Journal, During Fifteen Years' Captivity on that Island* and was long attributed to Daniel Defoe. A full examination of the authorship question is found in A. W. Secord, *'Robert Drury's Journal' and Other Studies*, Urbana, 1961, 1–45. This same quotation from Drury appeared in S. Kay, *Travels and Researches in Caffraria*, New York, 1833, 336, but there are no other references to an early slave trade out of Natal in these sources or in Drury. Drury further writes that six Africans from Delagoa Bay who had been taken aboard on a previous trip were left off at Port Natal and that the Natal slaves were left off in Madagascar, where 130 other slaves evidently of Madagascar origins were purchased and taken aboard. See *Madagascar; or Robert Drury's Journal*, ed. by P. Oliver, New York, 1969, 304–7.
14. Bannister, *Humane Policy*, xxxii.
15. Mr Fynn, 'From a Fragmentary Paper Written by Mr Fynn . . .', in J. Bird, comp., *The Annals of Natal: 1495 to 1845*, Cape Town, 1965, vol. 1, 73.

Bannister also collected the available evidence concerning all trade out of Delagoa Bay during the period of the Dutch settlement there, 1721 to 1729, and collated the information into an export table. During these nine years exports included 49 574 pounds (about 22 500 kilograms) of ivory, 288 slaves, and various quantities of tin, aloes, gold dust, ambergris, honey, copper and rice.[16] Because these statistics were based on official reports Bannister acknowledges that they may not be complete. However, the inclusion of slaves in this list, during an early period when there was no compelling reason to cover up the slave trade, suggests that the numbers are accurate and that the trade was indeed minimal, averaging 48 slaves per year and often amounting to fewer than 20 per year out of Delagoa Bay. It is highly unlikely that the export of people in these small numbers had a revolutionary impact on the sociopolitical structures of the societies where they originated.

The Dutch period in the 1720s was the high point of the slave trade in the eighteenth century. The evidence thus supports Smith's contention that only during the Dutch occupation was there a consistent effort to obtain slaves.[17] He notes that slavers avoided Delagoa Bay because it was not equipped to handle large numbers of captives, which they could obtain more easily at ports to the north.[18] A Dutch trader found that no slaves were available for purchase at Delagoa Bay in 1731 because, according to the Africans, there had been no recent wars to generate prisoners.[19]

In the 1750s and 1760s trade at the bay was dominated by the English, who were seeking ivory for their trade with India.[20] This orientation of trade at Delagoa Bay towards India and consequent interest in ivory persisted with the arrival of the Englishman John Bolts under the Austrian flag in the 1770s.[21] Smith estimates that in the late 1770s annual ivory exports from Delagoa Bay may have reached over 100 000 pounds.[22] The Portuguese drove away the 'Austrians' in 1781, and documents relating to the creation of a Portuguese establishment there in the next few years refer only to the value of trading in legitimate commercial goods, especially ivory.[23]

One of the few relevant documents of the late eighteenth century, 'Mr Penwell's account of Delagoa given me by Himself', states that slaves were not sold by the people living around Delagoa Bay (the 'Tembe, Mafuma and Matoll') because 'in battle they give no quarter, consequently no slaves'. This source informs us that

16. Bannister, *Humane Policy*, 144. Adding to the total exports the 25 slaves who were taken to the Cape in 1730 when the post was abandoned brings the total for slaves to 313; J.C. Armstrong's personal communication, citing C.G. Coetzee, 'Die Kompanjie se Besetting van Delagoa-baai', *Archives Year Book for South African History*, 9th Year, Pretoria, 1948, 269.
17. Smith, 'The Trade of Delagoa Bay', 176.
18. Smith, 'The Trade of Delagoa Bay', 177.
19. A.K. Smith, 'The Struggle for the Control of Southern Mozambique, 1720–1835', Ph.D. thesis, University of California, Los Angeles, 1970, 154.
20. Smith, 'The Struggle for the Control of Southern Mozambique', 162–5.
21. Smith, 'The Struggle for the Control of Southern Mozambique', 166–8, 176–97.
22. Smith, 'The Struggle for the Control of Southern Mozambique', 191.
23. For example see 'Carta dos Governadores Interinos ao Secretario de Estado, em 19 de Julho de 1785', Documento no.21, in A. Lobato, *História do Presídio de Lourenço Marques* vol.1: 1782–1786, Lisboa, 1949, 202–3.

'they traffick within Land for Teeth with what they get from the Europeans', confirming that the trade at the bay involved ivory and that there was no regular traffic in slaves.[24] On the other hand, a trickle of slaves nevertheless left the area. A Portuguese friar who lived in Mozambique for 17 years and resided at the bay in 1782 and 1783 reported that the chiefs there sold as slaves their enemies captured in wars.[25] Alexandre Lobato indicates that at this time the annual export trade from the 'two great commercial highways of the region', the Maputo and Nkhomati (Manissa) Rivers, included the equivalent of six to seven boatloads of ivory, rhino horn, hippo teeth, amber, gold, copper, agricultural products and slaves from wars.[26]

The Portuguese abandoned Delagoa Bay in 1796 after a French attack and did not reoccupy the area until 1799. As Smith notes, very little evidence at all bears on Delagoa Bay for the first two decades of the nineteenth century.[27] The lacuna itself suggests that there may have been little trade of any kind out of Delagoa Bay in this period, although such an absence of evidence is inconclusive. The Portuguese garrison, which was supposed to maintain a monopoly of trade in ivory and other specified goods, was too small to prevent a British ship from trading at the bay in 1801. The next time a British East India Company ship tried to trade was not until 1815, however, and this time the Portuguese succeeded in keeping the foreigners out. In the meantime, French and English whalers had been coming to the bay for provisions since 1789, and English and American whaling ships continued to resupply their ships there after the turn of the century.[28]

---

24. 'Mr. Penwell's account of Delagoa given me by Himself', no date, no name of person to whom given in G.M. Theal, comp., *Records of South-Eastern Africa*, Cape Town, 1964, vol.2, 455–65. Theal estimates the document is from the late eighteenth century; the contents, which refer to specific chiefs, indicate a date from the 1780s.
25. Lobato, *História*, vol.1, 21.
26. Lobato, *História*, vol.1, 21. Zimmerman concludes that 'the years 1785 to 1794 mark the peak of the French slave trade at Moçambique', which was brought to a halt by the British and never really revived. Except for the years 1789 to 1800 at the single port of Moçambique Island, trade in foreign ships was officially illegal, so foreign trade is almost impossible to trace. The complete absence of any references to French ships buying slaves at Delagoa Bay in Zimmerman and in Mettas is therefore not conclusive. See M. Zimmerman, 'The French Slave Trade at Moçambique, 1770–1794' M.A. dissertation, University of Wisconsin, Madison, 1967, 19, 21, and *passim*; and J. Mettas, *Repertoire des Expéditions Négrières Françaises au XVIIIe Siècle*, vol.2, Paris, 1978, 1984. On the other hand, in 1785 a French ship which had aided the Portuguese in a fight against Africans at Delagoa Bay subsequently went to Moçambique Island to purchase slaves, suggesting that slaves had not been available at Lourenço Marques; Lobato, *História*, vol.1, 127. Filliot attempted to compile a comprehensive statistical profile of the slave trade to the Mascarene Islands in the eighteenth century. He documents the trade from the Portuguese coast of Mozambique, but in his massive search he found no references to slaves from Delagoa Bay. Nevertheless this is inconclusive since he acknowledges that no use had been made by himself or his sources of the Portuguese archives at Lourenço Marques; J.M. Filliot, *La Traite des Esclaves vers les Mascareignes au XVIIIe Siècle*, Paris, 1974, 52. Although Dutch ships stopped occasionally at the bay looking for lost ships and had an ongoing awareness of activities there, the Dutch sources show no evidence of significant trade in slaves from Delagoa Bay during the late eighteenth century; J.C. Armstrong, personal communication. I am indebted to Armstrong for assistance with sources for this period.
27. Smith, 'The Trade of Delagoa Bay', 175–6. Smith's research included a search for all related materials in the Lisbon overseas archives, the *Arquivo Histórico Ultramarino*.
28. Smith, 'The Struggle for the Control of Southern Mozambique', 210–11, 225–7.

The most significant commercial development at Delagoa Bay at this time was the Portuguese establishment of a whaling company. Their first attempt in 1817 failed when their representative alienated the Tembe chief by neglecting to request permission to use Tembe land, and he and his men were killed.[29] Nevertheless the whaling company was successfully established in 1818, and to service it the Portuguese brought in both black harpooners (*harpoadores negros*) and specialised tools from North America.[30] It is highly unlikely that the Portuguese would have been interested in setting up a whaling station there had there been an extensive and lucrative slave trade out of the bay by 1818. Clearly, whaling activities and ivory exports still dominated the commercial scene at the bay as late as that date. Captain Owen wrote, during his survey trip of 1822–3:

> When the Sun is in the Northern Hemisphere, which is the Season for the Black Whale to Calve, this Bay is very much frequented by American and English Whalers, into which vessels many of the Natives engage themselves as Boat Crews for very trifling remuneration.[31]

Far from there being an extensive Portuguese slave trade, Owen observed a thriving commerce with Africans in legitimate goods. According to Owen,

> The Portuguese shew not the shadow of pretention to interference with any of these people, and indeed have great dread of them. The commerce of all these people is similar; that is beads, brass and cottons for Elephants' Teeth, Ambergris, Rhinoceros Horn, and Hippopotamus Teeth, they also barter their Cattle, Poultry, Pigs, Goats, and Grain, as also the skins of wild animals.[32]

Captain Nourse, an Englishman from the HMS *Andromache* who, as part of Britain's surveillance of slaving on the high seas, had no reason to want to hide any slave trade carried on at the bay, mentioned only ivory when discussing the activities of the Portuguese.[33]

Certainly thousands of slaves were already being taken from the coast of Mozambique by then, but from areas much farther to the north. An 1809 report of a British sea captain noted that French ships from the Ile de France and Bourbon preyed on the Portuguese, taking almost all of the Portuguese vessels trading along the coast in 'negroes, elephants' teeth, gold-dust, and specie'; but this activity ranged

---

29. Smith, 'The Struggle for the Control of Southern Mozambique', 225–6.
30. Visconde de Paiva Manso, *Memoria sobre Lourenço Marques (Delagoa Bay)*, Lisboa, 1870, 12.
31. Captain Owen, of HMS *Leven*, 'The Bay of Delagoa' in Theal, *Records of South-Eastern Africa*, vol. 2, 475. This article contains information not available in Owen's published journals.
32. Owen, 'The Bay of Delagoa', vol. 2, 474.
33. 'Extracts from a letter from Commodore Joseph Nourse to J. W. Croker, esq.', 15 Jan. 1823, in Theal, *Records of South-Eastern Africa*, vol. 9, 20.

as far north as Cape Delgado and cannot be pinpointed to Delagoa Bay.[34] The
Portuguese still had only small settlements at Correntes (the mouth of the Limpopo)
and Inhambane.[35]

A report from the Earl of Caledon in 1810 indicated that ships carrying slaves to
Brazil supplied themselves at the old, established slave ports farther north at
Moçambique Island and Inhambane and did not bother to stop at the smaller southern
port of Delagoa Bay:

> I understand there are but four ships regularly employed in the slave trade
> between Rio de Janeiro and the settlement of Mozambique [Island] and
> Inhambane and these I have reason to believe are bona fide Portuguese
> property . . . The usual course for the slave ships after receiving the cargo at
> Mozambique [Island] is to proceed to Rio de Janeiro.[36]

The Portuguese trade in slaves going to Brazil was by that time extensive, but it
was still originating further north according to all the evidence. An English visitor to
Mozambique in 1812 reported that

> There are regular ships come annually from Rio [de] Janeiro to Mozambique
> [Island] with supplies, and take in return slaves, ivory, gold dust, and gum. The
> Americans have always been in the habit of coming there, and still continue to
> do so every year in the months of June and July, and smuggle slaves to the
> Brazils and Spanish America. A brig also, lately from Seychelles, but
> belonging to the Isle of France, had been there and taken away two hundred
> slaves.[37]

This British captain also noted that 12 000 slaves were exported annually from
Portuguese settlements when the French had possessed the Isle of France. Thus,
although there is clear evidence of an extensive slave trade from the northern coasts
of Mozambique by 1812, not until ten years later did it reach as far south as Delagoa
Bay.

Owen's diary helps to pinpoint the date, late in 1823, at which the slave trade

34. 'Report to Captain J. Tomkinson, commanding His Majesty's sloop of war Caledon, to Vice-Admiral
    Albemarle Bertie', 7 June 1809, in Theal, *Records of South-Eastern Africa*, vol. 9, 1. Campbell has
    dealt with the early nineteenth century but has very little for the period before 1820, none of which
    refers to Delagoa Bay; G. Campbell, 'Madagascar and Mozambique in the Slave Trade of the Western
    Indian Ocean 1800–1861', in W. G. Clarence-Smith, ed., *The Economics of the Indian Ocean Slave
    Trade in the Nineteenth Century*, London, 1989, 166–93.
35. 'Report of Captain William Fisher, of His Britannic Majesty's Sloop of War Racehorse, to
    Vice-Admiral Albemarle Bertie', 17 Aug. 1809, in Theal, *Records of South-Eastern Africa*, vol. 9,
    11.
36. 'Letter from the Earl of Caledon to the Right Honourable Nicholas Vansittart, Cape of Good Hope', 27
    June 1810, in Theal, *Records of South-Eastern Africa*, vol. 9, 11–12.
37. 'Letter from Captain H. Lynne to Rear Admiral Stopford', 21 May 1812, in Theal, *Records of
    South-Eastern Africa*, vol. 9, 16.

began to afflict the Delagoa Bay area. On Owen's first trip to the bay, arriving in September 1822, he observed that the local people were 'accustomed to nothing but whalers and a few slave-ships . . .'[38] At that time the area was thickly inhabited, and the land was cultivated 'so that the natives were enabled to live in the greatest abundance and comfort'.[39] On the same trip Captain Owen wrote to George Thompson:

> The natives of Delagoa Bay are a timid race, and seemingly at peace with every body, but the Vatwahs treat them like a conquered people, and have lately overrun the country. They offer no objections to any one passing through their country.[40]

Owen's testimony confirms that slaves were exported from Delagoa Bay, but the numbers were few and the local societies had not yet been disrupted, nor was slave-raiding a normal, ongoing activity. As late as 1 May 1823, Captain Owen noted:

> Like all other African Nations all the countries around the Bay make Slaves of their enemies, but of the enemies only. There are however very few slaves exported from this place, and the natives have a decided aversion to the trade.[41]

Cobbing's argument rests on the assumption that the sources covered up a large trade before 1823. However, Owen made his observation that there were few slaves exported from Delagoa Bay, being fully aware that some slaves were being captured and sold, and so he did not minimise the numbers out of ignorance or deceit. He witnessed at one point the process:

> . . . the Portuguese Commandant had persuaded him [Chief Mayetta] to seize and sell a number of his own wretched and defenceless subjects for slaves, at the price of about a dollar and a half each, paid in valueless merchandise; and he had actually taken an expedition on foot for the purpose, as the Commandant was in daily expectation of the annual ships from Mozambique to take his living cargo . . . we afterwards learnt that he actually procured the number required by the Commandant, who exported them to Brazil.[42]

Owen was in fact eager to expose the extent of the slave trade from the Portuguese coast. He reported that

---

38. W. F. W. Owen, *Narrative of Voyages to Explore the Shores of Africa*, London, 1833, vol. 1, 148.
39. Owen, *Narrative*, vol. 1, 137, 141.
40. G. Thompson, *Travels and Adventures in Southern Africa*, Cape Town, 1967, vol. 1, 182 n.
41. Owen, 'The Bay of Delagoa', vol. 2, 465–79.
42. Owen, *Narrative*, vol. 1, 270.

Quilimane is now the greatest mart for slaves on the east coast . . . From eleven to fourteen slave-vessels come annually from Rio [de] Janeiro to this place, and return with from four to five hundred slaves each on average.[43]

Inhambane is by no means so rich as Quilimane, as from the small extent of its river it has not the same facilities for procuring slaves, the source of wealth to the latter place; those they do obtain are the spoils of war amongst the petty tribes . . . The trade of Inhamban[e] consists principally in ivory, and bees' wax, about one hundred thousand pounds of the former being annually conveyed to Mozambique.[44]

Owen explicitly observed the change by his later visits in 1823 and after:

In every succeeding visit since our first arrival at Delagoa we had observed that the natives were becoming still more unhappy; many, it appeared, had voluntarily sold themselves to slavery to avoid the miseries of starvation: for so great had been the ravages of the Hollontontes [Nguni-speakers] that even onions . . . had become exceedingly scarce. It likewise appeared that the French of Bourbon had opened a trade to this Bay for slaves . . .[45]

On another of his visits in late 1823 or in 1824 Owen learned that three French vessels had recently been to the bay. One from Bourbon left six weeks before his arrival and carried off 130 slaves, and he believed it had marked the beginning of a slave trade between the bay and the French of Bourbon. The other two hailed from Mauritius, and their notorious 'master' had kidnapped unsuspecting Africans whom he had plied with liquor to reduce resistance. Had there been a systematic slave trade ready to deliver slaves to ships arriving at Delagoa Bay, presumably the Europeans would not have had to resort to trickery nor would the Africans have been so trusting and so easily kidnapped. Owen concluded,

What a contrast did these poor people exhibit in their present situation with that in which we first found them [in 1822]! The little market, the fair exchange, the busy mercantile spirit, and the ardour of speculation had vanished, leaving only abject beggary and want of the mere necessaries of life.[46]

In October 1823 Owen reported that the trade from Mozambique port, in the north, included an estimated 15 000 slaves annually and that 10 000 slaves had been exported from Quelimane in the previous year. At this point the slave trade further

43. Owen, *Narrative*, vol. 1, 286–7.
44. Owen, *Narrative*, vol. 1, 301.
45. Owen, *Narrative*, vol. 2, 218. This observation supports the conventional view that slaves became readily available at Delagoa Bay as a result of the migrations from the south and that the slave trade expanded following these migrations, rather than the reverse.
46. Owen, *Narrative*, vol. 2, 218.

south was still minimal relative to the northern trade, though he noted that its negative effects were beginning to be felt internally:

> From Inhambane, however, the trade in slaves is very limited compared with that of Mozambique and Quilimane, the neighbouring tribes being very averse to it, nevertheless wars are excited solely to make slaves to pay for merchandize. The same also occurs at English River [Delagoa Bay] to a still smaller extent, yet sufficiently so to keep the neighboring tribes in a ferment and continual state of warfare.[47]

Captain Owen exposed the extensive slave trade at Portuguese ports farther north, and he had every reason to expose it in Delagoa Bay as well, because he was determined to find an excuse for the British to take over the area from the Portuguese. Nevertheless the most damning thing he could say in 1823 was not that the slave trade was then already extensive but that it might become so. In a letter dated 11 October 1823, Owen wrote that:

> It is to be lamented that our negotiation [between Great Britain and Portugal] was so unwise as to permit the slave trade to exist even as far as Delagoa Bay, where such trade had never before existed beyond the purchase of a dozen a year, but where by this permission means will be found to keep the whole country in a state of disorder and warfare, for the purpose of having slaves in greater numbers.
>
> The port is more convenient than any other for direct communication with Brazil, and if the temptation to make slaves be permitted to be held out to the natives, by opening a market for them, they will cut one another's throats without mercy, and the whole country will be depopulated in a very few years.[48]

Apparently the Portuguese were eager to take advantage of local conflicts that generated captives but were not well enough established to absorb large numbers of slaves when they first became readily available. Migrants from the south raided the Delagoa Bay area, disrupting food production and precipitating famine in a time of drought-induced scarcity. Owen indicated that as of 1823 the Portuguese at Delagoa Bay were still so isolated that they themselves were vulnerable to food shortages. This in turn suggests that visiting ships, which might have brought relief supplies, arrived very infrequently and that the Portuguese were still in no position to engage

---

47. 'Letter from Captain W.F.W. Owen to J.W. Croker', 9 Oct. 1823, HMS *Leven*, Mozambique, in Theal, *Records of South-Eastern Africa*, vol. 9, 32.
48. 'Letter from Captain W.F.W. Owen to John Wilson Croker, esq.', 11 Oct. 1823, HMS *Leven*, Mozambique', in Theal, *Records of South-Eastern Africa*, vol. 9, 37–9.

in an extensive slave trade as late as 1823.[49] In a letter dated 10 May 1825 Owen described the events of 1823 to the Portuguese Governor of Moçambique:

> It is, however, most strange that even through all this time [fighting and threats to the fort] the Commandant and officers of your fort traded with these very Vatwahs [Nguni-speakers], for their spoils and slaves taken from the people of Temby and Matoll, etc. etc. . . . The devastation of the Vatwahs, and consequent famine, brought slaves to the fort for almost nothing; but fortunately, the fort itself was in want, and could not sell food for slaves.[50]

The evidence from Fynn on his way to establish himself as a trader at Natal also suggests that the slave trade out of Delagoa Bay was still limited in scope in mid-1823. Fynn spent six months at Delagoa Bay, first arriving in mid-June 1823. There he met the priest at the fort who '. . . accompanied us to the cells, where we saw about 80 slaves in irons. They had been captured in fights between neighbouring tribes, and had recently been purchased.'[51] Fynn observed that in 1823 'the articles procurable by barter at the settlement were sea-cow and elephant ivory, also ostrich feathers. The principal objects for sale, however, were slaves.'[52] Here Fynn is not indicating a large-scale slave trade, however, for he states that there was only one trading ship per year, which took off all these goods at once. The message is rather that the sum total of trade, including slaves, was minimal in 1823, but relative to the other goods traded slaves had the highest value. Fynn provided some insight into the source of the slaves. According to him,

> The Chief who is the champion of Temby is named Mohambie . . . He is the only Chief at Delagoa who takes prisoners, which are conveyed across English River to the Portuguese to whom they are sold as Slaves for trinkets and cloth which he shares with his king. These Slaves are kept in the Fort until the annual vessel comes to carry them off.[53]

Although according to Fynn in 1823 only one ship a year picked up slaves, by the time of Owen's trips in late 1823 or early 1824 it appears that more ships had begun to arrive. Fynn also exposed the machinations of the Portuguese, who managed to

---

49. As of 1823 all trade with Delagoa Bay carried on Portuguese ships was still routed through Moçambique Island, but no Portuguese ships sailed between Moçambique and Delagoa Bay in the years 1821–23. Hence it does not appear that the Portuguese could have been exporting slaves from the bay in this three-year period. Hedges, 'Trade and Politics', 230–31; E. A. Eldredge, 'Delagoa Bay and the Hinterland in the Early Nineteenth Century: Politics, Trade, Slaves, and Slave-Raiding,' in E. A. Eldredge and F. Morton, eds., *Slavery in South Africa: Captive Labor on the Dutch Frontier*, Boulder, 1994.
50. 'Letter from Captain Owen to Senhor de Botelho, Governor of Moçambique, Leven', 10 May 1825, in Theal, *Records of South-Eastern Africa*, vol. 9, 57.
51. H. F. Fynn, *The Diary of Henry Francis Fynn*, ed. by J. Stuart and D. Mck. Malcolm, Pietermaritzburg, 1950, 39.
52. Fynn, *The Diary*, 40.
53. H. F. Fynn, 'Delagoa Bay', *Records of South-Eastern Africa*, vol. 9, 487.

foster warfare as a source of slaves, so he also was clearly not trying to cover up slaving activities:

> The various tribes in the vicinity of Delagoa, like all other native tribes of Africa, are constantly engaged in petty warfare, and, wherever there is a Portuguese settlement, these contests are encouraged, and not infrequently, one or the other of the rival parties is aided by Portuguese soldiers. The prisoners taken by each tribe are purchased by the Portuguese to become slaves. Mayetha, chief of the Tembe country at the time of my visit, had recently been defeated and many of his subjects sold into slavery.[54]

It would be incorrect to assume without further evidence that the Portuguese were involved not only in slave-trading in the immediate vicinity of the bay but also in damaging slave raids in the interior prior to the mid-1820s. There is contrary evidence that the outlying areas had not yet been ravaged by the slave trade and slave raiders in early 1823. When the Wesleyan missionary in Tembe, William Threlfall, first arrived in mid-1823, he observed that the people lived

> all along the coast to this bay, where the population is great indeed, in every quarter; not living in large towns but distributed in villages equally over the face of the country, for the advantage of cultivation; and the country, as far as I have seen it, is cultivated.
>
> I found the face of the country everywhere covered with the richest pasturage, and extensive fields of caffre and Indian corn.[55]

This scene of peaceful settlement indicated that there had not yet been the widespread disruption that would have resulted from extensive slave-raiding. Threlfall observed that many of the people in the Delagoa Bay area were in distress, but the causes did not arise from slaving. According to Threlfall, the migrating Nguni-speakers from the south, called 'Vatwahs' at Delagoa Bay, had laid waste all the neighbouring areas except for the southern half of the bay, 'Inyack and Mapota' (Nyaka and Maputo). The Vatwahs were apparently raiding only for food, for there is no mention of killing, only famine. Thus the people were being raided for food at a time when drought already had created scarcity, leading Threlfall to describe the area as 'beautiful and fertile in native productions beyond description generally; but for the last two or three years, with little rain – which, with the devastations of the Vatwahs, has produced famine'.[56] Drought combined with political disruptions to create a decade of misery from 1823.[57] By the late 1820s the slave trade out of Delagoa Bay had reached its full proportions, and the effects were disastrous.

54. Fynn, *The Diary*, 43.
55. 'William Threlfall, Village Sleugally, Tembe, Delagoa Bay, 1823', in Bannister, *Humane Policy*, lxvi.
56. 'Threlfall, Portuguese Fort, Delagoa Bay, 29 Nov. 1823', in Bannister, *Humane Policy*, lxvii.
57. M.D.D. Newitt, 'Drought in Mozambique, 1823–1831', *Journal of Southern African Studies*, 15 (1988), 14–35

Since Harries has accused Portuguese colonial officials and historians of covering up Portugal's participation in the slave trade, and Cobbing accepts his case, it is worth considering whether the lack of evidence of an extensive slave trade from Delagoa Bay before 1823 is in fact the product of a Portuguese conspiracy. Both the major nineteenth-century Portuguese sources on Mozambique and recent works by Portuguese historians have systematically exposed the trade in slaves. Harries himself conducted a thorough investigation and revealed the high level of the slave trade after 1823, but he did not find any evidence for a heavy slave trade out of Delagoa Bay before that year. If there is in fact a conspiracy of silence, it remains to be explained why the Portuguese would have felt free to expose and condemn trading out of Moçambique Island, Quelimane and Inhambane to the north and yet would cover up a similar trade out of Delagoa Bay.

Harries's evidence that the modern Portuguese historian Alexandre Lobato deliberately concealed extensive slaving out of Delagoa Bay rests on Lobato's statement that 'Lourenço Marques was one of the rare ports of Mozambique that did not export slaves.'[58] Harries neglects to mention, however, that in this passage Lobato is referring to the time period covered by the second volume of his collection, 1787–99; in volume 1, which covers 1782–86, Lobato reports the export of slaves from Delagoa Bay in those years, and he does not imply that an extensive slave trade out of Delagoa Bay never developed in the nineteenth century. In addition, Lobato is not covering up Portuguese slaving at all in the sentence cited, as it confirms that the Portuguese slave trade was extensive out of other Portuguese ports. According to official figures collected by Lobato, some 46 893 slaves were exported from Mozambique between 1781 and 1790, approximately half on Portuguese ships and half on foreign vessels. Lobato assumes that these official figures are low, noting that the illicit trade must have been large since the clandestine export of slaves was so easy along the coast north of Quelimane and especially north of Angoche.[59]

Nor can early Portuguese sources be rightly accused of systematically covering up the Portuguese slave trade out of Mozambique. Sebastião Xavier Botelho was Governor of Mozambique from 1825 to 1829, and in his book of 1835, the major primary source for the period, he exposed and denounced the slave trade out of Mozambique.[60] Botelho attributes the poverty of Quelimane by the 1830s to slave-trading, as compared to its prosperity before the slave trade increased there in about 1810. He readily acknowledges that 14 to 18 ships a year arrived in the northern Mozambique ports from Rio de Janeiro to transport slaves beginning in 1810. He also condemns later activities of public officials at Lourenço Marques, where governors

58. Lobato, *História*, vol. 2: 1787–1799, vol. 2, 356, quoted in Harries, 'Slavery, Social Incorporation and Surplus Extraction', 311.

59. Lobato, *História*, vol. 2, 356–7. Lobato does not elucidate the period 1800–30 since his work ends in 1799, but his exposure of the slave trade in the earlier period indicates that he was not part of a conspiracy of silence about the Portuguese slave trade out of Mozambique.

60. S. X. Botelho, *Memoria Estatistica sobre os Dominios Portuguezes na Africa Oriental*, Lisboa, 1835.

were not content to collect the fruits of spontaneous disagreements among the Caffres but who fomented them themselves, beginning wars among them in order to offer kindness, capture them and sell them . . . It is up to me to say that all these crimes have advanced here not only unsanctioned but also authorized because when vice begins with those in power, far from being strange or abhorrent, it is taken as an example and used to excuse other crimes.[61]

Other scholars studying the slave trade from Mozambique have tended to confirm that Delagoa Bay was late in entering the slave trade on a large scale. J. Capela and E. Medeiros trace the slave trade from Mozambique to the islands in the Indian Ocean between 1720 and 1902. They note the rise of Quelimane as the dominant port for slave exports after ships from that port became exempt from customs at Moçambique (Island) in 1814, but they did not find evidence of an extensive trade from Lourenço Marques until early 1827.[62]

We have ample evidence, then, from both Portuguese sources and outsiders about the Mozambican slave trade up and down the northern coasts. It is extremely unlikely that an extensive slave trade was being carried on, completely unrecorded, at Delagoa Bay. English, Dutch, French and Portuguese ships all frequented the coast, and all had conflicting interests in the area, which argues against a conspiracy of silence concerning slaving activities at Delagoa Bay. Sources which do expose the slave trade elsewhere but consistently portray Delagoa Bay as primarily a site of ivory exports and as a whaling station can be taken as implying the lack of extensive slave-trading and slave-raiding in the Delagoa Bay region prior to 1823. There is thus no evidence for Cobbing's assertion that the slave trade at Delagoa Bay reached the proportions of 1 000 slaves exported annually from 'about 1818', when all sources suggest that Owen was correct when he estimated the numbers prior to 1823 at about a dozen a year. The numbers of slaves who were exported from Delagoa Bay before 1822 or 1823 were therefore far too few significantly to disrupt the societies from which they hailed. The slave trade and slave-raiding cannot have been responsible for demographic upheavals among the northern Nguni-speakers between 1817 and 1822. Although the slave trade out of Delagoa Bay prolonged and intensified regional violence after 1823, it could not have originated dislocation far inland as early as 1817–22, and the explanation for early conflict there must lie elsewhere.

The Cape Frontier Slave Trade and Violence in the Interior

Sporadic fighting and demographic dislocation in southern Africa persisted into the 1830s, and the Zulu have long served as convenient scapegoats for the continuing violence. In fact neither the Zulu nor such related breakaway groups as the Ndebele

---

61. Botelho, *Memoria*, 92. Translation mine.
62. J. Capela and E. Medeiros, *O Tráfico de Escravos de Moçambique para as ilhas do Indico 1720–1902*, Maputo, 1987, 32–41. Their ship lists are far from complete, and these data are supplemented with evidence from a broad range of archival sources.

were ultimately responsible for most of the conflict in the interior of southern Africa. After an initial period of migration and localised struggles between various African chiefdoms, slave-raiding by Europeans and their agents played the primary role in fostering and exacerbating conflicts throughout the region.

What was the nature of slave-raiding in the interior, and who was responsible for it? Cobbing argues that most of the turmoil farther west, that is north-east of the Cape colony, was caused by white missionaries engaging in slave-raiding in that area. However, it was European settlers and their Griqua allies and not the missionaries named by Cobbing who raided for slaves. The Griqua were the main marauders in the area of the Orange River from the time they arrived there, and they had been a major cause of demographic dislocation among the Tswana before the Zulu kingdom was ever formed.

The white colonists were both directly and indirectly responsible for the activities of the Griqua. The slavery of the Cape spawned unified groups of people of Khoi and mixed-race descent who moved beyond the border and became known by various names: Bastaards, Kora, Korana and eventually Griqua and Bergenaar.[63] But traders in the Cape colony armed the Griqua and wanted them to supply legitimate goods acquired by hunting, such as ivory, skins and ostrich feathers. Colonial officials also wanted the Griqua to provide security on the northern frontier, eventually leading to an 1843 treaty. For both these reasons the white frontiersmen and the colonial government were happy to continue supplying the Griqua with guns, which the Griqua used to attack and raid their neighbours ruthlessly both for cattle and for the illicit item of commerce, slaves.

Cobbing is therefore correct to identify Europeans and their allies as the main instigators of violence across the Cape colony's frontier. However, Cobbing also accuses certain missionaries from the London Missionary Society of masterminding the slave trade in this area and of concealing their involvement in it, in spite of the fact that they actively tried to expose and stop the trade. Cobbing's accusations that white missionaries were systematically enslaving Africans for sale to the Cape colony rest on inadequate evidence, and there are data to suggest that his charges are false. Numerous missionaries condemned the immoral conduct of the white settlers, and Cobbing himself relies on their own writings for evidence of the slave trade. With competing mission groups vying for influence in the region and all seeking support from home, a conspiracy of silence covering up a missionary role in the slave trade is hard to credit. So many Sotho who had worked in the Cape colony returned to Lesotho in the 1830s and 1840s that had the missionaries been involved in enslaving them, and had they suffered direct enslavement, surely there would be recorded reports of it. The early missionaries in Lesotho were Protestants who hailed from France and had no direct connection with the missionaries from the London

---

63. See M. Legassick, 'The Northern Frontier to c. 1840: The Rise and Decline of the Griqua People', in R. Elphick and H. B. Giliomee, eds., *The Shaping of South African Society, 1652–1840*, Middletown, 1988, 358–420.

Missionary Society serving the Griqua nearby, and their copious reports beginning with their arrival in 1833 would certainly have revealed a scandal had one existed on a significant scale.

Cobbing begins his indictment of the missionaries as slavers by presenting a famous battle, a confrontation of various people at the Tlhaping town of Dithakong, as a missionary-led slave raid. Cobbing builds his case against the missionaries by claiming the supposed raid to be merely one of many. He depicts the battle as pre-planned by missionaries on the basis of only part of one European eyewitness account, disregarding contrary evidence from this same account and from other European and African witnesses. A survey of the historiography surrounding the Dithakong battle, to present the accepted version of events in this context, allows us to analyse Cobbing's use of the sources and to assess the plausibility of his reinterpretation.

The complicated confrontation at Dithakong occurred in the context of considerable demographic turmoil in the interior of southern Africa. The background events of 1822–3 have been fairly well described by scholars. Large-scale migrations in the interior began when the Hlubi of Mpangazitha crossed the Drakensberg from the east and attacked the Tlokwa under the leadership of their queen regent, 'MaNthatisi, in early 1822. The Sotho-speaking Tlokwa of 'MaNthatisi raided others for food, both cattle and standing crops, as they fled the Hlubi and eventually settled west of the Caledon River in about 1824. Subsequently they came into occasional conflict with their Sotho-speaking neighbours, who emerged after 1824 as the Sotho nation of Moshoeshoe. In 1853 they were finally defeated by Moshoeshoe and incorporated into his nation.

The Hlubi and Ngwane, under Matiwane, fought a decisive battle in 1825, and in the aftermath the Hlubi chief Mpangazitha was killed and his followers dispersed. This left ~~the Ngwane dominant in the area of the Caledon River~~ until they were disbanded in 1827. In the meantime their raids had dislodged various Sotho and Tswana-speaking groups further north, including the Fokeng under Sebetwane, the Phuthing under Tsowane and the Hlakwana under Nkarahanye. These were the three groups involved in the most famous battle of the time, the battle at the just-abandoned Tlhaping town of Dithakong (Lattakoo) on 24 June 1823. On that date, two Europeans, John Melvill and the London missionary Robert Moffat, accompanied the Tlhaping group of Tswana and a force of mounted Griqua armed with guns to defend the town. They managed to rout the Fokeng, the Phuthing and the Hlakwana, killing the chiefs Tsowane and Nkarahanye. The Tlokwa of 'MaNthatisi were not present.

This battle has come under close scrutiny by scholars in the past because of a dispute over the identity of the participants. European observers, including the traveller George Thompson, reported that rumours circulated widely beforehand among the Tlhaping Tswana at Kuruman that an infamous group of so-called Mantatees was invading the area. Subsequently this appellation stuck to both the 'invaders' and the refugees from the battle, leading later historians to assume that the 'attackers' at Dithakong had been the Tlokwa of 'MaNthatisi. Cobbing takes this confusion over the identity of the Africans at Dithakong, though it has long since been resolved, to indicate contradictions arising from a cover-up constructed around a battle that had not in fact occurred. On this false premise he reinterprets the events at Dithakong instead as a slave raid instigated by John Melvill and Robert Moffat, with the Tlhaping and the Griqua as their allies.

The identity of the participants has been adequately dealt with by Marion How and subsequently by William Lye, both of whom used a variety of independent sources, African and European.[64] Marion How corrected the version of the battle put forward by her grandfather D. F. Ellenberger, who had mistakenly described the encounter as two separate battles instead of one and placed the Tlokwa of 'MaNthatisi at the scene. Cobbing considers Ellenberger's mistakes to be sufficient reason to dismiss him as a source altogether. This ignores the fact that Ellenberger's work was based on oral testimony from dozens of African informants whose information he systematically cross-checked whenever possible with his colleague and translator (and son-in-law) J.C. MacGregor, who collected his own version of *Basuto Traditions.*[65]

To assume that this battle involving three identified African chiefs and their followers never took place just because Ellenberger was partially incorrect is to deny a voice to the African participants who left behind the oral traditions of the event that appear in MacGregor's work as well as Ellenberger's. Marion How and then Lye tied together the oral traditions and the written evidence, including that of the missionaries, to make a convincing case as to who was present.[66] In the written sources, we find that Moffat clearly identifies those present: the 'Maputee' ([Ma]Phuting) of 'Chuane' (Tsowane) and the 'Batclaquan' ([Ba]Hlakwana) of

---

64. M. How, 'An Alibi for Mantatisi', *African Studies*, 13 (1954), 65–76; and W. F. Lye, 'The Difaqane: The Mfecane in the Southern Sotho Area, 1822–24', *Journal of African History*, 8 (1967), 107–31. Historians have long since recognized that the colonists misidentified many Africans, indiscriminately calling otherwise unknown groups who originated from the north-east 'Mantatees'. The term 'Mantatees' was a catch-all name used for all non-Xhosa Africans of whom Cape colonists became aware during this period, either through hearsay or as incoming labourers. Cobbing's treatment of this issue (in 'The Mfecane as Alibi') illustrates why his work is so difficult for a non-specialist to read and criticize. Cobbing uses the term Mantatees beginning on page 492 to refer to captured, enslaved labourers sold into the colony, without initially explaining this use to the reader. He does not trace the origins of the term and its misuse in the sources until pages 514–15; and he never acknowledges that the distinction between so-called Mantatees and the people of 'MaNtatisi was recognized even when the term Mantatee was first in use and is widely understood by historians today. It is not until the reader reaches the discussion and footnotes on page 516 that we learn why Cobbing rejects the accepted view of events at Dithakong, found in the work of How and Lye. Even here he never addresses the evidence on which the accepted view is based, making it necesary to review this evidence briefly here.
65. J.C. MacGregor, *Basuto Traditions*, Cape Town, 1905. For further discussion of Ellenberger and MacGregor see E.A. Eldredge, 'Land, Politics and Censorship: The Historiography of Nineteenth-century Lesotho', *History in Africa*, 15 (1988), 191–209.
66. Unfortunately the renditions of How and Lye, like that of Ellenberger before them, read much into the material which they have only surmised and which is highly questionable, such as the attitudes and intentions of the participants. Many of the pejorative adjectives from the missionary sources which appeared in Ellenberger also appear in How and in Lye.

'Carrahanye' or 'Karaganye' (Nkarahanye), and that he specified that Tsowane's people had stayed in the town while the Hlakwana engaged in fighting the Griqua/Tlhaping force. Thompson referred to the presence of the 'Bacloqueeni' ([Ba]Hlakwana) and of 'Mahallogani' (Nkarahanye).[67] The European witnesses distinguished only two and not three groups by sight, but in the confusion this is not surprising: battlefield eyewitnesses are notoriously unreliable. There is no reason to assume that Sebetwane's Fokeng were not present, as Cobbing does, noting Edwin Smith's implausible explanation that they were hidden from view.[68] Both Sebetwane and one of his retainers told David Livingstone of their presence (leading the Fokeng) at the battle, and Nkarahanye's son Setaki was one of Ellenberger's informants. Since many Phuting and Hlakwana ended up in Lesotho and their descendants there are alive and well, they are hardly 'shadowy Caledon groups', as Cobbing calls them, questioning their very existence.[69]

It is in this context that Cobbing's conclusion that no battle occurred must be rejected. Cobbing presents his rendition of events without reference to previous analyses, making the novelty of his premises difficult for non-specialists to perceive, and he does not present the evidence directly for the reader's consideration. Hence the reader is asked to accept at face value that the confrontation at Dithakong was an organised, preconceived missionary slave raid. Cobbing asserts that

> the 'battle' of Dithakong was one such slave (and cattle) raid, unprovoked, on a still unidentified 'enemy', who became immortalized as mantatees. This is clear from the writings of Moffat, Melvill and Thompson, the former two of whom, both missionaries, were the instigators and organizers both of the raid and the disposal of the prisoners. This emerges best in Melvill's account.[70]

To build his general case against missionaries Cobbing mistakenly identifies Melvill as a missionary here. Melvill was still a government agent in 1823 and did not become a missionary until four years later. Cobbing further depicts the actions of these men in terms which suggest a conspiracy:

> It was Mr Melvill who brought the three most feared Griqua leaders of their generation – Waterboer, Adam Kok and Barend Barends – together, and organized the arms and powder. It was Moffat and Thompson who spied out the positions of the victims; and Moffat and Melvill who guided the army into 'battle' on 25 and 26 June.[71]

---

67. Lye, 'The Difaqane', 127–8. The difficulties of transcribing Tswana sounds account for the many variations of name spellings in early sources. For example, a sound which many foreigners have difficulty pronouncing can be rendered as 'hl' or 'tl' or 'cl'; another guttural consonant is rendered alternatively as 'r' or 'g' or 'h'.
68. Cobbing, 'The Mfecane as Alibi', 516.
69. Cobbing, 'The Mfecane as Alibi', 516n. In the text Cobbing refers to 'the Hlakwana and Phuting, whoever they were'.
70. Cobbing, 'The Mfecane as Alibi', 492.
71. Cobbing, 'The Mfecane as Alibi', 492.

Melvill and Moffat estimated that 400 to 500 of their opponents were killed, but Cobbing lowers this estimate to 200–300. The Europeans noted that the retreating Phuthing and Hlakwana burned the town of Dithakong, but since Cobbing does not accept that it was these outsiders who were attacked, he accuses the Europeans of claiming that the victims burned their own villages and asserts instead that the forces with the missionaries burned some villages.[72] Then Cobbing makes it plain that he believes that Melvill and Moffat were motivated solely by the prospect of profits:

> Thirty-three cattle were given to Melvill 'according to the custom of the country'. Moffat, Melvill and a mission labourer named Hamilton used armed Griqua to round up the women and children who were not dead or had not been able to escape. Over ninety prisoners were taken back to Kuruman on 25–27 June. There a squabble broke out between the missionaries and the Tlhaping chief, Mothibi, over their disposal. Griqua guns decided the issue in favour of the missionaries. During the next few days Melvill scoured the countryside and captured at least fifty more women and children. He avoided the men. Women and young males were what the Cape market preferred. Melvill immediately despatched fifteen Mantatees for sale to Graaff Reinet in the north-eastern Cape, for which he received payment in ammunition. At least thirty remained with the Griqua in Griqua Town. Moffat kept several at Kuruman, and took one boy as a personal servant who was 'affectionately domesticated in the family of his benefactor' [*sic*]. Others, including five women – who fortunately 'indicated nothing of cannibal ferocity' – and a 'fine boy', Moffat took with him for distribution in Cape Town in January 1824 to the applause of the local press. Almost certainly the rest were sent to various destinations in the Cape.[73]

Cobbing's case against Melvill and Moffat must therefore be interpreted in terms of the outcome – were these people enslaved? – as well as in light of their original intentions – did they plan and execute a slave raid? I conclude below that many of the people brought back after the battle did indeed end up as captive workers who could be called slaves, but this was an unintended outcome, and Moffat and Melvill never planned this expedition or any other as a slave raid.

Since Cobbing's case against the missionaries rests on a piece of evidence from Melvill, it is important to assess Melvill's credibility. John Melvill was alternatively known in the sources as Melville, leading to possible confusion. Melvill was appointed government agent in Griqualand on 21 March 1822; he was accepted as a missionary by the London Missionary Society in 1827 and remained stationed among the Griqua. Melvill was held in high regard by John Philip, who said that if

---

72. Cobbing, 'The Mfecane as Alibi', 492. Cobbing mistakenly says that Dithakong was the residence of the 'Maida' when in fact it had long been the main Tlhaping town, and the Maili (Maidi) lived among the Tlhaping near Dithakong.
73. Cobbing, 'The Mfecane as Alibi', 493.

any government agent had to be appointed to live among the Griqua, Melvill was 'the fittest man the government could have selected to fill the office'.[74] Cobbing's main source of information on Melvill and the slave trade was George Thompson, a businessman and traveller, and as Thompson never set up business in this area and was not connected to missionaries, he was perhaps an objective witness.[75] Thompson had a high opinion of Melvill as well:

> No one who is acquainted with Mr Melvill personally, can for a moment doubt the benevolence and disinterestedness of his character. Indeed his being here at all is a sufficient proof of these qualities. He formerly held an easy and respectable situation under Government in Cape Town, namely, that of Inspector of Public Buildings, etc, with an income of about 7000 rix-dollars per annum; but being a religious man, and zealous for the civilization and conversion of the heathen, he applied to the Government for his present appointment, and voluntarily resigned it for his lucrative situation, with the benevolent purpose of promoting Missionary operations.[76]

Thompson was not entirely convinced by Melvill's account of himself and his activities among the Griqua but respected his intentions nevertheless:

> How far Mr Melvill justly estimated his own qualifications for the arduous task of influencing a semi-barbarous people, may well be questioned, on witnessing the unhappy results of his interference with the affairs of the Griquas; but his praiseworthy motives and generous self-devotion must ever be respected. He now receives, as the Government agent here, a salary of only 1000 rix-dollars (£75); besides which he occupies a small house belonging to the London Missionary Society.[77]

Dismissing Melvill's and Moffat's explanations of their own activities, Cobbing suggests that instead of helping victims of the battle they were capturing slaves:

> The Missionaries tried to depict themselves as succouring the prisoners, and rescuing them from their evil chiefs and starvation (with all those cattle?). There is no doubt, however, that they were fully and consciously engrossed in what they were doing, i.e. collecting slaves, and that the cover of hypocrisy was intended to deflect the certain censure from the government in London and from their seniors in the London Missionary Society if it had leaked out that they were selling people into slavery.[78]

74. J. Philip, *Researches in South Africa*, New York, 1969, vol. 2, 79.
75. Thompson, *Travels and Adventures*.
76. Thompson, *Travels and Adventures*, vol. 1, 74.
77. Thompson, *Travels and Adventures*, vol. 1, 74.
78. Cobbing, 'The Mfecane as Alibi', 493.

There is no evidence to support this particular missionary slave-trading conspiracy, and the only evidence Cobbing cites to support his general argument comes from Melvill himself. But why would Melvill raise possible questions by implicating himself at all when he could have avoided all mention of receiving cattle or of 'disposing' of the captives? Melvill's account seems credible under the circumstances. This also is the only 'evidence' used by Cobbing to indict Moffat:

> The next morning a party of men were sent to bring them [the captured women and children] along, and most of them were then distributed among the Griquas to become their servants, which was considered to be the best way of getting them taken care of, and provided with food. With the apprehension, however, that the providing of victuals for those poor creatures might, after all, fall exclusively upon me, I applied for a share of the captured cattle, for myself and the Missionaries, on account of our having furnished the commando with ammunition. By this means I secured a supply of provisions for them, in any emergency, or for any other prisoners who might hereafter be taken. I had allotted to me thirty-three head of cattle, not choosing to receive any more than a regular share, according to the custom of the country, in order to prevent the Griquas from murmuring; at the same time I expressly stated to the chiefs, that I designed the cattle for the subsistence of the Mantatee prisoners.[79]

Cobbing questions Melvill's veracity by wondering how the women and children from the enemy could have been starving, as he described them, when there were so many cattle at hand.[80] Some of these women may have only recently joined these chiefdoms, however, and in times of insecurity and scarcity men often ate while depriving or casting off women and children. The traditional productive role of women was less important in mobile fighting groups, and their access to food was extremely limited. Men had a strong incentive to control women in the context of ongoing threats to life and the need for women's reproductive capacities, but they had no incentive to treat women well. When wealth and food was in the form of cattle, women had no guaranteed access to this food and were often left to fend for themselves, living on gathered grasses and seeds. It is therefore not inconceivable that this group of 'Mantatees' with large herds included women and children who were starving.

As for the disposal of these prisoners, their fates varied, but it is doubtful whether Melvill or Moffat profited. R.L. Watson discredits Cobbing's account of Moffat as supposedly 'distributing' six refugees in Cape Town by clarifying the import of his newspaper source, the *South African Commercial Advertiser*. The newspaper

---

79. 'Melvill's narrative of transactions after the battle, and of his excursion to rescue the women and children of the invaders', in Thompson, *Travels and Adventures*, vol. 1, 153.
80. Cobbing, 'The Mfecane as Alibi', 493.

indicated that Moffat was accompanied by seven Africans, identified two of them, and discussed them at greater length without referring to their distribution or sale.[81] In fact the group that accompanied Moffat to Cape Town included Chief Mothibi's counsellor, Thaiso, and son, Phetlu. Thompson repeats the newspaper account from the *South African Journal* about their trip, and they appear in several places in his diary of his travels; Phetlu died of anthrax in March 1825 after returning to Kuruman from Cape Town, apparently free to do so. Cobbing's insinuation that these people were sold into slavery by Moffat is unfounded.[82]

The essence of Cobbing's case is thus to argue that the missionaries deliberately planned and executed a slave raid (the battle at Dithakong), to imply without providing evidence of other slave raids that this event was part of a general pattern of missionary-organised raids and to misconstrue newspaper accounts to suggest that these missionaries regularly sold the captives into slavery for their own gain. It is true that Africans were continually being captured and sold into slavery and that some of the people who returned with Melvill and Moffat from the battle suffered such a fate. However, these instances are not proof that this battle was planned as a slave raid by these men nor that these missionaries or any others were systematically engaged in slave-raiding.

The presence of a forced labour system at the Cape which received captives from the frontier meant that many of the women and children brought back from the battle found themselves introduced into the colony as unwilling workers. Others remained, helpless, as servants to the Griqua. The acceptance of client status by people who lost their herds was routine, so that those who remained among the Griqua in this status would not have considered this form of oppression unusual. It is not inappropriate to characterise all these helpless victims as slaves: whether working for the Griqua or in the colony, they were captive and had no control over their own fates. However, those who went to the Cape colony did not necessarily end up as chattel slaves, as argued by Cobbing. Thompson explains:

> Within the last two years upwards of 1000 fugitives, mostly in a state of extreme destitution, have taken refuge in the Colony, – a circumstance wholly unprecedented in any former period. These refugees have been, by the direction of the Home Government, indentured as servants for seven years to such of the Colonists in the eastern districts as are not slave owners, and precautions have been adopted, (efficient ones, I trust,) to prevent any of those poor exiles from being ill-treated, or from hereafter merging into a state of slavery.[83]

The children captured for sale to the colonists by Griqua and Bergenaar must have been vulnerable to permanent enslavement, and no doubt that is why they were

81. R. L. Watson, *The Slave Question: Liberty and Property in South Africa*, Middletown, 1900, 19–20, 234n.
82. Thompson, *Travels and Adventures*, vol. 1, i, 86, 88, 92–3, 112, 115, 165–6; vol. 2, 48n, 223–4, 235.
83. Thompson, *Travels and Adventures*, vol. 1, 187.

preferred. Adults, such as the women sent by the missionaries, would have remembered their original homes and would not have been as easy to retain permanently. The Sotho who entered into colonial service during these years did indeed return to Lesotho in the late 1830s and early 1840s, bringing back with them the herds they had accumulated during their periods of service. This seems to indicate that the terms of indentured servitude described by Thompson may have indeed governed the relationship between some 'Mantatee' Sotho and their employers.

One reason that it is so surprising that Cobbing accuses Melvill of covering up his activities as a slave trader is that Melvill deliberately exposed the slave trade in his correspondence. Among his early records is a lengthy letter written when he was still a government agent, in 1824; parts of it were published by the missionary John Philip in his famous 1828 book criticising Cape colony policy, *Researches in South Africa*.[84] Subsequently Melvill's letter was published almost verbatim in an 1835 government report.[85] He exposed the violent raiding committed by the Bergenaar, who had broken away from the Griqua in 1821 and who captured cattle and slaves to sell to white settlers. Mellvill carefully distinguished between those renegade Bergenaar Griquas, who were guilty of destructive raiding, and the Griqua under Waterboer at Griquatown and under Cornelius and Adam Kok, who were maintaining the interests of the colonial officials. Melvill explained that the Bergenaar had attracted followers because they avoided colonial restrictions on commerce and thereby derived huge profits, while those who co-operated with the colonial authorities and their representatives, i.e. the Griqua under Andries Waterboer, suffered the disadvantages of restricted access to trade. Melvill specifically identified the colonists as complicit in fostering and promoting the destructive activities of the Bergenaar by selling firearms to them.[86] Melvill also explained the use of these guns by the Bergenaar for raiding neighbouring Africans such as the Sotho. In one instance some Sotho who were attacked by the Bergenaar did not fight, deciding it was useless, and many of them were enslaved:

> . . . four white men, different from the rest of the plunderers, joined the party, and having collected all the boys carried them off.[87]

84. Philip, *Researches*, vol. 2, 79–84. Original letter from John Melvill to Sir Richard Plasket, Secretary of Government, Cape Town, 17 Dec. 1824.
85. 'Extract from a Report by Mr. Melville [*sic*], Government Agent for Griqua Town, dated December 1824, relative to the State of the Griquas addressed to the Colonial Secretary', in *British Parliamentary Papers* (hereafter *BPP*), 50 (1835) XXXIX, 212–9, 'Papers Relative to the Condition and Treatment of the Native Inhabitants of Southern Africa within the Colony of the Cape of Good Hope or Beyond the Frontier of that Colony, Part I: Hottentots and Bosjesmen; Caffres; Griquas'.
86. 'Extract from a Report by Mr. Melville [*sic*], Government Agent for Griqua Town, dated December 1824, relative to the State of the Griquas addressed to the Colonial Secretary', in *BPP* 50 (1835) XXXIX, 215–6, 'Papers Relative to the Condition and Treatment of the Native Inhabitants'.
87. 'Extract from a Report by Mr. Melville [*sic*], Government Agent for Griqua Town, dated December 1824, relative to the State of the Griquas addressed to the Colonial Secretary', in *BPP* 50 (1835) XXXIX, 217, 'Papers Relative to the Condition and Treatment of the Native Inhabitants.

Apparently not only boys were enslaved, for 'one woman, however, resisted when one of the band attempted to drag her away'.[88]

Melvill took a tour with a fellow missionary, Kolbe, in 1828, with a view to discovering more about the neighbouring 'Bashutoos'. On this trip Melvill recorded more instances of Bergenaar depredations against the Sotho.[89] Melvill ended his journal notes from this trip with clear allusions to the complicity of the white settlers in this slaving, though these were deleted in publication. Melvill accused the 'haughty and unfeeling farmer' of 'unchristian-like acts according to his own selfish views', but the adjective 'unchristian-like' was edited out. More significantly, he asked, 'And why must these boers as if a superior race of beings deprive their poor fellow creatures of what God has given them?' The question was printed, but Melvill's next sentence was censored and can be found only in the original letter:

> We hesitate not to say that they [the Boers] are robbers of the oppressed. We are all pleading for the emancipation of slavery, – a christian-like work indeed! – but in Africa christians are daily making slaves.[90]

Again he emphasised a few sentences later:

> Govt is continually making regulations agreeable to justice, to punish the Bushmen and other plunderers of Cattle, but we trust the same Govt will prevent the farmers from plundering – we say plundering – the bushmen & Bassutoos.[91]

Melvill's evidence supports Cobbing's description of the Bergenaar as slavers, except that it does not implicate Melvill himself. Of course both Melvill and Philip, who quoted Melvill extensively, were interested in promoting the interests of 'their' Griqua under Waterboer and were not necessarily friendly to the renegade Bergenaar; however, there is no reason to suspect that their descriptions of them as slavers are incorrect. It is therefore surprising, given Melvill's role in exposing the slave trade, that Cobbing accused him of involvement in it. Cobbing has not provided any evidence that the missionaries condoned or participated actively in the slave-raiding in this area; on the contrary, they did not hesitate to condemn colonists

88. 'Extract from a Report by Mr. Melville [*sic*], Government Agent for Griqua Town, dated December 1824, relative to the State of the Griquas addressed to the Colonial Secretary', in *BPP* 50 (1835) XXXIX, 217, 'Papers Relative to the Condition and Treatment of the Native Inhabitants.

89. Extracts from the Journal of Messrs Melvill and Kolbe, addressed to the Revd Richard Miles, Superintendent of the Society's Missions in Africa, Philippolis, 25 Nov. 1828, Council for World Missions (London Missionary Society) Archives (hereafter CWM). An edited version of this was published as J. Melvill, 'Missionary Tour through the Country of the Bashutoos', *Transactions of the Missionary Society*, 52 (Oct. 1829), 123–8. Other extracts from Melvill appear in this journal.

90. School of Oriental and African Studies (hereafter SOAS) Council for World Mission Archives (hereafter CWM), Extracts from the Journal of Messrs Melvill and Kolbe, 25 Nov. 1828 (unpublished original letter).

91. (SOAS) CWM, Extracts from the Journal of Messrs Melville and Kolbe, 25 Nov. 1828 (unpublished original letter).

engaged in illicit activities, which included the enslavement of Africans. It would be a mistake, however, to dismiss Cobbing's emphasis on slaving on the northern Cape frontier because of his error in assigning responsibility for it. Although Cobbing's case against Melvill and the missionaries may be unsupportable, his case against the colonists stands.

Environment and Society: Sources of Competition and Conflict

Since there is compelling evidence that extensive slave-trading at Delagoa Bay did not precede the conflicts associated with political amalgamation and state formation in south-eastern Africa, this leaves open the question of what processes did generate the dramatic sociopolitical changes of the early nineteenth century. A number of theories have been put forward, some of which offer useful insights into the root causes for change in this period. Gluckman first proposed the possibility of overpopulation as a source of stress and an explanation for political consolidation and the emergence of the Zulu nation.[92] Not long after Alan Smith demonstrated that political change in south-eastern Africa was linked to the ivory trade out of Delagoa Bay.[93]

More recently, Jeff Guy pursued the idea of environmental influences by seeking to explain the rise of the Zulu kingdom in terms of 'stock-keeping and the physical environment of Zululand'.[94] He argued that in the area that became the Zulu state cattle needed access to varying types of grasses found in different areas, according to topography and rainfall, during the changing seasons of the year. The need for access to the whole range of pasture types governed the location of settlement sites and created an incentive for bringing more land under Zulu control.[95] According to Guy, deterioration of the land from over-use, combined with drought, produced famines in the late eighteenth century, which brought about conflict and political change and eventually led to state formation.

Guy's theory of overpopulation and environmental degradation in the Natal/Zulu kingdom area is problematic. The carrying capacity of land in terms of people is determined by the use that people make of the land. Guy attempted to assess the

92. M. Gluckman, 'The Rise of a Zulu Empire', *Scientific American*, 202, 4 (1969), 157–68. Omer-Cooper subsequently focused on the age-regiment system of Dingiswayo and argued that it was newly borrowed and adapted from the customs of his Sotho-speaking neighbours, but recent research indicates this was a false assumption; Omer-Cooper, *The Zulu Aftermath*. In the context of the historiography of South Africa in the 1960s, Omer-Cooper broke new ground in giving primary attention to the internal dynamics of African history in his book. Unfortunately, the very title of the book perpetuates the myth of Zulu responsibility for the violence of the period. By focusing only on the internal dynamics of these societies, Omer-Cooper ignored the fact that they were affected by external trade and other forms of European influence. Implicit in Omer-Cooper's book, in addition, is a 'great man' approach to history, as his focus tends to be on the character and innovations of leaders.
93. Smith, 'The Trade of Delagoa Bay'; and A.K. Smith, 'Delagoa Bay and the Trade of South-east Africa', in R. Gray and D. Birmingham, eds, *Pre-colonial African Trade*, London, 1970, 265–89.
94. J. Guy, 'Ecological Factors in the Rise of Shaka and the Zulu Kingdom', in S. Marks and A. Atmore, eds, *Economy and Society in Pre-industrial South Africa*, London, 1980, 102–19.
95. Guy, 'Ecological Factors', 105–12.

relationship of northern Nguni-speakers to their environment in terms of land use, but he looked at only the pastoral side of the production process and ignored cultivation. On this basis Guy proposed the hypothesis that 'by the end of the eighteenth century an imbalance had arisen between population density and the resources of the region' and that this contributed to the radical social changes which took place.[96] There is no evidence that environmental degradation had occurred, and Guy jumped to unfounded conclusions when he assumed that 'by the end of the eighteenth century, the physical resources were breaking down under existing systems of exploitation'.[97] The seasonal rotation he emphasises argues against unconscious misuse of pastures.

Furthermore, there is evidence that arable land was being used efficiently through cultivation practices that allowed for soil regeneration. To Guy's discussion of stock-keeping and pasture use must therefore be added an analysis of cultivation and arable land use. Cultivation represents intensified land use relative to pastoralism and produces much greater quantities of food in proportion to the amount of land used. Solving a problem of 'overpopulation' by increasing food production can therefore be accomplished either by acquiring more land for extensive pastoral use or by converting land already available to more intensive use through cultivation. Cultivation was as important to the people of south-eastern Africa as was stock-keeping, and grains, both sorghum and maize, were a critical component of their diet.[98] Because of the warm climate crops matured in only three months, and on well-watered fields with proper soils two or even three crops could be grown in a single field each year.[99] The Zulu were careful to ensure that the fertility of the soil was renewed: the stalks from the harvested grain were collected and burned, and the ashes scattered to serve as fertiliser in the fields.[100] Zulu recognition of the critical value of food crops was evident in the severity of the law under Shaka that no one was allowed to pick even a single ear of corn or head of sorghum without Shaka's permission, on pain of death.[101] In order to support a growing population with food, the acquisition of good, well-watered arable land with rich soil was critical.

Guy's interpretation stressing overpopulation, environmental degradation and the desire for pasture land is therefore incomplete. Had there been generalised overpopulation as postulated by Gluckman and Omer-Cooper, it is hard to explain in terms of production needs why the fertile tract of land in Natal south of the Zulu

96. Guy, 'Ecological Factors', 103.
97. Guy, 'Ecological Factors', 103.
98. Guy acknowledged the importance of cultivation in another article, but he did not attempt to revise his earlier thesis based on the recognition that 'cereal production was not only fundamental to the existence of these societies, but absorbed massive amounts of labour time dominating not only the productive processes, but profoundly affecting social life generally', J. Guy, 'Analysing Pre-capitalist Societies in Southern Africa', *Journal of Southern African Studies*, 14, 1 (1987), 29.
99. N. Isaacs, *Travels and Adventures in Eastern Africa*, Cape Town, 1936, vol. 2, 127.
100. Isaacs, *Travels*, vol. 2, 127.
101. Isaacs, *Travels*, vol. 1, 46 and vol. 2, 241.

kingdom, which was available for herding, was left unutilised by Shaka. Furthermore, if the population had increased to the point where it could no longer be supported by a primarily pastoral economy, it was still possible to grow more food by using the most fertile land more intensively in cultivation.

In light of these reservations, other arguments that Guy puts forward in support of environmental stress need to be reassessed. According to Guy, because of overpopulation the marriage of women was deliberately postponed, using female age-sets linked to male regiments in order to limit human reproduction and restrict the rate of demographic expansion. He argued that the Zulu king delayed marriage for both men and women to limit the rate of biological reproduction as well as the reproduction of homesteads through marriage, in order to solve the supposed problem of overpopulation.[102] In a later article Guy went so far as to assert that 'reproductive sexual relations however could only take place with the king's permission', assuming both popular compliance with the king's orders and a desire on the part of the king to limit reproduction.[103]

The evidence does not support this emphasis on limited reproduction. Although the marriage age of men was postponed under Shaka, the marriage age of women, the only factor relevant to birth rates, was not. Evidence referring to women remaining unmarried to the age of 30 used by Guy dates from a much later period and can in no way be convincingly projected backwards.[104] Although girls could not marry until released by Shaka, there is no evidence that he made them wait beyond the normal age of 15. The only contemporary reference to the age of marriage of women from the reign of Shaka indicated that women married ('were allowed to become wives') at the age of 14 or 15.[105] The young women in age-sets attached to military barracks were displeased when they were forced to marry older men instead of the men closer to their own age.[106] Men who were released to marry could take as many wives as they could afford, that is those for whom they could pay bridewealth.[107] Bridewealth at the time was very low outside the royal family: one or two head of cattle only.[108] Observers noted that married men were all polygamous, and it is unlikely that many girls remained unmarried for long. Shaka may have wanted to retain control over

---

102. Guy, 'Ecological Factors', 116.
103. Guy, 'Analysing Pre-capitalist Societies', 32.
104. Krige says marriage was also delayed for women in Shaka's time, but she has no source or evidence for this assertion, and elsewhere she tends to collapse evidence from different periods, a mistake Guy makes here as well by using Shepstone's evidence concerning delayed marriage of women in 1873, E.J. Krige, *The Social System of the Zulus*, Pietermaritzburg, 1957, 38; Guy 'Ecological Factors', 116.
105. Captain J.S. King, 'Some Account of Mr Farewell's Settlement at Port Natal, and of a Visit to Chaka, King of the Zoolas, etc.', in Thompson, *Travels and Adventures*, vol. 2, 251.
106. Krige, *The Social System*, 38.
107. Lunguza ka Mpukane, informant in C. de B. Webb and J.B. Wright, eds, *The James Stuart Archive*, Pietermaritzburg, 1976, vol. 1, 317.
108. Lunguza ka Mpukane in Webb and Wright, *The James Stuart Archive*, vol. 1, 317. Isaacs indicates that bridewealth was seldom more than ten cows: *Travels*, vol. 2, 237. Gardiner estimates it was four to six cows, but twenty to one hundred for a chief's daughter; A.F. Gardiner, *Narrative of a Journey to the Zoolu Country in South Africa*, London, 1836, 98.

young men through the military system, but reproductive rates would have been reduced only if the marriage age of women rose, which apparently did not happen. Competition for people remained a driving incentive for chiefdoms and nations in southern Africa throughout the early decades of the nineteenth century, and there is no reason to think that biological reproduction was limited deliberately.

Using dendroclimatology, Martin Hall reassessed timing in the environmental factor when he demonstrated that droughts in south-eastern Africa had long occurred in twenty-year cycles. He suggested that the carrying capacity of the land was increased by a steady rise in rainfall during the second half of the eighteenth century, which encouraged the use of formerly marginal land. This time of plenty was followed by a severe drought at the beginning of the nineteenth century, which brought about a crisis as the habitable lands decreased, food production fell and famine ensued.[109]

Philip Bonner accepted Hall's argument that drought could partly account for the revolutionary sociopolitical changes of the period even though cyclical droughts had recurred many times previously, and he offered an explanation for why those of the early nineteenth century were more radical than had been earlier, similar but 'less formidable' strains.[110] He concluded that dominant groups who exercised control through the new *amabutho* (age-regiments) had then emerged and that when drought and famine on this occasion led to shortages of manpower and cattle the new, more powerful aristocracy harnessed their control over both through use of the age-regiments. Bonner raised the question of why the process of political amalgamation occurred where it did as well as at the given point in time, but he did not pursue regional geographic variations, and his focus was limited to the Ngwane of Sobhuza.

Bonner's interpretation is a useful starting point for a successful reinterpretation of revolutionary demographic and political change in the early nineteenth century. In the late eighteenth century and probably considerably earlier, African societies in southern Africa were characterised by increasing socioeconomic stratification and correlated political amalgamation.[111] The Delagoa Bay ivory trade significantly

109. M. Hall, 'Dendroclimatology, Rainfall and Human Adaptation in the Later Iron Age of Natal and Zululand', *Annals of the Natal Museum*, 22 (1976), 693–703. Wright and Hamilton have asserted that 'the "environmental" argument is speculative and cannot by itself explain why conflict over resources should have begun when and where it did, nor why it should have produced the particular effects that it did.' This led them to emphasize an explanation based on trade, but they have admitted that trade also can account for state formation in the region only partially, since 'why these processes should have begun in these particular chiefdoms and not in others is more difficult to explain'; J. B. Wright and C. A. Hamilton, 'Traditions and Transformations: The Phongolo–Mzimkhulu Region in the Late Eighteenth and Early Nineteenth Centuries', in A. Duminy and B. Guest, eds, *Natal and Zululand From Earliest Times to 1910: A New History*, Pietermaritzburg, 1989, 61.

110. P. Bonner, *Kings, Commoners and Concessionaires: The Evolution and Dissolution of the Nineteenth-century Swazi State*, Cambridge, 1983, 21.

111. Bonner summarizes the interpretation of this process found in D. W. Hedges, 'Trade and Politics': Bonner, *Kings, Commoners and Concessionaires*, 10–23.

accelerated the process of economic growth and political consolidation in the area. As Smith notes, there is compelling evidence that 'until the second or third decade of the 19th century ivory was the most sought after, consistent, and important commodity to be exported from Delagoa Bay'.[112] The export of ivory generated a surplus of imported valuables which was expropriated by chiefs, who used their new-found wealth to consolidate their power, and wealth and power became mutually reinforcing.

The problem for the beneficiaries, however, lay in the limited nature of the herds on which the ivory trade drew. With extraction of large quantities of ivory the elephant population eventually declined and exports became scarce. The decline of the elephant population must have created a crisis in the economy and the polity: chiefs who had established themselves on the basis of wealth derived from the ivory trade had adopted systems of taxation and expropriation, but the trade had not promoted the intensification of land use or the generation of a surplus based on agriculture to support them from local production. As a result, local economies could not support high levels of extraction indefinitely, and chiefs must have found themselves competing for declining supplies.[113]

Neither the export of ivory nor the import of cloth and beads transformed local industries or the production of food. However, this trade was important because it served as a source of wealth which powerful people were able to control and manipulate to increase their own sway. Hence trade stimulated the emergence of socioeconomic inequalities. Socioeconomic inequalities fostered the unequal distribution of food in time of scarcity, both within societies and between chiefdoms, resulting in famine for those lacking access to productive resources.[114] Famine in turn provoked competition over scarce resources necessary for producing food (land and people), and the resulting conflicts led to political consolidation.

Droughts reduced the carrying capacity of both arable land and pastures, and increased competition over resources in the late eighteenth and early nineteenth centuries. Both written and oral sources confirm that south-east Africa suffered major droughts between 1800 and 1803, in 1812 and in 1816–18.[115] Some areas

---

112. Smith, 'The Trade of Delagoa Bay', 176; see also Portuguese sources, e.g. Manso, Memoria, 11–13, 66–9, 100–1, 118, 121, 131.
113. See also A. Smith, 'The Indian Ocean Zone', in P.M. Martin and D. Birmingham, eds, History of Central Africa, London, 1983, vol. 1, 233–6.
114. It is not sufficient to assert that drought must somehow have induced social stress without explaining the precise causal relationship: in well-managed systems of food storage and distribution through any form of social security system, drought need not cause food scarcity, famine, or social distress. As Amartya Sen has shown, it is politics and the distribution of food entitlements which determine the social impact of drought, i.e. whether or not drought leads to famine; A. Sen, Poverty and Famines: An Essay on Entitlement and Deprivation, Oxford, 1982. For an explanation of Sen and an analysis of drought and famine in nineteenth-century southern Africa using Sen's approach, see E.A. Eldredge, 'Drought, Famine and Disease in Nineteenth-century Lesotho', African Economic History, 16 (1987), 61–93.

suffered also from the destruction of crops by crop rust and from a cattle epizootic from 1816 to 1818. Given a situation of ongoing competition for land and cattle, these droughts explain the timing of overt conflicts between the Xhosa and white settlers in 1801, 1811–12, and 1818–19, and they correspond chronologically with periods of demographic and political turmoil among the northern Nguni-speakers, first under Dingiswayo and later under Shaka.

Increasing political amalgamation and socioeconomic stratification produced inequalities in access to productive resources between and within chiefdoms, resulting in famine in times of drought and provoking the political revolution among the Mthethwa and the Zulu in times of drought in the early nineteenth century. The changed sociopolitical context explains why strategies of famine resistance had broken down so that the drought of 1800 to 1803 had severe consequences, including widespread famine, even though dry periods had occurred in the past without similar consequences. In its earliest stages drought compelled herders from neighbouring societies to compete over pastures because the normally sufficient carrying capacity of the area for their herds declined dramatically. Without water or forage, animals died quickly, and stored grain provided the most secure food supply for people.[116] The production of surplus grain for storage in case of scarcity required access to fertile and well-watered land, and in extended droughts crop failure brought people into overt conflict either over grain stores or over riverine lands which supported minimal crops even in dry years and in normal years produced surpluses.

During droughts the wealthy and powerful took advantage of their greater access to food resources while the poor suffered disproportionately, provoking conflict. Drought provided an incentive and opportunity for the powerful to consolidate further their control over fertile and well-watered arable land at the expense of weaker neighbours. Furthermore, droughts made evident the extreme vulnerability of the poor and weak to food scarcity and increased their incentive to submit to political authority, even when extremely oppressive, because such submission promised security from starvation.

---

115. The great drought of 1800 to 1803 affected all southern Africa. Europeans in the Cape colony lost so many cattle from drought in 1800 that an expedition was sent north to acquire cattle from trade with the Tlhaping (Tswana); J. Barrow, *An Account of Travels into the Interior of Southern Africa*, London, 1801, vol. 2, 55. Numerous oral traditions about this drought and the associated famine have been recorded from the Tswana, Sotho, and Zulu. See 'Mabokoboko, ou une page d'histoire', *Journal des Missions Evangéliques* (1884), 420; H. Laydevant, OMI, 'La Misère au Basutoland', *Les Missions Catholiques* (1934), 333–7; N. S. Moshoeshoe, 'A Little Light from Basutoland', *Cape Monthly Magazine*, New series, 2, 10 (April 1880), 221–33, and 2, 11 (May 1880), 280–92; *Almanaka ea Basotho*, Selemo sa 1894, Khatiso ea A. Mabille, Morija, 1894; *Litaba Tsa Lilemo*, Morija, 1931. See also C. Ballard, 'Drought and Economic Distress: South Africa in the 1800s', *Journal of Interdisciplinary History*, 17 (1986), 359–78; Eldredge, 'Drought'; Guy, 'Ecological Factors'.
116. Nguni-speakers had the capacity to store large quantities of food for up to seven years in order to prevent famine in times of drought. Contrary to what Hall states, both grain pits and grain baskets were used by Nguni-speakers for storing huge quantities of grain, and although some would always be lost to rot and pests, the incentives for storing grain to avoid famine were very great in the nineteenth century. Hall, 'Dendroclimatology'.

There is considerable evidence that early conflicts involving the Mthethwa and
the Zulu were related to competition over arable lands. Both the Ngwane under
Sobhuza and the Ndwandwe under Zwide consolidated and expanded their areas of
control on the banks of the Phongolo River, and the major struggle between them
arose over arable lands there.[117] Among the regional soils, many were poor and
unsuitable for cultivation, and fertile arable land that was well-watered and
drought-resistant was relatively scarce.[118] Zulu military establishments were located
in very fertile areas, good for cultivation as well as herding.[119]

Intensive use of these fertile areas for cultivation necessitated mobilisation of
greater amounts of labour, provoking competition for people as well as land. The
process of state formation under Dingiswayo and during Shaka's early years was a
process of incorporation of people, not extermination. Women in particular were
highly valued both for reproduction and because they were the primary agricultural
producers. During Shaka's reign a Zulu chief explained that he spent much time
searching for refugees from Shaka, 'for the purpose of enriching himself by adding
their females to his establishment (who were a valuable property and disposable at
the will of the possessor)'.[120]

The conflicts generated during political consolidation under the Zulu must be seen
in the context of the ongoing competition for both land and people. Although Zulu
aggression under Shaka contributed significantly to the violence in the immediate
area, the majority of the Zulu people were victims of their circumstances and cannot
be held responsible for the violence which plagued the region. Growing vulnerability to famine in times of food scarcity drew people to any strong leader who could
provide them with a livelihood and protection. The expansion of arable production
was the best means of achieving food security in the long run, but gaining the
necessary labour and opening new lands was a long and tedious, even painful
process. Hence there arose the natural impulse to accumulate wealth more quickly
and directly. The employment of women in agriculture left men free to acquire
surplus directly through raiding and the accumulation of booty. The booty from raids
provided an easy way for chiefs to satisfy the needs and demands of their people in
order to keep followers from falling away. Some people were motivated to support
Shaka by the attraction of a share of the booty, as he kept only a portion of captured
cattle for his own herds and distributed the rest among his people.[121] The raiders
accumulated livestock much more rapidly than they could have through natural
increase, and military expeditions became the quickest route to wealth for the state
and the soldiers. As the Zulu military became important in generating state revenues,
over time the age-regiments were institutionalized and took on their own imperative,

117. Omer-Cooper, *Zulu Aftermath*, 49; J. B. M. Daniel, 'A Geographical Study of Pre-Shakan Zululand',
     South African Geographical Journal, 15 (1973), 29.
118. Isaacs, *Travels*, vol. 1, 85, 106, 149–52, 159, 161.
119. Isaacs, *Travels*, vol. 2, 171.
120. Isaacs, *Travels*, vol. 1, 110.
121. Isaacs, *Travels*, vol. 1, 180, 283.

fighting to support themselves as an end in itself and not merely for defensive purposes. Systematic raiding in turn fostered hostile neighbours and made protection a major incentive for further population concentration and political consolidation.

The sporadic conflicts that continued in the interior of southern Africa beyond the period of state formation in the years following 1822, associated with large-scale migrations and considerable human misery, also had environmental sources. The damaging European-armed raids of the Griqua can only partly account for these events, since massive migrations like those that converged at Dithakong in 1823 clearly resulted from other factors. In fact these conflicts on the highveld can also best be understood with reference to the appearance of drought at a time when political events undermined traditional strategies of avoiding famine. However, because the land was much drier and less fertile there than in areas east of the Drakensberg, soils and vegetation appear to have suffered permanent damage from human settlement over time.

There is evidence of gradual long-term environmental degradation in the southern African interior prior to the arrival of the missionaries in the early nineteenth century. Moffat reported that when they first arrived in 1820 'years of drought had been severely felt', prompting the Tlhaping both to blame the missionaries and to seek a famous rainmaker from the Hurutshe about 300 kilometres to the north-east.[122] The Tlhaping told Moffat their oral traditions of 'incessant showers', 'giant trees and forests which once studded the brows of the Hamhana hills and neighbouring plains' and impassable torrents in the Kuruman and other rivers in order to demonstrate that the land had been gradually drying up. Moffat noted the physical evidence that supported this:

> . . . the dry seasons had commenced at a period long anterior to the arrival of the missionaries. Independent of the fact being handed down by their forefathers, they had before their eyes the fragments of more fruitful years in the immense number of stumps and roots of enormous trunks of *acacia giraffe*, when now scarcely one is to be seen raising its stately head above the shrubs; while the sloping sides of hills, and the ancient beds of rivers, plainly evinced that they were denuded of the herbage which once clothed their surface. Indeed, the whole country north of the Orange River lying east of the Kalagare desert, presented to the eye of an European something like an old neglected garden or field.[123]

John Campbell, a fellow missionary from the London Missionary Society, also heard that the Kuruman River had been drying up over time. In 1820 he wrote:

> All the elderly people at this meeting asserted, that in their young days the Krooman [*sic*] was a great river, and as a proof of this, said that, sometimes it rose and continued high for so long a time, that women who happened to

122. R. Moffat, *Missionary Labours and Scenes in Southern Africa*, London, 1842, 307.
123. Moffat, *Missionary Labours*, 329–30.

be on the other side of the river, frequently lost all hope of being able to recross it, and married other men, they also asserted that great quantities of reeds grew in it. Much water they said used to come down from the Moloppo, which formed a junction near them, and from another river called the Mesaree, but that the Krooman does not now receive any supply from them . . . No stream now ever flows within its banks, but large pools are formed in its bed in times of much rain.[124]

Moffat attributed the environmental degradation of the area to human agency, since the Tlhaping and other Tswana with whom he was acquainted moved their huge towns periodically, and, when they chose a new site, they levelled every tree in sight in order to clear spaces for homes and fields and to acquire timber and poles for houses and fences. Moffat assumed that deforestation caused by people seeking building materials in turn had caused the drying up of both springs and rivers, since rain evaporates quickly without vegetation and does not feed the rivers and underground reservoirs for spring water.[125] Over time the loss of vegetation and diminishing water supplies would have decreased the carrying capacity of the land in terms of both livestock and people. Although Moffat's causation cannot be established, these early missionary observations offer evidence that significant environmental deterioration had been occurring in the region.

In this gradually deteriorating environment the Sotho- and Tswana-speakers of the interior, like their neighbours near the coast, experienced both migration and famine during the drought of 1800–3, and they subsequently faced crop rust and a cattle epizootic that destroyed both their crops and their herds between 1816 and 1818.[126] These disasters devastated people throughout the region, including the Tlokwa and the other Sotho- and Tswana-speakers, leaving them without stored grain or large herds. Drought was still evident when Moffat arrived in 1820. With little time to recover, the Tlokwa may already have been on the brink of famine in 1822, when their migration was first provoked by the arrival of the Hlubi. Evidence indicates that drought had been ongoing in the area for several years prior to 1824 and that it persisted into 1826.[127] These were precisely the years in which the massive

---

124. J. Campbell, *Travels in South Africa*, New York, 1967, vol. 2, 93–4.
125. Campbell, *Travels*, vol. 2, 332–3.
126. 'Mabokoboko ou une page d'histoire'; *Almanaka ea Basotho*, 1894; *Litaba Tsa Lilemo*, 1931.
127. In August 1824 Thompson encountered some Kora who were literally starving to death, and noted that they had been reduced to this state because of extreme drought. Thompson, *Travels and Adventure*, vol. 2, 30–3. Similarly Moffat noted that there had been 'several successive years of drought, during which water had not been seen to flow upon the ground; and in that climate, if rain does not fall continuously and in considerable quantities, it is all exhaled in a couple of hours'. This drought lasted several years prior to early 1826, when finally rain came, indicating that the drought dated back at least three years to 1823 if not earlier; Moffat, *Missionary Labours*, 315, 447. Sotho oral traditions also indicate that there was a severe drought during these years; 'Liketso tso etsagetseng Lesotho 1820–1870' [Events in Lesotho 1820–1870], *Leselinyana la Lesotho* (newspaper of the Paris Evangelical Missionary Society in Lesotho), (October 1871), 73–7; *Litaba tsa Lilemo*, 1931; Moshoeshoe, 'A Little Light from Basutoland'.

migrations of the interior were provoking such fear among the Griqua and Europeans on the border of the Cape colony. Before the rain finally came in 1826 Moffat observed that '. . . the cattle were dying from want of pasture, and hundreds of living skeletons were seen going to the field in quest of unwholesome roots and reptiles, while many were dying with hunger'.[128]

An uninhabitable landscape, then, was the context in which the competition for cattle and standing crops occurred on the highveld after 1822. Because the land to the west of the Drakensberg mountains is much drier than the land to the east, settlement patterns on the highveld have always tended to be highly concentrated around the rare sources of water. Hence the various Tswana towns found by the Europeans at the turn of the nineteenth century were huge. Dithakong had 10 000 to 15 000 Tlhaping inhabitants in 1801 and remained a huge and thriving town even after the chief moved some of his people 130 kilometres south-west to Kuruman, the new capital where the missionaries set up their mission in 1820. Kuruman itself had an estimated 8 000 to 10 000 inhabitants in 1823. These towns were of typical size for the area, so it stands to reason that were any single town routed by an invader, the refugees would constitute a huge group themselves. The entire populations of Fokeng, Phuthing and Hlakwana apparently converged at Dithakong. Thompson reported a conversation with Melvill who referred to the rumours about 'an immense horde, or nation', which was approaching from the north-east.[129] The term 'nation', perhaps borrowed here by Melvill from his Tswana informants, more accurately describes these groups, which included non-combatants, and reflects the fact that they had been complete societies prior to being uprooted. The numerical estimates of the size of groups involved in the confrontation at Dithakong do not seem so high in this context: if 10 000 to 15 000 Fokeng men, women and children were joined by similar numbers of Phuthing and Hlakwana, the total would have amounted to the 40 000 to 50 000 people estimated by Melvill and Moffat.

The otherwise mystifying convergence of three nations at Dithakong in 1823 must be viewed in this context. The generally dry environment of this region left its people highly vulnerable to food scarcity and famine in times of drought. Dithakong was different, however: the town was located near the Kuruman spring, which was reportedly the most abundant spring in South Africa and next to the 'Lattakoo' or Mashowing River.[130] The site was no doubt originally chosen for its capacity to support crops even during droughts, and its reputation for successful agriculture must have been widespread. Khoi accompanying the London missionary John Campbell to 'Lattakoo' were 'amazed at the extent of land under cultivation, having never seen so much before in one place'.[131] The old Tlhaping capital also had a great reputation for artisan industries, and success in producing agricultural surpluses on a

128. Moffat, *Missionary Labours*, 316.
129. Thompson, *Travels and Adventures*, vol. 1, 79.
130. Thompson, *Travels and Adventures*, vol. 1, 100, 107.
131. Campbell, *Travels*, vol. 1, 64.

regular basis would have been a precondition for the emergence of craft specialisation. Messengers sent to warn the Tlhaping were told that the invading people wanted crops as well as cattle.[132] Apparently even the people at Kuruman did not have good crops that year, for Thompson noted the superiority of the millet crop at Dithakong, which was flourishing because of the settlement's proximity to the spring and the river, although at that point even the Mashowing River 'was only a chain of pools'.[133] In the context of drought-induced food scarcity exacerbated by an unstable political climate, the search for food helps to explain the migration of entire chiefdoms and the confrontation at Dithakong.

A succession of distinct factors perpetuated violence among Africans west of the Drakensberg, like their neighbours to the east. The first disruptions associated with the migrations of Africans in 1822 from across the Drakensberg were apparently prolonged by pre-existing problems of food scarcity caused by drought and a cattle epizootic. These migrations and related conflicts ended in the 1820s, however, and it was the Griqua and Kora raiders, capturing cattle and slaves for their white frontier neighbours, who bore responsibility for intensifying the violence in the 1820s and prolonging it well into the 1830s. Their raiding activities predated this period but clearly intensified in the 1820s, as the white settler frontier moved outwards and provided a growing market for stolen cattle and captured children.

Conclusions

Trade-intensified competition over productive resources in an increasingly strained natural environment generated conflict among southern African societies in the early nineteenth century. The white colonists in the Cape and, after 1823, slave traders at Delagoa Bay fostered further conflict and violence by providing a market stimulus to open warfare and enslavement. Cobbing is right to absolve the Zulu from the responsibility for most of the regional conflicts of the 1820s and 1830s, and this is his abiding contribution. These disruptions were associated with attempts by Africans to cope with their environment, and they involved and were caused by Europeans as well as Africans.

History is political, and it has always been systematically distorted in South Africa to suit the ends of continued white domination, most notably in the historiography of the 'mfecane'. We must continue our search for a more sophisticated understanding of the historical processes involved and recognise the dilemmas that confronted all Africans when faced with the European presence in the region. It is a mistake, however, to assume that historical change in southern African societies was merely a reaction to the European presence. In discrediting the old 'Afrocentric' interpretations of the 'mfecane', Cobbing argues that there was no self-generated internal revolution in the societies of south-eastern Africa and that the Zulu state developed

132. Thompson, *Travels and Adventures*, vol. 1, 101.
133. Thompson, *Travels and Adventures*, vol. 1, 107.

only as a defensive reaction to the Delagoa Bay slave trade.[134] Not only does he reverse his chronology, but he also rejects generally the notion that dynamic internal forces generated change in African societies. Historians working throughout Africa have spent the last three decades challenging the racist assumption of exclusive European agency in African historical change and demonstrating the complexity of internally generated change over time in Africa. It is a step backwards to depict African history in South Africa again as a wholly reactive process and to deny to Africans their own history. Events and developments in this period in southern African history must be interpreted not only as African attempts to contain and resist the aggression of the Europeans but also as a reflection of the complex interplay of environment, society, and economy.

Acknowledgements

I would like to thank James C. Armstrong, R. Hunt Davis Jr., Robert Edgar, John Mason, Alan K. Smith, and Rick Watson for their comments and suggestions on an earlier version of this paper.

134. Cobbing, 'The Mfecane as Alibi', 517.

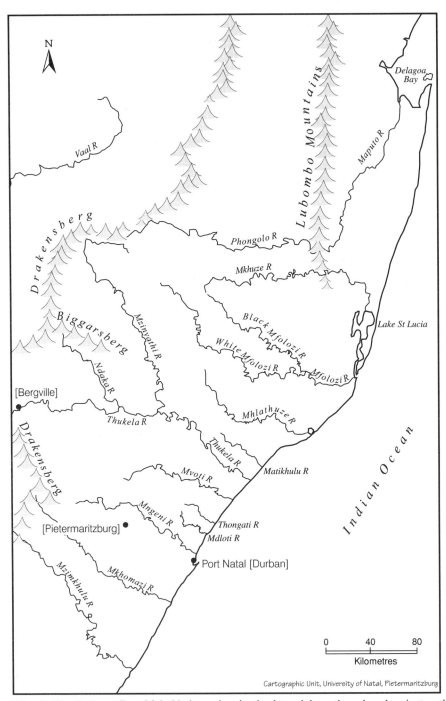

Map 3. The Delagoa Bay–Mzimkhulu region in the late eighteenth and early nineteenth centuries.

6 Political Transformations in the Thukela–Mzimkhulu Region
in the Late Eighteenth and Early Nineteenth Centuries

JOHN WRIGHT

This essay is the third in a series in which I seek to establish a new baseline for research into the history of the region between the Thukela and Mzimkhulu Rivers in the late eighteenth and early nineteenth centuries. In the first, I argue that the concept of the mfecane as it applies to this region is largely a product of colonial mythologising, and, in support of the critique of mfecane theory developed over the last few years by Julian Cobbing,[1] that the concept is of no analytical value and needs to be abandoned by serious scholars.[2] (By the mfecane I mean the notion that the series of wars and migrations which swept over much of south-eastern Africa in the 1820s was a result of the supposedly explosive expansion of the Zulu kingdom under Shaka.) In the second essay I argue that the standard account of the history of the Thukela–Mzimkhulu region before 1830, that which appears in A.T. Bryant's *Olden Times in Zululand and Natal*,[3] is also based largely on colonial-made myths and cannot be regarded as reliable.[4] In the present essay I go on to outline an empirical answer to the question of what to put in its place.[5]

Bryant's account of the history of the Thukela–Mzimkhulu area is scattered through his synthesis of the history of the broader Natal-Zulu kingdom region. This is based on a model which was first clearly articulated in the writings of settler and missionary historians in colonial Natal in the 1850s and 1860s.[6]

In terms of this schema, the region's history falls into four phases. In the first, the ancestors of the African population of Natal migrated into the region from further

---

1. Cobbing's critique has been advanced in a series of mostly unpublished papers. See also his article, 'The Mfecane as Alibi: Thoughts on Dithakong and Mbolompo', *Journal of African History*, 29 (1988), 487–519.
2. J.B. Wright, 'Political Mythology and the Making of Natal's Mfecane', *Canadian Journal of African Studies*, 23,2 (1989), 272–91.
3. First published in London in 1929.
4. J.B. Wright, 'A.T. Bryant and "the Wars of Shaka"', *History in Africa*, 18 (1991), 409–25.
5. The interpretation put forward in this essay summarizes some of the main findings of my Ph.D. thesis, 'The Dynamics of Power and Conflict in the Thukela-Mzimkhulu Region in the Late Eighteenth and Early Nineteenth Centuries: A Critical Reconstruction', University of the Witwatersrand, Johannesburg, 1990.
6. For an account of the development of this model see Wright, 'Dynamics', 1–6.

north in Africa. By Bryant's reckoning, this process had taken place during the period from about AD1500 to 1700.[7] The migrations were succeeded by a second phase, described by Bryant as a 'golden age',[8] during which the people, divided into numerous small patriarchal 'clans', lived in relative peace and plenty. The third phase began dramatically in the 1810s with the sudden rise of the Zulu kingdom under the 'tyrannical' rule of Shaka and the 'invasion' of the region south of the Thukela by his 'bloodthirsty' armies. In the space of a few years, the region was 'devastated' and 'depopulated'. This phase gave way to a fourth, the era of 'civilization', with the arrival in the Zulu kingdom of British traders from the Cape in the mid-1820s.

Since the rise of Africanist history in southern Africa in the 1960s, a number of academic writers have gone a long way towards reclaiming the history of the area north of the Thukela (i.e. what is now called Zululand) in the period under study from the domination which settler-orientated historiography has exercised over it for a century and a half. By contrast, the contemporary history of the region south of the Thukela has received very little attention from academic historians, and Bryant's account of it remains dominant. This essay aims to demonstrate that, on the basis of the existing evidence, a quite different interpretation can be put forward. For background material it draws on several of the recently produced academic studies of the history of the region north of the Thukela.[9] For empirical evidence it makes use particularly of the collection of oral traditions recorded by James Stuart in the first two decades of the twentieth century.[10]

The period which it covers begins in the 1770s and 1780s with the first impact on the territories south of the Thukela of the political conflicts which were then building up in the region north of the river. It ends when, in the later 1820s, a new set of historical forces, rooted in developments in the political economy of the Cape colony, began to make itself felt in these territories.

Intrusions from the North *c.1770–c.1815*

The notion that the first black inhabitants of south-east Africa migrated into the region within the last few centuries was firmly put to rest in the 1970s by the results of archaeological research into the history of its Iron Age farming communities.

---

7. A.T. Bryant, *Olden Times in Zululand and Natal*, London, 1929, chs. 1 and 2, and 232–5, 313–17.
8. Bryant, *Olden Times*, 71.
9. Especially D.W. Hedges, 'Trade and Politics in Southern Mozambique and Zululand in the Eighteenth and Early Nineteenth Centuries', Ph.D. thesis, University of London, 1978; and C.A. Hamilton, 'Ideology, Oral Traditions and the Struggle for Power in the Early Zulu Kingdom', M.A. dissertation, University of the Witwatersrand, Johannesburg, 1986.
10. Stuart's notes are housed in the Killie Campbell Africana Library, University of Natal, Durban. Translated and annotated renderings of the oral testimonies which he recorded are currently being published by the University of Natal Press in a series of volumes entitled *The James Stuart Archive of Recorded Oral Evidence Relating to the History of the Zulu and Neighbouring Peoples*. Four volumes, edited by C. de B. Webb and J.B. Wright, have so far been produced, Pietermaritzburg, 1976–86. Three more are planned.

Indications are that the first farmers established themselves on the coast of what became the Natal/Zululand area in the first few centuries of the AD era.[11] Whether they were migrants or indigenous hunter-gatherers who took to farming is a subject of debate.[12] Research into the area's Iron Age history has focused mainly on investigating subsistence patterns and settlement types and distribution, and little is known about the political and social structures of local communities until the mid-sixteenth century. From this period date the first written descriptions, made by Portuguese shipwreck survivors, of the region's inhabitants. Over the next two hundred years or so parties of European castaways and traders produced enough by way of written ethnographic evidence to indicate that at this time the Thukela–Mzimkhulu region was occupied by numerous small, politically uncentralised chiefdoms.[13]

This picture is consistent with one derived from recorded oral traditions, whose historical reach in this area extends back to about the mid-eighteenth century. Evidence from the traditions suggests that at this time there were several dozen or several score discrete chiefdoms in the region, the largest of which probably numbered no more than a few thousand people and extended over no more than a couple of thousand square kilometres. In some areas, neighbouring chiefdoms whose rulers claimed to be genealogically related constituted loose clusters, which can be called 'paramountcies', headed by a senior chief. The authority exercised by these figures seems to have been mainly formal in character, and there is no evidence for the existence at this period of politically centralised and socially stratified polities, or what can be called embryonic 'states'.[14]

Patterns of political change in the Thukela–Mzimkhulu region cannot be traced before the later eighteenth century, when the effects of conflicts which were taking place in the territories to the north of the Thukela began to make themselves felt. From about the third quarter of the eighteenth century, certain chiefdoms – notably the Thembe, Mabhudu, Dlamini, Ndwandwe and Mthethwa – in an area which extended from beyond Delagoa Bay to south of the Mfolozi River were beginning to expand in size and power, and increasingly to clash with one another and with their smaller neighbours. The causes of these developments are a subject of debate among historians of the period: the position taken here is that their initial dynamic, at least,

11. The evidence has recently been summarized in T. Maggs, 'The Iron Age Farming Communities', in A.H. Duminy and B. Guest, eds, *Natal and Zululand from Earliest Times to 1910: A New History*, Pietermaritzburg, 1989, 28–33.
12. See M. Hall, *The Changing Past: Farmers, Kings and Traders in Southern Africa, 200–1860*, Cape Town, 1987, ch. 3.
13. For a survey of the evidence see Wright, 'Dynamics', 19–22. For a sceptical analysis of these sources by an anthropologist see J. Argyle, 'An Evaluation of Portuguese Shipwreck Narratives as Sources for Nguni Ethnology', unpubl. paper, University of Natal, Durban, 1990.
14. J.B. Wright and C.A. Hamilton, 'Traditions and Transformations: The Phongolo-Mzimkhulu Region in the Late Eighteenth and Early Nineteenth Centuries', in Duminy and Guest, eds, *Natal and Zululand*, 57–9; Wright, 'Dynamics', 16–18.

seems to have been provided by the rapid expansion after about 1760 of an international trade in ivory at Delagoa Bay.[15]

Particularly significant in its import for political developments south of the Thukela was the expansion of the Mthethwa chiefdom in the area between the lower Mfolozi and the Mhlathuze Rivers.[16]

In what seems to have been a defensive reaction to the increase in Mthethwa power, the ruling groups in a number of chiefdoms along the lower Thukela sought to strengthen their polities by enlarging the territories which they dominated. The most successful in this aim seem to have been the rulers of the Qwabe chiefdom in the area between the Mhlathuze and the Thukela.[17] Chiefdoms further up the Thukela which seem to have begun expanding in the later eighteenth century were those of the Nyuswa, the Mkhize and perhaps the Chunu.[18] Inland, on the upper Mzinyathi River, the Hlubi chiefdom was responding in much the same way to the threat posed by the growth of the powerful Ndwandwe chiefdom to the east.[19]

The expansion of the Qwabe seems to have been the main factor in dislodging a group of Thuli from the upper Matikhulu area, and, sometime in the 1770s or 1780s, sending them migrating southwards across the Thukela. After forcing their way through a number of small coastland chiefdoms, the Thuli re-established themselves in what is now the Pinetown–Durban area. From there they proceeded to extend their domination over the inhabitants of a territory which reached perhaps fifty kilometres inland, and the same distance southwards to the Mkhomazi River. Several offshoot chiefdoms set themselves up further south between the Mkhomazi and the Mzimkhulu. Numbers of groups displaced by these incursions moved still further southwards to the region of the Mzimvubu River.[20] These movements, it is argued here, may have been a factor in stimulating the initial expansion of the Mpondo chiefdom, which, by the 1820s, dominated the area about the lower Mzimvubu.[21]

15. Pioneering research in this field was done in the 1960s by A. K. Smith. See his essays, 'The Trade of Delagoa Bay as a Factor in Nguni Politics 1750–1835', in L. M. Thompson, ed., *African Societies in Southern Africa*, London, 1969, ch. 8, and 'Delagoa Bay and the Trade of South-east Africa', in R. Gray and D. Birmingham, eds, *Pre-colonial African Trade: Essays on Trade in Central and Eastern Africa before 1900*, London, 1970, ch. 13. A more detailed investigation is that of David Hedges in his thesis, 'Trade and Politics', chs. 3, 6. See also the arguments in Wright and Hamilton, 'Traditions and Transformations', 59–62, and Wright, 'Dynamics', 27–33.

16. On the history of the Mthethwa chiefdom in the late 18th and early 19th centuries, see Hedges, 'Trade and Politics', 183–93; Hamilton, 'Ideology', 112–38.

17. On the expansion of the Qwabe see Hedges, 'Trade and Politics', 169–77; Hamilton, 'Ideology', 155–61; Wright, 'Dynamics', 35–6.

18. Wright, 'Dynamics', 36–7.

19. Wright, 'Dynamics', 37–9. On the expansion of the Hlubi see also J. B. Wright and A. Manson, *The Hlubi Chiefdom in Zululand-Natal: A History*, Ladysmith, 1983, 4–10. On the expansion of the Ndwandwe chiefdom see Hedges, 'Trade and Politics', 156–64; P. Bonner, 'Early State Formation among the Nguni: The Relevance of the Swazi Case', unpubl. paper, University of London, 1978; and P. Bonner, *Kings, Commoners and Concessionaires: The Evolution and Dissolution of the Nineteenth-century Swazi State*, Johannesburg, 1983, ch. 2.

20. On the migration of the Thuli and their establishment of a new paramountcy see Wright, 'Dynamics', 40–9.

21. W. Beinart, *The Political Economy of Pondoland 1860 to 1930*, Johannesburg, 1982, 9–10.

Sometime after the migration of the Thuli, the continued expansion of the Qwabe was instrumental in pushing the Cele too across the lower Thukela. Their ruling house settled on the lower Mvoti River, and subsequently supplanted the Thuli as rulers of the chiefdoms of the coastlands as far south as the Thongati–Mdloti area.[22]

The Thuli and Cele paramountcies were much larger than any of the historically known chiefdoms which had previously existed in the coastlands. Though there is no evidence surviving on the subject, the spheres in which they exercised political influence probably extended beyond the Mzimkhulu to the south, and into the Natal midlands to the west. But in both polities the central authority remained weak. In neither case were the rulers able to establish centralised institutions of government which gave them the degree of control over their adherents that was exercised by leaders in the Ndwandwe and Mthethwa chiefdoms. Both the Thuli and Cele polities remained loose aggregations of chiefdoms rather than budding states.[23]

In the first ten or fifteen years of the nineteenth century, pressures from the north and east on the polities along the line of the Thukela and Mzinyathi Rivers seem to have been increasing. In the coastlands, the Qwabe were seeking to expand southwards across the Thukela at this time. Further up the river, the Nyuswa may also have been doing so.[24] In the Hlubi chiefdom on the upper Mzinyathi, the authority of the paramount was weakening as subordinate sections of the ruling house sought to challenge his authority.[25]

The extent to which these developments were a response to external pressures is not clear, but it is likely that they were in some measure a product of intensifying conflict between the emerging states of the Thukela–Delagoa Bay region, particularly between the Mthethwa and the Ndwandwe. By the late 1810s these conflicts were coming to a head, with major consequences for the inhabitants of the territories to the south.

Upheavals in the Thukela Valley in the Later 1810s

The causes of the confrontation between the Mthethwa and the Ndwandwe towards the end of the 1810s are still being explored. One influential explanation, which derives from the work of Alan Smith and David Hedges, sees this conflict as a more or less inevitable outcome of a growing rivalry between the two chiefdoms for control of the local trade in ivory to the chiefdoms on the southern shores of Delagoa Bay.[26] More recently, Cobbing has pressed the argument that the fierce political

22. Wright, 'Dynamics', 53–6.
23. Wright, 'Dynamics', 50–6.
24. Wright, 'Dynamics', 164–8.
25. Wright, 'Dynamics', 177–8; Wright and Manson, *The Hlubi Chiefdom*, 10–11.
26. Smith, 'The Trade of Delagoa Bay', 185; Hedges, 'Trade and Politics', 165.

struggles which were building up in the Delagoa Bay hinterland, including the regions to the south, in the later 1810s and early 1820s were largely the product of a rapid increase after 1815 in a trade in slaves at Delagoa Bay.[27]

Cobbing's hypothesis is becoming the subject of a vigorous academic debate, but on the face of it, it seems possible that by the later 1810s the impact of the Delagoa Bay slave trade was increasingly being felt in the regions to the south. The trade in slaves from south-eastern Africa to Brazil was rising rapidly after 1810,[28] and was supplemented by a continuing trade to the French colony on Bourbon (Réunion) island and to the British colony on Mauritius.[29] The export of slaves from Delagoa Bay was well-established by the early 1820s,[30] and it is a reasonable supposition that it was already expanding in the later 1810s. As Cobbing suggests, the violent aggressions of the Ndwandwe against neighbouring chiefdoms, including the Mthethwa, at just this time may have been in part a response to pressures exerted by slaving groups nearer the bay, or possibly even the product of slaving operations on the part of the Ndwandwe themselves.[31]

The two hypotheses outlined above are not mutually exclusive. Whatever the precise explanation of the Mthethwa–Ndwandwe conflict, it is clear that its political consequences were felt over a wide area. As the struggle between them came to a head, some of the smaller chiefdoms caught up in it began to take to flight. One of the first to do so was the Ngwane chiefdom under Matiwane, which lay on the western borders of the Ndwandwe polity. After an attack by the Ndwandwe, Matiwane and many of his adherents made off to the westward.[32] Falling upon the ruling section of the Hlubi, they killed the paramount chief, Mthimkhulu, and seized his cattle. Upon this, the Hlubi polity, which was little more than a loose clustering of semi-autonomous chiefdoms, broke up into its constituent parts. Some remained in the

---

27. Cobbing, 'The Mfecane as Alibi', 503–7; J. Cobbing, 'Grasping the Nettle: The Slave Trade and the Early Zulu', in D.R. Edgecombe, J.P.C. Laband and P.S. Thompson, comps, *The Debate on Zulu Origins: A Selection of Papers on the Zulu Kingdom and Early Colonial Natal*, Pietermaritzburg, 1992.

28. J. Miller, 'Slave Prices in the Portuguese Southern Atlantic, 1600–1830', in P.E. Lovejoy, ed., *Africans in Bondage: Studies in Slavery and the Slave Trade*, Madison, 1986, 44, 59. See also the figures in D. Eltis, *Economic Growth and the Ending of the Transatlantic Slave Trade*, New York, 1987, 249, 250.

29. E. Alpers, *Ivory and Slaves in East Central Africa*, London, 1975, 214; M. Jackson Haight, *European Powers and South-East Africa: A Study of International Relations on the South-East Coast of Africa 1796–1856*, London, 1967 (1st ed. 1942), 158–62; B. Benedict, 'Slavery and Indenture in Mauritius and Seychelles', in J. Watson, ed., *Asian and African Systems of Slavery*, Oxford, 1980, 138; R. Beachey, *The Slave Trade of Eastern Africa*, London, 1976, 27–35; G. Campbell, 'Madagascar and Mozambique in the Slave Trade of the Western Indian Ocean 1800–1861', in W.G. Clarence-Smith, ed., *Economics of the Indian Ocean Slave Trade in the Nineteenth Century*, London, 1989, 166–93; M. Carter and H. Gerbeau, 'Covert Slaves and Coveted Coolies in the Early 19th-century Mascareignes', in Clarence-Smith, ed., *Economics of the Indian Ocean Slave Trade*, 194–208.

30. A. Smith, 'The Struggle for Control of Southern Moçambique, 1720–1835', Ph.D. thesis, University of California, Los Angeles, 1970, 350–1; Smith, 'The Trade of Delagoa Bay', 177.

31. Cobbing, 'Grasping the Nettle', 11–12.

32. The sources on the flight of the Ngwane are often contradictory. The argument put forward here is based on the analysis in Wright, 'Dynamics', 110–16, 178–9, 210–13.

Hlubi territory, some moved off to the west and north in bids to maintain their autonomy, some made their way to give their allegiance to neighbouring chiefs, and some submitted to Matiwane.[33]

To put a safe distance between themselves and the Ndwandwe, the Ngwane continued their migration south-westward across the Mzinyathi and the Biggarsberg into the valley of the upper Thukela. After establishing themselves near what is now Bergville, they began to bring the neighbouring Bhele and Zizi chiefdoms under their sway. Some groups of Bhele and Zizi sought to preserve their political independence by moving away southward to the Mzimkhulu region; others, unable to offer resistance to the Ngwane, had no option but to give their allegiance to Matiwane. Within a short time the Ngwane headed a paramountcy which dominated the upper Thukela basin.[34]

The migration of the Ngwane caused major political and social disruptions among the chiefdoms between the Mzinyathi and the Thukela, and brought a new set of pressures to bear on the polities south of the river. Soon afterwards, a major shift in the balance of power at the centre of conflict to the north sent more shock waves across the region. In an attack on the Ndwandwe, the Mthethwa army was defeated and driven back, and the Mthethwa chief, Dingiswayo, captured and killed.[35] These events effectively destroyed the loosely structured Mthethwa state, and confirmed the position of the Ndwandwe as the dominant power between the Black Mfolozi and Phongolo Rivers. To the south, the long-established Qwabe chiefdom and the newly rising Zulu chiefdom were left as the dominant polities in the area between the White Mfolozi and the Thukela Rivers.

The Zulu chiefdom at this time was headed by Shaka kaSenzangakhona, who, after the death of his father, had been set up as chief by his overlord, Dingiswayo, and encouraged to expand his chiefdom as a sub-agency of the Mthethwa power.[36] Following the defeat of the Mthethwa, the Ndwandwe launched several raids against the Zulu, which the latter survived only with difficulty. Faced with defeat and perhaps destruction, the Zulu leadership under Shaka moved rapidly to coerce or cajole neighbouring chiefdoms into a defensive alliance against the Ndwandwe.[37]

Through a combination of military aggression and political manoeuvring, Shaka first brought the relatively powerful Qwabe chiefdom under his authority, and then turned his attention to the other chiefdoms of the lower Thukela Valley. The Chunu under Macingwane were able to avoid the fate of the Qwabe by migrating across the Thukela, probably to the upper Mvoti region. The Mkhize under Zihlandlo submitted to Shaka without a struggle. The Nyuswa tried to resist, but were defeated by a Zulu force sent against them. To the west of the former Chunu territory, the Thembu chiefdom, which, under the leadership of Ngoza, was itself trying to expand

33. For an analysis of the evidence on the Ndwandwe attack on the Hlubi see Wright, 'Dynamics', 213–18.
34. Wright, 'Dynamics', 218–23.
35. Hedges, 'Trade and Politics', 193; Hamilton, 'Ideology', 136–7.
36. Hamilton, 'Ideology', 125–33, 225–7, 335. ff.
37. Hamilton, 'Ideology', 247 ff.

at this time, sought to maintain its independence by shifting westward across the lower Mzinyathi.[38]

The events described above completely transformed the political scene in the lower Thukela Valley and in the extensive territories between the upper Thukela and the Mzinyathi. The chiefdoms which had previously been jostling for influence along the lower Thukela were now subordinate to the expanding Zulu power. The Hlubi chiefdom, which had dominated the basin of the upper Mzinyathi, had fragmented. The Ngwane were consolidating a new chiefdom about the upper Thukela. Poised uncertainly between the Ngwane and the Zulu were the newly displaced Chunu and Thembu chiefdoms.

Zulu Expansion over the Lower Thukela in the Early 1820s

Zulu expansion towards the lower Thukela was primarily a defensive move undertaken to eliminate potential threats from the south, and to acquire the resources of cattle and labour which were urgently needed to strengthen the new and relatively weak Zulu state against Ndwandwe raids from the north.[39] Shaka so far succeeded in his strategy as to be able to defeat and drive off another Ndwandwe raiding force. Soon afterwards, the Ndwandwe state broke up into a number of separate groups, all of which shifted away to the northward. The Khumalo under Mzilikazi moved to what later became the south-eastern Transvaal, the Msane under Nxaba to eastern Swaziland, and the Jele (Jere) under Zwangendaba and the Gaza under Soshangane to the Delagoa Bay area. The Ndwandwe ruling house itself moved across the Phongolo into southern Swaziland.[40]

In the traditions of the Zulu ruling house, as rendered for instance by Bryant, the collapse of the Ndwandwe state came to be explained as the outcome of defeat at the hands of the Zulu. The Ndebele, Msane, Jele and Gaza, as well as the Ndwandwe ruling house, were portrayed as having 'fled' from Shaka.[41] The evidence from sources drawing on non-Zulu traditions (see the previous paragraph) points to a rather different explanation. While the rise of the Zulu power may well have been an important factor in the break-up of the Ndwandwe state, and in the shift of its offshoot chiefdoms northwards rather than in any other direction, it is unlikely to have been the only one. The most likely kind of explanation is that the state fell apart as a result of internal stresses which were exacerbated by external factors like the emergence of Zulu power and also, as Cobbing has argued, the expansion of the Delagoa Bay slave trade.[42]

38. Hamilton, 'Ideology', 160–75, 247, 252–3, 258–60, 476; Wright, 'Dynamics', 180–5, 223–8.
39. Hamilton, 'Ideology', 172–5.
40. On the Khumalo see J. Cobbing, 'The Ndebele Under the Khumalos, 1820–1896', Ph.D. thesis, University of Lancaster, 1976, 15–16; on the Msane see Bryant, *Olden Times*, 460; on the Jele and Gaza see G. Liesegang, 'Nguni Migrations between Delagoa Bay and the Zambezi, 1821–1839', *African Historical Studies*, 3 (1970), 317–23, and Smith, 'The Struggle for Control', 250–9; on the Ndwandwe see Bonner, *Kings, Commoners and Concessionaires*, 29.
41. Bryant, *Olden Times*, 206–9, 279–80, 422–3, 448, 459–60.
42. Cobbing, 'The Mfecane as Alibi', 506.

The break-up of the Ndwandwe polity and the consequent migration of several offshoot chiefdoms from the region north of the Black Mfolozi left something of a political vacuum in these territories. The prime strategic concern of the Zulu leaders was now to establish effective domination over the remaining groups in the area, and to secure their northern borders against possible raids on the part of groups in the turbulent regions beyond the Phongolo River. To this end the Zulu set up a number of military settlements between the Black Mfolozi and the Mkhuze Rivers.[43] Contrary to the stereotyped view, they did not at this stage have anything like the military or political capacity to extend their domination two hundred kilometres further north to Delagoa Bay.

Again contrary to the common view, it is clear that the emergent Zulu state was not strong enough to pursue a policy of active expansion to the southward either. In this direction, the main aims of its rulers were to establish a stable and secure border in the valleys of the lower Thukela and lower Mzinyathi. To this end they sought to break up or drive away chiefdoms which they regarded as posing a threat to the stability of the region, and set up three semi-autonomous client polities to maintain control over it.

The sequence of developments that took place in this area in the late 1810s and early 1820s is impossible to establish with any certainty, but the overall consequences of Zulu intervention are clear enough. To the south-west they sought to establish their authority over the Thembu, who, to avoid domination either by the Zulu on one side or by the Ngwane on the other, made off southwards through the Natal midlands and ultimately across the Mzimkhulu River. To maintain control over the area on either side of the lower Mzinyathi, Shaka established Jobe of the Sithole as ruler of a partly autonomous client polity.[44]

South of the Zulu heartland, Shaka set up Zihlandlo, ruler of the long-established Mkhize chiefdom, in a similar capacity. With Shaka's backing, Zihlandlo began expanding the area under his authority southwards across the Thukela towards the Mvoti, where the Chunu chiefdom had recently re-established itself.[45]

In the face of Mkhize expansion, and alarmed by the Zulu attack which finally triggered off the migration of the nearby Thembu, the Chunu once again moved off. After pushing their way through the small polities of the Natal midlands, they halted in the mid-Mkhomazi/mid-Mzimkhulu area, and once again sought to consolidate.[46] Not long afterwards, pressures exerted by the Sithole and Mkhize to the east and the Ngwane to the west sent a large group of Memela, Nhlangwini and others from the northern midlands migrating southward.[47]

South of the lower Thukela Shaka set up a third client polity to watch over Zulu

43. Wright, 'Dynamics', 188–9, 192. See also Hamilton, 'Ideology', 219–24; Hedges, 'Trade and Politics', 214–16.
44. Hamilton, 'Ideology', 253–5; Wright, 'Dynamics', 247–8.
45. Wright, 'Dynamics', 232–8, 251–2.
46. Wright, 'Dynamics', 242–7.
47. Wright, 'Dynamics', 249–51.

interests. Its core was formed by the Cele chiefdom, which had dominated the lower Mvoti region for several decades, and had submitted to Shaka's overlordship without resistance. Under the rule of Magaye, who had been placed in the chiefship by Shaka, the Cele were required to exercise dominion over the numerous smaller chiefdoms in the coastlands which had been forced to acknowledge Shaka's supremacy. To buttress Magaye's authority, and to enable him the more effectively to raid cattle from the territories further south on Shaka's behalf, the Zulu chief stationed in his chiefdom a force of armed men known as the iziYendane. Within a short while this force had broken up the Thuli paramountcy in the lower Mngeni–lower Mkhomazi area. To the leadership of the remnant Thuli chiefdom, Shaka elevated Mathubane, who belonged to one of its junior sections. Like other local chiefs, he came under the overall authority of Magaye.[48]

By the early 1820s the emerging Zulu state had established indirect domination over a belt of territory on its south-western and southern borders which extended from the lower Mzinyathi south-eastward between the Thukela and Mvoti Rivers to the coast, and thence south to the lower Mngeni–Mlazi area. But its authority in this region was not uncontested. To the west, the Ngwane chiefdom dominated the basin of the upper Thukela. To the south, the Chunu were seeking to establish their power between the middle Mkhomazi and the Mzimkhulu.

Upheavals in the Midlands in the Late 1810s and Early 1820s

Since it was first articulated in print by British settlers in Natal and the eastern Cape in the late 1820s and the 1830s, the idea that the region south of the Thukela River was devastated and depopulated in a series of bloody attacks by Shaka's armies has gained virtually universal acceptance in the literature. From the 1860s, when Theophilus Shepstone, Secretary for Native Affairs in the colony of Natal, first recorded evidence to this effect, some historians, including Bryant, have accepted that other groups from north of the Thukela were also instrumental in causing the political, social and economic upheavals which affected the territories south of the river soon after Shaka's rise to power.[49] But, again virtually without exception, these writers have portrayed these groups as having been 'driven out' by Shaka's armies. In their accounts the primary responsibility for the devastation of the Thukela–Mzimkhulu region which is supposed to have taken place continues to be attributed to the Zulu.[50]

A critical re-examination of the evidence points to a very different set of conclusions. The Zulu were not the main agents of the upheavals which took place south of the Thukela. The migrant groups which mainly caused them – the Ngwane, the Thembu, the Chunu, and the Memela and Nhlangwini – were not in any simple

---

48. Wright, 'Dynamics', 252–66; Hamilton, 'Ideology', 469–72.
49. See the discussion in Wright, 'Dynamics', 99–110.
50. See for example J.D. Omer-Cooper, *The Zulu Aftermath: A Nineteenth-century Revolution in Bantu Africa*, London, 1966, 156–7.

sense 'refugees' from the Zulu, and, in the case of the Ngwane, were not refugees from the Zulu at all. And neither these groups nor the Zulu universally devastated or depopulated the region south of the Thukela.

As far as the Ngwane are concerned, the evidence suggests, as indicated above, that they took to flight after an attack by the Ndwandwe in the late 1810s. Why they chose to flee rather than give their allegiance to the Ndwandwe, or, alternatively, why the Ndwandwe drove the Ngwane out instead of seeking to incorporate them into their own polity, are subjects which need to be explained, not glossed over. That 'flight' was necessarily the response to 'attack' cannot simply be assumed, as it usually is in accounts informed by the notion of the mfecane. The explanation in this case has much to do with the aggressiveness with which the Ndwandwe were waging war by the late 1810s. To the south they were confronting the Mthethwa, and to the north the Dlamini, and very probably slaving groups from the Delagoa Bay region as well. They may possibly have been engaged in slaving themselves: if so, this would help explain why they seem to have been less concerned with bringing the Ngwane chiefdom under their authority than with breaking it up.[51]

Little is known about the chiefdom which the Ngwane set about re-establishing on the upper Thukela. What evidence there is suggests that, far from simply massacring or 'driving out' the local Zizi and Bhele communities, as conventionally they are supposed to have done,[52] the Ngwane leaders sought to incorporate as least some of them as political subjects.[53] It made little sense for leaders who were constantly trying to augment the manpower and womanpower under their control to kill off the members of communities which they subjugated, even if one makes the assumption, which is dubious anyway, that they had the physical capacity to do so. *Pace* the specific case of the Ndwandwe cited above, most wars during the period of heightened violence which undoubtedly occurred in the late 1810s and 1820s were probably fought to capture cattle, to destroy the leadership structures of resistant chiefdoms, and to acquire more adherents, not to destroy populations.

Numbers of Zizi and Bhele gave, or were forced to give, their allegiance to Matiwane. Others made off to the southward across the Mzimkhulu River. Little is known about the impact of their migration on the chiefdoms of the Natal midlands; as their movement seems to have taken place through the sparsely inhabited uplands along the Drakensberg, it probably had little directly destabilising effect.[54]

A much more disruptive series of migrations took place through the midlands in the early 1820s, when, as has been described in the previous section of the essay, the Zulu were consolidating their hold on the lower Thukela Valley. The process of their expansion was watched with increasing consternation by the Thembu on the lower Mzinyathi to the west and the Chunu on the upper Mvoti to the south. Each of these large chiefdoms had already moved once before to remain outside the Zulu sphere of

51. See the discussion in Wright, 'Dynamics', 178–9, 210–13.
52. Bryant, *Olden Times*, 139, 357.
53. Wright, 'Dynamics', 220–1.
54. On the migration of Zizi and Bhele groups see Wright, 'Dynamics', 220, 302.

influence, but, given their size and strength, neither could expect to be regarded by the Zulu leaders as anything but a threat to the stability of their southern borderlands. There is some evidence that Shaka tried to secure the voluntary submission of the Thembu, but in the event their chief, Ngoza, refused to give it. A subsequent attack by a Zulu force was beaten off by the Thembu, but, to avoid further attacks, Ngoza made up his mind to migrate once again. With the Zulu to the east, the Ngwane to the west, and a country largely denuded of cattle to the north, the Thembu had little option but to head southwards. Pushing their way through the small chiefdoms of the midlands, and seizing cattle where they could, they eventually crossed the Mzimkhulu River and, on the margins of the Mpondo chiefdom's sphere of influence, set about trying to reconsolidate their chiefdom.[55]

At much the same time, the Chunu chiefdom under Macingwane on the upper Mvoti also decided to shift further southward. For some time they had been coming under pressure from the Mkhize chiefdom, which, with Shaka's backing, was expanding southwards across the Thukela. The Zulu attack on the Thembu triggered their decision to move off through the midlands. Like the Thembu, they broke up several smaller chiefdoms before coming to a halt between the Mkhomazi and the Mzimkhulu Rivers, some 150 kilometres from their starting point.[56] Soon after the Thembu and the Chunu came the Memela and Nhlangwini from the lower Ndaka (Sundays)–middle Thukela region. Under increasing pressure from the Ngwane to the west and the Sithole, another satellite chiefdom of the Zulu, to the east, the leaders of these chiefdoms also chose to move off to the south. Apparently acting in concert, they followed a route which converged with those previously taken by the Thembu and Chunu. Their migration ended across the Mzimkhulu, where they became one of the by now numerous polities which were struggling to reconstitute themselves as coherent chiefdoms and to survive in what was becoming an arena of rapidly mounting conflict.[57]

After these migrations the major powers between the Thukela and the Mzimkhulu were the three Zulu satellite chiefdoms – the Sithole, the Mkhize and the Cele – together with the Ngwane in the north-west and the relocated Chunu in the south. Between them they dominated the whole of the region. The independent small chiefdoms of the midlands and the coast had either taken to flight southwards, had given their allegiance to one or other of the emerging powers, or had been broken up and dispersed.

The 'Devastation of Natal' Reconsidered

The stereotyped view that in the 1810s and early 1820s the Zulu state was the only significant agency of change in the Thukela–Mzimkhulu region, and that the Zulu had the power to intervene more or less at will in the region's affairs, completely fails

---

55. Wright, 'Dynamics', 239–42.
56. Wright, 'Dynamics', 242–7.
57. Wright, 'Dynamics', 249–51.

to capture the complexity of the region's history in this period. So too does the notion that this history was mainly one of violence and destruction.[58]

There is no doubt that these years saw a great political, social and economic upheaval taking place south of the Thukela as migrant groups from the north pushed their way into it and disrupted established patterns of existence. But, contrary to the commonly held view, these groups used force not so much to wipe out populations as to seize the resources and, and at times, to destroy the political organisation of communities which stood in their way. In the process, a number of small chiefdoms, particularly in the south, where the paths of a number of the larger migrant groups converged, were so thoroughly broken up that they ceased to exist as political entities. Many, probably most, of their members, though, survived to give their allegiance, either as individuals or in groups, to other chiefs. Outside the south, most chiefdoms seem to have been able to retain a degree of cohesion, even if many lost some of their component sections through secession. Generally speaking, for smaller groups there were three main strategies of survival: to migrate as an independent unit; to remain *in situ* and wait for dangers to subside; and to give their allegiance to a new leader who could offer effective protection. Numbers of groups may have followed all three courses at different stages. Comparatively few had the resources needed for successfully pursuing the first and second courses, and over time most ended up taking the third.

The history of the period was characterised not so much by the destruction of peoples as by two other, interlinked processes: the displacement and migration of populations, and the fragmentation of political units and their reaggregation into new, enlarged entities. The numerous small polities which had previously existed were replaced by a handful of much larger chiefdoms, the cores of which were formed either by intruding groups – the Ngwane, Sithole, Mkhize, Chunu – or by local groups which, under varying circumstances, managed to maintain their cohesion – the Memela, Nhlangwini, Zelemu-Wushe (or Bhaca) and Cele.

Political reaggregation was accompanied by demographic concentration. The conventional view holds that if the inhabitants of the Thukela–Mzimkhulu region were not mostly massacred in the violence of the period, they were driven out, either on to the highveld or southwards across the Mzimkhulu. The available evidence indicates clearly that this was not so. Numbers of groups did migrate out of the region (including some which made off to the Zulu chiefdom, *pace* the notion of the Zulu as destroyers), and there may have been a temporary drop in the overall population as a result. But most of the previous inhabitants remained within the region, and a fall-off of population would to some extent have been offset by the advent of intruding groups like the Ngwane and the Mkhize. As significant as migrations inward or outward across what are in any case rather arbitrarily determined boundaries were the internal movements which took place.

---

58. This section of the essay draws on Wright, 'Dynamics', 266–77.

As numbers of people shifted into the territories dominated by the larger and more stable chiefdoms to find security, so these regions became relatively more populated, while other areas became relatively denuded of inhabitants. Regions in which concentrations of population formed were very likely the territories dominated by the Ngwane in the north-west, the Mkhize in the lower Thukela Valley, the Cele south of the lower Thukela, and the Chunu and other large chiefdoms about the Mzimkhulu. The intervening regions – the area between the Mzinyathi and Ndaka Rivers, the central midlands, the southern coastlands – probably experienced a drop in population. In these regions numbers of small groups clung on in the more broken or forested parts. They lived largely by gathering and hunting, and probably kept cultivation and herding of livestock to a minimum to avoid attracting the attention of larger groups. Others took advantage of the breakdown of previously established authority structures to turn to banditry.

The members of most of the communities described as 'cannibals' in the literature were probably bandits. The literary stereotype about the widespread existence of cannibalism in the Natal area in Shaka's time was very much a product of settler ideology and its exaggeration of a handful of recorded eye-witness accounts and traditions.[59] It is likely that in areas where agriculture and livestock production had collapsed some people took to cannibalism to stay alive. But in regard to traditions of cannibalism, the comments made by Peter Delius in his study of the history of the Pedi chiefdom of the eastern Transvaal region are pertinent. Such traditions, he suggests, functioned to show 'the dire consequences of the destruction of properly constituted authority'. They were thus liable to exaggeration in African society as well as by white commentators, and need to be treated with caution. Close investigation of his sources, Delius argues, shows that cannibal groups were 'principally distinguished by the fact that they secured their subsistence almost exclusively through raiding, and were thus seen as living on their fellows'.[60]

The scraps of evidence which exist suggest that south of the Thukela–Mzinyathi Valley such groups emerged in precisely those regions which had been most heavily raided by larger chiefdoms and had been partially denuded of population. Several traditions indicate that in the north the country between the Mzinyathi and the Ndaka Rivers was one such region. Others were the territory about the upper Mvoti, the

---

59. The making of this stereotype needs detailed research in its own right. Early writers like A. F. Gardiner, (*Narrative of a Journey to the Zoolu Country*, London, 1836, 185–6) and N. Isaacs (*Travels and Adventures in Eastern Africa*, Cape Town, 1970 ed., 1st publ. 1836, 78) mention the practice of cannibalism in the Natal region in passing, but it was not until the later nineteenth century that writers like T. Shepstone, ('The Early History of the Zulu-Kafir Race of South-Eastern Africa', in J. Bird, comp., *The Annals of Natal*, vol. 1, Pietermaritzburg, 1888, 159–60) began to portray it as a major consequence of 'Shaka's wars'. In the early twentieth century Bryant took delight in further embellishing the stories of Shepstone's informants about cannibals: see *Olden Times*, 58, 248, 348, 377, 410, 504, 552, 558–9.
60. P. Delius, *The Land Belongs to Us: The Pedi Polity, the Boers and the British in the Nineteenth-century Transvaal*, Johannesburg, 1983, 24.

broken country of the mid-Mngeni Valley and the coastlands from the Mngeni southward.

While the political map of the Thukela–Mzimkhulu region changed dramatically in the late 1810s and early 1820s, the process of change was not one of unmitigated destruction. The stereotype about the devastation of the Natal area by the Zulu which began to emerge in the literature in the late 1820s and 1830s, and which has been reproduced by generations of historians up to the present, was a product less of historical analysis than of ideological interpolation by colonial writers.

Consolidation of Zulu Domination South of the Thukela

By the early 1820s the emerging Zulu state was the most powerful political actor in the territories south of the Thukela, but it by no means completely dominated the region. To the west and south, the Ngwane and Chunu chiefdoms respectively exerted influence across considerable territories. There was nothing inherent in Zulu policy which necessarily entailed further expansion in these directions. But within a short space of time, political developments within the Zulu polity and on its northern borders set in train a process which saw Zulu domination extended westward to the Drakensberg Mountains and southward to the region of the Mzimkhulu.

The precise nature of these developments will not be known until the history of the early Zulu state has been studied in greater detail, but primarily they had to do with the growth of internal opposition to Shaka's rule at a time when his kingdom was facing increasing pressures from the north.[61] As a usurper, Shaka had from the beginning of his reign faced strong, if muted, opposition from within the Zulu ruling house. In addition, as the Zulu state expanded, its rulers faced continuing resistance from sections of powerful subordinate chiefdoms such as those of the Qwabe and the Mthethwa. Exacerbating the resultant internal tensions was, possibly, the threat of incursions into the northern borderlands on the part of raiding and slaving groups from the region round Delagoa Bay.[62]

One of the responses of the Zulu leaders to the internal and external problems of security which they faced was to shift their capital, kwaBulawayo, together with many of Shaka's *amabutho*, or age-regiments, from the mid-White Mfolozi area south-east to the Qwabe territory between the Mhlathuze and the lower Thukela. The move was made to suppress dissidence among the Qwabe, and perhaps also to put a greater distance between the state's nerve-centre and the unstable northern borderlands.[63] With this shift closer towards the lower Thukela, the territories south of that river became established as a zone of new strategic importance for the Zulu leaders. For the leadership as a whole, expansion to the southward presented a means

---

61. Carolyn Hamilton is the first writer to have paid close attention to the growth of resistance within the Zulu kingdom to Shaka's rule. See particularly the discussion in 'Ideology', 174–5, 184–6, 354–5, 362–3, 506–8.
62. Cobbing, 'The Mfecane as Alibi', 506–7.
63. Hamilton, 'Ideology', 184–6, 350–7, 361–2; Wright, 'Dynamics', 281–3.

of bringing new resources of cattle under its control. For Shaka and his party of supporters in particular, it also afforded the opportunity of establishing a separate power-base which could be brought more directly under their control than was possible in the regions north of the Thukela where their authority was being contested.[64]

To secure unimpeded access to the territories beyond the Thukela, it was necessary for the Zulu first of all to eliminate the rival Ngwane and Chunu chiefdoms. At some point in the early 1820s both were attacked by Zulu forces. Though they lost many of their cattle, the Ngwane succeeded in escaping across the Drakensberg and re-establishing their chiefdom in the Caledon Valley. The Chunu chiefdom, however, was broken up. The cattle seized from it were placed at new cattle posts erected by Shaka in the country of the Cele chief, Magaye, and guarded by the latter's *amabutho*. Other posts may have been established in the Sithole domain on the lower Mzinyathi for the cattle taken from the Ngwane.[65]

These campaigns extended Zulu power westward to the Drakensberg and southward to the vicinity of the Mzimkhulu. They were not, however, followed by effective occupation. While the Zulu state had the ability to mount occasional forays into these territories, it did not have the capacity to set up the permanent military presence which colonisation would have entailed. The area west of the Mzinyathi was vulnerable to raids by the Griqua and other mounted gunmen who, by the early 1820s, were raiding further and further from the west and south across the southern highveld.[66] Similarly, the territories about the Mzimkhulu were exposed to raids from the groups which, at this time, were struggling for domination in the region to the south (see below).

In the face of these dangers the Zulu leaders held back from occupying more territory south of the Thukela. Their policy was instead to consolidate their hold on the coastland region which they already controlled by proxy through Magaye, and to send armed parties to raid cattle further and further south beyond the Mkhomazi.[67] In 1824 a force of Zulu *amabutho* from north of the Thukela penetrated to the vicinity of the Mzimvubu River and seized cattle from the Mpondo. These were placed at posts set up in Mathubane's territory near Port Natal, and watched over by men of his Thuli chiefdom.[68] At no stage, as far as the evidence goes, did Zulu armies make the murderous sweeps through the Natal area which conventionally they are supposed to have done.

---

64. Hamilton, 'Ideology', 350–7, 474–5; Wright, 'Dynamics', 283–4.
65. Wright, 'Dynamics', 384–6.
66. Julian Cobbing has been the first to recognize the importance of the role played by these raiding bands in the upheavals which took place on the highveld in the 1820s. See his article, 'The Mfecane as Alibi', 496–500; and also J. Richner, 'The Withering Away of the "Lifaqane": Or a Change of Paradigm', B.A. Hons. essay, Rhodes University, Grahamstown, 1988, chs. 2–4.
67. Wright, 'Dynamics', 286–95.
68. Wright, 'Dynamics', 287–90.

Upheavals South of the Mzimkhulu in the 1820s

The conventional literature on the 'devastation of Natal' sees large numbers of 'refugees' from the region as having fled from roving Zulu armies southward across the Mzimkhulu River towards the Cape frontier. According to this view, most of these groups ended up as clients of the Thembu and the Gcaleka Xhosa, or as so-called Fingoes in the eastern Cape colony.[69] Recently Cobbing and Alan Webster have called this orthodoxy into question. Few Fingoes, they argue, originated in Natal; most of them were Xhosa who had been dispossessed by British cattle raids and land seizures across the eastern frontier of the Cape, particularly during the war of 1834–5. Stories that they had fled from the Zulu and become virtual slaves of the Gcaleka were to a large extent evolved by the colonial authorities to cover their seizure of large numbers of Fingo captives in the course of the war.[70]

The details of the arguments put forward by Cobbing and by Webster are open to debate, but a close examination of the evidence on political developments in the Thukela–Mzimkhulu region in the 1820s lends support to their general hypothesis that most Fingo were not of Natal origin. There is little doubt that numbers of groups displaced by the upheavals of the late 1810s and early 1820s migrated across the Mzimkhulu. But, contrary to the stereotyped view, most of these groups re-established themselves between that river and the Mzimvubu rather than moving on further south.

The first major group to move into these territories consisted largely of Bhele displaced by the Ngwane from the area south of the Biggarsberg. Sometime afterwards, the comparatively powerful groups of Macingwane's Chunu and Ngoza's Thembu arrived on the scene. They were followed by the Nhlangwini of Nombewu, the Memela of Mdingi and the Bhaca under Madikane. Besides these larger groupings, and the fragments of other polities which adhered to them, numbers of smaller parties from the Thukela–Mzimkhulu region also made their way southward.[71]

The groups which moved across the Mzimkhulu found themselves entering the sphere of influence of the larger and more powerful Mpondo paramountcy. This was located on either side of the lower Mzimvubu, and since 1820 or before had been ruled by Faku, son of Ngqungqushe.[72] To the south-west across the Mthatha were various groups of Thembu, most of which acknowledged the paramountcy of the

69. See for example Omer-Cooper, *The Zulu Aftermath*, chs. 10, 11.
70. J. Cobbing, 'The Myth of the Mfecane', seminar paper presented to the Department of History and the Institute for Social and Economic Research, University of Durban-Westville, 1987, 21–3; J. Cobbing, 'Jettisoning the Mfecane (with *Perestroika*)', seminar paper presented to the African Studies Institute, University of the Witwatersrand, Johannesburg, 1988, 13; A.C. Webster, 'Ayliff, Whiteside, and the Fingo "Emancipation" of 1835: A Reappraisal', B.A. Hons. essay, Rhodes University, Grahamstown, 1988; A. Webster, 'Land Expropriation and Labour Extraction Under Cape Colonial Rule: The War of 1835 and the "Emancipation" of the Fingo', M.A. dissertation, Rhodes University, Grahamstown, 1991.
71. Wright, 'Dynamics', 301–5.
72. Beinart, *Political Economy of Pondoland*, 9–10; J.B. Peires, *The House of Phalo: A History of the Xhosa People in the Days of their Independence*, Johannesburg, 1981, 86.

Hala section under Ngubengcuka, or Vusani. Though the polity under his authority seems to have been more loosely constituted than that of Faku,[73] it would still have represented a major obstacle for the migrant groups which were making their way south across the Mzimkhulu before and after 1820. For these groups, the choices were to make their submission to established and relatively powerful rulers like Faku and Ngubengcuka, to fight them for dominance, or to attempt to re-establish themselves on the edges of the Mpondo sphere of influence.

In the first instance most of the larger migrant groups seem to have chosen the latter course. Their sudden advent inaugurated a long period of political instability and violence in the territories south of the Mzimkhulu. What little is known of the region's history in the 1820s is largely about fights and raids. The first major conflict of the period was probably that between the Mpondo and Ngoza's Thembu. In the event, the Mpondo defeated the Thembu in battle, killed Ngoza and broke up his chiefdom. While numbers of his people probably gave their allegiance to local chiefs, many of them eventually made their way back northward and submitted to Shaka. Not long afterwards the Zulu made the first of a series of interventions in the politics of the region. As already described, they attacked and destroyed the Chunu chiefdom. The chief, Macingwane, disappeared, and numbers of his people returned to make their submission to Shaka.[74]

It is significant that, contrary to what the conventional view would lead one to expect, the remnants of the Thembu and Chunu retraced their footsteps to the north and gave their allegiance to Shaka rather than continuing further to the south. Several other smaller groups also returned northwards from the Mzimkhulu region at this time. All, it seems, preferred to join Shaka or to try to maintain an autonomous existence in the Zulu sphere of influence north of the Mzimkhulu rather than to remain in the zone of intensified conflict which was emerging in the south.[75]

The destruction of the Thembu and Chunu powers marked the end of one phase of conflict in the Mzimkhulu–Mzimvubu region and the beginning of another. In this, the protagonists were the Bhaca, the Memela, the Nhlangwini and the Mpondo. From the north, raiding parties from the Zulu domains made occasional forays into the coastlands south of Port Natal and, eventually, as described above, over the Mzimkhulu. By the end of the 1820s the dominant powers in the region were the Mpondo and Bhaca chiefdoms. More groups had moved out of the zone of conflict to settle north of the Mzimkhulu; others had moved away southward.[76]

The disruptions caused in the territories south of the Mzimkhulu in the 1820s by the intrusion of groups from the north were compounded by the effects of the conflicts and confrontations which were taking place at this time on the Cape eastern frontier and also on the southern highveld. The precise nature of these effects awaits

73. Peires, *House of Phalo*, 84–6; E. Wagenaar, 'A History of the Thembu and their Relationship with the Cape, 1850–1900', Ph.D. thesis, Rhodes University, Grahamstown, 1988, 1–4.
74. Wagenaar, 'A History of the Thembu', 305.
75. Wagenaar, 'A History of the Thembu', 305–6.
76. Wagenaar, 'A History of the Thembu', 306–9, 374–5.

further research. In spite of the size of the corpus of works, published and unpublished, on the history of the eastern Cape region, there is still no study which comprehensively assesses the far-reaching impact of British policies and the British presence on the African societies beyond the Cape colonial boundary in the eventful period of the 1810s and 1820s. Nor is there any work which does much to recognise, let alone to analyse, the overall impact on this region of raids and threats of raids from the other side of the Orange River.[77] In the absence of such studies, the most that can be said here is that the interactions between established chiefdoms like those of the Mpondo, Thembu and others with intrusive groups from north of the Mzimkhulu in the 1820s are likely to have been shaped in important ways by pressures which they were all coming under from the south and from the north-west.

Conclusion

The Zulu were still consolidating their domination over the territories south of the Thukela when, in the mid-1820s, a completely new set of political factors began to come into play in the region. These stemmed from the advent at Port Natal from 1824 onward of parties of British traders and hunters from the Cape colony. Their coming was a product of the growing interest which, after the end of the Napoleonic wars, merchants and officials in the Cape and Britain were showing in south-eastern Africa as a field of commercial enterprise. The traders were welcomed by Shaka as sources of manufactured goods, as potential intermediaries with the British authorities in the Cape, and as potential allies in his struggles against his opponents inside and outside his kingdom. By 1827 they had become an important factor in the politics of the Zulu state, and by 1829, with the backing of groups of merchants and missionaries in the Cape, were pressing for British intervention in the affairs of Port Natal and its hinterland.[78] For their part, the Cape authorities were by this time actively extending the colony's sphere of influence northwards towards the Mzimkhulu.[79] The field was becoming set for a struggle between the Zulu state and Cape-based interests, backed ultimately by imperial Britain, for control of the territories about Port Natal. The forces which, for more than half a century, had operated to lock the region south of the Thukela ever more firmly to the polities north of that river were now starting to be countered by forces which sought to pull it into the political and economic orbit of the Cape. A new era in its history was beginning.

---

77. Exceptions are Cobbing, 'The Mfecane as Alibi', 500–1; Richner, 'The Withering Away of the "Lifaqane"', 22–3.
78. Wright, 'Dynamics', ch. 7.
79. Wright, 'Dynamics', 369, 375–80.

7 'The Character and Objects of Chaka'

A Reconsideration of the Making of Shaka as Mfecane Motor

CAROLYN HAMILTON

In a series of papers and articles beginning in 1983, Julian Cobbing has offered a radical, and often provocative, critique of the mfecane as the pivotal concept of the history of southern Africa in the nineteenth century.[1] He asks vigorous new questions about everything from the identity of the 'Fingoes' in the south and the 'Mantatee hordes' on the highveld, to the extent of the slave trade around Delagoa Bay. Cobbing's work has stimulated a host of graduate studies on these topics, and has prompted a number of established students of the period to reassess aspects of their earlier work.[2] The sheer scope of the critique is, however, also the source of its greatest weakness. In particular, Cobbing may be criticised for misusing evidence and employing imprecise periodisation.

Nowhere are these criticisms more pertinent than in relation to a central element of Cobbing's thesis, namely, his view of 'Shaka-the-monster' as a European invention to mask illegal labour procurement activities and land occupation. In this essay, I focus on Cobbing's reconstruction of the making of the Shaka myth. My purpose is to disentangle the elaborate weave of Cobbing's powerful insights and implausible conspiracy theories. I suggest that while Cobbing's critique is extremely valuable, especially in the way that it forces historians to question many of the assumptions

1. J. Cobbing, 'The Case Against the Mfecane', seminar paper presented to the Centre for African Studies, University of Cape Town, 1983; in revised form 'The Case against the Mfecane', seminar paper given at the African Studies Institute, University of the Witwatersrand, Johannesburg, 1984; 'The Myth of the Mfecane', seminar paper presented to the Department of History and the Institute for Social and Economic Research, University of Durban-Westville, 1987; 'The Mfecane as Alibi: Thoughts on Dithakong and Mbolompo', *Journal of African History*, 29 (1988), 487–519; 'Jettisoning the Mfecane (with *Perestroika*)', paper presented together with John Wright's 'Political Mythology and the Making of Natal's Mfecane' to the African Studies Institute, University of the Witwatersrand, Johannesburg, in 1988 to a seminar entitled 'The Mfecane: Beginning the Inquest'; and most recently, 'Grasping the Nettle: The Slave Trade and the Early Zulu', in D. R. Edgecombe, J. P. C. Laband and P. S. Thompson, comps, *The Debate on Zulu Origins: A Selection of Papers on the Zulu Kingdom and Early Colonial Natal*, Pietermaritzburg, 1992.
2. See the work of Cobbing's students, notably J. Richner, 'The Withering away of the "Lifaqane": Or a Change of Paradigm', B.A. Hons. essay, Rhodes University, Grahamstown, 1988; A. Webster, 'Examination of the "Fingo Emancipation" of 1835', paper presented to the African Studies Seminar, University of Cape Town, 1990; and that of John Wright on the genesis of the mfecane myth in Natal, notably 'Political Mythology'.

with which they have for too long been extremely comfortable, he fails fundamentally to come to grips with the full complexity of his primary target, past
historical myth-making processes.

Cobbing identifies four key elements in the notion of the mfecane as most
commonly espoused: firstly, 'a self-generated internal revolution' within northern
Nguni-speaking societies which culminated in the 1820s in the regionally dominant
Zulu power led by a savage despot, Shaka; secondly, attacks by the Zulu on
neighbouring chiefdoms which forced the latter to flee their land and which, in turn,
displaced other chiefdoms still further afield; thirdly, a 'cataclysmic period of
black-on-black destruction' (including cannibalism) leading to the depopulation of
the interior of South Africa; with all of this culminating, fourthly, in the restoration
of security with the advent of the Europeans.[3] Cobbing's observation that this
explanation of the depeopling of much of the interior and for the arrangement of the
African inhabitants of southern Africa in a surrounding 'horseshoe' serves to
legitimate white occupation of the land and the ideology of separate development is
not new. But the case that he presents for the selection of its component elements,
and how the myth became established, is challenging.

The central claim of Cobbing's critique is that by making Shaka the motor of the
mfecane, white writers were able to ignore or cover up the devastating impact of
white penetration into southern Africa in the early nineteenth century. He suggests
that this included the effects of a massive demand for labour in the form of slaves or
variants thereof ('apprentices', 'refugees' and so on) from both the Cape colony in
the south, which was experiencing a labour supply problem following the ending of
the British slave trade in 1807, and from Delagoa Bay in the north, an increasingly
important slaving port in the 1800s.[4]

Cobbing argues that the various elements of 'mfecane theory' were established as
part of an 'alibi' by early missionaries like Robert Moffat and John Melvill, traders
like Henry Francis Fynn and Francis Farewell, and colonial officers like
H. Somerset, all anxious to obscure aspects of their activities and policies in relation
to the early nineteenth-century African inhabitants of southern Africa – in particular
their roles in resolving problems of labour supply. The components of 'mfecane
theory', he argues, were subsequently taken up, developed and combined by a
generation of settler historians like George McCall Theal, George Cory, Eric Walker
and D.F. Ellenberger, eager to argue the case for 'the empty land' in response to the
1913 Land Act. After the Second World War, Cobbing continues, the explanatory
scope of 'mfecane theory' was widened by apartheid historians to explain 'the
natural "pluralism" of black societies and how they self-sequestered themselves into
proto-Bantustans in the time of Shaka'.[5]

3. Cobbing, 'The Mfecane as Alibi', 487–8.
4. For the fullest and latest version of Cobbing's argument on the slave trade, see 'Grasping the Nettle',
5–20. This aspect of Cobbing's argument builds on the work of P. Harries, notably 'Slavery, Social
Incorporation and Surplus Extraction: The Nature of Free and Unfree Labour in South-East Africa',
Journal of African History, 22 (1981), 309–30.
5. Cobbing, 'The Mfecane as Alibi', 519.

Cobbing's energetic interrogation of the available sources and his wide-ranging, highly interconnected review of the central conflicts and forces at work across southern Africa offer a stimulating reinterpretation of early nineteenth-century southern African history. His demonstration of the 'spatial sequence' of population movements, and the absence of 'hard evidence for Zulu agency' for many of its key events, are convincing reasons for 'jettisoning' the 'Afrocentri[c] . . . macro-theory or macro-myth of the mfecane' as an explanation for the depopulation of the interior.[6]

But Cobbing's reconstruction of the making of the myth of the mfecane is as over-determined by white interests as the 'mfecane theory' is innocent of them. For Cobbing, the history of the period is entirely shaped by settler and capitalist forces, as is the manipulation of the past which he highlights. The burden of Cobbing's argument is that the construction of the mfecane as an 'alibi' for the more criminal of their activities, was determined by the interests and views of Europeans. The early travellers and traders, and their settler heirs, simply 'invented' the relevant components of the mfecane myth as they saw fit, and as best suited their needs.

But as any *aficionado* of crime literature knows well, a good alibi – one that excites little suspicion or is likely to hold up under investigation – is well-grounded in the facts as far as they can be determined and is invested with detail that is convincing. It appeals to the general preconceptions of its interrogators, its victims and its perpetrators, and it only deviates from the actual events in certain crucial respects. That the mfecane has been proved to be a good alibi is attested to by its resilience over time. This is not a result of simple-mindedness, but is a consequence rather of the embeddedness in the myth, and in its key features, of African views of the past, notably that of internal African agency.

By arguing that Europeans 'invented' the myth of the mfecane and its component elements, Cobbing assumes that the production of history in the nineteenth century was carried out by Europeans only, independent of the historical consciousness of the Africans with whom they were in daily contact. The implication of this assumption is that nineteenth-century Africans were without an intellectual history of their own and that they were unable, or at least failed, to produce history in the service of complex ideological objectives worthy of comparison with their European neighbours, nor significant enough for the latter to need to take cognisance of. In other words, Cobbing's case against the mfecane is doubly focused on European activities at the expense of those of Africans: both in terms of his characterisation of the events and forces of the time, and in terms of their production in historical discourse. In so doing, Cobbing repeats the separation of black and white history in as serious a way as the myth of the mfecane itself does. In effect, Cobbing simply replaces the master narrative of Shaka-as-cause-of-violence with that of slave trade-as-cause-of-violence. In so doing, he fails to harness his powerful insights

6. Cobbing, 'The Mfecane as Alibi', 517. See p.488 for the description of mfecane theory as Afrocentric.

regarding the mfecane myth in the service of an analysis that takes proper cognisance of regional developments and local particularities.

My case then, is not for the mfecane, but against aspects of the case as presented by Cobbing. In this essay, I challenge his assumptions about the European manufacture of the mfecane and the 'virulent anti-Shaka literature' of the 1820s as, among other things, an attempt 'to draw a curtain over the slave trade'.[7] I suggest that this invocation of conspiracy depends on an untenable notion of European interests as monolithic and as unchanging over time. I attempt to give substance to my challenge through exploration of a central element in 'mfecane theory', that of Shaka.[8] In so doing I address primarily the arguments advanced in Cobbing's single published article on the topic, 'The Mfecane as Alibi: Thoughts on Dithakong and Mbolompo', but I also comment on his widely cited paper, 'Grasping the Nettle: The Slave Trade and the Early Zulu', the main arguments of which have become the fundamental premises of a range of subsequent research projects.[9]

I focus in detail on the 1820s, the period in which Cobbing posits that the image of Shaka was established which became central to 'mfecane theory'. Cobbing asserts that, from the first, it was in the interests of the Port Natal traders to promote Shaka as a tyrannical despot. I try to demonstrate that this sweeping claim misses crucial changes in the circumstances of the early traders, and completely ignores the productions of Shaka taking place in contemporary African settings.

The essay examines the image of Shaka promoted in the Cape by the Port Natal traders in the 1820s and distinguishes between the versions sponsored by different factions within the Port Natal community. It looks at the way that these productions shifted during the period under review in response to specific developments in the traders' commercial ventures, and their relationships with the Zulu court and their African neighbours. In sharp contrast to Cobbing's argument, the essay suggests that before the Zulu king's death in late 1828, the traders' presentation of Shaka was that of a *benign patron*. There were two exceptions to this, and these arose in response to

7. Cobbing, 'The Mfecane as Alibi', 504. Cobbing goes even further in the invocation of a conspiracy, describing the European manufacture of the mfecane as the perfection by settler propagandists of 'their pièce de résistance, "the mfecane", combining partly contextualised facts, half-truths, and lies, both of commission and ommission' in 'Grasping the Nettle', 1.

8. In his 1989 article, 'Political Mythology', Wright aligned himself closely with the main points of Cobbing's arguments on the Natal/Zulu material under review in this essay. Following a warm debate on the topic at the Conference on Enlightenment and Emancipation, held at the University of Natal, Durban, 1989, at which both Wright and I presented papers, Wright has refined his arguments regarding trader politics, and avoids many of the errors and generalisations which characterise his own earlier article, and the work of Cobbing. For his revised position see his Ph.D. thesis, 'The Dynamics of Power and Conflict in the Thukela-Mzimkhulu Region in the Late Eighteenth and Early Nineteenth Centuries: A Critical Reconstruction', University of the Witwatersrand, Johannesburg, 1990, especially the final chapter.

9. See, for example, the papers presented by students or ex-students of Cobbing's at the recent colloquium, 'The Mfecane Aftermath: Towards a New Paradigm', University of the Witwatersrand, Johannesburg, 1991, notably J. Richner, 'Eastern Frontier Slaving and its Extension into the Transorangia and Natal, 1770–1843'; C. Gorham, '"A Blind Darkness": Knowledge, Trade, and the Myth of 1824: The Trading Settlement of Port Natal as Gateway to the "Mfecane"'; B. Lambourne, 'A Chip off the Old Block: Early Ghoya History and the Emergency of Moletsane's Taung'; as well as the essays by A.C. Webster and J.B. Gewald included in this collection.

the particular financial difficulties which one of the traders, James King, faced at two specific moments in time. The essay shows that in the Cape King came to be seen as manipulative and unreliable. His two negative depictions of Shaka were discredited in the eyes of the colonial administration and in the popular press, and did not, before 1829, succeed in establishing a negative image of Shaka in the colony.

As was the case with the traders' images of Shaka, different versions of Shaka were promoted by different interest groups within the Zulu kingdom and the Natal area, and these also shifted over time in response to changing circumstances. The essay locates the origins of Shaka's image as a tyrant both in versions of Shaka current among disaffected elements in the Zulu kingdom in the 1820s, as well as in the picture of a despot painted by the Zulu authorities themselves. It suggests that the traders' productions of Shaka were not simply manifestations of the view of Shaka that most directly suited their material interests, but were also shaped by the form and content of the various African views which they encountered and with which they intersected during their stay in Natal.

My proposition is that at various times, the Shaka in different European perorations took cognisance of the many Shakas that were heard in African voices, and vice versa. It was out of this process that emerged the 'Shaka' that became central to 'mfecane theory'.

European Productions of Shaka in the 1820s
The Image of Shaka before 1824

The first productions of Shaka to percolate down to the Cape colony were contained in the reports of visitors to Delagoa Bay, then the port nearest to the Zulu kingdom. In 1822 Henry Francis Fynn joined the *Jane*, a vessel belonging to the Cape mercantile concern, Nourse and Company, trading with Delagoa Bay. In a stay that overlapped with that of a British naval squadron under Captain W.F.W. Owen, Fynn spent some six months at Delagoa Bay, and undertook extensive exploration of its immediate surrounds. Fynn records that he heard of 'the Zulu tribe, under Shaka, [who] were a very powerful nation', and intrigued, arranged a visit to a Zulu homestead and would have continued on to Shaka's capital if the distance had not proved prohibitive. While much of Fynn's account of his visit to Delagoa Bay was written long after the event, and was extensively informed by subsequent information and attitudes which he acquired, it is evident that the impression of Shaka which he gleaned at Delagoa Bay excited his curiosity and was not threatening.[10]

By 1823 reports of the prospects of trade with the Zulus received from Nourse and Co. were so favourable that Francis Farewell was able to secure significant financial backing by Cape merchants for an exploratory voyage to Delagoa Bay and

10. H.F. Fynn, *The Diary of Henry Francis Fynn*, ed. by J. Stuart and D. McK. Malcolm, Pietermaritz-burg, 1950, see chapters one and two, and especially 42.

Natal. Farewell chartered two ships, the *Julia* and the brig, the *Salisbury*, under James King. When they arrived at Delagoa Bay, Owen's vessel, the *Leven*, was in port, and Farewell went aboard to interview Owen. The interview contained nothing to discourage him, and he and King immediately proceeded to the coast of Natal in an attempt to open communications with Shaka.[11] They failed to land successfully, and in the process sustained damage to their ships, lost two boats and a considerable amount of their trade goods.[12]

Undaunted, Farewell returned to the Cape, negotiated new financing with Messrs Hoffman and Peterssen, hired a large party to accompany him – including the young Fynn – and engaged two ships to transport the party and their cargo to Natal. In response to a request from the Governor of the Cape for information regarding his activities, Farewell reported that the prospects of trade from a base at Port Natal were excellent, the 'natives hav[ing] requested that we come and traffic with them . . .'[13]

By June 1824 both ships had landed their cargoes successfully, and Farewell and Fynn had travelled overland to meet Shaka themselves. In the first report from the Port Natal settlement to the Cape, Farewell confirmed the expectations that Shaka would make a good trading partner. He depicted the Zulu king as enthusiastic about the settlement, and well-disposed towards the British. He noted that his companions found the orderliness, manners and customs of the Zulu both 'astonish[ing] and pleas[ing]'.[14] Cape opinion of Shaka could not have been better. For the next two years not one single negative report concerning the king emanated from Port Natal.

11. See Fynn, *Diary*, 51–3, 56, n. 1; Cape Archives (hereafter CA) Government House Archives (hereafter GH) 1/39, 45–58, J. King to the Sec. for Colonies, the Earl of Bathurst, 10 July 1824; (CA) Notarial Protocols, Cape Districts (hereafter NCD) 35/8, 534–41 for details of Farewell's engagement of King. Owen's journal was edited and published as *Narrative of Voyages to Explore the Shores of Africa, Arabia and Madagascar*, 2 vols, London, 1833. However, the publication also includes material drawn from other sources, is heavily edited and cannot be treated as an accurate reflection of Owen's views in 1822. An account of Shaka, attributed to Farewell writing in 1825 is reproduced in Owen's text and must be treated with the same caution. It is most unlikely, for example, that Farewell would have referred to Shaka as 'the king of Natal, and of the Hollontontes'. One of Owen's officers, T. Boteler, also published an account of Owen's trip in 1835 (*Narrative of a Voyage of Discovery to Africa and Arabia, Performed in His Majesty's Ships Leven and Barracouta*, 2 vols, London, 1835). For some idea of what Owen's contemporary opinion of Shaka was like, see Public Record Office (hereafter PRO), Archives of the Colonial Office (hereafter CO) 48/62, John Philip's report to Acting Colonial Secretary, P.G. Brink, 13 Apr. 1824, believed to be based on Owen's information see (CA) GH 23/7, 144–5, Governor of the Cape, Lord Charles Somerset to Bathurst, 22 Apr. 1824) in which Philip comments optimistically on the prospects for trade with the interior.

12. The precise nature of this setback in commercial terms is difficult to assess. The venture was well-insured and substantial claims were made. Unfortunately, the extent of the final settlement is not known. In his letter to Somerset, 1 May 1824, Farewell noted that the earlier expedition 'sustained a most considerable loss', (CA) CO 211, 222–5. However, it is clear that for his next expedition Farewell was obliged to seek other financial backing. See (CA) NCD 35/9, 67–75, 117–26, 144–9, 573–8, 585–9.

13. (CA) CO 211, 222–5, Farewell to Somerset, 1 May 1824; NCD 35/9, 573–8, 585–9. It is not clear from Farewell's letter who precisely 'the natives' are, i.e. whether he means the Zulu authorities or the inhabitants of the bay area; for continued reports of Shaka's 'friendly disposition' arriving at the Cape in this period see (PRO) CO 48/62, W.H. Lys, Officer of Health, to P.G. Brink, 12 Apr. 1824.

14. (CA) CO 211, 650–1, 656–7, Farewell to Somerset, 6 Sept. 1824.

The Traders' Shaka, 1824–27

Cobbing's characterisation of the Port Natal settlement and the objectives of the traders is a central aspect of his wider thesis about the invention of the mfecane myth. His argument can be broken down into two parts: his reconstruction of what the traders were actually up to at Port Natal; and secondly, how they represented their actions and those of the Zulu king.

Cobbing claims that the Port Natal traders were slavers, and that all evidence of this aspect of their activities has been systematically excised from their accounts of the period.[15] He uses two arguments to support these assertions: firstly, he argues for the existence of a vibrant slave trade centred on Delagoa Bay and the involvement of chiefdoms between the Bay and Port Natal in slaving through the Portuguese port. He then locates the Port Natal trading entrepot firmly in this context. Secondly, he rereads the traders' narratives in search of hidden slaving activities.

Reconsideration of both of these arguments suggests that they do not support his conclusions. In challenging Cobbing's arguments, I do not necessarily reject the idea that the Port Natal traders may have been interested in, or on occasion, have participated in slaving activities of one sort or another. I do not accept, however, that there is as yet any conclusive evidence regarding their successful prosecution of a trade in slaves, and argue that other considerations were crucial in shaping both their relationship with the Cape and their depictions of Shaka.

I am critical of Cobbing's characterisation of the Port Natal traders as slavers on a number of grounds. Firstly, it cannot be assumed that the region was the slaving vortex that Cobbing implies. The cases which he makes for a slave trade of significant volume through Delagoa Bay and for the region to the south as a significant supplying area, while suggestive, are by no means well-established. The major problem is Cobbing's failure to consider sources which contradict his claims. One instance of this must suffice to make the point, though others are available for review:[16] Cobbing[17] claims that in the period after the Napoleonic Wars when slave

15. Cobbing, 'The Mfecane as Alibi', 504; 'Grasping the Nettle', 25.
16. See, for example, Cobbing's assertion that in 1827 Cane supplied slaves to a schooner at Delagoa Bay, 'Grasping the Nettle', 27. In my view the document cited as evidence is open to a very different reading. In such cases it is incumbent on the historian to discuss the quality of the evidence and the context of the document.
17. Cobbing, 'The Mfecane as Alibi', 504–6; 'Grasping the Nettle', 4–5. In the latter paper Cobbing claims further that in 1822–23 the main trading items moving through the bay were slaves. He cites as his sources 'the relevant evidence' in two volumes of G. M. Theal's *Records of South-East Africa*, without page references, and Fynn's *Diary*. The *Diary* is also cited in 'The Mfecane as Alibi' as a source of evidence for slaving at the bay (See note 101). The *Diary* is a source, like so many others, which Cobbing elsewhere (see, for example, 'The Mfecane as Alibi', note 120) thoroughly discredits. Dismissal of some of the major sources of the period as white 'forgeries', and subsequent citation of them, is a characterisitic feature of his argument, and is subject to two criticisms. The first is that such texts are significantly more complicated constructs, and are shaped by a more complex set of interests, than Cobbing allows. (See my more detailed discussion below of precisely the same problems in Cobbing's treatment of James Stuart.) The second is that, having indicted such sources, subsequent citation of them requires specific argumentation as to why they may be relied on in relation to a particular matter.

exports off the southern coast of Mozambique shot up, Delagoa Bay enjoyed pre-eminence as a supplier. His evidence for Delagoa Bay enjoying 'additional priority' in this period is a reference to a letter from Owen, captain of the *Leven*. In point of fact this letter does not assert that the slave trade at Delagoa Bay was especially active, but that it *might* become so in the future.

> The Port [Owen writes in 1823] is more convenient than any other for direct communication with Brazil, and if the temptation to make slaves *be* permitted to be held out to the natives, . . . they *will* cut one another's throats without mercy, and the whole country *will* be depopulated in a very few years [my emphasis added].[18]

The context of Owen's speculations and opinions regarding the slave trade are worthy of further consideration. This letter, and other of his communications,[19] take the form of strong motivations for the British government to oust the Portuguese from the southern Mozambiquan coast, as part of a strategy to secure British sea routes and the Cape colony. To this end, Owen emphasised the iniquities of Portuguese trading practices. In this context, his emphasis at one point on the relative lack of slaving at Delagoa Bay is noteworthy, an opinion not considered by Cobbing: 'There are,' Owen comments, 'very few slaves exported from this place.'[20] This remark demands Cobbing's consideration. Closer attention to specific sources, their tight periodisation and investigation of their contexts of production is clearly imperative in any attempt to assess the volume of the slave trade. They are essential prerequisites to the making of well-founded connections between the slave trade and wider regional politics and, more specifically, the trading activities of the Port Natalians.

Cobbing's argument that the Zulu, among others, were active slavers, is based on evidence even more tenuous.[21] The first source is the presence of Portuguese soldiers inland, on 'expeditions', which, Cobbing claims – without a shred of further evidence – 'can only have been for slaves'.[22] At the very least, Cobbing needs to consider the possibility that they were engaged in securing traffic in ivory and cattle, two items of trade extensively discussed in the work of earlier researchers.[23] The second source is evidence that Cobbing is in expectation of one day uncovering:

18. G.M. Theal ed., *Records of South-East Africa*, London, 1903, vol. 9, 37.
19. Theal, *Records of South-East Africa*, vol. 9, 32–5, 37–9.
20. Theal, *Records of South-East Africa*, vol. 2, 487.
21. Cobbing, 'Grasping the Nettle', 8.
22. Cobbing, 'Grasping the Nettle', 9.
23. D.W. Hedges, 'Trade and Politics in Southern Mozambique and Zululand in the Eighteenth and Early Nineteenth Centuries', Ph.D. thesis, University of London, 1978; A. Smith, 'The Trade of Delagoa Bay as a Factor in Nguni Politics, 1750–1835' in L.M. Thompson ed., *African Societies in Southern Africa: Historical Studies*, London, 1969, ch. 8.

> Other powerful Tsonga chiefs . . . had fearsome reputations and are likely to
> have been involved in the slave trade, although evidence has not yet come to
> my hand.[24]

Finally, Cobbing's argument regarding the slave trade as the context in which Port
Natal must be viewed is based on the level of warfare and violence in the region. This
is ascribed, without evidence beyond that already discussed above, to the
vicissitudes of raiding *presumably* for slaves'[25] (my emphasis). The teleology is
surely untenable, and casts serious doubts over Cobbing's methods more generally.
None the less, there are indications that some chiefdoms did trade prisoners taken in
war through Delagoa Bay, and this does warrant further investigation.[26] What is at
issue, and which remains to be established with any reliability, is the timing and
volume of this trade, and whether it was sufficient to constitute the slaving vortex
which Cobbing invokes as the appropriate context for the Port Natalians' activities.

What evidence does Cobbing present for involvement of the Port Natal traders
specifically in this supposedly vibrant regional slave trade? Cobbing sets the scene
by claiming that Port Natal was at the time of the traders' arrival 'already a fairly
well-known slaving port',[27] but gives no reference; of the traders' participation in
certain of Shaka's campaigns, he claims that 'there can be no doubt that these raids
were for slaves',[28] and again cites no evidence. Other scholars[29] have argued that
very different reasons underlay the traders' armed forays at Shaka's behest − such
as the growing insecurity of the Zulu rulers at this time leading Shaka to insist that his
clients, including the traders, provide military support − and again, it is incumbent
on Cobbing to consider these arguments.

Finally, Cobbing claims that '[s]hips calling at Port Natal in 1827–7 [*sic*] could
easily have taken out slaves'.[30] The claim is based on the arrival of ships at Port Natal
after the attacks (i.e. slave raids, in his terms) on the Ndwandwe and Khumalo. Not
only is there nothing to indicate that the traders returned to Port Natal with
prisoners,[31] but all evidence points to Shaka as controlling the timing of the two

24. Cobbing, 'Grasping the Nettle', 10.
25. Cobbing, 'Grasping the Nettle', 10.
26. See, for example, the comments on p. 48 of Fynn's *Diary* to this effect.
27. Cobbing, 'Grasping the Nettle', 26.
28. Cobbing, 'Grasping the Nettle', 27.
29. B. Roberts, *The Zulu Kings*, London, 1974, 100–3; C. A. Hamilton, 'Ideology, Oral Traditions and the
   Struggle for Power in the Early Zulu Kingdom', M.A. dissertation, University of the Witwatersrand,
   Johannesburg, 1986, 363.
30. Cobbing, 'Grasping the Nettle', 27.
31. Cobbing cites N. Isaacs, *Travels and Adventures in Eastern Africa, Descriptive of the Zoolus, their
   Manners, Customs, etc.*, ed. by L. Herrman and P. R. Kirkby, Cape Town, 1970, 95, and Fynn's *Diary*,
   128, as evidence that the traders took captives in raids against the Ndwandwe and Khumalo; 'Grasping
   the Nettle', note 215. Care needs to be taken in the interpretation of this evidence. Isaacs observes that
   when the Khumalo surrendered they agreed to 'give up cattle, and become tributary to the conqueror'.
   Isaacs goes on to comment that 'one of our seamen proposed that they should give ten young maidens
   by way of cementing their friendship by nuptial ties'. There is no indication that the women were given
   to the traders although it is not impossible. It is important to note that cattle with which the traders

attacks. One wonders how the traders managed to orchestrate the timely arrival of the two ships. In fact, the correlation in timing was not as neat as Cobbing claims it was. This Cobbing explains away as being the result of 'a scrambled chronology in Fynn's material . . . to prevent the historian from putting two and two together'.[32] No source of an alternative chronology is cited. In fact, Isaacs, another of the traders, confirms that the 'raid' cited took place in June 1826, while the arrival of the ship concerned can be dated to April 1826.[33] In other words, Fynn's chronology is borne out by other sources, and Cobbing's is incorrect. More importantly, at least one of the ships concerned was the *Helicon*, a British naval vessel!

Cobbing's persistent failure to consider the evidence against his case is the greatest weakness of his argument.[34] Although the evidence for the involvement of the traders in slaving activities is insufficient for it to bear the weight placed on it by Cobbing's argument, the possibility that the traders occasionally traded in slaves, and carefully eliminated all references to such activities, cannot be ruled out. Cobbing is right to stress that the traders' accounts of their activities cannot not be taken simply at face value. However, the manner in which historians seek to reread these accounts in search of inconsistencies and signs of cover-ups must itself be much more rigorous and cautious than is presently the case.

Furthermore, the assertion that the traders were heavily involved in slaving is inconsistent with the next element of Cobbing's argument, his claim that the traders, and their backers at the Cape, were keen to see the establishment of a colony at Port Natal: an official British presence would undoubtedly have nipped any slave trade in the bud.

It is my contention that not only is it unlikely that the traders were energetic slave hunters, but also that their lobby for the establishment of a colony at Port Natal only kicked off after 1828 in response to the changed circumstances that prevailed after the death of Shaka. Cobbing's misplaced assertion that the traders sought to persuade the British to annex the Natal region in the 1820s skews our understanding of contemporary relations between Port Natal and the Zulu kingdom. Cobbing posits that the desire to see a colony established in the Natal region was the reason for the

---

returned to Port Natal after this campaign, were not booty which they had seized, but a portion of the captured cattle awarded to them subsequently by Shaka. It seems likely that any captives taken in battle would also have gone directly to the Zulu king. The Fynn reference cited as evidence for the traders having taken captives in battle is even less conclusive. Fynn describes how, during the Ndwandwe campaign, Shaka interrogated a captured Ndwandwe mother and child, and then ordered them to be killed. Fynn then interceded on behalf of the child, asking that he 'might become my servant'. Although we have no way of proving it, this may well have been an opportunistic attempt by Fynn to acquire child labour, but it does not qualify as evidence of slave raiding.

32. Cobbing, 'Grasping the Nettle', note 217.
33. Isaacs, *Travels and Adventures*, 60; *Cape Town Gazette and African Advertiser*, 28 Apr. 1826.
34. Similarly, when he so suggestively draws our attention to the fact that after leaving Natal, one of the traders, Nathanial Isaacs, went on to become a slaver elsewhere, he should also tell us that another member of the trading party, John Ross, alias Charles Rawden Maclean, later in life became an avid *anti*-slaver. S. Gray, 'South African Fiction and a Case History Revised: An Account of Research into Retellings of the John Ross Story of Early Natal', *Researches in African Literature*, 19, 4 (1988), 473–4.

traders' obsessive discussions of the depredations of the Zulu king. While it is clear that after the assassination of Shaka at least some of the traders were eager to see the establishment of a colony, and that by that time they were unanimous in describing Shaka as a tyrant, in 1824–5, neither case prevailed. If Cobbing's attribution of motives to the traders is somewhat problematic, so is his argument that they demonised Shaka to promote their dual aims of slave trade and colonisation. In fact, the image of Shaka presented by the traders between 1824 and 1830 was nearly always benign – with two exceptions.

Cobbing describes Farewell's expedition as 'a large colonising party' which landed 'in the hope of creating a *fait accompli* for the only slightly interested Cape Government'.[35] Farewell's report to Somerset in 1824 contains references which, taken at face value, may lend themselves to this interpretation.[36] Farewell noted the circumstances of a 'grant' of land to the traders by Shaka, and described conditions conducive to settlement. He suggested that these benign conditions would provide a 'few families' from the distressed settler community in the Cape with a 'comfortable assylum [*sic*] . . . as a colony'. When placed in context, these comments resist interpretation as an insistent campaign for the colonisation of the Natal area.[37]

The context includes that of Farewell's preoccupation with creating a viable base for his trading venture. The small Port Natal community was experiencing a crisis over the cultivation of agricultural products for their own consumption, as well as a shortage of labour more generally.[38] While there is nothing to indicate that the traders feared Shaka, Farewell was sensible of the small settlement's vulnerability, and of the need for the traders to operate from a secure and relatively self-sufficient base. It was on Farewell's agenda to establish clearly in the minds of the Zulu the extent and nature of the traders' power and commercial interests.[39] Moreover, by September 1824, 20 members of the original party had left Port Natal, and still another 10

35. Cobbing, 'The Mfecane as Alibi', 490; 'The Myth of the Mfecane', 11–12; The *fait accompli* idea originates in the work of Roberts, *The Zulu Kings*, see p. 138 in particular. As evidence, Cobbing cites Farewell's first communication with Somerset, without noting that Farewell was not approaching Somerset but *responding* to a query from the Governor; he also cites Fynn's comments that in retrospect he realised that Farewell was going to stay longer than he said, but the remark does not necessarily connote a campaign for colonisation. Neither is the latter borne out by Farewell's contracts regarding the ships, which were for 15 months only. ((CA) NCD 35/9, 573–8 Notarised Affreightment Declaration, between James Gosling and F. G. Farewell, 15 Apr. 1824). In his discussion of Farewell and King's motives for going to Natal, Fynn makes no mention of colonisation.
36. (CA) CO 211, 650–1, Farewell to Somerset, 6 Sept. 1824. Cobbing does not, however, cite this document.
37. While I do not consider Farewell's aim in 1824 to be the establishment of a colony at Port Natal, I do recognise that Farewell was careful to try and secure official Cape recognition and support for his commercial venture. I am grateful to J. Wright for discussion on this point.
38. Lt. E. Hawes to C. R. Moorsam, Commodore of the British fleet at the Cape, 16 May 1825, (CA) CO 233, 245–6. For the published report see the *Cape Town Gazette and African Advertiser*, 4 June 1825.
39. Isaacs, *Travels and Adventures*, 15, 22, 24, 42, 52, 53, 71; also see King's comments, *South African Commercial Advertiser*, 11 July 1826; Farewell to Somerset, 6 Sept. 1824, (CA) CO 211, 650–1; also see correspondence between the commander of the *Helicon* and the Cape administration regarding the first Zulu visitor to the Cape (CA) CO 270, 202–4.

desired to go.[40] Farewell's suggestion that a 'few families' could prosper in the Natal region was not a move to encourage formal colonisation, but rather an attempt to maintain at Port Natal the infrastructure necessary for the prosecution of trade.

It would be equally problematic to read off from Farewell's claim to have received a land grant from Shaka a desire for British intervention in Natal.[41] Farewell had successfully negotiated access to the area around Port Natal with Shaka, although obviously not on the terms or in the form in which he represented it in his report. The 'grant' at this stage offered no inducement to colonisation in and of itself, but it did serve to underwrite the security and stability of the trading venture, and appealed to Farewell's backers in the Cape. In fact, the report of the grant was sent first to them, and then forwarded to Somerset.[42]

In the meantime, the traders enjoyed greater success in their trading activities than in the subsistence sphere. They acquired ivory directly from Shaka, from the Mpondo country and from the inhabitants in and around Port Natal.[43] In a report that was subsequently published in the *Cape Town Gazette and African Advertiser*, Lieutenant Hawes, the officer commanding the *York*, which called in at Port Natal in May 1825, observed that the traders were 'living on the best terms of friendship with the natives and under the protection of king Inguos Chaka', who, he noted, 'professes great respect for white people'. As Hawes reported, 'The success of the party in their mercantile speculations is believed to be the extent of their expectations.'[44]

But small storm clouds were gathering on the Port Natal horizon: Hawes also commented on the traders' lack of a boat and supplies.[45] Since their arrival in Port Natal, the traders had only once been able to use the *Julia* to replenish their supplies and transport their ivory before it was lost off the Natal coast. The cargo lost in the wreck of the *Julia* was worth more than its insured value. Coming on top of the previous losses (see p. 188), this latest disaster almost certainly meant that Farewell was beginning to experience financial pressures on top of his supply problems.[46]

It was at this point that James King re-entered the picture. Although he had been

40. (CA) CO 233, 103–4, J. Hoffman and J.S. Peterssen to Moorsam, 9 Mar. 1825.
41. Cobbing, 'The Mfecane as Alibi', 490.
42. (CA) CO 211, 650–1 and 656–7, Farewell to Somerset, 6 Sept. 1824.
43. Isaacs, *Travels and Adventures*, 18, 22, 31; Fynn, *Diary*, 110, 117.
44. (CA) CO 233, 245–6, Hawes to Moorsam, 16 May 1825. For the published report see the *Cape Town Gazette and African Advertiser*, 4 June 1825. Hawes's report was passed on to the Cape Governor, Somerset, (CA) CO 233, 244. Note also, for example, that when Farewell's backers, Hoffman and Peterssen, lost contact with him as a result of the wreck of the *Julia* in late September 1824, they were dilatory in contacting the authorities, and once they did, expressed no alarm on behalf of the party at Port Natal; (CA) CO 233, 103–4, Hoffman and Peterssen to Moorsam, 9 Mar. 1825. The authors of this letter comment that they returned from Natal because 'the country and natives were different from what was told them'. In the *Diary*, Fynn indicates that Peterssen was disappointed to find that Shaka's residence was not built out of ivory, and, being corpulent and temperamental, that he was not fitted for the rigours of Shaka's kingdom (ch.5). Also see Moorsam's comments about their dilatoriness, Moorsam to Hoffman and Peterssen, 17 Mar. 1825, encl. (CA) NCD 25/11, 765–83.
45. Hawes, *Cape Town Gazette*, 4 June 1825.
46. (CA) CO 233, 247; (CA) Hoffman and Peterssen to Moorsam, 9 Mar. 1825; (CA) CO233, 103–4, NCD 35/11, 765–83 and enclosures; (CA) NCD 35/9, 573–8.

on the earlier exploratory voyage with Farewell, he had done so in the latter's employ. He struggled to raise the necessary capital for a venture independent of Farewell.[47] In the loss of the *Julia*, however, King saw an opportunity for entering into the trade at Port Natal. The motivation for Cape capital to back him at this point consisted of two parts: the first was the commercial calculation that by arriving with much-needed supplies and a vessel, King would be able to take over the sea transport aspect of the trading venture, if not actually insert himself into the Port Natal trade itself; the second was the representation of the endeavour as the humanitarian succouring of Farewell's party supposedly cut off for some time from the colony.[48]

King's expectations were dashed when his vessel, the *Mary*, was wrecked on entering the bay at Port Natal in October 1825, and its cargo lost.[49] King's party suddenly found themselves entirely dependent on Farewell, even for their sustenance. Undaunted, King tried another tack. The new arrivals set up camp in a separate area of the bay and immediately set about building a ship. Their aim was not to be able to quit the shores of Natal, which they could have done on any one of a number of ships that called in at Port Natal during their sojourn there. Rather, the building of the ship offered a means of recouping losses and of gaining a hold over Farewell who still lacked access to a much-needed vessel.[50]

However, the building of a boat was a lengthy undertaking. Isaacs's account makes it clear that King's party, of which he was a member, soon began to run short of provisions. They had nothing much to trade for supplies, while Farewell's party was constrained to husband its resources. After King's first visit to Shaka, together with Fynn and Farewell, the traders came away with 107 head of cattle; one solution to the problem of supplies was to survive by Shaka's patronage. This King initially tried to do by salvaging gifts for the king such as the *Mary*'s figurehead, but when ingenuity in this area ran out, his party was faced with a stark choice: either to be cut off from Shaka's patronage or to become Zulu clients – a course of action which King realised involved military services.[51]

While the party hesitated over this issue, their conditions declined still further. It was at this time that relations between Shaka and the traders became especially strained, with the Zulu monarch seizing ivory which Fynn collected, apparently

47. (CA) GH 1/39, 45–58, King to Bathurst, 10 July 1824; Farewell to the editor, *South African Commercial Advertiser*, 31 Jan. 1829.
48. None the less, King's expedition was not heavily capitalised, and drew on credit as well as special concessions from the authorities. (CA) CO 3929, 136–9, King to Somerset, 9 Aug. 1825; also the response from the colonial authorities, CO 4853, 393, 409, Sir Richard Plasket, Chief Sec. to the Govt. to King, 12 Aug. 1825; also see CO 3929, 184–5; CO 243, 147–52; CO 235, 511–12; CO 4853, 453; CO 293, 1323–6.
49. Isaacs, *Travels and Adventures*, 13, 18.
50. Isaacs, *Travels and Adventures*, 25, 60; also see Farewell's comments in the *South African Commercial Advertiser*, 31 Jan. 1829; (CA) GH 1/39, 45–58, King to Bathurst, 10 July 1824. In fact, the building of a boat at Port Natal had been on King's agenda from the first, and to that end, he had taken with him to Port Natal the necessary tools and a shipwright.
51. Isaacs, *Travels and Adventures*, 60, 64, 66.

without royal permission.[52] Thus when, in April 1826, the *Helicon* arrived at Port Natal, King took passage aboard in order to proceed to the Cape to obtain a new cargo, leaving his comrades in what Isaacs describes as a 'miserable situation'.[53]

Cobbing argues that the traders promoted a negative image of Shaka at the Cape in order to encourage British intervention in Natal in the form of colonisation.[54] Although he generalises their source and timing, the images to which he refers arise out of this and a subsequent visit by King to the Cape.

Reports of the traders' circumstances which immediately preceded King's arrival in the Cape, and indeed, his own initial remarks, contain no negative references to Shaka or the Zulu. 'The natives' were described as 'harmless' and as behaving 'extremely well'.[55] So satisfied was the colonial administration with the intelligence at its disposal for Natal and the attractiveness of conditions there, that they had no hesitation in sanctioning proposed visits to the Natal area by botanists, missionaries and the like.[56] Thus, when King arrived in Port Elizabeth in April 1826, both the general public in the Cape and the colonial authorities had only heard praise of Shaka.[57] In his first public comments, contained in an article in the *South African Commercial Advertiser*, King continued in this vein, describing Shaka as obliging, charming and pleasant, stern in public but good-humoured in private, benevolent and hospitable.[58]

In the meantime, however, King's attempts to raise money for another ship and a cargo failed.[59] He was thus obliged to approach the colonial authorities for

---

52. *Cape Town Gazette and African Advertiser*, 6 Jan. 1826.
53. A section of King's party, under Norton, the mate of the *Mary*, gave up the shipbuilding exercise, and in defiance of King, departed for the Cape in the wrecked ship's longboat. Those who remained behind began to find it impossible to obtain food or porters without invoking Shaka's name as a threat. Things became particularly severe in the period immediately prior to the traders' crops being ready for harvest, Isaacs, *Travels and Adventures*, 27–8, 38, 41, 42, 47, 57, 64, 67–70; *Cape Town Gazette and African Advertiser*, 6 Jan. 1826 and 28 Apr. 1826; (CA) CO 293, 97–100, report of the mate of the late brig *Mary*, J.E. Norton, to Plaskett, 19 Jan. 1826.
54. The argument that the two stereotypes – 'depopulated Natal and Shaka-the-monster' – were designed to encourage settlement and British involvement in Natal is in itself not convincing. Both stereotypes can be seen as disincentives for colonisation. A good or better case can be made to the effect that the very opposite stereotype – a stable and orderly Zulu society under the firm hand of a powerful king on the borders of the proposed colony and the existence of a plentiful supply of labour, preferably rendered docile by the conquering Zulu (especially in the face of the turbulent Cape frontier and that colony's labour problems) – would have constituted a significantly more powerful inducement to the British authorities. However, even had the traders wished to encourage settlement, they could not have argued that labour was plentiful, for it was not.
55. (CA) CO 293, 97–100, Norton to Plaskett, 19 Jan. 1826; *Cape Town Gazette and African Advertiser*, 28 Apr. 1826.
56. See the requests of C.H. Wehdemann, 8 Nov. 1824, CO 2659, 693–4; granted 9 Nov. 1824, CO 2659, 691–2, 695; CO 4851, 487; (CA) Archives of the Magistrate of Uitenhage, (hereafter UIT) 15/9, 247 and James Whitworth and Samuel Broadbent, 4 Mar. 1825, CO 230, 375–8; and the response, CO 4852, 488, for permission to proceed to Natal.
57. *Cape Town Gazette and African Advertiser*, 6 Jan. and 28 Apr. 1826.
58. *South African Commercial Advertiser*, 6 June 1826.
59. In May King attempted to negotiate the purchase of a schooner on a two-thirds mortgage. Pointing out that his finances were precarious, King sought colonial aid with the financing by stressing that his object was to assist his wrecked crew, or failing aid, he requested the use of a government vessel. King

assistance. In his appeal he resuscitated the claim that he wanted to succour those left behind.[60] When he heard on 7 June that even this appeal had failed, King chose a new approach. In an article on 11 June in the *South African Commercial Advertiser*, King, for the first time, represented Shaka as a 'despotic and cruel monster'.[61]

On the basis of the threat posed by Shaka to the apparently vulnerable 'castaways' at Port Natal, King succeeded in rallying sufficient support to fit out another vessel, the *Anne*, for a 'rescue' mission, and, in this way, he returned to Port Natal with a cargo of trade items, and Mrs Farewell.[62] As Brian Roberts notes in a much-neglected study that focuses on the contradictions between the traders' pronouncements of Shaka's murderousness and their actions, Mrs Farewell's inclusion in the party makes 'one suspect the disparity between King's words and actions'.[63]

Thus King's second article in the *South African Commercial Advertiser*, which stands in marked contrast in content and style to his first, cannot be seen as a bid to encourage colonisation, nor as yet another instance in a stream of 'mendacious propaganda' about Shaka; it must rather be read as a highly specific strategy pursued at a particular moment. This image of Shaka contradicts his own earlier statements, as well as to the reports of the other traders, notably Farewell. The Cape authorities, however, clearly set little store by King's latest intelligence on Shaka, and continued to sanction trips to Natal.[64] Indeed, within months, King himself was obliged to try and repair the damage by convincing his backers in Cape Town that Shaka, although a despot, 'to do him justice, is for a savage the best-hearted of his race'.[65]

With King's cargo-laden return to Port Natal, the situation of his party improved dramatically.[66] But conflict immediately erupted between Farewell and King. The tensions between the two groups which prevailed before King's first trip to the Cape, and the open conflict which ensued after his return, are ignored by Cobbing in his arguments about the image of Shaka, but have implications for the specific views of

was not allowed to bring ivory with him on the *Helicon* from Port Natal, despite Mrs Farewell's request to the governor to allow an exception. (CA) CO 293, 619–22, King to Plaskett, 2 June 1826; (CA) CO 235, 946–9, Elizabeth Farewell to Somerset, 27 Dec. 1825. Amongst other things, King also heard at this time of the failure of another of his schemes to come to fruition. See (CA) GH 23/7, 401, concerning his lease on the Bird and Chaun islands. Note that the Ordnance storekeeper at the Cape was pressing his backer, Collison, for debt settlement, while Collison himself was petitioning the Lieutenant Governor of the Cape for relief, see (CA) CO 293, 1319; CO 219, 1317–18.

60. (CA) CO 293/138.

61. *South African Commercial Advertiser*, 11 June 1826; note that this is the same description that is ascribed to Farewell in J. Bird comp., *The Annals of Natal: 1495 to 1845 . . .*, vol.1, reprint Cape Town, 1965, 93, and which was quoted in G. Thompson, *Travels and Adventures in Southern Africa*, Cape Town, 1967, vol.1, 174–5.

62. On 22 July 1826, King, with the backing of one William Hollett, hired from John Thompson (Farewell's agent in the Cape), the *Anne*, and on the same day appointed Thompson his agent as well, (CA) NCD 25/14, 145–55, 156–9; (CA) NCD 25/11, 765–83.

63. Roberts, *The Zulu Kings*, 98.

64. Application by George Rennie and response, (CA) CO 293, 911–12; (CA) CO 4895, 60–1.

65. King to 'T', presumably Thompson, May 1827, published in *The Colonist*, 3 Jan. 1828.

66. Isaacs, for example, was able to resume the collection of curiosities, an endeavour he had been obliged for some time to forgo because of the lack of trade goods. See Isaacs, *Travels and Adventures*, 70–1.

the Zulu king which the traders subsequently promoted. Even writers on the affairs of the traders who have taken note of the split have failed to find a satisfactory explanation.[67] This is because the available evidence is not especially illuminating. Isaacs, one of the major sources on the quarrel, noted that it was over 'matters of a pecuniary nature', and elaborated on a particular tussle between the two over the question of under whose name trade goods sent to Shaka would proceed.[68] Farewell, in a letter to the *South African Commercial Advertiser* in January 1829, claimed that King had undermined him and attempted to exclude him from the trade.[69]

While it is difficult to say with any certainty what underlay the conflict, these remarks are consistent with the thesis that King had proceeded to the Cape on the understanding that he would there procure trade goods on Farewell's behalf, if not on his own as well. This enabled him to tap Farewell's superior credit at the Cape.[70] All along, it had been King's aim to enter the Port Natal trade on terms more advantageous to himself. Initially these had collapsed when he lost all his cargo in the wreck of the *Mary*. On his return to Port Natal in October 1826, King sought to hold Farewell to ransom over the question of supplies.

Farewell refused to co-operate with King, as did John Cane and Henry Ogle of his party, although Fynn, previously one of Farewell's party, now began to play an increasingly independent role. Again, the reasons for this are not hard to find when the trading, rather than colonising, interests of the traders are focused on. Fynn was one of the most active among the traders, particularly in the area south of Natal. He would have had none of Farewell's objections to 'buying' supplies from King, if not exchanging ivory for them, and perhaps a greater need for fresh supplies.

As has been argued above, the greatest difficulties experienced by the Port Natal traders concerned the maintenance of a direct import/export route to and from the Cape. The seas between Port Natal and the Cape are unusually treacherous,[71] while the financing of ships for the task involved considerable expense, a problem exacerbated by the succession of losses and the difficulty of negotiating the sand bar at the entry to Port Natal.[72] One option investigated by King was the location of an alternative port. The other was the opening-up of a route overland.[73] It was at this

67. Roberts, *The Zulu Kings*, 99, 103–4. Roberts suggests that King wanted to take over Farewell's grant of land from Shaka, but cites no evidence for this. Note that Cobbing's treatment of the split is confined to a discussion of divisions on the eve of Shaka's assassination, 'Grasping the Nettle', 28.
68. Isaacs, *Travels and Adventures*, 75–6.
69. Also see the report in the *South African Commercial Advertiser*, 27 Dec. 1828.
70. See note 62 above.
71. J.K. Mallory, 'Abnormal Waves on the South East Coast of South Africa', *International Hydrographic Review*, 51, 2 (1974), 99–129.
72. King faced an added problem when his shipwright downed tools. For evidence of continued problems of supply, see the journey of 'John Ross' to Delagoa Bay, and the traders' bartering for supplies with the *Buckbay Packet*. Isaacs, *Travels and Adventures*, 101, 102, 117.
73. See John Cane's deposition, 10 Nov. 1828, in which he asserts that Shaka 'wished government to procure him a road that his people might come along with their sticks in their hands without assegaay or any other weapon to see the white people' and that Shaka said 'he would send no more ivory by sea but would collect some and send them to Faka's kraal [en route to the Cape]. . . and deliver them to an officer who should be sent down and from whom he would expect a present in return . . .', (CA) GH 19/3, 388–415.

time that King and Fynn (the trader with the most southerly base) began actively to pursue a plan to open up a direct southern connection with the Cape.[74] This, I would argue, was the logic underlying King's next journey to Port Elizabeth with two ambassadors from Shaka, and the attacks at much the same time by Shaka and Fynn on the communities of Africans living in the area between the southern reaches of the Zulu kingdom and the colony.

This series of events has also been misinterpreted and little understood largely because of the obfuscation caused by the thesis that the traders desired to use Shaka's southern campaigns to generate fear at the Cape and in that way to push the British authorities into establishing a colony in Natal. John Wright argues that King went to the Cape to get recognition for his latest land concession from Shaka, and 'to agitate for the establishment of some kind of British authority at Port Natal to give his claims effect'.[75] In fact, King did not raise the issue of the land grant until 29 July 1828, that is, over two months after his arrival at the Cape, and, significantly, at the lowest point in his negotiations with the authorities. He used the grant to claim for himself the authority to negotiate on Shaka's behalf, something the authorities were expressly trying to avoid. Had King's primary objective been to obtain land grant recognition, he would surely have brought the original (or a supposedly original) document with him, but he did not. Instead he made a copy from memory – or so he claimed, for the existence of the original, and of an original land grant, was later strenuously denied by another of the traders, John Cane.[76]

King's plan, it seems, was less ambitious. A more likely reconstruction of his objectives at this time is that he aimed to have Shaka support Fynn in clearing the way between Port Natal and the colony; by establishing Zulu authority in the area – possibly at first through local chiefs forced to recognise a loose form of distant Zulu rule, and if necessary, the extension over time of a more direct form of Zulu administration – conditions more conducive to the prosecution of trade would be created. But King knew, of course, that any attempt by Fynn and Shaka to subdue the intervening communities would cause alarm at the Cape.

Shaka seems at this time to have started to work more closely with the traders than before. He began to supply the traders with ivory directly and eased the restrictions on their other trading initiatives.[77] He was interested in developing the southern reaches of his kingdom for other reasons. With the defeat of the Ndwandwe in 1826, the bulk of the Zulu army was freed for redeployment in the south. It has also been argued that internal disaffection at this time placed Shaka in a position of wanting to cement and monopolise the relationship with the traders, themselves based in the south. When Shaka mooted a plan to send ambassadors to the Cape so as to consolidate his position within the kingdom, King immediately agreed.[78]

74. By this time, moreover, Fynn's family had set up base in Grahamstown.
75. Wright, 'Dynamics', 358.
76. See G.H. 19/3, 473–5 and 376–84.
77. See, for example, Fynn, *Diary*, 131.
78. Isaacs, *Travels and Adventures*, 71; King to 'T', presumably Thompson, 27 May 1827, published in the *South African Commercial Advertiser*, 3 Jan. 1828.

The Cape's Shaka

The first move in the preparation of informed opinion at the Cape for the plan to open the overland route was the release by the traders' backers in Cape Town of a letter from Port Natal for publication in the *South African Commercial Advertiser*.[79] In the letter, King praised Shaka, spelled out his plan for a southern campaign and stressed that Shaka's intentions towards the colony were peaceful. Thus, if anything, when King set sail in the recently completed *Elizabeth and Susan* for the Cape, he did so with the aim of promoting a positive image of Shaka. On his arrival at Port Elizabeth on 4 May 1828, he continued to stress 'the friendly disposition of Chaka towards our nation', and the absence of any threat to the colony from Shaka's latest campaigns.[80]

However, King had made a significant miscalculation. In the period between his first (1826) and second (1828) visits, the colonial administration's policy shifted from a concern with the opening-up of new markets and strategic bases beyond the colony to one of stabilising the independent frontier chiefdoms and containing expansion. By late 1827 Bourke stated that official policy was

> to maintain those situated immediately on our front in possession of their country as long as by their friendly and peaceable conduct they prove themselves deserving of our protection. This will be easiest and cheapest way of preserving the colony itself from plunder and disquietude . . .[81]

In terms of this policy, the colonial authorities could not countenance Shaka's campaigns on or near the borders of the colony.[82] By the time King came to compose a detailed written statement for the authorities on the purpose of the Zulu embassy, he was acquainted with the new policy. In his statement he stressed the urgency of sending one of the ambassadors back to Shaka as soon as possible to apprise Shaka and Fynn of this unexpected policy shift. To his injunctions for speed, King added the puzzling comment that he had left hostages in Shaka's hand to guarantee the safety of the Zulu ambassadors. It is clear from the operations in the Mpondo country, of one of the claimed hostages, Fynn, that this was not the case.[83] However, King's claim lent an added impetus to the urgency of returning a messenger to Shaka, at the same time obscuring Fynn's role in a southern campaign which was increasingly showing the possibility of coming into direct confrontation with the British. It also contrived to suggest that the traders' role in Shaka's campaigns was

---

79. King to 'T', presumably Thompson, published in the *South African Commercial Advertiser*, 3 Jan. 1828.
80. (CA) GH 19/3, 30–3, King to J. van der Riet, Civil Commissioner, Uitenhage, 10 May 1828.
81. (CA) GH 23/8, 298–304, Richard Bourke to Lord Viscount Goderich, 15 Oct. 1827.
82. By 9 May, King had been in contact with military officials in Port Elizabeth from whom he would have learnt of this policy. See (CA) GH 19/3, 35–6, Commandant F. Evatt to Lt. Col. Somerset, 9 May 1828.
83. See the discussion in Roberts, *The Zulu Kings*, 129–36.

forced upon them.[84] Once this report was submitted, King waited to see whether his communication regarding Shaka's peaceful intentions towards the colony would result in a change in policy.

King was also waiting for the registration of the *Elizabeth and Susan* to be completed by the Port Elizabeth port authorities. He anticipated that the boat, once registered, would either begin plying regularly between Port Natal and the Cape, thus alleviating the supply problem, or alternatively, if disposed of, would provide him with the necessary capital to obtain a new cargo and transport it to Natal. During May, King was optimistic on both counts. His statement of Shaka's friendly intentions had filtered through to the frontier, while on the basis of his positive intelligence regarding Shaka, the authorities sanctioned the expedition of Messrs Cowie and Green to the Zulu kingdom. Likewise, the press assured the general public that there was nothing to fear from Shaka.[85]

When, however, it appeared that the registration of the boat might be in jeopardy, and the Cape authorities, already tardy in responding to the embassy, appeared to want Shaka to bring his campaign to a halt, King attempted, once again, to use the threat of Zulu hostility to achieve his ends. He declared that if his craft was not registered he would not risk sending it back to Natal with the one Zulu ambassador whose arrival Shaka was anxiously awaiting. If Shaka did not hear from his ambassador, he continued, the safety of the colony could not be guaranteed.[86] The threat fell on deaf ears.[87]

The colonial authorities refused to be drawn into what they recognised as King's machinations. A government representative, Major A.J. Cloete, was despatched to Port Elizabeth to circumvent King and to deal directly with the Zulu ambassadors. Cloete was instructed to inform the ambassadors that King enjoyed no status in the eyes of the British authorities.[88] Although at this time intelligence from the frontier indicated that Shaka's army was advancing on the frontier chiefs, there were no fears in the official mind that the colony was the object of Shaka's attacks.[89] What they did fear was that a war north of the frontier would send large numbers of refugees streaming into the colony. Cloete's subsequent discussions with the Zulus did not alter the picture of Shaka's intentions towards the colony as peaceful, and the tenor

84. King to Van der Riet, 10 May 1828; (CA) GH 19/3, 39–42, see also the emphases on haste, and in particular on the urgency of the return of one of the chiefs in King's anxious communication to Van der Riet, 24 May 1828; Fynn, *Diary*, 141, 153. Fynn subsequently made the same use of the hostage argument.
85. See (CA) CO 4888, 217; (CA) CO 4893, 249; (CA) CO 4895, 312–13; (CA) CO 359, 191–2, 198–9, D.P. Francis, Port Captain, to the Acting Secretary to Government, Lt. Col. Bell, 9 May 1828, and 23 May 1828; (CA) GH 19/3, 35–6, Evatt to Lt. Col. Somerset, 9 May 1828; *The Colonist*, May, June, 1828.
86. (CA) GH 19/3, 48–53, King to Bourke, 6 June 1828; (CA) GH 19/3, 66–9, King to Van der Riet, 6 June 1828; (CA) UIT 15/12, 45–7, Van der Riet to Bell, 7 June 1828.
87. (CA) CO 4322, 151–2. None the less Bell took sufficient cognizance of the threat to have the possibility of registration carefully checked out for a loophole. See (CA) GH 19/3, 54.
88. (CA) CO 4893, 255–357, Bell to Cloete, 14 June 1828.
89. Minutes of the Cape Council of Advice, 21 June 1828, A.C. 2, 453–60; (CA) GH 19/3, 88–9, Major Dundas to Bourke, 20 June 1828.

of the pertinent official correspondence over the next two months indicates that King's image of Shaka-as-monster had failed to take root. The policy of the colonial officials was to meet Shaka at the first possible opportunity and to explain their position with regard to the chiefdoms across the border, after which, they believed, he would withdraw.[90] Over the next two months, the Cape authorities only became more sceptical of King and what Cloete described as his 'determined perversion of facts'.[91] Likewise, reports in the press questioned the idea that Shaka was vengeful, describing him as 'amiable' and as a better diplomat than the British officials.[92]

King's strategies were by no means exhausted and, until his departure in August, he tried a range of other ploys to extort money out of the authorities as well as to shore up his position in the eyes of the Zulu envoys, but all these were blocked by the perspicacious Cloete. The latter also put considerable effort into exposing King's manipulations to the ambassadors, indicating that the British government dissociated itself from King and emphasising the colonial government's favourable disposition towards Shaka.[93]

Perhaps King's most outrageous manoeuvre was to approach the Chief Commissioner for Uitenhage, Van der Riet, in an attempt to circumvent Cloete, and on the basis of reports of Shaka's imminent advance on the Xhosa chief Hintsa, to offer to broker an accord between Shaka and the colony. With this ploy, King tried for the last time to invoke a threatening Shaka, claiming that if he did not intervene, both the Port Natal settlement and the colony would be attacked by the Zulu. Once again, the authorities remained unconvinced, with justification it seems, for in the same week, King was claiming Shaka as a 'friend of nearly three years' to whose 'humanity and kindness' he owed a great debt.[94] By August, as the situation on the frontier deteriorated, the colonial administration deemed it best to return the envoys to Shaka

90. See (CA) Archives of the Magistrate of Albany (hereafter AY) 8/79, 193–6, 189–99, Somerset to Dundas, 15 June 1828; (CA) GH 19/3, 85–7, W.J. Shrewsbury to Somerset, 12 June 1828, Somerset to Bell, 20 June 1828; (CA) GH 19/3, 88–91, Dundas to Bourke, 20 June 1828; and (CA) GH 19/3, 92–5, deliberations of the Council of Advice in Cape Town, 21 June 1828; (CA) CO 4888, 270–1, Bell to Dundas, 21 June 1828; (CA) GH 19/3, 96–103, Cloete to Bell, 27 June 1828. Also see (PRO) CO 48/124; (CA) GH 19/3, 92–5; (CA) CO 4888, 274–5.

91. Cloete to Bell, 11 July 1828, GH 19/3, 159–66. The colonial authorities were extremely suspicious of King and his motives in bringing the chiefs to the colony. They were also alert to the contradictions and shifts in the account of things that he promoted. See (CA) UIT 15/12, 45–7, Van der Riet to Bell, 7 June 1828.

92. *The Colonist*, May-July 1828.

93. (CA) GH 19/3, 125–6, King to Cloete, 4 July 1828; (CA) GH 19/3, 126–7, Cloete to King, 4 July 1828; (CA) GH 19/3, 115–24, Cloete to Bell, 4 July 1828; (CA) GH 19/3, 167–8, Cloete to King, 5 July 1828; (CA) GH 19/3, 169–172, King to Cloete, 5 July 1828; (CA) GH 19/3, 174–7, Cloete to King, 10 July 1828; (CA) CO 4895, 336, Bell to King, 11 July 1828; (CA) GH 19/3, 159–166, Cloete to Bell, 11 July 1828; (CA) GH 19/3, 212–15, King to Cloete, presumably 18 July, 1828; (CA) GH 19/3, 216, Cloete to King, 18 July 1828; (CA) GH 19/3, 248–63, Frances to Bell, 25 July 1828; (CA) GH 19/3, 258–63, Cloete to Bell, 29 July 1828; (CA) GH 19/3, 264–71, King to Cloete, 29 July 1828; (CA) GH 19/3, 198–203, Cloete to Bell, 18 July 1828; (CA) GH 19/3, 272–3, Cloete to King, 30 July 1828; (CA) GH 19/3, 274–81, King to Cloete, 30 July 1828; also see (CA) CO 4894, 18–19; (CA) GH 19/3, 178–81; (CA) CO 4893, 265–7, 291–2.

94. (CA) GH 19/3, 178–81, King to Cloete, 11 July 1828; (CA) GH 19/3, 206–9, King to Van der Riet, 13 July 1828.

with assurances of friendship and a clear statement of their determination not to countenance his southern attacks. The embassy, including King, was returned to Natal aboard a naval vessel, the *Helicon*. After their departure, the press continued to report favourably of Shaka. When British forces thought, mistakenly, that they had engaged the Zulu, an editorial in *The Colonist* accused the commanding officer, Dundas, of 'gross violation of the law of nations'.[95]

In fact, so 'civilised' was the press's view of Shaka, that it was speculated that he must be 'of white extraction'.[96] In the same edition one correspondent commented perceptively on the problem of interpreting Shaka:

> The character and objects of Chaka it is not to be expected should be favourably represented by the tribes he had ruined, or threatened to destroy, and considerable caution is therefore requisite in weighing the evidence only procurable through prejudiced channels; from sources of this kind the Invader is declared a determined, a systematic, and a practiced plunderer, raising no corn, breeding no cattle, and procreating no children.[97]

The same reservation was true for King's representation of Shaka, and, indeed, was widely held.

Thus, it is clear that my reading of government documents and press reports of the period is very different from that of Roberts,[98] whose account of wholesale panic at the Cape in response to scares about an invasion by Shaka is the root of Cobbing's mistaken periodisation of the image of Shaka.

On the mission's return to Port Natal, Shaka received the reports of his ambassadors, including the chronicle of King's deceits and manipulations, as well as the messages from the British authorities. Incensed by King's duplicity and foolishness, and anxious that he had come close to provoking the British into battle, Shaka promptly despatched a member of Farewell's camp, John Cane, overland to the Cape to affirm his peaceful intentions and his compliance with British requests. He also asked for an official British agent to the Zulu kingdom.[99] Through Cane Shaka stressed that he 'was no longer disposed to molest the frontier tribes of Caffers' and that his aim was 'free intercourse with the colony'.[100] The Cape authorities were highly receptive to this latest embassy and in November the *South African Commercial Advertiser* reported its belief that the 'frightful stories' sometimes told about Shaka were 'mere fabrications'.[101] As far as informed opinion at the Cape was concerned, in 1828, Shaka was no monster. Nor, for that matter, had there been anywhere a call for the Natal area to be colonised.

---

95. *The Colonist*, 26 Aug. 1828.
96. *The Colonist*, 19 Aug. 1828.
97. *The Colonist*, 19 Aug. 1828.
98. Roberts, *The Zulu Kings*, chs 2–6.
99. Isaacs, *Travels and Adventures*, 133; *South African Commercial Advertiser*, 31 Dec. 1829.
100. Report of Sir Lowry Cole, G.H. 23/9, 39–47.
101. *South African Commercial Advertiser*, 15 Nov. 1828.

Shaka Posthumously

Unbeknown to the *South African Commercial Advertiser* and its readers, however, both James King, the opportunistic purveyor of rumours of Zulu attack, and Shaka, the king who-was-not-a-monster, were already dead. The former died mysteriously on 7 September, and the latter was assassinated on 24 September. Cobbing argues on the basis of circumstantial evidence that Fynn was behind the assassination of the Zulu king.[102] The timing and circumstances of these deaths is odd, and Cobbing is correct to question the conventional interpretations. But his evidence for Fynn's involvement is not conclusive, and in his preoccupation with European agency and European sources Cobbing fails to take account of Zulu oral tradition on the event, in which there is no hint of involvement by Fynn. Oral traditions are notoriously permeable to such information, while the succession practices of local northern Nguni-speakers – which preclude an assassin from succeeding to the office of his victim – would have placed a high premium on the revelation by the contenders for the succession of any involvement by Fynn and Farewell. It should be noted, moreover, that the traders' response to the assassination was defensive. They improved their fortifications at Port Natal, readied their boat for an emergency departure and, indeed, Farewell and Isaacs left soon thereafter for Port Elizabeth.

It was only *after* the death of Shaka that the traders began for the first time to talk about the colonisation of Natal and consistently to employ a rhetoric critical of Shaka.[103] Their monopoly over the Natal trade, which had prevailed since 1824, was finally coming to an end. Their successful promotion of conditions in Natal had stimulated others to follow in their footsteps.[104] The traders had not yet established relations with the new Zulu king in the way that they had with the old, and circumstances in Natal in early 1829 were more volatile and less predictable than ever before. The traders had attempted repeatedly to make a go of the Natal trade on their own, and had failed. By 1829, and under these circumstances, colonisation offered the traders an excellent opportunity for making good their by now quite considerable losses. It was at this time that Farewell raised capital against his land grant in expectation of the rapid development of Port Natal.

The vilification of Shaka that began at this time was as specific to the conditions which prevailed in early 1829 as King's remarks in 1826 and early 1828 were specific to his particular circumstances at the time. On his return to the Cape, Farewell faced accusations that he had fought in the Zulu armies – an allegation not without substance. The thrust of his defence, an argument which was subsequently taken up by Fynn and Isaacs, was that the traders had been threatened by Shaka and

---

102. Cobbing, 'The Mfecane as Alibi', 512–13; 'Grasping the Nettle', 28–9.
103. See (CA) GH 19/3, 579–80, Farewell to Bell, 19 Feb. 1829; (PRO) CO 48/133, Farewell to the Chairman, Committee of the Commercial Exchange, Cape Town, 3 Mar. 1829; (CA) CO 3941, 403–4, S. Bannister to Bell, 28 Mar. 1829, and a host of other applications by Bannister. (PRO) CO 48/13 Note also the changed tenor of Farewell's communication to J. Barrow of 15 Mar. 1829.
104. (CA) CO 4895, 350, Bell to Mr Benjamin Green, 22 Aug. 1828; (CA) CO 3937, 323–4, Green to Bell, 11 Aug. 1828; (CA) CO 357, 400–1, Farewell to Bell, 4 Dec. 1828.

forced to participate in the campaigns.[105] At this point, precisely because the Zulu king was dead, the traders could malign Shaka to provide an 'alibi' for their own actions without undermining their own representations of the stability of conditions in Natal. In support of their case against Shaka, they drew on a stock of stories with which they had become acquainted in Natal, stories garnered from African informants.

Moreover, the traders were also aware that they could no longer monopolise the image of Shaka that prevailed at the Cape to the extent that they had previously done. The British authorities had resolved to send the agent requested by Shaka, and were highly suspicious of the traders. In addition, numerous other parties in the Cape announced their intention of proceeding north to the Zulu kingdom.

When these various groups arrived in Natal, they found that the image of Shaka as a tyrant which was gaining ground in the Cape in 1829 was strongly echoed in Zulu society. 'Shaka-the-monster' was no more the 'invention' of the traders in 1829 than it had been before that. Nor was a negative view of Shaka the only image that prevailed in Zulu society in 1829. Resistance to Shaka's assassin and successor, Dingane, ensured the continuity of positive productions of Shaka. It is to a brief examination of the various African productions of Shaka that the next section of this essay turns, so as to challenge another of Cobbing's generalisations: his view that there is, at best, a single 'Zulu' voice, that 'it' presented a view of the Zulu past that was essentially unchanged between 1820 and 1900, if not the present, and that white views of Shaka were impervious to that view.

Zulu Productions of Shaka in the 1820s
Domination and Resistance in the Zulu Kingdom under Shaka

Sometime before about 1820, in a controversial accession, Shaka kaSenzangakhona took over the leadership of the Zulu chiefdom with assistance from the local paramount power, the Mthethwa. The latter were subsequently defeated by the Ndwandwe, and, some time before the first traders arrived at Port Natal, the Zulu forces, considerably enlarged and reorganised, themselves repulsed an Ndwandwe attack and ultimately participated in the break-up of the Ndwandwe kingdom.

When the traders landed at Port Natal in 1824 they entered a relatively young and highly hetereogeneous polity which the new Zulu leaders were in the process of consolidating into a centralised state. But this process of centralisation was far from smooth. The new Zulu rulers faced opposition from within the ruling house that was to culminate in the assassination of Shaka in 1828. These internal disputes were, however, overshadowed by the ruling house's struggle to assert its hegemony in the wider region and to maintain Zulu ascendancy over neighbouring chiefdoms. In the mid-1820s, Zulu overrule was by no means well-entrenched. In particular, the Zulu rulers faced rebellion in two of the largest chiefdoms subordinate to their rule:

---

105. *South African Commercial Advertiser*, 27 Dec. 1828, 31 Jan. 1829; (CA) GH 23/9, 39–47, Farewell's report; (CA) GH 1/15, 665.

among the Qwabe in the south and the Khumalo in the north. Another festering sore was the Lala tributaries on the southern periphery close to Port Natal. Zulu control over these areas was maintained only with difficulty by a combination of force and persuasion. There were thus great inequalities within the Zulu kingdom, deep-seated divisions and considerable disaffection. Even after the collapse of Khumalo resistance in 1826, Shaka's position was by no means secure.[106]

Ongoing resistance in the areas mentioned, and smaller outbreaks of rebellion elsewhere, prompted continued coercive responses from the Zulu authorities. These included merciless campaigns and stern sentences for individual rebels. The effect of these actions was to invest Shaka with a reputation for harsh and arbitrary action. On the one hand, the Zulu authorities fostered this image through carefully managed displays of despotism and brutal justice at court, using terror as a basis for absolute rule across a huge kingdom. The displays were not designed only to inspire obedience from their subjects, they were also meant to strike fear into the heart of their enemies and to impress the traders with Zulu power.

This despotism was justified by the other component of Shaka's image, that of a leader of tremendous abilities, the great unifier and the hero in battle. Both components of this image are present in his praises. The Zulu king was reputedly one of the authors of his own representation, collecting praises that he liked for himself. According to the informant Mbokodo kaSokhulekile, Shaka took for himself the praise 'The one whose fame resounds even as he sits', after he heard it used in respect of the Mbo chief, Sambela.[107] Stuart's informant, Jantshi, recalled his father, Nongila, one of Shaka's most trusted spies, describing the Zulu king as a successful conqueror, but also one who frequently caused people to be put to death.[108] Nongila claimed that Shaka fed people to the vultures, but linked such acts to the maintenance of authority and discipline in the Zulu kingdom.[109] He related how Shaka would cut off a man's ears if he did not listen, i.e. obey, and he would pick out anyone wounded in battle and kill him for being a coward, for running away.[110] But as much as a reputation for harshness served Shaka's purposes, and was promoted actively by his supporters, so too did it form the basis of opposition to his rule. Qwabe accounts of Shaka vilify him as a tyrant, and Lala accounts depict him as a marauder, a destroyer and a 'madman', *sans* caveats about the maintenance of discipline.[111]

By 1826 the traders were firmly inserted in the Zulu kingdom, and were closely involved in the extension of Zulu rule south of the Thukela. They encountered these different views of Shaka in a range of contexts such as at his court in circumstances

106. King to 'T', presumably Thompson, 2 May 1827, in *The Colonist*, 3 Jan. 1828.
107. C. de B. Webb and J. B. Wright, eds, *The James Stuart Archive of Recorded Oral Evidence Relating to the History of the Zulu and Neighbouring Peoples*, Pietermaritzburg and Durban, 4 vols 1976– , vol. 3, 15, Mbokodo.
108. *James Stuart Archive*, vol. 1, 195, Jantshi.
109. *James Stuart Archive*, vol. 1, 195, Jantshi.
110. *James Stuart Archive*, vol. 1, 195, 201–2, Jantshi.
111. *James Stuart Archive*, vol. 2, 232, Maquza; vol. 3, 55–6, 65–7, Mcotoyi.

of his making, or through their independent contacts with the Qwabe, Khumalo, Cele and Mbo. They also heard reports of Shaka's depredations from elements of the African community at Port Natal who had previously been driven from their territories by Shaka.[112]

Shaka's supporters and opponents thus shared certain images of the Zulu king, and contested others. All these, and the struggles between them, and their shifting content in response to changing conditions, both during the reign of Shaka and subsequently, as well as the way in which they intersected with the views of the Port Natal traders, have been ignored by Cobbing. As a result, he has mistakenly concluded that 'Shaka-the-monster' was invented as a settler 'alibi'.

Listening for the Voices of Domination and Resistance

Cobbing is oblivious to these processes because he collapses the different, contending versions into a single 'Zulu voice', that, in recorded form, he conceives of as being contaminated.[113] Herein lies the reason for Cobbing's failure to come to grips with African views of Shaka. For Cobbing, there are none yet extant. He is deaf to the cacophony of conflicting images of Shaka contained in sources like the *James Stuart Archive*, for he dismisses them as fundamentally 'tainted' by their recorder. For Cobbing, Stuart, more than any other single writer, was responsible for the creation of the image of Shaka that sits at the heart of the mfecane stereotype. The *Archive*, in his view, is poisoned not only by Stuart, but also by earlier white writers of Zulu history who shaped the range of 'historical fantasies' that informed Stuart's approach, and, indeed, is further adulterated by the present editors.[114]

Cobbing is guilty of two significant oversights in his evaluation of the *Archive* and his discounting of its many Shakas. The first is that while it is indeed true that Stuart was fascinated by Shaka – he delivered dozens of lectures in Natal and in London on the subject of the Zulu monarch, and constantly directed his informants on to the topic of Shaka – the range of variant opinions in their statements, and the extent to which these statements differ from Stuart's own versions, are a strong indications of their integrity.[115]

The great well of bitterness towards Shaka, for example, which permeates the entire testimony of an informant like the Qwabe woman, Baleka, was no mere response to Stuart's promptings. The Qwabe chiefdom was in rebellion for much of the reign of Shaka and was subject to brutal repressive measures. Baleka's father, Mpitikazi, nearly lost his life at Shaka's hand. Baleka noted the details of Shaka's persecution of the Qwabe, and recounted a host of gruesome tales told to her by her

112. Fynn, *Diary*, 65–6, 130; Isaacs, *Travels and Adventures*, 18, 19, 24–6, 32, 37, 41, 63, 67, 70, 78, 83, 89–90, 140.

113. This view of Zulu oral tradition is spelt out at length by Cobbing in a review article on the *James Stuart Archive*, entitled 'A Tainted Well: The Objectives, Historical Fantasies, and Working Methods of James Stuart, with Counter Argument', *Journal of Natal and Zulu History*, 11 (1988), 115–54.

114. While Cobbing dismisses Stuart's informants' versions of Shaka, he does concede that the *James Stuart Archive* may yield historical data, 'Tainted Well', 116–17.

115. Stuart never published anything on Shaka beyond the accounts in his four Zulu readers, *uBaxoxele*, *uTulasizwe*, *uHlangakula* and *uVusezakiti*, London, 1923–26.

father on topics such as the inhumanity of Shaka, his wanton cruelty –
including stories of the cutting open of a pregnant woman, and the feeding of human
corpses to the vultures.[116] Her judgement of Shaka was harsh:

> That man used to play around with people. A man would be killed though he
> had done nothing, though he had neither practised witchcraft, committed
> adultery nor stole.[117]

For Mpitikazi and Baleka, Shaka was best summed up by this one of his praises, 'The
violently unrestrained one who is like the ear of an elephant'.[118] Finally, for them,
Shaka, who refused to father children, and whom they credit with having killed his
own mother for concealing a child of his, was an animal. 'A person like Tshaka is
like a wild beast, a creature which does not live with its own young, its male
offspring.'[119]

Secondly, Cobbing fundamentally misunderstands Stuart when he describes him
as 'a representative and influential product of an unpleasant generation', whose
'thought exemplifies the pathologies of colonial society . . .'[120] In fact, investigation
of the vast residue of the unpublished Stuart papers – his private correspondence,
draft manuscripts, and his notes to himself – reveals that Stuart was disenchanted
with prevailing 'native policies', that he objected to labour levies and the
dispossession of people from their land, and that he evinced a powerful commitment
to giving Africans a say in their own affairs, to allowing them to be heard in their own
words. In significant ways, Stuart was painfully at odds with the prevailing
sentiments of his fellow colonists. In terms strongly reminiscent of modern scholars
concerned with the view 'from below', yet also captive to the discourse of his times,
he objected to the keystone of paternalism:

> This question of the contact between the civilized and uncivilized races
> receives its expression almost entirely from the civilized themselves. The
> whole controversy is an *ex parte* affair – conducted by the civilized against
> one another, instead of by civilized and uncivilized. The uncivilized man's
> voice is never heard. In any case, it cannot be detected amidst all the Babel of
> talk that is constantly going on, most by people who know nothing of the
> situation as it is from the Native's point of view. In a question of this kind
> surely the voice of the people primarily concerned is of the greatest
> importance.[121]

---

116. *James Stuart Archive*, vol. 1, evidence of Baleka, especially 7–12.
117. *James Stuart Archive*, vol. 1, 12, Baleka.
118. *James Stuart Archive*, vol. 1, 8, Baleka.
119. *James Stuart Archive*, vol. 1, 8, Baleka.
120. Cobbing, 'Tainted Well', 120.
121. Killie Campbell Africana Library, Stuart papers, file 42, item xxi.

Cobbing claims that Stuart's motive for collecting so prodigious a body of oral tradition was to answer 'the central riddle [as to] how . . . the native [was] to be dispossessed of his land, set to work, administered, controlled, set apart, ordered around, treated as a child, impoverished, and dehumanised without the white man (and his wife) having their throats slit',[122] but this takes no account of the complexity of Stuart's career, nor of the highly contested development of colonial native policies of the early twentieth century and the tremendous ambiguity of the positions of their early formulators.

Full investigation of Stuart in such a way as to facilitate a proper reading of the recorded traditions merits detailed attention and is thus beyond the scope of this essay.[123] However, it is essential that we begin to challenge Cobbing's characterisation of Stuart's recording activities, as well as his wholesale dismissal of African versions of the past.

Cobbing is undoubtedly correct to reiterate Jan Vansina's seminal points concerning the need for scholars using information contained in collections of oral traditions to come to terms with the presences in the traditions of the collectors. But not only is Stuart's presence different from the stereotypical colonial functionary of Cobbing's depiction, the interests of the recorder of an oral text are not as all-determining as Cobbing supposes. Texts frequently say things over and above what their authors, their editors and even their 'collectors' intend. The informant from whom the tradition is recorded constitutes yet another presence, as do any interests which the informant and/or the collector intend the text to counter, avoid or neutralise.

Oral traditions thus require the reconstruction of their own histories. We need to know under what circumstances the oral text came to be transcribed, and by whom. We need to know all about the background, interests and experiences of the transcriber. We also need to know who the informants were, their backgrounds, interests and experiences. We need to establish how they gleaned the information provided, and we need to know all the same things about their sources. On the basis of all this information we need to make judgements about the production, its periodisation and its faithfulness in written form to the oral original. Where transmutations may have crept in over time we need to assess their likely content and scope. Finally, we need also to come to grips with the stylistic elements of the texts, the way in which their form changes over time, as well as with what is entailed in the transition from oral to written form.

Events internal to the Zulu kingdom were responsible for sharp debates over Shaka, not merely between his supporters and his detractors during his lifetime, but also subsequently as different Zulu interests drew on different Shakas to support

---

122. Cobbing, 'Tainted Well', 122.
123. For a further discussion of Stuart, see C. A. Hamilton, 'Authoring Shaka: Models, Metaphors, Historiography', Ph.D. thesis, The Johns Hopkins University, Baltimore, 1993, chs 7 and 8.

their actions in a changing world. In particular, different versions of Shaka emerged throughout the nineteenth century at times of succession disputes. Indeed, any attempt to discover the kinds of view of Shaka that prevailed in the 1820s in the Zulu kingdom must test the oral traditions for subversions or mutations that occurred subsequently.[124] With careful attention of this kind to the background and context of oral accounts, they can be used as sources of African views of Shaka and of Zulu history, and as such, cannot be ignored by historians seeking to understand the making of South African historiography.

Conclusion

This essay has shown that before 1829 the Port Natal traders were not trying to lure the British north using a vilification campaign against Shaka and the Zulu. 'Shaka-the-monster' and 'Zulu tyranny' had other sources. Both images, I have argued, have African origins. In the 1820s they were well-entrenched in the oral traditions of both Shaka's supporters and his enemies, although in different forms. In 1829, however, following his death, these images became for the first time the dominant images in both Cape Town and the Zulu kingdom.

History as Alibi; Alibi as Ideology

Cobbing is arguing a familiar case: that in South Africa, history is distorted to cover up past misdeeds and to legitimate conditions in the present. In that form, history becomes a component of the dominant ideology. The implication of Cobbing's particular 'case' is that this happens in a mechanical and reductionist fashion – that, to paraphrase his argument in a bald fashion for the sake of clarity, ideologues, in the guise of early travellers and later historians, 'invent' the version of the past that best serves white interests, and this 'invention' is then incorporated wholesale into the dominant ideology.

The argument presented in this essay is that like alibis, both histories and ideologies which are successful resonate in a body of information known to both their promoters and those whom they seek to persuade. Moreover, although any one version of the past may be the best known one, or any one ideology the dominant one, neither exists independently of other versions or views. Rather, the struggle between dominant and subordinate ideologies and versions of the past are part of each one's *raison d'être*.

New versions of the past, no less than the ideologies which they seek to underpin, must articulate different versions of the past in such a way that their potential antagonisms are neutralised and the argument is convincing. The various elements that make up a version of history that serves well any particular ideology must incorporate and neutralise the arguments of the opposition. Since any ideology is

---

124. For a detailed assessment of the various versions of the life story of Shaka that occur in the *James Stuart Archive*, and their dating, see Hamilton, 'Authoring Shaka', ch. 4.

always in a state of being struggled over, that is, is always 'in process', so too is the historical account constantly shifting to take account of the changing terrain of the struggle, the subtle elaborations and shifts in the argument of the opposition.

In ascribing the construction of a particular version of the history of early nineteenth-century southern Africa to settlers, and settler interests, and in assuming that once in place the 'alibi' thus established remained much the same into the present, Cobbing both misunderstands the relationship between history and ideology, and fails to come to grips with the full complexity of past processes of the construction of historical knowledge.

Acknowledgements

I would like to thank Gay Seidman, Philip Curtin, Norman Etherington, John Wright, Patrick Harries, Jürg Richner and Julian Cobbing for their comments on an earlier version of this article.

8 Matiwane's Road to Mbholompo
A Reprieve for the Mfecane?

JEFF PEIRES

The small and possibly smug world of precolonial southern African historians was rudely shattered in 1983 by the appearance of a brilliant polemic by Julian Cobbing entitled 'The Case Against the Mfecane'.[1] In a series of increasingly provocative papers and lectures, Cobbing challenged the existing conventional wisdom, first put forward by John Omer-Cooper in 1966, that the Mfecane was a 'revolutionary process of change from a single centre',[2] namely the rise of the Zulu kingdom. Omer-Cooper was much concerned to stress the Afrocentrism of his perspective. The Mfecane, he maintained, gave the lie to the view 'that African societies had no record of autonomous development . . . [The Mfecane] was essentially a process of social, political and military change, internal to African society and taking place with explosive rapidity.'[3]

Cobbing not only rejected Omer-Cooper's definition of the Mfecane, but he seriously questioned whether the event had taken place at all. He argued that the Mfecane was not an internally self-generated revolution occurring within northern Nguni-speaking society, but a convenient alibi, whereby succeeding generations of white historians rationalised and legitimated white seizure of black lands. The wars and dispossessions of the early nineteenth century were set in motion not by the rise of the Zulu state but by two chains of violence emanating from colonial aggression. One chain of violence, in the east, was initiated by Portuguese slave-trading from Delagoa Bay, which impacted directly on northen Nguni-speakers. Another chain of violence, in the west, was prompted by the labour needs of the Cape colony and augmented by the raiding activities of its armed and mounted surrogates, the Griqua.

It is not an exaggeration to say that the entire debate on the nature of southern African precolonial societies has been paralysed by Cobbing's intervention, and will continue to remain so until the crisis created by 'the Cobbing hypothesis' has been resolved. Fortunately, one of his articles has been published in an historical journal,

---

1. J. Cobbing 'The Case Against the Mfecane', seminar paper presented to the Centre for African Studies, University of Cape Town, 1983.
2. J.D. Omer-Cooper, *The Zulu Aftermath: A Nineteenth-century Revolution in Bantu Africa*, London, 1966, 7.
3. Omer-Cooper, *The Zulu Aftermath*, 168.

'The Mfecane as Alibi: Thoughts on Dithakong and Mbolompo',[4] thereby making it possible for serious historical debate to commence. I will confine myself to those aspects of 'The Mfecane as Alibi' which relate to my own area of specialisation, namely what became the eastern Cape/Transkei region. Much of what follows may seem negative and petty. It certainly lacks the broad sweep and wider political resonances which characterise Cobbing's work. But it is essential, I believe, after ten years of 'the Cobbing hypothesis', to get the debate down to specifics. And it does provide me with an opportunity to reassess the career of one of the most fascinating and under-studied figures in the history of South Africa: Matiwane, the chief of the Ngwane.

Matiwane is one of the forgotten men of South African history, but his ultimate failure does not permit us to ignore the power that was his in the days of his glory. Matiwane irrupted on to the highveld about 1822. He crushed the Hlubi, defeated the Tlokwa and compelled Moshoeshoe to pay him tribute. For five years or more, he dominated the southern highveld.

> Matiwane, the *gwalagwala* [lourie] bird with the red knees
> And the red eyes. He reddened his mouth
> By drinking the blood of men.[5]

In 1828, for reasons that are in dispute, Matiwane left the highveld and crossed the western extremity of the Drakensberg into the Transkei area. On 27 August 1828 he was utterly destroyed at the battle of Mbholompo by the combined forces of the Thembu, Xhosa and Mpondo kings, backed by the British army. Cobbing chose Mbholompo as a good case whereby the 'teleological and Afrocentric assumptions of mfecane theory' (p. 489) might be tested. It is as a test case that I will be reviewing Matiwane's road to Mbholompo; by means of it I hope to produce a concept of the Mfecane which is very different from Cobbing's.

The History of Matiwane

Since it is unlikely that the average reader will be aware of the rich African sources available for reconstructing the history of Matiwane, and since Cobbing – who is aware of at least some of them – has concealed their existence, it seems necessary to introduce them at some length.

Pride of place must undoubtedly go to the extraordinary oral tradition published in 1938 under the name of the *History of Matiwane and the amaNgwane Tribe, as told by Msebenzi to his Kinsman, Albert Hlongwane*.[6] Msebenzi, a grandson of

---

4. J. Cobbing, 'The Mfecane as Alibi: Thoughts on Dithakong and Mbolompo', *Journal of African History*, 29 (1988), 487–519.
5. N.J. van Warmelo, ed., *History of Matiwane and the amaNgwane Tribe as told by Msebenzi to his Kinsman Albert Hlongwane*, Pretoria, 1938, 63. My own translation, rather than Van Warmelo's somewhat euphemistic version.
6. Van Warmelo, *History of Matiwane*.

Matiwane, was born about 1850, some twenty years after his illustrious grandfather's death. His poetic talents were recognised while he was still a boy, and he was singled out by his father, the regent of the Ngwane, for training as an historian and praise-singer. About 1930 he paid a visit to his literate nephew, Albert Hlongwane, who transcribed the old man's traditions word for word. The text was subsequently translated and footnoted by Government ethnologist N.J. van Warmelo and published by the Department of Native Affairs in Pretoria.

This mode of publication, not unusual in the high colonial period, should not lead one to question the authenticity of the *History of Matiwane*. The text is entirely in Zulu, and is more than 100 pages long. Both the structure and the language of the narrative confirm its oral origins. It is full of repetitions, poetic images and archaic expressions, and includes 128 lines of Matiwane's praises. Van Warmelo, a Venda specialist, could not have fabricated any part of it, nor could he have had any conceivable motive for doing so.

The next most valuable source is 'The Story of the "Fetcani Horde" by One of Themselves', published in the *Cape Quarterly Review*.[7] The narrator is Moloja, a rank-and-file soldier of Matiwane. Unlike the *History of Matiwane*, this is not an oral tradition but an eye-witness account. Moloja fought against Shaka's Zulu at Ladybrand, and he participated in an expedition which reconnoitred the Transkei region the year before Matiwane's fatal decision to move south. He does not pretend to know anything about Matiwane himself, or about the councils of the chiefs, but he gives vivid and credible accounts of the events which he personally experienced. After the defeat of Matiwane, Moloja settled in Lesotho where he told his story to J.M. Orpen, a colonial official with a longstanding interest in African history. Although differences in wording do exist between the two printed versions of Moloja's text, these do not significantly affect the content of his story.

A third important source is 'A Little Light from Basutoland' by Nehemiah Moshoeshoe, the sixth son of the great Sotho king. This text was published in English,[8] but is based on a series of articles which first appeared in Sotho in *Leselinyana kaLesotho*. Matiwane is only one of the chiefs dealt with in Nehemiah's kaleidoscopic narrative, but the references are all the more valuable for being incidental and therefore obviously genuine. I have not been able to consult the numerous Sotho references to the history of Matiwane cited by P.B. Sanders,[9] but, judging from Sanders's text, they seem to be in general agreement with the other African sources detailed here.

'A Story of Native Wars' by 'an aged Fingo' named Platje Mhlanga[10] is another

---

7. The more complete version may be found in *Cape Quarterly Review*, 1, 2 (1881–2), 267–75. Differently worded extracts are quoted in D.F. Ellenberger, *History of the Basuto: Ancient and Modern*, London, 1912, 178–88 *passim*.
8. N. Moshoeshoe, 'A Little Light from Basutoland', *Cape Monthly Magazine*, New Series, 2, 10–11 (1880), 221–33, 280–92.
9. P.B. Sanders, *Moshoeshoe, Chief of the Sotho*, London, 1975, 30.
10. P. Mhlanga, 'A Story of Native Wars', *Cape Monthly Magazine*, New Series, 14, 84 (1877), 248–52.

eye-witness account, related by a Hlubi who served for a time in Matiwane's army. This text is relatively brief, but is still of historical interest as an independent confirmation of other sources.

More problematic is the account of 'The Amahlubi and the Amangwane' which W.C. Scully, the well-known magistrate and writer, composed for a series of ethnic histories which appeared in *The State*.[11] Scully's main informant was Dick Simanga, a half-brother of Matiwane, whom he interviewed in 1895. Alone of these five sources, this does not pretend to be a verbatim text and is liberally interspersed with Scully's own embellishments and assertions, some of them borrowed from G.M. Theal's questionable histories.

Whatever criticisms might be made of Scully's text, the other four African sources cannot easily be dismissed on the grounds of colonial influence or subjective bias. In each case the name of the original informant is known and the account is given verbatim in the informant's own words. The narratives of Msebenzi and Nehemiah, composed in Zulu and Sotho respectively, were obviously not susceptible to white influence. The other two appeared as isolated historical fragments in literary journals, and did not form part of any broader conceptual agenda by the white editors. The four texts are completely independent of each other, and each represents a distinct historical viewpoint: Ngwane royal (Msebenzi), Ngwane commoner (Moloja), Sotho (Nehemiah) and Hlubi (Mhlanga). Only one text (Msebenzi) is an oral tradition, subject to the normal distortions of oral tradition over time. Moloja and Mhlanga were participants and eye-witnesses of the events they describe, and Nehemiah got his information directly from participants and eye-witnesses. Nor do these African sources present a gilded or hagiographical portrait of Matiwane. As we shall presently discover, they depict him as a man who was capable of killing his brothers, betraying his army to the enemy and deliberately deceiving his people by concealing the reports of his spies. In sum, the four African texts on which the following section mostly relies are independent, consistent and reliable, and even if one cannot accept them at face value they should at least be taken into account.

Cobbing, however, makes no direct reference to any of these valuable sources. This is especially curious inasmuch as he is certainly aware of at least three of them. He refers to the archival documents which Van Warmelo appended to the *History of Matiwane*, but he does not use the *History* itself. He disparages D.F. Ellenberger's *History of the Basuto*[12] but he fails to mention that Ellenberger's version of Matiwane's story is explicitly drawn from Moloja and Nehemiah Moshoeshoe. The closest that Cobbing ever comes to acknowledging the existence of any of these African sources is footnote 110, which states:

> I do not regard the allegations either of Ellenberger or those in Van Warmelo as reliable. There is no evidence [of battles between the Ngwane and the Zulu or the Ndebele] from the Zulu or Ndebele sides. 'Zulu' meant any Nguni.

11. W.C. Scully, 'Fragments of Native History,' Parts 4 and 5, *The State*, (1909), 284–92, 435–41.
12. Ellenberger, *History of the Basuto*.

It is indeed an extraordinary turn of phrase to dismiss a 110-page Zulu text, probably the finest oral tradition ever recorded in the Zulu language, as an 'allegation'. There might not be any evidence of battles with the Ngwane from the Zulu or the Ndebele sides, though R.K. Rasmussen would disagree.[13] However, there is plenty of evidence from the Ngwane and the Sotho sides, and it would be absurd to argue that Moloja, who was personally engaged in these battles,[14] did not know whom he was fighting against.

Even if Cobbing does regard the five texts as unreliable, he has no right to conceal their existence. He has an obligation to discuss these texts and give reasons for his assessment. Unwary readers may well be predisposed to reject the 'allegations' of Van Warmelo (seemingly an Afrikaner) and Ellenberger (a missionary) as unreliable. They should not, however, casually dismiss the evidence of five authentic and unchallenged African witnesses.

Matiwane's Road to Mbholompo

Cobbing alleges towards the end of his article (p.509), that 'the Ngwane were first expelled from the Mzinyathi by the direct or indirect attention of the Delagoa Bay slavers'. He offers no evidence − indeed none exists − that the Delagoa Bay slavers ever came anywhere near Matiwane, so we must excuse the 'direct' part of 'direct or indirect attention' as a rhetorical flourish. In fact, Cobbing has nothing new to say about Matiwane's origins in the Natal region except that he lived on the Mzinyathi, which is a mistake.

Matiwane's home was on the White Mfolozi from which he was driven, possibly by the Ndwandwe leader Zwide, before the emergence of Shaka.[15] He fled south-west to Ntenjwa in the foothills of the Drakensberg, the original home of the Hlubi and the Zizi. This first invasion initiated his career as a conqueror and an overlord. Matiwane compelled defeated chiefs to give up their eldest sons and their fattest cattle in return for being left alone. The men were organised into age-regiments, but an ethnic hierarchy persisted and the Ngwane regarded the Hlubi as their 'servants'.[16]

When Shaka defeated Zwide and laid claim to sole authority in the northern Nguni-speaking region, Matiwane realised that he could no longer hold his ground. He decided to preserve his power by relocating it. According to Msebenzi, he explained his motivation as follows:

13. R.K. Rasmussen, *Migrant Kingdom: Mzilikazi's Ndebele in South Africa*, London, 1978, 55, states that 'Ndebele-derived evidence makes it clear that he [Matiwane] fought − and was defeated by − subjects of Mzilikazi.' Unfortunately, I have not been able to check Rasmussen's references.
14. Moloja, 'Fetcani Horde', 269–70. Every one of the five sources mentions the Zulu attack on Matiwane. See also footnote 20 below.
15. The sources are contradictory. Van Warmelo, *The History of Matiwane*, refers to a conspiracy between four chiefs, including Shaka, Dingiswayo and Zwide, to fall upon 'that little fly', 20; Moloja, 'Fetcani Horde' refers to an attack by Ndwandwe, the father of Zwide, 268.
16. On the relationship between Matiwane and his subject chiefs, see the crucial texts in Van Warmelo, *History of Matiwane*, 22, 46. On the Ngwane view of the Hlubi as their servants, see Moloja, 'Fetcani Horde', 268; and Mhlanga, 'A Story of Native Wars', 250.

> I am retiring in order to be further removed from Shaka, that he may not get at
> me while still well fed, it were better that he reach me when hungry. I shall
> climb over the mountains and get to the top and settle there.[17]

Strangely enough, he said nothing about the direct or indirect attentions of the
Portuguese slavers at Delagoa Bay.

Cobbing maintains that the interests of Matiwane and the other 'black groups' on
the highveld were essentially complementary. 'The Ngwane', he argues, 'expanded
more as a defensive organisation than an offensive one'. (p. 508) This view of
Matiwane's activities would certainly have surprised Chief Mpangazitha of the
Hlubi, whom Matiwane killed, Chief Sikonyela of the Tlokwa, whom he defeated,
and Chief Moshoeshoe, who was forced to pay him tribute.[18] It would also almost
certainly have offended Matiwane himself, who enjoyed being praised as the
gwalagwala bird whose lips were reddened by the blood of men. The recorded
sayings of Matiwane, such as 'the nation I make war on goes hairless' (shaved heads
being a sign of mourning),[19] do not evoke a chief of defensive and pacific
disposition. We would do well to remember that it is not only white sources which
depict the Mfecane as a time of unbridled and indeed praiseworthy ferocity.

The crux of Cobbing's argument, however, lies not with Matiwane's sojourn on
the highveld but with his decision to leave it. Cobbing can find no direct evidence
bearing on this question, and resorts to speculation:

> What at this stage drove the Ngwane south? . . . Before I undertook research
> for this article, the hypothesis that Griqua–Bergenaar attacks from the west
> were responsible had occurred to me . . . the Ngwane were far more exposed
> where they were, west of the Caledon . . . The contemporary evidence fully
> backs this hypothesis. The conclusion is inescapable. The Ngwane . . . had
> the misfortune to run into the Griqua in the Caledon who attacked them from
> the west for Mantatees and cattle. (pp. 508–9)

We will look at the Griqua in due course. But one is constrained to remark that had
Cobbing conceived his hypothesis after doing his research rather than before it, his
results might well have been very different. In particular, if he had consulted the five
African traditions discussed above, he would have found that they are all agreed on
the reasons for Matiwane's move south.

Matiwane's power on the highveld remained unchallenged until approximately
February 1827, when it began to unravel with frightening rapidity. The first blow fell
with a Zulu attack, which is confirmed by all five traditions and by the French
missionary T. Arbousset.[20] The best explanation of this attack is that given by

---

17. Van Warmelo, *History of Matiwane*, 22.
18. Sanders, *Moshoeshoe*, 29–30, 37–8.
19. Scully, 'Fragments of Native History', 290.
20. Moloja, 'Fetcani Horde', 269–70; Scully, 'Fragments of Native History', 435; Moshoeshoe 'A Little
    Light from Basutoland', 224–5; Mhlanga, 'A Story of Native Wars', 251; Van Warmelo, *History of
    Matiwane*, 26–8; T. Arbousset and F. Daumas, *Narrative of an Exploratory Tour to the North-East of
    the Colony of the Cape of Good Hope*, Cape Town, 1968 (1st published in 1846), 307.

Nehemiah Moshoeshoe, whose evidence is all the more trustworthy inasmuch as it comes from a disinterested outsider. Nehemiah writes that Shaka was summoned by the Hlubi chiefs Mehlomakhulu and Sidinane, after Matiwane had killed their father, Chief Mpangazitha. Moloja gives a vivid picture of the fighting:

> The Zulus had crossed the Caledon. It was many days since our cattle were taken [by the Zulus]. We were as numerous as they; they and the cattle were scattered. We had reached Viervoet (Kolonyana). The great regiment (of the amaNgwane) proposed that we should go in a body. The regiment of the white shields (the married men) refused. They went on [alone]. They wanted to capture many [cattle]. Ho! When the first Zulu rushed at them shouting the hullabaloo, they fled. We the Ushee [regiment], we fought at Lady Brand. We fought well. We killed all the Zulus there. We were tired out . . . We met the Zulu army returning from chasing the regiment of the white shields. There we fought with them. There Dingaan himself was stabbed in the chest by that small party of ours. He was serving in that army of his brother Chaka.[21]

The Ngwane held their ground. but they were unable to prevent the Zulu taking most of their cattle. Shortly after this incident, Matiwane began to think of moving south. He sent two regiments, the uShiyi and the inTsimbi, to spy out the land of the Thembu.

Before they could return, however, the Ngwane had suffered another, even more decisive, setback at the hands of the Sotho king, Moshoeshoe. Matiwane had made his alliance with Moshoeshoe the cornerstone of his policy, but there were many of his councillors who distrusted the Sotho leader. Rumours spread that Moshoeshoe had doctored the presents he sent to Matiwane with a medicine that caused the Ngwane chief to love him. At the same time, the councillors argued, Moshoeshoe was conspiring with Shaka. The *History of Matiwane* relates the story of a delegation of Ngwane who visited Moshoeshoe, only to discover a delegation from Shaka already there:

> When we filled our hemp-pipes to praise you [Matiwane], we heard Shaka's praises being recited on the other side of the fence. That mSuthu of yours about whom we spoke to you all these days, where are our lies now? [referring to Matiwane's refusal to believe that Moshoshoe was plotting against him]. We asked you: What does that mSuthu mean by continually standing over you?

When Matiwane still refused to take action against Moshoeshoe, the Ngwane commanders called out the army on their own authority:

> Arm yourselves! For Matiwane has abandoned his responsibilities! His father is now that Moshoeshoe.[22]

21. Moloja, 'Fetcani Horde', 270.
22. Van Warmelo, *History of Matiwane*, 40–1.

The Ngwane armies advanced up the single road leading to Thaba Bosiu, but the Sotho rolled boulders down on them, and they were defeated with great slaughter. More surprising is the assertion in the *History of Matiwane*, confirmed by Moloja, that Matiwane warned Moshoeshoe of the impending attack, thus ensuring the defeat of his own army.[23] This astonishing story becomes less incredible once one understands that Matiwane was concerned not so much with helping Moshoeshoe as with destroying his own rebellious generals.

After this unnecessary defeat, Matiwane gathered together the survivors and demanded to know who had called out the army without his permission. But the princes of the blood were equally furious, and replied:

> They [those of royal blood] replied, 'It [the army] was called out by us, but as to those that you enquire about [killed in battle] they were killed by you, by you yourself . . .'
>
> And the indunas spoke in the same strain. They said, 'As for you [Matiwane], what hinders us from killing you? Do you think that amongst the sons of Masumpa [Matiwane's father] you are the only one, that we cannot make another son of Masumpa chief? You despise us and listen more to Moshoeshoe than to us.'[24]

The relationship between Matiwane and the rebel regiments was still deadlocked when further troubles descended on him from outside. Chief Mehlomakhulu had resuscitated Hlubi power, and defeated three Ngwane regiments at Moolmans Hoek. At the same time, a formidable new enemy, Mzilikazi, raided deep into the southern highveld.[25]

Meanwhile, the scouting expedition had returned from the Transkei region. They reported that the country was rich in cattle, but that they had not been able to capture any. Moreover the rigours of the journey had reduced them to such a state of illness and starvation that Matiwane did not dare allow them to return home until they had fully recuperated. For it is clear from the records that the decision to move south was Matiwane's alone, and that he forced the other Ngwane to accept it.

> The great men, our fathers, said . . . 'We have been fortunate, we have conquered others, and settled in a country, let us stay and eat corn. Chaka has come and turned back. Mosilikatze has come and turned back. If they come another day we shall devise some scheme and fight them well.' But the chief refused to listen.[26]

Matiwane's brother, Hawana, was even more emphatic:

---

23. Van Warmelo, *History of Matiwane*, 40; Moloja, 'Fetcani Horde', 272.
24. Van Warmelo, *History of Matiwane*, 43–5.
25. Moloja, 'Fetcani Horde', 272; Rasmussen, *Migrant Kingdom*, 55.
26. Moloja, 'Fetcani Horde', 272.

There? Where? We have come a long way, we are not going anywhere else. We have already built here. Has this fellow eaten a sheep's lung? It is he who has been sent to destroy our nation.[27]

Such an insult could not be tolerated by Matiwane, especially in the light of his generals' threat to 'make another son of Masumpa chief'. He sent an army against Hawana, his own brother. After two days of fierce fighting, the loyalists prevailed and Hawana was killed. Another brother, Madilika, had already been killed for similar reasons.[28]

Resistance to Matiwane's tyranny collapsed after the death of Hawana and Madilika. 'We had better go', said Matiwane's mother, 'or he [Matiwane] is certain to kill us all.'[29] And so the Ngwane moved south to their eventual destruction at Mbholompo.

The answer to Cobbing's question, 'What at this stage drove the Ngwane south?' is abundantly clear. It was none other than Chief Matiwane himself, against the evidence of his own spies and the wishes of his own people. It was Matiwane himself who drove his people south, even though he had to kill his own brothers first. Buffeted by external defeats and shaken by internal rebellion, the *gwalagwala* bird with the red knees clearly felt that the only means of rejuvenating his waning authority was a brand-new start in a brand-new country.

It would not have been difficult to make this point in a much briefer space, but I have chosen to tell the history of Matiwane at length because it demonstrates the unusually rich and rewarding extent of the African sources which Cobbing has chosen to ignore. These sources demonstrate that an Afrocentric approach is neither ideological nor teleological; on the contrary, it is the only approach which is permitted by the historical evidence. Matiwane's movements cannot be explained merely in terms of external enemies, black or white. They can only be explained by an understanding of the internal dynamics of the Ngwane kingdom.

But what of the 'contemporary evidence' which Cobbing maintains 'fully backs' his hypothesis? (p. 508)

The first point to make is that none of the intrusive 'Mfecane' groups which invaded the Transkei region before 1827 (referred to by Cobbing on p. 500) had anything to do with Matiwane. The descent of the Cape Drakensberg was an arduous task which precluded the possibility of a lightning raid in the Transkei area by any of the highveld chiefdoms. The Mfecane of the early 1820s had nothing to do with Matiwane, but was the work of wholly unrelated invaders who had entered the Transkei region directly from Natal. Reverend John Brownlee refers, for example, to an attack by the 'Ficani' on the Mpondo about the middle of 1824 at a place far distant from either the Ngwane or the British imperialists.[30]

27. Van Warmelo, *History of Matiwane*, 30. According to Van Warmelo, eating a sheep's lung was supposed to turn a warrior into a coward.
28. Van Warmelo, *History of Matiwane*, 30–44.
29. Moloja, 'Fetcani Horde', 272.
30. G. Thompson, *Travels and Adventures in Southern Africa*, Cape Town (1st published in 1827), 1967–8, vol. 1, 180. Curiously enough, Cobbing fails to mention this reference.

The most famous of these invaders were the Bhaca, under their redoubtable chief, Madikane.[31] The March 1825 attack on the Thembu, to which Cobbing refers (p.500), was most probably carried out by the Bhaca. The raiders are described as people 'who never rear cattle, nor sow corn, but slaughter and devour'. This description fits the Bhaca, but not the Ngwane. The location of the raiders, on the Tsomo River, and the date of the attacks likewise fit in better with what we know of Bhaca movements at the time.[32] It is also barely possible that the mysterious invaders were the Sotho-speaking Hoja, some of whom were driven out of the Tarka by a Boer commando in 1824.[33] Moorosi's Phuti also raided Boer cattle.[34] There is no evidence anywhere in Cobbing's sources that the 'Mfecane' of 1825 were the soldiers of Matiwane.

What of the Griqua–Bergenaar attacks from the west which, Cobbing suggests, drove Matiwane south into what is today the Transkei? I do not pretend to any special expertise on the Griqua, and it is beyond the scope of this essay to examine the battle of Dithakong. Available evidence on the Griquas of 1827–8 indicates, however, that they posed very little threat to Matiwane if – as is extremely unlikely – they had any contact with him at all. The Dithakong alliance between Andries Waterboer, Barend Barends and Adam Kok was a one-off marriage of convenience, never again to be repeated. Waterboer and Barends remained in the deepest north-west Cape, hundreds of kilometres removed from Matiwane, and Adam Kok, who settled at the abandoned mission station of Philipolis in 1826, was by far the weakest of the three. Kok's humble request for a renewal of the missionary influence against which he had initially rebelled indicates his desire 'to regain the advantages of respectability and a settled existence'.[35] And, even though the old spirit of hunting and raiding was not altogether quenched, neither Robert Ross nor Martin Legassick mention any contact between the Griqua and Nguni-speaking people during this period. By 1827 Adam Kok's Griqua numbered no more than 60 families, with 200 Kora and Sotho families subordinate to them.[36] Finally, it is by no means a foregone conclusion that

31. See A.M. Makaula, 'A Political History of the Bhaca from Earliest Times to 1910', M.A. dissertation, Rhodes University, Grahamstown, 1988. Also D.Z. Makaula, *UMadzikane*, Cape Town, 1966.
32. Madikane was killed fighting the Thembu and the Qwathi at Gqutyini in the present-day Engcobo district. This occurred about the time of a solar eclipse that can be dated to 20 December 1824, M. Rainier, 'Madikane's Last Stand,' (unpublished manuscript, 1982). The key text is a letter, W.H. Rogers to Major Forbes, 27 May 1825, G.M. Theal, comp., *Records of the Cape Colony*, London, 1897–1905, vol. 22, 429–39. In addition to the passage quoted above, Rogers refers to the invaders as people who burned their enemies alive in their huts at night. Bhaca rebels murdered Chief Sonyangwe by this means.
33. Thompson, *Travels and Adventures*, vol. 1, 179–80. W.H. Rogers to Major Forbes, 27 May 1825, Theal, *Records of the Cape Colony*, vol. 22, 430, states 'they have a great dread of fire arms and relate that some few of their tribe attempted to plunder some people to the westward who had them (firearms) and were repulsed'. This fits the Hoja better than the Bhaca, but in any case it should be noted that this text hardly indicates a mass explusion.
34. Moloja, 'Fetcani Horde', 271.
35. R. Ross, *Adam Kok's Griqua*, Cambridge, 1976, 21.
36. M. Legassick, 'The Northern Frontier to *c*.1840: The Rise and Decline of the Griqua People,' in R. Elphick and H.B. Giliomee, eds, *The Shaping of South African Society, 1652–1840*, 2nd ed., Cape Town, 1989, 394.

Adam Kok could have driven Matiwane from the highveld, even with horses and guns. Mzilikazi, who crushed Barend Barends in 1831, was not afraid of guns and had nothing but contempt for the Griqua and their ilk:

> [The Griquas] were only a pack of thieves, and destitute of courage, for in no instance had they ever stood, or could stand, the brunt of battle. He had always destroyed and driven them with a handful of men and the mere striplings of his army.[37]

The only army that he feared, Mzilikazi added, was that of the Zulu chief, Dingane. There is no reason to believe that Matiwane felt any different.

Cobbing cites three specific pieces of evidence in support of his contention that the Ngwane were driven south by the Griqua. (p.508) We will examine each in turn:

- In 1829 the Revd William Shaw was told by two of the prisoners taken at Mbholompo: 'They had seen when far to the north some white people with horses, which we suppose to have been some of the Griquas.'

One should note to begin with that it was Shaw rather than the prisoners who identified the 'white people with horses' as Griqua. Mpini, a grandson of Matiwane's brother who got the story from one of Moloja's contemporaries, told Van Warmelo that the Ngwane 'were unfamiliar with guns but had already seen horses a few times on the Vaal. They had belonged to Boers.'[38] It is therefore quite possible that the 'white people' referred to were indeed white people. But even if the 'white people' were Griqua, Shaw's informants said nothing about firearms or fighting, which one might suppose were more memorable than horses. Moloja, who fought at Mbholompo, states explicitly that 'we had never seen horses or mounted men before [Mbholompo], and were sore amazed.' It is clear from this that the uShiyi regiment, at least, never encountered the Griqua.[39]

Shaw's informants did add that 'their nation are fond of War, and for many years they had been moving over an immense extent of country and had conquered and plundered many tribes both of Caffres and Bootshuanas'. This is hardly in keeping with Cobbing's image of a passive group of Africans trapped in the transcontinental crossfire of interrelated European plunder systems. Finally, one should note that the 'prisoners taken at Mbolompo' were prisoners no longer. They had indeed been captured by the British troops, but, less than one year after their capture, they were free inhabitants of the Transkei region.

---

37. Rasmussen, *Migrant Kingdom*, 81–4. It is also worth noting that Moshoeshoe defeated the Kora and the Newlanders on an open field in 1850, even though these were accompanied by 800 Rolong and a British artillery unit. Sanders, *Moshoeshoe*, 72–4.
38. Van Warmelo, *History of Matiwane*, 263.
39. Quoted in Ellenberger, *History of the Basuto*, 188. W. Shaw, *The Journal of William Shaw*, ed. by W. D. Hammond-Tooke, Cape Town, 1972, 160.

- Bannister heard from other prisoners that the Ngwane had been repelled by the Griquas about two years since, and twice they sought for a place to rest.

Saxe Bannister (not Shane Bannister, as Cobbing calls him) was a British publicist who never went anywhere near Mbholompo. His information came not directly from 'other prisoners', as Cobbing states, but third-hand, from a British officer, who had heard it from some Khoi, who had spoken to some prisoners. In considering this text, it is pertinent to quote some other extracts which Cobbing preferred to ignore.[40]
    In discussing their origins, the prisoners reportedly said:

> They were first driven from their houses by Chaca several years ago; then repelled by the Griquas about two years since; and twice they had sought for a place of rest. The Tambookies, they assert, first attacked them without provocation.

They gave the following description of the aftermath of the battle:

> [The Xhosa and the Thembu] fell upon the women and children in the most inhuman manner imaginable . . . A few men and numbers of women and children fell into our hands. Many have requested our protection, being afraid to remain as the Caffres would kill them. I hear the boers have taken several to the Colony, and the remainder were escorted by a party of cavalry into the track of the dispersed Maceesas [i.e. Ngwane].

At another point in his book, Bannister described Lieutenant-Governor Richard Bourke in the following terms:

> It is impossible to describe a person better disposed towards the native people than Major-General Bourke . . . His benevolent intentions are proved substantially by his public acts.

This is the same Major-General Bourke whom Cobbing maintains sent an army across the Kei River and deliberately instigated a massacre, purely to extract labour for the colonial farmers.
    Cobbing cannot have it both ways. If he accepts Bannister's authority concerning a Griqua attack on the Ngwane, then he must also accept, on the same authority, that Shaka attacked the Ngwane, that it was the Thembu not the British who initiated the battle of Mbholompo, that the Ngwane women and children voluntarily accepted British protection, that the British soldiers escorted the majority of captives back to their people, and that Lieutenant-Governor Bourke was a sincerely humane individual. Any one of these admissions would destroy his entire case.

---

40. S. Bannister, *Humane Policy; or, Justice to the Aboriginees of the New Settlements*, London, 1968, (1st edition published in 1830), 156–59.

- Finally, Andries Stockenstrom referred to 'great atrocities' committed by Adam Kok's Griqua on 'black fugitives' – and he meant the Ngwane – in the upper Caledon.

Stockenstrom did not identify the 'black fugitives' in question, and Cobbing has no right to state with such assurance that 'he meant the amaNgwane'. The passage is taken from some unrevised autobiographical notes that Stockenstrom wrote in 1856, nearly thirty years after Mbholompo. It occurs at a point in his narrative where he is trying to rationalise his harsh treatment of the Griqua and the Khoi.[41] On the very page that Cobbing alludes to, Stockenstrom confuses Adam Kok's mission station of Philipolis with the Kat River mission of Philipton. Elsewhere, he refers to the 'Fetcani' of Mbholompo as a branch of the 'Mantatee [i.e. Sotho] hordes'. In short, the extract is the casual remark of a confused and elderly politician trying to justify himself. Since it is far from certain that he was even referring to the Ngwane, I think we may discard this text.

In addition to these three unsatisfactory texts cited by Cobbing, there are two other references to contacts between the Ngwane and the Griqua. The first comes from W.C. Scully's version of his conversation with Dick Simanga:

> To westward lay the waterless desert on whose hither fringe dwelt the cunning yellow men who rode swift horses and spat death from iron tubes. Matiwane had met and been worsted by the Griquas on one occasion when he led his haggard horde across the wide plains, in the hope of being able to find a haven on the banks of the Vaal.[42]

Expressions such as 'cunning yellow men' and 'haggard hordes' demonstrate conclusively that there is more Scully than Simanga in the above passage, but even if we take it at face value, it means only that the Griqua blocked Matiwane's path westward; even Scully does not suggest that the Griqua chased Matiwane south. The best clue to the occasional Griqua references in the history of Matiwane is provided by the missionary Stephen Kay:

> This young man [a former follower of Matiwane] informed me that he was with the Mantatees, when the Matlhapees and Griquas attacked and shot so many of them near Lattakoo [Dithakong]. This fact, therefore, indubitably shows that Matiwane's forces . . . formed a branch of that powerful host.[43]

Kay's inference is understandable, but obviously incorrect. Matiwane never fought at Dithakong. The value of the quotation is to demonstrate that the young man in question did not accompany Matiwane all the way from the Natal region but joined his army on the highveld. Matiwane's army was, after all, a composite entity of

---

41. A. Stockenstrom, *The Autobiography of the late Sir Andries Stockenstrom, Bart*, ed. by C.W. Hutton, Cape Town, 1887, vol. I, 213, 278–9. It is also possible that Stockenstrom was thinking of an incident in which he supported a group of San against the Griqua leadership. See Ross, *Adam Kok's Griqua*, 24.
42. Scully, 'Fragments of Native History', 437.
43. S. Kay, *Travels and Researches in Caffraria*, London, 1833, 299–300.

diverse origins which contained remnants of all the nations he had conquered – Zizi, Hlubi and Sotho. I would suggest that the scattered and insubstantial references to the Griqua originate not with Matiwane or the Ngwane proper, but with some of his followers who had fought against the Griqua before attaching themselves to the Ngwane chief. The tenuousness of the evidence – no names, no places, no anecdotes –clearly indicates that the Griqua did not play a significant role in Ngwane history.

It is not as though we lack an explanation for Matiwane's decision to depart from the southern highveld. Shaka's army had defeated him, and his alliance with Moshoeshoe was broken. A new enemy, Mzilikazi, had appeared, just as an old one, Mehlomakhulu, was reviving. Matiwane had killed two of his brothers out of jealousy, he had betrayed his own soldiers to the Sotho king, and he held the remainder of his followers in subjection by fear alone. Matiwane did not need the Griqua to push him out of the highveld: he had no reason to stay.

The British Attack

Even if Matiwane's Ngwane were not driven south by the Griqua, the possibility remains that Cobbing's second major hypothesis is correct, namely that the British attacked Matiwane at Mbholompo in 1828 for the express purpose of acquiring labourers: 'Driven into the Transkei, the Ngwane were at once set upon by the British who were raiding for "free" labour in the aftermath of Ordinance 49'. (p.509) It is therefore to the behaviour of the British authorities that we now turn.

Cobbing argues, on the basis of Susan Newton-King's article, 'The labour market of the Cape Colony, 1807–1828',[44] that an acute labour shortage 'threatened the whole British settler scheme, and with it economic development and "defence" on the eastern frontier'. (pp.493–4) With the failure of attempts to import white indentured labour, and with the prospect of slave abolition in the near future, the Cape Government proposed to meet the need by importing black labour from beyond the colonial boundary. This was illegal in terms of existing legislation until the Governor passed Ordinance 49 'for the Admission into the Colony . . . of Persons belonging to the Tribes beyond the Frontier, and for regulating the manner of their Employment as free labourers in the service of the Colonists'. Cobbing continues: (pp.501–2)

> Bourke urged London to agree to the Colony 'inviting' in not merely emaciated individuals . . . but 'whole tribes'. But would they come?
>
> This was a grim moment for Africa. It was the first time in British colonial experience anywhere that the dilemma of how to 'attract' free labourers, to work at very low wages and in perhaps appalling conditions, had to be faced.

---

44. See S. Marks and A. Atmore, eds, *Economy and Society in Pre-industrial South Africa*, London, 1980.

The passing of an Ordinance permitting 'invitations' was unlikely to have much effect. Later more thorough strategies were devised and perfected in the Cape to force out free labour . . . But in 1828 the only way to obtain 'free' labour was to send in an army and fetch it out. As soon as Ordinance 49 permitting the issue of invitations was safely drafted, Bourke seized on the news of the Zulu invasion as a pretext to send his armies across the Kei to bring out some more labour.

It is my contention that Cobbing's interpretation of British policy is just as erroneous as his argument that Griqua attacks drove Matiwane south. I will begin by analysing the labour policies of the Cape colony during the administration of Acting Governor Richard Bourke. I will then question the contention that 'the only way to get free labour was to send an army and fetch it out'. Finally, I will compare Cobbing's version with the events leading up to the battle of Mbholompo with the historical record.

British capitalism had long outgrown the smash-and-grab phase of primitive accumulation by the time that Matiwane headed south. Those were the days when the ardent free trader, William Huskisson was President of the Board of Trade, and the *laissez-faire* principles of Adam Smith were the conventional wisdom of Britain's commercial ruling classes. As far as labour policy was concerned, the anti-slavery movement was approaching its zenith, and Britain was moving rapidly towards a code of social relations in which voluntary submission took the place of coercion, where masters were urged 'to employ a system of encouragement in vigorous exertion, instead of the dark code of penalties against crime'.[45]

In southern Africa, the new thinking was embodied in the so-called Commission of Eastern Enquiry, appointed in 1822, to root out the mercantilist detritus of the former Dutch colonies.[46] They produced a series of wide-ranging recommendations designed to break the feudalistic hold of the Cape Dutch oligarchy; to liberalise production, trade and land tenure; and to create a rational and impartial bureaucracy capable of administering a free market economy. They vigorously condemned all forced labour practices, believing that these rendered the Afrikaner masters indolent and unenterprising and discouraged the Khoi working classes. They lauded the achievements of properly salaried Khoi artisans, and confidently anticipated that free Khoi would boost the economic prosperity of the Cape as soon as their disabilities were removed.

Acting Governor Bourke, appointed precisely on account of his known Whig (i.e.

45. J.P. Kay Shuttleworth, quoted in M. Rayner, 'Slaves, Slave Owners and the British State: The Cape Colony 1806–1834', *Collected Seminar Papers,* Institute of Commonwealth Studies, vol. 12, 1981, 16. The points that I am making above are commonplaces of all recent writing on the abolition of the slave trade. See, for example, J.C. Armstrong and N. Worden, 'The Slaves, 1652–1795', in Elphick and Giliomee, *Shaping of South African Society, 1652–1840,* 164.
46. I have discussed the Commission of Eastern Enquiry and the revolution in government in detail in J.B. Peires, 'The British and the Cape, 1814–1834', in Elphick and Gilomee, *Shaping of South African Society, 1652–1840,* 490–9.

liberal) sympathies was fully committed to this 'Revolution in Government'.[47] His closest associates were the Cape's leading liberals, the Reverend John Philip, Landdrost Andries Stockenstrom and Judge Henry Burton. Ordinance 49, which opened the Cape's borders to foreign labourers, and Ordinance 50, which abolished forced labour for colonial Khoi, were the products of this partnership. Since Cobbing has sneered at the notion of 'invitations' it is perhaps important to stress that these ordinances were not intended as positive injunctions but were conceived as permissive legislation, situated within the classical liberal framework of removing all the artificial and unnatural impediments which hindered the free operation of market forces. The two ordinances were promulgated within three days of each other, and were certainly intended to operate in tandem, to free the Cape labour market from its dependence on forced labour. Cobbing's interpretation of Ordinance 49 – that it was introduced to facilitate the forced importation of servile black labour – is incompatible with the provisions of Ordinance 50, which freed the Khoi within the colony from involuntary servitude. It is not reasonable to suppose that any colonial administration would undertake the risky and complicated task of forcibly recruiting untrained, untamed and linguistically incomprehensible foreigners in order voluntarily to release the docile and thoroughly domesticated labour force which it already had at its disposal.[48]

Cape Government officials stationed on the frontier wholeheartedly endorsed the viewpoint that African labour should enter the colony voluntarily and without coercion. It is significant that they gave practical rather than moral reasons for their opinions.[49] Landdrost Andries Stockenstrom of Graaff-Reinet was adamant that Africans should not be 'decoyed' or 'enticed' into the colony, as forced labour was bound to desert and it would endanger the security of the frontier districts. Landdrost W. Mackay of Somerset East thought that 'compulsion is totally out of the question' and that employers who attempted coercion risked their lives. He issued orders that foreign labourers who wanted to leave their employers should not be forcibly prevented from doing so.

But the most interesting opinion is that of W.B. Dundas, the Landdrost of Albany. Dundas administered the district where the 1820 settlers resided and the labour shortage was most acute. Drawing on his experiences with the Mantatee (i.e. Sotho-speaking) refugees, Dundas declared that any form of indenture would cause

---

47. Despite his title of 'Acting Governor', Bourke's appointment was not meant to be temporary. He was only so named because the appeal of his predecessor, Lord Charles Somerset, was still pending. See H. King, *Richard Bourke*, Melbourne, 1971.

48. Bourke was under no pressure at home or abroad to pass Ordinance 50. Newton-King's argument on p. 197 of 'The Labour Market of the Cape Colony, 1807–1828', in Marks and Atmore, *Economy and Society*, cannot be sustained. The reasons for the passage of Ordinance 50 are those which she gives on p. 198.

49. Newton-King, 'The Labour Market', 194; W. Mackay to R. Plasket, 20 Feb. 1827, Theal, *Records of the Cape Colony*, vol. 34, 271–3; W. Dundas to R. Plasket, 10 Apr. 1827, Theal, *Records of the Cape Colony*, vol. 34, 395–8. The only frontier Landdrost who approved of forced labour was the veteran J.C. Cuyler of Uitenhage, who was dismissed shortly afterwards on the recommendation of the Commissioners of Enquiry.

potential labourers 'to resist and leave us'. The relationship between settlers and Mantatees was mutually beneficial. On the one hand, the Mantatees were anxious to get cattle which they could no longer obtain in their own country. On the other hand, the settlers appreciated Mantatee labour, and their fear of losing it led them to treat the Mantatees relatively well. He himself employed Mantatee labour at a rate of four cattle per family per year, and he was fully satisfied with the results. Like his brother landdrosts, Dundas was convinced that it was absolutely impossible to police coerced labour in a frontier situation:

> When satisfied with their treatment, they are cheerful, obliging and obedient, and though hard labour . . . is irksome to them, they have no objection to make themselves generally useful; but on the contrary, if the naturally hasty temper of the savage is excited by ill usage of any kind, they become sullen and resolutely indifferent . . . they invariably leave their employers, and frequently the Colony altogether.[50]

It was this same W. B. Dundas, a considered advocate of free labour, who was to lead the first commando against Matiwane some eighteen months later.

We come now to the question of whether it was indeed urgently necessary for Bourke to send an army into Xhosaland to bring the labour out. Cobbing has no doubt that it was urgent in the extreme:

> As soon as Ordinance 49 permitting the issuing of invitations was safely drafted, Bourke seized on the news of the Zulu invasion as a pretext to send his armies across the Kei to bring out some labour. (p.502)

'As soon as Ordinance 49 . . . was safely drafted' is a curious formulation. It implies that Cobbing is aware of a hole in his argument, namely that Bourke's instructions to his 'armies' (21 June 1828) were issued *before* the promulgation of Ordinance 49 (14 July 1828). Leaving this aside, however, Cobbing is clearly indicating that Bourke seized the first possible opportunity 'to bring out some labour'. But did he?

In fact, he did not. Bourke had received permission from the British government to recruit Xhosa labour as early as 26 October 1826. Ordinance 49 had been 'safely drafted' ever since 30 June 1827 – more than a year before the battle of Mbholompo.[51] Clearly the labour shortage, though chronic, was not so urgent as all that.

And that is not all, Ordinance 49 was already 'safely drafted' by 24 August 1827, when Bourke himself arrived on the frontier in response to a war scare unintentionally generated by Matiwane's initial scouting party.[52] On his arrival, he

---

50. W. Dundas to R. Plasket, 10 Apr. 1827, Theal, *Records of the Cape Colony*, vol. 34, 395–8.
51. R. Bourke to Lord Bathurst, 30 June 1827, Theal, *Records of the Cape Colony*, vol. 32, 53–4.
52. R. Bourke to Viscount Goderich, 15 Oct. 1827. British Parliamentary Papers (hereafter BPP) 252 of 1825, 21–22. Bourke further went out of his way to 'convince them [the Xhosa chiefs] of the necessity of defending their country against all invaders, and of the utter impossibility of receiving them into the Colony'.

found that 3 000 of Chief Bawana's Thembu had entered the colony as refugees. Not only did the allegedly labour-hungry Bourke fail to enslave this first instalment of Ngwane invaders, but he actively compelled the 3 000 Thembu already in the colony to depart from it immediately. If the labour crisis was as serious as Cobbing suggests, why did Bourke pass up this fine opportunity to acquire Thembu labourers? The Thembu were regarded as 'a quiet and inoffensive race, and for a long period of time upon friendly terms with the Colony'. To accept Cobbing's thesis is to believe that the colonial administration preferred the 'fierce and less civilised' Ngwane beyond the colony to the 'quiet and inoffensive' Thembu already inside it. This is absurd. The fact is that Bourke, like the governors who followed him, was more concerned about the military security of the frontier than about the labour problems of the settlers.

'Would they come?' asks Cobbing, referring to black peoples 'invited' in by Ordinance 49. Indications are that they certainly would. Even if one accepts that the Mfecane was set in motion by the Portuguese and the Griqua, it would still be true that there were tens of thousands of starving, homeless and desperate people roaming about southern Africa seeking work and refuge. Peace, security and four head of cattle per family per year does not sound like a bad deal, especially since one could always run away from ill-treatment. Cattle-clientage was a common practice among any southern African peoples; indeed it was the foundation of the Mfecane kingdoms of Moshoeshoe and Sekwati. In the early years of interracial contact before the 1811–12 Frontier War, even though the Xhosa still possessed land in abundance, many of them willingly served white farmers in exchange for cattle. As Chiefs Chungwa and Ndlambe, both noted opponents of white domination, put it in 1803, 'the colonists were such rich people, that [the Xhosa] should be glad to come among them and gain a day's wage now and then'. After the 1811–12 war, however, all Xhosa residing to the west of the Fish River were expelled; and a strict policy of 'non-intercourse' was adopted which effectively prevented white farmers from employing Xhosa labour until the passage of Ordinance 49.[53] The labour shortage, to which Newton-King and Cobbing allude, was to a very considerable extent artificial, and owed its origins to the Cape Government's refusal, for security reasons, to permit the Xhosa enemy within the colonial gates.

By 1828 the stick of increased landlessness and the carrot of imported commodities had combined to make the Xhosa ever more willing to enter colonial service. Farmers had little difficulty in recruiting labour, as this passage from a missionary's diary attests:

> We have frequent visits from Dutch Boors, who come in order to engage
> Caffres in their service, the Govt having lately issued an Ordinance allowing

---

53. H. Lichtenstein, *Travels in Southern Africa, in the Years 1803, 1805 and 1806*, trans. by A. Plumptre, 1812–5; repr. Cape Town, 1928–30, vol. 1, 386. See also J. B. Peires, *The House of Phalo: A History of the Xhosa People in the Days of their Independence*, Johannesburg, 1981, 104; B. Maclennan, *A Proper Degree of Terror: John Graham and the Cape's Eastern Frontier*, Johannesburg, 1986, 59–61.

the Natives beyond the Colonial boundaries to enter into the service of the Colonists. Here are three Boors here today for this purpose, and I have had to write passes for several Caffres who have agreed to go with them. I am sorry to say that Mama has been induced by their flattering promises to enter into the service of one of them, and will thus be removed from the means of grace.[54]

Three days later, the missionary again remarked that he was 'busy writing passes for Caffres to go to the Colony'. So many Xhosa voluntarily availed themselves of the opportunity offered by Ordinance 49 that the chiefs themselves objected to it, and the Commandant of the Frontier called for an end to 'the great influx of Caffres into the Colony at the present moment'. Far from struggling to attract free labour, the colony attracted more than it could safely manage, and Ordinance 49 was suspended in August 1829, little more than a year after its proclamation.[55]

Having established, first, that Bourke's administration genuinely preferred free labour to coerced labour, and second, that a sufficient, uncoerced labour supply was readily available, we pass on to the events leading up to the battle of Mbholompo. My argument here is a simple one, namely that the traditional explanation of Mbholompo is essentially correct, and that the capture of refugees by Colonel Somerset was a by-product of the battle rather than its cause. To establish this important point, it is necessary, albeit tedious, to go through the events item by item, contrasting Cobbing's interpretation with the evidence provided by the historical sources.

Cobbing begins by asserting that 'Bourke seized on the news of the Zulu invasion as a pretext to send his armies across the Kei to bring out some labour'. (p.502) He produces no evidence to support this interpretation, and he makes no effort to locate or quote the instructions given by Bourke to his representatives on the spot, Major Dundas and Colonel Henry Somerset. Detailed evidence on this point is, in fact, available in the Cape Archives, but it appears that Cobbing has never consulted it.

The story begins with the arrival at Algoa Bay in May 1828 of a deputation from Shaka to inform the colonial authorities of his intention to attack the Mpondo and other trans-Keian peoples, and to assure them of his friendly disposition towards Britain. Almost simultaneously, the colonial authorities received information from the missionaries in the area that later became the Transkei, that the Zulu forces had crossed the Mzimvubu River and were heading for the Great Place of Hintsa, virtually adjacent to the colonial boundary.[56] Fearing another massive influx of

54. Shaw, *The Journal*, 141.
55. Stockenstrom, *Autobiography*, vol. 1, 304; H. Somerset to W. Dundas, 12 Aug. 1829, BPP 252 of 1835; C.F.J. Muller, *Die Oorsprong van die Groot Trek*, Cape Town, 1974, 105–12.
56. Government House Archives (hereafter GH) 19/3 Statement of James King, 10 May 1828; GH 19/3 W. Shrewsbury to H. Somerset, 12 June 1828. The Zulu deputation to the Cape, as well as their invasion of Mpondoland, are amply attested in Zulu and Mpondo sources. See, for example, C. de B. Webb and J. Wright, eds, *The James Stuart Archive of Recorded Oral Evidence Relating to the History of the Zulu and Neighbouring Peoples*, vol. 2, Pietermaritzburg, 1979, 61, 167; V.P. Ndamase, *AmaMpondo: Ibali ne-Ntlalo*, Lovedale, n.d., 9.

Xhosa refugees, Bourke instructed Major Dundas to visit Hintsa and the other Xhosa chiefs, to encourage them to 'unite their forces and oppose a resolute resistance to the invasion of their country'. Bourke was most anxious to avoid any fighting, however, and the chief purpose of Dundas's mission was not to 'bring out some labour', but to secure a personal interview with Shaka and to persuade him to withdraw from the Transkei region. When, eventually, Dundas did get involved in some fighting with Matiwane (see below), Bourke officially reprimanded him for it.[57]

Cobbing ignores all this and proceeds:

> In July 1828 a commando under the military commandant of Albany, Major Dundas, hurried to Vusani's Tembu to prepare them for an attack on the Ngwane or Fetcani. While the Tembu were mobilising, Dundas rode on to the Mpondo and discovered that the 'Zulu' army was in fact that of H.F. Fynn and his fellow Natal adventurers. (p. 502)

One might begin by noting that Major Dundas was not a military commandant, that Vusani's real name was Ngubengcuka, and that the correct spelling of 'Tembu' is 'Thembu', but these are small matters. What is more important is that Dundas's commando did not hurry to Ngubengcuka's Thembu to prepare them for an attack on the Ngwane, nor did he leave them mobilising. Dundas, in fact, went nowhere near the Thembu at all, but touched at Hintsa's and then headed straight for the Mpondo because he had been informed that there was a Zulu delegation at King Faku's place. Faku informed Dundas that the Zulu had plundered his country for a month and a half, and that he had accepted cattle from Shaka's ambassadors as a token of Mpondo submission to the Zulu king. Faku did refer to 'Henry Fynn and his small party with Chaka's army',[58] but to state, as Cobbing does, that the army which attacked the Mpondo belonged to Fynn and not to the Zulu, is to state that Faku did not know whom he was fighting with, or whom he had negotiated with, or whom he had submitted to.[59] It is quite clear from Faku's statement that he was attacked by a Zulu army, and that Fynn's party was only a small adjunct to it. Cobbing continues:

> Dundas's commando then doubled back and reached Vusani again on 24 July. The white and Hottentot gunmen and the by now fully mobilized Tembu moved east of the Mbashe and surrounded the Ngwane villages before dawn on 26 July. The Tembu climbed the ridges behind the *imizi* [homesteads] and

---

57. Cape Archives, Colonial Office Archives 4888, J. Bell to W. Dundas, 21 June, 27 June, 18 July 1828.

58. Van Warmelo, *History of Matiwane*, 243. Cobbing omits to mention both this phrase, and Faku's later reference to 'Chaka's people, who had been accompanied by a party of armed Englishmen'. Both phrases clearly indicate that Fynn's group was an appendage to the main Zulu army, and nothing more than that.

59. Both Cobbing and I rely on Dundas's report of 15 Aug. 1828, reprinted in Van Warmelo, *History of Matiwane*, 241–9. I invite the reader to consult the original and decide which summary is the more accurate. Ndamase, *AmaMpondo*, 9, confirms that the Zulu invaded Mpondoland and that Shaka gave cattle to Faku, though he insists that this did not imply Mpondo subordination to the Zulu.

drove the awakening victims on to the British guns . . . There was now no realistic Fetcani problem to the east of the Tembu.

One is puzzled by Cobbing's gratuitous reference to 'Hottentot' gunmen, but again that is a minor point. More important is the fact that an examination of the evidence to which the above passage refers makes it quite clear that it was the Thembu king Ngubengcuka, and not Major Dundas, who was quite literally calling the shots. The Ngwane's own version of their arrival in Thembuland confirms this:

> Through these mountains we came to the country of the Abatembu. Tshaka had already been there. We found that the people of many villages had fled, and their cattle had been taken. We attacked the villages that remained and took many cattle. (Mhlanga)

> After this, the Ngwane and their chief Matiwane simply went on and on, making no halt until they reached Mbholompo. When he reached the territory of other chiefs, and found that they had crops standing, he attacked and conquered them, taking their grain, thus becoming 'the lazy one who consumes the grain of those who work hard' (one of Matiwane's praises). (*History of Matiwane*)

> We descended these mountains again. We came towards the people of Kubencuka. We saw there peaceful people . . . We captured cattle in all directions, even to the Umzimvubu . . . The Tembus called from a distance: 'Wait, in a month we shall be among you.' We did not know they had gone to call whites. We settled down nicely. The first time the Tembus came alone to attack us, and they were not so many, and it was open country, and we killed them nearly all. (Moloja)[60]

The Ngwane themselves thus confirm that they invaded the Thembu country, attacked the Thembu and seized their cattle. One of Dundas's volunteers described the scene as 'all desolation, all dead men, women and children, cattle and dogs. Everything was laid waste, and the whole country burnt black'.[61] There can be no doubt that the Thembu were faced with a serious military crisis that was quite unrelated to the Cape colony's labour problems. They had no need to be mobilised by Dundas or anyone else; they had already mobilised themselves:

> There were five or six, the oldest and most important among the [Thembu] people, who spoke. The invasion of their country by the Fickanies, the loss of

60. Mhlanga, 'A Story of Native Wars', 251; Van Warmelo, *History of Matiwane*, 46; Moloja, 'Fetcani Horde', 273.
61. 'Extracts from the journal of Bertram Egerton Bowker', in I. Mitford-Barberton, ed., *Comdt. Holden Bowker: An 1820 Settler Book Including Unpublished Records of the Frontier Wars*, Cape Town, 1970, 58.

their cattle, the destruction of their corn, the murder of their women, and their children carried away from them, were the great subjects of their harangues, and all in their turn urged a determination to resist, and that their insulted country called for vengeance on the intruders.[62]

Both Mpondo and colonial sources show that it was the Thembu king, Ngubencuka, and not Major Dundas, who was the architect of the anti-Matiwane coalition. Chief Victor Poto states clearly that his forefather King Faku 'was requested by Ngubencuka to come and help him in the battle with Matiwane at Mbolompo'.[63] The settler Thomas Philipps, who had a personal grudge against Dundas, placed full responsibility on the Thembu king:

> Major D. was deceived by the Tambookie Chief Vasanie and suffered himself and a little retinue to be led by that scoundrel to slaughter innocent individuals.[64]

Even Reverend Kay, a severe critic of Dundas, lays part of the blame on Ngubencuka:

> Statements, therefore, the most exaggerated were got up by the different Chieftains with a view of inducing Government to send out an armed force to their help.[65]

Cobbing maintains that 'it is inconceivable that the Anglo-Tembu intelligence system did not know that their victims were the Ngwane' (p. 502n). In fact, it is not so inconceivable as all that. The evidence of Mhlanga quoted above confirms that the Ngwane had settled in country recently traversed by the Zulu. Faku had informed Dundas that the Zulu had headed towards Thembuland. Dundas was, as he admitted himself, confused by 'the various and contradictory reports respecting Chaka which are daily received'.[66] Even more important is Mhlanga's revelation that Matiwane deliberately concealed his true identity:

> Matiwane did not wish his name to be known by those people. We were commanded therefore to call ourselves Magagadlana.[67]

Let us return to the role of the British in the battle of Mbholompo. It will be recalled that Acting Governor Bourke had sent Major Dundas on a mission to negotiate directly with Shaka or his ambassadors. He was still on that mission when he was contacted by Ngubengcuka's messengers who gave him 'certain information

---

62. Report of W. B. Dundas, 15 Aug. 1828, quoted in Van Warmelo, *History of Matiwane*, 248.
63. Ndamase, *AmaMpondo*, 10.
64. T. Philipps, *Philipps, 1820 Settler; His Letters*, ed. by A. Keppel-Jones, Pietermaritzburg, 1960, 350.
65. Kay, *Travels and Researches in Caffraria*, 328.
66. For example, Dundas was informed by two young Thembu girls, prisoners of Matiwane, that 'they were undoubtedly Chaka's people', Van Warmelo, *History of Matiwane*, 239, 244, 246.
67. Mhlanga, 'A Study of Native Wars', 251.

respecting the advance of the Zoolas'. En route to Ngubengcuka's Great Place (which, *pace* Cobbing, he had not yet visited), Dundas was disturbed by Thembu war-cries announcing Matiwane's advance. On his arrival at the Great Place, Dundas found approximately 5 000 Thembu warriors already armed and assembled without any suggestion, let alone assistance, from himself. It was only at this point that he assumed a leading role. Even so, Cobbing's description of the skirmish is suspect:

> The Tembu climbed the ridge behind the *imizi* and drove the awakening victims on to the British guns. About seventy Ngwane were shot dead and 25,000 cattle plundered. There was now no realistic Fetcani problem to the east of the Tembu. (p.502)

It is not clear why Cobbing refers to the 'awakening victims', when the battle took place well after dawn. The number of 70 killed is also probably an exaggeration.[68] But, again, these are small matters. More important is Cobbing's statement that there was no longer a 'realistic Fetcani problem east of the Tembu', which implies that the second, and more significant, allied attack was launched against a beaten and defenceless enemy.

Nothing could be further from the truth. Moloja relates that only seven 'bands' of the Ngwane fought against Dundas, and that the mighty uShiyi regiment remained entirely intact. The Ngwane followed up the retreating Thembu, attacked them and recaptured all the cattle which had been lost. Moloja's statements are confirmed by Reverend Kay, who added:

> [Matiwane] vowed vengeance against his opponents, declaring that he would pay them a visit when they least expected him . . . Fear and revenge, therefore, gave rise to a hue and cry, which put the whole of Kafferland in commotion.[69]

Revengeful or not, the Ngwane now firmly established themselves in the heart of Thembuland, near the sources of the Mthatha River, where they began to erect dwellings and plant gardens. It is in this context that the battle of Mbholompo was fought on 27 August 1828. Mbholompo was no gratuitous assault on a beaten enemy but a calculated attack initiated by the Thembu king Ngubengcuka in concert with his allies, namely the Gcaleka, the Mpondo and the British.

Having established this context, there is no need to quarrel with Cobbing's description of the battle itself. The allies attacked the Ngwane before dawn, attempting no negotiation and giving them no opportunity to withdraw peacefully. The British cavalry swooped on the sleeping Ngwane in their huts, and continued to

---

68. Dundas in Van Warmelo, *History of Matiwane*, 239, refers to 10 am; B. Bowker, 'Journal', has 'daylight'; Moloja, 'Fetcani Horde', 273, has 'early morning'; Mhlanga, 'A Study of Native Wars', 251, refers to the battle taking place in the afternoon. Bowker refers to 16 killed on each of the Thembu and Ngwane sides; Kay, *Travels and Researches in Caffraria*, 329, refers only to 'several' shot.
69. Moloja, 'Fetcani Horde', 273; Kay, *Travels and Researches in Caffraria*, 330.

attack them as they struggled to escape. When some of the Ngwane rallied and tried to make a stand, the British opened up with cannons. Many fled to the neighbouring forests, some of which apparently caught fire, though there is no evidence to suggest that the British deliberately 'raked the Ngwane escape routes'. (p. 502) The Thembu and Gcaleka armies participated unrestrainedly in the carnage:

> While the military were routing Matuwane and his warriors, [the Xhosa] busily employed themselves in driving off all the cattle they could find, and in murdering the women and children . . . the field presented a scene indescribably shocking: old decrepit men with their bodies pierced, and heads almost cut off; pregnant females ripped open; legs broken, and hands likewise severed from the arm, as if for the purpose of getting the armlets or some other trifling ornament.[70]

All the sources used by Cobbing justify Somerset's decision to take possession of more than 70 Ngwane children in terms of the above atrocities. This may or may not be true, but it is beside the point. I have had previous experience with Colonel Henry Somerset's lying and self-serving dispatches.[71] It was Boer practice, and Somerset's practice also, to entice Boer volunteers to military service with easy pickings in cattle and child servants. I have little doubt that Somerset allowed the Boers to take as many children as they could get.

My dispute with Cobbing concerns not what Somerset actually did, but with the historical significance that should be attached to it. Cobbing sees this raiding of children as 'the primary objective of Somerset's commando' (p. 503), as part of the 'trans-continental crossfire of interrelated European plunder systems'. I reject this, and I reject the idea that the British were 'raiding' for 'free labour' in the aftermath of Ordinance 49. Somerset's Boers were not raiding for new-style 'free labour' but for old-style 'forced labour', as they and their fathers had been doing for decades. It was precisely this kind of labour relationship that Ordinance 49 was intended to replace. Even if Ordinance 49 failed to prevent the battle of Mbholompo, it nevertheless cannot be labelled as the ultimate cause of the battle. Mbholompo was a contradiction of current British policy, and not its manifestation.

A Reprieve for the Mfecane?

Cobbing rejects not only the concept of the Mfecane but even the very word itself. 'Walker coined the word "mfecane" in 1928. Walker's neologism, meaning "the crushing", has no root in any African language'. (p. 487) This is an astonishing claim. Any Xhosa dictionary will inform one that '*imfecane*' is derived from the root '*-feca*', meaning 'to crack, bruise, break down the maize or sweetcorn stalks'.[72]

---

70. Kay, *Travels and Researches in Caffraria*, 332; Bannister, *Humane Policy*, 156–9. Another relevant extract is quoted on p. 21 above.
71. Peires, *House of Phalo*, 227 n.95.
72. A. Kropf, *A Kaffir-English Dictionary*, Lovedale, 1899, 100.

Contemporary English sources habitually refer to the invaders as 'Fetcani' or 'Fetcanie', and the word '*imfecane*' appears in a Xhosa-language newspaper as early as 1863.[73] The word originally seems to have meant a military unit, as indicated, for example, in the statement of one Ngwane, 'we sent out Fetcanie, beat the Tambookies often, and took their cattle'.[74] *Imfecane* refers to people who are crushing others, rather than to people who are themselves crushed. It appears to be part of an extended metaphor, in which the marauding bands see themselves as crushing their wealthy and ineffectual opponents; in the words of Platje Mhlanga, '*ladla impakata nodiza*' (they consumed the corn-cob and the stubble as well).[75]

It must, however, be conceded that the Xhosa use of the word '*imfecane*' applies not to the historical event itself but to some of the people who participated in it. Thus a Hlubi descendant of Mehlomakhulu refers to this period as '*iimfazwe yeMfecane*' (the wars of the Mfecane), rather than 'the iMfecane'. To that extent, the use of 'Mfecane' as a portmanteau word denoting the whole of the historical event is indeed a coinage, a neologism. But that does not necessarily imply that we should reject it.

The term 'feudalism' was unknown during the feudal era. The term 'Renaissance' was invented by Jacob Burkhardt in 1840. History, like any social science, should aim at generalisation, and if we can think of a suitable term and if we can agree on its interpretation, we are certainly entitled to use it. The term 'Mfecane' undoubtedly has its attractions. First of all, it is already well established in the historical literature. More important, it appears not only in Xhosa and Zulu, but in Sotho as well. Finally, the term was used in its own time not as a synonym for a specific ethnic group, but as a generic term for any group of aggressive 'crushers', regardless of their ethnic origin. But given the divisions that the Cobbing hypothesis has already aroused, the essential consensus necessary for the preservation of the term has almost certainly disappeared. Even those of us who are still attracted by the old paradigm will need to dig out our trusty inverted commas, and refer henceforth to the Mfecane as 'the Mfecane' or 'the so-called Mfecane' just to prove that we are hip to current trends.

Killing off the term 'Mfecane' is, however, a pretty hollow victory unless one has also killed off the old paradigm. It is this old paradigm rather than the word 'Mfecane' which I would like to defend in these final paragraphs. It is quite adequately summed up in Omer-Cooper's phrase 'a revolutionary change proceeding from a single centre'.[76] This formulation is broad enough to encompass both Omer-Cooper, who sees the change as essentially political and military in nature, and those influenced by mode-of-production theory, such as Jeff Guy, Philip Bonner and David Hedges, who emphasise the social and economic transformation

73. Thompson, *Travels and Adventures*, vol.1, 180; Van Warmelo, *History of Matiwane*, 235; J. Mazamisa, 'Izizwe za-Mamfengu', *Indaba* 1 (1863), 171n.
74. Van Warmelo, *History of Matiwane*, 235–6.
75. Mhlanga, 'A Story of Native Wars', 249.
76. Omer-Cooper, *The Zulu Aftermath*, 7.

embodied in the regimental system.[77] The single centre is not, of course, the Zulu kingdom alone but the whole of the area inhabited by northern Nguni-speakers. The concept of a single centre does not in any way exclude the influence of trade from Delagoa Bay or elsewhere. Primary sources as different as H.F. Fynn and Thomas Mofolo have stressed the importance of Dingiswayo's links with the Portuguese, as have such diverse historians as Alan Smith, Henry Slater and Hedges. All these concur in viewing trade as an external factor which impacted on the internal structure of the Zulu state, transforming it into something new and essentially different.

Cobbing sees neither revolutionary change nor a single centre. All rhetoric aside, he is indeed proposing a new paradigm. He sees no dynamic initiative, no creative tension, no social transformation occurring within the African societies themselves. African societies are reduced to the status of hapless and passive victims, mere billiard balls crashing into each other, propelled around the table by infinitely more cunning and sinister forces. And in place of an internally generated trajectory, he proposes two chains of externally sourced violence: one proceeding from the Portuguese at Delagoa Bay, and the other from the British and their Griqua surrogates at the Cape. Let us not reduce the debate on the Mfecane to a mere quibble about words. Let us choose between these paradigms.

Although credit is certainly due to Julian Cobbing for rekindling interest in the early nineteenth century and for postulating a bold new paradigm, it must also be said that his use of evidence is sufficiently reckless to undermine his credibility among all those with the patience to check his footnotes. Even more questionable than his tendency to stretch and distort historical information to suit his own purposes is his determination to ignore all sources which contradict his hypotheses. The interests of the new paradigm would be far better served by discussing its weaknesses fully and frankly, and by treating contradictory sources with due consideration rather than by trying to rubbish and belittle them. Instead of opening the road to a new consensus on early nineteenth-century history, Cobbing's, aggressive tone and dubious methods have created new obstacles to our understanding that were not there before.

In conclusion, I would like to suggest that the new model paradigm is an even greater misrepresentation of the truth than the old Mfecane stereotype. I think I have shown that there is hardly a single statement anywhere in Cobbing's version of the history of Matiwane that can stand up to detailed examination, and I am led to believe that the same can be said for the other two props of his argument, namely the battle of Dithakong and the trade of Delagoa Bay. We should not therefore be panicked into discarding the old paradigm until we have a better idea of what the iconoclasts are proposing to put into its place.

The correct response to Cobbing's provocation, in my view, is to resume our unfinished attempts to establish the material content and context of the history of

---

77. For further discussion on this point, see J. B. Peires, 'Paradigm Deleted: The Materialist Interpretation of the Mfecane', *Journal of Southern African Studies*, 19 (1993), 295–313.

African societies in southern Africa, rather than to rush down a blind alley, grubbing for colonialists behind every dirt bin. Let the faddists, the lemmings and the kamikazes take flight in their new-look, new paradigm hot-air balloon, if they so desire. The rest of us must lose no time in getting the old paradigm off the scrap-heap and back on to the road. It should be an interesting race.

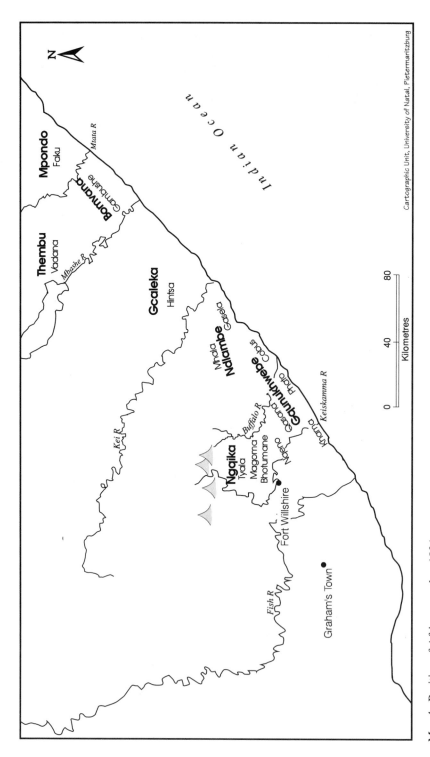

Map 4. Position of African peoples, 1834

9 Unmasking the Fingo
The War of 1835 Revisited

ALAN WEBSTER

'Mfecane' historiography has separated the advent of the Fingo[1] from the war of 1835 (the so-called Sixth Frontier – or 'Kafir' – War).[2] Its Afrocentric explanation of the arrival of the Fingo revolves around the claim that all Fingo were Natal refugees from the devastation of Shaka's 'mfecane', who fled south. They were rescued in May 1835 from the oppression of their Gcaleka hosts by the coincidental arrival of British troops in Butterworth. How the Europeans happened to be 300 kilometres from the colonial border is explained in white history as a defence of the Cape colony in the Sixth Frontier War. Both these compartmentalised histories – 'mfecane' and 'settler' – are based on myth. The identity of the Fingo in 1835 and the events of the war are intertwined: each is dependent upon a re-examination of the other.

The events of 1835 must be explained within the context of the early nineteenth-century expansion of the Cape colony into Rharhabe territory – approximately the area bounded by the Fish and Kei Rivers, the Amatola Mountains and the Indian Ocean. The burgeoning European population demanded more land and labour, and the Rharhabe were increasingly pressurised into reacting to their inexorable dispossession. In late December 1834, after decades of trans-frontier raids by the colonists, the men of Maqoma, Tyali, Nqeno and Bhotumane[3] attacked farmers in the Koonap River area, and the southern Albany region. The Albany settlers panicked, describing these retributive raids in dramatic hyperbole, and called for help from Cape Town. Governor Sir Benjamin D'Urban and Colonel Harry Smith then took the opportunity to subdue the 'Kafir' chiefs,[4] seize most Rharhabe land, capture cattle and control the recalcitrant Gcaleka paramount, Hintsa. This was achieved by sending to the frontier a large force of British soldiers and colonists, who marched with relative impunity through Gcaleka and Rharhabe territory, plundering and burning as they went.

---

1. I have used the term 'Fingo' rather than the modern version 'Mfengu', as the latter seems merely to be a recently 'Africanised' word for a people created by British tribalisation. Fingo was the word in contemporary usage, and should be retained.
2. This war has also been called the 'War of Hintsa', the 'War of Maqoma' and the 'War of D'Urban'. None of these terms is sufficiently encompassing and I have opted for the neutral 'War of 1835'.
3. Cf. J. B. Peires, *The House of Phalo: A History of the Xhosa People in the Days of their Independence*, Johannesburg, 1981, ch. 4 for the Rharhabe genealogy.
4. This is not the place to debate the issue, but the term 'Xhosa' cannot be applied to the Gcaleka and the Rharhabe of the 1830s who were politically and socially more fractured than the single term implies. 'Kafir' indicates the colonial perception of a unified, threatening *intermensch* east of the frontier.

Along with the seizure of land and cattle came the capture of Rharhabe and Gcaleka (mainly women and children), who were taken back into the labour-starved eastern Cape to work on the settler farms.[5] Such slavery was illegal so they were described as an oppressed people rescued by British humanitarianism and given the name 'Fingo'. Included under the identity 'Fingo' was a range of other groupings which entered the colony during 1835. Their diverse origins were elided and were replaced by a single provenance as supposed refugees from Shaka who were settled at Peddie.

The War of 1835

The Settler Orthodoxy on the War of 1835

The settler version of the events and causes of the war of 1835 is encapsulated in the work of Robert Godlonton, the chief shaper and voice of settler opinion.[6] He claimed that war on the colony was fomented and planned from early 1834 by the Rharhabe chiefs, under the leadership of the paramount, Hintsa. The colony was then allegedly attacked simultaneously over the entire eastern frontier by over 10 000 Africans in December 1834. They overwhelmed the inadequate colonial defences and gained control of most of the area between the Sundays and Keiskamma Rivers. Their dominance was maintained for nearly a month, during which time the districts of Albany and Somerset were looted and denuded of colonial stock, innumerable European houses were destroyed, and innocent settlers were killed. Governor D'Urban informed the Colonial Secretary of State, Lord Spring-Rice, in January 1835:

> I cannot adequately point out to you the devastation and horror which these merciless barbarians have committed, this fertile and beautiful Province is almost a desert, and the murders, which have gone hand in hand with this work of pillage and rapine, have deeply aggravated its atrocity.[7]

The colony responded, according to Godlonton, and troops moved into Rharhabe territory in January 1835. In April the Gcaleka were attacked. Godlonton said that this was in punishment for their alleged involvement in the 'irruption', and he accused Hintsa of hiding all the colonial stock that had been taken in December

---

5. The first suggestions that labour seizures were being performed in 1835 came from Julian Cobbing, in lectures at Rhodes University in 1987, and in J. Cobbing, 'The Mfecane as Alibi: Thoughts on Dithakong and Mbolompo', *Journal of African History*, 29, (1988), 514.

6. R. Godlonton, *A Narrative of the Irruption of the Kafir Hordes into the Eastern Province of the Cape of Good Hope*, 1834–35, Graham's Town, 1836. For an analysis of Godlonton, see B. A. Le Cordeur, 'Robert Godlonton as Architect of Frontier Opinion', M.A. dissertation, Rhodes University, Grahamstown, 1956.

7. *British Parliamentary Papers* (hereafter *BPP*) 252 (1835), 132, D'Urban to Spring-Rice, 21 Jan. 1835. In 1812 Cradock had used almost the same description for the Rharhabe attacks on Albany, which had supposedly 'rendered desert the most fertile part of His Majesty's Settlement'; see *Cape Town Gazette and African Advertiser*, 6 June 1812.

1834. Hintsa was shot while escaping from his captors, which the settlers explained as justice for his complicity in the 'irruption'. Godlonton claimed that the settlers lost enormous numbers of stock, for which they were compensated with cattle taken from the Rharhabe and Gcaleka, and with grants of Rharhabe land. He alleged that the war of 1835 was 'a war of necessity, and not of choice',[8] and was deserved punishment for the 'unprovoked aggression' of December.

Background to the War

The settler interpretations of the events of 1835 are not only untenable, but they need to be inverted. It was the colony that invaded; it was the colony that took forced labourers; it was the colony that secured land for further settler farms. The key to understanding the war lies in the power of the Cape colony to expand and the ability of the Cape authorities to answer the needs of the colonists, which were largely for land, labour and security. Relations between the colonial authorities and the settlers in the Cape – and especially those in the eastern districts – fluctuated. The governors of the early nineteenth century were not always supportive of settler demands – as evidenced by Henry Somerset's battle with the Albany settlers – but in general needs were met. The governorships of Cole (1829–32), Wade (1833) and D'Urban (1834–7) were marked by an increased official sanction of settler demands. The relations between Cape Town and Graham's Town, and the way in which they changed, need further analysis. Slave labour had formed the backbone of the Cape economy from the mid-seventeenth century. But with the abolition of the maritime slave trade in 1807, the banning in the colony of African labour in 1809 and the denial of slave labour to the English settlers in Albany, an alternative stable labour supply had to be found to combat the severe labour shortage in the eastern districts in the 1820s and 1830s.[9]

The land and labour seizures of 1835 were not without precedent, as the colonists had previously tried various methods of dispossessing and controlling first the Khoi, and then the Africans. Legislation in the form of Hottentot Codes was passed to tie Khoi to colonial farms, in the hope that the labour shortage would be solved. These codes – promulgated by Governors Caledon and Cradock in 1809 and 1812 – stipulated that Khoi must either own land, which was forbidden to them in the colony, or find employment with Europeans. The regulations of 1812, which allowed for the apprenticeship – in other words, the forced retention – of orphaned or destitute children until the age of 18, were exploited, as the landdrosts who were

---

8. Godlonton, *Narrative of the Irruption*, 229.
9. See R. Shell, 'Adumbrations of Cape Slavery: Other Forms of Labour', seminar paper, Rhodes University, Grahamstown, 1989. See also R. Elphick and V.C. Malherbe, 'The Khoisan to 1828', in R. Elphick and H.B. Giliomee, *The Shaping of South African Society, 1652–1840*, Cape Town, 1989, ch. 1; C.C. Crais, 'Some Thoughts on Slavery and Emancipation in the Eastern Cape, South Africa, 1770–1838', Seminar Paper presented to the Conference on Slavery, University of Cape Town, Cape Town, 1989.

empowered to prosecute the legislation were the same who benefited from it.[10] The term 'apprenticeship' had none of its traditional connotations of learning a trade, with the employer's educational and social obligations; it was applied merely as a legal cover for child labourers. A child could easily be captured and described as an orphan; there could be no record of his real history. As John Agar-Hamilton put it, most of the colonists saw it 'as merely a veil required by an unintelligible convention to cover the exploitation of child labour'.[11]

Vagrancy clauses were included in the codes, and were then extended in specific vagrancy ordinances that allowed colonists to force any Khoi they deemed 'idle' to labour for them. The vagueness of the wording meant that any Khoi in the colony could be forcibly indentured by a colonist merely on the grounds of the European's claim that he was a 'vagrant'.[12] The notion of vagrancy hardly involved security at all, but was an attempt (usually successful) to force the aboriginal population into labour.[13] A 'vagrant' was defined as a non-European who did not possess land or a job. As the indigenous population was denied property ownership, the majority were automatically 'vagrants'. 'Vagrancy' remained a useful method of enforcing labour: Cole in 1831, and Wade in 1833, when showing concern about the colonial labour shortage, proposed vagrancy laws as the best method of solving the problem.[14]

These attempts to force Khoi into work did not satisfy the colonial labour needs. There was a tension within government policy following the expulsion of Africans from the colony in 1809: there was a need to keep Africans out to ensure frontier stability; but the government had to provide labour for its colonists. A possible answer to this dilemma was for the authorities to turn a blind eye to the highly illegal capture of labourers, mainly women and children. Explanations for the arrival of these Africans were manufactured to appease the Cape and London authorities: farmers claimed that they were 'apprentices'; alternatively they were described as 'Mantatees', with the explanation that they were a tribe of refugees from the devastation of the 'mfecane'.[15]

10. J.B. Peires, 'The British and the Cape', in Elphick and Giliomee, *The Shaping of South African Society*, 493.
11. J. Agar-Hamilton, *The Native Policy of the Voortrekkers*, Cape Town, 1928, 171. He exposes many of the euphemisms employed in labour seizure in the Boer republics, and the way in which the practices of the 1850s had very distinct roots in the 1820s and 1830s.
12. S. Newton-King, 'The Labour Market of the Cape Colony, 1807–1828', in S. Marks and A. Atmore, *Economy and Society in Pre-industrial South Africa*, London, 1980, ch.7, provides seminal work on labour and the attempts to control the Khoi during this period.
13. Cape Archives (hereafter CA) Clerk of the Legislative Council (hereafter LCA) 6, Comments of Philip, June 1834, and Campbell, 4 July 1834. The latter said that a vagrancy ordinance would force the Khoi to work, to the benefit of the wealthier settlers. Fairbairn's disapproving views on vagrancy laws can be found in H.C. Botha, *John Fairbairn in South Africa*, Cape Town, 1984, 97–104. Analyses of the intentions of vagrancy ordinances are provided in W.M. Macmillan, *The Cape Colour Question*, London, 1927, ch.16; Peires, 'The British and the Cape', 501.
14. Macmillan, *The Cape Colour Question*, 234.
15. For a discussion of the term 'Mantatee', see Cobbing 'The Mfecane as Alibi' and A.C. Webster 'Land Expropriation and Labour Extraction under Cape Colonial Rule: The War of 1835 and the "Emancipation of the Fingo"', M.A. dissertation, Rhodes University, Grahamstown, 1991, 47–8.

The commando system was a powerful method of enforcing white authority, and augmenting stock numbers. By the time the British took over, the system allowed for the summoning of a commando by the local field cornet upon the reporting of stock theft, and the following of the trail to the nearest homestead across the border, whereupon up to ten times the number of cattle reported stolen were seized.[16] The avenues for abuse of the system were numerous. Examples abound of these legal commandos becoming mere opportunities for the plunder of the Rharhabe in the 1820s and 1830s, sometimes all the way up to the Kei River.[17]

But commandos were not only used to seize cattle and subdue the Africans; they were exploited to seize labour for the colonists. In the first few decades of the nineteenth century the practice of seizing labour became more and more common, and by 1835 there was a long-standing precedent of illegal trans-frontier raids, and the capture of men, women and children to work on colonial farms.[18] In the late eighteenth and early nineteenth centuries labour-raiding was focused on the northern frontier.[19] As the European population moved towards the Fish River and consolidated there in the 1820s, the attention of raiders turned towards the Rharhabe.

J.B. Peires and M.G. Donaldson provide evidence of the capture of Africans across the Fish River.[20] In 1818 Rharhabe offered captives to white farmers, in exchange for European commodities.[21] Revd John Philip described an instance in 1820 when Ngqika women and children, who had settled on the Fish after moving

16. A summary of the system can be found in (CA) A1480, Read to Fairbairn, 13 Apr. 1834; *BPP* 279 (1836), 62, Glenelg to D'Urban, 26 Dec 1835. For descriptions of its injustices see (CA) Government House Archives (hereafter GH) 1/97, 68, Stanley to Cole, 27 Nov. 1833; *BPP* 50 (1835), 175–7, Moodie, Dec. 1823; J.C.S. Lancaster, 'A Reappraisal of the Governorship of Sir B. D'Urban at the Cape of Good Hope, 1834–1835', M.A. dissertation, Rhodes University, Grahamstown, 1980, ch. 5.
17. *BPP* 50 (1835), 183–4, Pringle to Commission of Enquiry, Jan. 1826; T. Pringle, *Narrative of a Residence in South Africa*, London, 1835, 325–6; (CA) A50/4, Read to Fairbairn, 12 Apr. 1833; *BPP* 503 (1837), 151, Somerset to D'Urban, 26 Sept. 1834; (CA) A1480, Read to Fairbairn, 13 Apr. 1834, and Read to Fairbairn, 27 June 1834.
18. The practice of labour seizure on commando continued for decades. In 1840 a commando of Natal Boers attacked the Bhaca and captured cattle and many women and children, explaining unconvincingly that these captives were taken by their Mpondomise allies, and that the Boers were outraged at the idea. They then 'apprenticed' most of them; see G.M. Theal, *The Republic of Natal: The Origin of the Present Pondo Tribe, Imperial Treaties with Panda, and Establishment of the Colony of Natal*, Cape Town, 1961, 19–20.
19. For numerous examples and analyses of labour raiding on the northern frontier, see G. Thompson, *Travels and Adventures in Southern Africa. Comprising a View of the Present State of the Cape Colony, with Observations on the Progress and Prospects of the British Emigrants*, 2 vols, London, 1827, Reprint edition, Cape Town, 1967, vol. 2, 7; G.M. Theal, comp., *Records of the Cape Colony*, London, 1904, vol. 25, 386–7; *BPP* 50 (1835), 56, Report of Stockenstrom, 1817, and 29–30, Maynier's replies to the Commission of Enquiry in 1825, and 144; Crais, 'Some Thoughts on Slavery', 11; S. Newton-King, 'The Enemy Within', Seminar Paper presented to the Conference on Slavery, University of Cape Town, 1989; Elphick and Malherbe, 'The Khoisan to 1828'.
20. J.B. Peires, 'A History of the Xhosa, *c.*1700–1835', M.A. dissertation, Rhodes University, Grahamstown, 1976, 101, 170; M.E. Donaldson, 'The Council of Advice at the Cape of Good Hope', Ph.D. thesis, Rhodes University, Grahamstown, 1975, 341.
21. C.C. Crais, *The Making of the Colonial Order: White Supremacy and Black Resistance in the Eastern Cape 1770–1865*, Johannesburg, 1992, 96.

from the Kat, were fraudulently contracted to Boers in Uitenhage (on the understanding that they were being taken home), while their men were sent to Robben Island.[22] On his arrival in Port Elizabeth in 1820, Thomas Pringle saw a number of Rharhabe women and children who were to be placed in servitude in punishment for allegedly having crossed the colonial boundary.[23] Thomas Stubbs recalled how a large number of Rharhabe women, who had come to collect clay at Clay Pits near Graham's Town in 1822, were seized by the neighbouring settlers, taken to Graham's Town and hired out to farmers.[24] There was an internal slave market at the Cape; Clifton Crais estimates that approximately 500 to 750 people were enslaved from beyond the colonial borders between 1807 and 1834.[25] Robert Shell shows that there were 5 000 Negroes – slaves confiscated by the British from Portuguese and French ships – who had been diverted, and were working in the Cape in 1800–40.[26]

The battle of Dithakong resulted in workers for the colony. At least 179 women and children were seized as labourers and sent as far south as Graaff-Reinet.[27] The same occurred at Mbholompo in 1828, under the guise of aiding the Gcaleka and Thembu – the British officially seized 25 women and 64 children, some of whom were given to officers, and the rest distributed as workers in Fort Beaufort.[28] The actual total was higher, as a large number of women and children ended up in Graham's Town where they were redefined as 'Fingo'.[29] In 1831 John Bigge, Commissioner of Inquiry at the Cape, showed concern at the continuing illegal slave trade.[30] Boers were still getting slaves clandestinely from the interior in 1833.[31] Pringle complained in 1834 that British troops and settlers attack the Rharhabe 'and carry the children into captivity'.[32]

But by 1834 there was still an acute labour shortage in the eastern districts. It was exacerbated by the failure of Ordinance 49 (1828) to attract African labourers into the colony. It was never expected that authoritarian colonial employment would be attractive to Africans, but the ordinance gave permission for Africans to be in the

22. J. Philip, *Researches in South Africa: Illustrating the Civil, Moral, and Religious Condition of the Native Tribes: Including Journals of the Author's Travels in the Interior; Together with Detailed Accounts of the Progress of the Christian Missions, Exhibiting the Influence of Christianity in Promoting Civilization*, London, 1828, 191–2; Pringle, *Narrative of a Residence*, 15, describes a similar incident.
23. T. Pringle, *African Sketches*, London, 1834, 133.
24. J. Cock, *Maids and Madams: A Study in the Politics of Exploitation*, Johannesburg, 1980, 199.
25. Crais, 'Some Thoughts on Slavery', 15.
26. Shell, 'Adumbrations of Cape Slavery'.
27. J. Richner, 'The Withering Away of the "Lifaqane": Or a Change of Paradigm', B.A. Hons essay, Rhodes University, Grahamstown, 1988, 8; see Cobbing, 'The Mfecane as Alibi', for a reinterpretation of the events at both Dithakong and Mbholompo.
28. (CA) 1/AY/8/18, Bell to Campbell, 24 June 1829.
29. R.A. Moyer, 'A History of the Mfengu of the Eastern Cape 1815–1865', Ph.D. thesis, London University, 1976, 605, Evidence of Jacob Tunyiswa.
30. L.C. Duly, *British Land Policy at the Cape, 1792–1844: A Study of Administrative Procedures of the Empire*, Durham, 1972, 146.
31. (CA) Archives of the Colonial Office (hereafter CO) 2744, Letter from Campbell, June 1833.
32. *Graham's Town Journal*, 4 Sept. 1834, Letter from Pringle.

Cape. The crisis was worsened by the overturning of a vagrancy ordinance (which had been designed to force the Khoi into service) by London in 1834, and the imminent emancipation of the colony's slaves in December 1834.

That there was a labour shortage in the 1820s and 1830s (especially in the eastern Cape) is indisputable. Bathurst in 1833 had a mere 140 Khoi and Mantatees to provide labour for the 900 Europeans,[33] although this was an improvement from the complete lack of servants in 1824. The population figures for the late 1820s show the eastern Cape with 86 non-whites (42 in Albany) to every 100 whites, compared with the western Cape median of 134 to 100. The labour shortage was regularly a subject of concern to the eastern colonists: 'W.G.' wrote to the *Graham's Town Journal* in 1833 to describe the scarcity of labour as 'the cause of all our troubles'.[34] The 1836 Cape Blue Book is vague as to the number of 'aliens' (Fingo, Mantatee and Bechuana) in Albany and Somerset, but makes it clear that 'Great numbers of these are in the service of the farmers.'[35] It lists 1 575 aliens working for farmers in Graaff-Reinet. By 1838 there were officially over 6 000 Fingo in the colony (3 517 in Albany), which inverted the figures to 134:100 in the east, and 119:100 in the west. In summary, in Albany in 1828 there was a ratio of 43 non-whites (potential labourers) to every 100 whites. In 1838 there were 141 to every 100 whites. The war of 1835 thus completely inverted the labour situation in Albany.

With the need for labour came a colonial desire for land. And dispossession in turn produced displaced Rharhabe for labour. In 1811–12 British troops cleared the 'Zuurveld' area between the Sundays and Fish Rivers of its Ndlambe inhabitants.[36] Troops moved in again in 1819, this time seizing a swathe of territory between the Fish and Keiskamma Rivers (the Neutral/Ceded Territory) from the British ally, Ngqika. The Zuurveld – now called Albany – was then filled with British settlers, who soon began to demand further land annexation. At first the Cape administration was unwilling to accede to settler demands, but from 1829 Cole's government proved very supportive of the Albany settlers, and the military and civil administration in Graham's Town was particularly pro-settler. In 1829 much of Maqoma's land was taken away on a pretext manufactured by Duncan Campbell, Civil Commissioner for Albany and Somerset.[37] It was given to Khoi to form the

---

33. (CA) Lieutenant Governor of the Eastern Cape (hereafter LG) 7, Population Returns for Bathurst, 1833.

34. *Graham's Town Journal*, 14 Feb. 1833, Letter from 'W.G.'.

35. Cape Blue Book, 1836, 201.

36. See B. MacLennan, *A Proper Degree of Terror: John Graham and the Cape's Eastern Frontier*, Johannesburg, 1986, for a vivid description of this process.

37. Campbell, in Graham's Town, was the real instigator of expansionism. He disliked the 'Kafirs' intensely, and it was he who insisted on many of the Rharhabe expulsions in the 1830s – see *BPP* 503 (1837), 104, Campbell to Bell, 27 Feb. 1834; (CA) 1/AY/9/19, Letter from Campbell, 20 Apr. 1834; (CA) 1/AY/9/7, 41, Letter from Campbell, 7 June 1834; C.L. Stretch, *The Journal of Charles Lennox Stretch*, edited by B.A. Le Cordeur, Cape Town, 1988, 164 n.41; (CA) A50/4, Read to Fairbairn, 7 Dec 1833.

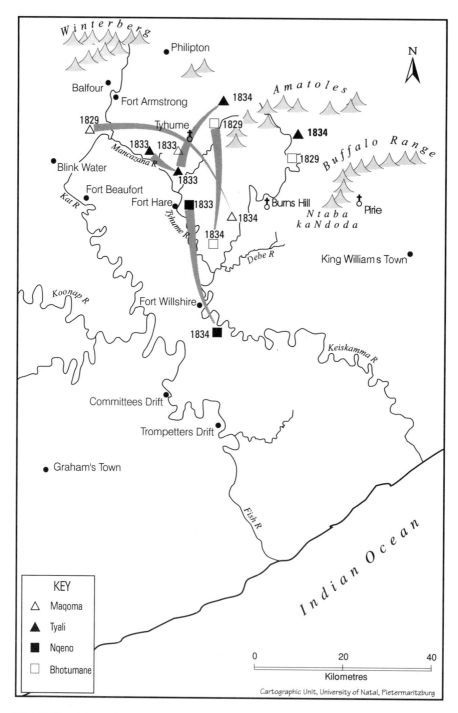

Map 5. Expulsions of Rharhabe, 1829–34

buffer Kat River Settlement,[38] and to white soldiers between the Kat and Koonap Rivers. Between September and November 1833 Maqoma, Tyali, Bhotumane, Nqeno and Qasana's people were driven eastwards.[39] Again in March 1834 Maqoma and Tyali were evicted from their new land and driven east by British troops armed with guns and cannon who burnt crops and huts, and seized cattle. Their bleak position, at the onset of winter without crops was further aggravated by the fact that the area to which they were expelled – around the Keiskamma – was subject to frequent droughts, one of which occurred in 1833–4.[40] In March and April 1834, 38 farms were surveyed along the Koonap River and allotted to colonists by Campbell; one of them comprised 80 hectares of Maqoma's old *komkhulu* (place of the chief).[41] Again in November and December 1834 the colonial troops attacked Tyali and Nqeno, burning crops and huts, wounding a chief, and forcing their people off their land for the third time in 14 months.[42] Philip described in November how the British troops had laid waste to 20 miles of Ngqika's crops and huts along the Tyhume River valley.[43]

By the end of 1834 the Rharhabe had little option but to respond. Not surprisingly, it was the people of Maqoma, Tyali and Nqeno who made the counter-attacks in December. For two decades they had been repeatedly forced off their land, their cattle had been raided, women and children captured, their possessions and dwellings burnt by commandos, and their autonomy threatened. As Reverend James Read of the London Missionary Society (LMS) had noted in 1833:

---

38. Analyses of the Kat River Settlement are limited. C.C. Crais, 'Beasts of Prey: Capitalism and Resistance in the Eastern Cape', Seminar Paper presented to the Centre for African Studies, University of Cape Town, 1989, summarises the progressive dispossession and destruction of the Settlement in the 1830s and 1840s; and T. Kirk, 'Progress and Decline in the Kat River Settlement, 1829–1854', *Journal of African History*, 14 (1973), 411–23, deals mainly with the lead up to the rebellion of 1851. But work still needs to be done on the early settlement. For a description of the rapid development of the Settlement, see *BPP* 252 (1835), 55–6, Report of Judge Menzies, Sept. 1830.

39. For a clear description of the evictions see (CA) A50/4, Read to Fairbairn; Chalmers to Stretch, 21 Nov. 1833, in U. Long, ed., *An Index to Authors of Unofficial, Privately-Owned Manuscripts Relating to the History of South Africa 1812–1920*, London, 1947, 81–4; (CA) A50/4, Read to Fairbairn, 7 Dec. 1833.

40. (CA) A50/4, Read to Fairbairn, 12 Apr. 1833; Read to Fairbairn, 7 Dec. 1833; *BPP* 503 (1837), 113, Somerset to Campbell, 5 Mar. 1834; Peires, 'A History of the Xhosa', 201. See M.D.D. Newitt, 'Drought in Mozambique 1823–1831', *Journal of Southern African Studies*, 15 (1988), 14–35 for a comparative study of the social tensions produced by drought.

41. (CA) LG 7, Bell to Commissioner-General, 1834; (CA) LG 587, 179–80. See (CA) Maps M1/2451–3 for distribution of farms and the number of Boer farmers on the Kat and Koonap Rivers.

42. Two patrols in early December in particular, those led by Sparkes and Sutton, contributed to the heightening of frontier tension. For the settler attempts to exonerate them of blame, see J. Heavyside, *Abstract of the Proceedings of the Board of Relief for the Destitute*, Cape Town, 1836, 88–9 and G. Cory, *The Rise of South Africa*, London, 1919, vol. 3, 55–60. For a more accurate assessment, see *BPP* 503 (1837), 158–60, Somerset to D'Urban, 12 Dec. 1834; (CA) A1480, Philip to Buxton, 1 May 1835; J.H. Soga, *The South-Eastern Bantu*, Johannesburg, 1930, 172; C.P. Brownlee, 'The Old Peach Stump', in *Reminiscences of Kaffir Life and History and Other Papers*, Lovedale, 1896.

43. (CA) A1480, Philip to Buxton, 1 May 1835. Philip gives a very clear picture of Rharhabe confusion and anger at the arbitrary and destructive actions of the colony. D'Urban's explanations of the causes of the war in *BPP* 503 (1837), 56–7, D'Urban to Glenelg, 9 June 1836, bear little resemblance to reality.

> There have been a number of the most aggravating circumstances possible, and
> every method contrived to agitate the Caffres with a view we think to have a
> pretext to take more land from them.[44]

The Events of 1835[45]

The counter-attacks of late December 1834 and early January 1835 were undertaken
by a minority of disgruntled Rharhabe, who attacked specific areas and farms in
Albany in groups, rather than a huge attack on the entire frontier.[46] In the last ten days
of December the Rharhabe managed to infiltrate into much of Albany east of
Graham's Town, although there was no mass onslaught of the type suggested by
Somerset's panicky estimates of 10 000 to 20 000 Rharhabe simultaneously
attacking along the length of the Fish River.[47] A Boer, Delport, described in February
how he had been attacked at his farm near the Fish River on 23 December by one
thousand 'Kafirs', and how he and his 13-year-old son, whose gun did not work, had
held them at bay.[48] Stories like this abounded, and it is upon these fictional accounts
that the settler version of 1835 is based. The Rharhabe parties of the first two weeks
seem to have consisted regularly of a hundred or more men, but by mid-January they
had shrunk to an average of about ten.[49] Such groups posed little real threat to the
armed colonists but were elusive and frustrating for the patrols.

They took cattle (although nothing like the number claimed), burnt selected
farmsteads, and killed 25 men, leaving women and children alone. It was not a mass
'Xhosa' response, planned well in advance by conniving chiefs, and masterminded
by the paramount Hintsa. It was a series of attacks by some of the frontier Rharhabe
(on a smaller scale than 1819) who, after the settlers put up such a weak initial
defence, were joined by many of the eastern Ndlambe (see map 5). The main
participating Rharhabe chiefs – Maqoma, Tyali, Bhotumane, Nqeno and Qasana –
did not wish a major confrontation with the militarily superior Europeans, but
wished to bring to the attention of the whites their anger at their loss of land and
increasing military impotence.

The two main areas attacked were that centring on the Koonap River – a tributary
of the Fish, north-east of Graham's Town – and that south of Graham's Town,
breaching the lower Fish south of Trompetter's Drift. These two regions contained

---

44. (CA) A50/4, Read to Fairbairn, 7 Dec. 1833. See also M. Wilson and L. Thompson, eds, *A History of South Africa to 1870*, Cape Town, 1982, 252.
45. For a full explanation of the events of 1835 see Webster, 'Land Expropriation', chs. 3, 5.
46. See also A.C.M. Webb, 'The Immediate Consequences of the Sixth Frontier War on the Farming Community of Albany', *South African Historical Journal*, 10 (1978), 38.
47. The Fish River was also in flood on 21–22 December – see Cory Library (hereafter CL) PR 3563, Reminiscences of H.J. Halse. Halse is not generally a reliable source, but is corroborated on this point by J.B. Scott, 'The British Soldier on the Eastern Cape Frontier, 1800–1850', Ph.D. thesis, University of Port Elizabeth, Port Elizabeth, 1973, 187–90.
48. (CA) 1/AY/8/86, Evidence of Delport, 23 Feb. 1835.
49. (CA) 1/AY/8/86, Report of P. Retief, 16 Jan, 1835; (CA) 1/AY/8/55, Report of Ziervogel, 8 Apr. 1835.

relatively dense colonial populations, the former chiefly Boer and the latter English. There were complaints by the Rharhabe about their ill-treatment at the hands of these frontier inhabitants. In 1830–1 farms had been issued to one hundred discharged white military personnel between the Koonap and the Fish (the area vacated by the Ngqika in 1819) to act as an additional buffer. It was the colonists in this area who were attacked, for reasons not difficult to comprehend.

Boer and settler patrols retained control in most areas throughout the period of the 'irruption'. By mid-January the Europeans had control of most of the territory west of the Keiskamma River, and the Rharhabe warriors were retreating from the Ceded Territory. D'Urban and British troop reinforcements arrived between 13 and 23 January, not to protect Albany, but to carry the war into Rharhabe territory and claim their spoils. D'Urban, who had only been in the colony for six months, was a conservative, officious, military man, who was firm in his belief in asserting military control. His views coincided with those of the 'Graham's Town faction' – a powerful group of settler leaders from fields of business, media, military, church, agriculture and the administration – who were in favour of expansion.

The armed response of the Rharhabe provided the opportunity for the amelioration of the settler demands for land and labour, and the chance to ensure the recognition of British hegemony by all 'Kafir' chiefs. The Mpondo and Thembu were prepared to acknowledge and aid the British, but the Gcaleka were recalcitrant. The settler view of the war, which was endorsed, supported and in many respects created by D'Urban, gives the impression that the army operations of April and May were relatively haphazard, and that the invasion of Gcaleka territory in particular was a decision of the moment, as was the 'emancipation' of the Fingo and the annexation of the Queen Adelaide Province. These three events, though, were the specific objectives of the colonial forces, and were in fact performed as part of a well planned and carefully conducted campaign.[50]

After a period of preparation in Graham's Town a massive force of British soldiers, colonists and Khoi made its way through Rharhabe territory, burning huts and crops, taking cattle, killing men and capturing women and children. Hintsa was commanded to side with the British. He vacillated, and the army continued straight into his territory in April. The failure of Hintsa to meet D'Urban's ultimatum for the Gcaleka actively to aid the colony led to a full-scale war on the Gcaleka. They, too, had their homes destroyed, their cattle taken, and their women and children captured. After surrendering to the overwhelming power of the British, Hintsa was imprisoned and murdered two weeks later. The power and effect of the British troops is clearly outlined in D'Urban's summary of the war. The Rharhabe loss, he said,

---

50. For the clear outlines of this plan, see G. M. Theal, ed., *Documents Relating to the Kaffir War of 1835*, London, 1912, 10–14, Smith to D'Urban, 14 Jan. 1835; *BPP* 279 (1836), 26–7, D'Urban's Orders, 22 Feb. 1835; (CA) A519/18, 51, D'Urban to Bell, 27 Feb. 1835.

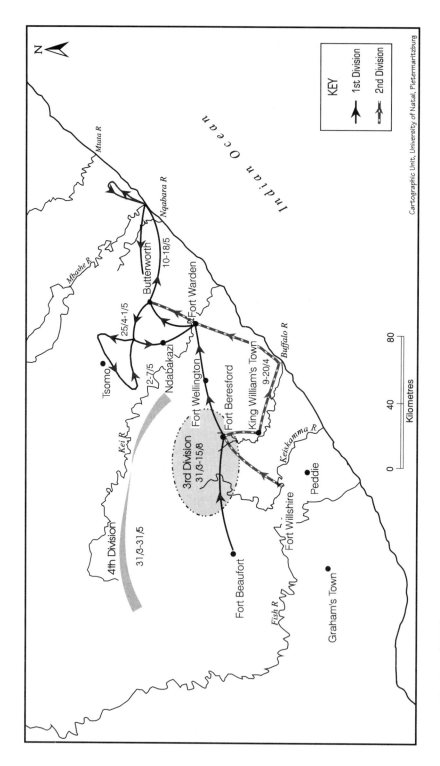

Map 6. The War of 1835

amounted to 4 000 of their warriors or fighting men, and among them many captains. Our's fortunately has not in the whole amounted to 100, and of these only 2 officers. There have been taken from them also, besides the conquest and alienation of their country, about 60 000 head of cattle, almost all their goats, their habitations every where destroyed, and their gardens and cornfields laid waste. They have, therefore, been chastised not extremely, but sufficiently.[51]

The Fingo

Settler Orthodoxy on the History of the Fingo

Parallel to the imbedding of the settler interpretation of the war of 1835 came the development of the history of the Fingo. The arrival of the Fingo in the colony was the most important event of the year 1835, and the one most shrouded in mystery. The central work on the history of the Fingo remains *The History of the Abambo*, written in 1912 under commission of the Methodist Synod by the Revd Joseph Whiteside,[52] a contemporary of George McCall Theal and George Cory. Whiteside, who drew partly on the personal writings of the Revd John Ayliff, claimed that all Fingo were refugee members of the Hlubi, Zizi, Bhele, Relidwane and Kunene from the Mzinyathi River region in what is now north-western Natal, where they had all been part of what he called the Mbo tribe. Whiteside's history of the Fingo is rooted in the orthodox explanation of the 'mfecane' as the central factor in all African movement in the sub-continent in the 1820s and 1830s.[53] This holds that the rise of Shaka and the overwhelming military power of the Zulu state in the late 1810s resulted in the rapid geographical expansion of the Zulu, accomplished by sundry deaths and destruction. One of the groups Shaka attacked was the Mbo. Ayliff's computation of the number of deaths that resulted from this attack is enough to preclude him from consideration as an accurate source. He assumed without any basis that there were 12 Fingo tribes: a biblical derivative. He then estimated, arbitrarily, that there must have been 60 000 in each tribe, thus totalling 720 000 people. Basing his calculations on his count of 30 000 Fingo in the colony in 1853, he then seriously concluded that Shaka killed 690 000 Fingo.[54]

The survivors of Shaka's attack managed to flee south along the coast to Hintsa, as refugees. Hintsa initially welcomed them in 1827–8, Whiteside continues, but soon forced them into oppressive slavery. Ayliff was the missionary with Hintsa at Butterworth from 1831 to 1835, and was described as the 'Father of the Fingo',[55]

---

51. (CA) GH 1/108, 122–3, D'Urban to Glenelg.
52. (J.Ayliff and) J. Whiteside, *History of the Abambo, Generally Known as Fingo*, Butterworth, 1912. I have referred to this book throughout under Whiteside's name, as Ayliff wrote none of it, and was merely inaccurately paraphrased for a small section of it.
53. As outlined in J.D. Omer-Cooper, *The Zulu Aftermath: A Nineteenth-century Revolution in Bantu Africa*, London, 1966.
54. (CL) PR 3826, Rough Notebook of Ayliff, 5.
55. See for example Gedye's comment in *Graham's Town Journal*, 1875, on 'the late revered, now sainted John Ayliff', who 'is still remembered by many of the now aged Fingos as their father'.

as the Fingo supposedly flocked to him for protection and to be converted. Whiteside claimed that it was Ayliff who organised the 'rescue' of these oppressed people from their Gcaleka overlords, and that when the colonial troops entered Gcaleka territory in April 1835, the same 16 800 surviving Fingo were rescued by the British and were given land and all settled around Peddie, in the ceded territory.[56] The Fingo were so grateful that they became allies of the colony and supporters of the Church and education – promises outlined by the Fingo chiefs in Peddie on 14 May 1835.

Whiteside's descriptions have been accepted in almost all respects by subsequent historians. As Richard Moyer said: 'Although some have interpreted the material differently or have embellished upon it, few have added more to our knowledge of the Mfengu.'[57] Yet *The History of the Abambo* is a book full of contradictions, exaggeration and myth, based marginally upon some of the writings of Ayliff (claimed posthumously as co-author), with an infusion of Victorian conviction and imagination.[58] In his first two chapters, supposedly describing all the Fingo in Natal, Whiteside draws extensively from Eugene Casalis, who was describing the movements of the Ngwane, not the Fingo.[59] Many of his descriptions of the 'Mbo', and their numbers and movement, are adapted from W.C. Scully's writing on the Hlubi and Ngwane.[60] Ayliff is not a reliable source on Fingo history either, even if quoted accurately. The evolution of his descriptions of their history shows his inadequacy as a historical source. The first 'history' of the Fingo was sent to D'Urban by Ayliff in May 1835, wherein he mentioned nine chiefs and the histories of the people.[61] From 1830 to 1837 Ayliff had written a daily diary of his life in Butterworth.[62] In this diary, he made scarcely any mention of Fingo, which suggests that he had little contact before 1835 with those people he termed Fingo.

In August and September 1835 Ayliff wrote three articles for the *Graham's Town Journal*, providing a rough summary of 'Fingo history',[63] that was to go into Whiteside's text. In 1851 and 1853 he wrote progressively more sophisticated 'histories' of the Fingo, with a strong anti-Gcaleka tone.[64]

In these later essays, Ayliff at no stage wrote independently on Fingo history, despite his supposed familiarity with his 'charges'. Having rambled for 90 pages about the destruction caused by Shaka, he contradicted himself by concluding that he

56. In 1819 the Fish River was redeclared the boundary of the Cape colony and the area between the Fish and Keiskamma Rivers was pronounced 'Neutral Territory'. By 1823 this area was known as the 'Ceded Territory' as white settlers slowly appropriated land in it.
57. Moyer, 'A History of the Mfengu', 9.
58. A.C. Webster, 'Ayliff, Whiteside, and the Fingo "Emancipation" of 1835:A Reappraisal', B.A. Hons essay, Rhodes University, Grahamstown, 1988, 2–20.
59. Whiteside, *History of the Abambo*, chs. 1 and 2; E. Casalis, *The Basutos or Twenty-three Years in South Africa*, London, 1861.
60. W.C. Scully, 'Fragments of Native History', *The State* (1909), 285.
61. (CA) A519/2, D'Urban Papers, Ayliff to D'Urban, 1 May 1835.
62. (CA) A80, Papers of John Ayliff. The only part of this collection that has been used is his diary between 1830 and 1838. All subsequent references to A80 allude only to the diary.
63. *Graham's Town Journal*, 20 Aug., 3 Sept., 17 Sept. 1835.
64. (CL) PR 3826, Rough Notebook of Ayliff, *c*.1851; (CL) MS 15,543, Sketch of Fingo History for Cathcart, Ayliff, *c*.1853. These, significantly, were written during the War of Mlanjeni.

was 'inclined to fear that the hellish practice of the slave trade thus begun on this [Natal] coast, was the origin of those wars which have nearly produced the entire extinction of the African Tribes of this Continent.'[65] In this manuscript Ayliff borrowed extensively from missionary journals, government and military literature, letters and contemporary explorers, sometimes employing verbatim quotes in order to write the history of the Fingo.[66]

Ayliff (and Whiteside) described the 'country of the Fingoes' as 'a country rich in pasturage and in wood, healthy, well watered and abounding in game of all sorts . . . The climate appears to be, generally speaking, temperate.' But this is an unacknowledged quotation directly from Thomas Arbousset, who had in fact been describing the country of the 'Zula'.[67] The missionary John Edwards wrote in 1836 about the 'Mantatees', and how 'the accounts of their wars and bloodshed would affect the most hard-hearted . . . [and how] Thousands of human skulls strew the land.'[68] Ayliff borrowed these descriptions, but used them to describe the sufferings of the Fingo. Ayliff was also influenced by the lamentations of T.L. Hodgson on the savagery of Africa, and the latter's hope that the English would bring civilisation and peace. Ayliff used the same phrases in his descriptions of the natural state of Africans and the tribulations of the Fingo.[69]

Ayliff even misquoted himself. In the 1853 manuscript, for instance, he described the ill-treatment of a 'Fingo' girl,[70] whom he had described as 'Kaffir' in his diary.[71] The propagandistic idea that the Fingo were Gcaleka slaves was suggested by D'Urban after similar claims by Godlonton in previous years,[72] which Ayliff awkwardly wove into his 1853 manuscript. The history of the Fingo thus does not come from the eye-witness Ayliff, but evolved in enigma, myth and military propaganda, from which Ayliff himself copied. Yet Ayliff and Whiteside are still uncritically accepted as authorities on the history of the Fingo.

The Creation of the Fingo

All previous studies of the Fingo have viewed them as a single group – with diverse Natal backgrounds – who were homogenised by 1835 and who entered the colony

65. (CL) PR 3826, 1; cf. R. Drury, *The Adventures of Robert Drury During Fifteen Years Captivity on the Island of Madagascar*, London, 1743, Reprinted in 1807, 442.
66. In (CL) MS 15,543, Sketch of Fingo History, Ayliff did not describe the movements of the Fingo in May in his own words. He merely transcribed Dutton's Notice, Ndabakazi, 3 May 1835.
67. T. Arbousset and F. Daumas, *Narrative of an Exploratory Tour to the North-east of the Colony of the Cape of Good Hope*, translated from the French by J.C. Brown, Cape Town, 1846, 133; (CL) MS 15,543, Sketch of Fingo History, 4–5; Whiteside, *History of Abambo*, 2.
68. *The Wesleyan-Methodist Magazine*, 15 (1836), 789, letter from Rev. J. Edwards, 17 Mar. 1836.
69. (CL) PR 3826, Rough Notebook of Ayliff, 5, makes specific reference to the 4 Aug. 1823 entry in Hodgson's diary; cf. T.L. Hodgson, *The Journals of the Reverend T.L. Hodgson, Missionary to the Seleka–Rolong and the Griquas, 1821–1831*, ed. by R.L. Cope, Johannesburg, 1977.
70. (CL) MS 15,543, Sketch of Fingo History, 46.
71. (CA) A80, Diary of Ayliff, 6 Aug. 1834.
72. D'Urban, Government Notice, 3 May 1835. See Peires, *The House of Phalo*, 225; Soga, *The South-Eastern Bantu*.

as a unit and remained together under their traditional chiefs, largely at Peddie. The evidence on Fingo identity and history is too piecemeal to support a full explanation of 1835, and much research is still needed to clear up the details. But two overriding points about the Fingos are clear: there was no homogeneous group in 1835 (nor for decades later), and few of the Fingo had similar backgrounds. Further, their existence was owed to the British devastation in the war of 1835, not to Shaka. Four distinct, and very different, categories of Fingo can be distinguished. First, there was a group of mercenaries who fought for the colonial army in 1835 and who claimed the name. Second were three groups of opportunist Rharhabe, Gcaleka, Mpondo and Thembu from the trans-Fish Wesleyan missions who were granted land at Peddie, Tyhume and King William's Town by the government. They were joined there by a scattering of Natal refugees from the Caledon River area, who were appointed by D'Urban as Fingo chiefs.

The third and fourth groups are not clearly delineated and the evidence on their identity is scanty. One resulted from the constant trickle of Rharhabe who entered the colony from 1835 to seek employment as their only means of survival after the destruction of their means of subsistence during the war. The fourth group – the most important for this essay – was one of Rharhabe, Gcaleka and Bomvana (mainly women and children) who were seized by the British troops in 1835 and channelled forcibly on to eastern Cape farms. The exact number of these forced labourers is unclear, and my hypothesis on their movements is built largely on circumstantial evidence. These four Fingo groups were elided under the same name and identity in 1835, and after a few decades developed a homogeneity that led to the present ethnic identity. Before the detail on these four groups is presented, though, we need to explore the origins of the term 'Fingo'.

Evidence of the Fingo before 1835

The etymology of the term Fingo is not clear. There were people called Fingo scattered, as individuals, families or groups, in the area between the Sundays and Mzimvubu Rivers before 1835. In 1827 the traveller Cowper Rose described a group of refugees gathered around Butterworth, who were called Fingo.[73] William Shaw described them in June 1827 as

> Africans of several distinct nations, who, in consequence of wars and commotions in the interior, have been scattered and driven from their native countries, and have sought refuge in the country of Hintsa, who has treated them kindly, and allowed them to settle among his people.

He noted that some came 'from the neighbourhood of the Portuguese settlements on the east coast', in other words from the vicinity of Delagoa Bay.[74] A month later

---

73. C. Rose, *Four Years in Southern Africa*, London, 1829, 93–5.
74. *The Report of the Wesleyan-Methodist Missionary Society, for the Year Ending December, 1827*, 42, Letter from W. Shaw, 19 June 1827.

William Shrewsbury claimed that there were five to six thousand Fingo at Butterworth, all of whom had been 'subdued by Chaka'.[75] Given subsequent evidence, Shrewsbury's estimate of Fingo numbers is probably too high. Shaw's evidence is crucial in three respects, which contradict Shrewsbury and Ayliff: he says that some Fingo moved originally from near Delagoa Bay; he stresses that Hintsa treated them well, as custom dictated for strangers; and he notes that they came, not from the coast, but from the interior.

There is much material to show that those Fingo who were refugees came into the colony via the interior – what became the Orange Free State and western Lesotho region – rather than south through Natal. Ayliff mentioned on a number of occasions that the Fingo were refugees from wars in the interior.[76] The Revd Brownlee met a group of people at Hintsa's residence (Butterworth) in 1822 who had been there for a number of years. He assumed that they were Bechuana (Tswana) or Damara, as they came from north-west of Lattakoo (Dithakong).[77] Somerset said in 1833 that the Fingo came from the north; that they had lived with the 'Goes' north of the Bastards, and had been driven south into the colony.[78] In October 1835 Judge Menzies, while travelling through the districts of Albany, Uitenhage and George, found 'many *"Natives of the Interior of Africa"*, called, or calling themselves, Fingoes'.[79]

This evidence is consistent with Cobbing's general hypothesis that there was a movement, among others, from Delagoa Bay (away from slavers), into the Caledon area, and then south after Griqua attacks. These 'wars of the interior' were not fratricidal holocausts generated by Shaka and raiding bands. It was the dislocation which resulted from the penetration of Griqua and Kora slavers and raiders that produced the upheavals in the trans-Orangian interior referred to. Movement in the interior had been dictated partly by intra-African hostility, but largely by European penetration in search of forced labour. Portuguese slave traders and their African middlemen had begun to have a major impact on the Delagoa Bay–northern Natal hinterland from the 1810s.[80] This increased disruption forced weaker groups – such as the Ngwane, Hlubi, Bhele and Zizi on the Mzinyathi and upper Thukela Rivers – to move, while the stronger groups like the Zulu and Dlamini (Swazi) were able to grow as defensive states.

75. *The Report of the Wesleyan-Methodist Missionary Society*, 45, Letter from W. Shrewsbury, 12 July 1827.
76. (CL) MS 15,543, Sketch of Fingo History; (CL) PR 3826, Rough Notebook of Ayliff.
77. Thompson, *Travels and Adventures*, vol. 2, 219; cf. Philip, *Researches in South Africa*, vol. 2, ch. 10. Reverend Kay made mention of the Fingo he had found with the Thembu, who were refugees from the interior; see S. Kay, *Travels and Researches in Caffraria, Describing the Character, Customs, and Moral Condition of the Tribes Inhabiting that Portion of Southern Africa*, London, 1833, 133–4, 293–4.
78. (CA) GH 1/97, 125, Report of Somerset. It is not clear to whom Somerset was referring, but is likely to have been the Ghoya, who were in what became the northern Orange Free State area.
79. (CA) 1/AY/8/24, Judge Menzies to D'Urban, 3 Oct. 1835. Original stress.
80. Cobbing, 'The Mfecane as Alibi', 504–7; and J. Cobbing, 'Grasping the Nettle: The Slave Trade and the Early Zulu ', in D. R. Edgecombe, J. P. C. Laband and P. S. Thompson, comps, *The Debate on Zulu Origins: A Selection of Papers on the Zulu Kingdom and Early Colonial Natal*, Pietermaritzburg, 1992, 8–19.

Components of the weaker groups moved south-west into, among other places, the Caledon River area, attempting to escape the disruption caused by the slave-raiding. But here again there was no safety, as by the early 1820s bands of armed Griqua and Kora raiders were penetrating the area from the west, in search of women and children to be captured and sold to colonial farmers as 'apprentices' or 'Mantatees'. A similar collision between raiders and dislocated groups again occurred, and from here there was a gradual flow of refugees moving south throughout the 1820s. They moved individually in different directions, to settle with varying acceptance among the peoples from the Thembu to well into the western parts of the colony, and were called 'Fingo'. Those who moved south into African polities were incorporated within them with varying status. Almost all Fingo who moved to the colony became labourers.[81]

The earliest documentation of a Fingo that I have found was in 1824, and by the mid-1830s they were to be found scattered throughout western Rharhabe territory. There were 'Fengus' at Pirie mission station in 1824,[82] who had come from the north where they had apparently been dispossessed by 'Mantatees'. Mrs Ross, wife of the missionary at Pirie, made a distinction between Fengus and Zizi refugees. The latter she also described as 'Mantatees', an ironic elision in view of Whiteside's assertion that the Zizi were 'Fingo'. By 1833 there were 120 Fingo at the Kat River Settlement,[83] and Fingo nearby with Bawana of the Winterberg Thembu.[84] Laing spoke of Fingo living near Anta on the upper Keiskamma, and in the Gaga and Buffalo River areas in 1832.[85]

The only group to have maintained cohesion in the move southwards was the Ngwane. In his movements into the Caledon and then south over the Drakensberg, Matiwane had gathered refugees, who became part of his doomed state and assumed the Ngwane identity. A clear case of the elision of the terms Fetcani, Ngwane and Fingo occurred in 1829, when two Fingo came to Butterworth to be married by the Revd Stephen Kay, Ayliff's predecessor. The man had been with the Mantatees at Dithakong, whereafter he fled south-east and joined the Ngwane in the Caledon area, whom the woman had already joined. [86] This group of Matiwane's was then forced south by the Griqua dislocation in the area, and was scattered by the British in 1828 at Mbholompo.[87] It must be stressed that the couple in question did not see

---

81. Campbell commented on a number of occasions that the 'devastating wars of the interior' were providing 'a valuable supply of servants' to Albany and Somerset. See, for example (CA) LCA 6, evidence of D. Campbell, 4 July 1834, in reply to Philip's complaints about the proposed vagrancy bill.
82. (CL) MS 2642, Letters of Mrs Ross, Apr. 1824.
83. (CA) 1/AY/9/7, 38, Population of the Kat River Settlement, 7 June 1833. There were also 426 Tswana.
84. (CL) MS 17119, 35, Testimony of Sihele.
85. (CL) MS 16, 579, Diary of Laing, entry for 18 Sept. 1833; (CL) MS 9037, 261, 280, Minutes of Presbyterian Meetings. See also (CL) Diary of Kayser, 19 and 22 Feb., 12 April, 31 May, 25 July, 4 Aug., 11 Sep., and 17 Oct. 1834 for references to Fingo near Burns Hill mission station.
86. Kay, *Travels and Researches in Caffraria*, 299–300.
87. Cobbing, 'The Mfecane as Alibi', 500–3.

themselves as Fingo until they came into contact with whites in 1829, and their original identities are unknown. There were many Ngwane who ended up as labourers in the colony after 1828. Most were subsequently termed Fingo.[88] Many of the Ngwane captured in 1828 were taken to Graham's Town involuntarily, from where they 'were distributed amongst the farmers in the Graham's Town District. From there they were distributed amongst the Fingos on the border and in the Eastern Cape.' They were then redefined as Fingo.[89]

It is clear that the orthodox view that all Fingo moved south from the Natal region to Butterworth via the area that is today the Transkei is completely misleading. John Wright's work on the Zulu kingdom and Natal shows convincingly that there is virtually no evidence for a large-scale flight of refugees southwards from the Natal region into the eastern Cape region in the 1810s and 1820s.[90] The process of Fingoisation in the 1820s and 1830s needs a close study. What was the precise motor of movement in the central and northern Transkei region in the period? What factors other than capture caused groups like the 'Mantatees', Bhele, Zizi and Ngwane to enter the colonial ambit? What was happening to the African polities and their internal dynamics that resulted in the alienation of so many people?[91]

It is very difficult to assess how many Fingo there were in 1835. The orthodoxy claims that there were 16 800 – a figure derived from the estimate of one of the British troops.[92] But this figure fails to differentiate between the different Fingo groupings. D'Urban's estimates in May 1835 vacillated between 5 000 and 15 000 Fingo. The elision of different types of Fingo has resulted in confusion as to their total number. By late 1835 there were definitely 700 at Peddie, 2 000 at Tyhume and 2 000 at King William's Town, most of whom came from the collaborator and military groups. A likely estimate of the number labouring in the colony – both voluntary and involuntary – would be up to 10 000. It is unclear how many Fingo came from Butterworth into the colony in May. It is possible there were 16 800 – all four groups mixed and separated again once in the colony – but it seems unlikely that there were so many.

88. For examples of the Fingo-Ngwane elision, see (CA) 1/AY/8/86, Statement of Umjojo, Graham's Town gaol, 22 Feb. 1835; Kay, *Travels and Researches in Caffraria*, 333.
89. Moyer, 'A History of the Mfengu', 605, Evidence of Jacob Tunyiswa. See also J. Bird, comp., *The Annals of Natal, 1495 to 1845*, Pietermaritzburg, 1888, vol. 1, 123, Evidence of H.F. Fynn to Native Commission, 1852; Cory, *Rise of South Africa*, vol. 3, 165n. interviewed an old Ngwane man who called himself Fingo, and who gave a brief synopsis of Ngwane history, and described all Ngwane as Fingo.
90. J.B. Wright, 'The Dynamics of Power and Conflict in the Thukela–Mzimkhulu Region in the Late Eighteenth and Early Nineteenth Centuries: A Critical Reconstruction', Ph.D thesis, University of the Witwatersrand, Johannesburg, 1990, 301–9. See also J.B. Wright, 'Political Transformations in the Thukela-Mzimkhulu Region of Natal in the Late Eighteenth and Early Nineteenth Centuries', in this volume.
91. I am indebted to John Wright for his comments and discussions on these questions.
92. *BPP* 279 (1836), 37, Estimate of Trotter, 14 May 1835.

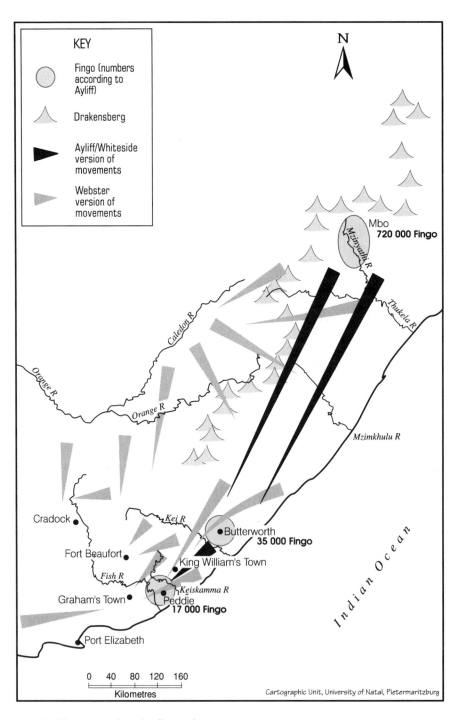

KEY

Fingo (numbers according to Ayliff)

Drakensberg

Ayliff/Whiteside version of movements

Webster version of movements

N

Mbo
720 000 Fingo

Mzinyathi R

Thukela R

Caledon R

Orange R

Orange R

Mzimkhulu R

Cradock

Kei R

Butterworth
35 000 Fingo

Fort Beaufort

King William's Town

Fish R

Graham's Town

Keiskamma R

Peddie
17 000 Fingo

Port Elizabeth

Indian Ocean

0   40   80   120   160
Kilometres

Cartographic Unit, University of Natal, Pietermaritzburg

Map 7. 'Fingo' entry into the Cape colony

Fingo Labourers

The unclarified third and fourth Fingo groups – the voluntary and involuntary labourers – shall be dealt with first. D'Urban made it clear that a chief reason for bringing Fingo into the colony was that of 'furnishing a supply of hired servants to the colonists',[93] and a substantial percentage of Fingo ended up as labourers.[94] The 'arrival of the Fingoes', wrote Ayliff, 'conferred an invaluable boon on the Colonists, who at that time were greatly suffering from the want of labour'.[95] The missionary at Bethelsdorp commented in 1837 that 'there has not been the same demand for labourers as formerly, a great number of Fingoes having come into the Colony, who are employed at lower wages than those usually given to Hottentots.'[96] In the same year a group of 80 Fingo (with families) were prepared to sell their cattle in order to ensure employment at Slaai Kraal.[97] Moyer noted the large number of Fingo workers in Port Elizabeth in the 1840s who were ousting the Khoi as cheap labour.[98] By 1842 there were several thousand Fingo and Tswana working in Cradock alone.[99] It is significant that the myth of the Fingo was generated in the region which stood to gain most from their arrival – Albany – and which received generous support from the whole eastern Cape, to which they were such a boon.

The first extensive group of Fingo brought in to work was that accompanying Somerset (who had organised the Mbholompo affair) in May 1835. They were, according to Ayliff and Whiteside, settled at Peddie but the Fingo census of October 1835 shows quite clearly that they were not. This group seems to have consisted of both free and unfree labourers. Some were retained at Fort Wellington[100] and Fort Warden[101] to work on the buildings, and at least 200 accompanied Somerset to Graham's Town, where they were immediately indentured.[102] In his attempt to explain why there were Fingo employed in the colony, Ayliff wrote that most of the Fingo at Peddie wanted to work in the colony.[103] It seems that many of the Fingo moved immediately to Graham's Town, where a location was set up on the outskirts of town. Fingo awaiting employment were to reside there, from where the Graham's

93. (CA) 1/AY/8/24, D'Urban to Campbell, 14 Oct. 1835.

94. (CA) LG 420, 124–7, Report of W. Fynn, 1 Nov. 1835.

95. (CL) PR 3826, 2, Rough Notebook of Ayliff. Ayliff pinpoints Ordinance 50 and the emancipation of the slaves as most harmful to the labour situation, but says that the abundant Fingo labour solved it.

96. Macmillan, *The Cape Colour Question*, 253.

97. (CA) 1/AY/8/50, Hudson to Campbell, 22 July 1837.

98. Moyer, 'A History of the Mfengu', ch.4. See J.C. Chase, *The Cape of Good Hope and the Eastern Province of Algoa . . .*, London, 1843, 238, for Fingo surf labourers at Algoa Bay.

99. Long, *An Index to Authors*, 261.

100. (CL) MS 951, Diary of T.H. Bowker, entry for 22 May 1835. There were 20 men, 40 women and 50 children.

101. J.E. Alexander, *Narrative of a Voyage of Observation Among the Colonies . . . and of a Campaign in Kaffer-land, 1835*, London, 1837, vol.2, 215; (CL) MS 951, Diary of T.H. Bowker, entry for 10 May 1835. There was still a large number there in 1836, see (CA) LG 420, 124–7, Report of W. Fynn, 1 Nov. 1835.

102. A.C.M. Webb, 'The Agricultural Development of the 1820 Settlement Down to 1846', M.A. dissertation, Rhodes University, Grahamstown, 1975, 209; see also (CA) CO 2756, Jarvis to Campbell, 26 May 1835.

103. *Graham's Town Journal*, 17 Sept. 1835, Ayliff article.

Town residents eagerly took labourers.[104] There were so many Fingo entering into contracts in Graham's Town with colonists that an extra clerk was appointed in July to countersign the service contracts.[105] In the same month Godlonton complained that the area around Graham's Town was 'teeming' with unemployed Fingo.[106] The majority of the Fingo were employed on farms as far afield as Graaff-Reinet, but the magistrate's records do show Fingo women working as domestics in Graham's Town.[107]

When the Fingo were brought under military escort to Graham's Town in May, Colonel England took a list of their names and those of the Boers to whom they were being indentured, and distributed it to all civil commissioners.[108] This list is obviously crucial to identifying Fingos and tracing their lives, but no copy has been found, although 10 were made. One list of Fingo labourers would have completely undermined D'Urban's explanation of their origins if it had somehow come to the attention of the Colonial Office. Did D'Urban order them to be destroyed?

During the attacks on the Amatole Mountains in early April a number of Rharhabe women were captured and brought into camp[109], but very little was said of them, as was the case with women and children captured in the Fish River bush in February and March.[110] T.H. Bowker reported that 50 women joined the British during the attack on Ntaba kaNdoda on 7 April, and that the following day many women – apparently Nqeno's people – came to the camp.[111] No further mention is made of them, and they were presumably either employed for the pleasure of the troops or taken into labour. The Rharhabe women around Burnshill were advised by the 3rd Division to move out of the bush, but they refused, as those who had fled to D'Urban's camp had been raped.[112] On 7 April Smith led a patrol into the bush around the Pirie mission where he 'captured 2 500 cattle[,] 15 women and a hottentot of the name of Lewis Arnoldus'.[113] Bowker's diary provides oblique references to the capture of Gcaleka women and children in late April while his patrol was hunting for Hintsa.[114]

104. (CA) CO 2756, Jarvis to Campbell, 26 May 1835.
105. (CA) 1/AY/9/62, W. Smith to Campbell, 4 July 1835. Aldwin was appointed.
106. *Graham's Town Journal*, 28 July 1835, Godlonton editorial.
107. For example, (CA) 1/AY/1/4, Magistrate's Records, Graham's Town, 11 Jan. 1836.
108. England wrote to D'Urban from Graham's Town on 20 May 1835 – (CA) A519/2, 24 – saying that he had made lists and made them available. Despite an extensive search, I have not been able to locate a copy in the Cape Archives.
109. J. Goldswain, *The Chronicle of Jeremiah Goldswain, Albany Settler of 1820*, edited by U. Long, Cape Town, 1946, 94–5; Alexander, *Narrative of a Voyage*, vol. 2, 80.
110. A.L. Harington, *Sir Harry Smith: Bungling Hero*, Cape Town, 1980, 30.
111. (CL) MS 951, Diary of T.H. Bowker, entries for 7 and 8 Apr. 1835.
112. Stretch, *The Journal*, 61.
113. Natal Archives (hereafter NA) A96, Shepstone Diary, entry for 7 Apr. 1835. See also Alexander, *Narrative of a Voyage*, 80. A similar description is given by Goldswain, *The Chronicle*, 94–5, who mentions that one of the women had given birth the previous day but had been forced to walk five miles.
114. (CL) MS 951, Diary of T.H. Bowker, entries for 26 Apr. 1835: 'catch several horses, and some Kafir women and children, these latter were let go as useless'; they moved on and 'find some more women and children'; 28 Apr. 1835: shot a woman by mistake 'and return without taking her'; 6 May 1835: 'Maqoma and Tyali's cattle and women and children have not been found and taken'.

The evidence for the seizure of Rharhabe women and children west of the Kei in 1835 is clear, but that for the taking of captives east of the Kei more circumstantial. The fact that there was definitely capturing of Rharhabe by the troops, although the evidence for it has always remained intentionally hidden, merely emphasises the extent to which this illegal behaviour was taking place and being covered up. There was no question that the Colonial Office would have launched a high-level inquiry, with very serious consequences for the Cape authorities, had it been known that Africans were being captured and forced to labour and that the British administrators were actively involved in planning this. D'Urban had planned for the invasion of the territory of the innocent Gcaleka before April, and by May he brought 17 000 'Fingo' into the colony, most of whom were labourers. Had he planned a general labour seizure to deal with the colonial demand? It was not coincidental that this solved the acute labour shortage in the eastern districts. There had been a long precedent of the capture of African women and children outside the colony and brought in under euphemistic labels such as 'Mantatee' and possibly 'refugee'. Labourers were being captured west of the Kei in 1835. The reasonable conclusion is thus that most of the 'Fingo' were Gcaleka (and Rharhabe) women and children captured illegally, and that the methods and accounts of capture were censored in official documents and excluded from private papers.

The seizure of women continued. Charles Bailie returned to King William's Town from the Pirie area on 21 June with a large patrol, having killed eight Rharhabe and 'captured 100 Caffre women with as many children'.[115] Was his death in the same area three days later[116] retaliation for these captures? Godlonton described this patrol as 'most judiciously and spiritedly conducted', but neglected to mention the captives.[117] A second patrol was sent out westwards from King William's Town to the Debe Flats, also on 21 June, under William Sutton and Charles Granet. They returned with four women and sixteen children.[118] A party of military Fingo chasing the Ndlambe eight miles outside King William's Town on 2 July seized twenty women, who were brought back with the other plunder.[119] They were presumably sent to Boer farms as forced labourers. Charles Stretch received a complaint from an elderly Ndlambe man in 1836 that his son had been forcibly seized from his garden on the Keiskamma by D'Urban's forces returning to the colony, and made to work on the farm of a Boer named O. Niekerk.[120]

It is important to remember that women and children were the preferred labour

---

115. Stretch, *The Journal*, 98, 22 June 1835.
116. The hagiography of the death of Bailie and his patrol is similar to that accorded the Wilson patrol in Matabeleland in 1893. For the settler version, see Godlonton, *Narrative of the Irruption*, 195–202. For a more accurate account, see (CA) A519/27, D'Urban Papers, 65–70, Information on Fingo women, 23 July 1835; Stretch, *The Journal*, ch. 4.
117. Godlonton, *Narrative of the Irruption*, 196.
118. Godlonton, *Narrative of the Irruption*, 197.
119. (NA) A96, Shepstone Diary, entry for 2 July 1835.
120. (CA) LG 420, 57, Report of Stretch, 1836.

captures, as the women were pliable and the children young enough to be subdued and trained to fulfil colonial labour demands. Men could defend themselves.[121] Susan Newton-King provides similar explanations for the majority of labour captives in the Graaff-Reinet district being women and children.[122] As shown above, there was a long precedent of labour seizures, and a serious need for them in the eastern districts in 1835. According to the official records, 88 per cent of the Fingo who came into the colony in May were women and children. It is probable that the British seizure of cattle in Rharhabe territory – from the Amatole, Keiskamma and Buffalo areas – and Gcaleka territory (especially in the week of 17–24 April in Butterworth) was accompanied by the capture of Africans, who were brought back to work. Why else would the Fingo have needed the entire 2nd Division (including military Fingo) to 'protect' them on their journey into the colony, when Henry Warden needed only a small patrol to ferry 600 people through Gcaleka territory? A fake history would then have been necessary to cover the actions.

The 'labour Fingo' were supplemented in mid-May by one thousand 'Fingo' taken by Smith in a raid on the Bomvana. He claimed that they were under Gcaleka oppression, and said that they were Fingo 'who, from their remote situation, had been unable to join their country men now under British protection'.[123] The pursuit of these Fingo seems to have formed an important reason for his attack past the Mbashe River. These Fingo were gathered at Smith's camp on the Guada River on 14 May, but little information is offered as to their identity or background. Given the general use of the term 'Fingo', and the fact that on 13 and 14 May, while Smith was chasing cattle within sight of the Mtata River, most of his force had remained at the mouth of the Mbashe,[124] as well as the precedency of labour seizure, it can be reasonably assumed that these were Bomvana and eastern Gcaleka, taken by a whirlwind commando to work in the colony.

All of these people were called 'Fingo' and most were placed temporarily in the King William's Town Fingo location where Smith found them useful.[125] From here a number were distributed in the colony. Frederick Rex, Assistant Quarter-Master at King William's Town, sent a group of 10 Fingo to his sister in Knysna in August, delivered to her by some Khoi taking leave: another 20 went to his parents, also in Knysna, in September, after his father had written to him in June to ask for Fingo labourers.[126] Rex had chosen his group because they were the 'best-tempered' of the many available in King William's Town. He felt 'that having them driven to the

---

121. See for example the arguments proposed by the Advisory Council in 1827, *BPP* 252 (1835), 12, when discussing the implementation of Ordinance 49. The civil commissioners from around the country had suggested that children be used as the main labour supply because of their obedience and inability to protest or rebel.
122. Newton-King, 'The Enemy Within'.
123. General Order No. 18, Smith, Fort Waterloo, 21 May 1835; Cory, *Rise of South Africa*, vol. 3, 157.
124. For Smith's description of the patrol, see *BPP* 279 (1836), 48–51, 18 May 1835.
125. *BPP* 279 (1836), 109, D'Urban to Smith, 12 Nov. 1835.
126. Long, *An Index to Authors*, 195, G. Rex to son, Knysna, 11 June 1835; 174–7, F. Rex to sister, King William's Town, 28 July 1835; F. Rex to father, 28 Aug. 1835.

Island [at Knysna] and back again once a day may have a good effect upon their scabby old legs'.[127] He also contemplated sending some to a friend as a present, with the warning that some Fingo needed to be flogged to ensure productivity.[128] In September, after reports from the town of George about the laziness of Fingo, George Rex asked that his son send him only women and children, with the explanation that civilisation would thereby be spread.[129] These facts all point to the assertion that forced labour was being distributed throughout the colony from a base in King William's Town.

The war caused a flood of 'voluntary' – forced by circumstance – workers too. From July 1835, the eastern civil commissioners complained of 'Fingo vagrancy' – Fingo moving around armed with assegais and refusing service.[130] These were largely dispossessed and alienated Rharhabe who entered the colony in search of subsistence. Over 600 were reported in the Winterberg area in August,[131] although it is not clear whether they originated outside or inside the colony. As early as July, Ziervogel had complained to Campbell that there were Fingo, armed with assegais, wandering around Somerset district, to which Campbell replied that they were to be arrested and transported to Graham's Town.[132] A complaint came from the Graaff-Reinet civil commissioner that there were many Fingo, Bechuana and Mantatee wandering around his district, and causing a disturbance by stealing cattle and refusing to enter service under the Boers.[133] The civil commissioners of Uitenhage and George reported similar situations.[134]

Integral to D'Urban's plans for the colony was that there were to be no unemployed Africans in the colony, as they would pose a security threat – much the same argument used in favour of vagrancy ordinances. The pass laws for 'Kaffirs' were to remain the same, and all Fingo must be controlled too. He thus ordered the 'apprehension' of all wandering, unemployed Fingo, Bechuana and Kaffirs, to be sent to Fort Beaufort or Cradock, from where they were to find employment, settle in a location near a town or in the new Ceded Territory locations, or leave the colony.[135] Although D'Urban's orders were carried out and many Fingo arrested, there were still disturbances throughout 1836 from wandering Fingo and Mantatees, and from armed Africans from the interior.[136] Captain Armstrong was in charge of placing the

127. Long, *An Index to Authors*, 177, F. Rex to father, 28 Aug. 1835.
128. Long, *An Index to Authors*, 180, F. Rex to Duthie, 25 Sept. 1835.
129. Long, *An Index to Authors*, 195–6, G. Rex to son, 18 Sept. 1835.
130. (CA) 1/AY/8/24, O'Reilly to Campbell, Cradock, 22 Sept. 1835; 1/AY/9/19, Campbell to D'Urban, Graham's Town, 24 July 1835.
131. (CA) 1/AY/8/86, Report from Field Cornet, Winterberg, 7 Sept. 1835.
132. (CA) A519/6, 95, Ziervogel to Campbell, July 1835.
133. (CA) A519/3, 194, Bell to D'Urban, 4 Dec. 1835.
134. (CA) A519/17, 156, W. Smith to Campbell, 1 Dec. 1835.
135. (CA) A519/17, 121–4, D'Urban to all civil commissioners, 14 Oct. 1835. Somerset was sent out to oversee the implementation: see A519/3, 65, Somerset to D'Urban, 23 Oct. 1835; A519/3, 97–100, Somerset to D'Urban, Oct. 1835.
136. (CA) A519/6, 99, Campbell to Hudson, 16 Apr. 1836; LG 420, 105, Report of Bradshaw, Bathurst Field Cornet, 21 Sept. 1836; 1/AY/8/49, Hudson to D'Urban, 19 Nov. 1836; 1/AY/8/50, Report of Stockenstrom, Mar. 1837; 1/AY/8/56, Ziervogel to D'Urban, 15 Nov. 1836.

captured Fingo in the Fort Beaufort location, from whence many were distributed as labourers. He noted that:

> I have held out every encouragement to the farmers to take the Fingos into their service and have already disposed of about 20 families in this way. I have also apprenticed several children to the farmers. The Graff Reynet and Beaufort burghers are desirous of taking a number of Fingos to their districts as servants, and I hope to dispose of a good many of them in this way.[137]

With Graham's Town and Fort Beaufort acting as bases, Fingos were distributed wherever they were needed. A total of 352 women and 567 children were taken from Graham's Town to King William's Town in June, against their will.[138] The civil commissioner for Graaff-Reinet complained in October of a labour shortage, whereupon surplus Fingo from Albany, Somerset and Uitenhage were sent there.[139] Part of a group of 33 Fingo families being transported to work in Uitenhage in November escaped in the night and returned to Graham's Town.[140] Most of these Fingo movements were accompanied by armed military patrols, which indicates that the Fingo were not moving voluntarily. With this threat of enforced removal to farms, any unemployed Fingo in Graham's Town rapidly found service, if only carrying firewood and water in town.[141] A prospective Cape Town employer, on the advice of J.C. Chase, asked Campbell to send him 60 to 80 male Fingo, aged 12 to 20.[142] In 1837 there were a thousand applications for Fingo workers from Cape Town alone.[143]

There are few case studies of Fingo who worked in the colony in the 1830s. But the evidence available supports the hypothesis that in 1835 there were many Rharhabe, Gcaleka and Bomvana who entered the colony – either at the point of a gun or to find food – to work, and who were then classified as Fingo. They formed the bulk of Fingo numbers, but virtually disappeared from official sight.

Military Fingo in the Colonial Army

A thousand men joined the British army in 1835 and accompanied the force across the Fish and Kei. D'Urban said that they were Fingo men who wished to aid the British. A number acted as messengers,[144] and the others were particularly effective

137. (CA) CO 2756, Armstrong to Campbell, 19 Oct. 1835.
138. (CA) A519/23, 269, D'Urban to Smith, 30 June 1835. D'Urban commented that 'many of the women are by no means willing to come'. I am grateful to Julian Cobbing for this reference.
139. (CA) A519/17, 156, W. Smith to Campbell, 1 Dec. 1835; (CA) CO 2756, Orders from Campbell, 4 Dec. 1835; A519/6, 98, Campbell to Graaff-Reinet civil commissioner.
140. (CA) A519/3, 189–90, Campbell to D'Urban, 27 Nov. 1835; (CA) 1/AY/9/19, Campbell to D'Urban, 29 Nov. 1835.
141. (CA) 1/AY/9/8, Campbell to D'Urban, 11 Mar. 1836.
142. (CA) 1/AY/8/86, Letter to Campbell, 30 Oct. 1835.
143. Webb, 'The Agricultural Development', 209.
144. (CA) A519/1, 201, Somerset to D'Urban, 26 Apr. 1835.

in capturing cattle.[145] Of those used in Gcaleka territory, 50 were sent to Clarkebury, 40 helped to ferry cattle between the Tsomo River area and Butterworth, and 130 aided Smith in the Tsomo mountains in late April.[146] It seems unlikely that these men merely appeared, as the military reports claimed; the British army was not in the habit of summarily adopting untrained, untrusted locals to aid in its operations. Most importantly, these men were given guns by the British.[147] These men must have been trained prior to the war – Halse reported that the provisional battalions, the Khoi divisions used in the army, included many Africans.[148] These mercenaries were then described as Fingo, and included in the history ascribed to all Fingo. The Fingo military group was given land at King William's Town after hostilities ceased and was settled under the charge of William Fynn, who received a farm on the Keiskamma River in payment.[149]

Fingo Mission Collaborators

The primary group to assume what was to become the identity of the Fingo was a 'collaborator' group. Most of them were from the trans-Fish mission stations, and they formed the basis of the settlements at Tyhume and Peddie. Ayliff claimed that all Fingo (16 800) were settled at Peddie in May 1835, where they remained. The Peddie location, according to D'Urban, was to encompass almost half the Ceded Territory,[150] and act as a buffer between the white colonists and their neighbours. D'Urban made a further suggestion in July that all the land between the Fish and Keiskamma Rivers, between Fort Willshire and Peddie, be allocated to Fingo in small fortified villages. He indicated that a list had been made of all Fingo settled there, and their locations.[151] Somerset reported that he had followed orders and placed the Fingo in the entire area.[152]

But these statements differed from what was happening on the ground. The Peddie location consisted in reality, not of an extensive buffer system, but of a small settlement of less than 100 square kilometres, clustered around the protection of the fort and the Boers stationed there.[153] An 1835 map shows the Fingo in two small

145. (NA) A96, Shepstone Diary, entries for 24–28 Apr. 1835. For Smith's view on the cattle-capturing ability of the Fingo, see W. Brinton, *History of the British Regiments in South Africa*, Cape Town, 1977, 51.
146. (NA) A96, Shepstone Diary, 31.
147. (CL) MS 15,543, Ayliff's Sketch of Fingo history, 80; (CL) MS 951, Diary of T. H. Bowker, entry for 30 Apr. 1835; (NA) A96, Diary of Theophilus Shepstone, 28a.
148. (CL) PR 3563, Reminiscences of Halse, 15.
149. (CA) LG 420, 124–7, W. Fynn to D'Urban, 1 Nov. 1836.
150. (CA) GH 19/4, 953, D'Urban to Campbell, 4 May 1835; (CA) A519/17, 25–31, Letter from D'Urban, 12 July 1835; *BPP* 279 (1836), 38–40, Somerset to D'Urban.
151. (CA) A519/17, 28, Letter from D'Urban, 12 July 1835. I have been unable to trace this list either.
152. *BPP* 279 (1836), 39–40, Somerset to D'Urban.
153. (CA) Map M3/379; (CA) 1/AY/8/24, Sketch of Fingo at Peddie; (CA) 1/AY/8/86, J.M. Bowker to Campbell, 2 June 1835; *BPP* 279 (1836), 109, Letter from D'Urban, 12 July 1835.

settlements on the Clusie (near Peddie) and Tyhume Rivers, not in any extended settlement.[154] By October 1835 there were a mere 698 Fingo at Peddie.[155]

And hardly any of these 'Fingo' at Peddie came from the Natal region. In late April Captain Warden had been despatched to Clarkebury with a patrol (which also included military Fingo) on a twofold mission. He was to organise a Thembu attack on the Gcaleka, and he was to fetch the trans-Kei missionaries and traders gathered there. The Europeans (including Ayliff) were brought to the British camp on the Ndabakazi on 5 May, along with 524 'station people'. The larger, but quite separate mass of 'Fingo' had already been collected there by the 1st and 2nd Divisions in the previous week. The whole Clarkebury group tagged along with the 'Fingo exodus', which left on 9 May, and arrived at Peddie on the 14th. The rest of the 'exodus' ended as labourers in the colony. These 524 'station people' came from the missions at Morley, Buntingville, Clarkebury and Butterworth,[156] where they had been faced in 1835 with the choice of white or traditional allegiance, and chose the more powerful. Given the low success rate of the missions, very few are likely to have been actual converts.[157] It is vital to note that this group from Clarkebury was enumerated on the official list specifically as Gcaleka, Mpondo and Thembu.

It was this small group that was settled around Fort Peddie on the Clusie River, under government agents John Mitford Bowker, Captain Halifax, Lieutenant Moultrie and Ayliff.[158] But in the population census of October 1835, these same people were no longer described as Thembu, Mpondo or Gcaleka. They now came under the designation 'Fingo'.[159] To this group there had been added 62 Hlubi, 30 Bhele and 32 Relidwane. Of all the Fingo at Peddie, there were, therefore, only 124 men, women and children from the Natal area. Mhlambiso, chief of this Hlubi group, with a mere 16 male followers, had been appointed overall chief, on the orders of D'Urban, from a recommendation by Bowker.[160] Ayliff's attempt to create a Fingo history is clearly exhibited here. In May 1835 he correctly described the people at Peddie as 'Native Inhabitants to the number of 500, who from attachment

154. See (CA) Map M1/2728. For the extent of the locations in 1835 and 1855 see (CA) Map M3/379; see also (CA) 1/AY/8/24, Sketch of the Fingo at Peddie, for the distribution of the Fingo from the missions at Peddie.
155. (CA) A519/3, 29–34, Census of Fingo at Peddie, 5 Oct. 1835. The Fingo commissioners complained to D'Urban that the group at Peddie were particularly troublesome – (CA) A519/3, 26–8, D'Urban Papers, 5 Oct. 1835. This is in marked contrast to Ayliff's descriptions of a happy, co-operative settlement.
156. *BPP* 279 (1836), 38, List of persons removed from Clarkebury, 3 May 1835.
157. For a report on the state of the missions and conversions, see (CL) MS 15,704, Minutes of the AGMs of the Wesleyan Methodist preachers in the Albany District. In 1834 there were 22 converts at Butterworth and 92 attending school; at Clarkebury there were 12 converts and 29 at school; at Morley there were 24 converts and 330 at school; and at Buntingville there were 11 converts and 329 at school. Laing noted, (CL) MS 16,579, entry for 28 Dec. 1834, that many Ngqika who used to reject the station were coming to him for protection, or to get the advantages it offered.
158. (CA) A519/3, 26–8, Fingo Commissioners to D'Urban, Peddie, 5 Oct. 1835.
159. (CA) A519/3, 29–34, Census of the Fingo at Peddie by Fingo Commissioners, 5 Oct. 1835. But cf. (CA) 1/AY/8/24, Sketch of Fingo at Peddie, where they are still described as Gcaleka, Mpondo and Thembu, and the land apportioned to them is indicated.
160. Albany Museum (hereafter AM) SM 1176, J.M. Bowker to D'Urban, 2 July 1835.

to the Missionaries, or dread of the Kafirs, had accompanied them [Warden].'[161] Yet in his restructured notes of 1851, he described this same group as Fingo who had lived for many years with the Thembu.[162] Ayliff and D'Urban were wholly misleading in their descriptions of Peddie. The majority of the small settlement was 'Kaffir', who had been 'formed' or 'altered' by the missionaries.[163] A small Natal group was placed with them, and a loyal chief was appointed by the government.

A second settlement, along the lines of that at Peddie, was created in the Tyhume River area in late August 1835, under government commissioners Captain Armstrong, Thomson and Dr Minto. A total of 2 014 men, women and children were settled around Fort Thomson, with adjacent land reserved for European farmers, as well as a possible Khoi settlement and an area for Fingo from the Kat River Settlement.[164] The identity of these Fingo is again unclear, but the settlement seems to have been of similar composition to that at Peddie. Five 'Natal chiefs' who had a sprinkling of followers were placed in charge. The rest were most likely Rharhabe from the missions, or defectors from Maqoma and Tyali. In 1836 Maqoma asked for his defectors to return to him from this Tyhume settlement. A third Fingo settlement was created at King William's Town in August and had 2 000 inhabitants. This too had 'Natal chiefs', but the majority were Fingo mercenaries and their families, granted land in exchange for their war services. The balance was made up of Gcaleka and eastern Rharhabe, held in transit to await placings in the colony.

The Fingo at all three locations, some as collaborators and buffers[165] and others as labourers, were provided with goats, implements, food and seed corn until 1837,[166] and were encouraged to plant gardens and establish themselves. There was a separate Fingo location at Fort Beaufort on the town commonage, although the size is unknown. Some Fingo waited at Fort Beaufort until land could be apportioned to them at Tyhume, while others waited to be sent to farms to work, and this transitional location was growing by late 1835.[167] The Fingo locations there and at King William's Town were not included in the detailed official maps of the towns drawn

161. *Graham's Town Journal*, 22 May 1835. The collaboration between D'Urban and the missionaries is evident in the fact that D'Urban had described the same event in precisely the same words a week previously; see (CA) CO 4381, D'Urban to Campbell, 15 May 1835. A similar description had been given by Reverend Davis, Wesleyan missionary at Clarkebury, *BPP* 503 (1837), 225, 19 Apr. 1835.
162. (CL) PR 3826, Rough notes of Ayliff, 14.
163. 'Fingo' is a Latin term, which means 'to form/shape, or to alter/change (with the intention of untruth)' – see C. T. Lewis and C. Short, *A Latin Dictionary*, Oxford, 1966. Another interesting definition of 'Fingo' can be found in J. L. Döhne, *A Zulu-Kafir Dictionary*, Cape Town, 1851; he says that it means 'to force, urge'.
164. (CA) 1/AY/8/24, D'Urban to Thomson, Armstrong and Minto, 24 July 1835; (CA) A519/3, 73, D'Urban to Fingo Commissioners; (CA) 1/AY/8/24, Fingo Commissioners to D'Urban, 29 Aug. 1835.
165. As outlined in *BPP* 279 (1836), 16, Letter from D'Urban; (CA) 1/AY/8/24, D'Urban to Thomson, Armstrong, Minto, 24 July 1835.
166. (CA) CO 4381, Fingo Commissioners' letters 21 Aug. to 21 Nov. 1835; (CA) LG 14, 173–4, Palmer to Campbell, 2 Nov. 1835; (CA) A519/7, 21, Bowker to Campbell, 20 Oct. 1835.
167. (CA) A519/3, 154–5, Armstrong to D'Urban, 14 Nov. 1835.

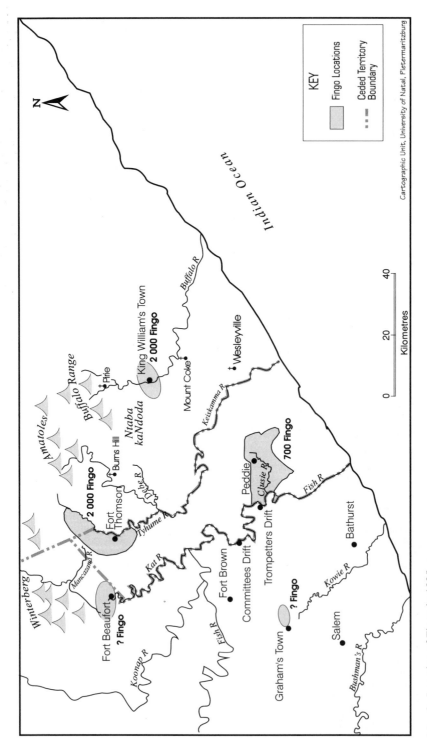

Map 8. Location of Fingo in 1835

in late 1835,[168] because they were probably labour camps. The Fingo commissioners at Fort Beaufort reported in November that the Tyhume settlement was growing, with huts erected, crops sown and more people, and suggested that more land be allotted to Fingo at Tyhume.[169] A similar progress report was made three months later.[170] By July 1836 Laing was describing sixty-seven 'Fingo hamlets' in the area around Fort Thomson, where Lovedale was to be placed.[171]

By October 1837 the Fingo settlement on the west bank of the Tyhume was twice as densely populated as when the Ngqika lived there. The population had risen to approximately 3 000, with well over 3 000 cattle and a similar number of goats. The precise identity and role of these Fingo is not clear, but it seems that most were defectors from Maqoma who were given land. With the disannexation of the Queen Adelaide Province in early 1837, the colony needed to bolster its buffer regions, the most important of which was in the Tyhume area. It is plain that the Fingo were acculturating rapidly to colonial farming techniques and society, as they worked particularly hard in clearing and cultivating the area, selling a corn surplus after their first year. The shedding of traditions is obvious in the way in which men and women had begun to share in agricultural operations by 1837.[172] In 1835 Fingo women had done the work alone, as custom dictated.

What was the plan behind these three Fingo locations? As can be seen, the evidence on Fingo in 1835 is scanty and piecemeal. It does show distinctive categories within the term 'Fingo', and it does give glimpses of movement and hints of a general policy. There are certain consistencies between and features common to Tyhume, Peddie and King William's Town. Each settlement had elements of each type of Fingo: labourer, collaborator (peasant farmer) and military.[173] The Tyhume complex included Fort Beaufort, where there was a large Fingo camp on the commonage, from where Fingo were distributed as labourers in southern Somerset and northern Albany. There were land-owning collaborators around the Tyhume, and a military contingent at Fort Thomson, in the centre of the settlement. Peddie regularly sent labourers into the colony; it had a gradually weakening collaborator settlement and a military force in Fort Peddie. King William's Town provided many labourers for the colony, as far west as Knysna, and had its share of collaborators who had land. Because it was furthest into African territory it had the largest military force, with a fort, Khoi soldiers and most of the Fingo military. Each of the settlements was attacked on a number of occasions by local Rharhabe.

168. See (CA) Maps M1/2729 and M1/2730 respectively.
169. (CA) A519/3, 156, Minto and Thomson to D'Urban, 13 Nov. 1835.
170. (CA) A519/4, 38–41, Fingo Commissioners to D'Urban, 2 Feb. 1836.
171. The information on the Fingo in 1837 comes from an informative report from Thomson to D'Urban, (CA) A519/7, 176–8, 23 Oct. 1837.
172. The gender delineation over labour was commented on by the Fingo Commissioners, (CA) LG 14, 15–6, Fingo Commissioners to Hudson, 11 Nov. 1835.
173. I have used the terms 'collaborator' and 'opportunist' for temporary convenience; they are intended to be descriptive, not judgemental. Analyses of their motives and the forces at work in the new Fingo groups and the Rharhabe polities are only beginning.

A further feature common to all three was the placing of settler farms in their immediate vicinity in 1835, after the annexation of the Queen Adelaide Province. A substantial number of farms were granted along the Buffalo River, near King William's Town, and the Fingo commissioners at both Tyhume and Peddie had instructions to intersperse the Fingo land grants with European farms, which were surveyed in late 1835. It is unlikely that African peasant farmers would be set up in direct competition with white farmers. The locations seem to have been specifically engineered as agriculturally self-supporting and militarily self-defending units situated strategically in the newly conquered territory. They extracted local labour for the colonial market and provided the adjoining new settler farms with a permanent labour supply. In other words, they were the basis of a consolidation of the expanded settler farm land, in terms of both security and labour, and a rural labour pool for colonial farms.

Fingo Chiefs and Tribalisation

Because there was no such thing as a 'Fingo tribe' before and during 1835, it was impossible for there to be natural chiefs. If the Fingo were being amalgamated and tribalised, there had to be African men in charge of them, apart from the white commissioners. Whiteside claimed that the Fingo chiefs were all from Zizi, Hlubi, Bhele and Relidwane royal lineages, and that when they were with the Gcaleka they had pretended not to be chiefs, in order to avoid victimisation. But the evidence suggests that they were collaborators and opportunists, who were prepared to follow British orders on the management of the Fingo.[174] The collaborators from the missions were placed under them, and it was claimed that the labourers who had disappeared from the farms also fell under their control. The chiefs changed fairly rapidly.[175] In 1854 the only two left of the original nine were Jokweni and Matomela.[176] Within two decades, the entire chiefly hierarchy had changed, presumably as a result of the dismissal of chiefs not meeting British expectations.

The chiefs at Tyhume in August 1835,[177] were not those whom Ayliff had listed as chiefs in May 1835.[178] They in turn differed from Theophilus Shepstone's list of April,[179] where the Fingo totalled merely 1 120. Shepstone had said on 19 April that there were only three Fingo chiefs, and that it was they who offered 970 military men.[180] Jokweni, who by the 1850s was one of the wealthiest Fingo chiefs, was no

174. See the changes from (CA) A519/2, Ayliff to D'Urban, Clarkebury, 1 May 1835; to (CA) A519/3, 29–34, Census of Fingo at Peddie, 5 Oct. 1835 and (CA) 1/AY/8/24, Thomson to D'Urban, 29 Aug. 1835; to (CA) GH 19/5, Treaty between Maitland and the Fingo chiefs, Jan. 1845.
175. Moyer, 'A History of the Mfengu', 595–8.
176. Moyer, 'A History of the Mfengu', 595–8.
177. (CA) 1/AY/8/24, 129, Fingo Commissioners to D'Urban, 29 Aug. 1835.
178. (CA) A519/2, Ayliff to D'Urban, 1 May 1835.
179. Moyer, 'A History of the Mfengu', 90c. Moyer commented on the dissimilarities in the various lists of chiefs made between 22 April and 9 May, which is when D'Urban was choosing whom he was to recognise, 190.
180. (NA) A96, Shepstone Diary, entry for 19 Apr. 1835.

hereditary chief, but because of his post-1835 importance, ethnographers like A.T. Bryant inserted him into the Zizi royal genealogy.[181] Makalima had lived near Ayliff for a while before 1835, and his loyalty could thus be trusted.[182] It is significant that when Ayliff listed the 'Fingo chiefs' in May 1835, Makalima was not among them.[183] It was decided to appoint him as a chief only once he had arrived in the colony. Mabanthla was also recognised as a chief for the first time when inside the colony. Both became Fingo chiefs with British backing. Veldman Bikitsha later commented that Mkwenkwezi, Jokweni and Mhlambiso did not appear in the respective Bhele, Zizi and Hlubi royal genealogies.[184] If this is correct, not one of the men given land in 1835 and appointed as chiefs had any claim to a position, apart from their loyalty to the British. They were all collaborators.

It is hardly surprising that the chiefs had little power and less respect,[185] as there was little bond between the newly-created tribe and the appointed collaborator leaders. Less than a month after their settlement, Bowker sent a batch of letters complaining about the Fingo at Peddie, and the way in which they were divided and fighting – even killing – each other. There were clearly problems in getting the Fingo to unify and accept the chiefs, and some Fingo refused to acknowledge chiefly authority and remained independent. Bowker had to arrest and remove a Khoi, Hermanus, as he was attracting Fingo away from the chiefs.[186] This view is far from the mystical tale of spontaneous Fingo unity and joy given by Veldman Bikitsha and Whiteside later in the century.[187] In order to entrench the appointed chiefs as leaders, they were given suits and knives by the British;[188] they also received and distributed land, which their followers were unhappy about.[189]

The Fingo chiefs fulfilled the role of sub-magistrate, under the Fingo commissioners, in order to create a structure of control over the Fingo, as suggested to D'Urban by Bowker.[190] In 1836 Makalima was appointed veld commandant at Tyhume, and Mhlambiso at Peddie. Others were appointed to the posts of veld cornet[191] on the recommendation of the Fingo commissioners in order that the chiefs 'would possess a more defined authority over their people than they do at present'.[192] This system of appointment became increasingly widespread in the Stockenstrom period after 1836, and had proved an effective method of subjugation by the 1850s.

181. Moyer, 'A History of the Mfengu', 184n.
182. (CA) 1/AY/8/24, Fingo Commissioners to D'Urban, 29 Aug. 1835.
183. (CA) A519/2, Ayliff to D'Urban, 1 May 1835.
184. (CA) NA 623, Evidence of Veldman Bikitsha to Lagden Commission, 1905.
185. (CA) 1/AY/8/86, J.M. Bowker to D'Urban, 4 June 1835.
186. (CA) 1/AY/8/86, J.M. Bowker to D'Urban, 5 and 9 June, 20 Oct. 1835; (AM) SM 1176, J.M. Bowker to D'Urban, 2 July 1835.
187. (CA) NA 623, Evidence of Veldman Bikitsha to Lagden Commission, 1905.
188. (CA) A519/3, 103, J.M. Bowker to Campbell, 10 Nov. 1835.
189. *Graham's Town Journal*, 17 Sept. 1835, Ayliff article. They were also given cattle to distribute to their followers, see (CA) GH 34/5, 21, Campbell to D'Urban, 14 July 1835.
190. (AM) SM 1176, J.M. Bowker to D'Urban, 2 July 1835.
191. Moyer, 'A History of the Mfengu', 197. A similar system was applied to the Ndlambe; Mhala and Mqhayi became Field Commandants, and Siyolo and Qasana Field Cornets.
192. (CA) A519/4, 40, Fingo Commissioners to D'Urban, 2 Feb. 1836.

The destruction of Rharhabe livelihood was one of the keys to the increase in Fingo numbers from the end of 1835. Apart from the three categories of Fingo in 1835 – collaborator, military and labourer – there were many Africans who came into the colony to seek work as the only means of survival. They either called themselves Fingo or were subsumed by the colonial authorities within the name. Apart from the Fingo forced to become labourers, there were a number of African peoples who moved into the colony, either attracted by employment or pressured by poverty in 1835 and the period following it. The immense destruction of Rharhabe food and livelihood by the troops in 1835, coupled with the seizure of the Queen Adelaide Province, produced landlessness and poverty, to which colonial indenture provided some solution. The German missionary Kayser noted in 1836 that the formerly well-populated areas around the Keiskamma were poverty-stricken, and that 'the Kaffers are now very much seeking work to get only food for payment'.[193] Even some of Phato's people undertook indenture.[194] While 1835 was not on the scale of the dislocation caused by the cattle-killing of 1856–7, it forced a large number of Rharhabe into the Cape. Because of the multi-faceted, vague nature of the 'Fingo' these people were easily subsumed as members of it. The mechanics of the tribalisation process that created the Fingo have yet to be explored. What were the forces that caused Rharhabe and Gcaleka to leave their homes and forgo their history and culture – even their clan names – and adopt a foreign culture? What social adhesive bonded the diverse amalgam of 1835 into the homogeneous ethnic grouping of the twentieth century? When and why did the 'Fingo' identity begin to take popular root?

Conclusions

Who thought of applying the general Fingo story to the labourers? As shown, there were occasional references to Fingo refugees in the late 1820s and early 1830s. When Ngwane women and children were captured at Mbholompo in 1828 and taken into the colony to work, they were called Fingo. A precedent was thereby created where people seized illegally to labour were described as Fingo. By the early 1830s there were a number of 'Fingo' working in Albany and Somerset, and the equating of the Fingo with labour came again in 1833, when Godlonton complained of the labour shortage. He suggested that the 'Fingoos' and 'Mantatees', who were living 'under the most despotic control of the Caffers', should be encouraged to enter colonial service, as their 'industry is almost proverbial'.[195] D'Urban was centrally involved with the Fingo in 1835: he was at the head of the invading forces in April and May, he appointed the Fingo chiefs, he organised the creation of the collaborator settlements. By portraying the Fingo as slaves being rescued by the British, it would be possible to escape Colonial Office censure. He and the colonists, in their public statements,

193. Kayser to Ellis, 4 Jan. 1836, quoted by Crais in 'Ambiguous Frontiers', 43–4.
194. F. Rex to Duthie, 25 Sept. 1835, in Long, *An Index to Authors*.
195. *Graham's Town Journal*, 16 May 1833, Godlonton editorial.

constantly equated the 'Fingo rescue' with 'the true spirit of the sweeping emancipation made by the mother country',[196] thereby inverting the identity of the captured labourers. D'Urban thus made use of an entrenched settler myth to cover the actions of his troops, putting his official stamp on the history of the Fingo.

Ayliff then wrote the 'Fingo history', probably with the aid of D'Urban and Godlonton. The scattered reports from the missions in the 1820s of Natal refugees were taken and interwoven with the contemporary myths of the destruction of Shaka. To this were added elements of each category of Fingo: that some fought in the army, some settled at Peddie, and some were refugees. All of this was amalgamated into one history, so that every Fingo supposedly had the same origins. Automatically, the thousands of illegal labourers had an identity that was acceptable to London. The story was polished when Ayliff was in Graham's Town – not ministering to the Fingo, as Whiteside claimed – between May and September. He published the new history in August and September, and reworked it again in the 1850s. But Ayliff never met D'Urban's expectations, and D'Urban (who in 1835 and 1836 had control of mission appointments) removed him from both of the important Fingo settlements, Peddie and Tyhume. His confused efforts at explaining Fingo history seem to have annoyed D'Urban, who complained to Smith that 'Mr Ayliff was a very improper person to send to Butterworth, imbecile, timorous and weak. Mr Boyce and Mr Palmer [actively pro-settler Wesleyan missionaries] both described him thus to me, and said that he was unfit for any post of trial.'[197] Ironically, Ayliff's 'history' was so effective that it has not been challenged for a century and a half.

It must be stressed that the orthodox history of 1835 and the Fingo is based largely on uncritical interpretations of military reports, and of the writings of settler apologists. Yet there are numerous proven cases of these reports and accounts being not only factually inaccurate, but specifically designed to mask the real events. D'Urban, in a colourful overstatement, described Albany as a barren and devastated desert before he had even arrived in the district. He blamed Hintsa for organising the attacks of December before he could have had any evidence of it. The report on the Smith patrol past the Mbashe River in May lied about the intentions of the patrol, about who suggested it, about the circumstances of Hintsa's death and about the identity of the 'Fingo' taken. D'Urban later claimed that he had only decided to annex the Queen Adelaide Province on 8 May, when it had been planned since January. D'Urban regularly alleged that the Fingo were slaves of the Gcaleka, when he knew that they were not. He also said that he had settled 16 800 Fingo around Peddie; a mere 700 were placed there, most of whom were 'Kafirs' from the Wesleyan missions. He deliberately misled the Colonial Office about the size of the 'Kaffir' force, about the effectiveness of his own troops, and about the length of the

---

196. For examples, see (CA) CO 4381, D'Urban, Official Notice, 3 May 1835; *BPP* 503 (1837), 181, D'Urban; *BPP* 503 (1837), 181, Address from Port Elizabeth residents.
197. (CL) MS 2033, D'Urban to Smith, 10 June 1836. See also A. T. C. Slee, 'Some Aspects of Wesleyan Methodism in the Albany District between 1830 and 1844', M.A. dissertation, Rhodes University, Grahamstown, 1946, 49.

hostilities. The settlers, with the collaboration of D'Urban and the Cape colonial authorities, exaggerated their losses and the destruction of late 1834. These are all crucial aspects of the war and the identity of the Fingo, and are demonstrably incorrect.

In summary, the orthodox interpretations of 1835 and the Fingo are seriously flawed. The 'Kafirs' were not the aggressors in the war of 1835; colonial expansion was. The 'irruption' of December 1834 was exaggerated by the settler press, and the impact of the invading colonial troops was underplayed. The colony did not suffer extensive stock and human loss, but it did take at least 60 000 cattle (apart from the number of goats) from the Rharhabe and Gcaleka for daring to attack the whites. The troops also wreaked mayhem with Rharhabe and Gcaleka livelihood, destroying crops and homesteads, and seizing almost all Rharhabe land for settler colonisation.

One of the major results of this large-scale conflict was the creation of the Fingo. The indigenes faced a choice between co-operation and conflict in 1835, and many of those who chose the former became Fingo. Fingo consisted of mission collaborators, mercenaries, refugees and voluntary labourers, all of whom were subsumed within this new identity. And included by the authorities was a large number of Gcaleka and Rharhabe women and children who had been captured during hostilities and who were forced to work on settler and Boer farms to alleviate the chronic labour shortage. It was this heterogeneous conglomeration that formed the Fingo, and not a refugee Natal ethnic unit who escaped from Shaka's rapacity.

This revision has important ramifications for 'mfecane' theorists. It is clear that the orthodox explanation of all Fingo as Natal refugees is highly inaccurate, and an important strut of the general 'mfecane' theory thus falls away. A number of areas of nineteenth-century history must now be reviewed in the light of this revision of 1835, among them the orthodoxies on the Great Trek, labour history and African proletarianisation, on the power of settler propaganda, and of course, on the later history of the Fingo.

Acknowledgement

I am indebted to the Human Sciences Research Council and the Ernest Oppenheimer Memorial Trust for funding which made this research possible.

This essay is derived largely from my MA dissertation: 'Land Expropriation and Labour Extraction under Cape Colonial Rule: The War of 1835 and the "Emancipation" of the Fingo', Rhodes University, Grahamstown, 1991. My intention has been to summarise the most important findings of the dissertation: to review the identity of the Fingo in the light of a reconstruction of the history of the war. I would like to thank Julian Cobbing and Jürg Richner for their unceasing support and ideas over the last four years, without which this work would probably not have been done. I am also indebted to John Wright for his many constructive and critical comments.

10 The Mfecane Survives its Critics

JOHN OMER-COOPER

The term Mfecane has come to be widely accepted as a name for the process of political change and the accompanying wars and migrations which began in the area between the Thukela River and Delagoa Bay during the later part of the eighteenth century. *Inter alia*, this process resulted in the emergence of the Swazi and Zulu kingdoms, the founding of the Gaza kingdom in southern Mozambique, and the migrations and state-building activities of the Ndebele and of the Maseko and Zwangendaba's Ngoni.

The Mfecane as a Process of African State-building

In *The Zulu Aftermath*[1] the Mfecane was presented as a positive process of political change in the direction of enlarged state power through improved military organisation and increased centralisation, and the expansion of the scale of political organisation through the rapid incorporation and assimilation of members of previously separate political communities. It was characterised as an essentially African revolution, the achievement of African leaders employing and modifying traditional institutions, values, weapons and tactics, rather than borrowing external models or techniques, in building their new kingdoms. It thus illustrated the capacity of African leaders for creative statecraft and the adaptability of traditional African institutions to new purposes. It demonstrated that the nineteenth-century history of Africa could not be adequately discussed simply in terms of external, predominantly European, forces acting on essentially passive African societies, but that it must be seen as a much more complex pattern involving reciprocal interaction between European and African initiatives.

The process of political change in the area inhabited by northern Nguni-speakers was described as beginning in the latter half of the eighteenth century in response to an intensification of intercommunity conflicts probably arising from heightened competition for grazing and garden land consequent upon population growth beyond

---

1. J.D. Omer-Cooper, *The Zulu Aftermath: A Nineteenth-century Revolution in Bantu Africa*, London, 1966. As Julian Cobbing has maintained that it was this publication (together with the chapter on the topic in M.H. Wilson and L.M. Thompson, eds, *The Oxford History of South Africa*, vol.1, Oxford, 1969) which gave the term common currency (e.g. Cobbing, 'The Case against the Mfecane', seminar paper presented to the Centre for African Studies, University of Cape Town, 1983), I have taken the account given in that work as the basis of discussion.

277

what could be comfortably sustained within the area by traditional food production practices.[2] The process involved an initial phase, dominated by Dingiswayo's Mthethwa and Zwide's Ndwandwe, in which the conversion of the corporate initiate-mate system to a means of military organisation and a device facilitating the incorporation of young males from other communities was implemented. The potential of this development, however, was not completely realised, in that the *amabutho* only assembled for fairly brief periods of active campaigning. This phase saw the movement of Sobhuza into the area of modern Swaziland and the first inception of what was to become the Swazi kingdom. It thus marked the beginning of the spread of the Mfecane beyond its original nuclear area.

As described in *The Zulu Aftermath* this first phase of the Mfecane gave way to the emergence of the Zulu kingdom under Shaka which marked the culmination of the process of political change in the sense that the military and political potential of the age-mate system was achieved with the introduction of continuous service, the conversion of royal homesteads into military barracks and the adoption of tactics involving close-formation fighting with the use of the short-handled stabbing spear. To the emergence of the Zulu kingdom was ascribed a great intensification of the Mfecane. It resulted in massive conflict and upheaval in Natal. It triggered the northward migrations of Soshangane, Nxaba, Zwangenbaba and the Maseko. Later Mzilikazi and the Ndebele broke away from Shaka's kingdom to carry both devastating warfare and the process of state formation to the trans-Vaal highveld and subsequently, after their defeat by the Boer trekkers, to western Zimbabwe. A Zulu attack also drove Matiwane and his Ngwane on to the trans-Orangian highveld where they greatly intensified the upheavals initiated by the intrusion of Mpangazitha and the Hlubi.

A further Zulu attack, together with conflict with forces of Mzilikazi's Ndebele and the failure of an assault on Moshoeshoe's stronghold of Thaba Bosiu, led Matiwane to abandon the Caledon Valley and lead his people across the Drakensberg into the Thembu country. Here they were attacked and broken up at Mbholompo by a British force which mistook them for an invading Zulu army.

The careers of Sobhuza (and of his successors, especially of course Mswati), Soshangane, Zwangenbaba, the leaders of the Maseko and their successors, and of Mzilikazi, constituted a series of experiments in state building involving the rapid assimilation of political, linguistic and cultural aliens and the development of a sense of common identity and loyalty within the new rapidly aggregated composite communities. The creation of such new communities as the Ndebele in what is now Zimbabwe or Mpenzeni's Ngoni in modern Zambia were seen as not only remarkable achievements with important consequences for the subsequent history of

---

2. See Omer-Cooper, *The Zulu Aftermath*, 24–7. My views on this as well as the detailed interpretations of many other aspects of the Mfecane have, of course, been significantly modified in the light of more recent research. See e.g. *The Cambridge History of Africa*, vol.5, Cambridge, 1976, 319–52; J.D. Omer-Cooper, *A History of Southern Africa*, London, 1987, 52–66.

those areas but as having universal significance in terms of our understanding of the formation of corporate political loyalties.

The series of state-building experiments undertaken by these leaders all involved a common set of institutions including the corporate age-mate system of military organisation, the use of royal households as military and administrative centres and the employment of appointed officials in key roles. The elements in this common package were none the less developed and employed in very different ways in reaction to the various situations faced by the individual leaders and their followers. The spread of the Mfecane, however, created both the need and the opportunity for the leaders of other peoples to build enlarged and strengthened political systems. In this task some, like the Hehe in Tanzania, borrowed some elements of the package, while others – like Moshoeshoe in the building of the Sotho kingdom – relied on the traditional institutions of their own societies, and alternative military tactics.

The Mfecane, it was maintained, had a major impact on the history of southern, central and east Africa.[3] It led to the creation of a whole series of new communities, some at a huge distance from their founders' original homes. Two of these, Lesotho and Swaziland, evolved into internationally recognised independent nations, while others remained significant centres of self-identification and political loyalty within the wider state structures created by colonialism. The migrations and military activities of the Ngoni, interacting in complex ways with the upheavals arising from the contemporaneous expansion of the east coast ivory and slave trade, had a major impact on east African societies and at least temporarily modified the distribution of population in some areas.

In southern Africa, the wars and upheavals of the period resulted in a general tendency for people to concentrate in and around areas of rugged country which offered greater defensive opportunities, leaving much of the more open country on the trans-Vaal and the trans-Orangian highveld temporarily largely depopulated. In Natal, apart from the area around Port Natal, much of the land lay temporarily empty as the population fled south under the impact of the migrations of a series of groups set in motion by the rise of the Zulu and subsequently by the Zulu *izimpi* themselves. This population accumulated in the extreme south of the Natal region and the northern section of what became the Transkei, in the neighbourhood of Faku's Mpondo, awaiting the return of more secure conditions which would allow them to reoccupy their earlier homes. In the meantime the northern Transkei region was a crucible of multiple and complex conflicts.

The disruption of the earlier pattern of population distribution, becoming known in the Cape through the reports of English traders in Natal and of travellers, traders and missionaries on the highveld, appeared to offer opportunities for the easy acquisition of desirable grazing land. This taken together with the strength of Xhosa resistance on the east coast, helped to explain the diversion of the main stream of white settler expansion away from its initially preferred route to that of the Great

---

3. An account of the impact of the Mfecane as I then understood it is set out in *The Zulu Aftermath*, 168–82.

Trek through trans-Orangia into Natal and what became the Transvaal. It thus helped to explain the positioning of the new nuclei of white land expansionism created by the Great Trek, and so contributes to an understanding of how the subsequent pattern of white and vestigial African land-holding in South Africa came about.

The Mfecane Debate: The Slave Trade Hypothesis and Afrocentricity Debate

An important measure of the value of any historical study is the extent to which it stimulates new empirical research and interpretative analyses. It is gratifying that the publication of *The Zulu Aftermath* has been followed by such a quantity of new research and speculative reinterpretation. In the development of knowledge, however, there are occasions when hypotheses which have long served as the starting points for the search for new data and the formulation of new questions can no longer sustain the weight of new evidence and are replaced by new postulates. With a paper delivered in 1983 entitled 'The Case Against the Mfecane', followed by a string of others, Julian Cobbing has proclaimed the need for such a major change of perspective, a paradigm shift with regard to the Mfecane. He and John Wright who has followed him in this regard have argued that the entire concept of the Mfecane should be scrapped.[4]

At times they seem to be arguing that it is all a myth and that the wars, migrations and so forth never really happened. Thus, in an article in the *Canadian Journal of African Studies*,[5] Wright acclaims Cobbing for formulating a sweeping critique of the notion that the Mfecane ever happened. Later in the same article in relation to the Mfecane in the Natal region, Wright claims, 'The Natal Mfecane is, therefore, the prototype of all other regional Mfecanes. Knock down the notion that it actually happened and the whole edifice of Mfecane theory is likely to come tumbling down.'

Further reading, however, soon reveals that this is not really what they mean. In spite of the remarks just quoted, Wright does not intend to deny that a process of political change in the direction of strengthened and expanded political organisation, accompanied by heightened military conflict and involving the military use of the *amabutho* system, developed in the area between the Thukela River and Delagoa Bay in the course of the eighteenth century. He accepts that the pace of the process

---

4. Cobbing, 'The Case against the Mfecane', University of Cape Town, 1983; 'The Case Against the Mfecane', seminar paper presented to African Studies Institute, University of the Witwatersrand, Johannesburg, 1984. 'The Myth of the Mfecane', seminar paper presented to the Department of History, University of Durban Westville, 1987; 'The Mfecane as Alibi: Thoughts on Dithakong and Mbolompo', *Journal of African History*, 29 (1988), 487–519; 'A Tainted Well: The Objectives, Historical Fantasies and Working Methods of James Stuart with Counter-argument', *Journal of Natal and Zulu History*, 11 (1988), 115–53; 'Grasping the Nettle: The Slave Trade and the Early Zulu', in D.R. Edgecombe, J.P.C. Laband and P.S. Thompson, comps, *The Debate on Zulu Origins: A Selection of Papers on the Zulu Kingdom and Early Colonial Natal*, Pietermaritzburg, 1992; 'Rethinking the Roots of Violence in Southern Africa, *c.*1790–1840'; 'Overturning the Mfecane: A Reply to Elizabeth Eldredge', papers presented to the Colloquium on the Mfecane Aftermath, University of the Witwatersrand, Johannesburg, 1991.

5. J.B. Wright, 'Political Mythology and the Making of Natal's Mfecane', *Canadian Journal of African Studies*, 23, 2 (1989), 287.

was subsequently intensified with the conflict between the Mthethwa and Ndwand-we and the emergence of the Zulu kingdom.[6] Neither he nor Cobbing denies the northward migrations of groups originally associated with the Ndwandwe into Mozambique and, in the case of Zwangenbaba's and the Maseko Ngoni, subse-quently on through Zimbabwe and Malawi as far as Tanzania. Cobbing does not deny that the Hlubi and Ngwane were driven across the Drakensberg on to the trans-Orangian highveld or that their intrusion into the area contributed to heightened insecurity there. Still less does Cobbing dispute the migrations of the Ndebele led by Mzilikazi on to and within the Transvaal region and after defeat by the trekkers into the Zimbabwe region, or his state-building achievements in the Transvaal and Zimbabwe regions; these formed the subject of Cobbing's own doctorate.[7]

Their criticism, then, is not aimed at disputing that the processes of political change, migrations and state-building activities of those involved in them actually occurred; rather it directs itself to three key issues which they believe to be crucial to the concept of the Mfecane.

The first of these issues is the causation of the process of political change in the direction of stronger and more extensive state systems in the area between Delagoa Bay and the Thukela. They reject the idea that it may have started in response to an ecological crisis, heightened competition for grazing land (perhaps specifically sweetveld late summer and winter grazing) to satisfy the needs of growing herds − a problem which might have been intensified by the onset of a cycle of relatively dry years after a number of exceptionally good ones.[8] Instead they follow Alan Smith, D. W. Hedges and Philip Bonner[9] in ascribing the original impulse to trade, probably initially mainly in ivory, with the Portuguese at Delagoa Bay. They modify this hypothesis, however, by arguing on the basis of work by P. Harries and G. Liesegang[10] on the slave trade at Delagoa Bay that an initial prolonged phase of

6. See J. B. Wright, 'Political Transformations in the Thukela–Mzimkhulu Region of Natal in the Late 18th and Early 19th Centuries', seminar paper, University of Anatananarivo, 1991, 8–12.

7. J. Cobbing, 'The Ndebele under the Khumalos, 1820–1896', Ph.D. thesis, University of Lancaster, 1976.

8. A possibility examined by J. Guy in 'Ecological Factors and the Rise of Shaka and the Zulu Kingdom', in S. Marks and A. Atmore, eds, *Economy and Society in Pre-Industrial South Africa*, London, 1980.

9. A. K. Smith, 'The Trade of Delagoa Bay as a Factor in Nguni Politics 1750–1835', in L. M. Thompson, ed., *African Societies in Southern Africa*, London, 1969; 'The Struggle for the Control of Southern Mozambique 1720–1835', Ph.D. thesis, University of California, Los Angeles, 1970; D. W. Hedges, 'Trade and Politics in Southern Mozambique and Zululand in the Eighteenth and Early Nineteenth Centuries', Ph.D. thesis, University of London, 1978; P. Bonner, 'The Dynamics of Late 18th-Century Northern Nguni Society: Some Hypotheses', in J. Peires, ed., *Before and After Shaka: Papers in Nguni History*, Rhodes University, Grahamstown, 1981, 74–81; P. Bonner, *Kings, Commoners and Concessionaires: The Evolution and Dissolution of the Nineteenth-century Swazi State*, Cambridge, 1982.

10. P. Harries, 'Slavery, Social Incorporation and Surplus Extraction: The Nature of Free and Unfree Labour in South-East Africa', *Journal of African History*, 22 (1981), 309–30; G. Liesegang, 'A First Look at the Import and Export Trade of Mozambique, 1800–1914', in G. Liesegang, H. Pasch and A. Jones, eds, *Figuring African Trade. Proceedings of a Symposium on the Quantification and Structure of the Import and Export and Long Distance Trade in Africa 1800–1913*, Berlin, 1986, ch. 5.

relatively slow change was succeeded by a sharp escalation of violence resulting from a massive increase in the slave trade from the bay. This resulted, they believe, in aggressive raiding especially by Zwide's Ndwandwe which, *inter alia*, drove the Ngwane south into northern Natal and the Hlubi over the Drakensberg. It also resulted in the Ndwandwe–Mthethwa conflict and, after the destruction of the Mthethwa kingdom, in the emergence of the Zulu kingdom as an essentially defensive reaction against slave-trade-prompted aggression from the north.[11] The acceptance of this hypothesis, they believe, would destroy the thesis that the Mfecane was an essentially African phenomenon.

There is no doubt that this postulated explanation is both plausible and intellectually attractive. The trade hypothesis offers the possibility of detecting a common dynamic linking the beginnings of state formation south of Delagoa Bay in the eighteenth century with the very much earlier emergence of substantial state systems at Toutswemogola, Mapungubwe and subsequently Great Zimbabwe.[12] It also offers a possible link between the emergence of enlarged states in the Phongolo–Mzimkhulu region and the eighteenth-century emergence of the Rolong paramountcy on the highveld, the alleged state-building career of Motlomi in trans-Orangia and most of all the creation of the Pedi paramountcy – though it might be noted that Peter Delius has reservations as to the validity of the trade hypothesis in this which might be thought to be the most clear-cut example of it.[13]

The suggestion that it was the expansion of the slave trade which brought the process of change to a head offers a very reasonable explanation for the emergence of militarism and the greatly intensified violence of the period. It must be noted, however, that the evidence for the growth of a substantial slave trade from Delagoa Bay relates to the period after 1823.[14] Though speculation to the effect that large-scale slave exports noted after that date might have begun a decade or more earlier is not, on the face of it wholly implausible, the burden of contemporary evidence as demonstrated by Elizabeth Eldredge[15] overwhelmingly supports the view that the slave trade at the bay before the 1820s was far too small to have produced the wide-ranging consequences attributed to it. What is more, contemporary accounts of the expansion of the trade when it did occur clearly point to the upheavals and famine resulting from the invasions of the Vatwah (a term used by the Portuguese for the Nguni-speaking intruders) as the cause of its growth. It is clear, then, that as Harries thought, the Mfecane was cause rather than effect of the expansion of the Delagoa Bay slave trade.[16]

11. See Cobbing, 'Grasping the Nettle'; Wright, 'Political Transformations'.
12. This point is raised by M. Hall, *The Changing Past: Farmers, Kings and Traders in Southern Africa*, 200–1860, Cape Town, 1987.
13. P. Delius, *The Land Belongs to Us: The Pedi Polity, the Boers and the British in the Nineteenth-century Transvaal*, Johannesburg, 1983, 11–19.
14. See Harries, 'Slavery, Social Incorporation and Surplus Extraction'.
15. E. A. Eldredge, 'Sources of Conflict in Southern Africa, *c.*1800–1830: The Mfecane Reconsidered', in this volume, especially p. 126–39.
16. Harries, 'Slavery, Social Incorporation and Surplus Extraction'.

This does not in itself invalidate the view that external trade in ivory and cattle was the sole cause of the upheaval. Indeed, Martin Hall's recent work suggests that there was no ecological crisis in the coastal zone capable of producing the upheaval.[17] Nevertheless, the possibility that competition for grazing land, involving perhaps intrusion by communities from the overgrazed upland areas on to the richer pastures nearer the coast and brought to a head in drought years, may have played a role in the matter is by no means ruled out.[18] Indeed, some combination of changes arising from involvement in external trade and highlighted territorial conflicts resulting from pressures on grazing and garden lands in times of drought remains the most probable explanation.

However, even if the hypothesis that external trade was the sole cause of the process were accepted, and the hypothesis that the slave trade in particular was the catalyst which initiated the development of highland militarism had not proved unfounded, the Africanist thesis would not be destroyed. It still remains the case that the series of experiments in state building was undertaken by African leaders, employing existing institutions of their own societies in new ways in the light of the critical situations in which they found themselves, rather than borrowing alien European models. Referring to these new political systems as reactive or in some cases defensive, does not alter the case. Of course, they were reactive in the sense that they developed in reaction to situations of great violence and insecurity[19] whether that situation of heightened conflict was initially caused by struggles over grazing lands or by the impact of the slave trade. They were also from one point of view defensive though that does not mean that they were not also from other perspectives aggressive and predacious. It is not the cause of the insecurity which provoked the process of political change at the heart of the Mfecane but the nature of the process itself which constitutes its Africanness.

The Role of the Zulu Re-examined

The second main argument of the critics of the Mfecane concerns the role of the Zulu – the Zulucentricity – which they see as essential to the whole concept of the Mfecane. First, they insist that it was not the emergence of the Zulu which initiated the process of state building and started the series of migrations out of the area between Delagoa Bay and the Thukela. Rather the Zulu kingdom was merely one of the products of a process which had started much earlier during the century.

According to John Wright, it was the emergence of the Ndwandwe and Mthethwa paramountcies which encouraged a number of other chiefdoms including the Qwabe and the Cele to start building similarly enlarged political units. It was during this

17. Hall, *The Changing Past*, 126.
18. On this see J. Gump, 'Origins of the Mfecane: An Ecological Perspective', paper presented to the Colloquium on the Mfecane Aftermath, University of the Witwatersrand, Johannesburg, 1991.
19. This point is made in J.D. Omer-Cooper, 'Aspects of Political Change in the Nineteenth-century Mfecane', in Thompson, *African Societies in Southern Africa*, 207–29.

period that southwards migrations into and through Natal were first set in motion. It was as a result of power rivalry between Zwide and Dingiswayo that the Ngwane and Hlubi were driven from their original homes.[20] It was the Ndwandwe who drove Sobhuza into the Swaziland area. (Cobbing lays more emphasis on the Ndwandwe – whom he believes to have been in the slave trade – as the motors of political and demographic change in the area.[21]) When the Ndwandwe had defeated the Mthethwa and the Zulu under Shaka emerged to challenge them, it was not Shaka's victory over Zwide's forces (or, as Wright would have it, not that alone) which resulted in the break-up of the Ndwandwe paramountcy and the northward migrations that followed: rather it was tensions within that enlarged confederacy and possibly (Cobbing thinks definitely) the pressures and opportunities resulting from the slave trade which had this result.[22] The migration of Mzilikazi's Khumalo (subsequently known as the Ndebele) on to the trans-Vaal highveld was not the consequence of rebellion against and defeat by Shaka but of conflict with the slave-trading Ndwandwe.[23] Cobbing, indeed, would stretch the impact of groups of slave raiders from Delagoa Bay very much further than this, believing them to have been responsible for driving Mzilikazi from the north-eastern trans-Vaal.[24] Shaka and the Zulu were not therefore responsible for the great chain of migrations into Mozambique and on through Zimbabwe into Malawi, Tanzania and Zambia, on to the trans-Vaal highveld and thence in Mzilikazi's case into Zimbabwe; neither did the leaders of these migrations borrow their ideas on organisation and tactics from the Zulu. Their state-building experiments were independent of and parallel to that of Shaka in the Zulu kingdom. After his initial repulse of Zwide's forces moreover, Shaka's kingdom remained relatively weak, Wright believes, and the positioning of a series of his military settlements can best be explained in terms of the need to establish a defensive cordon along his northern border against possible renewed Ndwandwe invasion. It was only after the defeat of Zwide's heir Sikhunyana in 1826, made possible by the support of the British traders with their guns, that the Zulu were placed in a dominant position with regard to the territory between the heartland of their kingdom and Delagoa Bay.

Similarly, with regard to Natal the Zulu and chiefdoms owing allegiance to them initially dominated only a very restricted area. The disruption of traditional settlement patterns was primarily due to the activities of other groups. It was only

20. Wright, 'Political Transformations'. That the Mfecane began with the emergence of the Mthethwa and Ndwandwe was made clear in Omer-Cooper, *The Zulu Aftermath*, and the idea that the Ndwandwe played the most crucial role has also been suggested earlier; see e.g., Bonner, *Kings, Commoners and Concessionaires*. John Wright's work, however, takes us significantly further along the road to a full understanding of the complex chain of events preceding and accompanying the emergence of the Zulu kingdom.
21. See Cobbing, 'Grasping the Nettle'.
22. Compare Cobbing's trenchantly expressed conviction on this point in 'Grasping the Nettle' and 'Rethinking the Roots of Violence', with Wright's much more cautious argumentation in 'Political Transformations'.
23. Cobbing, 'Grasping the Nettle', 7.
24. Cobbing, 'Grasping the Nettle', 10.

during the 1820s when Shaka moved the centre of his kingdom southward in reaction to internal political problems, and possibly also because of insecurity on his northern frontier, that the Zulu established themselves as the dominant power between the Thukela and the Mzimkhulu. Though Zulu forces did pass through Natal across the Mzimkhulu and the Mzimvubu to raid the Mpondo in 1824 and subsequently launched sporadic raids into the area between the Thukela and the Mzimkhulu before Shaka's major campaign into Pondoland in 1828, the Zulu were still not the only or main cause of insecurity in the Natal region.[25] Here again Cobbing takes a much more radical view. He argues that the disruption of life in the Natal area was not the work of the Zulu but of the English traders and their African followers who he believes were also involved in the slave trade.[26]

Some of these arguments are very convincing. Wright's work on the Zulu and on the dynamics of the situation in Natal taken together with Carolyn Hamilton's study of ideology and power struggles in the Zulu kingdom, constitute, I believe, a major advance in our understanding of the internal dynamics and external relations and impact of the Zulu state.[27] They certainly do show that the role of the Zulu has been significantly exaggerated. On the other hand, while modifying the earlier accepted picture, they by no means completely destroy it. That the emergence of the Zulu kingdom was not the beginning of the political transformations in the area between Delagoa Bay and the Thukela, but was itself the product of a chain of events which had started earlier and had previously seen the emergence of the Ndwandwe and the Mthethwa, was always clear. That the migration of Sobhuza to the Swaziland area and the initial dislocation of the Hlubi and Ngwane and thus the beginnings of the spread of the Mfecane also belonged to this period, has likewise long been accepted.

Wright successfully demonstrates that the role of the Zulu in Natal has been seriously exaggerated; he accepts that life there was greatly disturbed by groups moving south initially to avoid incorporation in the Ndwandwe or Mthethwa paramountcies and subsequently by others seeking to avoid a similar fate at the hands of the Zulu or their satellites. The Zulu themselves, moreover, did ultimately establish their predominance over most of Natal; they did drive the Ngwane on to the highveld, and their forces did campaign south as far as Faku's Mpondo.

Whether the migrations of Soshangane, Zwangenbaba, Nxaba and the Maseko

---

25. Wright, 'Political Transformations'; also his, 'A. T. Bryant and "The Wars of Shaka"', *History in Africa*, 18 (1991), 409–25.

26. The theme of the destructive role of the white traders in Natal was expounded in 'The Mfecane as Alibi', where Cobbing suggested, *inter alia*, that they may have been involved in the murder of Shaka. The idea that they were involved in the slave trade is set out in 'Grasping the Nettle' and further developed in 'Rethinking the Roots of Violence'.

27. J. B. Wright, 'The Dynamics of Power and Conflict in the Thukela–Mzimkhulu Region in the Late Eighteenth and Early Nineteenth Centuries: A Critical Reconstruction', Ph.D. thesis, University of the Witwatersrand, Johannesburg, 1990; C. A. Hamilton, 'Ideology, Oral Traditions and the Struggle for Power in the Early Zulu Kingdom', M.A. dissertation, University of the Witwatersrand, Johannesburg, 1986.

were or were not the direct result of the defeat of Zwide's forces by the Zulu, is far less clear. The claim made by Mayinga that the Gaza scattered before any attack by the Zulu[28] cannot be taken as any more definitive than the Zulu sources on which Bryant relied in maintaining that they had fled in reaction to Shaka's victory. It is not improbable that there were strong centrifugal tensions within Zwide's extensive paramountcy. It is not difficult to imagine that involvement in the slave trade might have increased these. Certainly, the Gaza and Zwangenbaba's Jere did subsequently participate in selling captives to the Portuguese.[29] Unfortunately for this thesis, however, the fact that the slave trade at Delagoa Bay seems only to have assumed significant dimensions after the intrusion of the Nguni-speaking groups who broke away from Zwide's paramountcy eliminates it as a probable cause of their initial secession. On the other hand, the fact that these migrations began coincidentally with the shift of the Ndwandwe headquarters across the Phongolo River into the southern Swaziland area just as the Zulu kingdom was successfully establishing itself, suggests that the defeat may well have been the precipitating cause which brought internal tensions to a head.[30] Wright's view that the failure of Ndwandwe forces against the Zulu is likely to have been a factor but not to have been the only cause, seems very fair.[31]

With regard to the Ndebele of Mzilikazi, the situation is similar. While the previous association of the Khumalo with the Ndwandwe in the period of Mzilikazi's father, Matshobane, has never been disputed, neither Cobbing's arguments based on the different way that the Ndebele employed the *amabutho* system,[32] nor the original evidence of members of the Ndebele kingdom, decisively disprove that they were for a time associated as a vassal chiefdom with Shaka's nascent kingdom and that their migration on to the trans-Vaal highveld was the result of attack and defeat by Zulu forces.[33] Indeed, an examination of the employment of the *amabutho* system by the Ndebele in comparison with the other Nguni-speaking groups who used it as a key element in their military and political organisation suggests the opposite conclusion. Of all these groups, only the Ndebele and the Zulu practised the system of keeping the *amabutho* in continuous service in settlements built for the purpose – an innovation which seems quite clearly attributable to

28. C. de B. Webb and J. B. Wright, eds, *The James Stuart Archive of Recorded Oral Evidence Relating to the History of the Zulu and Neighbouring Peoples*, vol. 2, 251, quoted by Cobbing, 'Grasping the Nettle', 11.
29. Harries, 'Slavery, Social Incorporation and Surplus Extraction'.
30. Peter Delius has suggested that Zwide moved his headquarters much further than has previously been thought in response to the defeat. He believes that he retreated as far as the Pedi country where he, rather than Mzilikazi, was responsible for the defeat of the Pedi. If this is confirmed by further research, the view that defeat by the Zulu was the catalyst for the secessions of the Gaza, Jere etc. and their northward migrations will be significantly strengthened. Delius, *The Land Belongs to Us*, 22–3.
31. Wright, 'Political Transformations', 13.
32. J. Cobbing, 'The Evolution of Ndebele *Amabutho*', *Journal of African History*, 15, 4 (1974), 607–31.
33. In 'The Case Against the Mfecane', 1983, Cobbing still held that Mzilikazi's migration had been precipitated by conflict with the Zulu.

Shaka. True, in the Ndebele kingdom the *amabutho* retained a corporate identity after their members had completed their initial period of military service and assumed adult status evolving into permanent administrative divisions of the kingdom, a development without parallel in the Zulu state.[34] This, however, can be readily explained in terms of the different circumstances in which Mzilikazi's migrant kingdom developed in comparison with that in which the Zulu state was placed.[35] It does not detract from the very close similarities in military organisation in the two kingdoms or require us to accept that such closely similar systems, practised by two leaders who started out in close proximity to one another were wholly independent inventions.

The evidence cited by R. Kent Rasmussen to the effect that Mzilikazi was for a time a vassal of Shaka and that his migration into the north-eastern trans-Vaal started in response to defeat by his overlord is too substantial to be cavalierly ignored. If Mzilikazi did break away in this manner and in so doing escaped with some of his paramount's cattle, it would help to explain his continuing dread of a Zulu attack; it would also help to explain why Dingane sent two expeditions to such a great distance for this purpose. Finally, Cobbing's alternative hypothesis that Mzilikazi was driven on to the trans-Vaal highveld by slave raiders is not supported by any substantial evidence.[36]

More important than these details, however, the re-evaluation of the role of the Zulu in the Mfecane in no way implies that the concept itself must be abandoned. Even if the effect of the emergence of the Zulu kingdom in intensifying and accelerating the spread of the process of change which had begun in earlier days has been exaggerated (and if one accepts Wright's version it is clear that their impact in this regard was nevertheless very considerable), it remains true that a process of change in the direction of strengthened and enlarged political organisation did take place in the course of the eighteenth century between Delagoa Bay and the Thukela, and that a whole series of migrations subsequently set out from this area carrying a common package of institutions. The various groups, in very different situations, employed these institutions in divers ways to build substantial states incorporating large numbers of previous outsiders. It is equally clearly the case that these activities had very significant consequences for the history of a large part of Africa. This is the essence of the Mfecane, not the extent to which it was, or was not, driven solely by Shaka's Zulu *izimpi*.

The third main focus of attack on the concept of the Mfecane relates to the extent of its impact. How extensive was the disruption of community life and the

---

34. This development was sketched in outline in Omer-Cooper, *The Zulu Aftermath*, 148–9; but has been examined in much more detail and clarity by Cobbing in his thesis on 'The Ndebele under the Khumalos'.

35. I still believe this argument, sketched in *The Zulu Aftermath*, 148–9, to be basically correct.

36. The chronology of the expansion of the Delagoa Bay slave trade as established by Elizabeth Eldredge seems to rule this out and to render implausible the view that he was subsequently driven from the north-eastern Transvaal region by the Delagoa Bay traders.

dislocation of population resulting from the upheavals of the period and who was responsible for such disruption as did occur? In relation to the Natal region, as has been noted above, Wright argues that the role of the Zulu in disturbing the pattern of life and settlement there has been very significantly exaggerated and that the main cause of this was the southward migration of a series of other chiefdoms. He also insists that the Natal region was never anything like wholly depopulated and that at least some segments of a large proportion of the communities that had been living in the territory survived within it throughout the period of upheaval. He does accept, however, that the pattern of life and settlement was very seriously upset by the successive migrations through the area; that substantial parts of the country were very largely depopulated and that there was a temporary concentration of population owing allegiance to a number of different leaders in the area between the Mzimkhulu and the Mzimvubu which became a cockpit for a complex series of conflicts.[37]

The Mfecane as Alibi: Griqua and Colonial Slaves

Cobbing's arguments are much more far-ranging. He concentrates his attention mainly on the areas of the highveld of trans-Orangia and trans-Vaal, though, as has been mentioned, he does also concern himself with the Natal region; also there he holds the English traders and their African followers, who he believes were engaged in slave trading, responsible for the disturbances. He also directs his attention to the zone beyond the Cape's eastern frontier. With regard to trans-Orangia he argues that while the activities of the Ngwane of Matiwane were no doubt disruptive, their consequences were short-lived and far less significant than those of the firearm-wielding Griqua raiders who were essentially agents of the expanding white settler capitalist economy of the Cape. It was actually the Griqua rather than the Zulu and the Ndebele who drove Matiwane and his people from the Caledon Valley to meet their fate at the hands of British troops at Mbholompo. In addition to raiding cattle to supply markets in the colony these mounted brigands were also engaged, he believes, in an extensive slave trade to satisfy the Cape farming economy's insatiable appetite for cheap African labour. The concept of the Difaqane (the Mfecane on the highveld) is essentially an alibi, claims Cobbing, created by white settlers, officials and missionaries to conceal these slave-raiding and -trading activities in which they were all implicated.[38]

As an instance of this he examines the well-known expedition of mounted Griqua organised by Moffat supposedly to save the Tlhaping settlement near Dithakong which was threatened by the advance of a number of wandering and plundering bands. Basing himself on the account of the incident given by the government official Melvill who accompanied the expedition, Cobbing claims it was really a cynically disguised slave raid. Following this general argument he maintains that the

---

37. See Wright, 'Political Transformations'.
38. Cobbing, 'The Mfecane as Alibi'.

accepted accounts of 'Mantatee' refugees entering the Cape to escape the devastations of the Difaqane and providing a much-needed temporary source of labour for farmers in the eastern districts, are a deliberate falsification. In fact, these 'Mantatees' were the victims of the Griqua slave raiders brought forcibly into the Cape and sold into forced labour, proceedings which were concealed by an extensive conspiracy of silence.[39] The activities of the Griqua slave raiders, believes Cobbing, extended into the trans-Vaal region where their disruptive consequences complemented those of the Delagoa Bay-based raiders. Mzilikazi's kingdom was essentially a defensive state which attempted to gather different communities together and offer them protection against these raiders.[40] Just as Mzilikazi had initially been driven on to the highveld as a consequence of the slave trade and subsequently out of the north-eastern trans-Vaal by Delagoa Bay-based raiders, so he was driven north from the vicinity of the Orange River to the central trans-Vaal and thence to take refuge in the west of this region by the cattle- and slave-raiding Griqua. Finally, it was the trekkers, with Griqua allies, who broke up his composite kingdom in the trans-Vaal region and forced him on his last great migration to Zimbabwe.

Officially sanctioned but concealed slave raiding extended to the Cape frontier zone also, Cobbing maintains. The military expedition which attacked and dispersed the Ngwane of Matiwane at Mbholompo allegedly to protect the Thembu and Xhosa from Zulu forces for which the unfortunate Ngwane were mistaken, was really, in his view, a huge official slave raid undertaken in the light of the labour crisis in the Cape's eastern districts.[41]

Not only were the disturbances on the highveld primarily the work of slave-raiding bands rather than migrations of the Mfecane but the consequences of these disturbances have also, in Cobbing's opinion, been exaggerated and misrepresented. The area of the later Free State and Transvaal was never wholly depopulated. Communities living in the area had always occupied widely separated settlements leaving substantial empty land between them. Population was never driven by the disturbances of the period into the precise areas of the subsequent 'homelands' of apartheid legislation. The idea that these were the creation of the Mfecane subsequently merely legitimised by white authority is another Mfecane myth. Lesotho, Cobbing argues further, was not really the creation of Moshoeshoe responding to the challenge and opportunities provided by the Mfecane. It was rather the result of peoples being driven together and concentrated by the pressure from Griqua raiders and land-grabbing Boers exerted over a prolonged period. Its survival as a distinct polity was the result of the fortuitous action of the Governor of the Cape. In the same way, the Mfecane cannot be said to have fathered Swaziland which has to be seen as the creation of Anglo-Boer rivalry and diplomacy. The Bechuanaland

39. Cobbing, 'The Mfecane as Alibi'.
40. Cobbing, 'Grasping the Nettle', 13; 'Rethinking the Roots of Violence', 25–6.
41. Cobbing, 'The Mfecane as Alibi'.

Protectorate (now Botswana) was even more clearly the creation of British policy rather than the Mfecane.[42]

With respect to the Natal region, Wright's argument that the role of the Zulu has been exaggerated and that the main agents of disruption were the various southward-migrating chiefdoms which passed through the area, is almost certainly correct. While it significantly modifies and greatly clarifies the previously accepted picture of what happened in the Natal area, it by no means totally transforms it.[43] His view that the depopulation of the region as a result of the upheavals of the Mfecane was far from total and that severe depopulation was restricted to part of the territory only, is also almost certainly right. These arguments taken together, however, in no way amount to a proof that the Mfecane in the Natal region never happened as he suggests in his article in the *Canadian Journal of African Studies*. On the contrary, they show quite clearly that it did.

Cobbing's theory that the white traders in the Natal area were engaged in the slave trade on a substantial scale, however, is at present without significant evidential support. The same must be said of the predominant role he ascribes to them in the disruption of life in the Natal area; and his assertion that it was Fynn rather than Shaka who organised and led the campaign into the Mpondo country in 1828 clearly flies directly in face of the available evidence.[44] On the face of it, the great power which Cobbing believes was wielded by these traders and their African followers in relation to that of the forces available to Shaka does not seem wholly convincing when one remembers how Dingane's *impi* overwhelmed the followers of the Natal whites at a time when his forces were also involved in the struggle with the Boer trekkers.

With regard to the highveld, Cobbing is right, of course, to draw attention to the plundering activities of the various Khoi and part-Khoi mounted gun-carrying raiders that he refers to as Griqua. That their depredations preceded the intrusions of the Hlubi and Ngwane and that they continued and intensified after the departure of Matiwane to what is today the Transkei, has long been established. No doubt he is right in stressing the need to take serious account of their role in the disruption of settled life in trans-Orangia and to a lesser extent some areas of the trans-Vaal.

It is when one comes to the extent of the role Cobbing ascribes to them and the chronology of their impact that doubts arise. Before the 1820s there is little evidence to suggest that the raiding activities of Jan Bloem and his Kora associates, of De Buys and his *volk* or of the Griqua-Bergenaar rebels resulted in any widespread disruption of African community life, albeit their impact should not be dismissed as insignificant.[45] In the case of the trans-Vaal, the Griqua raiders certainly repeatedly

42. See Cobbing, 'The Case Against the Mfecane'.
43. See Wright, 'Political Transformations'; and 'A.T. Bryant and "The Wars of Shaka"'.
44. See J.B. Peires, 'Matiwane's Road to Mbholompo: A Reprieve for the Mfecane?', in this volume.
45. See Margaret Kinsman, '"Hungry Wolves": The Impact of Violence on Rolong Life, 1823–1836', in this volume; Guy Hartley, 'The Battle of Dithakong and "Mfecane" Theory', in this volume.

harried Mzilikazi's Ndebele. He found their raids a serious menace and very difficult to deal with. He may well have shifted his headquarters from the vicinity of the Orange to the central Transvaal region in the hope, subsequently disappointed, of gaining immunity from them. His subsequent move to the Marico Basin may also have been, at least in part, a response to this menace. On the other hand, it should be recalled that the Griqua were only able to undertake major attacks on the Ndebele with the aid of African allies. The major onslaughts that they did undertake, moreover, all ended in disaster at the hands of the Ndebele forces.[46] To speak of Mzilikazi's kingdom as a defensive state is also, from one point of view, correct. The expansion of the core of his following and the extension of his authority over other communities was no doubt undertaken largely in search of security and under threat of attack from Griqua raiders, Zulu expeditions etc. It is, however, surely absurd to suggest that the rapid incorporation of large numbers of Sotho/Tswana speakers in the Ndebele community, the establishment of their paramountcy over other groups, the repeated campaigns against the Ngwaketsi, the expulsion of Moletsane and his followers across the Orange etc. were undertaken without great violence and disruption of normal life in the area of the trans-Vaal in which the Ndebele armies operated.

In trans-Orangia likewise, there seems no conclusive evidence to show that the impact of the Griqua was greater than that of the intrusions of the Hlubi and Ngwane and the predations of the Tlokwa and others set in motion thereby. Nor is there sufficient evidence to disprove the view that Griqua raiding escalated to a level at which it constituted a major cause of disruption in trans-Orangia in response to the chaotic circumstances arising from the intrusions across the Drakensberg. On the contrary, all the evidence suggests that Griqua raiding expanded to serious proportions only after 1823 and was largely confined to areas in the modern Free State where settled life had been already severely disturbed as a consequence of the chain of migrations initiated by the intrusion of the Hlubi and Ngwane.[47] There is no evidence that the Griqua had anything to do with the migrations of the Tlokwa or of the Phuthing, Hlakwana and Fokeng of Patsa who converged on Dithakong in June 1823.[48] The evidence also makes it quite obvious that Cobbing is wrong in asserting that it was the Griqua who drove Matiwane from the Caledon Valley. It is clear that his migration did follow encounters with Zulu and Ndebele forces and a failed assault on Thaba Bosiu, though it may have been precipitated by a power struggle within his own community.[49]

In the period following Matiwane's departure the Griqua certainly did become the

---

46. On this see R.K. Rasmussen, *Migrant Kingdom: Mzilikazi's Ndebele in South Africa*, London and Cape Town, 1978, 27–132.
47. See Hartley, 'The Battle of Dithakong', 10–11; also Kinsman, '"Hungry Wolves"'.
48. The weight of the evidence here clearly supports the view that these migrating groups were involved. See Hartley, 'The Battle of Dithakong', 9–15; Eldredge, 'Sources of Conflict in Southern Africa', 25–6.
49. See Peires, 'Matiwane's Road to Mbholompo'.

main disruptive force in trans-Orangia. Their raiding undoubtedly did contribute in a major way to the dislocation of life in the area and to the concentration of people in the neighbourhood of Moshoeshoe's nascent Lesotho kingdom. It was the activities of these raids also that drove Moshoeshoe's followers to adopt the tactics of mounted gunmen and induced the chief to invite the French Protestant missionaries to his realm.

With regard to the large-scale slave trading activities in which Cobbing believes the Griqua to have been engaged, there is no reason to doubt Saxe Bannister's claim that the Griqua gained control of a number of Sotho/Tswana and that they sold some of them into the colony.[50] Their own raiding activities and the general situation of acute instability and insecurity in the area would have made it very easy for them to get control of people in this way, and indeed made it difficult not to acquire responsibility for captives, abandoned children, destitute refugees, etc. That such people would have been exploited as dependent clients (a form of slavery perhaps) or have been disposed of to other Griqua or to colonists can hardly be doubted.

Afrikaner farmers, moreover, needed to be able to acquire small numbers of dependents who could be acculturated to their society and incorporated at least partially and in an inferior dependent capacity, in their families, to provide domestic services and serve as overseers of labour, These were to be retainers who could be trusted with firearms to defend the stock, and even to participate in military expeditions along with their masters.[51] It is difficult to doubt that the Griqua would have been a convenient source of such 'apprentices' or that the prospect of obtaining such tradable captives may have been an incentive to some of their raiding.

It is another thing, however, to maintain that the very large numbers of so-called 'Mantatees' who entered service with farmers in the Cape at this time were all captured by the Griqua and brought into the colony as slaves. To accept that such a large-scale operation with caravans of slaves moving under armed guard could have gone on without comment or criticism assumes a unanimity of interest, opinion and cynical indifference to considerations of humanity among missionaries, officials, farmers and traders that is frankly incredible. It is all the more difficult to believe in the face of the criticisms which were raised over aspects of the Mbholompo campaign.[52]

Certainly the evidence which Cobbing reveals in relation to the Dithakong campaign does little to establish his case. He finds it suspicious that Moffat should have broken off his journey to the Ngwaketse and hurried back to organise the expedition 'on the basis of unsubstantiated rumours of a Mantatee presence',[53] but the rumours were in fact essentially correct. Groups of wandering displaced people were approaching Dithakong. Would Moffat have acted more responsibly if he had

50. Quoted in Cobbing, 'The Mfecane as Alibi'.
51. An excellent account of the Afrikaner farmers' need for such '*inboekselings*' and of the roles they performed, is given by Delius, *The Land Belongs to Us*, 34–7, 136–47.
52. Noted in Cobbing, 'The Mfecane as Alibi', 513.
53. Cobbing, 'The Mfecane as Alibi', 492.

ignored these rumours? Cobbing's view that no such threat existed and that the accounts of the 'Mantatee' hordes were merely a blind to conceal an attack on the inhabitants of Dithakong itself, goes directly against the evidence. There is, in fact, quite sufficient evidence to establish that the Phuthing and the Hlakwane were definitely involved and strong indications that the Fokeng of Patsa (later known as the Kololo) were also.[54] If he and Melvill had really planned the whole expedition as a large-scale stock and slave raid, why did Moffat go off to the Ngwaketse and have to come dashing back? Was this perhaps all a devious subterfuge to conceal his criminal intentions?

After the battle about 150 women and children were brought to Kuruman. According to Moffat and Melvill, this was done to give them protection and save them from starvation. If capturing slaves was one of the main purposes of the campaign, why were the numbers small? The Griqua, with their firearms, were apparently in a completely dominant position, killed two to three hundred of the Mantatees and burnt their villages and had horses to help them round up any who might attempt to flee. The direct evidence of slave trading alleged against Moffat consists, firstly, in the fact that he kept one of the boys as a personal servant 'affectionately domesticated in the family of his benefactor';[55] and secondly, that he took 'some others, including five women and a fine boy, and placed them in the service of white families in the Cape'. In the case of Melvill, the gravamen of the charge is that he took 15 of the survivors of the battle who had come under his control, to Graaff-Reinet and placed them with white families there, receiving some ammunition in return.

However critical one may be of these transactions they scarcely provide justification for describing the whole campaign as a deliberately organised slave raid or indeed for doubting the general outlines of Moffat's account of it. When it is pointed out, moreover, that Moffat took great care in selecting the households with whom he left the people he took to the Cape to ensure that they did not end up in permanent servitude; that one of these households was that of the outstanding liberal, humanitarian missionary John Philip; and that the ammunition which Melvill received was probably not in return for the captives he placed in Graaff-Reinet but issued to him to further the discharge of his official duties,[56] Cobbing's accusations can be seen to be not just unfair but frankly preposterous.

While it is highly probable then that whites in the Cape did acquire some servants, probably mainly women and children, by trade or barter from the Griqua, a substantial part of the large number of 'Mantatees' who came into the Cape at this time probably did come as refugees from the situation of war and general insecurity on the trans-Orangian highveld, seeking safety, shelter, food and the means to acquire the cattle essential to establish or re-establish autonomous homesteads. This

54. See note 48 above.
55. Cobbing, 'The Mfecane as Alibi', 492–3.
56. See Hartley, 'The Battle of Dithakong'.

presumption is strengthened by the fact that so many of these 'Mantatees' subsequently left the colony with the cattle they had acquired to settle under Moshoeshoe.[57] The argument that the Mbholompo campaign was simply a huge slave-raiding expedition is also difficult to credit. According to Cobbing's account, the expedition involved about 16 000 men, including 531 gun-armed whites, constituting one of the largest armies yet seen in Africa. It had overwhelming fire-power and surrounded the Ngwane encampment before opening fire. Yet only between one and two hundred prisoners and about 47 women and 70 children were to be brought back to the Cape as workers.[58] The evidence concerning the Mbholompo affair as assembled by Jeff Peires clearly demonstrates Cobbing's account of this matter to be as baseless as his treatment of Dithakong.[59]

The Impact of the Mfecane Debated

Looking at Cobbing's criticisms of the alleged impact of the disturbances, it is easy to agree that the extent of depopulation should not be exaggerated. Probably no substantial area was ever even temporarily wholly depopulated. Some of the former inhabitants probably always remained, hiding in hilly or bushy areas and showing the good sense to keep out of sight of parties of mounted and armed men. Much of the more open highveld country may never have held a very dense population anyway. The idea that the entire area subsequently legislatively defined as exclusively belonging to whites had been vacated and that Africans had confined themselves to those very areas subsequently constituted 'homelands' is quite absurd. It is also obviously true that Moshoeshoe's kingdom might well have broken up if it had not been for the external pressure of land-hungry whites and that in the last resort its survival as a separate British colonial territory could not have come about without the actions of Governor Wodehouse. In the same way Cobbing is of course right to maintain that Swaziland as a high commission territory owed its existence to British policy as did the Bechuanaland Protectorate.[60]

On the other hand, neither Swaziland nor Lesotho would have become high commission territories or become the kind of states that they are now if they had not been part of the territories of two African kingdoms which owed their origins to the period of the Mfecane. In the same way, the native reserves were clearly residual areas of African land-holding which happened to survive the process of white land expropriation long enough for the value of their retention as breeding grounds of cheap migrant labour to be appreciated, rather than the direct creations of the Mfecane. Nevertheless, in some cases at least (such as Thaba Nchu), it is necessary to look back to the Mfecane to explain why the area concerned had a relatively

---

57. See e.g. P. Sanders, *Moshoeshoe: Chief of the Sotho*, London, 1975, 60–74.
58. Cobbing, 'The Mfecane as Alibi', 502–3.
59. Peires, 'Matiwane's Road to Mbholompo'.
60. The accounts of the Swazi and Lesotho kingdoms given in Omer-Cooper, *The Zulu Aftermath* made this quite clear.

concentrated African population and ended up as such a vestigial reserve and to account for the composition of its population. Finally, although the highvelds of trans-Orangia and trans-Vaal were never depopulated, Cobbing does not deny that life there was gravely disrupted and settlement dislocated; he merely suggests that responsibility for this should be placed mainly on the Griqua and Delagoa Bay slave raiders rather than on Mzilikazi and Matiwane. It still seems probable, therefore, that the upheavals of the time did encourage the movement of the trekkers into those areas and facilitate their initial settlement and the beginnings of the process of further expansion and land expropriation from their first nuclear settlements. If so, then they do form part of the explanation of the eventual pattern of land-holding that was to emerge.

Failure of the New Paradigm and the Value of the Debate

From the foregoing, it is clear that Wright's carefully researched critique which is confined to the Phongolo–Mzimkhulu area does not require the abandonment of the idea of the Mfecane or even drastically transform our understanding of it. Cobbing's much more broad-ranging arguments are another matter. Taking the implications of his arguments to their logical conclusion, the heightened demand for cheap forced labour in the Cape, South America, Indian Ocean Islands, the Middle East, etc. arising from the expansion of European capitalism must be seen as the ultimate effective cause of all the violence, upheavals and political changes in African societies in precolonial southern, central and east Africa in the nineteenth century. This grand scenario brings the activities of Delagoa Bay-based slavers and of the Mozambican super-*prazeiros* of Arab, Swahili and Nyamwezi leaders of slave caravans in eastern and central Africa, of Griqua bandits on the highveld, English traders in Natal and of British troops beyond the Cape colonial frontier as well as the creation of the Zulu, Swazi and Ndebele kingdoms and the migrations of the Gaza, Ngoni, etc. within a single explanatory framework. Within this scenario, the kingdom-building of Shaka, Mzilikazi, Soshangane, Zwangendaba *et al.* must be seen simply as a series of reactions to the expanding slave trade. Even if this attractive grand hypothesis were fully accepted, however, and Cobbing's assertions about the slave raiding activities of Griqua, Natal traders and British troops all proved fully substantiable, it would still be the case that the state building achievements and migrations of the Zulu, Swazi, Gaza, Ngoni, etc., the essence of the Mfecane, constitute an important theme in nineteenth-century African history. Though it would not require the abandonment of the Mfecane, however, it would place it in a significantly different context, and in this sense one could perhaps speak of a new paradigm. It is quite apparent, however, that not only is positive evidence for this grand new hypothesis lacking but there is quite sufficient negative evidence to demonstrate its falsity.

For Cobbing and Wright, however, the Mfecane is not seen only as an explanatory account of a process of change in African societies accompanied by widespread migrations which contributes to our understanding of the historical causation of some features of the more recent situation in southern, central and eastern Africa. Rather, as the tone and in certain cases the titles of some of their papers make clear, the real object of attack is the abuse of the Mfecane as a myth to lay the blame for the overwhelmingly greater part of the violence against Africans in South African history on Africans themselves to justify apartheid and to provide a basis for extreme Zulu nationalism. The Mfecane which they are attacking is thus not primarily that which has been portrayed and discussed by serious historians in recent years but caricature versions by pro-apartheid propagandists deliberately designed to provide a rationale for that monstrous system of race oppression and territorial segregation, and fed to young minds through school textbooks.

It is these versions in which the Zulu have the extreme centrality in the Mfecane, and which often look back to much earlier accounts such as those of the negrophobe Theal, that come to be depicted as the wars of Shaka, the mad monster. It is in these accounts that the violence in nineteenth-century history is attributed to the insensate ferocity of blacks massacring one another while the trekkers appear as benign bringers of peace and security. It is in these accounts that it is claimed that Africans coralled themselves in the exact areas later proclaimed as 'homelands', leaving entirely vacant the whole of the areas subsequently legislatively defined as for white ownership only.

With attacks on such pernicious rubbish one must of course have the greatest sympathy. The gross factual errors about the location of African communities in the period of the Mfecane and of the way that white expansion took place should be, and can easily be, decisively refuted. That white expansion was accompanied by great violence, cruelty and deceit should no doubt be made clear to dispel the fatuous myths of univeral white benignity if they still have any credence. The overwhelming institutional violence involved in the whole dreadful system of race domination and oppression should also be pointed out if there are still any who do not recognise this.

None of this, however, requires the abandonment of the Mfecane. On the contrary, it is from the study of that process itself that the best evidence for refuting these false inferences can be derived. The careers of the great leaders of the Mfecane, for example, decisively refute the view of African incapacity for originality and creative statesmanship, a foundation myth of white supremacist ideology. The study of the Mfecane demonstrates the importance of African initiatives undertaken in pursuit of their own ends not just in reaction to white activities in the making of southern African history. It thereby restores the dignity of Africans as persons and positive actors in that history which an excessively Eurocentric view destroys.

The state-building activities of these leaders, moreover, decisively give the lie to the concept of the immutability of ethnic identity and the impracticality of developing a common society from multicultural components which is the fundamental basis of the apartheid ideology. They show indeed that such communities as the Zulu and Swazi, for example, are nothing like the primordial organic nations with inherently different cultural propensities and divinely ordained destinies required by apartheid theory. Rather they originated very recently as hastily aggregated political units embracing many previously independent communities, and in the case of the Swazi, brought Nguni- and Sotho-speaking peoples together in a common political framework and loyalty. It was their incorporation within these political structures and the subsequent pressures of white attitudes and policies which gave them the sense of identity they now display. The successes of Mzilikazi, and of Zwangenbaba and the other Nguni leaders in so rapidly creating new communities from members of such extraordinarily heterogeneous linguistic and cultural groups makes these points even more forcibly.

Study of the Mfecane period of course also destroys such myths as that of the inherent militarism of the Zulu. Clearly, as they were simply a hastily and arbitrarily assembled grouping of some of tne northern Nguni-speaking peoples, any special military qualities they displayed must be the result of the militarist system in which they were incorporated rather than of any inherent propensities. Far from providing a support for apartheid, the study of the Mfecane explodes its entire intellectual foundations. The false and exaggerated statements made about the extent of land vacated at the time of the Mfecane are also most easily refuted from the detailed study of that chain of events.

The proper study of the Mfecane is then the best approach to the refutation of the false interpretations peddled by apartheid apologists and no new model to replace it is needed for this. If such a model were needed, moreover, that which Cobbing proposes seems hardly suitable for the purpose. In his extraordinarily Eurocentric account African initiatives are for the most part reduced to mere reactions to those of whites. Africans are portrayed as incapable of any effective resistance at any stage of southern African history to the overwhelming forces of white capitalism. The contribution of African rulers even to the creation of such states as Lesotho and Swaziland is written off as trivial. Furthermore, how satisfactory a means of absolving Africans from responsibility for violence in the Mfecane period is it to argue that they were acting as mercenary agents of white slavers?

The attack on the Mfecane for its supposed value to apartheid propagandists is open, moreover, to even more serious objections. To turn away from any major historical development because we object to the propaganda use to which its study may be put is to risk embarking on a road which leads away from the assessment of historical statements on cognitive grounds and towards their evaluation for their political utility to the causes we favour. That road must soon leave all honest scholarship behind. Some of the more rhetorical phrases in Cobbing's and Wright's papers do seem to suggest a teetering rather near the brink of this fateful slope.

Not only is the whole basis of the attack on the Mfecane for its supposed value to apartheid ideology intellectually worrying but the actual lines of attack are also in some cases seriously concerning. For example, to invest so much in attacking the notion that whites found empty land to occupy in what became the Orange Free State and the Transvaal, risks implicitly accepting the basic racist assumption that if they had been found empty by the trekkers the creation of a system of segregation, excluding blacks from owning land in these areas would have been justified. Of course the factual errors in the apartheid theorists' mythologised versions of the Mfecane and who occupied what land at the time of the Trek should be corrected. These facts, however, are not of fundamental significance in exposing the moral invalidity of apartheid.

In the same way, aspects of Cobbing's arguments about responsibility for violence seem to me to come dangerously close to accepting the idea that attempting to assess responsibility for violence on a racial basis is a significant exercise. Unless we accept the racist assumptions of apartheid, of course this is not so. No racial or ethnic group can be said to be inherently more violent than any other, and if members of one group appear to have acted more violently than those of another, we must assume that the others would have done just the same if their total historical situations had been reversed.

Much of the argument in this debate seems to me to illustrate the extreme difficulty (even for those of the purest intentions) of extricating themselves from the web of racial categories and the racist assumptions of the system in which they have been living.

Though the work of Cobbing and Wright has not destroyed the Mfecane or established any new paradigm, it should not be dismissed as trivial. It has drawn renewed attention to the possible role of long-distance trade from Delagoa Bay in the causation of the Mfecane. Wright's work in particular helps provide a much clearer picture of the Zulu state and of the role of its forces and those of the other groups involved in the dislocation of community life in the Natal region. Cobbing's work has usefully focused our attention on the role of Griqua raiders in trans-Orangia and given new emphasis to the appreciation that in this area the activities of such migrant groups as the Hlubi and the Ngwane overlapped and interacted in complex ways with disruptive influences stemming from the expansion of the Cape white settler economy. Most important of all, the Cobbing critique has reaffirmed the validity and the importance of the Mfecane and by raising new questions and stimulating new research has ensured that it will continue to occupy a prominent place in the historiography of southern and eastern Africa.

PART THREE

The Interior

'The time of troubles'
Difaqane *in the Interior*

NEIL PARSONS

Difaqane: **Evolution of the Word**

For the last thirty or forty years the term *difaqane* has been used very broadly by historians, for the wars of the 1820s and 1830s west of the Drakensberg. This usage, covering Sotho/Tswana/Pedi areas as a cognate of the term *mfecane* used for areas inhabited by Nguni-speakers, was taken up by Monica Wilson and Leonard Thompson in the first volume of their *Oxford History of South Africa* (1969). *Difaqane*, like *mfecane*, was then perpetuated and popularised even into apartheid state ideological pronouncements and school textbooks. Eccentric spellings such as 'difakane' and 'defikane' have also crept in, attempting to indigenise the word for linguistic areas where the concept had not previously been used.[1]

The word and concept of *difaqane* have a history that long predates their use in twentieth-century 'liberal' or apartheid historiography. The word itself, spelt *lifaqane* in southern Sotho orthography (though still pronounced the same as *di-*), goes back at least to the 1890s – and quite possibly half a century earlier in Lesotho historiography. Certainly, the fundamental assumptions behind the use of the term in the traditional historiography of Lesotho go back to the 1830s.

Lifaqane – as the plural form of *faqane*, meaning 'wandering horde' – appeared in print at least as early as 1892 in an article by the prolific Lesotho poet, playwright and historian Azariel Sekese (1849–1930), in a copy of the newspaper *Leselinyana la Lesotho*. The term *lifaqane* was then taken up by other historians of the southern Sotho, notably James Macgregor and Daniel Frederic Ellenberger, who extended its usage to apply to the wars caused by 'wandering hordes' around Lesotho in the 1820s – rather than just to the 'hordes' themselves.[2]

---

1. Major historians have assumed that *difaqane* is a straight translation from the Nguni word *mfecane* – see J. D. Omer-Cooper, *The Zulu Aftermath: a Nineteenth-century Revolution in Bantu Africa*, London, 1966, 5; L. M. Thompson, *Survival in Two Worlds: Moshoeshoe of Lesotho 1786–1870*, Oxford, 1975, 34n. For a textbook using *mfecane* and *difaqane* to justify apartheid land distribution see B. J. Vorster, J. Schoeman and A. P. J. van Rensburg, (*New Structure) Active History Form III*, Pretoria, 1976, 90ff. For 'Defikane' see J. Comaroff, *Body of Power, Spirit of Resistance: the Culture and History of a South African People* (Tshidi-Rolong of Mafikeng), Chicago, 1985, *passim*. (There is no word beginning with 'de-' in any Tswana dictionary that I have seen.)
2. P. Sanders, *Moshoeshoe: Chief of the Sotho*, London, 1975, 27n; L. B. J. Machobane, 'Mohlomi: Doctor, Traveller and Sage', *Journal of Southern African Historical Studies*, 2, (1976), 26 n.57; G. Haliburton, *Historical Dictionary of Lesotho*, Metuchen, 1977, 47, 90–1, 97, 160. I do not know if the word *lifaqane* was used in articles about the 1820s by Nehemiah Moshoeshoe published in *Leselinyane la Lesotho* a dozen years earlier than Sekese.

This all begs the question of when and how the word *lifaqane* emerged. Sekese or a predecessor could have got it direct as an existing Sotho word from oral sources, or as a back-formation into Sotho from English and Xhosa language publications. As Jeff Peires shows, the word 'ficani' was used in George Thompson's *Travels and Adventures in Southern Africa* as early as 1827, in an account of Matiwane's Ngwane and Hlubi. (Variant spellings in English, such as 'fetcani', can be accounted for as attempts to get to grips with the word's central click consonant.) The Xhosa word *imfecane* − later taken up by Eric Walker and other historians − was being used in Xhosa language publications from 1863.[3]

We know that the word 'fikani' was being used on the northern highveld in 1829. Mzilikazi kaMatshobane Khumalo used it, in the vicinity of present-day Pretoria, when he told Robert Moffat that 'he had received the Fikani who had been driven by the white men and Kaffirs' (i.e. from Mbholompo by British and Xhosa), and that the 'Fikani' had also told him of the artillery used by the whites. Mzilikazi was probably talking to Tswana-speaking Moffat in a cognate dialect of eastern Sotho, or his words were being interpreted through such a dialect.[4]

Difaqane: Evolution of the Concept

Whatever the origins of the word itself, the southern Sotho historical folklore of *lifaqane* was in place by the late 1830s. Writing from oral traditions recorded in 1836, the missionary Thomas Arbousset outlined the *lifaqane* concept's basic assumptions in a book published in French in 1842. He told the story of a time of peace − personified by the great 'doctor, traveller and sage' Mohlomi − followed by a time of war, started by the invasions of Nguni-speakers from the north-east. The period of stress was eventually settled and redeemed by Mohlomi's pupil in the arts of peace, Moshoeshoe.[5]

This was the pattern taken up by the first popular survey of southern Sotho history to appear in print, Joseph Orpen's 'History of the Basutos of South Africa', published in the *Cape Argus* in 1857. Orpen portrayed Mohlomi ('Motlumi') as having directly predicted Moshoeshoe's greatness, and then outlined the main steps of the *lifaqane* which are nowadays considered conventional. Mohlomi's death 'about 1815' was followed by

> convulsions produced by Chaka, which shook all South Africa . . . and dislodged the Amanguani Zooloos under Matoana [Matiwane] the Amatluibi Fingoes under Pacarita [Mpangazitha], from the district of Natal, and the Mantatees from Harrismith. All these fell promiscuously upon the Basutos like a deluge, while they were disunited . . . while Moselikatse, flying also from

3. See Jeff Peires's essay in this book, notes 29, 70 and 71.
4. R. Moffat, *The Matabeleland Journals of Robert Moffat*, ed. by J.P.R. Wallis, 2 vols, London, 1945, Reprint Salisbury, 1976, 16 and 28.
5. T. Arbousset and F. Daumas, *Narrative of an Exploratory Tour to the North-East of the Colony of the Cape Good Hope*, Cape Town, 1846 and 1968, 270–84. See also Machobane, 'Mohlomi'.

Dingaan, ravaged the country to the north, and almost exterminated the Bataungs, Molitsane's tribe.[6]

This narrative reached mature form in the Revd D.F. Ellenberger's *History of the Basuto, Ancient and Modern*, Volume One, published in 1912 − the main repository of 'what we call Sotho tradition', which had also become Christian mission tradition. Modern revaluation of the *difaqane* was also begun by writers within the missionary tradition. By the 1950s missionary historians had extended the term (with a minor orthographic change to *difaqane*) beyond Lesotho to the rest of the highveld and southern Kalahari, and were using it to mean 'the Time of Troubles . . . following the rise of the Zulu power under Shaka'. It was Ellenberger's granddaughter Marion How who first deconstructed accounts of the 1823 battle at Dithakong in a seminal article of 1955 entitled 'An Alibi for Mantatisi'.[7]

It is not difficult to see that the concept of *lifaqane*, as originally formulated, served the interests of the ruling monarchy of Lesotho − by portraying Moshoeshoe as the choice of destiny and expunger of misrule. Nor is it difficult to see how the concept could be adapted to serve missionary and settler interests, portraying Christianity and/or whites as the harbingers of peace after chaos. But such 'interests' do not invalidate the concept of *difaqane*; they merely alert us to how it has been and can be manipulated.

Difaqane: Revised Versions

Major deficiencies in the historiography of *difaqane* have been identified by historians writing since 1974. They have challenged the chronology of the *difaqane* wars as beginning around 1822 and ending around 1837, and they have challenged the idea of the wars being exclusively between African peoples.

For a start, it is impossible to unscramble the *difaqane* wars from prior, concurrent and subsequent wars with Afrikaner trekkers from the south coast. In an influential though unpublished seminar paper of 1974 Colin Webb recognised this by re-christening the 'Great Trek' as the 'White Difaqane'.[8]

There is also the problem of there being no sharp distinction between wars in the interior before and after 1822. As the present writer put it in an article published in 1974 the *difaqane* on the highveld 'was not merely a spin-off from "Shaka's wars"

---

6. J.M. Orpen, *History of the Basutus of South Africa*, Mazenod, 1979, 20–2. On chiefly oral traditions in the context of Sotho–Nguni conflict and literate missionary mediation, see I. Hofmeyr, 'No Chief, No Exchange, No Story', *African Studies*, 48, 2 (1989), 132–55; I. Hofmeyr, 'Jonah and the Swallowing Monster: Orality and Literacy on a Berlin Mission Station in the Transvaal', *Journal of Southern African Studies*, 17, 4 (1991), 633–53.
7. E.W. Smith, 'Sebetwane and the Makololo', Appendix A in his *Great Lion of Bechuanaland: The Life and Times of Roger Price, Missionary*, London, 1957, 267–8; Marion How, 'An Alibi for Mantatisi', *African Studies*, 13, 2 (1955), 65–76.
8. Colin de B. Webb, 'Of Orthodoxy, Heresy and the Difaqane' unpublished paper presented to Teacher Conference on African History, University of the Witwatersrand, May 1974, modified by me to 'Afrikaner Difaqane' in recognition of 'non-white' Oorlam-Afrikaners in N. Parsons, *A New History of Southern Africa*, London, 1982, 91.

and Boer-British antagonisms far to the east and south; it was the climax of local conflicts of many decades'.[9]

The inseparability of *difaqane* from the effects of Afrikaner trekking is a theme taken up by the essays in the third section of this book by Margaret Kinsman, Guy Hartley and Jan-Bart Gewald. The other critique of *difaqane* is taken further by the three contributions by Simon Hall, Neil Parsons and Andrew Manson, which follow this introduction. Together they show that the *difaqane* was preceded by up to two centuries of increasing unrest and intercommunal stress, expressed in sporadic but cumulative violence.

Difaqane: **The Current Critique**

Simon Hall's essay immediately after this introduction, opens up new perspectives for historians through the findings of recent archaeological research on the Later Iron Age in the area that became the Transvaal. His essay falls into two parts; the first is mainly concerned with the evidence of intensive trans-Vaal Ndebele hilltop settlements on the Waterberg plateau of the west-central Transvaal, dated from about AD 1650. This is matched with evidence of the rapid growth in size of Tswana villages in the southern Transvaal region in the eighteenth century, suggesting an alternative defensive settlement strategy in times of strife. The second part of the essay is a discussion of cave sites occupied by Tswana refugees from the *difaqane* in the 1820s – in particular a scaled-down village built within a cave near present-day Potchefstroom. Such material remains of everyday life indicate cultural resistance to the depredations of the *difaqane*.

My essay, which follows Hall's, attempts further to bridge the gap between 'prehistory' and history. Comparison between historical (oral) traditions and archaeological research on the seventeenth and eighteenth centuries not only develops a chronological framework but also offsets evidence of the scale and complexity of cattle-based chiefdoms. The rising tide of violence can be explained by increasing population density and shifts in the mode of production because of the demands of east coast trade. Competition for ivory, south and north of the Limpopo, prompted raiding and movements of both defensive and predatory migration. A 'pre-*difaqane*' period in the seventeenth and eighteenth centuries, associated with 'Tebele' or trans-Vaal Ndebele predatory migrations over the highveld towards the upper Limpopo, may be distinguished from a 'proto-*difaqane*' period from the 1750s or 1770s onwards, merging with the *difaqane* proper in the early 1820s.

Andrew Manson develops in more detail the analysis of escalating violence among the western Tswana in the 'proto-*difaqane*' period between about 1750 and 1820. He focuses on the breakdown of Hurutshe hegemony in the western Transvaal

---

9. Later I developed the ideas of 'Tswana-Sotho States in Crisis, *c*.1770–1820' and of 'Ivory Wars' starting around 1750 and extending from the Zimbabwe plateau to the Cape frontier. See N. Parsons, 'The Economic History of Khama's Country in Southern Africa', *African Social Research*, 18 (1974), 647; Parsons, *A New History*, 48–51; N. Parsons, *Focus on History, Book One*, Harare, 1985, 77.

area, as tributary Kwena and Kgatla groups broke away and came to blows with the Hurutshe and each other over croplands, cattle and the products of hunting. This period also saw the rise to power and wealth of Ngwaketse hunter-warriors west of the Hurutshe, and of the Tlhaping state exploiting the breakup of Rolong hegemony in the area that later became the western part of the Transvaal. The success of certain Tswana chiefdoms can be seen in their aggregation of human population in the 'wards' of large new towns from about 1750, and in their access to and control of trade in ivory, metals and cattle. The predominant direction of trading and raiding was to the east coast until soon after 1800, when south coast trading and raiding grew ever more important.

Two essays by Guy Hartley and Margaret Kinsman respectively, which follow that of Manson, investigate aspects of the *difaqane* proper in the area of the northern Cape. Hartley looks anew at the battle of Dithakong in June 1823, challenging the conclusions of Julian Cobbing and of Jan-Bart Gewald[10] that it was a slave raid by Cape officials and/or Bergenaar trekker brigands who then left a false record to make it look like a repulsion of eastern invaders – the so-called 'Mantatees'. Eye-witness accounts are examined. Hartley concludes that the women and children 'enslaved' were the by-products of the battle rather than its intended victims. There is also no doubt that the 'Mantatees' existed, even if their exact identity was not elucidated until 130 years later.[11] We cannot simply attribute the *difaqane* wars of trans-Orangia to non-African predators mostly from the south, as Cobbing would have us do, but we should recognise that such predators had a significant and increasing impact.

Margaret Kinsman investigates the effects of the *difaqane* wars on the social and economic life of Rolong people in the northwest between about 1823 and 1836.[12] In doing so she lays out much of the historical evidence that forms the background to Sol Plaatje's classic novel *Mhudi*.[13] The first three or four years saw confused brigandage by small and highly mobile groups of hungry *difaqane* attackers and defenders. Such confusion was replaced by Mzilikazi's Ndebele state in the western trans-Vaal, with inner tributary and outer raiding zones separated by a depopulated middle 'march'. But this uneasy peace gave space for regrouping of scattered Tswana chiefdoms on the periphery, allying themselves with Griqua and Boer brigands from the south. Kinsman outlines the impact of persistent violence, famine

10. J. Cobbing, 'The Mfecane as Alibi: Thoughts on Dithakong and Mbolompo', *Journal of African History*, 29, 4 (1988), 487–519; J.-B. Gewald, 'Mountaineers as Mantatees; A Critical Reassessment of Events Leading Up to the Battle of Dithakong' M.A. dissertation, University of Leiden, 1989.

11. How, 'An Alibi for Mantatisi'. The term 'Mantatee' being or becoming, like 'Matebele', synonymous with African rather than European or Eurafrican raiders. Kalanga (south-west Shona) traditions collected *c*.1900 by W.C. Willoughby refer to the 'Mantatee' as 'Matebele [who] came from Dithakong'; C. van Waarden ed., *Kalanga Retrospect and Prospect*, Gaborone, 1991, 90.

12. Two other papers on Tswana and Sotho responses to the *difaqane* wars were presented to the colloquium on the Mfecane Aftermath, University of the Witwatersrand, Johannesburg, 1991; A. Manson, 'The Hurutshe, the Difaqane and the Formation of the Transvaal State 1820–1875'; B. Lambourne, 'A Chip off the Old Block: Early Ghoya History and the Emergence of Moletsane's Taung'.

13. S. Plaatje, *Mhudi*, Lovedale, 1930.

and uncertainty – scattering people and destroying the agricultural base of the economy – and how people resisted by adapting and reconstructing their lives.

The final essay in this section, by Jan-Bart Gewald, opens up research on a geographical area much further west – the Namibian coast. Gewald traces the growth of maritime trade along the coast in the seventeenth and eighteenth centuries, focusing on trade by Atlantic ships and the extension of the Cape mercantile system northwards – demanding cattle and slaves, as well as whaling and sealing along the coast. In the early nineteenth century, Oorlam-Afrikaner trekker conquerors from the Cape opened up communications between the interior of central Namibia and the ports of Angra Pequena (later Luderitz) and Walvis Bay. Thus trading and raiding for cattle and slaves, for both the Atlantic and Cape markets, were extended further north and west towards the Okavango/Cubango River by the mid-nineteenth century.

Present research on the interior of southern Africa in the seventeenth and eighteenth and early nineteeenth centuries can be likened to archaeologists uncovering a great mosaic. The part of the pattern which is emerging most clearly is the western trans-Vaal. Its connections south to the Cape have also become clearer. But too little is known of the northern trans-Vaal area and its connections with the east coast and north towards the Zambezi. More revaluation is needed of the traditions of *difaqane* origins along the highveld margins of the Drakensberg.[14] Gewald and others have begun to mark out the connections between Namibia and the western Kalahari with the rest of the region, including the mercantile network of the southern Angolan (Mossamedes) coast.[15]

The concept of *difaqane* may lose persuasiveness the further it is abstracted from its origins in southern Sotho folk historiography. But its relevance as far west as Namibia and north of Zambia is demonstrated by the career of Sebetwane, born 20 km from the Lesotho border, who fought battles within 200 km of both Walvis Bay and Lusaka.

14. See Sanders, *Moshoeshoe*, 28n; Lambourne, 'A Chip off the Old Block'.
15. See especially E. Wilmsen, *Land Filled with Flies: A Political Economy of the Kalahari*, Chicago, 1989. Current research brought to the symposium's attention was that of Professor Morton of Indiana University, studying the previously ignored supply of slaves – along with ivory and cattle – between the Okavango delta (Ngamiland) and the Transvaal area in the century up to about 1877.

11 Archaeological Indicators for Stress

in the Western Transvaal Region between the Seventeenth and Nineteenth Centuries

SIMON HALL

Lepalong is a Tswana name, recounted in oral records collected by Paul-Lambert Breutz,[1] for a large natural cavern system in the vicinity of modern Carletonville and Potchefstroom. Lepalong was an extreme choice for a home, made, so the oral records say, by displaced Kwena people who had fled southwards away from Mzilikazi. This cavern was occupied between 1827 and 1836, and the record of that occupation is preserved in the substantial remains of what must have been a complete underground village. The value of this archaeological site is that it provides a record of social history and evidence for one kind of extreme strategic response to the strife of that period which, in the shifting matrix of what might be called the 'difaqane' historiography, provides a concrete expression of what life was like.

Julian Cobbing's critique of settler 'alibi' historiography and liberal interpretations of the difaqane locates causality for this strife and turmoil away from purely internal African agency and exposes the potential role of imperial Europe and its slaving agents.[2] Central to his critique is a demythologising of the role of the Zulu kingdom as the prime catalyst and epicentre from which all disruption and turmoil ultimately emanated. It may be that Cobbing's analysis has swung the historiographic pendulum rather violently, and detailed regional investigations may find his general hypotheses out of step with the evidence. It is the aim of this essay to introduce archaeological material into the debate about the difaqane as an additional source from which a more detailed history for the period may be constructed. Cobbing's analyses extend the range of possibilities for assessing the archaeological evidence as it currently exists and as more comes to hand.

It seems that the present archaeological data contribute to a history of the period of upheaval labelled the difaqane in several ways. Firstly, and in the case of the western

---

1. P-L. Breutz, *The Tribes of Rustenburg and Pilansberg District*, Pretoria, 1953, 219.
2. J. Cobbing, 'The Mfecane as Alibi: Thoughts on Dithakong and Mbolompo', *Journal of African History*, 29 (1988), 487–519; 'Grasping the Nettle: The Slave Trade and the Early Zulu', in D. R. Edgecombe, J. P. C. Laband and P. S. Thompson, comps., *The Debate on Zulu Origins: A Selection of Papers on the Zulu Kingdom and Early Colonial Natal*, Pietermaritzburg, 1992.

trans-Vaal, it helps untangle multiple causes by pointing out potential relationships between changes within Sotho/Tswana settlements during the late eighteenth century and an expanding northern Cape frontier as well as other tensions.[3] By looking back further in time through the archaeological record at these changes, the explanatory focus for them can, in part, be more specifically located and moved away from the Natal area and the east coast. Secondly, whatever the causes, individual archaeological sites such as Lepalong provide the detail of African strategic responses to strife – responses which are locally evolved. Primary documents on the whole do not record the necessary detail and, consequently, archaeology provides an alternative source for constructing that uniqueness. This perspective may be lost by working through a predominantly white, written record. The archaeological record, by its very nature, focuses attention on the texture of the African experience of that period.

In the rest of this essay I discuss Iron Age data from both pre-written and written contexts that are relevant to a wider view of the period.[4] I follow a chronological progression starting in about AD 1650, then move to the eighteenth century and end by looking specifically at archaeological material in the written context of the nineteenth century. This temporal transect spans the methodological transition from 'prehistoric' archaeology – that period which, for most of the Transvaal region, can only be accessed through the study of material culture – through to historical archaeology, which seeks effectively to combine archaeological materials with written sources. Such an approach can be powerful because of its potential to command several domains of human behaviour.[5] Preserved behaviour (archaeological materials) can be combined with the written word, with the spoken word and

---

3. T.N. Huffman, 'Archaeological Evidence and Conventional Explanations of Southern Bantu Settlement Patterns', *Africa*, 56 (1986), 280–98.

4. The Iron Age is the term used by archaeologists to refer to the last 1 800 years of southern African history. Unlike the use of the term in the European context, it does not imply preceding Copper and Bronze Ages. The Iron Age in southern Africa marks the appearance of Bantu-speaking people possessing a village-based mixed farming economy in which domesticated sorghums and millets and cattle and sheep/goats provided the subsistence base. The period is subdivided into the Early Iron Age and the Late Iron Age, with the break coming at about AD 1200. The crop economy possessed by Iron Age people required summer rainfall conditions and consequently, Iron Age people did not choose to move beyond the summer rainfall boundary. Early Iron Age sites are found in relatively low-lying mixed bush and grass areas of present-day Botswana, the Transvaal, Natal and the Transkei. In the Late Iron Age the first settlement of the highveld took place. The advent of the Iron Age in southern Africa did not bring the Stone Age hunter-gatherer way of life to an end. Hunter-gatherers shared the landscape with Iron Age farmers in a complex series of interactions. See C. Campbell, 'Images of War: A Problem in San Rock Art Research', *World Archaeology*, 18 (1986), 255–68; S.L. Hall, 'Pastoral Adaptations and Forager Reactions in the Eastern Cape', *South African Archaeological Society, Goodwin Series*, 5 (1986), 42–9; A.D. Mazel, 'People Making History: The Last Ten Thousand Years of Hunter-gatherer Communities in the Thukela Basin', *Natal Museum Journal of Humanities*, 1 (1989), 1–168; and T.A. Dowson, 'Hunter-gatherers, Traders and Slaves: The 'Mfecane' Impact on Bushmen, their Ritual and Art' in this volume.

5. R. Schuyler, 'The Spoken Word, the Written Word, Observed Behaviour and Preserved Behaviour: The Contexts Available to the Archaeologist', *Conference on Historic Sites Archaeology Papers*, 10 (1977), 99–120; K. Deagan, 'Avenues of Inquiry in Historical Archaeology', *Advances in Archaeological Method and Theory*, 5 (1982), 151–77.

even with observed behaviour (ethnography). The simultaneous use of written documents and archaeological data allows direct correlation of specific event and context with archaeological pattern. In this regard, historical archaeology is not simply a 'handmaiden to history' but can play the role of critical foil and spoiler for the documents.

Settlement Change

The time depth provided for the Iron Age by the archaeological record in the western trans-Vaal indicates that strife and stress were not confined to the early nineteenth-century period known as the difaqane. A brief examination of some archaeological evidence for earlier Iron Age social and economic stress helps put in perspective the scale of Late Iron Age reaction in the late eighteenth and early nineteenth centuries. Three strategies are visible in the archaeological record. These are hilltop defensive settlement locations, the aggregation of communities into larger towns and the use of underground cavern systems such as Lepalong. The evidence indicates that while the first two strategies were used periodically throughout the Iron Age, the use of cavern systems for large-scale occupation is peculiar to the nineteenth century.

Hilltop Defensive Settlements

The identification of Sotho/Tswana Late Iron Age sites from about AD 1600 onwards is relatively easy. From this time the cattle byres, boundary walls and hut enclosures of settlements in what later became the Transvaal, Orange Free State and Botswana were built from stone and are easily located on aerial photographs.[6] It is from this period that examples of the settlement changes are taken.

In the Waterberg of the central-west trans-Vaal, Late Iron Age stone wall sites built by Sotho/Tswana speakers (radiocarbon dated to AD 1650) were placed in easily defended hilltop positions. Rooikrans is an excavated example of such a site (Map 9).[7] This defensive position can be linked to some form of regional stress through the analysis of the bone food waste from the site, which shows abnormally low frequencies of cattle.[8] Although speculative, the defensive settlement strategy at

6. S. L. Hall, 'Excavations at Rooikrans and Rhenosterkloof: Late Iron Age Sites in the Rooiberg Area of the Transvaal', *Annals of the Cape Provincial Museums*, 1 (1985), 131–210; J. H. N. Loubser, 'Ndebele Archaeology of the Pietersburg Area', M.A. dissertation, University of the Witwatersrand, Johannesburg, 1981; J. H. N. Loubser, 'Buffelshoek: An Ethnoarchaeological Consideration of a Late Iron Age Settlement in the Southern Transvaal', *South African Archaeological Bulletin*, 142 (1985), 81–7; T. M. O'C. Maggs, *Iron Age Communities of the Southern Highveld*, Pietermaritzburg, 1976; R. Mason, 'Transvaal and Natal Iron Age Settlements Revealed by Aerial Photography and Excavations', *African Studies*, 27 (1968), 167–80; R. Mason, *Origins of Black People of Johannesburg and the Southern Central Western Transvaal AD 350–1880*, Johannesburg, 1986; M. O. V. Taylor, 'Late Iron Age Settlements on the Northern Edge of the Vredefort Dome', M.A. dissertation, University of the Witwatersrand, Johannesburg, 1979.
7. Hall, 'Excavations at Rooikrans and Rhenosterkloof', 138.
8. I. Plug, 'The Faunal Remains from Rooikrans and Rhenosterkloof, Two Iron Age Sites from the Central Transvaal', Appendix 2 in S. L. Hall, 'Iron Age Sequence and Settlement in the Rooiberg, Thabazimbi Area', M.A. dissertation, University of the Witwatersrand, Johannesburg, 1981, 184–206.

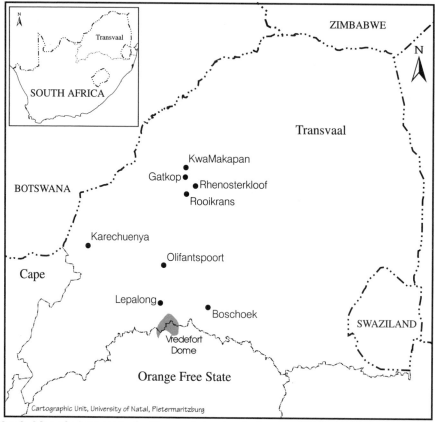

Map 9. Map of what became the Transvaal showing the location of sites mentioned in the text

this time may have been a response to increased raiding between communities in which cattle numbers among raided people declined. The stock enclosures at Rooikrans are small and suggest that they may have in fact only been used for sheep and goats. In contrast to Rooikrans, faunal remains from Rhenosterkloof (a valley floor Late Iron Age site) (Map 9) shows that the herding part of the economy was fully intact.

At the time of the Rooikrans excavation and interpretation, no explicit cause could be identified for the hilltop defensive settlements. However, more recent work in the Waterberg by J.A.N. Aukema provides a specific historical context for these defensive Sotho/Tswana settlement patterns.[9] Also about AD 1650, there was an inflow of new people into the Waterberg. This event can be recognised by the appearance of markedly different settlement layouts, house form and material

9. Reported in T.N. Huffman, 'The Waterberg Research of Jan Aukema', *South African Archaeological Bulletin*, 45 (1990), 117–19.

culture. These new migrants are identified as an early movement of Nguni-speaking 'Ndebele' who are not to be confused with the later nineteenth-century Ndebele of Mzilikazi. Independent genealogical extrapolation of the Langa Ndebele by A.O. Jackson gives a similar date to that established archaeologically.[10] Two examples of these Ndebele sites (Molore and Ndorobe within the Laphalala drainage) were built on top of extremely steep-sided hills, which must have been a defensive response to already established Sotho/Tswana Iron Age communities in the region, which, as noted above, reacted in the same way. This defensive posture against regional insecurity was strengthened by the aggregation of people into larger settlements enclosed by stone perimeter walls.

The combination of hilltop settlement with aggregation also occurred in the late nineteenth century. In the southern Waterberg, the 1870 to 1880 Sotho/Ndebele site of KwaMakapan is a good example (Map 9) while C. Van Waarden has recorded a similar late nineteenth-century site near the confluence of the Limpopo and Matloutse Rivers.[11] In these cases the settlements were located for defence against the colonial presence. With this background in place, we now turn specifically to the late eighteenth and early nineteenth centuries.

Aggregation of Communities

The Waterberg seventeenth-century aggregation response is of a much lower order in comparison to the 'anomalously large' populations observed in historic Sotho/Tswana towns.[12] The chronology of this Sotho/Tswana aggregation is critical in the context of the difaqane in the area. Prior to the eighteenth century, Sotho/Tswana sites in the Vredefort Dome region were single homestead units[13], and small relative to the historically well-known Tlhaping town of Dithakong and the Hurutshe capital of Karechuenya, visited by both W.J. Burchell and John Campbell.[14] Radiocarbon dates from a similar eighteenth-century 'megasite' at Olifantspoort, in the present-day Rustenburg area (Map 9), indicate that although the site was first occupied in the sixteenth century,[15] the large-scale increase in its size occurred in the eighteenth century, perhaps from AD 1750 onwards.[16]

The large size of Sotho/Tswana towns contrasts markedly with the dispersed homesteads of Nguni-speakers. Traditional explanations for this difference have emphasised environmental conditions and cultural preference. Environmental determinism can be discounted because arid areas such as present-day Botswana and

10. A.O. Jackson, ed., *The Ndebele of Langa*, Pretoria, 1983, 4.
11. C. van Waarden, 'Archaeological Investigation of Leeukop: A Functional Approach', *Botswana Notes and Records*, 12 (1980), 151–64.
12. Huffman, 'Archaeological Evidence', 289.
13. Huffman, 'Archaeological Evidence', 287; M.O.V. Taylor, 'Late Iron Age Settlements', 10–14.
14. W.J. Burchell, *Travels in the Interior of Southern Africa*, vol. 1, London, 1822; J. Campbell, *Travels in South Africa Undertaken at the Request of the London Missionary Society; Being the Narrative of a Second Journey in the Interior of that Country*, London, 1822.
15. Mason, *Origins of Black People*, 367–9.
16. Huffman, 'Archaeological Evidence', 291–2.

the western trans-Vaal contain the remains of dispersed homesteads dating throughout the Iron Age, whereas the large settlements are a recent phenomenon. Some of these dispersed sites were inhabited by Sotho/Tswana-speakers, and therefore cultural preference could also not have caused aggregation.[17] Similarly, social stratification can be discounted because prior to the growth of urban centres the general pattern of social stratification was the same among Nguni- and Sotho-speakers.

The combination of Sotho/Tswana aggregation from about AD 1750 and the association of these large settlements with hills suggests, as with the Waterberg example, that these changes are a result of specific historical events and are not ecologically determined or due to some general cultural preference. A range of alternatives can be isolated, some of which may be interlinked.

It is possible that this response was generated through increasing competition between Tswana chiefdoms for a slice of the growing European trade market.[18] Perhaps implicated in this would have been an increasing threat from the northern Cape in the form of armed and mounted Griqua and Kora raiders. As Andrew Manson also points out, it is not improbable that the European market may have simply temporarily exacerbated well-entrenched smaller scale competition between Tswana traders. Consequently, the eighteenth-century trend towards aggregation may have its roots well outside direct European intervention. One archaeological test for these propositions would be to examine the amount of reciprocal European trade goods, such as glass beads, which would have accrued from this trade. Excavations in the late eighteenth-century deposits at Olifantspoort yielded 'a mere 11 glass beads' and no other trade goods from 83 huts and 15 ash middens.[19] By archaeological standards, this excavation marks a relatively complete sampling of the settlement. Further excavations by Revil Mason at the eighteenth-century site of Platberg further to the south produced no beads at all.

Another factor which may have had the potential to exacerbate further the growing tension of the late eighteenth century is the introduction of maize. Tim Maggs has dated the presence of maize at Mgonduyanuka, a Late Iron Age site in the interior grasslands of Natal, to AD 1770, with the possibility that it could have been introduced even earlier in the seventeenth century.[20] There is no reason why the greater yields afforded by this crop did not increase population levels. Serious demographic stress may have resulted, however, from the interplay between a growing dependency upon the new crop and fluctuations in rainfall levels at the end

---

17. J. Denbow, 'Iron Age Economics: Herding, Wealth and Politics along the Fringes of the Kalahari Desert during the Early Iron Age', Ph.D. thesis, Indiana University, Bloomington, 1983; Huffman, 'Archaeological Evidence', 284.

18. A. Manson, 'Conflict in the Western Highveld/Southern Kalahari c. 1750–1820', in this volume.

19. Mason, *Origins of Black People*, 438.

20. T.M.O'C. Maggs, 'Mgoduyanuka: Terminal Iron Age Settlement in the Natal Grasslands', *Annals of the Natal Museum*, 25 (1982), 87.

of the eighteenth and beginning of the nineteenth centuries.[21] As potential complicating factors in the dynamics of the period, they should not be ruled out.

The archaeological record demonstrates that the combination of aggregation and hilltop sites has been a regular response in the Iron Age of the Transvaal region to extreme social tension. It has been suggested that Sotho/Tswana aggregation during the eighteenth century could have resulted from a number of different causes. More archaeological work is required, particularly in refining the chronology of the aggregation response but initial assessments suggest that causality cannot be linked directly to events in the Natal area.

Lepalong

There are a limited number of cavern systems in the trans-Vaal and elsewhere which preserve evidence of Iron Age occupation. Cavern occupation indicates that the 'choice' to use them was made under extreme duress because this option is completely atypical of normal Iron Age settlement preferences. The Boer siege in 1854 of an Ndebele/Sotho group in the Makapansgat Valley is the best-known example.[22] Other less well-documented occupations exist in the Dwarsberge and at Gatkop in the southern Waterberg.[23]

The chronology of the Lepalong occupation is established from oral histories collected by Breutz who indicates an 1820s and 1830s date.[24] Although no excavations have been undertaken at Lepalong (Map 9), there is nothing in the remains which suggests any occupation before this time. Not only do the dates mentioned in the oral records provide a general contextual backdrop against which the archaeology can be interpreted, but they also identify the occupants and their place of origin.

These records refer to the Kwena ba Modimosana ba Mmatau under Maselwane who moved to the cavern system in 1827 from the Rustenburg area seeking refuge from Mzilikazi, who had moved into the western trans-Vaal in the late 1820s. Maselwane's relationship with the Ndebele seems to have been equivocal. According to the records, he returned northwards for an undisclosed reason, but again moved back to Gatsrand (Lepalong) after narrowly avoiding a trap laid by Mzilikazi. On his way south, Maselwane raided some Ndebele cattle and, pursued by Mzilikazi, he had to move further to the south into the present-day Free State. Here he met Boer trekkers under the leadership of Andries Potgieter and became known to them as Selon. He joined Potgieter and guided him to Mzilikazi, who was defeated at Vegkop in 1836.

Maselwane's occupation of Lepalong is more explicitly mentioned in the oral records of another Kwena group, the Phiring, who under Mabalane left the

21. M. Hall, 'Dendroclimatology, Rainfall and Human Adaptation in the Later Iron Age of Natal and Zululand', *Annals of the Natal Museum*, 22 (1976), 693–703.
22. I. Hofmeyr, 'No Chief, No Exchange, No Story', *African Studies*, 48, 2 (1989), 131–55.
23. G.H.J. Teichler, 'Some Historical Notes on Derdepoort/Sikwane', *Botswana Notes and Records*, 5 (1973), 125–30; Hall, 'Excavations at Rooikrans', 133–5.
24. Breutz, *The Tribes of Rustenburg*, 108.

Zwartruggens area, again because of harassment by Mzilikazi. As with Maselwane, the Phiring appear to have had an erratic relationship with Mzilikazi. Before 1836 Mabalane and his followers returned to the Marico district, where they became subjects of Mzilikazi and were entrusted with some of his cattle and sheep herds. When Mzilikazi was under threat from both Boer trekkers and Dingane, the Phiring again left and moved south to Lepalong. Here they found the cavern already occupied by Maselwane's people who nevertheless also allowed them to use the cavern. The Phiring records give the only detail concerning the actual caverns. The informants told Breutz that the only way to gain access to the cavern system was with ladders, which were removed if the 'enemy appeared'.[25]

These records depict Mzilikazi as the specific agent responsible for the Kwena occupation of Lepalong. One can detect, though, an ambiguous tone in the records – that of 'formidable local raiders . . .' and 'a haven for refugees'.[26] The reference to the occupation of the Lepalong cavern, however, provides a specific agency; it is against this background that the archaeology must be compared.

Lepalong is made up of two physically separate parts, one above ground and the other in the cavern system. The relationship between the two is discussed at the end of this section. As already mentioned, no excavation has yet been undertaken at either component and therefore statements are at best tentative and preliminary. Complete mapping of the above-ground site has been completed and mapping of the below-ground component is under way. Parts of the underground site are extremely well preserved, and a major concern is to make a record of the site before further deterioration takes place. A descriptive report on the site has been published,[27] and the site was declared a National Monument in 1964.

The above-ground site runs for about 200 metres in a north/south direction and is 150 metres across at its widest point (Figure 1). The site is composed of 47 hut floors, some of which are loosely associated with a few small stock byres. The two larger stone wall byres at Lepalong are probably not associated with the rest of the site. These are connected to some square walls and appear to be associated with a 1930s settlement to the north-west.

The positions of the hut floors can be identified because of upright slate foundation stones arranged in circles of no more than 3 metres in diameter. The entrances and hence orientations of the huts are marked by a break in the foundation stones as well as larger upright monoliths on either side of the door. In some cases there are smoothed slabs at the foot of the doorway, evidence for a sliding door arrangement similar to those of Late Iron Age in the Magaliesberg.[28]

A point made earlier was that the archaeology has the potential to examine the details of African response to social turmoil. Written documents and oral testimony

25. Breutz, *The Tribes of Rustenburg*, 219.
26. Cobbing, 'Grasping the Nettle', 7.
27. E.J. Haughton and L.H. Wells, 'Underground Structures in Caves of the Southern Transvaal', *South African Journal of Science*, 38 (1942), 319–33.
28. Mason, *Origins of Black People*, 383–97.

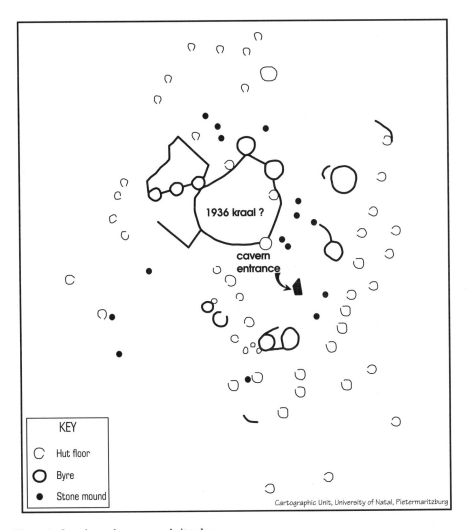

Figure 1. Lepalong above-ground site plan

do not generally refer to these day-to-day patterns. One way of investigating these is through a spatial analysis of settlements. Spatial organisation among Bantu speakers in southern Africa is a physical metaphor for economic, political and religious relationships as well as expressing values concerning status. Spatial organisation therefore reflects a world view, and there is nothing random or haphazard about how a settlement is planned. The link between this world view and its spatial expression is derived from the ethnography of Nguni- and Sotho/Tswana-speakers and is referred to as the Central Cattle Pattern. This ethnographically derived model is used as a baseline and analogue for the interpretation of settlement plans in the Iron Age past. I

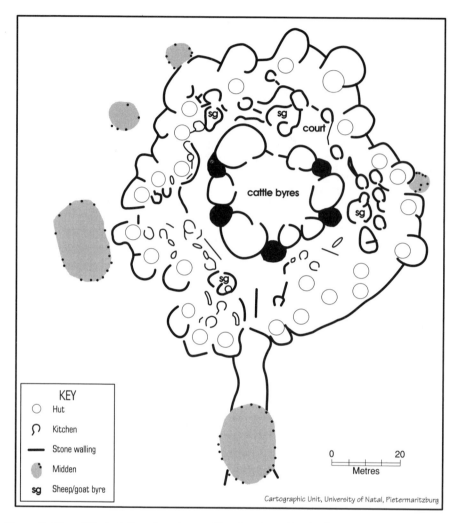

Figure 2. Plan of the Late Iron Age stone wall settlement at Boschoek

illustrate some of the main features of the Central Cattle Pattern using the ground plan of Boschoek, a late eighteenth-century Iron Age site at Suikerbosrand south of Johannesburg (Figure 2).[29]

29. T. M. Evers, 'Sotho–Tswana and Moloko Settlement Patterns and the Bantu Cattle Pattern', in M. Hall *et al.*, eds, *Frontiers: Southern African Archaeology Today*, Oxford, 1984, 236–47; T. N. Huffman, 'Archaeology and Ethnohistory of the African Iron Age', *Annual Review of Anthropology*, 11 (1982), 133–50; A. Kuper, *Wives for Cattle: Bridewealth and Marriage in Southern Africa*, London, 1982.

At the centre of the Boschoek hamlet is a series of cattle byres which are surrounded by a roughly circular arrangement of huts. Both the byres and the scalloped perimeter wall are built of stone, and consequently boundaries and edges between areas within the site and between the inside and outside of the site are clearly expressed. The centrality of the cattle byres reflects the importance of cattle as the major source of wealth and power and the medium through which a man accumulates wives and children. It is also by means of the slaughter of cattle that a man can invoke his ancestors. The central byre is a male area reserved for economic, ritual and political activity. Senior men are often buried in the byre or under the byre walls.[30] The byres may also serve as the *kgotla* (court), where men meet to settle disputes and judge cases. Alternatively, the *kgotla* may be outside the byre but still directly linked to it, and if the ground upon which the settlement is built is sloping, the *kgotla* will be above the byre.

Height is an expression of rank, and the senior man's hut will be positioned close to the *kgotla* but again further upslope, usually at the highest point in the settlement. People of lower rank would be placed lower down in the hut arc. At Boschoek the senior man's hut would have been directly up from the *kgotla* (Figure 2). The position of the senior man's hut also marks the back of the settlement, while the lowest part of the settlement would have been the front; this would often be the point at which cattle were herded in and out. Front and back also express secular and sacred areas. It is at the back of the settlement, usually the courtyard behind the senior man's hut, that rainmaking rituals would be performed. The scalloped back courtyards behind all the other huts would also have been sacred and private areas for the people occupying those huts.

A comparison between the normal and coherent Central Cattle Pattern described at the late eighteenth-century site of Boschoek (Figure 2) and the early nineteenth-century site of Lepalong (Figure 1) shows a number of significant differences. There is no central cattle byre at Lepalong and therefore, no symbolic focus around which the rest of the site is organised. The small enclosures are of a size used to keep sheep and goats. The absence of any cattle byres obviously suggests that this important part of the economy had been seriously undermined by the turmoil of the period. This is not surprising, and is also backed up by the oral records cited above. It should not be ruled out, however, that cattle herds were intact but were not kept at the site. A better defensive strategy may have been to corral them at stock posts on the Gatsrand hills to the south and to keep moving the cattle regularly between them.

Another distinctive feature at Lepalong is the absence of a surrounding perimeter wall or any walls which define the back and front courtyards of individual huts. As a result, any distinction between the front and the back of the settlement, if in fact it existed, cannot be readily made. The highest point in the settlement is to the north, but there is nothing in that area which demonstrates a senior status. It is also not possible to distinguish a *kgotla*; again this may not have been formally defined.

30. Mason, *Origins of Black People*, 427, 429.

Figure 3. Huts in the Lepalong cavern system. Note the raised platform in front. The upright sticks mark post-holes and the previous position of a wood and thatch fence.

Furthermore, the distribution of huts at Lepalong is loose and scattered with a linear straggle of huts in the east as well as several extremely disconnected outlying huts to the south and north. The only discernible pattern is several distinct hut clusters associated with small sheep/goat enclosures (Figure 1). These clusters are defined by the shared direction of the hut entrances, which are orientated towards the byres.

When compared to the spatial organisation at Boschoek, there are no clear patterns at Lepalong. The overall impression is one of a loose, fragmented community. This is not to say that the world view was not intact, but that its spatial expression had been expediently pruned to a minimum. While it is not particularly informative to correlate this with the general turmoil of the period, future work with the ethnography, written records and oral testimony may provide more specific ways of interpreting difaqane sites and for 'seeing' structure which is not readily apparent using the normal Central Cattle Pattern model. It may be, for example, that spatial structure is fragmented and not particularly well developed because the 'community' was made up of many unrelated and geographically disparate people. In this regard, the oral records cited above may be misleading in their emphasis upon specific Kwena groups.

The above-ground site clusters directly around the cavern entrance and indicates that it was built to provide immediate and direct access to the cavern system below (Figure 1). The two components are therefore chronologically contemporary. The cavern entrance is a fissure in the ground, 5 metres by 2 metres, and provides the only access to the underground site. As the oral records indicate, ladders are needed to enter the cavern. The main part of the cavern is a long solution cavity with smaller chambers leading off it.

Over 70 stone and daub huts are preserved, and very little of the cavern floor has not been built upon. The back of the huts often incorporated the sides of the cavern. The hut walls were built to a maximum height of about 1,5 metres and were not roofed (Figure 3). Construction in the cavern also includes features such as internal and external benches, platforms and steps as well as low walls which may have functioned as dykes for water control. Wood and thatch fences are indicated by post holes and in some of the deeper sub-chambers sheep and goat byres were built. A sump at the end of the main chamber retains a continuous pool of water.

Clearly, the restraint on space makes the search for macro-settlement organisation in terms of the centre/surround of the Central Cattle Pattern a meaningless exercise. Considerable structure is evident, however, at smaller spatial scales, particularly at the level of linked hut clusters and low walls which define these. Edges and boundaries which define what may be extended family units are more apparent than in the above-ground site. These features separate private space from well-defined public walkways that provide access through the clusters to the deeper chambers. A well-preserved hut cluster in one of the highest, and consequently, driest areas in the cavern system may have been for a senior man. Access to the byre chambers is through this area, and it also preserves the best evidence for granaries. In contrast to the above-ground component, upper and lower grindstones, as well as pottery, are relatively common in the cavern.

Unfortunately, early visitors to the site removed considerable amounts of metal work. There is a report that two wooden tinder boxes were also taken from the cavern site. Tinder boxes, along with beads, were traded and used as gifts by the Revd T. L. Hodgson among the Seleka Rolong in 1823,[31] so their presence at the site is not unexpected. A hand-stitched leather shoe and belt were found in the course of a recent photographic survey in the cavern. Their preservation over a 160-year period is also not unusual.

The labour invested in the cavern village shows that occupation was not ephemeral. This is in keeping with Maselwane's and, later, Mabalane's occupation of Lepalong, a period of considerable and sustained social and economic stress which, on present evidence, is directly linked to Mzilikazi and the less benevolent side of his presence in the region.

As mentioned, the close proximity between the above-ground site, the cavern entrance and the below-ground village suggest that both components are directly linked and, consequently, chronologically contemporary. One can only speculate upon the exact relationship between the components. The oral records tell us that when Mabalane moved to Lepalong, Maselwane was already there but was allowed to stay.[32] The above-ground site may have been used by one group, who were then allowed below if this was required. Alternatively, the two sites may have been used by a single community as local conditions required. If this was the case, then the disparity between the hut numbers (47 above to 70 below) could indicate that other people in the region may also have been allowed into the cavern during periods of direct threat.

Whatever the case, the above-ground village would have been highly visible. This emphasises the prime role of the cavern as a defensive refuge position and not specifically as a hideaway. There is no evidence, however, that the site was ever seriously threatened. Burnt villages are archaeologically recognisable, and there is nothing to show that the above-ground site was ever fired. A further consideration is the defence of sorghum, millet and maize granaries below gound as well as any domestic stock the community still owned. Another cavern system at Lindeques-drift, some 47 kilometres to the south-east of Lepalong, preserves the remains of baskets and maize.[33] Complete pots in the Dwarsberge caverns may also have been for cereal storage,[34] and the cavern at Gatkop in the southern Waterberg preserves wooden pole stock byres.[35] More specific economic information and interpretation will only be forthcoming once both components at Lepalong have been excavated.

31. T. L. Hodgson, *The Journals of the Reverend T. L. Hodgson, Missionary to the Seleka–Rolong and the Griquas 1821–1831*, ed. R.L. Cope, Johannesburg, 1977, 153.
32. Breutz, *The Tribes of Rustenburg*, 219.
33. Haughton and Wells, 'Underground Structures', 327.
34. Teichler, 'Some Historical Notes', 125, 128.
35. Hall, 'Excavations at Rooikrans', 133, 134.

Conclusion

The time depth of the archaeological record gives perspective to the scale of response in the later eighteenth and nineteenth centuries in the western and south-western trans-Vaal. The level of Sotho/Tswana aggregation is unprecedented in the archaeological record of the region and strongly underlines that a range of additional causes are sought. The increasing impact towards the end of the eighteenth century of the northern Cape frontier provides one possibility. The archaeological record, however, retains an independence and potential to highlight the plausibility of one, several, or none, of the causal agents currently proposed in the literature.

The second aspect of this essay has been a preliminary look at the archaeology of the extreme defensive cavern site of Lepalong and the oral evidence relating to it. No hard and fast conclusions have been drawn which directly feed the difaqane debate because the orientation at this archaeological scale is more towards a social history rather than a history of specific events, an aspect which is overlooked in most work on the difaqane.

Lastly, I have an uneasiness that no matter what history in terms of cause is constructed for the difaqane, the dominant image of African response will remain one of passive resignation to an all-embracing chaos. It cannot be denied that extreme strategies were adopted in order to cope with the stress of the period, and the case of Lepalong is a stark reminder of this, but this response nevertheless was still actively structured in relation to prevailing circumstances. This preliminary examination of the archaeology of the period makes a start towards investigating that structure which by the very nature of the data focuses specifically on the African experience of that period.

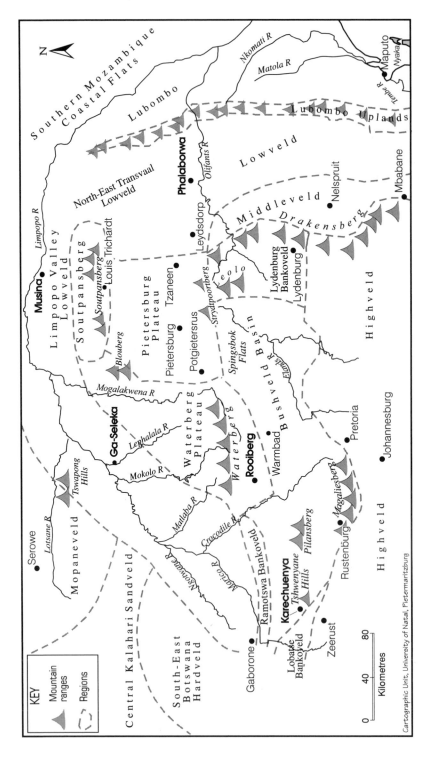

Map 10.   Main geographical regions of the trans-Vaal interior.
Note The tsetse fly belt covered most of the Lowveld and Coastal Flats in the eighteenth and nineteenth centuries.

Cartographic Unit, University of Natal, Pietermaritzburg

12

Prelude to Difaqane
in the Interior of Southern Africa
c.1600–c.1822

NEIL PARSONS

> . . . the eighteenth century in South Africa appears to have been a period of general restlessness and instability – of fissions, splinterings and hivings off. It seems to have been the beginning of the *volkerwanderung* that reached its crescendo with the more dramatic encounters and upheavals of the *Difaqane* during the first half of the next century. In such an environment of restlessness and uncertainty, it was the soldier kings or rulers that tended to succeed.
>
> LEONARD DINISO NGCONGCO
> 'Aspects of the History of Bangwaketse to 1910'

The *difaqane* wars around the area of the later Transvaal/Orange Free State are usually assumed to have begun in about 1822, after invasions from the east across the Drakensberg. But general restlessness and instability began much earlier – as Ngcongco indicates above – with a rising tide of violence from the later eighteenth century that cannot be clearly distinguished from the beginnings of the so-called *difaqane* in about 1822.

This essay looks at ways in which historians can use the findings of oral traditions and archaeology to reconstruct 'pre-*difaqane*' and 'proto-*difaqane*' periods of increasingly general crisis from the seventeenth up to the early nineteenth century. Understanding of these 'pre-' and 'proto-' periods should not only increase our understanding of the so-called *difaqane/mfecane*, but should also help to push back the frontiers of history – the continuous story of identifiable people – into the misty realms of prehistory.

Available oral traditions of the seventeenth and eighteenth centuries were mostly collected from Sotho/Tswana/Pedi-speaking elders, by European missionaries or officials and African intellectuals, before 1940. They tell of the growth of royal lineages, the spread of small states and small migrations of people. Mid-twentieth-century historians, drawing on the perspectives of anthropology and nuclear physics, saw these traditions as evidence of structural processes of 'fission' and 'fusion' at work in precolonial societies. Later twentieth-century historians, drawing on the perspectives of archaeologists and environmentalists, have emphasised the importance of climatic changes in determining political-economic developments. 'Droughts were the major cause of fission,' argue Thomas Tlou and Alec Campbell,

'Groups split up to find water or pasture.' Ngcongco has even correlated three major sets of Sotho/Tswana fission with droughts reported for Zimbabwe in 1450–80, 1561–63 and 1625–60.[1]

Following previous advances in Zambia and Zimbabwe, the Iron Age archaeology of what became the Transvaal/Orange Free State and Botswana has become much better understood in the past twenty years. Study of the distribution and dating of Iron Age pottery has been refined by research on Iron Age ecology and patterns of human settlement.

Archaeologists have adopted the concept of a 'Central Cattle Pattern' to explain the 'structural relationship' between settlement patterns and culture of Iron Age societies in the interior of South Africa. This pattern is evident in the ground plan of villages built around cattle byres, and in patterns of patriarchal male dominance based on wealth in cattle – marriage and inheritance through *lobolo/bogadi* (i.e.wives-for-cattle), systems of allegiance based on *mafisa* cattle (i.e. 'cattle-feudalism'), and even patterns of burial (male elders in the cattle byre, etc.).

The 'Central Cattle Pattern' is evident in Iron Age societies of the western/central trans-Vaal area as early as the fourth century, spreading south-east over the Drakensberg – with the superimposition of a royal pattern of 'divine kingship', derived from Zimbabwe, evident in the northern trans-Vaal region from the fifteenth and sixteenth centuries.[2]

The archaeologist Thomas Huffman has pointed out that societies based on the 'Central Cattle Pattern' developed in scale with new levels of political authority. Patriarchal family heads were grouped and subordinated to a second level of ward head; ward heads were under a third level of petty chief; petty chiefs sometimes under a fourth level of senior chief; and senior chiefs much more rarely under a fifth level of paramount ruler. Each level of political authority had its own court and cattle byre, and a defined settlement unit – such as the homesteads, wards and sections of a Tswana town.

South-eastern Bantu languages recognise three levels of political authority from family head through headman to chief, with the fourth level as 'great chief' – 'chief' being *ishe* (Shona), *hozi* (Tsonga), *kgosi* (Tswana) or *nkosi* (Zulu). Scholars have also demonstrated the incorporative or federative nature of political development by reference to four different levels. Homesteads combined into wards, wards into chiefdoms, and chiefdoms into states – though the latter were rare before 1800. Huffman's main insight therefore has been to spot a fifth level – the early empires of

1. M. Legassick, 'The Sotho–Tswana Peoples before 1800', in L. M. Thompson, ed., *African Societies in Southern Africa: Historical Studies*, London, 1969, 86–125; T. Tlou and A. Campbell, *History of Botswana*, Gaborone, 1984, 62; L. D. Ngcongco, 'Aspects of the History of Bangwaketse to 1910', Ph.D. thesis, University of Dalhousie, Halifax, 1977, 41, 47–9, 63.
2. The term 'Central Cattle Pattern' (abbreviated to CCP) dates from Thomas Huffman's works of 1987–88, originating as (Southern) 'Bantu Cattle Pattern' in his 1982 response (see 'Archaeology and Ethnohistory of the African Iron Age', *Annual Review of Anthropology*, 11 (1982) 133–50) to Adam Kuper, *Wives for Cattle: Bridewealth and Marriage in Southern Africa*, London, 1982, 140–56.

Mapungubwe and Great Zimbabwe and, later, the handful of nineteenth-century super-states led by Shaka, Mzilikazi, Mswati, Khama, and Moshoeshoe.

Archaeological data show that second-level polities rarely exceeded a hundred people, and third-level polities a thousand people. These were critical population numbers around which Iron Age polities seem to have had the options of fusion into a greater polity, or fission into smaller units. Why such population figures were critical remains to be elucidated.[3]

Such a hierarchy of political growth fits neatly – almost too neatly – with ideas about modes of production developed among historians in the 1970s and 1980s. The ownership of wealth and mode of production in homesteads (level one) is often referred to as 'primitive communist' (i.e. simple communal), alternatively 'patriarchal'. The economy of wards and lesser chiefdoms (levels two and three) corresponds with the 'lineage mode of production', which the archaeologist Martin Hall sees emerging in farming and, possibly, in herding societies by about AD 900. The economy of greater chiefdoms, states and super-states (levels three to five) corresponds with the 'tributary mode of production', which the economic historian Edward Alpers sees emerging in southern Africa under the impact of world mercantile penetration from around 1500.[4]

Distinguishing such modes of production helps to elucidate the 'relations of exploitation' at the heart of state growth. For example, Jeff Guy has argued that the fundamental cleavage in precolonial societies was between seniors (married men) and juniors (women and youths), rather than between classes of rich and poor.[5] This was arguably so with the small second- and third-level polities in the Natal and Lesotho areas before 1800. But it is more difficult to argue this for fourth- and fifth-level polities north of the Vaal, which included a significant subordinate class or classes.

The contrast between gender and class in south and north explains the commentary on the role of women in pre-1800 Lesotho society made by the early historian Joseph Orpen: 'there being no balalas (enslaved tribes), as among the northern tribes, wives supplied the place of household servants'. Among the Kwena north of the Vaal, indeed, aristocratic women were so divided from others of their

---

3. See T.N. Huffman, 'Archaeological Evidence and Conventional Explanations of Southern Bantu Settlement Patterns', *Africa*, 56, 3 (1986), 280–98. Cf. M. Fortes and E.E. Evans-Pritchard, eds, *African Political Systems*, London, 1940; T.O. Ranger, ed., *Aspects of Central African History*, London, 1968. On critical population density theory see Huffman, 'Archaeological Evidence', 283; W. Allan, *The African Husbandman*, Edinburgh, 1967, ch.7; M. Gluckman, 'The Rise of a Zulu Empire', *Scientific American*, 202, 4 (1963), 159–69.

4. M. Hall, 'Archaeology and Modes of Production in Pre-colonial Southern Africa', *Journal of Southern African Studies*, 14, 1 (1987), 1–17; E.A. Alpers, 'State, Merchant Capital and General Relations in Southern Mozambique to the End of the Nineteenth Century: Some Tentative Hypotheses', *African Economic History*, 13 (1984), 22–55.

5. J.J. Guy, 'Analysing Pre-capitalist Societies in Southern Africa', *Journal of Southern African Studies*, 14, 1, (1987), 18–37.

gender by class that they 'knew little about agriculture because most of the actual labour was done by their servants'.[6]

Historians working on southern Mozambique and Swaziland have suggested how trade with the east coast promoted general transition from a dominant lineage mode of production to a dominant tributary mode of production from about the seventeenth century. When chiefs began to act as entrepreneurs, they supplied products for export by exploiting and extending their tributary rights over labour and commodities.

Such 'expansion of luxury commodity production', in the forms of communal hunting and mining and agriculture, under the control of seniors headed by a chief, intensified the exploitation of the labour of juniors. The need for female and/or servant labour in communal agriculture was increased by the wants of, and by the withdrawal of, male labour. The labour of young males and servants was regimented into hunting and herding, and – together with young women – into mining, while craftwork was dominated – though not exclusively – by senior males.

Chiefs also exploited their ritual status as 'little gods' representing the senior lineage ancestors of the state, and thus embodying the nation and its territory. Alpers quotes the French anthropologist Maurice Godelier's observation on emergent dominant classes using prior control of the 'invisible forces of production' to take control of the material means of production. Thus privileged intercession by the chief with his royal national ancestors over rainfall might be used to take control of harvests. Mystical identification with the soil in which his ancestors lay also justified the tribute to the chief of the 'ground tusk' – the first tusk of a dying elephant to hit the ground.[7]

Perhaps most important of all 'invisible forces' was the mystique given to chiefly families in control of adolescent initiation into adulthood, and of the resulting male and female age-sets. Age-sets, ritually led by members of the royal lineage, were the structural cement which bound together – in common loyalty to one state – people

---

6. J. M. Orpen, *History of the Basutos of South Africa*, Mazenod, 1979 (reprint of 1857 edition), 21; G. Y. Okihiro, 'Hunters, Herders, Cultivators and Traders: Interaction and Change in the Kgalagadi, Nineteenth Century', Ph.D. thesis, University of California, Los Angeles, 1976, ch. 3 as quoted by Alpers, 'State, Merchant Capital', 45. Evidence of tributary and probably servile hunters within a state dates back at least to the *c.* 11th–12th century Mapungubwe culture site of Bosutswe – Edwin Wilmsen, personal communication.

7. M. Godelier, 'Infrastructures, Sociétés, Histoire', *Dialectiques*, 1 (1977), 50–3, quoted in Alpers, 'State, Merchant Capital', 28–9. The tributary custom of the 'ground tusk' has ancient but unstudied roots in the lower Zambezi and on the north-eastern Zimbabwe plateau – cf. D. N. Beach, 'The Shona Economy: Branches of Production' in R. Palmer and N. Parsons, *Roots of Rural Poverty in Central and Southern Africa*, 1977, 52; A. E. Alpers, *Ivory and Slaves in East Central Africa*, London, 1975, 18. I recall references in contemporary documents to the 'ground tusk' being taken as tribute in trade with the Portuguese on the north bank of the Zambezi in the 16th–17th centuries, but have not been able to locate my original source. For the 'ground tusk' in nineteenth-century southern Africa see E. C. Tabler, *The Far Interior*, Cape Town, 1955.

of the same age and gender otherwise divided by divergent class and ethnic identities. Age-sets were the instruments of communal tributary service in agriculture, hunting and other labour projects, and provided regiments for fighting.[8]

The Pre-*difaqane* Period *c.*1600–*c.*1750

The idea of a 'general crisis' developing from about the turn of the seventeenth century onwards is supported by an outline of major events in and around the interior of southern Africa up to the mid-eighteenth century.

Outline of Major Events

ZIMBABWE REGION

(a) The Rozvi army conquered 'Butwa', i.e. the south-western Zimbabwe plateau, in the 1680s. By the eighteenth century the Singo, who were possibly related to the Rozvi, had migrated from the eastern plateau southwards across the Limpopo to the Venda and Pedi on the Soutpansberg and Pietersburg plateaux.

(b) In the eighteenth century there were numerous small migrations of Karanga people from the eastern Zimbabwe plateau southwards.

(c) Pedi/Venda groups, such as the Nswazwi, migrated from the northern trans-Vaal region through the north-east of modern Botswana to become tributaries of the Rozvi in 'Butwa'.

(d) Gold exports were declining, and ivory exports rising – mainly through the Portuguese at Inhambane on the Indian Ocean.[9]

SOUTHERN MOZAMBIQUE REGION

(a) In the seventeenth century the warlike Thembe kingdom arose and dominated the other southern Tsonga (Ronga) chiefdoms around Delagoa Bay; and some Nguni chiefdoms to the south.

(b) Tsonga waged wars with the Pedi inland and expanded northwards towards Inhambane.

(c) Ivory and slave exports from Inhambane reached a peak in 1762, with the Portuguese treating Delagoa Bay merely as a feeder to Inhambane.

(d) The Dutch trading station at Delagoa Bay (1721–9) established the Bay's trading importance for ships of other European nations.[10]

8. Alpers, 'State, Merchant Capital', 41. For adolescent initiation and state growth see T.M. Evers and W.D. Hammond-Tooke, 'The Emergence of South African Chiefdoms: An Archaeological Perspective', *African Studies*, 45 (1986), 37–41. Fifth to seventh-century Lydenburg culture pottery heads may have represented ancestors of the royal lineage in initiation dances – cf. M. Wilson, 'The Sotho, Venda, and Tsonga', in M. Wilson and L.M. Thompson, eds, *The Oxford History of South Africa*, vol. 1: *South Africa to 1870*, Oxford, 1969–1971, 161 on masked initiation dances.

9. See D.N.Beach, *The Shona and Zimbabwe 900–1850: An Outline of Shona History*, Gweru, 1980; D.N. Beach, *Zimbabwe Before 1900*, Gweru, 1984; D.N. Beach, 'The Zimbabwe Plateau and its Peoples', in D. Birmingham and P.M. Martin, eds, *History of Central Africa*, vol. 1, London, 1983, 245–77; S.I.G. Mudenge, *A Political History of Munhumutapa, c.1400–1902*, Harare, 1988; W.G.L. Randles, *The Empire of Monomotapa*, Gweru, 1979. See also note 11 below.

10. A.K.Smith, 'The Peoples of Southern Mozambique: An Historical Survey', *Journal of African History*, 14, 4 (1983), 568–80; A.K. Smith, 'Delagoa Bay and the Trade of South-east Africa', in R. Gray and D. Birmingham, eds, *Pre-Colonial African Trade: Essays on Trade in Central and Eastern Africa Before 1900*, London, 1970, 265–89; A.K. Smith, 'The Trade of Delagoa Bay as a Factor in Nguni Politics, 1750–1835', in Thompson, *African Societies*, 171–90; Alpers, 'State, Merchant Capital'. See also D.W. Hedges, 'Trade and Politics in Southern Mozambique and Zimbabwe in the Eighteenth and Early Nineteenth Centuries', Ph.D. thesis, University of London, 1978.

(a) Singo rulers from north of the Limpopo dominated the Venda in the new Dzata kingdom by 1730.
(b) Pedi/Venda migrations occurred eastwards towards Inhambane and north-westwards across the Limpopo Valley through the Tswapong hills into Rozvi country.
(c) Ndebele from the trans-Vaal region dispersed and settled on the Waterberg plateau from the south-east; and crossed the Limpopo to the Tswapong hills of east-central modern Botswana.
(d) Some Hurutshe migrated from the central/western trans-Vaal region to dominate Gananwa north of the Waterberg plateau; and some Kgatla moved in to dominate the Pedi of the Lydenburg plateau.[11]

CENTRAL/WESTERN TRANSVAAL AND EASTERN BOTSWANA REGIONS

(a) Ndebele of the trans-Vaal region migrated north-westwards from their heartland east of Tshwane (Pretoria).
(b) Following the Hurutshe civil war *c.*1600, Kwena and Kgatla chiefdoms from the Tswana heartland in the western trans-Vaal region scattered in all directions:
     (i) east: some Kgatla went to the Lydenburg plateau (as above);
     (ii) south: Kgatla (Tlokwa) and Kwena migrated across from the upper Vaal, and Rolong settled across the middle Vaal;
     (iii) west: some Kwena moved as far as the south-east of modern Botswana to live among Rolong-dominated Khalagari groups;
     (iv) north: some Hurutshe migrated to Gananwa (see above); other Hurutshe (Khurutshe) moved to the Shoshong hills in the east-central region of modern Botswana.[12]

11. For 'Venda' history see N.M.N. Ralushai and J.R. Gray, 'Ruins and Traditions of the Ngona and Mbedzi Among the Venda of the Northern Transvaal', *Rhodesian History*, 8 (1977), 1–11; T.N. Huffman and E.O.M. Hanisch, 'Settlement Hierarchies in the Northern Transvaal: Zimbabwe Ruins and Venda History', *African Studies*, 46, 1 (1987), 79–116; T.M. O'C. Maggs and G. Whitelaw, 'A Review of Recent Archaeological Research on Food-Producing Communities in Southern Africa', *Journal of African History*, 32, 1 (1991), 23, citing J.H.N. Loubser, 'Archaeological Contributions to Venda Ethnohistory', Ph.D thesis, University of the Witwatersrand, Johannesburg, 1988. For 'Northern Sotho' history see: D. Hunt, 'An Account of the Bapedi' *Bantu Studies*, 5 (1931), 287–9; J.D. Krige, 'Traditional Origins and Tribal Relationships of the Sotho of the Northern Transvaal', *Bantu Studies*, 11 (1937), 321–56; N.J. van Warmelo, *Die Tlokwa en Birwa van Noord Transvaal*, Pretoria, 1953; Wilson 'The Sotho, Venda and Tsonga', 163–4; Q.N. Parsons, 'On the Origins of the BamaNgwato', *Botswana Notes and Records*, 5 (1973), 82–103; Smith, 'The Peoples of Southern Mozambique'. See also note 29, below.
12. For central/western Tswana see note 1 above, especially references in Legassick, 'The Sotho–Tswana Peoples', to works by Isaac Schapera, Paul-Lambert Breutz, etc.; R. Mason, *Origins of Black People of Johannesburg and the Southern Central Western Transvaal AD 350–1880*, Johannesburg, 1986; R. Mason, *Origins of the African People of the Johannesburg Area*, Johannesburg, 1987; Okihiro, 'Hunters, Herders, Cultivators and Traders'; Parsons, 'On the Origins'; B.P. Shaw, 'State Formation, Nation Building, and the Tswana of Southern Africa', M.A. dissertation, Duquesne University, Pittsburgh, 1975. The most detailed guide to the histories of Botswana peoples is I. Schapera, *Ethnic Composition of Tswana Tribes*, London, 1952. See also A. Manson, 'Conflict on the Western Highveld/Southern Kalahari *c.* 1750–1820' in this volume.

NORTHERN CAPE REGION

(a) The build-up and then break-up of Rolong kingdom under Taung; Nama-related Kora herder chiefdoms around Dithakong had come under Rolong rule from the east by *c*.1700.

(b) Rolong migrated north-west to Khalagari (Kgalagadi people) and Mbandu (i.e. proto-Herero) as far as the central Namibian region; north to Shoshong hills (Kaa) of east-central modern Botswana; south-east across the middle Vaal (Kubung); and south to the lower Vaal (Tlhaping).

(c) Groups of Tlokwa (Kgatla) migrated from north of the Vaal at Tlokwe (Potchefstroom) – see above.[13]

FREE STATE/LESOTHO REGIONS

(a) Nguni-speakers (Zizi etc.) settled through the Drakensberg passes on the south-east edge of the highveld.

(b) Nama-related Kora herder chiefdoms retained their independence in the Kalahari/Karoo around the Vaal-Orange confluence.

(c) Rolong moved across the middle Vaal to Kubung (i.e. Kroonstad); and further small parties of Kgatla/Kwena people migrated across the upper Vaal to Ntsuanatsatsi (near Vrede) southern Sotho heartland.

(d) Sotho (i.e. Fokeng/Kgatla/Kwena) lineages spread over the southern highveld – overlapping with Kubung and Zizi etc. – as far south as the lowlands of the upper Caledon Valley.[14]

Such an outline indicates the increasing scale and intensity of migrations and state-growth, with a heartland of Tswana growth in what is today the central/western Transvaal pushing out Sotho/Tswana/Pedi expansion in all directions. No doubt there was some accompanying violence and disruption, but the two major military powers in southern Africa, the Rozvi and the Thembe, were limited to the northern

13. For south-western Tswana see references in Legassick, 'The Sotho–Tswana Peoples'. For *c*.1450–1700 Khoisan herder occupation of Dithakong see P. B. Beaumont and J. C. Vogel, 'Spatial Patterning of the Ceramic Later Stone Age in the Northern Cape Province, South Africa', in M. Hall *et.al.*, eds, *Frontiers: South African Archaeology Today*, Oxford, 1984, 80–95; and contributions by P. B. Beaumont in *South African Archaeological Society Newsletter* (later retitled *The Digging Stick*), 3, (1980), 2–3; 4, 1 (1981), 1–2; 6, (1983), 1. For later Kora and Tswana history see C. C. Saunders, 'Early Knowledge of the Sotho: Seventeenth and Eighteenth Century Accounts of the Tswana', *Quarterly Bulletin of the South African Library*, 20 (1965), 60–70; R. Elphick and H. B. Giliomee eds, *The Shaping of South African Society, 1652–1840*, Cape Town, 1989, (especially chapter by M. Legassick, 'The Northern Frontier to *c*.1840: The Rise and Decline of the Griqua People', 358–420). See also M. Kinsman, '"Hungry Wolves": The Impact of Violence on Rolong Life, 1823–36' in this volume.

14. For 'Southern Sotho' and related Tswana and Khoisan see T. M. O'C. Maggs, *Iron Age Communities of the Southern Highveld*, Pietermaritzburg, 1976, P. W. Laidler, 'The Archaeology of Certain Prehistoric Settlements in the Heilbron Area', *Transactions of the Royal Society of South Africa*, 23 (1935), 54, 57; J. Walton, 'Early Bafokeng Settlement in South Africa', *African Studies*, 15 (1956), 37–43; Legassick, 'The Northern Frontier'; Wilson, 'The Sotho, Venda, and Tsonga'; L. B. J. Machobane, 'Mohlomi: Doctor, Traveller and Sage', *Mohlomi, Journal of Southern African Historical Studies*, 2 (1976), 5–27; B. Lambourne, 'A Chip Off the Old Block: Early Ghoya History and the Emergence of Moletsane's Taung', paper presented to the Colloquium on the Mfecane Aftermath, University of the Witwatersrand, Johannesburg, 1993.

and eastern peripheries of the trans-Vaal region. The outline above also suggests that migrations were directed along and towards trade-routes such as the major river valleys or across thirstlands, to areas with good cattle grazing which produced ivory and furs or metals for export trade. The main direction of such trade was towards the east coast, but there was also trade with the south coast and even in the direction of the west coast from the interior of southern Africa.

Evidence of trade, and of production for trade, as the main stimulus for migrations and state growth is, however, lacking in oral traditions. These record vivid stories of political conflict rather than economic activity, and anyway need to be read for symbolic rather than literal truth.[15] Taken at face value, oral traditions indicate that disputes over ritual leadership, and inheritance in status or cattle wealth, or over wives and children, were much more important than competition for tribute in trade goods.

Archaeological evidence of trade is patchy. As yet no seventeenth- or eighteenth-century sites are known on the trans-Vaal plateau with the wealth of evidence – in the form of trade beads or goods produced for trade – that has been found in some prime earlier sites around the middle Limpopo Valley. This may be taken as evidence of the dispersed and uneven impact of trade in the seventeenth and eighteenth centuries, or possibly as evidence of the declining importance of trade in developing internal economies. But the existence of such communications with the coasts is confirmed by the fact that the Dutch at the Cape of Good Hope in 1661, nine years after their arrival, received indirect intelligence of the Tswana (no doubt Rolong) north of the Orange River, 'living in stone houses built with cow dung and clay'.[16]

The most remarkable development in seventeenth-century trans-Vaal archaeology is the movement of settlements up to hill-top defensive locations. Simon Hall, in his essay in this book, shows this happening at Rooikrans, a small stone-walled Sotho/Tswana/Pedi site on the Waterberg plateau north-west of the Witwatersrand. A similar development from around the same time can be seen at Bruma on the Linksfield ridge in Johannesburg.[17]

A parallel sequence has yet to be established further west along the line of the Witwatersrand and the Magaliesberg, where Tswana settlement was concentrated. Well-known archaeological sites of Kwena settlement, Molokweni (Selonskraal) and Olifantspoort near Rustenburg, date from the sixteenth and seventeenth centuries but were built on low-lying lands. According to oral traditions, the Hurutshe founded their hill-top village of Chuenyane (Tshwenyane or Witkoppies) near Zeerust in the early sixteenth century; but then moved downridge to a larger

---

15. Cf. I. Hofmeyr, 'Jonah and the Swallowing Monster: Orality and Literacy on a Berlin Mission Station in the Transvaal' [Kekana-Ndebele of Mokopane], *Journal of Southern African Studies*, 17, 4 (1991), 633–53.
16. Saunders, 'Early Knowledge', 63.
17. Mason, *Origins of Black People*, 539.

twin settlement, Karechuenya ('Kurrichane' or 'Kaditshwene') during the reign of Menwe who died in about 1670.[18]

While the evidence from the western trans-Vaal area suggests more or less a continuum of state growth, the evidence from the central Witwatersrand and the Waterberg plateau suggests disruption and displacement among petty chiefdoms around the seventeenth century. The history of seventeenth-century Tswana state growth in the west, with the rise of Kwena and Kgatla dynasties followed by an eighteenth-century diaspora, is relatively well known. The history of militant trans-Vaal Ndebele expansion from the south-centre to the north-west has yet to be studied in detail, but its main features are identified below.

The Trans-Vaal Ndebele (Tebele) Diaspora

In his essay in this book, Hall suggests that sixteenth- and seventeenth-century Waterberg plateau settlements on hill-tops were defensive positions of existing Sotho/Tswana/Pedi-speaking groups against incoming brigands. People living on the hills with their cattle also cultivated red loam patches down the Motlhabatsi tributary of the Limpopo.

Settlement on high ground is not necessarily evidence of defensive or aggressive intentions. Hills can be vantage points for hunting, for protection for livestock from predators or tsetse-fly on the plain, as well as symbolic physical elevation of dominant groups overlooking inferior groundlings. Hill-tops also have associations with rain-making cults. But in the case of the sixteenth- and seventeenth-century Waterberg plateau the brigands can be identified from the material culture of their sites, including stone-corbelled dome housing, and from oral traditions, as groups of trans-Vaal Ndebele. These people, known among Sotho/Tswana/Pedi-speakers as 'Matebele', chose for themselves the steepest hills for their hill-forts around the Waterberg plateau.[19]

The southern trans-Vaal Ndebele, represented by the Manala/Ndzundza and Po/Tlhako groups and the Ndebele of Mabhogo (Mapoch), spread over the eastern Witwatersrand highveld adjoining the Drakensberg, up to the vicinity of Tshwane (Pretoria) by the seventeenth century. Oral traditions are clear about the origins of southern trans-Vaal Ndebele. They trace their ancestry to one Musi, 'somewhere between 1630–70', whose son Tshwane is commemorated by Pretoria's older name.

Oral traditions are less clear about the northern trans-Vaal Ndebele, who settled to the north-west around the Waterberg plateau possibly as early as the sixteenth century. While the Hwaduba trace themselves from Musi, and the Laka (Langa)

---

18. Mason, *Origins of Black People*, 52, 220, 463–551, 657–8; Maggs and Whitelaw, 'A Review', 21–2. For a note on the name Karechuenya see p. xiii of this book.
19. T. N. Huffman, 'The Waterberg Research of Jan Aukema', *South African Archaeological Bulletin*, 45 (1990), 118.

trace separate origins from the Natal area, the Malete/Seleka may be traced back to origins in the south-eastern heartland even earlier than Musi's reign.[20]

The antiquity of the name 'Matebele' north of the the Vaal may be judged by the fact that the name 'Motebele' was given to a Tswana (Kwena) prince in the western trans-Vaal region, datable to the later sixteenth century. He received the name because considerate 'Matebele' raiders gave him milk-goats at birth, instead of firing the house where his mother lay.

The origins of the Sotho/Tswana/Pedi word 'Matebele', from which the Nguni version 'Ndebele' is almost certainly derived, are not definitely known — though there are various semantic glosses for the term, such as derivation from go tebela (to 'strike or knock about with a fist'). But it was probably derived from another, even earlier, Tswana (Hurutshe) prince named Motebele.

Hurutshe oral traditions relate how Motebele, deposed by his brother Motebejane around the beginning of the sixteenth century, fled south-east from the western trans-Vaal to the Vaal. He returned with Nguni-speaking mercenaries to attack Motebejane's new capital at Chuenyane unsuccessfully. He and his followers (the 'Matebele') then blazed north to beyond the Waterberg plateau — founding the chiefly line of the Gananwa, a group of Pedi/Venda origin, in the northern trans-Vaal. These Nguni or early trans-Vaal Ndebele must have been the Malete, who regard themselves as senior relatives of the Gananwa chiefs.[21]

The Malete, and their Seleka offshoot, spread across the central trans-Vaal bushveld basin towards the middle Limpopo Valley. They even crossed the Limpopo to the Tswapong hills and the vicinity of Serowe in what is today eastern Botswana. The hill-fort on top of Swaneng hill near Serowe is said to have been of Seleka origin. Meanwhile other trans-Vaal Ndebele, the Laka and Hwaduba, occupied the Waterberg plateau which, as we have seen, has been well studied by archaeologists in the past twenty years.

20. N.J. van Warmelo, ed., *Transvaal Ndebele Texts*, Pretoria, 1930, 19; N.J. van Warmelo, ed., *A Preliminary Survey of the Bantu Tribes of South Africa*, Pretoria, 1935; N.J. van Warmelo, ed., *The Ndebele of J. Kekana: The Bahwaduba*, Pretoria, 1944, 14–25. Ngcongco in 'Aspects of the History of Bangwaketse', 60–1, dates the reign of the original chief Malete as *c.* 1385–1415, adding that Tshwane was named after the black cow (*kgomo e tshwana*) successfully sacrificed to bring rain to break the drought *c.* 1450 which had caused the Laka and Seleka etc. to break from the Malete.

21. For the Kgabo–Kwena prince Motebele a Kgabo, see J.T. Brown, *Among the Bantu Nomads*, London, 1926, 229–30; though Brown suggests these 'Matebele' were Shona rather than Nguni, the use of the word being generic for raiders rather than for a specific ethnic group. For the Hurutshe prince Motebele a Mohurutshe/Lehurutshe see P-L. Breutz, ed., *The Tribes of Marico District*, Pretoria, 1953–4, 19–21; Ngcongco, 'Aspects of the History of Bangwaketse', 48; Krige, 'Traditional Origins', 354; Transvaal Native Affairs Department, *Short History of the Native Tribes of the Transvaal*, Pretoria, 1905, 11–12. Before going north to the Gananwa, Motebele left his son Lesele in south-eastern Botswana with the people who became known as Khurutshe in the north: see I. Schapera, 'The Early History of the Khurutshe', *Botswana Notes and Records*, 2 (1970), 1–5; Chief Ramokate, 'Notes on the Khurutshe', *Botswana Notes and Records*, 2 (1970), 14; J. Mpotokwane, 'A Short History of the Bakhurutshe of King Motebele, Senior Son of King Mohurutshe' (or Queen Lehurutshe), *Botswana Notes and Records*, 6 (1974), 37–45; Parsons, 'On the Origins', 95.

Trans-Vaal Ndebele in the heartland, notably the Manala/Ndzundza, clung on to and revived their separate cultural and linguistic identity. Others in the north and west eventually became part of Sotho/Tswana/Pedi-speaking societies, and had lost their distinctive language and culture by the nineteenth century. The two most notable examples are the Po/Tlhako whose chief, Mogale, gave his name to the hills since garbled into 'Magaliesberg', and the Malete today living at Ramotswa in the south-eastern region of modern Botswana.[22]

Among the Sotho/Tswana/Pedi-speaking people the word 'Matebele' became almost synonymous with mercenaries and brigands, as well as with any Nguni-speaking immigrant. But the historical achievements of trans-Vaal Nguni groups were ultimately as much mercantile as military.

Associations with metallurgy in trans-Vaal Ndebele history seems to have been initially as customers for weapons of war. The Laka may have been drawn to settle on the Waterberg plateau by well-established local production of iron, copper and tin. The Waterberg also dominated the western trans-Vaal head of the Limpopo Valley, the major trade route to the coast.[23]

The archaeologist Jan Aukema has suggested that the Laka of the Waterberg managed to suppress local tin production around the seventeenth century, rather than to benefit from trade in it. But by the nineteenth century the Laka had a reputation as smelters of 'iron, copper, and tin, and in the manufacture of ornaments know how to mix the tin & copper so as to form an amalgam'. They spun local cotton, made splendid leopard karosses, and traded in tobacco inland and in ivory towards the sea. They were so 'rich in cattle' and trade goods that a chief in his twenties already had 48 wives. The Laka also had a distinctive dialect of Pedi/Sotho that seems to have still been suffused with their original Nguni dialect, including click-consonants.[24]

22. P-L. Breutz, *Tribes of Rustenburg and Pilansberg Districts*, Pretoria, 1952–3, 21–22, 175–79, 252, 286–90; A. Sillery, *The Bechuanaland Protectorate*, Cape Town, 1952, 160–5 (drawing on V. E. Ellenberger); Ngcongco, 'Aspects of the History of Bangwaketse', 60–1; Parsons 'On the Origins', 89–90. The 'many wandering and many splits' between Po/Tlhako of Mogale, Malete of Mokgosi, Seleka/Malete, etc. need to be sorted out.

23. Cf. F. R. Paver, 'Trade and Mining in the Pre-European Transvaal', *South African Journal of Science*, 30 (1933), 603–11; H. M. Friede, 'Notes on the Composition of Pre-European Copper and Copper-alloy Artefacts From the Transvaal', *South African Institute of Mining and Metallurgy*, 75, 7 (1975), 185–91; H. M. Friede and R. H. Steel, 'Notes on Iron Age Copper Smelting Technology in the Transvaal', *South African Institute of Mining and Metallurgy*, 76, 4 (1975), 221–31; R. H. Steel, 'Ingot Casting and Wire Drawing in Iron Age South Africa', *South African Institute of Mining and Metallurgy*, 76, 4 (1975), 232–7; H. M. Friede and R. H. Steel, 'Tin Mining and Smelting in the Transvaal During the Iron Age, *South African Institute of Mining and Metallurgy*, 76, 12 (1976), 461–70; Wilson, 'The Sotho, Venda, and Tsonga', 114 (quoting V. E. Ellenberger); Parsons, 'On the Origins', 90.

24. Huffman, 'Waterberg Research of Jan Aukema'; D. Livingstone, *Missionary Correspondence 1851–1856*, ed. by I. Schapera, London, 1961, 97–8; D. Livingstone, *David Livingstone: Letters and Documents 1841–1872*, ed. by T. Holmes, Bloomington, 1990, 24–5; D. Livingstone, *David Livingstone Family Letters 1841–1856*, ed. by I. Schapera, London, 1959, 243; D. Livingstone, *Missionary Travels and Researches in South Africa*, London, (Minerva Library ed.), n.d. [c.1900], 513; Okihiro, 'Hunters, Herders, Cultivators, and Traders', 211, quoting D. Livingstone to B. Pyne, (National Library of Scotland, Edinburgh, Ms. 10769).

It is not difficult to see how such small groups of well-armed mobile people, based in a string of hill-forts around the upper Limpopo Valley, could have been petty raiders with their spears as well as petty traders. If so, they were not the first or last to mix a little theft with pursuit of profit.

The argument is supported by an oral tradition of Malete/Seleka penetration across the Limpopo and settlement in the Tswapong hills. They were said to have been attracted to the iron-rich hills as 'customers' of long-established Pedi/Venda craftworkers 'who manufactured . . . asseghais, battle-axes, hoes, musical instruments'. But Malete/Seleka 'cupidity' in seizing tribute 'was in reality killing the goose that lay the golden eggs', leading to the decline of Tswapong metal crafts. The Malete/Seleka subsequently settled down to a less warlike life-style in the middle Limpopo Valley, developing chiefly skills in rain-making and in cattle trade from hill to hill across tsetse-infested countryside.[25]

Other Malete, trading in iron implements, moved to the Ngotwane and Taung Rivers of what is today south-eastern Botswana, settling as *bafaladi* (alien minority) miners and ironsmiths, initially paying tribute to local Tswana/Khalagari chiefs. By the eighteenth century they had built up their own cattle herds, and had adopted Tswana language and culture to an extent that they could assert political autonomy as an independent Tswana chiefdom or state.[26]

The Malete and Po/Tlhako account for some or many of the 'ruins of innumerable towns, some of which were of amazing extent . . . [with] stone fences, averaging from four to seven feet high' noted by Robert Moffat in 1829–30, travelling along the northern fringes of the Magaliesberg hills between modern Rustenburg and Pretoria. Moffat's Tswana-speaking informant told him about the Po, rich in cattle, whose boasting 'in their spears' had led to their defeat by Mzilikazi. The Po chief, Mogale, was referred to as 'Chief of the Blue Cattle'. Moffat's informant added how populous the country had been and how it had 'trafficked abundantly with the tribes farther in the interior'.[27]

The sixteenth- to eighteenth-century diaspora of the trans-Vaal Ndebele is a topic of great potential for further research. Its effects were not limited to south of the Limpopo. Some oral traditions identify Tumbare, the great general and kingmaker of the Rozvi kingdom in western Zimbabwe, as a later seventeenth-century Nguni-speaking immigrant doctor from the south. The concept of a trans-Vaal Ndebele diaspora also helps to explain otherwise mysterious oral traditions. Rozvi battles of the seventeenth and eighteenth centuries are recorded in oral tradition as being with

25. Parsons, 'On the Origins', 90, 100n. quoting 'Moozoongoo' as told to Douglas M'Intosh, *South Africa: Notes of Travel*, Glasgow, 1876, 25.

26. V. Ellenberger, 'History of the Ba-ga-Malete of Ramoutsa (Bechuanaland Protectorate)', *Transactions of the Royal Society of South Africa*, 25 (1937–38), 1–72; ('Di robaroba matlhakola –tsa ga Masodi-a-Mphela', 36–42). See also note 21 above.

27. R. Moffat, *The Matabele Journals of Robert Moffat 1829–1860*, ed. by J. P. R. Wallis, 2 vol., Salisbury, 1976, 9–10; R. Moffat, *Missionary Labours and Scenes in Southern Africa*, London, 1842, 523. Cf. Breutz, *Tribes of Rustenburg*, 21, 175–95, re. Lotlhokane (destroyed *c.* 1816–17) and neighbouring Tobong (Wolhuterskop near Hartbeespoort Dam).

the Ngwato in the south. But as the Ngwato were not yet in existence the conflicts seem to have been with Pedi/Venda groups impelled northwards by the trans-Vaal Ndebele.[28]

The trans-Vaal Ndebele diaspora one to three centuries earlier can easily be confused with the *difaqane* in oral traditions. (The confusion is compounded by Mzilikazi's Khumalo taking on pre-existing Ndebele identity.) This comes out clearly in an oral tradition recorded and published in 1991 from among Kalanga people whose ancestors were Pedi/Venda. They had been chased across the Limpopo by Malete/Seleka during that seventeenth-eighteenth-century rehearsal for the *difaqane*:

> We originate from Pietersburg (South Africa) some 100 years back. We are originally Pedi who during the Zulu troubles [*ka nako ya dintwa tsa Mazulu*] began moving to Rhodesia. We came through Tswapong.[29]

The Proto-*difaqane* Period *c.*1750–*c.*1822

While the impact of the trans-Vaal Ndebele diaspora died down, one can date an 'almost continuous jostling for ascendancy among the Tswana from about the middle of the eighteenth century, and a series of small wars growing ever more intense after the turn of that century. Elsewhere I have referred to the period of increasing violence about 1770–1820 from the Zambezi southwards as 'ivory-and-cattle-and-fur wars', to which might be added '-and-wives'.[30] In this essay we will limit ourselves to the Sotho/Tswana/Pedi-speaking societies in and around what became the Transvaal/Free State region.

Outline of Major Events

CENTRAL/WESTERN TRANSVAAL REGION

The Hurutshe state dominated the western highveld in the eighteenth century; but was challenged by surrounding Tswana states and progressively lost power around 1800. Andrew Manson has explored this elsewhere in this book.[31]

NORTHERN CAPE REGION

The Tlhaping state took over Rolong supremacy in the south-eastern Kalahari in the eighteenth century; but it came under increasing threat from Kora and Oorlam intruders from the Cape frontiers.

---

28. H. von Sicard, 'The Origin of Some of the Tribes of the Belingwe Reserve', *Salisbury Native Affairs Department Annual*, 25 (1948), 99; F. W. T. Posselt, *Fact and Fiction: Short Account of the Natives of Southern Rhodesia*, Bulawayo, 1978, 145. See also note 30 below.

29. Ahmed el Amin, 'Masunga, Village of the Man-Made Drought', *Kutlwano*, 29 (1991), 15, quoting Egbert K[g]ang Masunga, aged 64 'carrier of the family and Masunga [village]'s history'. Cf. Schapera, *Ethnic Composition*, 74–5, 78–9; N.M. Holonga, 'Overview of the History of the Bakalanga of Botswana' [pp.35–37] in C. van Waarden, ed., *Kalanga Retrospect and Prospect*, Gaborone, 1991, 35.

30. N. Parsons, *Focus on History, A Lower Secondary Course for Zimbabwe. Book One*, Harare, 1985, 77.

31. Manson, 'Conflict on the Western Highveld'.

EASTERN TRANSVAAL REGION

The Kgatla–Pedi state rose to power by conquest on the Lydenburg plateau. By the 1780s the Kgatla–Pedi, under the rule of Thulare, were raiding – if not trading – as far inland as modern Rustenburg and south of the Vaal.

NORTHERN TRANSVAAL REGION

(a) Kgatla and Tsonga incomers challenged Venda and Lobedu power around the Soutpansberg plateau.
(b) Tsonga from the south-east pushed the lowveld Pedi both westwards (e.g. Birwa), and north-eastwards to the Mozambique flats beyond the Limpopo from about 1730.[32]

EASTERN BOTSWANA REGION

(a) The Ngwaketse state dominated modern south-eastern Botswana, fighting with Hurutshe in the east and Tlhaping in the south.
(b) Kaa and Khurutshe fought over the Shoshong hills; Khurutshe raided as far north as the Luyana in what is today western Zambia.[33]
(c) Kwena, Ngwato and Tawana groups quarrelled and migrated as far north-west as the Okavango delta.

FREE STATE/LESOTHO REGION

Monaheng-Kwena chief Mohlomi 'distinguished himself much by personal bravery and generalship, and, by these means, and his peculiar political system . . . soon raised himself to great power'. After his death, about 1815, 'the country soon became distracted with feuds' – in which Moshoeshoe's Mokoteli–Kwena and Moletsane's Taung made their names as cattle-raiders.[34]

Growth of Towns

The two outstanding features of later eighteenth- and nineteenth-century Tswana states were the size of their capital towns and their inclusivity of ethnically diverse wards.

Archaeologists debate about the date when the 'mega-sites' of the Tswana emerged – the large towns, with populations between ten and twenty-five thousand, noted by nineteenth-century travellers. Some archaeologists now argue that such aggregation in size or traditional 'urbanization' dates only from about 1750.

Archaeological sites near modern Parys on the Vaal indicate that small settlements expanded into multi-ethnic communities only after the mid-eighteenth century. This has been taken as evidence of the 'fluid ward system of the Tswana', studied by Isaac Schapera and others in the twentieth century, 'whereby foreigners [were] incorporated into patrilineal decision-making groups'.[35] But the post-1750

32. Krige, 'Traditional Origins', 322, 352; also Legassick, 'The Sotho–Tswana Peoples', 111 n.74. Junod thought north-eastward Pedi migrations were explained by their following the retreat of wildlife to the lowveld: cf. Von Sicard, 'The Origin', 94; Smith, 'The Peoples of Southern Mozambique'.
33. See H. H. Johnston's comments in D. W. Stirke, Barotseland: Eight Years Among the Barotse, London, 1922, 3–4, 38. Harry Johnston claimed that the name 'Barotse' originated as a shortened version of 'Bahurutshe' c. 1800, after their invasion of the Zambezi. See note 21 above on Khurutshe origins and history.
34. Orpen, History of the Basutus, 20–1. See also note 14 above.
35. J. H. N. Loubser, 'Buffelshoek: An Ethnoarchaeological Consideration of a Late Iron Age Settlement in the Southern Transvaal', South African Archaeological Bulletin, 40, 1 (1985), 81.

aggregation thesis remains to be proven for the mega-sites of the western trans-Vaal region. We need to know, for example, where and when new wards of populations were added to the towns of Olifantspoort south of modern Rustenburg and Karechuenya north of modern Zeerust.

State growth seems to have gone hand in hand not only with 'urbanization' but also with increasing violence in the half century or so before the era known as the *difaqane*. This violence took the forms of forced migrations, dynastic quarrels and conquests.

One level of explanation is indicated by 'general crisis' theory, along lines suggested not only by Huffman's hierarchy but also by Max Gluckman's 'rituals of rebellion'.[36] Violence is seen as the inevitable consequence of general structural change from level-three chiefdoms to level-four states – like an engine being crashed into higher gear with gnashing and stripping of cogs.

Another level of explanation is suggested by focusing on the specifics of violence at strategic locations on the landscape – areas of heightened competition for resources. Two such strategic locations for further study are offered as examples – the Lydenburg plateau, and the Shoshong/Tswapong hills.

The Lydenburg plateau was a strategic location for controlling local production and eastern trade routes from the trans-Vaal to Delagoa Bay in 'ivory, horns, cattle and furs'.[37] Martin Legassick suggests this as the motive for the 'rise to hegemony' of the Kgatla–Pedi state. Peter Delius outlines more complex processes of cattle-centred state growth among the Kgatla–Pedi, adding that 'in the latter half of the eighteenth century these relatively peaceful processes of change were overtaken by a marked escalation of conflict' – which Delius attributes to population pressure, drought and competition for shrinking trade.[38]

The Shoshong/Tswapong hills were a stategic location for controlling production and trade in ivory and furs from the Kalahari to the upper Limpopo Valley, being taken from there to the coast. Competing Kaa and Khurutshe chiefdoms, ruling over Khalagari and Kalanga wards, were overtaken by a growing Ngwato polity in the last decades of the eighteenth century.

The Ngwato chiefdom was rationalised along state lines under the rule of Kgari (*c*.1817–28). Schapera has shown how Kgari developed a new system of vassal

---

36. M. Gluckman, *Rituals of Rebellion in South-east Africa*, Manchester, 1954.
37. For trade in 'ivory, horns, cattle and furs' between the Pedi and Delagoa Bay *c*..1836, see T. Arbousset and F. Daumas, *Narrative of an Exploratory Tour to the North-east of the Colony of the Cape of Good Hope*, Cape Town, 1968 (1st publ. in 1846), 180. The prehistory of north-eastern Transvaal trade is covered by N.J. van Warmelo, *The Copper Miners of Musina and the Early History of the Zoutpansberg*, Pretoria, 1940.
38. P. Delius, *The Land Belongs to Us: The Pedi Polity, the Boers and the British in the Nineteenth-century Transvaal*, Johannesburg, 1983, 13–19; Legassick, 'The Sotho–Tswana Peoples', 107–8. Unfortunately Legassick never published, nor have I yet seen, his 'Notes on Sotho–Tswana Long-distance Trade' (*c*.1970).

sub-chiefdoms, known as the *kgamelo* system. The *kgamelo* system was subsequently adopted by the Tawana state in the north-west of modern Botswana in the 1830s–1840s, and parallel innovations were achieved among the Kgabo–Kwena of the south-eastern Botswana region in the 1820s–1840s. (In the Ngwato case, in ways I have shown elsewhere, the polity was further developed into a super-state between 1875 and 1896).[39]

The acceleration of violence after about 1750 begs many questions about the people who initiated it and kept it up – violence by those that stood to gain, and between those that stood to lose. The essays in this section suggest some of the questions that need to be asked. Manson points to 'land shortage for grazing', and to a 'sudden demand for ivory'. Simon Hall refers to population growth, and mercantile expansion from the coast 'compressing people on the landscape' of the interior.

Population Growth and 'Land Shortage'

The emergence of Tswana towns and of numerous chiefdoms-cum-states on the trans-Vaal plateaux suggests a take-off in human population numbers around the mid-eighteenth century, though such dating is as yet very tentative.

The precondition or corollary of such a spurt in demographic growth was probably an increase in agricultural productivity. How was this achieved? Productivity and population levels were probably raised by the introduction of maize to higher rainfall areas. It is also possible that larger-scale political organization 'improved' the management of communal and vassal labour and cattle keeping under chiefly control and 'ownership'.

In wet years, three times as much maize as traditional sorghum and millets might be harvested. Improved grain supplies increased population density by ensuring that more children survived to become reproductive adults. But, as we have again in the early 1990s learned to our cost, maize fails in drought years, leading to famine and social unrest.

In Iron Age sites of the trans-Vaal archaeologists have found widespread distribution of heavy 'bird-bath' grindstones, suitable for grinding the tough bulky grains of maize. We do not yet know when and how and where maize was introduced into the trans-Vaal area. But maize became the staple crop of upland Natal areas during the eighteenth century, and perhaps earlier. It may have spread from the Inhambane/Delagoa coast to the eastern trans-Vaal even earlier than to the Natal

39. Isaac Schapera, *Tribal Innovators: Tswana Chiefs and Social Change 1795–1940*, London, 1970, 78, 79–80; Okihiro, 'Hunters, Herders, Cultivators and Traders', 48, 94; N. Parsons, 'The Economic History of Khama's Country in Botswana, 1844–1930', in Palmer and Parsons, *The Roots of Rural Poverty*, 119–20.

40. See T. M. O'C. Maggs, 'The Iron Age Farming Communities', in A. H. Duminy and W. R.Guest, eds, *Natal and Zululand from Earliest Times to 1910*, Pietermaritzburg, 1989, 43. Maize was recorded at St Lucia Bay in 1756 – S. Bannister, *Humane Policy: Or, Justice to the Aborigines of the New Settlements*, London, 1830, (reprinted 1968), appendices xxxii. M. Wilson, *Oxford History*, 142, denies maize had reached the middle Vaal by 1822.

area.[40] But its adoption would have been uneven and limited to higher rainfall areas. As of about 1840, 'mealies had never been seen' in the Shoshong hills of eastern Botswana.[41]

The intensification of the tributary mode-of-production in agriculture is illustrated by the Kgabo–Kwena, who conquered and incorporated many Khalagari vassals in the south-east of modern Botswana during the eighteenth century. Production of grain crops was intensified for essentially political reasons. The size of a ruler's grain basket was an essential public indicator of his power and prestige as a chief, lineage head, and household head.

The economic historian Gary Okihiro estimates that the combination of six vassal women hoe-workers, working in line, cultivated for the chief in two or three days the same area as one Kwena woman would have cultivated for her own household in a year – up to six 'Sekwena acres' or 0,4 hectares. Kwena chiefs also used their powers to summon female age-sets to cultivate ever larger chiefly tribute fields. Homesteads and lineage wards recruited extra labour by such devices as sponsored work-days (malaletsa) and by recruiting contract workers paid in food or goods. [42] The exploitation of women as women, and of young men as expendable youth, was increased by their use in age-sets as regiments for tribute labour and hunting or war.[43]

There is plentiful evidence in Tswana oral traditions of the incorporation of new populations in the form of lineage wards into Tswana chiefdoms in the period immediately before the difaqane. Such traditions indicate a range of strategies for incorporation, both peaceful and belligerent. While these traditions merit much more comparative study, two objects of chiefly accumulation and conflict and complication are outstanding – wives and cattle.

The obvious way for a chief to attach 'the underchiefs to himself and his government', as David Livingstone remarked among the Kgabo–Kwena, was 'by marrying . . . their daughters, or inducing his brothers to do so'. This in turn led to disputes over dynastic succession, which Manson calls the main 'detonator' of conflict among Tswana chiefdoms before difaqane.[44]

41. For uneven adoption of this reddish maize in Natal uplands see J. B. Wright and A. Manson, The Hlubi Chiefdom of Zululand–Natal: A History, Ladysmith, 1983, 7. On over-cultivation on Lydenburg plateau and the plains north of the Magaliesberg, see M. E. Marker and T. M. Evers, 'Iron Age Settlement and Soil Erosion in the Eastern Transvaal, South Africa', South African Archaeological Bulletin, 31, 123–24 (1976), 153–65. For the Shoshong hills see 'Khama's Own Account of Himself' [1901], ed. by Q. N. Parsons, Botswana Notes and Records, 4 (1972), 139.
42. Okihiro, 'Hunters, Herders, Cultivators and Traders', 69–73. It may be argued that wars are plots by patriarchs to kill off young male sexual rivals and to increase the supply of young wives – in conspiracy with matriarchs who benefit from the labour power of younger wives and daughters-in-law or adopted daughters.
43. Cf. Schapera, Ethnic Composition, passim; and works by Breutz.
44. Livingstone, Missionary Travels, 13. The poet L. D. Raditladi has demonstrated the epic literary qualities of stories of the pre-difaqane 'wars of the roses' in his classic play Motswasele II: Historical Drama in Tswana, rev. and ed. by D. T. Cole, Johannesburg, 1970. Such stories also show women as protagonists of events, rather than as mere objects of male competition.

Chiefs who accumulated more cattle could marry more wives, thus giving rise to more competitors for succession between children of greater and lesser wives. Disputes over bridewealth – *lobolo* or *bogadi* wars – grew more frequent as royal polygyny increased.

The increase in royal polygyny, with monarchs marrying more wives as more and more wards and sections were incorporated into the polity, is indicated by oral traditions as well as by the logic of Huffman's hierarchy in cattle-centred societies. The necessity to marry widely and well – 'contrary to the previous custom of the Basutus whose chiefs had seldom had more than three or four spouses' – was one of the main mysteries of peaceful statecraft passed on from Mohlomi to Moshoeshoe.[45]

Oral traditions of the later eighteenth century indicate increasing conflict over cattle. There was certainly raiding of cattle-for-wives, to finance marriage payments. Cattle-raiding was also a method of impoverishing rival lineages and chiefdoms, to then incorporate them as subject wards herding royal cattle. The Kgafela–Kgatla even record how they impoverished and incorporated a rival chiefdom in the bushveld north of the Pilanesberg about 1780 by deliberately planting tsetse flies to kill off their rivals' cattle.[46]

The changes in human demography and political conflict in the seventeenth and eighteenth centuries, which became more critical in the later eighteenth and early nineteenth centuries, can be matched by evidence of changing bovine demography. The distribution and increase in cattle numbers, and the opening up of new pastures, would have had dramatic effects on the competition between cattle-centred chiefdoms-cum-states.

The determinants of cattle population growth are complex. But new and improved pastures boosted fertility, while drought and disease caused morbidity. The main limiting factor on cattle distribution in the region north of the Vaal was tsetse fly. Cattle grazing was impossible in the tsetse belt, except on hills above the belt and at night when the flies slept. People also suffered and died from *nagana* or sleeping-sickness, as well as from malaria within the belt. People pushed back tsetse-infested bush by burning and clearing it for crop cultivation and cattle pasture.[47] But their burning and over-grazing, as well as natural factors such as climatic change, then brought back bush encroachment and tsetse-infestation.[48]

45. Orpen, *History of the Basutus*, 20; Machobane, 'Mohlomi'.
46. I. Schapera, *A Short History of the Bakgatla BagaKgafela of the Bechuanaland Protectorate*, Cape Town, 1942 and Mochudi, 1984.
47. Cf. C. Fuller, *Tsetse in the Transvaal and Surrounding Territories*, Pretoria, 1923; B.H. Dicke, 'The Tsetse Fly's Influence on South African History', *South African Journal of Science*, 29 (1932), 15–35; J. Ford, *The Role of the Trypanosomiases in African Ecology*, Oxford, 1971; L. Vail, 'Ecology and History: The Example of Eastern Zambia', *Journal of Southern African Studies*, 3, 2 (1977), 129–55; H. Kjekhus, *Ecology Control and Economic Development in East Africa: The Case of Tanganyika 1850–1950*, London, 1977.
48. Seleka/Malete and Birwa/Gananwa made a living by trading cattle across the Limpopo Valley via tsetse-free hilltops – cf. J. Mackenzie, *Ten Years North of the Orange River*, Edinburgh, 1871, 367.

This dynamic relationship between human settlement and tsetse infestation can be seen in archaeological evidence of cattle-keeping in the area of the Kruger National Park. Early Iron Age people opened up pasture grassland in former tsetse belts, but tsetse-infested bushveld took over again after 1000. Later Iron Age people then opened up pasture once more from about 1500 up to about 1800; then tsetse reigned again till around 1900 when they were cleared out by rinderpest killing off their wildlife hosts.[49]

This evidence in the Kruger Park suggests that the sixteenth, seventeenth and eighteenth centuries saw increasing settlement and population growth by cattle and people, followed by a period of crisis in the later eighteenth century when bush encroachment and tsetse-infestation pushed them back to higher land. The good rains of the later eighteenth century, interrupted by periodic droughts after the 1790s, are also likely to have had dramatic effects on other cattle pastures.[50]

How far can this situation from the Transvaal-Mozambique border lowveld be generalized elsewhere? A parallel case has been made for the Motlhabatsi Valley, feeding into the Limpopo from the Waterberg. Early Iron Age clearance and re-infestation by tsetse was succeeded by agricultural resettlement in the seventeenth century. The dating of the next re-infestation is not known, but nineteenth-century maps mark the area within the tsetse-belt – and the Kgafela–Kgatla tale of collecting tsetse to plague their enemy, referred to above, suggests that the belt was in the vicinity by about 1780.

By the 1860s, when it was mapped by cartographers, the tsetse-belt extended from the Mozambique lowlands up the Limpopo and Olifants Valleys, on to both the northern and eastern margins of the central trans-Vaal bushveld basin. Given that this situation emerged a century earlier, there is a good case for arguing 'compression on the landscape' or 'land shortage' on higher land in the north of the Vaal during the later eighteenth and early nineteenth centuries – pushing people towards increased conflict and violence.

A 'Sudden Demand for Ivory'

The evidence for Manson's 'sudden demand for ivory' in the eighteenth century has still to be pieced together. An indication of the demand can be found in the official Portuguese export figures from the Sofala (mid-Mozambique) coast which peaked at 165 000 kilograms of ivory in 1762 (from 24 000 in 1758), and still totalled 47 000 kilograms in 1806. These figures were no doubt underestimates and did not necessarily include Delagoa Bay, where many non-Portuguese ships operated.

49. A. Meyer, 'A Profile of the Iron Age in the Kruger National Park, South Africa', in Hall, *et al*, *Frontiers*, 214–27; I. Plug, 'Aspects of Life in the Kruger National Park during the Early Iron Age', *South African Archaeological Society, Goodwin Series*, 6 (1989), 62–8.
50. T. N. Huffman, 'Broederstroom and the Origins of Cattle-keeping in Southern Africa', *African Studies*, 49, 2 (1990), 1–12; Huffman, 'The Waterberg Research', 117. See T. Baines, *The Gold Regions of South Eastern Africa*, London, 1877, 153–4. 'The fly is extremely local . . . it shifts with the migration of game, and, therefore, the knowledge of the guide ought to be recent'.

David Hedges identifies a boom in ivory exports from Delagoa Bay after the 1750s – though this dwindled and was overtaken by sales of cattle and foodstuffs to European whaling ships in the last decade of the eighteenth century.[51]

Nor should our focus be limited to ivory. Furs such as leopard skins and the tailored pelts known as karosses, as well as feathers, were also exported across the Indian Ocean and increasingly into the Atlantic. David Livingstone, a member of a missionary society with branches in China as well as Africa, attested in the mid-nineteenth century that 'many' karosses from the Kalahari 'find their way to China'.[52]

We know from the archaeology of Toutswe and Mapungubwe that ivory and other 'products of the chase' were being produced in the middle Limpopo Valley lowveld, and from as far west across the Kalahari as the Boteti/Okavango region, from at least the eleventh century. Evidence of hunting for trade may be seen in the form of ostrich eggshell beads in Toutswe sites, and from ivory shavings left over from bangle manufacture at the pre-Mapungubwe site called Schroda.[53] But can we find any evidence of an increased scale of hunting from such areas in the eighteenth century?

Okihiro has shown how people in the eastern Kalahari tended to settle near good hunting lands, where game could be caught in the pit-traps known as *hopo*. In the eighteenth century the Kgabo–Kwena settled near salt-licks which attracted game. They conducted communal hunting drives – down lines of bush fencing sometimes more than a kilometre long – into a *hopo* pit that might be 120 metres square. A start has been made on the archaeology of pit-traps, but more research is needed to show whether they increased in size in the eighteenth century.[54]

The increase of Tswana hunting in the Kalahari in the eighteenth century is suggested by Tswana migrations across what became Botswana from the middle of the century. The new Tswana chiefdoms demanded tribute in the form of hunting from their vassals. These migrations followed in the tracks of Khalagari hunters and herders from the south-eastern Botswana region to the elephant-rich areas, north of the Shoshong and Tswapong hills and along the Boteti River to the lands around the Okavango marches. Khalagari groups and the Khoisan-speaking Teti, famous for

---

51. Randles, *The Empire of Monomotapa*, 79–80; P. L. Bonner, *Kings, Commoners and Concessionaires: The Evolution and Dissolution of the Nineteenth-century Swazi State*, Johannesburg, 1983, 20–1, (citing Hedges, 'Trade and Politics'). Whaling ships on occasion became slaving ships – cf. Baines, *The Gold Regions*, 107.
52. Livingstone, *Missionary Travels*, 43.
53. T.N. Huffman, verbal contribution at Colloquim on the Mfecane Aftermath, University of the Witwatersrand, Johannesburg, 1991.
54. N. Walker, 'Game Traps: Their Importance in Southern Africa', *Botswana Notes and Records*, 23 (1991), 235–42. Okihiro, 'Hunters, Herders, Cultivators and Traders', 66, mentions a *hopo* trap 20 metres by 6 metres square and 7 metres deep at its lowest point – served by a funnel of two *magora* brush fences up to a kilometre and a half long (and three-quarters of a kilometre apart at the mouth) through which thousands of animals were chased.

their skill and bravery in hunting elephants with spears, were reduced to vassalage.[55]

The eighteenth-century growth of Ngwaketse and Kwena states in the south-eastern Botswana region may be attributed to their incorporation of local Khalagari chiefdoms, who not only had 'enormous herds of the large horned cattle' but were compelled to give tribute in the furs and skins of jackals, wild cats, and antelopes. Evidence of the penetration of market values can be seen in the fact that Tswana chiefs were careful to organize hunting and tribute-taking from hunters during the March–May autumn season when pelts were thickest and glossiest.[56]

The organization of hunting by age-sets and even whole communities, ranging over hundreds of kilometres, suggests the scale of operation of chiefdoms-cum-states, rather than mere lineages and petty chiefdoms. Our assumption, until faulted, must be that this scale of hunting did not predate the mid-eighteenth century in the interior south and west of the Limpopo.

Mercantile Contacts with the Coasts

The penetration of coastal trade deep into the interior of southern Africa has a long history. Excavations in the Tsodilo hills in the centre of the sub-continent have produced shells from Atlantic trade as early as the sixth century, and shells from Indian Ocean trade as early as the eighth century. But there is very little evidence of direct penetration of the interior by coastal traders until the mid-eighteenth century, when they came equipped with firearms.

The earliest traditions of Tsonga traders from the southern Mozambique coast penetrating up the Limpopo Valley lowveld, as far as Mapungubwe, are associated with the migration traditions of 'Ba-Haole' i.e. Kwena–Pedi who settled there at an as yet undetermined time in the seventeenth or eighteenth centuries. But Dutch failure at Delagoa Bay to obtain information about the interior in the 1720s suggests that coastal Tsonga were not penetrating the plateau hinterland of the eastern trans-Vaal. The initiative for trade still appears to have been with Kgatla–Pedi and Phalaborwa–Pedi trading from inland.[57]

This position seems to have been reversed as southern Tsonga chiefdoms grew more militant. The Maputo lineage was established in power at Delagoa Bay by about 1750.[58] By the 1780s, as Elizabeth Eldredge shows in her essay in this book, six or seven boatloads of ivory, etc. were reaching Delagoa Bay annually down the

---

55. Parsons, 'On the Origins'; Okihiro, 'Hunters, Herders, Cultivators and Traders', 64–5, 105, 120, 159; Ngcongco, 'Aspects of the History of the Bangwaketse', 118 (citing *The Journals of Andrew Geddes Bain*, ed. by M.H. Lister, Cape Town, 1949, 61–4).
56. Paver, 'Trade and Mining', 604; Okihiro, 'Hunters, Herders, Cultivators and Traders', 64–5.
57. The Kgabo-Kwena chief Motswasele I (born *c.* 1715–45; ruled *c.* 1770–85) 'was a great traveller, and the first that ever told the Bakwains of the existence of white men' – Livingstone, *Missionary Travels*, 12. His travels were presumably before he reigned. The Ngwato broke away from the Kwena during his reign.
58. Maggs, 'Iron Age Farming Communities', 42, quoting Hedges 'Trade and Politics'.

Nkhomati and Maputo Rivers in the 1780s. Presumably this refers to larger boats than canoes, sailed by coastal traders. The expansion of tsetse-infestation up the Olifants and Limpopo Valleys in the later eighteenth century would also have given a biological advantage to coastal lowland hunters and traders in the lowveld, with partial immunity or tolerance to *nagana* and malaria.

Oral tradition about Dingiswayo's youth in the north of the Natal region around the 1780s tells of Qwaqwa–Sotho traders from the Bethlehem area west of the Drakensberg passing through Mthethwa country on their way to Delagoa Bay.[59] This suggests that the area north of the Orange River which saw the later rise of Sebetwane's Kololo was already in contact with the coast four decades earlier. But there is as yet no firm evidence of slave-trading to support Cobbing's thesis on the origins of the Kololo.[60]

Meanwhile the mercantile economy of the Cape colony was pushing trade progressively northwards. Indirect contacts across the Orange River were made as early as 1661 by the Dutch station at the Cape founded in the 1650s. What Simon Hall calls 'compression on the landscape' seems to have begun with Kora groups of Khoisan herders being pushed northwards in the seventeenth century. What is still very unclear is how this was linked to other Kora/Nama-related herders being pushed south by the Tswana kingdom of the Rolong. The Dithakong culture of stone-walled Khoisan herder sites, in the area south of modern Botswana, is dated approximately 1450–1700; while the similar 'Type-R' culture, in the Orange-Vaal triangle is dated approximately 1350–1600.[61]

Competition between Kora and Rolong north of the Orange River took a turn in favour of the Kora around 1760. The Kora of Matsatedi (Taaibosch) attacked as far north as the Ngwaketse in the south-eastern Botswana region. They were joined by Oorlam–Afrikaner trekkers, who became established as hunter-trader-raiders north of the Orange by the 1770s. Kora and Oorlam shared a common trekker culture based on firearms, horses and ox-wagons, as well as the common language of Afrikaans in the making.[62] The 1770s–90s saw bitter 'Bushmanland' wars between Khoisan and Boers on the Cape frontier south of the Orange River. The first official Dutch envoy on the Orange, Robert Gordon, mapped it and re-named it in 1779, and reported what he heard of southern Tswana trade with the Portuguese on the east

59. J. Argyle, 'Who were Dingiswayo and Shaka? Individual Origins and Political Transformations', in *Collected Seminar Papers on the Societies of Southern Africa in the 19th and 20th Centuries*, University of London, Institute of Commonwealth Studies, vol. 7, 1975–76; A. T. Bryant, *Olden Times in Zululand and Natal, Containing Earlier Political History of the Eastern-Nguni Clans*, London, 1929, 88–9.
60. J. Cobbing, 'Grasping the Nettle: The Slave Trade and the Early Zulu', in D. R. Edgecombe, J. P. C. Laband and P. S. Thompson, comps, *The Debate on Zulu Origins: A Selection of Papers on the Zulu Kingdom and Early Colonial Natal*, Pietermaritzburg, 1992.
61. See note 13 above; Maggs, *Iron Age Communities*, 293–4.
62. Legassick, 'The Northern Frontier'; Saunders 'Early Knowledge', 68–9; J–B. Gewald, '"Mountaineers" as Mantatees: A Critical Reassessment of Events Leading up to the Battle of Dithakong', M.A. dissertation, University of Leiden, 1989, 7–18. Ngcongco ('Aspects of the History of Bangwaketse', 86) remarks that *c.* 1800: 'Total warfare was not yet a characteristic feature of military conflicts in Southern Africa'.

coast. From about this time the northern trekkers were joined by European brigands – notably the Swede Hendrik Wikar, the German Jan Bloem (Blum), the Polish-Greek Stephanos, the Dutch-Huguenot Coenraad de Buys, and the Boer brothers Jacob and Carel Krieger (Kruger) – as well as by missionaries-cum-traders like the Scotsmen Robert and William Anderson.

Bloem founded his own Kora chiefdom and dynasty (hence many modern place-names, including Bloemfontein). He led his troops north to attack the Ngwaketse in 1798–99, embroiling the Kora further in western Tswana politics and war. Kora, Griqua and sometimes Boers were known collectively as the 'Masetedi' among Tswana-speakers in the nineteenth century.[63]

Official expeditions from the Cape, seeking to facilitate trade, were pushed northwards – Truter and Somerville[64] in 1801, Cowan and Donovan in 1808. The first two reached Dithakong; the second two tried to make it via the south-eastern part of modern Botswana into the Limpopo Valley trade route to the east coast. Though much mystery surrounds their fate, it is most likely that Cowan and Donovan perished from fever on the Limpopo in Laka country west of the Waterberg.[65]

Buys joined the Ngwaketse and Hurutshe around 1818, after previous polygynous sojourns among the Xhosa, Tlhaping and Rolong. He was an active participant in the rising violence, helping the Hurutshe to attack the Po/Malete of the Magaliesberg, earning a series of praise-names by which he was remembered.[66] In 1818 Buys was

63. Cf. Saunders, 'Early Knowledge', *passim*; Parsons, *New History*, 94–5; and works cited in notes 64 and 65 below. Isaac Schapera thinks 'Masetedi' was derived from *basetedi* i.e. bastards, the name by which Griqua then called themselves – personal communication.

64. For Truter and Somerville see J. Barrow, *A Voyage to Cochinchina in the Years 1792 and 1793 . . .To which is annexed an Account of a Journey made in the years 1801 and 1802 . . . To the Residence of the Chief of the Booshuana Nation . . .*, London, 1806; J. Barrow, *An Account of Travels into the Interior of Southern Africa*, London, 2nd ed, 1806; P. B. Borcherds, *An Auto-biographical Memoir of Petrus Borchardus Borcherds*, Cape Town, 1861; G.M. Theal, comp., *Records of the Cape Colony*, vol. 4, London, 1899, 77; W. Somerville, *William Somerville's Narrative of His Journeys to the Eastern Cape Frontier and to Lattakoe 1799–1802*, Cape Town, 1979. See also S. Daniell, *African Scenery and Animals*, London, 1804–5 (reprinted London, 1831; Cape Town, 1976); S. Daniell, *Sketches Representing the Native Tribes, Animals and Scenery of Southern Africa*, London, 1820.

65. For Cowan and Donovan see G. Thompson, *Travels and Adventures in Southern Africa*, Cape Town, 1967–68, (1st publ. in 1827), 210–11; S. Kay, *Travels and Researches in Caffraria Describing the Character, Customs and Moral Conditions of the Tribes Inhabiting that Portion of Southern Africa*, London, 1833, 219–20; Moffat, *The Matabele Journals*, 18–19; Livingstone, *Missionary Travels*,12; Brown, *Among the Bantu Nomads*, 233; A. Smith, *The Diary of Dr. Andrew Smith, Director of the Expedition for Exploring Central Africa, 1834–6*, ed. by P.R. Kirby, Cape Town, 1939–40, vol. 2, 162; Ngcongco, 'Aspects of the History of Bangwaketse', 93, 94. The story of the death of Cowan at the hands of the Ngwaketse in 1806–7 may be a confusion with the death of the cattle-raider Frans Krieger or Kruger Danster in 1809 – R. Wagner, 'Coenraad de Buys and the Eastern Cape Frontier', University of London, School of Oriental and African Studies Seminar, 1972, 5 (citing Moodie's *Record*, vol. 23).

66. Buys's Hurutshe friends called him 'Moro', presumably based on his habitual morning greeting to others (though the word came to mean 'coffee grounds' in Tswana); his Malete enemies remembered him as 'Diphafa', referring to the feathers in his hat – alternatively 'big beer-pots', referring to a booming voice or the bang of a gun; cf. J.T. Brown, *Secwana Dictionary*, Tiger Kloof, 1939, 73, 59, 246; Sillery, *The Bechuanaland Protectorate*, 161; Ngcongco, 'Aspects of the History of Bangwaketse', 95. He later became 'Sekgobokgobo' to the Birwa, Van Warmelo, *Tlokwa en Birwa*, 47.

joined by the escaped Cape slave Joseph Arend. Arend was told by Kwena allies of
the Hurutshe in the central trans-Vaal about the 'Macuas (or white people) residing
beyond them . . . on the opposite side of a wide water, which they cross on rafts'.
Presumably this referred to the village at Lourenço Marques fort, reached from the
west across the wide Matola River or Espirito Sancto estuary. Arend and one of
Buys's sons tried to take the eastern route – through the Drakensberg by the Olifants
Valley – in order to buy gunpowder at Delagoa Bay. But their way was blocked by
the hostility of the Pedi kingdom in the complex small wars that beset states and
chiefdoms from the Kalahari to the Drakensberg.[67]

In 1820 the missionary-traveller John Campbell reached the Hurutshe capital at
Karechuenya in the western trans-Vaal. He noted that Hurutshe trading connections
were almost entirely with the north-east and east – in the words of Breutz's
summary, 'beads, copper, iron, silver, rain-medicine and vaccine in return for ivory,
skins and cattle'.[68] Campbell was also told that Tsonga traders came to the Hurutshe
from near the coast to trade beads for ivory, arriving from both the plateau in the east
and the Limpopo Valley in the north-east.[69]

In about 1820 Buys moved along the north-eastern trade route – down the
Limpopo Valley – as far as the Tswapong hills, where he and his sons settled among
local Birwa. The motive of the move was possibly to be nearer gunpowder supplies;
the timing of the move was probably to avoid the arrival of John Campbell – as Buys
was an outlaw trying to hide from the Cape authorities.[70] The Ngwato of the
east-central Botswana region, living near the Tswapong hills, record Buys as

67. Legassick, 'The Sotho–Tswana Peoples', 108 quoting J. Campbell, *Travels in South Africa
    Undertaken at the Request of the London Missionary Society: Being a Narrative of a Second Journey in
    the Interior of that Country*, London, 1822, vol. 2, 356–9; Thompson, *Travels and Adventures*, 209–10
    outlines Arend's itinerary. Legassick speculates on a Pedi kingdom monopoly of trans-Drakensberg
    trade blocking Arend. Legassick's quote as well as mentioning 'Macuas' (see note 69 below), goes on
    to talk about a white woman trader living among brown-skinned long-haired people on the netherbank
    of the river. Might this be a conflation with knowledge of the Portuguese *prazero* settlements on the
    Zambezi? Travelling in the Orange Free State area only ten years later Arbousset (*Narrative*, 183) was
    amazed to find that people there knew about Lake Marabai, i.e. Malawi, beyond the Zambezi. Another
    Kwena tradition relating to the early nineteenth century refers to a 'Portuguese' with oxen coming from
    the direction of Angola across the Kalahari via Ghanzi to south-eastern Botswana – L. Knobel, 'The
    History of Sechele', *Botswana Notes and Records*, 1 (1968), 52.
68. Campbell, *Travels . . . Second Journey*, vol. 1, 239–41; vol. 2, 351, 358–59; Breutz, *The Tribes of
    Marico District*, 14–25; Okihiro, 'Hunters, Herders, Cultivators and Traders', 187–9, 198.
69. Tsonga traders were given various names in the interior, such as Malukwe, Malokwana, and Makwapa
    (Ma-Gwamba) – with translations such as Knopneusen/Knobnose and Stutterer, referring to facial
    scarification and barbarian language (comparable with the insulting terms *makwerekwere* now applied
    to Africans from beyond the Zambezi). Tsonga or Afro-Portuguese were also called *mahalaseela*, i.e.
    ma-hale-tsela or people from down the road (Paver, 'Trade and Mining', 609; R. Wagner,
    'Zoutpansberg: The Dynamics of a Hunting Frontier', in S. Marks and A. Atmore, eds, *Economy and
    Society in Pre-Industrial South Africa*, London, 1980, 342–3). Kwena/Hurutshe tradition also refers to
    their mythical founding chief, Thobega, as Morwa Mogaloa-tsela – Transvaal Native Affairs
    Department, *Short History*, 1905, 11; (cf. Breutz, *The Tribes of Marico District*, 68, 111, 171, 182–3; J.
    Ramsay, 'Native Myths', *Mmegi/The Reporter*, 9, 34 (10 Sept. 1992), 140.
70. W. C. Willoughby, 'The First White Man in Khama's Country'. (W. C. Willoughby Papers, Selly Oak
    Colleges, Birmingham – file No. 795); Peter M. Sebina, 'The Lost City' MS dated 1962 (Botswana
    National Archives, Gaborone – S312/5).

'Mokgowa' and as the first *mohibidu* (red person) that they had seen.[71] In 1843, after visiting the Ngwato, Livingstone reported that Buys 'after committing many acts of injustice & murder among the Southern tribes proceeded to the north-east of the Bamangwato, and there fell a victim to fever'. Ngwato traditions add that Buys died of fever in the Tswapong hills.[72] He left behind an infant son there, called Mmegale, presumably with his Birwa mother, who was brought up locally and was initiated into the Ngwato state as an adolescent in about 1834.

Buys's older sons – known as Kadise, Toro, and Toronyane – disappear from Ngwato traditions. But they reappear on the opposite side of the Limpopo valley in the traditions of other Birwa groups living in the Blouberg hills: 'Coenrad, Michael and Boris Buys, who came from the direction of Bechuanaland, and entered this country, all of them red people quite unlike the natives, and possessing guns . . . When the guns were fired, all the people fled to the hills.'[74] People had good reason to be afraid. The Buys–Birwa were to play their part as armed trader-raiders in the Tsonga–Portuguese ivory and slave trades. They were also the *voor-voortrekkers* for the Trichardt/Van Rensburg and Potgieter groups of Boers who were soon to arrive from the Cape colony.

In 1829–30 the missionary Robert Moffat, touring in the central trans-Vaal, received direct evidence of Delagoa Bay from an Ngwato traveller who had actually been there. The traveller described trade in ivory in exchange for beads and linen cloth, and denied the existence of either a slave trade or white influence beyond the Bay. He described trade in ivory and copper, and tin or zinc, with traders in boats that came up the Limpopo as far as the north-eastern trans-Vaal; and described warlike people with spearheads as large as spades, presumably Laka/Tlhako of the Waterberg, living in the hills around the rivers.[75]

71. The suggested origins of 'Makgoa'/'Makgowa' are various: (a) Sebina, 'Lost City', says derivation from *go Kgowa* ('to peel with a knife') describing the peeled red look of the visitors' skin; (b) W.J. Burchell, *Travels in the Interior of Southern Africa*, London, 1822–24, vol. 2, 312 – cited by J. Comaroff, *Body of Power, Spirit of Resistance: The Culture and History of a South African People*, Chicago, 1985, 37, thought it derived from the resemblance of people on horses to *makgoa mashweu*, 'white bush lice'; (c) references to 'Macuas' on the Mozambique coast as in Campbell, *Travels . . . Second Journey*, vol. 2, 356–9; and reference in 1779 to the Limpopo rather than the Vaal (Lekoa/Lekwa) was the wide 'Koang' River full of canoes; Saunders, 'Early Knowledge', 68–9, also give credence to derivation as an ethnic name from Afro-Portuguese traders originating among the Makua of northern Mozambique.
72. I can find no reference to Buys's residence or death in the Tswapong hills in Roger Wagner's three University of London, School of Oriental and African Studies African History Seminar papers (17 May 1972, 24 Jan. 1973 and 8 May 1974), or in his 'Coenraad Buys in Transorangia', *The Societies of Southern Africa in the 19th and 20th Centuries*, University of London: Institute of Commonwealth Studies Collected Seminar Papers, vol. 4, 1972–73, 1–8.
73. On Buys's son Mmegale, see Livingstone, *Missionary Correspondence*, 38–9, portraying him as the heathen servile gardener of a Ngwato master, with two more brothers 'he informed me . . . in servitude to another tribe'; Anon. ('A British Official'), 'In Khama's country', *Monthly Review*, 7 (June 1902), 115–16. Mmegale would have been a member of Malekantwa age-regiment, initiated about 1834.
74. Wagner, 'Transorangia', 5 – quoting Van Warmelo, *The Copper Miners*, 105. Wagner dates Coenraad de Buys as 1761–?1822, and his sons Gabriel as 1808–55, Theodorus Cornelis as 1810–?51, and Michael as 1812–88, 'Zoutpansberg', 338–9.
75. Moffat, *Matabele Journals*, vol. 1, 17–18.

Literary references to trade in ivory and beads from the Limpopo/Marico headwaters down the great valley to the sea grow more frequent after 1830. By 1835 it appears that individual Portuguese as well as Tsonga traders were reaching the western trans-Vaal with pack oxen. East coast traders were reaching as far inland as 'Ghoya' (i.e.Taung) country in what became the northern Free State, where they bargained in the 'silent trade' manner reminiscent of Portuguese elsewhere in Africa.[76]

In 1841 Laka/Tlhako traders were seeking feline furs in the western trans-Vaal for export to the sea, but Tsonga from the north-east were still the main traders. Tsonga traders were admired for their strength: they 'bear their ivory away on their shoulders'. This observation implies they had no need for slave-carriers, but did not preclude the development of slave trading in the northern trans-Vaal in the 1830s.[77]

Conclusion

In general this essay supports the conclusions of Andrew Manson, in this volume, that there was 'a continuum of change' among the chiefdoms of the highveld before the era termed the *difaqane*, perhaps 'hastened by the impact of European traders and raiders' in the last decades of the eighteenth century. That such processes were already under way, Manson adds, can be seen in the 'speed and success with which many Tswana communities transformed themselves into autonomous and independent "states"' immediately after the interruption of the *difaqane* wars.

The disruption of the *difaqane* wars far exceeded the normal birth pangs of violence that accompanied previous phases of constitutional change, as lineages grew into chiefdoms and chiefdoms grew into states. What marks off the *difaqane* wars after *c*.1820–22 is the scale and intensity of violence, and the extraordinarily predatory and mobile nature of the chiefdoms and states involved. Only children and women were incorporated into the new chiefdoms of the 1820s; adult men in chiefdoms conquered at this time were killed off.

This new scale and intensity of war on the interior plateaux were of external origin. There is no escaping the fact that oral traditions record invasion by northern Nguni-speaking people from across the Drakensberg – in other words a spill-over of what is called the *mfecane* in history books.

The historical experience of the interior lands west of the Drakensberg offers a reference model against which to compare developments east of the Drakensberg. Both areas had essentially similar cattle-centred homestead and lineage systems. But the processes of state-formation seem to have gone back to the sixteenth century or

---

76. Arbousset, *Narrative*, 179–80, 278–80; Smith, *Diary*, 42 on 'silent trade'; Moffat, *Matabele Journals*, 17–18, shows that the Portuguese forbade African traders to approach them directly; Livingstone, *Family Letters*, 44, relates how Sechele was redeemed by beads from MaLokwana *c*.1830.
77. See Okihiro, 'Hunters, Herders, Cultivators and Traders', 187–9, 211. On Tsonga strength, see H.H. Methuen, *Life in the Wilderness*, London, 1846, 146–9 (cited in Okihiro, 'Hunters, Herders, Cultivators and Traders', 187).

earlier in the area north of the Vaal, while they rapidly developed only from the later eighteenth century in the northern Natal area. In Natal, if we may pick up a previous analogy, polities were crashing through two or three 'gears' at once, from second gear lineages up to fifth gear super-states in just a few decades.

Mfecane states, and their *difaqane* imitators, were marked by an extraordinary degree of militarism and chiefly autocracy. Where did these trends come from? John Omer-Cooper and Philip Bonner have suggested that 'larger initiation schools and permanent age-groupings with a military role' were 'Sotho borrowings' among states established by northern Nguni-speakers.[78] But the obvious precedents for militarist autocracy lie in the Thembe and other states of the southern Mozambique region in the eighteenth century, whose subjects included northern Nguni-speakers, and also further back in the Rozvi super-state of the late seventeenth-century Zimbabwe region.

The Thembe case draws our attention to the impact of coastal trading and slave-raiding, as a factor in such predatory state growth. The Rozvi case draws us back to the nature of cattle-based southern African polities. The new polities remained unstable and liable to erupt in civil war so long as they depended on military predation for their patterns of accumulation and consumption of wealth. But after a generation or so they reverted to the confederative model of civil society, binding lineages and chiefdoms together with cattle-centred relationships – which redistributed wealth rather than merely consuming it.[79] As it had been among the Rozvi, so it was also to be among *mfecane* and *difaqane* states after the middle of the nineteenth century. But a new phase of external impact then began with the penetration of colonial 'industrial capital' into Africa.

78. J.D. Omer-Cooper, *The Zulu Aftermath: A Nineteenth-century Revolution in Bantu Africa*, London, 1966, 27; Bonner, *Kings, Commoners and Concessionaires*, 24–5; Smith, 'Delagoa Bay'; Smith 'The Trade of Delagoa Bay'.
79. Cf. D.N. Beach, 'Ndebele Raiders and Shona Power', *Journal of African History*, 15 (1974), 633–51.

13 Conflict in the Western Highveld/Southern Kalahari
c.1750–1820

ANDREW MANSON

The intention of this essay is to establish that the period from about 1750 to 1820 was a time of conflict on the western highveld and in the adjacent southern Kalahari characterised by warfare and raiding. It should be noted that the notion of the outbreak of 'Tswana wars' in the late eighteenth century is not new – it was mentioned by Neil Parsons in his *New History of Southern Africa* (1982).[1] This essay constitutes a fresh look at the evidence on which some of Parsons's conclusions were based – most notably, the ethnological surveys of Paul-Lambert Breutz. It also draws on my own research into the Hurutshe, and on theses by Leonard Ngcongco and Gary Okihiro on the Ngwaketse and Kwena. All of these works owe much to the pioneering work of Isaac Schapera, though his findings have not been exempt from critical evaluation.[2] I attempt to reconcile and periodise oral traditions collected by Breutz, and to flesh out some economic aspects of the conflict only suggested in the works of Schapera and Ngcongco. I also refer to Legassick's innovative work on the emergence of the Sotho/Tswana.

The essay then examines the causes of the violence and offers a discussion of the processes of state-formation among these communities. Finally, this analysis is related to the re-evaluation of the difaqane initiated by Julian Cobbing. The intention is not to contest his wide-ranging critique, but rather to stress that conflict and violence engulfed regions in southern Africa other than the Natal/Zulu kingdom area where the origins of the difaqane are said to have been.

The peoples whose history is recorded here were the inhabitants of the Tswana chiefdoms (the Kgatla, Fokeng and Kwena) located in the present-day Rustenburg district and, directly to their west, the Hurutshe in the Marico, and the Ngwaketse

---

1. N. Parsons, *A New History of Southern Africa*, London, 1982.
2. See P-L. Breutz, ed. *The Tribes of the Rustenburg and Pilanesberg Districts*, Pretoria, 1953; *The Tribes of Marico District*, Pretoria, 1953–4; A.H. Manson, 'The Hurutshe in the Marico District of the Transvaal, 1848–1914', Ph.D. thesis, University of Cape Town, 1990; L. Ngcongco, 'Aspects of the History of Bangwaketse up to 1910', Ph.D. thesis, Dalhousie University, 1976; G.Y. Okihiro, 'Hunters, Herders, Cultivators and Traders: Interaction and Change in the Kgalagadi, Nineteenth Century', Ph.D. thesis, University of California, Los Angeles, 1976. For I. Schapera's work most reference is made to his *A Short History of the BaKgatla bagaKgafela of the Bechuanaland Protectorate*, Cape Town, 1942.

351

and Kwena in the Kanye and Molepolole regions of southern Botswana. Reference will also be made to the Rolong and Tlhaping whose activities impinged on the affairs of the Hurutshe and Ngwaketse.

Major Conflicts and Political Shifts Between 1750–1820

In the years leading up to 1750 the Hurutshe chiefdom, based in what is today the Rustenburg-Marico area, seems to have been pre-eminent among the Tswana communities in the region. They appear to have contained their Ngwaketse neighbours to the west.[3] They were widely accepted as the 'senior tribe of the Bechuana'.[4] This seniority was given ritual respect in ceremonies where Hurutshe chiefs were recognised as the highest in rank.[5]

While there were periods of Hurutshe political dominance over their neighbours, the chiefdom was also subject to processes of fission and sudden economic disaster that moderated the extent of this dominance.[6] After about 1750, however, attempts were made by a range of subordinate chiefdoms to break Hurutshe hegemony in the region. Traditional ceremonial rights usually granted to the Hurutshe were ignored by the Fokeng. This led to a battle in which Thebe, the son of the Fokeng chief, Diale, was killed.[7] Around the same period the Ngwaketse began to challenge the Hurutshe. They intervened directly in Hurutshe affairs by placing a client chief, Tirwe, in control of their neighbours, and sought ways of expanding to the west.[8] These developments heralded the waning of Hurutshe ascendency among the Tswana, and conflict among groups previously controlled by the Hurutshe.

From about 1790 the Fokeng, living a little north-west of modern Rustenburg, became involved in a twenty-year hostility with the Tlokwa. The Fokeng 'warrior chief', Sekete, was killed in a skirmish with the Tlokwa in about 1800.[9] In the reign of his successor, Thethe (*c*.1805–15), war broke out between the Fokeng and the Kgatla. Simultaneously Thethe faced a challenge from his two brothers, Nameng and Noge, and sought the assistance of the Pedi. Fokeng traditions mention that Sekwati was the Pedi ruler but it was almost certain to have been Thulare, who was widening the authority of the Pedi polity in this period.[10] According to Fokeng

3. For this see Manson, 'The Hurutshe', 41; M. Leggasick, 'The Sotho-Tswana Peoples before 1800', in L. M. Thompson, ed., *African Societies in Southern Africa: Historical Studies*, London, 1969, 100.
4. G. P. Lestrade, 'Some Notes on the Political Organisation of the Bechuana', *South African Journal of Science*, 35 (1928), 427–32.
5. See I. Schapera, *Ethnic Composition of Tswana Tribes*, London, 1952, 8; F. H. W. Jensen, 'Note on the Bahurutshe', *African Studies*, 6 (1949), 41.
6. This occurred in the middle of the seventeenth century when a large faction of the Hurutshe under Mangope moved away from the main Hurutshe house at Karechuenya. See Manson, 'The Hurutshe', 41.
7. See Breutz, *The Tribes of Rustenburg*, 61.
8. Manson, 'The Hurutshe', 51; I. Schapera, 'A Short History of the Bangwaketse', *African Studies*, 1 (1942), 3.
9. Breutz, *The Tribes of Rustenburg*, 63.
10. See P. Delius, *The Land Belongs to Us: The Pedi Polity, the Boers and the British in the Nineteenth-century Transvaal*, Johannesburg, 1983, 15.

tradition, Thethe sent karosses and tobacco to the Pedi; in return they dispatched a force under Thulare's son, Maleku, which devastated the followers of Nameng and Noge.[11] Captives and cattle were taken back to Pedi country. Thethe's overture helped to induce the Pedi to attempt to win control over the hinterland on which their trade was based.[12] By 1830 when the Ndebele arrived in the area, the Fokeng appear to have been weakened and divided.

Similarly, the Kwena baMagopa, settled north-east of present-day Brits, were locked in a state of conflict with the Kgatla and the Po, a trans-Vaal Ndebele or 'Tebele' offshoot living at Wolhuterskop aboout 40 kilometres east of present-day Rustenburg. The foremost 'warrior chief' in Kwena traditions was the regent, More, who ruled from c.1750–1770. When More refused to hand control of the Kwena back to the rightful heir, Tsoku, the community divided. More settled west of the Pienaars River and several other sections of the Kwena went their own way after about 1770. Tsoku's Kwena were no match for the Kgatla, and after a major defeat Tsoku sought the assistance of his rival, More. Towards the end of the eighteenth century, the Kwena regrouped and consolidated under More.[13] Around 1820 the Kwena ba Magopa were assailed by a large combined army of the Kgatla, Hwaduba and Tlhako from the east. Heavy, though indecisive, fighting occurred. This was followed by Pedi cattle raids. By 1822 the Pedi seem to have taken control of Kwena affairs for they allocated land for settlement by the various Kwena fragments.[14] In 1834 Andrew Smith was informed by the Kwena ruler that they had lost their cattle to the Pedi in the early 1820s, before the Ndebele arrived on the highveld.[15]

The traditions of the Kgatla bagaKgafela, residing in the eighteenth century near modern Northam, north-east of the Pilanesberg, emphasize a prolonged war with the Fokeng.[16] The Kgatla became rich in cattle from these wars but in the last quarter of the century dissension arose in the community over the distribution of captured cattle. Mmagotso, previously regent of the Kgatla and uncle of the rightful heir, moved away from the new chief Pheto, and gave allegiance to the Kwena. Mmagotso attacked Pheto with support from the Kwena under Legwale but was defeated and captured. Pheto successfully centralised the Kgatla before his death in 1805. More booty fell into the hands of the Kgatla bagaKgafela shortly after his death when they assisted the Kwena to beat off an attack from the Ngwaketse.[17] Kgatla power was, however, sapped by internal rivalries between 1810 and 1824, which left them vulnerable when Sebetwane's Kololo swept on to the western highveld from 1824.[18]

11. Breutz, *The Tribes of Rustenburg*, 63.
12. Legassick, 'The Sotho–Tswana Peoples', 109.
13. Breutz, *The Tribes of Rustenburg*, 85–7.
14. Breutz, *The Tribes of Rustenburg*, 89.
15. See A. Smith, *The Diary of Dr. Andrew Smith*, ed. by P.R. Kirby, Cape Town, 1939–40, 110–11.
16. Breutz, *The Tribes of Rustenburg*, 254; Schapera, *A Short History of the BaKgatla bagaKgafela*, 12–15.
17. Breutz, *The Tribes of Rustenburg*, 254.
18. J.D. Omer-Cooper, *The Zulu Aftermath: A Nineteenth-century Revolution in Bantu Africa*, London, 1966, 94–5.

In addition to losing sway over the Tswana to the east, which gradually allowed
the Pedi to dominate affairs in the region, the Hurutshe had to deal with pressure
from the Tshidi-Rolong to the west and, from the late eighteenth century, with
rivalry from the Tlhaping who entrenched their hold over mercantile trade
emanating from the Cape colony.[19] Rolong-Hurutshe dissension is indicated by the
mention in Rolong traditions of the loss of two of their chiefs at the hands of the
Hurutshe between about 1790 and 1818. None the less, according to Rolong
traditions, large numbers of cattle were captured from the Hurutshe during raids
conducted in the late eighteenth century.[20]

Ngwaketse attempts to intercede in Hurutshe politics in about 1750 have been
alluded to. The Ngwaketse were key players in the transformations taking place in
the region under study. Isolated from the trade arteries to the east and south, they had
to assert themselves politically to gain a larger share in mercantile affairs. Their
aggrandisement occurred initially under the rule of Moleta when he defeated and
turned the Kgwatheng-Kgalagadi into tributaries. The significance of this was that it
broke the stranglehold that the Tlhaping and some Kora groups had exerted over
trade in the southern Kalahari. It was, however, the chieftainship of Makaba II
(*c.*1790–1824) that clearly marked the rise of the Ngwaketse to a position of great
prominence in the Tswana world. '. . . Makaba was a warrior chief and during his
reign fought nearly all of the chiefdoms surrounding him.'[21]

Makaba moved to Kanye hill, a position he could fortify against attack. From there
he raided the Kwena in order to seize cattle and to 'regulate . . . the frontiers of his
geographical and political control'.[22] This tendency continued for some time and in
1808 the Ngwaketse under Makaba II became involved in conflict with the Kgatla
ba Mmanaana, tributaries of the Hurutshe residing a little to their north. Makaba
inflicted a defeat on the Kgatla and siezed most of their cattle. The Kgatla then
offered allegiance to the Ngwaketse. Somewhat reluctantly (given the growing
military prowess of the Ngwaketse) the Hurutshe attempted to re-assert authority
over their former tributaries. In a confrontation with the Kgatla/Ngwaketse the
Hurutshe were defeated and their chief, Sebogodi, was killed. The Kgatla then
moved eastwards and were incorporated into the Ngwaketse.[23]

This was followed by further raids by the Ngwaketse on the Hurutshe which
prompted the Hurutshe finally to enter into a defensive alliance with the Tlhaping,
Kwena, Kgatla bagaKgafela and some Kora groups.The so-called 'war of Moabi'
(after Makaba's uncle who defected to the alliance) followed.[24]

Shortly after 1815 Coenraad de Buys, one of the growing trickle of settlers from
across the Orange River, arrived among the Hurutshe, earning the name 'Moro',

19. For a thorough account of economic developments among the Tlhaping see G. Y. Okihiro, 'Precolonial
    Economic Change Among the Tlhaping', *International Journal of African Historical Studies*, 17, 1
    (1984), 59–79.
20. See S. M. Molema, *Montshiwa 1815–1896: Barolong Chief and Patriot*, Cape Town, 1966, 8.
21. Ngcongco, 'History of Bangwaketse', 85.
22. Ngcongco, 'History of Bangwaketse', 89.
24. Ngcongco, 'History of Bangwaketse', 90.

presumably an adulteration of his first salutation, *Môre* (Afrikaans for 'Good morning'). In 1818, at the Tholwane River in the Rustenburg district, De Buys assisted the Hurutshe in an attack on the Malete, another group of recalcitrant tributaries, who had allegedly been a 'thorn in the eye' of the Hurutshe. The Malete were defeated, their capital destroyed and they were placed under the control of Senose, a powerful Hurutshe ward head.[25] De Buys then moved over to the Ngwaketse. De Buys's intervention may have been of some consequence, but it is significant that he did not initiate this friction – it had existed prior to his arrival and continued after his departure.[26]

In 1798–99 the Ngwaketse were able to beat off an attack from the Kora and Griqua under Jan Bloem. In the first decade of the next century the aggression of the Ngwaketse gave rise to the counter-action by the surrounding communities that was mentioned earlier. This forced Makaba temporarily to relocate his people closer to the Rolong, his only allies in the region. (It was only from 1817 that the Rolong fully threw their support behind Makaba after one of their raiding parties had been intercepted and routed en route to Kwena territory.) The Ngwaketse increased in numbers during this time, attracting various splinter groups from other upheavals, including some Rolong clans.[27] In 1818 a combined Ngwaketse/Rolong army attacked the Hurutshe who escaped losses by hiding their cattle before the raiders appeared.[28]

Makaba's enterprises were not confined to military activities. He followed a dual, though contradictory, policy by seeking to appease some of his neighbours. He sent cattle to Mothibi, the Tlhaping chief, and despatched envoys to the Hurutshe in 1820 to try and establish friendly relations.[29] These overtures were generally treated with suspicion, and both the Hurutshe and other Ngwaketse leaders vehemently propounded Makaba's untrustworthiness to any European visitors to their capitals. According to Ngcongco 'it was probably partly exasperation that his efforts (of reconciliation) were being thwarted by Mothibi and the Bahurutshe that led Makaba to recommence his attacks on these people'.[30]

We turn now to a consideration of the Kwena of the Kweneng district of present-day Botswana. Processes of centralisation began later in this community than in other Tswana groups in the region. Moreover, the Kwena were still primarily hunters and herders when most of their neighbours were active in long-distance trading. They did, however, obtain metals by exchanging skins and cattle with the Hurutshe and Rolong.[31] By the turn of the century the Kwena on the margins of the

25. See *The Marico Chronicle*, 16 Mar., 1912. Letter from F. Jensen.
26. See Diary of Revd J. Campbell, South African Library (hereafter SAL), Cape Town; J. Campbell, *Travels in South Africa Undertaken at the Request of the London Missionary Society: Being a Narrative of a Second Journey in the Interior of that Country*, vol. 1, London, 1822, 251.
27. Ngcongco, 'History of the Banwaketse', 90.
28. Breutz, *Tribes of Rustenburg*, 31–2.
29. See Campbell, *Travels in South Africa, Undertaken at the Request of the London Missionary Society*, 247, 264; Campbell, *Travels . . . Second Journey*, vol. 1, 266.
30. Ngcongco, 'History of Bangwaketse', 94.
31. Okihiro, 'Hunters, Herders, Cultivators and Traders', 187.

Kalahari had entered a period of rapid transformation. They began to shift from a 'small, mobile hunting and herding group to a large-scale settlement of townsmen, farmers and traders'.[32] The process of subordinating various Kgalagadi peoples of the desert reached its peak later in the nineteenth century. These servants, the Bolangwe and Shaga especially, 'were conscripted to hunt fur-bearing animals for Bakwena masters',[33] presumably to increase access to metals through trade. In the early nineteenth century there is also clear evidence for an accretion of chiefly power when the chief Motswasele 'arbitrarily confiscated the peoples' cattle to enable him to satisfy his desire for newly introduced goods'.[34] A civil war ensued in 1821 and the Kwena divided into two factions. At this time the Kwena were also attempting to break the Hurutshe stranglehold over trade, for the Revd J. Campbell's account makes frequent reference to the aggression of the Kwena towards the Hurutshe. He records in his diary that the Kwena were about to attack them on the day of his departure from the Hurutshe capital at Karechuenya.[35]

Accounting for the Conflict

From the preceding discussion it is absolutely clear that the Tswana in the west were embroiled in struggles which mirrored the political turmoil among the Ndwandwe, Qwabe, Mthethwa and Ngwane in the same period. What caused this conflict on the highveld? Firstly, a desire to increase holdings of cattle through raiding frequently led to war, particularly in the Rustenburg area. Traditions point to a rise in the level of cattle raiding. The question that follows is why should cattle raiding have increased at this time? There are two likely answers. The first is that during the middle decades of the eighteenth century the Tswana-speaking population was growing, probably due to the availability of a stable supply of food, caused, as in the eastern coastal region, by a period of consistently good rainfall. At much the same time these communities had access to fewer and fewer areas suitable for occupation. The southern Kalahari prevented expansion westwards, and to the north-east lay the Limpopo River and the tsetse fly belt so unsuited for cattle or human habitation. In this bounded context, localised fluctuations caused by the need to gain access to land for settlement and grazing would have severely disrupted local relations. The second reason for increased cattle raiding lay in the need to gain desirable trade goods which could be obtained by cattle exchange.

The seizure of women and captives constituted a further motive for the increased conflict. Captives (*malata*) and foreigners were assimilated with relative ease in to local communities through the ward system which minimised problems of administration and discontent by allowing a considerable degree of social and political independence to incorporated people. Cattle provided the basis for

32. Okihiro, 'Hunters, Herders, Cultivators and Traders', xvi.
33. Okihiro, 'Hunters, Herders, Cultivators and Traders', xvii.
34. Okihiro, 'Hunters, Herders, Cultivators and Traders', 190.
35. See Campbell *Travels . . . Second Journey*, vol. 2, 1822, 251, 260; (SAL) Diaries of Revd J. Campbell, 26.

exchange in Tswana society, as they did in many other African societies at a similar period. The exchange of wives for cattle, and of cattle for labour and loyalty, provided the basis of political life. Chiefs and powerful men accumulated cattle to distribute and thus to raise their social standing and maintain their power. The accumulation of cattle and women through raiding allowed certain chiefs to attract more followers and bind them into stronger relations of dependence.

The frequent incidence of fission taking place within chiefdoms has long been recognised by commentators as a major source of friction among the Tswana. The fission is usually ascribed to the Tswana kinship system. Though the Tswana had, in theory, well-defined rules of succession to the chieftainship, in practice, successions were bedevilled by several factors. The 'great' wife was not neccessarily the same person as the 'first' wife, leading to competition for legitimacy between the eldest sons of these two wives. In addition, the practice of levirate whereby a brother or uncle of a chief who died without issue could father a child with the 'great' wife, also led to rivalry between half-brothers.[36] Consequently the patrilineal principle of succession, coupled with the practice of polygyny, led to contests and frequently to fission.

A fourth cause of tension among these Tswana chiefdoms relates to the drought of the last decade of the eighteenth century. Coupled with land shortage and an increase in cattle this drought is likely to have had a severe effect on the Tswana chiefdoms spread in autonomous units across the western highveld region.

A final reason lies in competition over trade. The extent and range of Tswana precolonial trade is now so well documented in the archaeological and historical record that it needs no futher elaboration here.[37] The main directions of trade contact were east to Maputo Bay, north-west into the Okavango and central Namibia,and south with the Kora on the Orange River.[38] The main difficulty facing the Ngwaketse was that they were barred from the important trade routes by the Rolong in the south, and by the Hurutshe to the east, a problem they tried to remedy by adopting a policy of 'southward orientation' during the rule of Makaba.[39] The main trade goods were furs, feathers, metals (copper, iron and tin) fashioned into ornaments and tools, and tobacco. It is likely that certain groups such as the Tlhaping and Hurutshe competed strongly over trade in metals, especially copper, as there was a keen local demand for these items. The cultivation and exchange of tobacco was monopolised by the

36. See I. Schapera, *A Handbook of Tswana Law and Custom*, London, 1955, 55–6.
37. It was observed by early travellers such as Lichtenstein, Burchell and Campbell. More recently scholars have outlined in greater detail the prevalence of trade among the Tswana. See Okihiro, 'Precolonial Economic Change'; B.P. Shaw, 'State Formation, Nation Building and the Tswana of Southern Africa', M.A. dissertation, Duquesne University, Pittsburg, 1975; T. Tlou, *A History of Ngamiland 1750–1906*, Gaborone, 1985; M. Wilson, 'The Sotho, Venda and Tsonga', in M. Wilson and L.M. Thompson, *The Oxford History of South Africa*, Oxford, 1969–1971.
38. For a summary see J. Denbow, D. Kiyaga-Mulindwa and N. Parsons, 'Historical and Archaeological Research in Botswana', in R. Hitchcock, N. Parsons and J. Taylor, eds, *Research for Development in Botswana*, Gaborone, 1987.
39. The phrase is Ngcongco's. See 'History of Bangwaketse', 105.

Hurutshe.[40] Most crucial of all, was the ivory trade which occupied the attention of all the communities under discussion.

Trade goods were relayed through 'trade mates' (marts) from one district to the next.[41] The increased volume of ivory and copper through Quelimane from 1760 suggests the growing importance of the east coast trade.[42] The Hurutshe knew the names of all their trading partners as far as the Tsonga on the east coast,[43] a distance of over a thousand kilometres. In exchange for their copper, tobacco, ivory and other goods the Tswana received beads, cloth, buttons and livestock. The principal beneficiaries were the existing power-holders who were in the best position to secure a monopoly over this trade. By accumulating wealth chiefs could attract new followers and clients. The logical outcome of this argument is that attempts to control trade led to competition and conflict. Thus the Tswana-speaking communities on the western highveld were aware of the new demand for, and availability of trade goods and, building on established trade routes and practices, bound themselves into the international trade network on the best terms they could.

Two points should be emphasised here. Firstly, this trade was in goods and not in people. According to Campbell in 1820, the Hurutshe 'knew of no nations who sold men' – a suggestion that they had no knowledge of slaving taking place in the region.[44] Secondly, the escalation in trade would not have severely disrupted communities geared to an exchange economy, but when combined with factors mentioned – drought, succession disputes, land shortages and so on – its impact was significant.

To conclude this section we need to order these factors into some meaningful pattern. A shortage of land for grazing and agriculture, coupled with the sudden demand for ivory, raised competition and conflict in the region to a new pitch. The effect on these communities was to bring to an end the period of fission that characterised the period up to about 1770–1780. Larger military and political alliances began to proliferate around the end of the century (viz. the Kgatla/ Hwaduba/Tlokwa in the Rustenberg-Pilanesberg area, the Tlhaping/Kwena/ Hurutshe and the Ngwaketse/Rolong further west). From the early nineteenth century, fusion, as many historians of the Tswana now agree, became the dominant process among Tswana chiefdoms.[45] From the last decades of the eighteenth century the number of new wards in which previously independent groups came together escalated.[46] The problem of chiefly succession continued to counter this process, but was eventually outweighed by the declining availability of good lands which put a brake on expansion and fission, except at the expense of one's neighbours.

40. Campbell, *Travels . . . Second Journey*, vol. 1, 226.
41. The evidence for this is contained in Campbell, *Travels . . . Second Journey*, vol. 2, 274.
42. Campbell, *Travels . . . Second Journey*,. vol. 2, 274.
43. Campbell, *Travels . . . Second Journey*, vol. 2, 240–1.
44. Campbell, *Travels . . . Second Journey*, vol. 2, 242.
45. The idea was articulated with most precision by Legassick in 'The Sotho–Tswana Peoples', 106–107.
46. See Schapera, *Ethnic Composition*.

Consequently, as Basil Sansom has noted, a 'tendency to predation prevailed once chiefdoms became embattled within boundaries'.[47] The process of amalgamation was uneven and incomplete by the time that the first of the desperate victims from the south – the Fokeng, Phuthing and Hlakwana – arrived in the area. The Ngwaketse had welded themselves into a polity strong enough to withstand these new pressures, but the Kwena, Fokeng and Kgatla of the Rustenburg district, who were weak and still in the process of being drawn into the orbit of Pedi dominance, succumbed with little resistance.[48] The once powerful Hurutshe clung precariously to their severely diminished base at Karechuenya. Their fortunes took a turn for the worse when in mid-1820 a large section under Senose seceded to form the Hurutshe boo-Mokgathla.[49]

From this discussion of the Tswana chiefdoms in the western highveld/southern Kalahari region prior to 1820, the following conclusions can be drawn. Firstly, in this period all the chiefdoms attempted either to expand the territory they controlled and to bring other communities under their control, or they sought to attach themselves to chiefdoms which could offer protection. To facilitate expansion and the incorporation of new followers, certain ruling factions had to increase their authority by centralising the various organs of state power.

Secondly, bureaucratic structures were developed at all levels of Tswana society to cope with the process of amalgamating 'separate communities into larger confederations'.[50] As B.P. Shaw put it in his study of state-formation amongst the Tswana, 'Tswana polities had a . . . well developed, centralised political organisation with . . . power concentrated in the hands of the chief.'[51] While the causes of this state-formation were similar to those that scholars suggest for the emergence of centralised states in the eastern coastal region,[52] these processes amongst the Tswana chiefdoms were not as far advanced as they were among Nguni-speakers such as the Mthethwa and Ndwandwe.[53] The signs of the acquisition and retention of power by certain Tswana chiefs were visible in the development of agencies and institutions that served to order and rank Tswana society. This was reflected in the political and social hierarchy that prevailed in Tswana chiefdoms and which so impressed the early European writers on the Tswana. Recent research has also revealed the level of economic stratification caused by differential access to resources. Margaret Kinsman, for example, has analysed the position of women and dependant groups,

47. B. Sansom, 'Traditional Economic Systems', in W.D. Hammond-Tooke, ed., *The Bantu-speaking Peoples of Southern Africa*, London, 1974, 258.
48. The process was probably slowed down by the death of Thulane in 1822 and the subsequent civil war between his sons. See Delius, *The Land Belongs to Us*, 15.
49. Manson, 'The Hurutshe', 58.
50. Legassick, 'The Sotho–Tswana Peoples', 106.
51. Shaw, 'State Formation', 94.
52. These have been put forward by Hedges, Bonner, Wright, Smith and Guy, amongst others.
53. For a clear discussion of events among the Nguni-speakers at this time see J.B. Wright, 'Political Transformations in the Thukela–Mzimkhulu Region of Natal in the Late Eighteenth and Early Nineteenth Centuries', in this volume. The hypotheses outlined by Wright rest on a vast body of work which principally examines the rise of the Zulu kingdom under Shaka.

showing that their subordination lay in legal circumscriptions and property relations which denied them ownership of cattle.[54]

Thirdly, the 'Tswana wars' severely reduced the cohesion and economic independence of certain groups (for example, the Kwena ba Magopa and Fokeng) who were in the process of being incorporated into larger political units. The economic and political insecurity of such communities was due almost entirely to intra-Tswana rivalries and political developments that pre-date and owe little to non-African intervention in the region. There is no doubt, however, that individuals such as Buys, Bloem and their Griqua and Kora allies added to the general insecurity of the period. The ease with which the Ndebele settled the highveld was due as much to the fact that the Tswana were caught up in a process of profound political change, leading to the emergence of new alignments and states, as it was due to the growth of Ndebele power. The defeat of the Pedi by the Ndebele (or the Ndwandwe) allowed the victors to take over, with relative ease, those communities formerly under Pedi authority.

Given these three points it seems that we cannot talk of the violence of the 1820s as having one source, or even several centres. These arguments do not discount the possibility of pressure from the coastal regions associated with the rise of big trading states, nor of enormous demands for labour which Cobbing sees as emanating from the Cape colony and Delagoa Bay. However there is also a need to look at the view offered on the horizon of the western highveld where, as this essay has demonstrated, dramatic developments took place in the last decades of the eighteenth century. The picture that begins to emerge is that there was a more generalised 'time of troubles' sweeping the entire western (and probably central and northern) highveld. It was the result of ongoing processes that were not initiated by the impact of European traders and raiders though they may have been hastened by them. These changes and transformations originated many decades before white penetration of the area. Thus the situation was not entirely comparable to that south of the Thukela River, where, by the 1820s, as John Wright has shown, the Zulu and British mercantile interests were competing directly for control over the territories around Port Natal.[55]

Furthermore, a look at the situation prevailing among the Tswana communities suggests that we should not approach this period from the point of view of counter arguments about 'Zulucentrism' and 'Eurocentrism', but from a wider perspective that includes societies beyond these confines. The heightened violence and upheavals of the 1820s should be seen as an event, albeit profound, in a continuum of change that engulfed chiefdoms on the western highveld. It did not represent a major break from the past heralding the dawn of capitalism into southern Africa. The speed and success with which many Tswana communities transformed themselves into

---

54. For a discussion of this see M. Kinsman, 'Notes on the Southern Tswana Social Formation', in K. Gottschalk and C. Saunders, eds, Collected Papers, Centre for African Studies, vol. 2, University of Cape Town, 1981; and M. Kinsman, 'Beasts of Burden: The Subordination of Southern Tswana Women, *ca*. 1800–1840', *Journal of Southern African Studies*, 10, 1 (1983), 39–54.
55. Wright, 'Political Transformations'.

autonomous and independent 'states' from the 1840s suggests that the process of state formation was under way by the late eighteenth century. The stimuli of external pressures and threats, of mercantile capital and of new technology hastened and shaped this transformation, but did not introduce it. Cobbing would appear to be overstating his case, otherwise credible in many respects, by asserting that African societies were simply 'broken down and exploded by the (capitalist) system', or that this same system 'jolted them into life'.[56] As this contribution has indicated, these societies were very much alive and robustly kicking.

56. See J. Cobbing, 'Jettisoning the Mfecane (with *Perestroika*)', seminar paper presented to the African Studies Institute, University of the Witwatersrand, Johannesburg, 1988, 15.

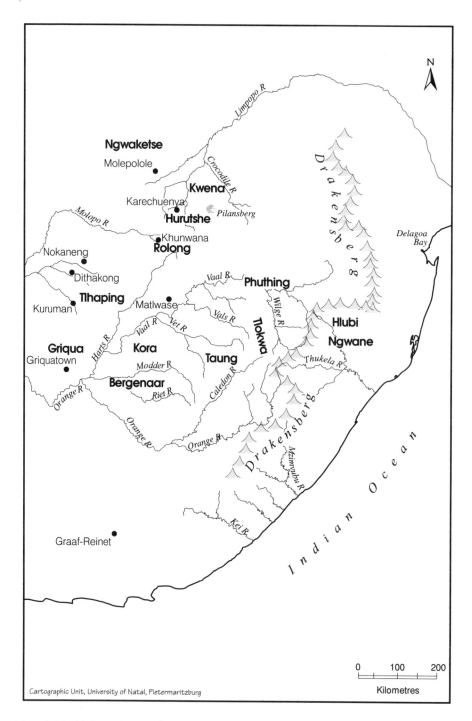

Map 11. The highveld in the early nineteenth century

14 'Hungry Wolves'
The Impact of Violence on Rolong Life, 1823–1836

MARGARET KINSMAN

Since the publication of John Omer-Cooper's *The Zulu Aftermath* in 1966 much has been said in textbooks and lecture theatres about the Difaqane on the highveld. Yet, despite this acclaim, so little research has been done on the subject that historians actually know very little about its dynamic or impact. They tend to describe what happened on the highveld through reference to old and very confusing military maps, criss-crossed with diverse paths of warfare. To explain the map, a confusing list of raiders' names is usually offered, accompanied by a description of the battle of Dithakong, which is cited as a typical event of the period. Generalised comparisons are the next level of explanation. Typical of these is the claim that the Sotho were able to build confederations, while the Tswana were not – which, incidentally, is not true.[1]

So superficial is our knowledge of the period that it quite easily lends itself to erroneous interpretations. The old myth of the 'emptied land', although still held by arch-conservative ideologues, has long since been discredited and needs little more comment here. Similarly, the nineteenth-century notion of naked barbarism and unlimited blood-letting on the highveld has also been overthrown. Yet the ongoing silence about what actually happened on the highveld in the 1820s and 1830s and the continuing void in analysis still leads to confusion.

The latest proposition, put forward by Julian Cobbing, is that the Difaqane on the highveld did not occur at all, but was a carefully crafted myth used to cover up the violence of Cape-based slavers. Cobbing has sought to disprove the Difaqane on the highveld by discrediting contemporary missionary reports on the battle of Dithakong.[2] His analysis, however, is highly problematic. To begin with, his reading of specific documents is biased and gravely distorts the process of historical reconstruction.[3] He further neglects to state that the battle was part of a larger regional movement of people, witnessed and recorded by a number of Europeans and Africans. Documents storing these observations were produced at different

1. See, for example, T.R.H. Davenport, *South Africa: A Modern History*, Johannesburg, 1987, 18–21; J.D. Omer-Cooper, *A History of Southern Africa*, London, 1987, 59–66; or, K. Shillington, *History of Southern Africa*, Harlow, 1987, 47–51.
2. J. Cobbing, 'The Mfecane as Alibi: Thoughts on Dithakong and Mbolompo,' *Journal of African History*, 29 (1988), 487–519.
3. See G. Hartley, 'The Battle of Dithakong and "Mfecane" Theory' in this volume.

times and places, and reflect the experiences of a wide range of individuals. These documents go far beyond the eye-witness accounts of missionaries which Cobbing singled out for criticism. They include the writings of European hunters and the diaries of missionaries from competing mission societies – who, incidentally, would have been quick to pick up any misconduct on the part of the Dithakong missionaries. They include the contemporary statements and later oral recollections of African participants in, and victims of, the raids. Moreover, they include group memories of the period as they were later encoded in African oral traditions and praise poems. Scattered and problematic though these sources are, they combine to support the argument that the raids which textbooks attribute to the Difaqane did in fact take place.

Yet the question still remains: if what we now call the Difaqane did in fact occur, what was its dynamic? What was its historical significance?

The example of the Rolong allows one to put forward new propositions about the nature of the Difaqane on the highveld and its long term significance. What is now called the Difaqane by historians was actually a string of superficially disconnected raids, which continued between 1822 and 1836. Significantly, it was not one raid or even scattered raiding which splintered community life. It took persistent raiding and continued displacement over a number of years finally to break African communities apart. One can conclude that it was not the physical violence of the period that led to community breakdown, but the loss of vital economic resources which had formerly underpinned extended settlements.

This essay examines the impact of raids in the 1820s and 1830s on a group of related Rolong communities which lived between the Molopo and Vaal Rivers in the southern highveld. The Rolong had long built towns in the area, basing town life on mixed agriculture and extensive hunting and trade networks.[4] The raids of the 1820s and 1830s profoundly challenged Rolong communities with repeated displacement and often stark destitution. Town life was interrupted as raids put communities to flight. The forced abandonment of sown fields, the loss of herds, as well as the often unsuccessful search for secure lands, tore at the fabric of Rolong society. Poverty and insecurity drove many families from their historic communities. Some sought shelter with old allies like the Kora or even with the militant bands disrupting the region, while others found refuge in the old hunting districts. Remnant communities continued to cluster around different chiefs, but these were driven by the hard times to search out new ways of surviving. Even in chiefs' settlements an increasing number eked out a living through hunting and collecting, while some turned to migrant labour and commodity production to get the resources needed to rebuild town life.

The disintegration of town life signalled the beginning of deep social change. Chiefs, community elders and even fathers had previously used their control over

---

4. See Q.N. Parsons 'Prelude to *Difaqane* in the Interior of South Africa, *c*.1600–*c*.1822', in this volume.

livestock to secure their control over subordinates and sons. The severe livestock losses of the 1820s limited the extent to which they could continue to do this. Increasingly the youth and the poor looked to new avenues – outside the direct control of elders and chiefs – for acquiring the livestock they needed.

The Difaqane coincided with the expansion of Cape-based trade and European settlement in the region and, in turn, facilitated it. Increasingly, African men could seek wealth outside the networks of subordination which operated within their own settlements by involving themselves in migrant labour and peasant production. The 1820s and 1830s, then, saw the beginning of slow, complex and profound social processes of social and economic transformation in African communities on the highveld, These changes would play an increasing role in shaping African interaction with European merchants and settlers.

It is difficult to establish with clarity what happened to the Rolong in the the 1820s and 1830s. They were raided by what may appear to be a confusing variety of groups. To make matters worse, each raiding party had its own internal structure and purpose, which meant that each affected the Rolong in slightly different ways. To make sense of the material, I have divided the events in two, dealing with the period between 1823 and 1826 first, and then moving on to the decade between 1826 and 1836. The period between 1823 and 1826 was characterised by unpredictable raiding undertaken by a variety of small communities who were largely in search of resources for consumption or production. Like the Rolong they were looking for survival. The second period, between 1826 and 1836, was quite different. It was dominated by the introduction and expansion of the Ndebele state on the western highveld. Ndebele raiding had a geopolitical intent. As a result, it was more predictable, but far more destructive.

In order to clarify what happened during each period, I start by describing the raiders. Identifying their composition and motivations begins to explain the impact they had on the Rolong communities. I then move on explore that impact in detail.

The Turmoil of 1823–26

Between 1823 and 1826, the Rolong of the western highveld experienced a series of intermittent, small-scale raids by parties bent on acquiring subsistence resources. The chronology of the raiding is complex and often confusing. Figure 1 summarises the events of 1823, the most difficult period.

In 1823 the Rolong fell victim to a series of raids undertaken by the Phuting, the Hlakwana, and possibly also the Fokeng,[5] all of whom had fled their homelands in

---

5. Cobbing, 'The Mfecane as Alibi', argues that the Hlakwana and Phuting were not involved in this early raiding in the west. Rather, he argues that the battle at Dithakong, usually ascribed to the two groups, was in fact a slave raid, mounted by the Griqua and supported by the missionaries. Cobbing, however, based his interpretation on a limited number of texts and was quite biased in his analysis. A careful review of evidence suggests that these groups were indeed involved.

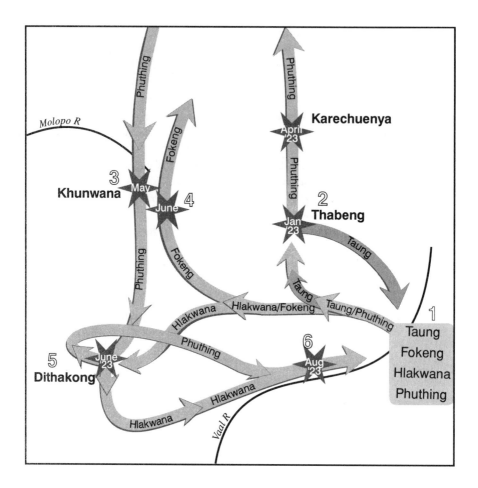

Figure 1. Movements of raiders in 1823

1. By the second half of 1822, turmoil and widespread raiding in the eastern highveld put numerous communities on the move, including the Phuthing, Hlakwana, Fokeng and Taung.

2. By December 1822, and in January 1823, various groups reached the Vaal River and then moved off in different directions. The Phuthing went far north to raid in the western highveld; the Taung occupied Thabeng and then returned east; the Hlakwana and Tokeng continued west.

3. The Phuthing swung south to raid Khunwana and then moved south towards Dithakong.

4. The Fokeng occupied Khunwana and then moved north, returning to raid the Rolong in June.

5. The Hlakwana and Phuthing joined at the battle of Dithakong, but, once defeated, retreated separately.

6. The Phuthing and Hlakwana retreated along the Vaal.

the east shortly before. Although they caused widespread devastation, these groups had abandoned the region by September 1823. Between 1824 and 1826, however, more effective bands, consciously organised for brigandage, raided in the region. In the east, far more disciplined bands under the leadership of the Taung raided the Rolong under Sefunela, while in the west, the Fokeng raided Rolong communities under Tawane and Gontle.

It is important to consider the situation of the aggressors, for their own impoverishment and bewilderment begins to explain the wreckage and dislocation which occurred during this period. The task is difficult. At most, scraps of evidence remain regarding the background and development of the raiding parties. It is particularly difficult to reconstruct the experiences of the Fokeng. Still, sufficient details remain about the Phuthing, Hlakwana and Taung to enable us to reconstruct in a very cursory way the circumstances which drove them to plunder.

The History of the Raiders

It seems that prior to the 1820s, the Phuthing and Hlakwana were self-sufficient subsistence producers, residing on the eastern highveld. Practising mixed agriculture, they probably settled in clusters of villages which shared common families of notables in loosely knit confederacies.[6] The Phuthing, living further east, seem to have been the first to be displaced in raids and to have splintered. One Phuthing fragment, for example, took to arms, and according to Hlakwana traditions, attacked the Hlakwana. The Phuthing were defeated and tradition says they were driven into a river to drown. Another surviving Phuthing section, still reeling from a previous raid, was attacked by the Ngwane. They fled their homeland, as did the Hlakwana who, according to tradition, were also then attacked by the Ngwane: 'They first fought the Matabel [Ngwane]: and upon being conquered by them fled and all the tribes they approached fled.'[7]

Robert Moffat, citing information gained from Phuthing and Hlakwana stragglers, reported that the two communities were forced to abandon sown fields and were stripped of their herds. 'Like many pastoral people,' he noted, 'when robbed of their cattle they have nothing left.'[8] Forced, then, to depend for their livelihood on plunder, they fled the turmoil of the eastern trans-Vaal for the west.[9] To the astonishment of the southernmost Tswana, 'their object seems not so much to war, as

6. Information regarding the early structure of these groups is particularly scanty, but this is the impression left in existing accounts of the period. See, A. Smith, The *Diary of Dr. Andrew Smith*, vol. 1, P. R. Kirby ed., Cape Town, 1939–40, 136. For the following accounts of the two groups, see D. F. Ellenberger, *History of the Basuto*, New York, [1969], 139. Ellenberger is undoubtedly a problematic source, but until more research is undertaken on the history of these groups, his account is the best one available.
7. Smith, *Diary*, vol. 1, 391–2.
8. M. Moffat and R. Moffat, *Apprenticeship at Kuruman*, I. Schapera, ed., London, 1951, 102 and 372 (quote from 372); and R. Moffat, *Missionary Labours and Scenes in Southern Africa*, London, 1842, 360.
9. University of London, Wesleyan Methodist Missionary Society Archives (hereafter WMMS), Broadbent, Maquassi, 8 June 1823. The quote is from a diary entry dated 25 Jan. 1823.

to devour the produce of the land of which they get possession'.[10] And the extremity of their deprivation came to characterise them in southern Tswana eyes as 'hungry wolves'.[11]

It was not the military capacity of the Phuthing and Hlakwana which overwhelmed their victims, rather their sheer numbers. Melvill, who witnessed their attack on Dithakong in June 1823, guessed the Phuthing and Hlakwana to be roughly 30 000 in number.[12] Moffat placed their combined followings at 50 000.[13]

Yet each was a motley amalgam with disparate traditions. At the core of each group were either Phuthing or Hlakwana refugees – men, women and children – who had fled together as a group at the time of the Ngwane incursions.[14] None the less, they 'increased their numbers as they have travelled, conquering different tribes, living by plunder'.[15]

It is likely that few, if any, of the refugees understood the background of their new leaders. A Tswana woman who joined the Phuthing, for example, could say little of their origins, other than that they came from a distant land.[16] Rather, it would seem that they joined the plundering groups in panic. Four Hurutshe women taken after the battle of Dithakong rationalised their joining the marauders in the shrill tones of desperation: 'The Bahurutse [Hurutshe] are no more . . . Kureechane [Karachuenya, the principal Hurutshe settlement] is destroyed. Many of its inhabitants, including Leeuwqueeling [Diutwileng] the regent, are killed and the remainder scattered in the fields without cattle.'[17] The account is an exaggeration and, perhaps more than anything else, reflects the fear of indigency which drove the victims to seek security with the victimisers. The first response of both Melvill and Moffat to the testimony of the prisoners taken after the battle at Dithakong was that the Phuthing and Hlakwana had become quite heterogeneous, their followings bringing with them disparate experiences.[18] Their first impressions possibly better described the Phuthing and Hlakwana than all their subsequent efforts at historical reconstruction.

Little security could have been found with the aggressors, however, for their relentless impetus for raiding remained hunger. The Phuthing were known to pillage both the garden grounds and the herds of the communities they overcame. Still, such stores were insufficient to support the group, and the Phuthing left in their wake a scattering of wounded, enfeebled, and starving stragglers. S. Broadbent and

10. Moffat and Moffat, *Apprenticeship*, 77.
11. Moffat and Moffat, *Apprenticeship*, 78.
12. The comment regarding the strength of sheer numbers is drawn from the information taken from messengers about the fall of Khunwana. Moffat and Moffat (1951), *Apprenticeship*, 78. For Melvill's estimate see National Archives, Cape Town Depot (hereafter CA), CO 185, Melvill.
13. Moffat and Moffat, *Apprenticeship*, 95.
14. Smith, *Diary*, vol. 1, 391–2.
15. WMMS 300/2/10, Hodgson, Maquassi, 9 Aug. 1823.
16. Moffat, *Missionary Labours*, 355.
17. Moffat and Moffat, *Apprenticeship*, 95.
18. (CA) CO 185, Melvill; Hodgson forwarded Moffat's opinions. WMMS 300/2/10, Hodgson, Maquassi, 9 Aug. 1823.

T. Hodgson, for example, encountered several small Phuthing parties in the bushy koppies near Thabeng after the departure of the main body in January 1823.[19] Melvill reported that after the battle at Dithakong and eventual evacuation of the Phuthing from the Tlhaping area in August 1823, hundreds of women stragglers remained at Dithakong, Kuruman and Nokaneng.[20] Melvill and Moffat attempted to collect them together, but only a small number would come. The remainder stayed behind when they encountered food of any kind.[21] Finally, the Phuthing retreat past Thabeng in the east in September 1823 must be counted as one of the most wretched scenes of the period. Broadbent learned from Rolong scouts that 'small parties here and there' had strayed behind the main Phuthing body, 'and they appeared in a most wretched plight from want of food'.[22] Moroka, the Rolong chief's son, closely watched the movements of the Phuthing and reported that stragglers were 'chiefly women' and many had 'died of hunger and fatigue'.[23] So enfeebled were the parties that the Rolong 'were cutting off scores of the poor stragglers'.[24] When considering the impact of the lumbering multitude, one must remember this degree of destitution.

Like the Phuthing and Hlakwana, the Taung suffered greatly as a result of the devastating raids on the eastern highveld. According to the Taung chief, Moletsane, it was a time of 'confusion and desolation', and the Taung 'saw themselves ruined'.[25]

Yet, unlike the Phuthing and Hlakwana who suffered severe losses of their herds, the Taung abandoned their homelands before falling victim to direct raids.[26] Like some of their western Ghoya neighbours, they seem to have maintained some semblance of corporate unity, and with this cutting edge organised raiding parties amongst themselves, apparently attempting through brigandage to regain sufficient cattle to reconstruct their former village life.

The Taung, who squatted in the abandoned town of Thabeng in January 1823, seemed more interested in finding refuge than in plunder. The Rolong had been able to remove their herds when evacuating the town, but the Taung eventually consumed the settlement's harvest.[27] Little is known of the structure of the Taung at this time, but the ease with which the Rolong defeated them in February 1823 suggests that

19. See, for example, South African Library (hereafter SAL), Methodist Missionary Archives (hereafter MMS), XIII, Hodgson, Journal 7, 24 Jan. 1823.
20. (CA) GR10/2, Melvill, Griqua Town, 21 July 1823. They were found as far south as Tlosi Fountain, two days journey south of Kuruman. See Moffat, *Missionary Labours*, 367.
21. (CA) CO 185, Melvill.
22. S. Broadbent, *A Narrative of the First Introduction of Christianity Amongst the Barolong Tribe of Bechuanas, South Africa*, London, 1865, 67.
23. (SAL) MMS XIII, Hodgson, Journal 11, 9 Aug. 1823; WMMS 300/2/10, Hodgson, Maquassi, 9 Aug. 1823.
24. Broadbent, *Narrative*, 67.
25. R. Germond, ed., *Chronicles of Basutoland*, Morija, 1967. Germond quotes a letter from Moletsane dates 8 January 1852. It is also found in G.M. Theal, ed., *Basutoland Records*, vol.1, Cape Town, 1883, 517.
26. Tradition had it that they even retained the poles and mats with which they made houses. Ellenberger, *History of the Basuto*, 165.
27. (SAL) MMS XIII, Hodgson, Journal, 20 June 1823.

they still used decentralised, village-based methods for organising raids. A party of 50 to 60 Rolong fighters attacked the Taung, killed 20 and captured a Taung 'captain'.[28]

Between 1823 and mid-1824, however, Taung military organisation seems to have undergone a fundamental change. In December 1823 the Taung headed a confederacy of raiding parties from six villages which began military operations in the present-day Orange Free State.[29] In early 1824 this body threatened the Rolong chief, Sefunela, and, in slightly reduced form, attacked the chief's settlement in May 1824, ostensibly for revenge.[30] After the town was taken, however, the confederacy split. According to a Rolong man taken prisoner by the Taung, 'a savage and bloody battle ensued'.[31] Thereafter, the main body of the Taung with its Ghoya allies returned to their home base along the Vals and Sand Rivers,[32] while a smaller splinter group followed the Rolong to Phitsane, raiding Kora and Tlhaping settlements on their way.

This splinter raiding group went through a significant transformation in the process. According to the Rolong prisoner, the Taung commando which followed Sefunela was 'not so numerous, but bold'.[33] It adopted forced marches, utilised complex stratagems to entrap townspeople in their settlements, and now struck in pre-dawn raids.[34] Raiding had become the focal point, the central item of discussion of the commando.[35] And Moletsane, who took control over this section of the Taung after the battle at Phitsane, recalled that he was 'carried away with his success', and determined to continue raiding north of the Molopo River.[36] From this time onwards, Moletsane's Taung began to attract a variety of local ruffians, so that by 1827 the group was a mixed bag of brigands.[37]

Unlike the Phuthing and Hlakwana, the Taung were less interested in immediate consumption, than in amassing herds which could be brought back to their home villages. The Rolong prisoner taken in 1824 noted that the Taung 'have at present many fat cattle and a few sheep', and would 'eventually return to their own country when they are completely enriched with spoils'.[38] In the eyes of the Taung, such raiding may have been necessary for restoring village life, and when raiding to the north was obviated by the Ndebele presence in the late 1820s, the Taung turned to migrant labour in the Cape colony.[39]

---

28. (SAL) MMS XIII, Hodgson, Journal, 22 Feb. 1823.
29. The entry implies that women and children were not active in fighting, unlike the Phuthing and Hlakwana parties. (SAL) MMS, Hodgson, Journal 12, 26 Dec. 1823.
30. The militias were led by Moletsane's father, Mophethe, and another Taung leader, Mokhedi, as well as by three Ghoya headmen. WMMS 300/1/2, Edwards, Griqualand, 8 Jan. 1826; Theal, *Basutoland Records*, vol. 1, 517.
31. Moffat and Moffat, *Apprenticeship*, 150.
32. Theal, *Basutoland Records*, vol. 1, 517.
33. Moffat and Moffat, *Apprenticeship*.
34. Moffat and Moffat, *Apprenticeship*, 147.
35. Moffat and Moffat, *Apprenticeship*, 150.
36. Theal, *Basutoland Records*, vol. 1, 517.
37. WMMS 300/2/21, Hodgson, Platberg, 23 June 1827.
38. Moffat and Moffat, *Apprenticeship*, 150.
39. 'A Sketch of Native Traditions', *Diamond Fields*, 10 Aug. 1871.

The Impact of Early Raids on Sefunela's Rolong

The seemingly perpetual upheaval of these years tore at the fabric of Rolong society. Chiefly power, supported by the chief's ownership of large herds and his ability to loan cattle to his followers, nearly collapsed as a result of the large-scale losses in livestock. Similarly, the extended family structure, as well as the ward system, were severely threatened by livestock losses and by repeated forced abandonment of sown fields.[40] With the very basis of its subsistence production so reduced, Rolong society was shaken to its core.

Social and economic disintegration, however, were not caused by a single raid or a single evacuation, but resulted from the continued attrition of resources over the years, which sapped Rolong social life, though it did not totally extinguish it. The process of fragmentation occurred in three ways: forced displacement, impoverishment of town residents, and the shedding of households as families sought subsistence elsewhere. It is to the study of this fragmentation that we must now turn.

The Chronology of Raiding

The Rolong community under Sefunela was repeatedly forced to abandon its settlements between 1823 and 1826. The Phuthing attack on their town at Thabeng in January 1823 forced the Rolong to evacuate the settlement and to seek shelter in open land to the west. The Taung occupied the town until March, persuading the Rolong to pause before resettling at Matlwase in April 1823. They enjoyed only a short-lived peace, however, for the Taung expelled Sefunela's following from Matlwase in May 1824 and followed them in their flight west. And, although Sefunela led his community to the Vaal River in the hopes of negotiating a refuge with the Griqua to the south, the chief's unhappy encounter with the Griqua captain, Andries Waterboer, convinced him to join other Rolong communities on the Molopo River. Though raided yet again by the Taung at Setlagoli, Sefunela imposed forced marches on his following and joined the Rolong at Phitsane in August 1824. Once again Sefunela's community fell victim to Taung brigandage, after which it retired along the Molopo River.

Sefunela made numerous excursions east between February and June 1825, attempting to forge an alliance with various Griqua and Kora bands to force the Taung from the Matlwase area. Even though these efforts failed, Sefunela's community made preparations to resettle Matlwase in June 1825, and the rebuilding of the town began in July. The failure of a Rolong raid against the Taung in September 1825, however, resulted in the Rolong abandoning the town, and Sefunela took up a migratory life along the Vaal River. Clearly, the continued displacement gradually drained Sefunela's Rolong of their economic viability.

---

40. For a more detailed study of the southern Tswana social formation, see M. Kinsman, 'The Social Formation of the Southern Tswana', paper presented to the African Studies Seminar, University of Cape Town, 1980.

The Impact of Violence on Sefunela's Rolong between 1823 and 1826

The advance of the Phuthing along the Vaal River in December 1822 and January 1823 caused widespread alarm, and communities over a wide strip of territory abandoned their settlements. Hodgson and Broadbent rummaged through the debris of several deserted villages when travelling up the Vaal at this time. Hodgson noted of one village formerly occupied by Kora and Tswana families:

> Here was seen a Bechuana house left half built; and there were scattered about part of the sticks and mats of which the Coranna houses are formed, and which they usually convey with them . . . Here lay a dish, and there a spoon, etc., clearly indicating the distress and agitation of mind under which the inhabitants fled.[41]

Broadbent described another Koran village, where fighting had clearly taken place.

> In some parts, houses were broken and partly burnt. Here and there were strewn wooden utensils, and sometimes skeletons who had been slain in the assault, or of children who had been left by their friends, and had been killed by the enemy, or perished from want.[42]

Despite the appearance of a helter-skelter evacuation of the region, the Phuthing had already become so numerous and their march sufficiently slow to forewarn communities of their approach. Thus, although fighting between Sefunela's men and the Phuthing occurred, the majority of townspeople seem to have escaped with whatever they could carry and, more significantly, with the great bulk of their herds.[43] Sefunela, Moroka (the heir apparent), and possibly a majority of the townspeople fled north-west, while the chief's brother, Tshabadira, and a large number of fighters stayed behind, probably to protect the main body's retreat. They later regrouped in refuge.[44]

The community sheltered near present-day Wolwespruit and occupied a series of temporary camps, moving as pasture or water resources were exhausted or when new hunting sites were spotted.[45] It was an awkward itinerancy. Sefunela's camp alone consisted of 482 households. Surrounding it were cattle posts, lying anywhere

---

41. A. Hodgson, *Memoirs of Mrs. Anne Hodgson*, W. Shaw, comp., London, 1836, 135.

42. Broadbent, *Narrative*, 37.

43. W.G.A. Mears, *Wesleyan Barolong Mission in TransOrangia, 1821–84*, Cape Town, 1968. Broadbent gave a rather beautiful description of the Wesleyan missionaries' encounter with Tshabidira: 'we saw clouds of dust ascend into the air, then heard the lowing of hundreds of cattle, bleating sheep and goats, driven by a mixed multitude of men, women, and children, accompanied by a host of armed soldiers', Broadbent, *Narrative*, 28.

44. Broadbent, *Narrative*, 37.

45. While journeying to visit Sefunela, Hodgson passed through one of the chief's camps which had already been abandoned. (SAL) MMS, Hodgson, Journal 8, 9 Feb. 1823. According to Hodgson, the community moved again on 16 Mar. 1823, 2 Apr. 1823 and 5 Apr. 1823.

from a half-day's to a day's journey away, where were found 'sufficient numbers' of people 'to protect the cattle in case of attack'.[46]

However, it was most probably the sheer size of Sefunela's following that forced it to remain on the move: having abandoned their gardens, the Rolong were dependent on wild foods and milk, supplemented by game meat, and all three resources (pasture, wild plants and game) in any one locality were likely to be rapidly exhausted by the community.

When considering resettlement, the prospect of a lost grain harvest continued to preoccupy Sefunela.[47] Grain was critical to the Rolong food supply, particularly in the dry season between August and October, when the withering of grass curtailed milk supplies and there were few wild fruits. The Taung, it was known, had taken refuge in the abandoned town of Thabeng. And, perhaps more than anything else, it was the news brought back by Rolong messengers – that the ousted Taung had left their grain standing – which convinced Sefunela to begin moving his camps east and to prepare for rebuilding.[48]

Rebuilding, indeed, began in April 1823, though at a new site, Matlwase. And, although a party of fighters which had been sent to Thabeng to harvest grain for seed reported the devastating news that the Taung had somehow robbed them of their harvest,[49] it was none the less to be a time of regrouping. Sefunela was joined by a 'considerable number of Marolongs [Rolong]', and by January 1824 the new town's population was 'much larger' than the five hundred or so households which had fled with Sefunela.[50]

Unlike the Phuthing attack, the Taung raid against Matlwase in May 1824 took the Rolong completely by surprise. Soon after abandoning the town, Sefunela told the missionary, Edwards, that

> a powerful army of natives . . . came quite unexpectedly upon his town . . . After having made all the resistance in his power he was obliged to retreat, leaving the Town and much cattle in the hands of the enemy.'[51]

Hodgson, who revisited Matlwase in August 1825, wrote:

> Most of the houses which I left occupied by inhabitants peacefully living together were burnt down, the cattle kraals, gardens, etc., were destroyed and here a broken pot and there a broken spoon, etc., indicated the haste in which the Barolong had deserted their residence.[52]

46. (SAL) MMS XIII, Hodgson, Journal 8, 9 Feb. 1823; WMMS 300/2/10, Hodgson, Maquassi, 9 Aug. 1823. The quote comes from the latter.
47. WMMS 300/2/5, Hodgson, Maquassi, 8 June 1823.
48. (SAL) MMS XIII, Hodgson, Journal 9, 22 Feb. 1823.
49. (SAL) MMS XIII, Hodgson, Journal 10, 20 June 1823.
50. WMMS 300/3/2, Broadbent and Hodgson, Maquassi, 1 Jan. 1824.
51. WMMS 301/1/2, Edwards, Griqualand, 8 Jan. 1826.
52. (SAL) MMS XIV, Hodgson, Journal 14, 6 Aug. 1825.

The Taung, who had threatened to attack since March 1824, held off their raid until the Rolong fields had ripened.[53] Thus, for a second year running, the community under Sefunela was stripped of its harvest. Moreover, while a substantial number of livestock were lost by the Rolong at Matlwase[54] their losses were greatly increased during Sefunela's long and circuitous flight to Phitsane. Not only did the Griqua confiscate 630 head of cattle from the beleaguered chief, but shortly afterwards Sefunela's following suffered two more devastating raids on the part of the Taung at Setlagoli and again at Phitsane.[55]

Although Sefunela's following had managed through its ordeals to retain at least some of its herds, the community as a whole was greatly impoverished. Sefunela complained that 'many of his people died of hunger' during the long march from Matlwase to Phitsane.[56] And Moffat, who met the community near Phitsane, reported of Sefunela, 'Poor man, his people as well as his cattle are greatly reduced. They seem only to possess the few skins on which they sleep.'[57] This was exaggeration, although Sefunela's following as well as its livestock were greatly depleted. Hodgson perhaps best described the impact of the repeated Taung raids by noting: 'all . . . have reduced the King's army considerably – diminished his means of support, eclipsed his authority'.[58]

The rapacity of the Taung raids of 1824 seem to have broken the back of the Rolong. Although 327 households returned with Sefunela to Matlwase in 1825, it was clear that the permanence of the settlement was dependent on expelling the Taung from the region.[59] The Rolong subsistence base was simply too fragile to withstand further raiding. When the Rolong attack against the Taung failed in September, the community splintered. Sefunela informed Broadbent that 'it was more probable that his enemies would follow up the advantage they gained, that he was not in a situation to give them battle, and that therefore, it became imprudent to remain at Makuassie [Matlwase]'.[60] Rather, the community would 'seek a safer residence at a greater distance from that part of the Interior so much disturbed by war'.[61] Thus, they began an itinerant life along the Vaal River.

53. WMMS 301/12/3, Edwards, Griqualand, 8 Jan. 1825.
54. The approximate number of cattle stolen by the Taung, or its relative proportion to the Rolong herds as a whole is unknown. Though contemporary reports agreed it was sizeable, Edwards heard from Sefunela that the Rolong had lost 'much cattle'. WMMS 301/12/3, Edwards, Griqualand, 9 Jan. 1825. Sefunela was the primary informant of Hodgson and Broadbent. Hodgson recorded that the Rolong had suffered 'much loss' in the raid. (SAL) MMS XIV, Journal 15, 25. Broadbent wrote that Sefunela's community lost a 'vast number of cattle'. WMMS 300/2/45, Broadbent, Griqua Town, 1 July 1824. Moffat tended to downplay the number taken, but he spoke with Sefunela only after even more devastating raids were undertaken against the community's herds at Setlagoli. Moffat and Moffat, *Apprenticeship*, 146.
55. Moffat and Moffat, *Apprenticeship*, 145 and 146.
56. Moffat and Moffat, *Apprenticeship*, 146.
57. Moffat and Moffat, *Apprenticeship*, 150.
58. WMMS 302/1/53, Hodgson, Vaal River, 4 Oct. 1825.
59. WMMS 302/1/67, Hodgson, Vaal River, 12 Nov. 1825 and WMMS 302/1/53, Hodgson, Vaal River, 4 Oct. 1825.
60. Broadbent, *Narrative*, 169–70 and WMMS 302/1/53, Hodgson, Vaal River, 4 Oct. 1825.
61. WMMS 302/1/67, Hodgson, Vaal River, 12 Nov. 1825.

It was not so much the physical distance from the Taung, but rather temporary abandonment of town life based on agriculture that granted the Rolong asylum from raids. According to Hodgson, the community under Sefunela 'change their residence every two or three weeks and live in the bushes'.[62] The aged witness, Mooi, later recalled that the Rolong did not sow during this period, 'because we had plenty of cattle and sufficient milk'.[63] The circumstances, however, were not so bountiful. Although the Rolong had begun to replenish their herds by trading the worked skins of wild game to the Griqua,[64] their livestock suffered badly from the sour pasture near the Vaal River.[65] The community remained in large part dependent on the Kora for milk supplies.[66] Moreover, the loss of the staple grain rendered it all too dependent on *veldkos*, or wild plants. *Veldkos*, it is true, was abundant along the river, particularly in the rainy season. Yet, such supplies fluctuated greatly, and in the dry season they dwindled.[67] With such uncertain food supplies, the community under Sefunela began to crack. When he settled at Platberg in 1826, only 230 households remained in his following.[68]

It is important to note that it was not so much the actual violence of raids which reduced Sefunela's following. The erosion of the community – from a number 'much larger' than 500 households in 1823, to 327 households in 1825 and finally to 230 households in 1826 – did not take place all at once. Moreover, although undoubtedly some did die in battle and others from starvation, the shedding of households was rather the result of the attrition of agricultural resources. Raiding did have the effect of isolating small groups of families from the main body of the Rolong.[69] Equally, however, significant were those who consciously left the community in search of food elsewhere.

This type of scattering involved anything from whole wards to small numbers of families. Travelling along the Vaal River towards Matlwase in July 1825, for example, Hodgson met Sefunela's half brother, 'Maquarri'. Complaining of the Taung raids in 1824, the headman 'mentioned the deplorable state of poverty to which the tribe of the Barolongs were reduced'. Hodgson noted that 'Maquarri' with several Rolong followers were 'yet dispersed amongst the Koranas'.[70] Just to the north resided 'Rampi Kuntsi, a captain under Sibbonel', who had taken shelter with another Kora village.[71] Similarly, another 'respectabale under captain', Motsegare,

62. (SAL) MMS XIV, Hodgson, Journal 18, 30 Oct. 1825.
63. (CA) Griqualand West Land Commission (hereafter GWLC) 67, vol. E, 14.
64. (SAL) MMS XIV, Hodgson, Journal 21, 29 Nov. 1927.
65. (SAL) MMS XIV, Hodgson, Journal 18, 1825. Hodgson frequently complained during this period of losses of livestock; the difficulty most frequently involved sheep. See his journal extracts for 14 Jan.–30 Jan. 1826.
66. (SAL) MMS XIV, Hodgson, Journal 18, 26 Nov. 1825.
67. (SAL) MMS XIV, Hodgson, Journal 21, 25 Nov. 1827 and Journal 18, 23 Jan. 1826.
68. WMMS 302/2/41, Hodgson, Vaal River, 18 Aug. 1826.
69. Hodgson and Broadbent encountered a number of individuals stranded near Thabeng after the Rolong evacuation of the town in 1823. See Broadbent, *Narrative*, 38 and T. L. Hodgson, *The Journals of the Reverend T. L. Hodgson*, R.L. Cope, ed., Johannesburg, 1977, 127 and 130.
70. (SAL) MMS XIV, Hodgson, Journal 17, 26 July 1825.
71. (SAL) MMS XIV, Hodgson, Journal 17, 27 July 1825.

had been 'reduced almost to want' in 1824 and took refuge among the Kora either in 1824 or 1825.[72] Finally, at least one other major party of a hundred households abandoned Sefunela's following in late 1825, seeking refuge with the Rolong further west.[73] The attribution of the titles 'captain' and 'under captain' to the notables encountered along the Vaal, and in the last instance the size of the group migrating, suggest that the clusters of exiles described were fragments of wards, or possibly even whole wards, which were able to cling together through the diaspora. It is likely that smaller groups of families or individuals also scattered but survived. Little is known of these. Many may have been integrated into Kora and Griqua settlements, or, like the characters in Sol Plaatje's historical novel, *Mhudi*, managed eventually to rejoin their former communities.[74] Others, it should be noted, drifted as far as the Cape colony, to become the first generation of black labourers on colonial farms.[75]

The Impact of Early Raiding on the Western Rolong

Only fragments of evidence remain illuminating the experiences of the western Rolong during this period. Little, if anything, can be said of the Rolong under Matlabe. Documentary evidence and oral traditions shed somewhat better light on the communities under Tawane and Gontle. Moffat left notes of his visit to the two leaders in October 1824 as did Andrew Bain in August 1826, but the two-year interlude is not covered by any documentation. Oral traditions provide some insights into the period, yet these, as well as oral recollections collected in the late nineteenth century and praise poems focus almost exclusively on the royal clan. Little is said of the complex process of dispersal which seems to have occurred. Sufficient evidence does exist, however, to allow some reconstructions to be made. Moreover, available evidence suggests that although the experiences of the western Rolong settlements differed in detail from those of Sefunela, the general process of impoverishment and social disintegration they underwent paralleled that occurring in Sefunela's community.

---

72. (SAL) MMS XIV, Hodgson, Journal 17, 19 Sept. 1825. Even with Motsegare's move to Platberg in 1827, Hodgson felt 'pained at his poverty in cattle compared with the flocks he had when in his former power at Maquassi'.
73. WMMS 303/1/27, Archbell, Platberg, 9 Sept. 1830.
74. S. Plaatje, *Mhudi*, London, 1978. Ostensibly the work is an historical novel, and Plaatje undoubtedly used a good deal of freedom in portraying the struggles of his main characters. Yet Plaatje's choice of theme, his sympathy for the characters, as well as the details from various passages in the book suggest that he went far further than existing European sources to research the book, and used as a main historical source oral traditions maintained by local African communities. Unfortunately, Plaatje did not give details of his sources, and we can get, at best, only an impressionistic idea of what he drew from other African experts on the period and what he drew from his own imagination. Notwithstanding this problem, the novel would be a wonderful way into the period for high school and university students.
75. This is studied in greater depth in M. Kinsman, 'Between Two Stones', paper presented to the African Studies Seminar, University of Cape Town, 1982.

The Chronology of Raiding: The Western Rolong, 1823–26

Like Sefunela, Gontle and Tawane and the western Rolong were repeatedly displaced from their settlements between 1823 and 1826. The Phuthing raided their combined settlement in May 1823. Although most of their followers found refuge north of the town, the Rolong fell victim to a Fokeng raid in July 1823. By the middle of 1824, Tawane and Gontle had resettled with their people at Phitsane, northwest of Khunwana. Yet, as described earlier, once joined by Sefunela's Rolong, they were exposed to Taung raids. No less than three Taung raids occurred, all apparently in August 1824. Although the Taung were largely unsuccessful in their aggression, the combined Rolong communities re-occupied Khunwana. They were forced, however, to abandon the site, not so much because of military threat but because of drought later in the year. Sefunela, as noted earlier, began his move back to Matlwase, while Tawane and Gontle moved to Morokweng near the Molopo River.

The new site offered little refuge. The Fokeng attacked the Rolong in December 1824, forcing Gontle to remove to Kongke, in the old hunting grounds south of the Molopo River. The news of repeated disturbances north of the Molopo River – first in June 1825 and then in August the same year – continued to unsettle the Rolong under Tawane but they suffered no direct raids until March 1826. Then, after being raided by the Fokeng, Tawane's following moved further west along the Molopo River, entering the Kalahari. Tawane's tattered following experienced yet another raid by the Fokeng in October 1826. Eluding the Fokeng raiders, Tawane's Rolong fled south. They settled first at Dithakong and then at Taung. By this time they had become an impoverished, crippled community.

The Impact of Raiding: The Western Rolong, 1823–26

Although only impressionistic accounts remain regarding the fate of Gontle's and Tawane's followers, they suggest that the disintegration of the communities was gradual and, as with Sefunela's following, often led to the abandonment of mixed agriculture for the comparatively more secure life of hunting and collecting. The Phuthing attack on Khunwana seems to have destroyed the settlement. After engaging in two battles with the Phuthing – one lasting three days – the Rolong fled.[76] The Phuthing subsequently ravaged the town's food supplies, probably including the maturing grain crop.[77] Moreover, although Tawane and Gontle found refuge in the north, large numbers of their followers were stranded in isolation, some in the vicinity of the town and others in full flight as far south as Kuruman.[78] The silence of Rolong oral traditions regarding the Fokeng raid in July 1823 suggests that the Rolong found it relatively inconsequential compared to that of the Phuthing.

76. Moffat, *Missionary Labours*, 340–2; Moffat and Moffat, *Apprenticeship*, 73, 77–8 and 83–5.
77. Moffat and Moffat, *Apprenticeship*, 77 and 86.
78. (CA) CO 185, Melvill.

Although the tumult created during the Phuthing sack of Khunwana convinced many individuals and families to seek refuge in the south – in the hunting districts between the Molopo and Mashowing Rivers, in Tlhaping precincts like Kuruman and possibly even as far south as the Cape colony[79] – it by no means extinguished the communities under Tawane and Gontle. In 1824 Tawane complained bitterly of the hunger resulting from the Phuthing 'scourge' of Khunwana in 1823.[80] None the less, he and Gontle not only resettled a substantial part of their following at Phitsane in 1824, but also provided shelter for a large number of Ngwaketse and Hurutshe refugees who had fled the warfare occurring north of the Molopo River. According to Moffat's estimation, Phitsane housed well over 20 000 residents in August 1824.[81]

The Taung raids against Khunwana in August 1824 jarred the settlement. Still, after three pitched battles during which a considerable number of Rolong fighters were killed, the Rolong were able to limit their losses to only a small number of herds.[82] Rather, it was the repeated raids of the Fokeng that finally shattered the communities under Tawane and Gontle.

In December 1824 Gontle brought the news to missionaries at Kuruman that he had again been raided by the Fokeng, adding that his people had 'suffered a very considerable loss'.[83] His inability to acquire Tlhaping military support at the time may have convinced him to take refuge at Kongke, between the Mashowing and Molopo Rivers. It was to become a rather bleak existence. Andrew Geddes Bain, who visited the site in 1826, described the settlement as falling under the authority of the chief, Molala, who was known to have 'very considerable' herds. Included in the settlement's population were

> a great number of people . . . Barolongs, Baklara [Tlharo from near the Kuruman River] and Basana [most likely poor hunters] who had been living near the Molopo River at different parts but had lately come together under Mallala [Molala] at this place on account, as they said, of the approach of the Mantatees [Fokeng].[84]

Among these was the Gontle, with his remaining following.[85] The change from town life based on mixed agriculture to a life in refuge was profound. At Kongke the Rolong lived in scattered villages which seem to have lacked gardens. Moffat noted

79. Moffat and Moffat, *Apprenticeship*, 281.
80. Moffat, *Missionary Labours*, 415.
81. Moffat, *Missionary Labours*, 388.
82. In the first attack, the Rolong abandoned Phitsani, only to resettle the town shortly after. In the second there was a bitter loss of life, particularly amongst Rolong notables. Still, the hunters under the Griqua captain Barend Barends broke up a Taung contingent west of the settlement, and in a larger battle near the town, the Rolong and the Griqua recaptured most of the Rolong livestock which had been stolen. In the third skirmish, the Taung seem to have succeeded in capturing a large number of herds, but Moroka, an active fighter at the time, later recalled that the Rolong gave chase and regained herds of all but one 'kraal' (ward). Moffat and Moffat, *Apprenticeship*, 144 and 148; (CA) GWLC 67, vol. e, 30.
83. Moffat and Moffat, *Apprenticeship*, 172.
84. A. Bain, *The Journals of Andrew Geddes Bain*, M. Lister ed., Cape Town, 1949, 33.
85. Bain, *Journals*, 35; Moffat and Moffat, *Apprenticeship*, 266.

the prospects for residents were all but pleasing. 'They have few cattle and grass is scarce. They place some dependence on locusts, which is very precarious, for it is now a fortnight since any were seen.' However, game was occasionally killed.[86] Conditions were sufficiently harsh to throw off at least one satellite settlement to Tswaing by 1827. At Tswaing and at Setabeng, twenty miles away, 'a great number of Barolongs . . . dwelt'. The village at Tswaing 'was not a proper town, but a comparatively temporary abode',[87] or rather 'cattle posts',[88] where residents relied on the products of their remaining herds or on hunting.

Tawane's fate in the dry reaches of Morokweng may have been little better. Unfortunately no contemporary description of his settlement there remains. It was not until the Fokeng raid of early 1826 that his community shattered.[89] News of the battle reached Kuruman in March, and reports spread that the Fokeng 'surrounded Tawane and his people during the night, and at daylight rushed on the unconscious inhabitants, killed a great number, and took nearly all their cattle'.[90] Driven from their town, Tawane's remaining following moved west up the Molopo River, where they met the trader, Bain.[91] Like Sefunela and Gontle before him, Tawane was forced to give up cultivation, and, possibly shedding a large proportion of his following, took up an itinerant life. According to Bain's description, Tawane's new settlement was far from permanent, but rather seems to have been one of a series of camps which were evacuated when the scanty water supplies were exhausted. At the time of Bain's visit, the chief resided in 'a thick wood on the northern side of the river'; no fields had been cultivated, and the Rolong lived in 'a temporary town where no houses were built, but some bushy screens were erected here and there to shelter the inhabitants from the winds'.[92]

The impact of the final Fokeng (or Kololo) raid on Tawane in October 1826 is obscure. He fled, with what was probably only a semblance of his former following and a portion of his former herds, first to Dithakong and then to Taung. No description of his settlements there remains, although the difficulties of life experienced were summarised by Tawane, who said he had 'no news but drought and hunger' while remaining on the Harts River.[93]

As with the Rolong under Sefunela, then, it seems that the repeated raids impoverished the Rolong along the Molopo River. Mixed agriculture was temporarily foresaken, and refugees sought shelter in scattered settlements in the former hunting reserves. Though remaining herds may have in some cases supported

---

86. Moffat and Moffat, *Apprenticeship*, 251–3. The quote comes from 252–3.
87. Moffat, *Missionary Labours*, 458.
88. Moffat and Moffat, *Apprenticeship*, 241.
89. Moffat and Moffat, *Apprenticeship*, 252.
90. Moffat and Moffat, *Apprenticeship*, 212 and 215. The quote is from 215.
91. University of the Witwatersrand (hereafter WITS): Molema Papers, A979 Cc1, Historical Notice; and (WITS) John MacKenzie Papers, C79, Montsioa, Declaration, Bloemhof, 1871.
92. The first quote is from Bain, *Journals*, 40 and the second is from Andrew Bain, 'Extracts from the Journal of Mr. Andrew Geddes Bain', *South African Quarterly Journal*, 1, 4 (1830), 415.
93. Moffat and Moffat, *Apprenticeship*, 258.

some semblance of former wards, in others, family groupings were forced to abandon their settlements, to seek subsistence on their own. Economic collapse resulting from raids generated social disintegration.

The Ndebele Period, 1826–36

The presence of the Ndebele on the western highveld from 1826 to 1838 introduced a period of ambiguous peace. The Ndebele cleared the area of the brigands, who had destabilised Rolong settlements with their unpredictable raiding, and replaced these with a stronger, more centralised state. The Ndebele were a far more effective military power than the former brigands, and when the geopolitics of the state required, they easily crushed local communities. The uneasy stability brought about by their presence was sufficient, however, to allow the Rolong to begin reconstructing their former communities. As will be shown elsewhere, reconstruction was based partially on commodity production and migrant labour, and it stimulated slow but far-reaching change in the communities which were regathering.

The Ndebele State

Central to understanding this period is a discussion of the Ndebele state. The Ndebele were caught in the conflicts between emerging states in present-day KwaZulu/Natal in the 1810s and 1820s, but moved west in the early 1820s, crossing the Drakensburg and possibly settling first in the eastern highveld.[94] The Ndebele were probably initially small in number and relatively weak, yet they embarked on a period of state building in the mid-1820s which refigured the geopolitics of the central highveld. The process of state building is still little understood, but it seems that Ndebele expansion was based, at least in part, on raiding local communities. Although numbers of indigenes may have been killed or fled into open country, the Ndebele absorbed members of the conquered communities and their herds. They adopted many Zulu institutions, including the isolating of young men into regiments and the centralisation of cattle holdings under the king. Thus the Ndebele incorporated the defeated communities either as warriors in the regiments, as servants in the central settlements, or as client communities on the outskirts of the kingdom.[95] Impressionistic evidence would suggest that between 1826 and 1832 the Ndebele had established a polity which controlled roughly the same area as what became the Transvaal.

The lack of detailed historical studies of the Ndebele during this period greatly handicaps our understanding of the state. A cursory examinination of available evidence, however, suggests that the Ndebele domains were organised in four belts of territory. Towards the centre of the polity was a series of large Ndebele

---

94. An excellent discussion of early Ndebele history is found in R.K. Rasmussen, *Migrant Kingdom: Mzilikazi's Ndebele in South Africa*, London, 1978.
95. J.D. Omer-Cooper, *The Zulu Aftermath: A Nineteenth-century Revolution in Bantu Africa*, London, 1966, 133–6; University of London, London Missionary Society (hereafter LMS) Correspondence, Matabeleland, I/1/a, Moffat, Kuruman, 24 Nov. 1836.

settlements which were closely controlled by the Ndebele ruler, Mzilikazi. These appear to have housed the military regiments and the core Ndebele population, with its domestic servants. Such settlements covered only a small area of land controlled by the Ndebele. Andrew Smith noted that Mzilikazi was 'in the habit of concentrating his population wherever he may be himself . . . almost the entire of his country is without inhabitants only a few old men and the women being dispersed here and there to take charge of the enormous herds of cattle'.[96] Surrounding the core settlements and covering an extensive area were districts reserved for pasturing livestock. Smith's comment that women and old men were left to herd cattle is hyperbole. He estimated elsewhere that roughly half the Ndebele men were involved in watching the herds and in other productive activities.[97] Interspersed along the outskirts of the pastoral districts were client chieftainships, made up of indigenous communities which, because of conquest or voluntary assignation, accepted the overlordship of the Ndebele state. These were semi-autonomous. Though separate from the Ndebele socially, they often accepted Ndebele representatives in their towns, the Ndebele supervising the political activities of the residents and local trade.[98]

Moreover, the subject communities often paid tribute to Mzilikazi. One Rolong community, for example, came to provide worked skins and beads for the Ndebele. Similarly, one Hurutshe subject community paid tribute in the form of both new and worked skins, and another gave grain.[99] Beyond these, the Ndebele cleared a wide area which functioned as a march. Smith noted when travelling from Dithakong to the Ndebele capital in 1834:

> We met with few inhabitants till we reached the country of the Matabili [Ndebele], distant about two hundred miles in a north-east direction. In former days this intervening district was inhabited by Batlapi [Tlhaping] and the Barolong [Rolong]; but at present it is only the resort of the poor of those tribes and of the Baharootzie [Hurutshe].[100]

A similar march was established to the south east of the Ndebele.[101] American missionaries living in a client chieftainship explained the march thus:

> In the vicinity of the Molopo River there is fine grazing land, as well as much that might be cultivated with and without irrigation; but the country being open

96. (CA) Government House Archives (hereafter GH) 19/4, Andrew Smith, (n.p.), 12 Dec. 1835.
97. (CA) GH 19/4, Andrew Smith, Philippolis, (n.d.).
98. LMS Correspondence, Matabeleland I/1/a, Moffat, Kuruman, 20 Nov. 1836; and J.C. Chase, 'Substance of the Journal of Two Trading Travellers', *South African Quarterly Journal*, 1, 4 (1830), 404.
99. (CA) GWLC 66, vol. c, 373–4 and 378.
100. A. Smith, 'Report of the Expedition for Exploring Central Africa', *Journal of the Royal Geographical Society*, 6 (1836), 403.
101. Smith, 'Report of the Expedition', 406.

and exposed to Moselekatzie's enemies on the south of him, is left to be transversed by the beasts of the field.[102]

Though the Ndebele re-organised large areas of the central highveld – the area which became the core of the state – they left communities like the Rolong under Tawane and Sefunela largely unmolested, until movement of the capital required that certain regions be cleared to establish the march further west.

The Uneasy Peace, 1826–1833

The presence of the Ndebele in the central highveld brought, early on, a period of some harmony to the Rolong area. Possibly because the Ndebele were moving their capital from the eastern highveld to the headwaters of the Crocodile River to the west, they forced both the Fokeng and the Taung from the western highveld by 1827. Though little is known of Ndebele relationships with the Fokeng, the Fokeng chief, Sebetwane, later told David Livingstone that it was Ndebele raids which drove him from the highveld.[103] Similarly, the Taung chief, Moletsane, testified that Mzilikazi's regiments persuaded him to abandon raiding the western highveld and to retreat to the Vaal River.[104]

Granted this period of relative security, various scattered Rolong communities began to resettle. Sefunela, who was 'wearied of removing from place to place with the Corannas',[105] and who was 'yet desirous of settling some place where he can sow corn',[106] agreed to settle at Platberg near the Vaal River in July 1826.[107] Similarly, Tawane, who had suffered considerable privation while on the Harts River, had returned to the headwaters of the Molopo River by 1830. By 1831 both Tawane, who had settled at Khunwana, and Gontle, who had abandoned Kongke for Setlagoli, had rebuilt substantial towns. The French missionary, Rolland, estimated in 1831 that Gontle's town housed three to four thousand residents.[108] And the

102. D.J. Kotze, ed., *Letters of the American Missionaries, 1835–1838*, Cape Town, 1950, 125.
103. E. Smith, 'Sebetwane and the Makololo', *African Studies*, 15, 2 (1956), 53.
104. The period between 1825 and 1827 was one of great insecurity for the Taung. Hodgson, who interviewed Taung visitors to the Vaal River in December 1825 noted, 'It appears that the country further in the interior is much disturbed by war'; the Taung were considering moving towards the Vaal. (SAL) MMS XIV, Hodgson, Journal 18, 20 Dec. 1825. In January 1826 Hodgson's wife wrote that Moletsane intended to settle at Matlwase. A. Hodgson, *Memoirs*, 176–7. In March, however, the Taung were moving in a series of camps near Thabeng hoping to return to their homeland. The Taung were, for the moment, however, north of the Vaal, 'to increase the difficulty of the Matebeli should they suddenly advance upon them.' (SAL) MMS XIV, Hodgson, Journal 19, 4 Mar. 1826. In July they took possession of Matlwase. (SAL) MMS XIV, Hodgson, Journal 19, July 1826. The Ndebele did not raid the Taung until 1827. Then they chased the Taung to the Modder River, just below present-day Bloemfontein, attacked them there, captured a number of cattle and killed many of Moletsane's following. The Taung divided, half fleeing up the Modder River and the other half fleeing down. The Ndebele pursued the latter and seized all its herds. (CA) GWLC 66, vol. c, 348–9. Moletsane, who had fled down the Modder River, took up residence along the Vaal. He was attacked by Griqua under Adam Kok, however, and stripped now of all of his herds, he followed Kok to Philippolis a broken and impoverished man, (CA) GWLC 67, vol. 1, 5.
105. WMMS 302/2/23, Hodgson and Archbell, Vaal River, 6 June 1825.
106. (SAL) MMS XIV, Hodgson, Journal 19, 23 June 1826.
107. WMMS 302/2/41, Hodgson, Vaal River, 18 Aug. 1826.
108. Germond, *Chronicles of Basutoland*, 78.

missionary, Lemue, who visited Khunwana in 1832, remarked that as far as the eye could see there were 'corn fields dotted over the carefully cultivated country-side'.[109]

It was an uneasy peace, however. News of devastating Ndebele raids against groups to the north continued to shake Rolong confidence in their newly found security. Ndebele attacks on the Ngwaketse in 1828 reportedly drove the community into exile; despite Ndebele promises to establish peaceful relations with their neighbours, they again attacked the Ngwaketse in 1830, killing many people and plundering them of cattle. Survivors of the attack took up a harsh exile in the Kalahari desert.[110] The Hurutshe, who had split into two communities at the time, found their subordinated position less than secure. The Ndebele had snatched Hurutshe youth in open country and attached them as servants to Ndebele notables.[111] Moreover, the Hurutshe chief, Makhatla, who paid a 'large part of his crops' as tribute to the Ndebele, was refused permission in 1830 to sow in his own country and forced to cultivate sites nearer the Ndebele capital.[112] Though the Rolong along the Molopo River agreed to pay tribute to the Ndebele, there were signs that the belligerency of the Ndebele would spill over into their region. Ndebele commandos reportedly attacked the herds of Moletsane, who had resettled along the Vaal River, having taken possession of the livestock of local Kora groups and even Tawane.[113] Sefunela, at his now burgeoning settlement at Platberg, refused to consider moving back to the more fertile grounds of Matlwase: the threat of war perpetuated by the Ndebele presence kept the community from returning north.[114]

From 1829, then, efforts were made to build a military confederacy which would oust the Ndebele from the highveld. The first was undertaken under the leadership of the Kora brigand, Jan Bloem, in early 1829. Haip, a Kora leader who was a major participant in the raid, explained that having suffered (alongside Moletsane) from Ndebele cattle raiding, he and Moletsane decided that 'some decisive effort was needed for protection.' 'Not being confident of their own powers',[115] they approached Jan Bloem, who agreed to assemble a commando against the Ndebele. The raid itself was initially successful: Bloem and his militia carried off a number of cattle. They were attacked, however, 'by an endless multitude of [Ndebele] warriors', who retook the herds and killed 50 Kora.[116] The raid, though unsuccessful, was the first of a series of incidents which led to the organisation of a massive commando against the Ndebele led by the Griqua captain, Barend Barends.

109. Germond, *Chronicles of Basutoland*, 86.
110. Germond, *Chronicles of Basutoland*, 86; (WITS) Mary Moffat Papers, A669f, M. Moffat, Lattakoo, 18 Dec. 1828; (LMS) Correspondence, South Africa, XII/1/b. Baillie, New Lattakoo, 30 Sep. 1830.
111. (LMS) Matabeleland, I/1/a, Moffat, Kuruman, 20 Nov. 1836.
112. Germond, *Chronicles of Basutoland*, 76.
113. Smith, *Diary*, vol. 1, 158; (WITS) MacKenzie Papers, C 79.
114. WMMS 303/3/28, Archbell, Platberg, 10 Aug. 1832.
115. A. Smith, *Andrew Smith's Journal of His Expedition into the Interior of Southern Africa*, Cape Town, 1975, 125.
116. LMS Correspondence, South Africa, XI/3/b, Hamilton and Moffat, New Lattakoo, 6 Mar. 1828. See also the evidence of Nicholaus Kruger, (CA) GWLC 67, vol. m, 6.

Barends was perhaps the most interesting (although least studied) of the Griqua captains. The first to settle north of the Orange River early in the nineteenth century, he was the most adventurous of the Griqua hunters and explorers. He remained something of a Griqua nationalist. Fearing the encroachment of oppressive colonial regulations north of the Orange River, he refused to co-operate in any way with Cape colony directives. Similarly, he provided a haven for runaway slaves and 'Hottentot' servants who fled the colony in the 1810s and 1820s. None the less, latent in his attitudes was a staunch paternalism towards local black communities. Though initially angered at Bloem's raid on the Ndebele, Barends was gradually persuaded to undertake a similar expedition himself.[117]

The first factor operating to change Barends's mind may have been the Ndebele threat to obstruct Griqua hunting north of the Molopo River. Though Barends hunted and traded in the Hurutshe area in the late 1820s, Mzilikazi 'signified his intention last year [1830] of prohibiting Barends and a party from hunting in the country where he now resides'.[118] Yet Barends's goal came to be couched in much more visionary terms:

> Barend Barends [was] labouring under an unaccountable delusion that he was destined to sweep Moselekatse and his gang of blood thirsty warriors from the fine pastures and glens of Bakone country [the highveld] and thus emancipate the aborigines from their thraldom.[119]

Barends agitated and lobbied from Khunwana to Philippolis and between 1830 and 1831 collected heterogeneous groups which were unanimous 'in their enmity to the Matabele king'.[120] This included not only his own followers, but Griqua from Griqua Town, Campbell and Philippolis – some threatened by the lost hunting grounds, some seeking to restore herds stolen from them, and many, undoubtedly, out for the booty.[121] It included Kora, like Haip, who sought to put an end to the raiding of their herds.[122] It included Tlhaping and Rolong contingents who, 'Alarmed at Motselekatse's hostile dispositions', agreed to march at the end of the summer season.[123] Estimates of the size of the commando vary from 900 to 1 300. Of these, anywhere from 280 to 550 (according to the informant) were Griqua and Kora, and the remainder were Rolong and Tlhaping.[124]

The commando set out in June 1831. The cattle-raiding undertaken by the party was particularly successful: overcoming several cattle posts, the combined army

---

117. LMS Correspondence, South Africa, XI/3/b, Hamilton and Moffat, New Lattakoo, 6 Mar. 1828.
118. LMS Correspondence, South Africa, XII/4/d, Wright, Griqua Town, 3 Nov. 1831.
119. Moffat, *Missionary Labours*, 166–7.
120. Moffat, *Missionary Labours*, 166.
121. 'The Late Griqua Raid,' *Grahamstown Journal*, I/2 (6 Jan. 1832); LMS Correspondence, South Africa, XII/4/d, Wright, Griqua Town, 3 Nov. 1831.
122. Smith, *Diary*, vol. 1, 159.
123. Germond, *Chronicles of Basutoland*, 76. This describes a meeting with the Tlhaping, but seems equally relevant to the Rolong.
124. (CA) CO 2728, Kolbe, Philippolis, 7 Oct. 1831, enclosed in Van Ryneveld, Graaff Reinet, 28 Oct. 1831.

may have captured as many as 6 000 head of livestock, and this with little resistance from Ndebele regiments.[125] On its return home, however, the commando was overtaken by Ndebele warriors. By report, great carnage followed. The Ndebele apparently surrounded Barends's camp at night and initiated a surprise attack in which 'nearly all [were] massacred without resistance'.[126] According to contemporary reports, the Ndebele killed 400 Griqua and 'cut off a great many Corana and Bechuanas'.[127]

It should be noted that although Rolong participation in Barends's raid may have proved somewhat disastrous, the community under Tawane took up an even more defiant stance, apparently in 1832. The Ndebele sent two representatives to Khunwana to oversee the town. Acceptance of the representatives would have meant formal subordination to the Ndebele. Also, the Rolong distrusted Ndebele motives. According to oral traditions, the messengers had been sent to 'take their children as tribute'.[128] The tradition reflects the widespread fear of Ndebele treachery during the period. Andrew Smith learned from Tswana subjects of Mzilikazi in 1835:

> the Tswana subjects of Mzilikazi often become his victims through ruse. The Ndebele would move into the vicinity of a settled village and pretend friendship until the people felt easy. Then, most usually by cover of night, they would surround the village and attack it at night . . . After capturing the village, Mzilikazi would usually move the older men and women to a distance . . . The younger women and men would be taken to the Ndebele kraals where they would be integrated into the ruling elite.[129]

According to Tawane's successor, Montsioa, the arrival of the representatives coincided with a rumour that Khunwana was to be attacked.[130] Tawane gave orders for the men to be killed. And it was this incident which, according to contemporary reports, brought about a devastating Ndebele attack in 1833.[131]

The Ndebele Dispersal of the Western Rolong

In 1833 earlier Rolong fears of Ndebele treachery and intermittent raids were exacerbated by threats of direct attack. Ndebele aggression was precipitated by a perception that their capital in the central Transvaal region was far too vulnerable. Barends's commando and the Rolong murder of Ndebele officials may have been vexatious enough. Still, contemporary rumours had it that the Ndebele were also

125. 'The Late Griqua Raid', *Grahamstown Journal*, 1832.
126. 'Smallpox', *South African Commercial Advertiser*, VIII/477, 7 Jan. 1832.
127. 'The Griquas', *South African Commercial Advertiser*, VII/462, 16 Nov. 1831.
128. University of Cape Town, Lestrade Papers, BC 255, AC, folder 9. 'Dico Tsa Secwana. Tales about the Bechuana tribes.'
129. Paraphrased by W. Lye in Smith, *Andrew Smith's Journal*, 265.
130. (WITS) MacKenzie Papers, C79. 131. See, for example, S. Plaatje, *Mhudi*, which I believe was based on Plaatje's extensive collection of oral recollections and traditions.
131. (LMS) Correspondence, South Africa, XIII/4/e, Moffat, Kuruman, 10 Jan. 1833; Germond, *Chronicles of Basutoland*, 104.

threatened by the Zulu. In any case, the Ndebele moved west, establishing a new capital at the headwaters of the Marico River.[132]

It is arguable that as part of this move west, the Ndebele determined to push the march south and west as well. Though previously the Molopo River was recognised as the border area between independent polities and the Ndebele, the latter now cleared a wide area of major settlements, which extended from the Ndebele capital to the Mashowing River. Between 1833 and 1834, then, both the Hurutshe and the Rolong were ousted from the area in a series of most devastating raids.

The Rolong under Tawane at Khunwana were the first to be attacked in 1833. According to contemporary reports, the Ndebele surrounded the town at night and launched a surprise, pre-dawn attack:

> . . . the slaughter was so great that men, women, and children were lying promiscuously among the stones of the neighbourhood. People who visited the spot two days later, saw starving children sucking, but in vain, the breasts of their lifeless mothers. We saw the rest of the tribe wandering in the wilderness. Their number did not exceed 300, and no women or children were among them.[133]

According to S.M. Molema, the attack was remembered as a 'terrible deluge'. 'Many Barolongs perished and much cattle was taken.'[134] Montsioa recalled that the Ndebele killed, amongst others, his mother and brother, 'and all my father's house'.[135] The figure of 300 survivors most likely reflects only those who fled in the immediate company of Tawane, for it seems that many of the survivors of the raid scattered as in earlier flights. By May 1833 it was reported that 'The whole country about the Vaal River and Philippolis together with the intermediate country, is full of Bechuanas who have fled form the north, being driven from their own country by Masselikats [Mzilikazi].' Tawane, it was noted, was resident 'but a short distance from the Vaal'.[136] Though it is difficult to determine whether Gontle's settlement was also attacked, he moved with Tawane's following and the remaining herds first to the salt pans near Logageng and then to Taung. From Taung, the two chiefs and their followings joined Sefunela's community, which at the time was moving to Thaba Nchu.

As in the mid-1820s, the Rolong of Khunwana dispensed with town life, and gave up mixed agriculture to seek subsistence through other means. Abandoning Taung for Thaba Nchu, Tawane left behind two of his brothers, Masheka and Moroi. The

132. (SAL) George Stow Papers, G. Stow, 'The Invasion of the Stronger Races', vol. 1, 181; Omer-Cooper, *The Zulu Aftermath*, 138–44.
133. Lemue, 'Narrative', *South African Commercial Advertiser*, IX/603, 23 Mar. 1833.
134. (WITS) Molema Papers, A979, Cc1. Molema's history, however, confuses the incident with the Ndebele retaliation on Barends's raid. The path of retreat, however, clearly identifies it as the Ndebele raid on Khunwana.
135. (WITS) MacKenzie Papers, C 79; the reference to 'house' refers to his father's relatives. Tawane, himself, survived.
136. 'The Tribes to the North', *Grahamstown Journal*, II/86, 15 Aug. 1833.

two 'had many people. It was a large town, and [there were] many outposts of
Bakalaharis and Bushmen [referring to hunter clients of the Rolong].'[137] Though
Masheka apparently left Taung for Dithakong, both rejoined Rolong settlements
when they were re-established on the Molopo River in the 1840s.

Though surviving oral recollections provide only a partial picture of the dispersal
of Tawane's following, travellers' accounts indicate that the march between the
Molopo and Mashowing Rivers was scattered with impoverished refugees. The
hunter, W.C. Harris, encountered between the Meritsani and Molopo Rivers an
'extensive stone town, which once contained its "busy thousands" but now presents
a heap of ruins'.[138] Though Harris believed the region was de-populated, Smith
found 'two or three hamlets' of Hurutshe refugees there. He noted, 'They have the
appearance of half starved persons, having no cattle . . . Trust entirely to the
spontaneous productions of the ground and what game they can procure.'[139] Passing
near the Setlagoli River, Harris noted, 'We passed many extensive villages totally
deserted: rude earthen vessels, fragments of ostrick egg-shells, and portions of the
skins of wild animals, however, proving that they had been recently inhabited.'[140]
Smith encountered in the vicinity a motley collection of 'poor natives' who had
either lived in the region prior to the 1820s or had taken shelter there since.[141]
Tawane's son, 'Rabokatlou', remained behind at Tswaing to the south, living with
his grandparents.[142] Near the lake bed at Tswaing itself lived families from a variety
of communities, though they were largely Tlharo (people living south-west of the
Tlhaping) and Rolong. Here, they mixed with the Lala – paupers – 'since the
almost total disorganisation of the tribes'.[143] And of the region between the
Mashowing and Setlagoli Rivers, Bain noted:

> The natives scattered about this part of the country are the remains of various
> Bechuana tribes, such as Baharutsie, Wanketzie and Barolongs . . . These
> poor people live in very small communities, scattered over the face of the
> country, but have not a single head of cattle to live by, their whole dependence
> and only food being locusts, or such game as chance may direct to their
> pitfall.[144]

As occurred in the mid-1820s, these people survived the destruction of their
agricultural base by adopting a more scattered settlement pattern and by subsisting
on hunting and collecting.

---

137. (CA) GWLC vol. E, Evidence of Baikhaki, 45.
138. W.C. Harris, *Narrative of an Expedition into Southern Africa*, Bombay, 1833, 83.
139. Smith, *Diary*, vol. 2, 38.
140. Harris, *Narrative of an Expedition*, 67.
141. Smith, *Andrew Smith's Journal*, 208 and 209.
142. (CA) GWLC 67, vol. J, 13.
143. Smith, *Andrew Smith's Journal*, 191.
144. Bain, *Journals*, 140.

The Regrouping under Sefunela

Just as the community under Tawane had regrouped during the peaceful hiatus between 1826 and 1833, the Rolong communities south of the Ndebele march regathered, using the peaceful years to attempt a more permanent reconstruction of community life. This is particularly demonstrated by Sefunela's community which settled at Platberg on the Vaal River.

As discussed earlier, Sefunela's community had abandoned Matlwase in 1825. Greatly impoverished by repeated raids, they took up a migratory life on the Vaal River and were dependent largely on Kora milk supplies. In 1826 the missionary, Hodgson, negotiated an uneasy truce between Sefunela and the Taung, who were themselves fleeing from Ndebele raids. This achieved, Hodgson persuaded Sefunela to join two Rolong headmen at Platberg in July 1826.[145] The settlement was small, numbering 230 households, and impoverished. The chief, for example, was dependent to some extent on the livestock of missionaries for survival.[146] Moreover, the uncertainty of permanence and the continued fear of losing remaining herds persuaded the Rolong to forsake the outpost system for pasturing livestock: livestock was to be compounded nightly in the town.[147] Small parties continued to settle at Platberg. In January 1827 Sefunela was joined at Platberg by the impoverished headman, Motsegare. By March Hodgson reported that three more headmen with their followings had settled with the new community.[148] And in 1829 still another Rolong leader with a following of a hundred households moved to the town.[149] By late 1829 the population at Platberg had grown from 230 to 500 households.[150]

According to Broadbent, at the base of resettlement was 'the prospect of quiet habitation and secure dwelling places'.[151] Still, it is clear from Hodgson's journals that resettlement was predicated upon the expanding surpluses in subsistence goods. The Rolong, it seems, traded with the Sotho to restore their seed stores.[152] It is likely, too, that repeated surpluses from harvests also provided the provisions necessary for feeding the new residents of the town. Similarly, it appears that residents of Platberg became quite active in trade to rebuild their herds. Sefunela's brother, for example, traded rings and worked skins with the Griqua for sheep in 1827. He purchased sheep again at Philippolis in 1828.[153] Small parties probably went to trade with farmers along the northern boundaries of the Cape colony.[154] And from at least 1828, colonial

---

145. The local Rolong name for the site is Motlana Pitse ('horse's jawbone'). 'Sketch of Native Traditions', Diamond Fields; WMMS 302/3/1935, Hodgson and Archbell, Platberg, 30 Sept. 1827; (SAL) MMS XIV, Hodgson, Journal 19, 31 July 1826.
146. (SAL) MMS XIV, Hodgson, Journal 20, 42.
147. WMMS 302/3/11, Hodgson and Archbell, Platberg, 31 Mar. 1827.
148. WMMS 302/4/15, Hodgson, Platberg, 19 Mar. 1828; (SAL) MMS XIV, Hodgson, Journal 20, 18 Jan. 1827.
149. WMMS 301/5/46, Archbell, Platberg, 31 Dec. 1829.
150. WMMS 301/5/46, Archbell, Platberg, 31 Dec. 1829.
151. Broadbent, *Narrative*, 180.
152. WMMS 303/4/30, Archbell, Platberg, 4 Sept. 1830.
153. (SAL) MMS XIV, Hodgson, Journal 21, 29 Nov. 1827 and 15 Mar. 1828.
154. R. Godlonton, *A Narrative of the Irruption of the Kaffir Hordes*, Cape Town, 1965, 147.

traders began to make regular visits to Platberg. In fact, by 1831 a colonial trader settled permanently at the station.[155]

Pre-eminent among Rolong trade goods were hides, and it is a testament to a certain genius that a commodity as plentiful as skins caught locally in the hunt could, through trade, ultimately revitalise the community's economy. The town's population continued to grow, as scattered family groups and headmen continued to resettle with Sefunela. In 1832 the population was estimated to be between three and four thousand and by 1833 it had grown to as much as eight to ten thousand.[156] The traditional layout of the Tswana town reasserted itself with the adoption of the cattle post system. And by 1830 it was already evident that the resources at Platberg were simply too scanty to support the town's population.

As much as half the town's population temporarily abandoned Platberg in 1831 – 'some for the colony, and others to different mission stations, and to people unconnected with any missions, but who could render them provisions'.[157] The problem persisted until the community moved to Thaba Nchu in 1834. Archbell noted in 1833, with the population at Platberg then growing by roughly a hundred households a year, 'the land capable of cultivation, and the water' had become relatively speaking 'very scarce'. The community would either have to move to more fertile grounds, or split apart.[158] They found a wide girth for expansion at Thaba Nchu, in the fertile western foothills of the Maluti mountains. Indeed, expand they did, for when settling there in 1834, they were joined by the now tattered communities of Tawane and Gontle, as well as a third strife-torn chief, Matlaba.

Conclusions

The case study of the Rolong allows us to critically assess Cobbing's proposals about the violence experienced by African communities on the highveld in the 1820s and 1830s, and, where Cobbing's arguments fail, to suggest new avenues for research or to offer new explanations. Cobbing's proposals were indeed innovative. He dismissed Omer-Cooper's argument that violence was part of African state-building during this period. Cobbing criticised the very concept of the Difaqane, saying it did not really occur, but was a methodically designed myth, perpetuated initally by Cape-based slavers and colonial land-grabbers to cover up their actions. The true cause of violence, he argued, was the expansion of European capitalism in southern Africa, in the form of white, Griqua and Kora slavers in the Orange River area, white colonial aggressors on the eastern frontier, and European slavers from Delagoa Bay in the far north. Cobbing argues that the increasing convergence of their activities in southern Africa created a vortex of violence. In order to survive, African people

155. (SAL) MMS XIV, Hodgson, Journal 21, 16 Apr. 1828 and 14 June 1828; WMMS 303/2/28, Archbell, Platberg, 28 Feb. 1831.
156. WMMS 303/3/36, Edwards, Bootshuaap, 5 Nov. 1836; WMMS 304/4/18, Platberg, 27 May 1833..
157. WMMS 305/1/46, Archbell, 'A Summary of the Wesleyan Bechuana Mission', 1834.
158. WMMS 303/3/18, Archbell, Platberg, 27 May 1833.

responded by setting up a variety of 'defensive' or 'reactive' states, ranging from new 'San' and 'Khoi' formations to the Zulu state itself.[159]

Cobbing's work makes a number of very significant contributions. His emphasis on early slaving north of the Orange River re-awakens us to the (often violent) process of colonial expansion which occurred on the so-called northern frontier. Indeed, the Griqua civil wars in the 1820s and the increasing penetration of labour-hungry white colonists from the Cape from the late 1820s signalled a new chapter in the history of the region north of the Orange River. Yet his central argument that contacts with the Cape had overwhelming and traumatic effects on the interior is not valid. To clarify this point, it is important to examine Cobbing's arguments about the causes of violence and its perpetrators, and finally to examine the results he implies.

Cobbing attributes the violence in areas north of the Orange River to the activities of Griqua and Kora raiders who were supplying the Cape slave trade. This focus forces him to view local African communities as relatively passive. He does not look at long-term or even recent historical changes in African communities in the region. As a result, he lacks any yardstick by which to gauge the impact of Griqua or Kora immigrants in the area.

Cobbing admits that Cape-based trade had occurred in the region for forty years as had slaving.[161] (I would argue that this was very limited.) What he does not say is that such contacts were notable, not for their success in transforming African societies in the region, but for their failure. Despite arguments to the contrary[162] Cape-based trade made little impact on highveld trade networks before 1820. Neither did the occasional raiding of miscreants like Coenraad de Buys seriously disrupt local black communities.[163] Finally, as we have seen in this case study, the Kora and Griqua were not the initiators nor the main perpetrators of violence, particularly in the early 1820s.

159. J. Cobbing, 'Jettisoning the Mfecane (with *Perestroika*)', paper presented to Centre for African Studies, University of Cape Town, 1989.

160. These changes are discussed in Q. N. Parsons, 'Prelude to *Difaqane* in the Interior of South Africa' in this volume. For a discussion of the archaeological evidence supporting the idea of Parsons' 'Ivory Wars', see S. Hall, 'Archaeological Indicators for Stress in the Western Transvaal Region between the Seventeenth and Nineteenth Centuries' in this volume.

161. J. Cobbing, 'Rethinking the Roots of Violence in Southern Africa *c.* 1790–1840', paper presented to the Colloquium on the Mfecane Aftermath, University of the Witwatersrand, Johannesburg, 1991, p.10; and J. Cobbing, 'The Mfecane as Alibi', 496.

162. M. Legassick, 'The Northern Frontier to 1820: The Emergence of the Griqua People', in R. Elphick and H. B. Giliomee, eds, *The Shaping of South African Society 1652–1820*, Cape Town, 1979, 255–9.

163. Cobbing's imagery of the Griqua before 1820 is not well founded. 'Griqua raids for slaves and cattle,' Cobbing argues, 'had been going on for years', Cobbing, 'Re-thinking the Difaqane', 496. Periodic violence did break out, particularly with local hunter-collectors. However, this usually concerned water rights. More critical in the acquisition of labour was the process of dispossession, where Griqua colonists usurped the grounds of local hunter-collectors. More often than not, local bands became tied to Griqua households as what would become bonded labour. But in so absorbing local groupings, the Griqua imitated the system of bonded or client labour used by indigenous Tswana and Kora groups. Although the resulting labourers were tied to Griqua households, they were by no means 'enslaved'. See M. Kinsman, 'Populists and Patriarchs: The Transformation of the Captaincy at Griqua Town, 1804–1822', in A. Mabin, ed., *Organisation and Economic Change*, Johannesburg, 1989, 2–3.

The main raiders were undoubtedly African communities: the Phuthing, the Fokeng, the Taung and later the Ndebele. There is no evidence to suggest that the Kora or Griqua caused these African communities to raid. Although the Kora and Griqua did eventually take up raiding (including slave raiding), this was from the mid-1820s, and they may have been capitalising on turmoil, rather than initiating it. Moreover, although they appeared as occasional interloping raiders in the north in the 1820s, they focused their aggression on a band of territory far to the south, stretching from Dithakong through the flats of what became the southern Free State to the Caledon River Valley.

In seeking explanations for the causes of violence in the 1820s and 1830s, one gains far deeper insights by looking at communities living north of the Rolong rather than at the Griqua and Kora. Although far too little is known about the history of African communities on the highveld before the nineteenth century, the scattered studies which exist suggest that a dramatic process of state-building had recently occurred. Chiefs in the central highveld embarked on a process of political centralisation and, particularly from the late eighteenth century, on territorial expansion.[164] Communities on the periphery, like the Taung and the Rolong, were displaced, fragmented and destabilised by seemingly continuous low-intensity warfare when looked at in this context, the Difaqane was perhaps not an historical anachronism, but the intensification of an ongoing process. Possibly what was most historically distinctive about the period that became known as the Difaqane on the western highveld was that the main perpetrators of violence were no longer the strong states in the centre, but the former victims on the periphery, like the Taung.

To return to the thesis of African state-building does not mean a return to Omer-Cooper's original hypothesis. For too long, historians have sought explanations for the Difaqane exclusively in the rise of the Zulu state. It is time that the causes of violence were attributed to a range of far-reaching historical changes occurring throughout the sub-continent.

Much work needs to be done here. Communities on the highveld were involved in significant change in the centuries before 1800. A number of factors seem to have been at work. Increased dependence on cattle-keeping on the highveld, as described by Martin Hall, probably had important effects in re-shaping social relationships.[165] Similarly, the intensification of participation in long distance trade may also have played a major role in stimulating change. Although the impact of trade needs to be more fully researched, there is evidence to suggest that it had significant economic and social effects. It is now urgent that Neil Parsons's

---

164. Two very important contributions, here, are Q.N. Parsons, 'Prelude to *Difaqane* in the Interior of South Africa', in this volume; and T.N. Huffman, 'Archaeological Evidence and Conventional Explanations of Southern Bantu Settlement Patterns', *Africa*, 56 (1986), 280–98. See also Hall, 'Archaeological Indicators for Stress'.

165. M. Hall, *The Changing Past: Farmers, Kings and Traders in Southern Africa, 200–1860*, Cape Town, 1987, 46–54.

proposition about the 'Ivory Wars' on the highveld in the late eighteenth century be taken up and developed.[166]

Regional specialisation of production for trade seems to have occurred, with the Sotho, for example, specialising in grain production, the Rolong and Tlhaping in worked skins, and the Hurutshe and Ngwaketse in ironware. This, in turn, is likely to have stimulated deep-rooted social change. Southernmost Tswana men, for example, abandoned their control over cultivation, to focus their attention on working skins for trade. This would have fundamentally altered the basic division of labour in southern Tswana settlements, leaving women in control of cultivation and harvests. Correspondingly, it may have altered, and strengthened the position of women in town life. These kinds of factor may have underlain state-formation.

Consideration of details like these will allow historians to stop *describing* African societies on the highveld and, with the assistance of archaeology, to begin *analysing* their dynamics.

The case study of the Rolong shows that in order to restore community life, they used trade to acquire new herds. Yet, the highveld networks, particularly after Ndebele settlement of the area, had disintegrated. The breakdown of the northern trade routes forced local communities to refocus their activities and for the first time to participate seriously in Cape-based trade networks. What we call the Difaqane was not caused by the extension of Cape-based trade networks in the region, rather the disruption of the period facilitated the expansion of these networks.

Finally, one must tackle Cobbing's argument about how societies re-constituted themselves. Cobbing argues that when agricultural communities re-emerged, they were not '"pre-colonial" at any moment'. Indeed, he claims the new chieftainships were 'brought into being by capitalism'.[167] This implies that the demands of capitalism worked to restructure African societies.

But the process was much more complex. The withering of economic resources as a result of continuing raids and displacement caused communities to disintegrate gradually, as families were forced to seek subsistence in other, non-agricultural ways. Yet, as soon as they could, it seems that most refugees rejoined their communities. They re-structured community life around the old principles of patriarchy, re-instituting the authority of the chief and ward elders, and the extended family.

The critical consideration in community restructuring was regaining the resources – the seeds and the livestock – needed for survival in an agricultural community. Surpluses from harvests as well as the natural increase of herds may have gone some way in providing these resources once peace prevailed. The Rolong also used trade to gain access to seeds and livestock.

Rolong involvement in trade was not revolutionary. They had long worked skins for long-distance trade. It was in one aspect providential that the tumult of the 1820s

166. Parsons, 'Prelude to *Difaqane*'.
167. Cobbing, 'Re-thinking the Difaqane', 15.

had forced them to intensify their dependence on hunting for survival, for it also gave them increased access to their major trade product. In this sense, economic deprivation did not force the Rolong to take up new productive activities, but to expand the use of existing alternatives. Moreover, once sufficient economic resources were accumulated, the Rolong shifted production, adopting mixed agriculture once again.

Labour migrancy may have been the exception here. Working for wealthy men to gain livestock was not new in Rolong society: it had long persisted in the form of temporary clientship. White settlement of the area, however, created new opportunities for individuals to earn wealth and new conditions for labour. The impact of labour migrancy during this early period seems to have been minimal, although detailed studies in the future might prove otherwise.

It would seem, then, that the re-constitution of community life did not require radical changes. But as communities regrouped, social relations were set on a slightly new footing. This was not the result of raiding, itself, but of the extent of raiding and the massive loss of livestock suffered by chiefs and community elders. Chiefs, ward heads and family elders were able to re-assert their authority through livestock loans, yet their capacity to do so was limited. Livestock holdings were just too small.

One can propose that this shook loose the fabric of Rolong society. Initially, the youth or the poor may have been forced to seek wealth, and particularly livestock, outside their community. Yet, over the years, the ability of these groups to acquire wealth independently, outside the structures of subordination which operated within Rolong communities, may have created new conflicts. These conditions permitted the creation of new groups: peasant farmers, migrant workers and small-scale traders. Although initially peripheral in community life, they seem to have increased in number and power over the course of the nineteenth century, eventually to challenge existing forms of patriarchal control.

The long-term significance of the Difaqane, then, was that it unleashed a deep, slow and multi-directional social transformation which over the course of the nineteenth century would break existing social formations apart. The new emergent social groups – the peasant producers, the share-croppers, the migrant workers – would tie African communities to the European-dominated capitalist structures surrounding them.

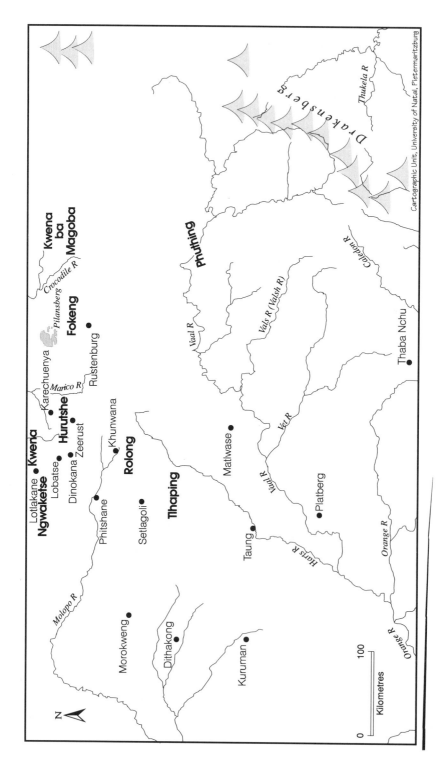

Map 12.   The central and northern highveld

15 The Battle of Dithakong and 'Mfecane' Theory

GUY HARTLEY

This essay aims to explore the relationship between the battle of Dithakong (1823) and 'mfecane' theory in the context of the growing critique of the theory led by Julian Cobbing. The essay seeks to establish the original version of events at Dithakong, and argues that with particular reference to the upheavals west of the Drakensberg in 1822–4 certain aspects of the theory may be tenable.

Up to the present, 'mfecane' theory has dominated the literature of early nineteenth-century history of the southern African interior, emphasising the self-generated and Afrocentric nature of the immense upheavals within black society during the 1820s. Ever since Cobbing questioned whether the 'mfecane' occurred in this sense, and suggested rather that the destabilisations sprang from European penetration,[1] there have been efforts both by himself and his students to give his ideas academic credibility. Key events within the 'mfecane' diaspora have been identified and explained in terms of the larger suppositions of European expansionism and labour demands, and without reference to African agents involved in a knock-on process from the east. Dithakong is one such case study that stands at a critical juncture for these ideas with particular respect to the chains of violence west of the Drakensberg. Consequently, there has been a range of interpretations of the battle of Dithakong that seek to incorporate it within the broader theoretical framework proposed by Cobbing.[2]

Dithakong is situated on the western fringe of what has been termed the 'blank space' – the Vaal-Caledon region – which was supposedly devastated by numerous 'hordes' in the years 1822–3. Few literate reporters had penetrated this area by 1823. At the moment of the disruptions, then, there are few eyewitness accounts of

---

1. See J. Cobbing, 'The Case Against the Mfecane', seminar paper presented to the Centre for African Studies, University of Cape Town, 1983; revised version with same title presented to African Studies Institute, University of the Witwatersrand, Johannesburg, 1984; 'The Myth of the Mfecane', seminar paper presented to the Dept. of History, University of Durban-Westville, 1987; 'Jettisoning the Mfecane (with *Perestroika*)', seminar paper presented to the African Studies Institute, University of the Witwatersrand, Johannesburg, 1988; 'The Mfecane as Alibi: Thoughts on Dithakong and Mbolompo', *Journal of African History*, 29 (1988), 487–519.
2. Julian Cobbing began the re-examination on Dithakong in 'The Mfecane as Alibi'. Similar critiques have been forwarded by students who at some time have worked under Cobbing. See J. Richner, 'The Withering Away of the "Lifaqane": Or a Change of Paradigm', B.A. Hons. essay, Rhodes University, Grahamstown, 1988, 7–10; J-B. Gewald, '"Mountaineers" as Mantatees: A Critical Reassessment of Events Leading up to the Battle of Dithakong', M.A. dissertation, Rijks Universiteit, Leiden, 1989.

contemporary events. However, the occurrences at Dithakong on 25–27 June 1823 stand as one key exception with the eyewitness narratives of three Europeans. Dithakong, therefore, constitutes a locality of relatively sure empirical ground with regard to the nature of violence in the interior and so is catalyst to the very heart of the broader issues at stake.

In the past, the battle of Dithakong has been viewed as a defence against the threatening advance of a vast and destitute 'mfecane' migratory grouping. However, latest versions interpret the events in terms of a slave- and cattle-raid on an unprovoked and unaggressive people. These alternative analyses have obviously not been arrived at independently or in isolation, but need to be considered as a whole in relation to the Cobbing thesis. Although recognising the advances made by the revisionists, it will be argued that – with regard to Dithakong – their analyses have been forced and suited to meet the demands of their larger suppositions, which ultimately brings their singular Eurocentric theory of violence into question.

The Original Accounts

The original reporters described Dithakong as a defensive battle against the 'Mantatee', a desperate, foreign migratory grouping that had come from the east. For many months prior to this confrontation, there had been numerous rumours concerning the approach of this 'Goth-like army' which was reported to have destroyed many communities in its advance. The 'horde' was depicted as 'hungry wolves', whose object appeared 'not so much to war, as to devour the produce of, the land of which they [got] possession'.[3] Believing these reports to have little foundation, Robert Moffat, the missionary at Kuruman who lived amongst the Tlhaping, continued to carry out his intentions to journey northwards to the Ngwaketse, a Tswana grouping, in the hope of establishing amicable relations. Before reaching his destination, however, on the basis of the convergence of informants' accounts from a range of different groupings – which included eyewitness reports from Rolong recently engaged in battle – Moffat made a hurried return to Kuruman fearing for the safety of the place, given the advance of the 'Mantatee' southwards.

A meeting was held amongst the leaders of Mothibi's Tlhaping to consider what line of action to adopt. It was decided to seek the aid of the Griqua, who resided to the south and whose possession of firearms could save Kuruman from possible destruction. Judging it best to confront the 'Mantatee' at a distance from Kuruman to avoid involving the Tlhaping wives and children, the war party set out for Dithakong. After Moffat had failed to reach an agreement of peace with the 'Mantatee', the Griqua and Tlhaping entered into battle for their very lives on 26 June 1823. Eight hours later, the 'Mantatee' had been dispelled, and Kuruman had been saved.[4]

---

3. M. Moffat and R. Moffat, *Apprenticeship at Kuruman. Being the Journals and Letters of Robert and Mary Moffat*, ed. by I. Schapera, London, 1951, 77, 78.
4. For the above events, see Moffat and Moffat, *Apprenticeship*, 73–95.

The Recent Accounts

A hundred and sixty-five years later, the revisionists suggest that the original accounts have been uncritically accepted. Both Cobbing and Jürg Richner attempt to situate Dithakong in terms of the colonial demands for labour. Cobbing argues that an *in depth* reading of the evidence reveals the battle of Dithakong was no more than a slave and cattle raid organised by Moffat and John Melvill, the government agent of Griqua Town who was present at the conflict, to meet the colony's labour problem. The 'Mantatee' threat was a mere alibi for the raid.[5]

Richner has clearly struggled to reconcile the integrity and compassion of Moffat with the appellation of slave trader. He has continued to present Dithakong as a raid but without implicating Moffat. In what he ingeniously calls the Tlhaping 'commercial jealousy scare', Richner argues that the trade monopoly of the Tlhaping was in danger of being undermined when Moffat ventured to the Ngwaketse. In order to prevent Moffat from reaching the Ngwaketse, the Tlhaping chief, Mothibi, used the 'Mantatee' scare and fed him messages about 'Mantatee' movements that frightened Moffat into returning home. By this stage, Moffat completely believed the 'Mantatee scare' and made a hurried journey to Griqua Town to seek Griqua support. Mothibi's new 'commercial jealousy scare' had now developed a momentum of its own. Fearing that the Griqua would take his cattle if there was no 'horde', Mothibi was forced to designate a victim people who unfortunately comprised the inhabitants of Dithakong. Once again, then, Dithakong was a raid for cattle and slaves that took place under the cover of the 'Mantatee' myth.[6]

Jan-Bart Gewald continues in the genre of Dithakong-as-raid. He treats the slaving aspect as a side issue, but his thesis is also an explicit attempt to explain the events without reference to African agents involved in a knock-on process from the east. He argues that Dithakong resulted from a 'complex of factors' related to 'tensions internal to and between, the Orange River outlaws, the Tlhaping polity, the Griqua polity and the missionaries'. He suggests that the 'raid' constituted the logical conclusion of the development of events in Transorangian history, which particularly involved the quest for socio-economic-political stabilisation on the part of the Tlhaping, Griqua and missionaries.[7]

The Recent Accounts: An Analysis
The Perception of the Eyewitness Narratives

Although the revisionist accounts differ vastly in terms of detailed explanation, they display a number of common features. Firstly, they show extreme scepticism towards the eyewitness narratives of the events, which are emphatic about Dithakong being a defensive battle against the 'Mantatee horde.' Moffat, Melvill

---

5. Cobbing, 'The Mfecane as Alibi', 492, 493.
6. Richner, 'The Withering Away of the "Lifaqane"', 7–8.
7. Gewald, '"Mountaineers" as Mantatees', ch. 1, p. 7, ch. 7, p. 1–2.

and George Thompson, a Cape Town merchant who had undertaken a journey into the interior and happened to arrive at Griqua Town shortly before Moffat's hurried appeal there, constitute the main literate reporters of the events.[8] In the final analysis, with the odd exception,[9] the original reporters are presented as outrageous liars who deliberately deceived the public as to their real intentions.

Elsewhere, I have argued that the eyewitness accounts have yet to be proved unreliable.[9] Their narratives agree well with one another in both sequence and occurrence, and appear unlikely to be attempts at collusion. By examining each reporter's frame of reference and basic presuppositions about life, I have argued that what they state is consistent with their characters. If they had been lying, in each case the reporters would have displayed complete incompatibility with what is known about the rest of their lives.[10]

Moffat lived remarkably closely in line with his basic conservative, evangelical assumptions formed abroad. In fact, I argued that his experiences in southern Africa further convinced him of his Christian presuppositions as he showed ever-increasing concern for the 'lost'. In his role as missionary, he attempted to function so that his words and deeds accorded with revealing the truth of the saving grace of the gospel. His understanding of true spirituality was set within a total social context. All aspects of life were required to accord with the tenor of the gospel. His deep sense of humanity and compassion is continually manifest. Anything detrimental to the gospel needed to be approached with caution. For this reason, Moffat was strongly condemnatory of his predecessors' self-interested involvement in trading, which he

8. For Moffat's account, see his letters and journal in *Apprenticeship*, 73–111, see also R. Moffat, *Missionary Labours and Scenes in Southern Africa*, London, 1842, ch. 21–22; for Melvill's, see G. Thompson, *Travels and Adventures in Southern Africa*, Cape Town, 1962, (originally London, 1827), 174–85; for Thompson's, see Thompson, *Travels and Adventures*, 87–129. Whereas Moffat and Melvill were present at the battle, Thompson had already returned to the colony to give 'speedy information' with respect to the 'Mantatee' threat. The importance of Thompson's account lies in the fact that he established the reports about the existence of the 'Mantatee' by being an eyewitness to their advance. Whilst war preparations were being made at Kuruman, he proceeded to Dithakong in order to establish the reports about the numerous grouping. He found Dithakong deserted and a few miles onwards, confronted the immense 'horde' in a valley below. He watched their advance on the old Dithakong site before returning to Kuruman. For further sources of the events, see the *South African Commercial Advertiser*, 7 Jan. 1824, reprinted in G.M. Theal, *Records of the Cape Colony*, London, 1902–05, vol. 16, 497–505; T.L. Hodgson, *The Journals of the Reverend T.L. Hodgson*, ed. by R.L. Cope, Johannesburg, 1977, 180–2.

9. Richner, for example, suggests that Moffat, rather than lying, was deceived. However, this is a difficult position to sustain. Moffat had met the inhabitants of Dithakong on previous occasions. That he should mistake the local community for an aggressive fifty-thousand strong group of foreigners is difficult to accept. His descriptions of the grouping contrasted sharply with the people of his area. To be consistent, either Moffat was lying or stating the truth. Gewald suggests that Thompson, too, was deceived in identifying the 'Mantatee' as a local community in the area. Again, this position is not easy to maintain. Note the vast difference for Gewald's precedent – see '"Mountaineers" as Mantatees', ch. 6, p. 10, note 42 – in relation to Thompson's account, *Travels and Adventures*, 121–5.

10. For a more thorough account of what can only be dealt with here in summary concerning the portrayal of Moffat, Thompson and Melvill, see G.F. Hartley, 'Dithakong and the "Mfecane": A Historiographical and Methodological Analysis', M.A. dissertation, University of Cape Town, 1992, chapters on the reporters.

believed caused their downfall.[11] He was also careful to separate his central task of preaching the Word from the realm of state affairs.[12]

Moffat consistently displayed a high view of the worth and dignity of humankind, revealing a longing for the reconciliation of the individual with the loving, personal God of the Bible, and, consequently, reconciliation amongst human beings.[13] These were the biblical sanctions which Moffat steadfastly upheld as his primary objective point of reference. When offered many cattle by Tshosa a few months before Dithakong to assist him in leading a commando against his father, Makaba, chief of the Ngwaketse, with whom he had seriously clashed, Moffat, true to his convictions responded, 'that such conduct was contrary to the Laws of God, and as the servants of God it was impossible for us to accept the invitation, no, not for all the cattle in Africa'.[14]

Yet at Dithakong, according to Cobbing, Moffat uncharacteristically metamorphoses into a slave and cattle raider, collaborating as an agent of conquest to meet the demands of the colony's labour problem.[15] In this way, Cobbing's critique appears to be a reversion to the Majeke thesis of the 1950s, which argued that the primary role of the missionaries was to assist the government in the subjugation of the African and herald a capitalist Christian civilisation.[16] In the case of Moffat, whatever his cultural trappings and personal limitations, it is difficult to view his missionary zeal in terms of British imperialism. Instead, he needs to be placed within the theological context of his conversion and the evangelical revival in Britain.

Thompson, too, deviated little from his 'liberal' notions. He was involved in the circle of society that supported the ardent libertarians, John Fairbairn and Thomas Pringle, and he was engaged in many 'liberal' pursuits.[17] He was an energetic proponent of free market ideology and continually called for the annihilation of slavery. Thompson strongly reflected ideas of nineteenth-century British liberalism and the demands of industrial capital. He believed a coerced and immobile body of workers was economically irrational. Slave labour was too expensive and uninventive. He was convinced that a free labour force encouraged to work by the incentive of wages was far cheaper and more efficient.[18]

His call for the abolition of slavery was not just economically motivated, but also

11. Moffat, *Missionary Labours*, 216–17.
12. Moffat and Moffat, *Apprenticeship*, Robert Moffat to James and Mary Smith, 20 Aug. 1822, 61–3; Robert Moffat to James and Mary Smith, 15 Nov. 1825, 204–05; J. S. Moffat, *The Lives of Robert and Mary Moffat*, London, 1885, 77.
13. See Moffat, *Missionary Labours*, 134, 135, 174, 325; Moffat and Moffat, *Apprenticeship*, 60, 131, 134.
14. Moffat and Moffat, *Apprenticeship*, Robert Moffat, journal, 12 Jan. 1822, 42.
15. Cobbing, 'The Mfecane as Alibi', 492–3. As noted, Richner exonerates Moffat. Gewald is not explicit on Moffat. He suggests that Moffat was either deceived or that he deliberately attempted to assert his authority in the region. See Gewald, '"Mountaineers" as Mantatees', ch. 6, p.8, ch.7, p. 2.
16. N. Majeke (pseudonym for Dora Taylor), *The Role of the Missionaries in Conquest*, Johannesburg, 1952.
17. H. C. Botha, *John Fairbairn in South Africa*, Cape Town, 1984, 36, 141.
18. Thompson, *Travels and Adventures*, 327, 353, 369.

inspired by the British humanitarian movement, which, itself, was influenced by Nonconformist Christianity. Fundamentally, humanitarianism stressed the moral equality of all people. The goal of ending slavery was not only a liberal and economically rational objective, but also a humane and moral one. Thompson was profoundly affected by these ideologies. Christian morality instilled in him the humane and philanthropic spirit so fundamental to the anti-slavery crusade. While in the Roggeveld, Thompson was informed of the many commandos in which numerous San were killed and their children forcibly taken into the colony as labour. Thompson was horrified by what he described as 'these massacres', and by the coercive extraction of the children into servitude.[19] He was also strongly condemnatory of the Boer commando at Tarka that had shot thirty San. He responded, 'This is certainly lamentable work, whatever be the cause of it − that we should be under the necessity of hunting down our *fellow-men* like the wild beasts of the field' (my emphasis).[20]

For Thompson, a fervent liberal steeped in Christian notions, slavery went against his very being. The inseparability of Thompson's commitment to anti-slavery from his economic and moral objectives precluded him from involvement in the forcible extraction of labour. His adherence to the free market ideology based on voluntary submission, together with the moral overtones, worked against the 'smash-and-grab' policy of primitive accumulation that Cobbing proposes. Yet at Dithakong he is implicated in the 'raid' for 'slaves' by acting as the spy seeking out the positions of the enemy,[21] and by handing over the gunpowder.[22]

Melvill is the final case in point. A deeply religious man, Melvill had long displayed sympathy for the cause of missions. It was his strong religious convictions that drove him to consider the position of government agent amongst the Griqua. Having journeyed into the region inquiring into Griqua affairs, he resolved to forsake his position as inspector of buildings, for which he received the handsome sum of 7 000 rixdollars per annum, for the government agency at Griqua Town at a salary of only 1 000 rixdollars. He had been deeply disturbed by the unfortunate conditions of the Griqua, and had determined to help them by attempting to convert them to Christianity, and by aiming to bring to them the benefits of western civilisation.[23] A number of people, including the fervent humanitarian, Dr John

19. Thompson, *Travels and Adventures*, 221–3.
20. Thompson, *Travels and Adventures*, 42.
21. Cobbing, 'The Mfecane as Alibi', 492.
22. Gewald, '"Mountaineers" as Mantatees', ch.6, p.8–11. Gewald, however, is not explicit on Thompson. Either he deliberately planned the raid or was deceived. Richner is not certain about Thompson's role and offers little explanation. Richner, 'The Withering Away of the "Llifaqane"', 8.
23. For his background, see M. Legassick, 'The Griqua, the Sotho–Tswana and the Missionaries, 1780–1840: The Politics of a Frontier Zone', Ph.D. thesis, University of California, Los Angeles, 1969, 296–7; Thompson, *Travels and Adventures*, 81–2; C.J. Beyers, ed., *Dictionary of South African Biography*, Durban, 1981, vol.4, 357–8.

Philip, held Melvill in high regard, noting his sincerity and good intentions.[24]

Although recognising the 'benevolent purposes' and 'honourable intentions' of Melvill, both Thompson and Moffat believed that he did not possess the necessary qualifications to deal with the political affairs of such a divided and unstable polity. His very nature restricted him from a clear analysis of Griqua affairs.[25] As government agent, his interferences often led to further conflict and dissension. However, Melvill continued in the sincere belief that he was acting for the good of the Griqua, and he was not beyond offering some contribution.[26]

His instructions involved the establishment of law and order, and the suppression of illegal trading. He consistently crushed lawlessness. His efforts to enforce regulations even led to the departure of lawless elements from Griqua Town, who would augment the growing, unruly Bergenaar grouping. In the future, the Bergenaars would provoke much disorder by raiding for both cattle and human beings to trade illegally with colonial frontiersmen. Melvill vehemently condemned their illicit activities and was quick to expose the immoral conduct of both the Bergenaars and the white settlers.[27] Yet at Dithakong, again, according to Cobbing and Richner, he is unexpectedly engaged in illegal trading that everywhere else he condemned.[28]

The distinctive outworkings of the reporters' commitment to their specific evangelical and liberal *Weltanschauungen* make for their presentation as slavers and outrageous liars no easy assignment. Their involvement in an armed raid would fundamentally militate against their adherence to the basic moral responsibilities of world views to which they held with remarkable consistency in both words and deeds for the rest of what is known about their lives. Rather, their consistency of character in line with their basic presuppositions suggests the authenticity of their accounts on Dithakong.

Yet Cobbing, Richner and Gewald have tended to dwell upon certain incidental details that cause them to question the historical reliability of the narratives. They give a central position to these incidental historical details and attempt to seize hints of 'suppressed evidence'. While they exaggerate such evidence, they downplay

24. J. Philip, *Researches in South Africa*, London, 1828, vol. 2, 79; S. Broadbent, *A Narrative of the First Introduction of Christianity Amongst the Barolong Tribe of Bechuanas, South Africa*, London, 1865, 132; Thompson, *Travels and Adventures*, 82; *British Parliamentary Papers* (hereafter *BPP*), Shannon, 1970, 70 vols, Papers Relative to the Condition and Treatment of the Native Inhabitants of Southern Africa Within the Colony of the Cape of Good Hope or Beyond the Frontier of That Colony, part 1, London, 1835, Evidence before Government Commission, April 1824, 128.
25. See *BPP*, Papers Relative to the Condition . . ., 128; Thompson, *Travels and Adventures*, 82.
26. For an in-depth discussion on Melvill's involvement in Griqua affairs, see Legassick, 'The Griqua, the Sotho–Tswana and the Missionaries', 298–306.
27. *BPP*, Papers Relative to the Condition . . ., Extract from a report by Melvill relative to the state of the Griqua, Dec. 1824, 214, 219.
28. Cobbing, 'The Mfecane as Alibi', 492–3; Richner, 'The Withering Away of the "Lifaqane"', 8. Gewald suggests that Melvill's involvement derived from a predetermined attempt to consolidate his position amongst the Griqua, perhaps coupled with a self-interested preoccupation with trading. Gewald, '"Mountaineers" as Mantatees', ch. 5, p. 11, ch. 7, p. 2.

whatever does not suit their position. It is interesting that they accept as much of the reporters' accounts as they find convenient, then ignore or repudiate other parts of the same documents which contradict their notions. Their selection of what is 'authentic' and what is 'unauthentic' in the accounts is often quite arbitrary, based on a preconceived bias and supported by previous arbitrary conclusions.

Probably the major reason for their scepticism concerns the events surrounding the aftermath of the battle. Once the 'Mantatee' had been put to flight, the Griqua rounded up over a thousand cattle, 33 of which were later given to Melvill. A number of women and children, who had been left on the battlefield were collected and taken to Kuruman, from where they were later distributed amongst the Griqua or sent into the colony. For Cobbing, this suggests that Moffat and Melvill were 'consciously engrossed' in collecting slaves to meet the labour demands of the colony. The 33 cattle and the 'payment' in ammunition received for the 'sale' of the 'slaves' to the colony, are the imagined fruits of the raid for Melvill. Moffat is supposed to have kept several 'slaves' at Kuruman whom he later distributed to various destinations in the Cape.[29]

Without refuting the interpretations given to the events by the reporters, the revisionists completely ignore and reject their internal testimonies. In all fairness, however, the fact that prisoners and cattle were taken on 27 June 1823 does not necessarily imply a raid, but can more rationally be explained in terms of the inevitable aftermath of a victorious, defensive battle.

The reporters wrote that the women and children left on the battlefield were completely destitute and famished. Having wandered across the interior for many months, they now appeared exhausted, broken and distressed with hunger. Alone on the battlefield, they were prey to the depredations of the Tswana who during the battle had only too clearly shown their intentions. Whilst the Griqua were putting the 'Mantatee' to flight, the Tlhaping had set about slaying the women and children left on the battlefield, as Moffat related, 'for the sake of a few rings, or of being able to boast that they had killed some Mantatee'.[30] In conformity with his biblical views concerning the dignity and worth of every individual human being, Moffat displayed his fierce disapproval of the unnecessary bloodshed by riding in amongst the Tlhaping and preventing them from killing the innocent. Out of compassion, the missionaries collected the women and children to provide them with protection, and a number were taken to Kuruman.[31] Many others, however, chose to remain on the battlefield, and as they sought to reach their defeated peoples were later murdered by

29. Cobbing, 'The Mfecane as Alibi', 492–3. See also Richner, 'The Withering Away of the "Llifaqane"', 8. Gewald is not as concerned with the slaving aspect and does not deal with it in much depth. See '"Mountaineers" as Mantatees', ch. 8, p. 1.
30. Moffat, *Missionary Labours*, 361.
31. For a detailed account of these events, see: Moffat and Moffat, *Apprenticeship*, 95–100; Thompson, *Travels and Adventures*, ch. 16, headed: 'Mr. Melvill's Narrative of Transactions after the Battle, and of His Excursion to Rescue the Women and Children of the Invaders', 174–85. Note the compassionate response of Moffat, Hamilton and Melvill as opposed to their depiction as slavers.

vengeful Tswana.[32] This was the realisation of the well-founded fears that had induced the missionaries to provide sanctuary to the defenceless.

It was considered that the refugees might best be provided for under the supervision of the Griqua. However, since the Griqua seemed more concerned with the cattle they had gained than the people, Melvill applied for a share of the captured cattle, perceiving that the task of providing food might rest exclusively on him. He was allotted the 33 head of cattle[33] and the Revd T.L. Hodgson, a Methodist missionary, on visiting Griqua Town in July 1823, alludes to them being used for the said purpose when he relates, 'Mr Melvill sent off this morning to Graaff-Reinet fifteen female prisoners, some of whom I saw most eagerly eating the dung of the oxen killed for their support.'[34]

With regard to the 'Mantatee' sent to Graaff-Reinet, it was claimed by Melvill that this was done with the refugees' best interests in mind. The Griqua were finding it difficult to accommodate them in the face of a severe drought and food shortage. For some, there were just too many refugees for which to provide. On account of the harsh material conditions, but also, fundamentally, as a result of the indifferent and uncaring attitude of the Griqua, it would appear that the initial scheme for the 'Mantatee's' provision seemed to be thwarted. Melvill seriously believed, then, that they would be looked after best in the houses of the colonists. He wrote accordingly to Andries Stockenstrom, the *Landdrost* at Graaff-Reinet, noting how 'badly off' the 'Mantatee' were amongst the Griqua.[35] At the same time, Melvill understood the advantages of the refugees being used as labour in the colony.[36] However, he never intended them as a slave labour supply. His attempt to relocate the women and children in the Cape was a by-product of and pragmatic end to the battle, and not its cause. Similarly, Moffat was at great pains to ensure that the six women and the boy he distributed in the colony were well-cared for, and that their freedom was guaranteed. He left two of the women in the care of John Philip.[37] It is difficult to sustain the thesis that both Moffat and Melvill were consciously selling the prisoners into slavery.

The ammunition Melvill received need not be interpreted as payment for the

---

32. Moffat and Moffat, *Apprenticeship*, Robert Moffat to Mary Moffat, 13 Aug. 1823, 107; and Mary Moffat to James and Mary Smith, 1 Sept. 1823, 109; Hodgson, *Journals*, 190.

33. Thompson, *Travels and Adventures*, 176–7. Melvill is also unjustly charged with taking 'his customary cut of 30 cattle' in a 'raid' against Sefunela's Rolong in 1824. Cobbing's account in 'The Mfecane as Alibi', 497, is based on conjecture and misrepresents the contextual evidence. Melvill neither took the 30 cattle, nor can the events be construed as a raid. For detail on the whole episode, see: Moffat and Moffat, *Apprenticeship*, 145–54, 198–200, 206; Broadbent, *Narrative*, 130–3, 158, 173; Hodgson, *Journals*, 9, 246, 322; D.F. Ellenberger, *History of the Basuto: Ancient and Modern*, London, 1912, 167; Legassick, 'The Griqua, the Sotho-Tswana and the Missionaries', 307–10, 338.

34. Hodgson, *Journals*, 182.

35. *BPP*, Papers Relative to the Condition . . ., Melvill to the *Landdrost* of Graaff Reinet, 31 July 1823, 226. See also Somerset to the Commissioners of Inquiry, 227; Government Archives, Cape Town (hereafter CA) CO 1/GR 16/12 Stockenstrom to Bird, 16 Oct. 1823.

36. *BPP*, Papers Relative to the Condition . . ., 226.

37. *BPP*, Papers Relative to the Condition . . ., 129.

prisoners. Below is a portion of the letter from the Colonial Secretary to Stockenstrom, that alludes to the ammunition:

> Sir,— I have had the honour of submitting your letter of the 11th Instant with its enclosure from Mr Melvill to His Excellency the Governor. It appears to be desirable that Mr Melvill should be supplied with a larger portion of ammunition, than what had been sent to him at the period of your letter, and His Excellency does not imagine there will be any difficulty in so doing, now that it is understood that you can receive adequate supplies at Graham's Town.[38]

Cobbing fails to mention the fact that Melvill was the government agent at Griqua Town. It is clear from this letter and from the instructions on his appointment as government agent,[39] that ammunition would be forwarded from the colony for the necessary administration of the territory. Bearing in mind that the supply of gunpowder had been exhausted since its distribution to the Griqua before the battle, it is understandable that more ammunition was needed for the protection of the area, especially in the face of further threatened raids from the 'Mantatee', as well as from the Bergenaars, who continued to assert themselves in the ongoing civil war. On receiving the intelligence about the 'Mantatee' threat from Thompson and Melvill, the colonial authorities were quick to respond with the ammunition supply, as they were deeply distressed about the stability of the frontier region and feared that the colony would be overrun.[40] To conclude that the acquisition of ammunition compounded a business transaction for the sale of slaves is unwarranted, and remains at best conjectural.

The Perception of the 'Mantatee'

The second common feature of the revisionist versions of the battle of Dithakong is dissatisfaction with the way in which the 'Mantatee' have been described. The original reporters were certainly emphatic about the existence of a foreign, threatening people. Moffat noticed how distinctively they contrasted with the Tswana of his area in dress, ornaments, weapons and behaviour.[41] However, the recent critics tend to suppose that the 'Mantatee' were 'mythical beings', invented as an alibi for the raid. Indeed, according to them, it was the local community at Dithakong who were the unfortunate and innocent people attacked.[42]

---

38. Theal, *Records of the Cape Colony*, vol. 16, Bird to *Landdrost* of Graaff-Reinet, 27 Aug. 1823, 223.
39. *BPP*, Papers Relative to the Condition . . ., Instructions to Melvill, 21 March 1822, 212.
40. (CA) CO 1/GR 16/12 Stockenstrom to Bird, 2 July 1823; and Stockenstrom to Melvill, 12 Sept. 1823; Thompson, *Travels and Adventures*, 161.
41. Moffat and Moffat, *Apprenticeship*, R. Moffat, journal, 25 June 1823, 95.
42. Cobbing is uncertain as to the precise identification of those at Dithakong. The fact that Dithakong had been a Maidi residence prior to 1823 suggests to him that they were the ones attacked, but Moffat mentions that Hurutshe women amongst the prisoners as well, which indicates to Cobbing that they, too, were victims. For Richner, the innocent involved included the Maidi, Hurutshe and Kwena. For Gewald, it was the Maidi and the Rolong-Mariba. See: Cobbing, 'The Mfecane as Alibi', 514; Richner, 'The Withering Away of the "Lifaqane"', 8; Gewald, '"Mountaineers" as Mantatees', ch. 7, p. 1.

A number of factors have led to this conclusion. Firstly, it is believed that the upheavals to the north-east of Kuruman in the months leading up to Dithakong can be explained without reference to the existence of the foreign grouping. For Cobbing, this is demonstrated in terms of Kora/Taung/Griqua attacks. He attempts to show continuity of such dislocations caused before and after Dithakong.[43] But this interpretation reveals critical shortcomings in periodisation. The majority of examples are drawn from the post-Dithakong period, the impact and extent of which are well established. However, in the years prior to Dithakong, there is evidence only of occasional depredations in this region by certain Griqua and frontier ruffians, that were sporadic and transitory. For the months prior to Dithakong when the first reports about the devastations of the 'Mantatee' were being received, Cobbing can only produce one example of a Kora/Taung/Griqua attack which lacks little substance in itself. The example involves the Kora raiding the Hurutshe at Karechuenya in 1822–3. Nowhere in his footnotes is there given explicit reference to this attack.[44] He has yet to demonstrate his opinions convincingly. It appears that it was only after Dithakong that the Bergenaars and Kora penetrated this region causing significant disturbances.

The second reason for the conclusions of the revisionists relates to the great confusion surrounding the etymology and composition of the term, 'Mantatee'. Since Moffat, Melvill and Thompson referred to the vast 'horde' as the 'Mantatee', many have identified 'MaNthatisi's Tlokwa of the Vaal-Caledon region as the grouping at Dithakong. Earliest writers of African history such as George McCall Theal, G.W. Stow and D.F. Ellenberger all succumbed to this interpretation.[45] However, Marian How has since convincingly shown that the Tlokwa never crossed west of the Vaal.[46] Cobbing and Richner have therefore tended to draw the neat conclusion that there was no massive grouping west of the Vaal. The 'Mantatee' were merely 'invented beings'. The word was simply coined as a euphemism for forced labour (Cobbing) or derived from the misheard 'Matabele' (Richner).[47]

Curiously, this was the conclusion of neither How nor subsequent writers such as William Lye, John Omer-Cooper, Isaac Schapera and Martin Legassick.[48] On the testimony of the original reporters, these scholars determined that Dithakong was in fact overrun by a foreign migratory grouping, who were not in the first place 'Mantatee'. Moffat, for example, wrote on the testimony of the prisoners that they

43. Cobbing, 'The Mfecane as Alibi', 496–8.
44. Cobbing, 'The Mfecane as Alibi', 497, 514, notes 54 and 141.
45. G.M. Theal, *History of South Africa*, 11 vols, London, 1915, vol. 5, 442. Theal did, however, recognise that the 'Mantatee horde' was composed of many different groupings, which included the Tlokwa. G.W. Stow, *The Native Races of South Africa*, London, 1905, 460; Ellenberger, *History of the Basuto*, 136–9.
46. M. How, 'An Alibi for Mantatisi', *African Studies*, 13, 2 (1954), 65–76.
47. Cobbing, 'The Mfecane as Alibi', 493; Richner, 'The Withering Away of the "Lifaqane"', 9.
48. W.F. Lye, 'The Difaqane: The Mfecane in the Southern Sotho Area, 1822–24', *Journal of African History*, 8 (1967), 107–31; J.D. Omer-Cooper, *The Zulu Aftermath: A Nineteenth-century Revolution in Bantu Africa*, London, 1966, 86–98; Moffat and Moffat, *Apprenticeship*, xxiv; Legassick, 'The Griqua, the Sotho–Tswana and the Missionaries', 328–41.

themselves disclaimed the appellation of 'Mantatee' given to them. Instead, he was informed that they consisted of a mixture of peoples, comprising essentially the 'Maputee' and the 'Batclaquan', under the chiefs 'Chaane' and 'Carrahanye' respectively.[49] Thompson was similarly informed. On his return to Cape Town, he confronted a Rolong refugee at Griqua Town who had fled the interior. The man had been driven from his territory by invaders he called 'Batcloqueene' under chiefs 'Malahanye' and another he could not recall.[50]

Whereas Gewald just ignores this evidence, Cobbing and Richner are quick to dismiss it. How and subsequent historians have translated Moffat and Thompson's references as the Phuting of Tsowane and the Hlakwana of Nkarahanye. This was substantiated on the basis of Ellenberger's independent identification of these groupings under the said leaders in his *History of the Basuto*, long considered the main source of Sotho oral tradition.[51] In a short footnote, without explanation, Cobbing proposes such a conclusion is 'extremely dubious' and 'unwarranted'.[52] Both Cobbing and Richner believe Ellenberger's information to be derived from Moffat's sources. Richner goes so far as to say that since there is little other independent evidence for the existence of such groupings, they can be safely rejected.[53] But conforming to the consensus of the day, Ellenberger placed 'MaNthatisi's Tlokwa at Dithakong. Surely if he had obtained his information from Moffat's sources, he would rather have identified the Phuthing and Hlakwana at Dithakong? Clearly, he had been informed by old men of the groupings, as he

49. Moffat and Moffat, *Apprenticeship*, Robert Moffat, journal, 21 July 1823, 102–3. All the references to *Apprenticeship* used in this essay have been checked with copies of originals in the National Archives of Zimbabwe located at the University of Cape Town Archives – BCS 36 D75/55, BZA 80/87–80/90 – to counter Gewald's argument that Moffat's original documents have been significantly altered with regard to 'mfecane'-related passages. The transcriptions by Schapera used here can be relied upon: he also directly noted differences between the original documents and later versions; see Moffat and Moffat, *Apprenticeship*, 75; Gewald, '"Mountaineers" as Mantatees', ch. 6, p. 8.

50. Thompson, *Travels and Adventures*, 137.

51. Ellenberger, *History of the Basuto*, 34–7, 70–2, 121, 351. Although much of his evidence derives from oral traditions, Ellenberger also used documentary sources. He did not always note his sources, which makes it difficult at times to critique his work.

52. Cobbing, 'The Mfecane as Alibi', 516, note 154. Interestingly, in his latest article, Cobbing has since found it necessary to refute the references in an exhaustive critique. Many of his arguments hinge on the same assumption that Ellenberger derived his information from Moffat. For example, Cobbing argues that Ellenberger, believing Moffat's 'Batclaquan' to be his Hlakwana, fictionally inserted his people of the Vaal-Caledon region into the northern Cape. Cobbing's reason for this intrepretation revolves around the fact that Ellenberger does not mention the presence of the Hlakwana west of the Vaal in the sections that focus on the grouping, and does so only in passages related to the northern Cape. However, apart from the question of why Ellenberger did not place the Hlakwana at Dithakong, it is clear that the sections on the Hlakwana only deal with their history up to 1822, when they resided in the Vaal-Caledon region. Ellenberger divided his book into three sections, the first of which covered the ancient history of the Sotho. The second period describes the 'Lifaqane Wars', which Ellenberger has beginning around 1822. For this reason, Ellenberger does not mention the advance of the Hlakwana west of the Vaal until the second section on the 'Lifaqane Wars'. See J. Cobbing, 'Overturning the Mfecane: A Reply to Elizabeth Eldredge', paper presented to the Colloquium on the 'Mfecane' Aftermath, University of the Witwatersrand, Johannesburg, 1991, 26–31; Ellenberger, *History of the Basuto*, viii. For further discussion, see Hartley, 'Dithakong and the "Mfecane"', 74–7.

53. Richner, 'The Withering Away of the "Lifaqane"', 9.

himself states, about the existence of the Phuthing and Hlakwana under Tsowane and Nkarahanye respectively, but had not been specifically told that they were represented at Dithakong. Interestingly, on the testimony of Setaki, a son of Nkarahanye, he placed the Phuthing and Hlakwana across the Vaal at this time, where they suffered a great defeat.[54]

Ellenberger himself harboured grave doubts whether the Tlokwa had ever crossed the Vaal, and became convinced that the Phuthing and Hlakwana were at Dithakong. Regrettably, he did not have the opportunity to pursue further sources in order to corroborate his own opinions, and, therefore, contradict historians of the day such as Theal.[55] Of course, had Ellenberger had access to Moffat's private journals, he would have been provided with the ideal and necessary proof.[56]

The existence of the Phuthing and Hlakwana cannot be denied. Today their descendants dwell in Lesotho. Further oral testimonies point to their involvement at Dithakong. From old men of the Phuthing, D.F. Ellenberger's son, Rene, confirmed that 'Tsooane, chief of the Maphuthing, was killed by Makulukama (Coloured people, Griquas) in a fearful fight beyond the Vaal River.'[57] The Revd Daumas, too, writing on behalf of Moletsane, chief of the Taung in the 1820s, documented that Tsowane and his people were defeated near Dithakong by the Griqua.[58] Breutz in the 1940s indicated from Kwena-Modimosana oral traditions that they remembered the 'BaTlhakwane' war of 1823–4.[59] The Hurutshe also recalled the advance of the 'BaTlhakwane' through their territory.[60] In addition, on 3 October 1857, on a visit to Mzilikazi, Moffat was introduced to a foreigner who, on enquiry, was found to be one of 'Chuane's people' defeated at Dithakong. The man mentioned that three great chiefs had fallen that day, namely, 'Chuane, Kharaganye and another.'[61] That Moffat was securing his alibi created 34 years previously, certainly requires a stretch of the imagination.

The only other recorded material by inhabitants of the zone of conflict during this

---

54. Ellenberger, *History of the Basuto*, 139.
55. How, 'An Alibi for Mantatisi', 75.
56. Although the relevant sections of Moffat's private journals were printed in a London Missionary Society publication, *Quarterly Chronicle of Transactions*, 3, London, 1829, and his public memoirs, published in *Missionary Labours and Scenes in Southern Africa* (1842), mentioned the chiefs though not the names of the foreign groupings at Dithakong, it appears that Ellenberger had either no access to them or overlooked the references to prove his ideas. It was only through the publication of Moffat's private journals and letters in Schapera's *Apprenticeship at Kuruman* (1951) that the consensus of the day changed as to who was represented at Dithakong.
57. How, 'An Alibi for Mantatisi', 68.
58. G.M. Theal, *Basutoland Records*, vol. 1, Cape Town, 1883, 517. Notice that Daumas writes, 'Tsuane, Chief of the Bafokeng (who were improperly confounded with the Mantatis)'. R. Ellenberger (D.F. Ellenberger's son) thinks Daumas either misunderstood Moletsane, for he knew little Sotho history, or he cut Moletsane short. Instead of speaking of the Fokeng of Sebetwane and the Phuthing of Tsowane, he collapsed them together. Ellenberger was led to this conclusion, for there has never existed a Fokeng chief called Tsowane. See How, 'An Alibi for Mantatisi', 75.
59. P-L. Breutz, ed., *The Tribes of Rustenburg and Pilansberg Districts*, Pretoria, 1953, 430.
60. P-L. Breutz, ed., *The Tribes of Marico District*, Pretoria, 1953, 7.
61. R. Moffat, *The Matabele Journals of Robert Moffat 1821–1860*, ed. by J.P.R. Wallis, London, 1945, 81.

period was that of Hodgson and S. Broadbent, pioneer missionaries into the upper-Vaal region.[62] Lye has shown that their accounts, taken from a different perspective, dovetail favourably with Moffat's with respect to the approach and retreat of the numerous and desperate grouping.[63] Although the precise nature of movement of the 'Mantatee' prior to Dithakong cannot be held with exact certainty, it seems difficult to deny the existence of the vast foreign grouping in retreat from Dithakong eastwards towards Matlwase.

The contemporary evidence appears to confirm the existence of the foreign grouping,[64] consisting primarily of the Phuthing and Hlakwana. Although Moffat does not mention Sebetwane's Fokeng of Patsa, there does exist a small amount of evidence to suggest that they were also represented at Dithakong. David Livingstone learnt from Sebetwane, shortly before the latter's death, that his people had been part of the vast grouping driven back by the Griqua from Kuruman in 1824.[65] The reference would appear to relate to Dithakong, but is open to interpretation. Ellenberger also situated the Fokeng of Patsa in the neighbourhood of Dithakong.[66] Perhaps Sebetwane was the forgotten third chief? It is difficult to know with any certainty.[67] Moffat did, however, note that the 'Mantatee' at Dithakong also

62. See Hodgson, *Journals*, 101–90; Broadbent, *Narrative*, 20–77; W. Shaw, comp., *Memoirs of Mrs. Anne Hodgson*, London, 1836, ch.7.

63. Lye, 'The Difaqane', 112, 123–9. For further discussion, see Hartley, 'Dithakong and the "Mfecane"', 78–81.

64. Note that Griqua oral tradition also recounts uniform reference to a foreign grouping that came and warred over the African nations of their quarter. See Bloemhof Arbitration Court, *Evidence Taken at Bloemhof Before the Commission Appointed to Investigate the Claims of the South African Republic, Captain N. Waterboer, Chief of West Griqualand, and Certain Other Native Chiefs, to Portions of the Territory on the Vaal River, Now Known As the Diamond Fields*, Cape Town, 1871, evidence of Kruger, 4, 7, 8; evidence of Jansen, 12.

65. D. Livingstone, *Missionary Travels and Researches in South Africa*, London, 1857, 84.

66. Ellenberger, *History of the Basuto*, 137. Ellenberger even describes a battle involving the Patsa at Dithakong a few days before 26 June. In this case, it is difficult to know from where he derived his information.

67. Much concerning the Patsa is open to speculation. In his latest papers, Cobbing argues that the 'known facts' about the Patsa migration path rule against them being near Dithakong. He relates that they first fled eastwards 'probably' from the Griqua or 'perhaps' the Taung. They then came into contact with Portugese slavers 'perhaps somewhere' in the modern Fouriesberg-Bethlehem area. From there, the survivors crossed the southern, central and western Transvaal region towards the Molepolole area via an 'unknown migration path'. The very language Cobbing uses, suggests that his 'known facts' are not well established. It is difficult to demonstrate that either the Griqua or the Taung moved the Patsa groups eastwards from their homelands near modern Virginia. There is mention of the Fokeng chiefs, Sebetwane and Ramabusetsa, coming into contact with slavers, but the evidence suggests that the Patsa fled north-east for the east coast, where they were confronted by the slavers somewhere between Port Natal and Delagoa Bay. The reference derives from oral tradition, a rare instance where Cobbing uses such evidence, and is open to many different readings regarding timing and the nature of the participants. Since it stands alone, it cannot be accepted unreservedly. Certainly the movement of the Patsa prior to their arrival in the Molepolole area in 1824 remains open to speculation, leaving the remote possibility that they were at Dithakong. See Cobbing, 'Jettisoning the Mfecane', 14, 31; Cobbing, 'Rethinking the Roots of Violence in Southern Africa, *c*.1790–1840', paper presented to the Colloquium on the 'Mfecane' Aftermath, University of the Witwatersrand, Johannesburg, 1991, 11–12.

included Hurutshe refugees, who had been absorbed into the conquering 'horde' as it marched through the interior.[68]

It seems strange that many of the early writers believed 'MaNthatisi's Tlokwa were represented at Dithakong, when the reporters clearly illustrated this was not the case. If the etymology of the term Mantatee is considered, however, this designation becomes understandable.

From the earliest reports, it is especially clear that the word did indeed refer to 'MaNthatisi and her Tlokwa. The first messages Moffat received depicted the 'horde' as 'Mantateesa', and always spoke of her in the feminine.[69] Later the word 'Mantatee' became more frequently heard, and the original references never again appeared in European accounts. The very word 'Mantatee' that was adopted and used broadly by Moffat, Thompson and others, has also inextricable links with 'MaNthatisi's Tlokwa. When the first literate European observers entered the Vaal-Caledon region in the 1830s, they discovered that the Tlokwa, indeed, identified themselves as the 'Mantatee'. They did not make the 'Mantatee'/ 'MaNthatisi elision as Cobbing suggests.[70] It was already in place. Andrew Smith, for example, stated explicitly that their principal name was the Tlokwa, 'though at different times it has been called after some of its more remarkable chiefs upon the same principal as it has lately been styled Mantatees, or in other words, the people of Mantatee.'[71] With reference to the Tlokwa/Mantatees, Smith described in 1836 how this had occurred:

> any remarkable instance of prosperity, or any occurrence which is calculated to raise a tribe in the estimation of the others around it, is sometimes considered by the tribe itself as best to be recorded by the adoption of a new name, and on such occasions the name assumed is generally made to refer either to the occurrence or to the ruler under whose government it happened. The other means by which changes are produced, namely, the influence of strangers, operate principally during warlike movements, when bodies come in contact who are unacquainted with each others previous designations. On such occasions the one speaks of the other as the people of such and such a chief, and by perseverance in that system often eventually succeed, at least to a certain extent, in establishing names hitherto unknown in the country.[72]

68. See examples of incorporation in Thompson, *Travels and Adventures*, 107–8. For the Hurutshe refugees, see Moffat and Moffat, *Apprenticeship*, R. Moffat, journal, 21 July 1823, 102.
69. Moffat and Moffat, *Apprenticeship*, R. Moffat, journal, 16 May 1823, 77.
70. Cobbing, 'The Mfecane as Alibi', 515.
71. A. Smith, *Andrew Smith's Journal of His Expedition into the Interior of South Africa: 1834–36*, Cape Town, 1975, 92. See also T. Arbousset and F. Daumas, *Narrative of an Exploratory Tour to the North-East of the Colony of the Cape of Good Hope*, Cape Town, 1968, (originally publ. in 1846), 31.
72. Theal, *Basutoland Records*, vol. 1, Extracts from the report of the expedition for exploring Central Africa from the Cape of Good Hope, under the superintendence of Dr. A. Smith, 13.

Through a combination of these two processes, then, the Tlokwa had come to be known as the 'Mantatee'. It would appear 'MaNthatisi had gained infamy as the leader of a warlike grouping, and, given the extent of her power, her name became the epithet by which other warlike bands were characterised. This interpretation seems to be placed beyond doubt when Moffat writes:

> The prisoners also inform us that they are not the Mantatees; but that numerous and powerful tribes bearing that name are also, according to report, infesting the interior, plundering, etc.[73]

The fact that Moffat continued to use the term 'Mantatee' to denote peoples he knew were not in actuality the 'Mantatee', seems to have been the cause of much of the confusion in the past. Moffat used the word in a similar way to the Tswana for whom it signified 'Invader' or 'Marauder', describing wandering foreigners stemming from the east.[74] As was the practice, then, Moffat applied the word to foreign invaders other than those at Dithakong as well.[75] Similarly, the word acquired a generic meaning within the Cape colony, by which refugees of the interior were designated, including groupings of Tswana.[76] Over time, Moffat's initial identifications became obscured, and later writers, removed from the events in both space and time, uncritically made the Tlokwa/Mantatee elision with the 'Mantatee' of Dithakong.

The Battle of Dithakong and the Chains of Violence in the West

Given that there did indeed exist a numerous and destitute migratory grouping at Dithakong, it becomes necessary to reconsider the revisionist explanations for the upheavals in the interior in the early 1820s. In the final section of this essay, then, some broader implications of the battle will be considered, with particular reference to the conflicts west of the Drakensberg in the years 1822–4.

The revisionists attempt to establish the chains of violence in the trans-Orange region in terms of forces stemming from that zone itself, arguing that the raiders originated in the south and that the dominant flow of violence was from west to east, or south-west to north-east.[77] To suggest, however, that Griqua-Kora-renegade European raids, such as the alleged one at Dithakong, were the cause of the destruction of African communities in the west in the years 1822–3, rests upon shaky empirical ground. A review of their evidence indicates that Griqua-Bergenaar-Kora

---

73. Moffat and Moffat, *Apprenticeship*, R. Moffat, journal, 21 July 1823, 103.
74. Thompson, *Travels and Adventures*, 204. See also evidence of this in the vernacular histories, *Dico tsa Secwana* and *Ditirafalo tsa merafe ya BaTswana*, cited in E. W. Smith, 'Sebetwane and the Makololo', *African Studies*, 15, 2 (1956), 53 n. 1.
75. Moffat and Moffat, *Apprenticeship*, 132–3, 144–52.
76. (CA) CO 1/GR 15/71 Graaff-Reinet Register 1826–7: 'Apprentices of the Mantatee Nation'. See also, Lye, 'The Difaqane', 122 note 94.
77. Cobbing, 'The Mfecane as Alibi', 498–9; Richner, 'The Withering Away of the "Lifaqane"', 3.

raiding played an important role in the conflicts from late 1823 onwards, but cannot be easily maintained for the period prior to Dithakong.[78]

The imagery of the Griqua before 1823 as slave and cattle raiders whose attacks 'had been going on for years'[79] is difficult to validate. The majority of Griqua were restrained from illegal trading and raiding by the leading families, in whose interests it was to dominate, specifically, the ivory trade and stabilise the region.[80] Most of Cobbing and Richner's examples involve small, autonomous bands of Griqua who often aligned themselves with exceptional, unruly frontiersmen such as Coenraad Bezuidenhout, Cobus Vry and Coenraad de Buys. Their impact, however, was sporadic and transitory, and did not seriously disrupt local communities. Breakaway groups such as the Bergenaar played a more significant role. Towards the end of 1822, the renegade Bergenaar grouping that was to be the cause of much devastation in the future, began to penetrate the south-eastern fringe of southern Sotho settlement. Given their small numbers and initial disorganisation, they appear only to have become effective raiders towards the end of 1823.[81] It can only be speculated what the extent of their role was before Dithakong. By no means, however, did their reach extend so deep into the Vaal-Caledon region by the end of 1822 as to cause the population migration of the Phuthing and Hlakwana from their homelands along the Wilge River west of the Drakensberg on to the highveld. Neither has it been established that their attacks set in motion groups closer to their home base who, in turn, devastated areas further afield by this time.[82]

Towards the end of 1823 a number of forces that changed the situation were unleashed. One such force was the dislocation on the highveld caused by the 'Mantatee' together with the growth of the Bergenaar who were free from any restraint.[83] Another was the increase in guns and the possibilities of illicit trading,[84] which fostered raiding on the Sotho/Tswana that proved devastating over the years. Cobbing and Richner have illuminated well the nature and impact of these raids. Yet

78. See Cobbing, 'The Mfecane as Alibi', 496–8, especially notes 49–51; Richner, 'The Withering Away of the "Lifaqane"', 2–7.

79. Cobbing, 'The Mfecane as Alibi', 496; Richner, 'The Withering Away of the "Lifaqane"', 8.

80. M. Legassick, 'The Northern Frontier to 1820: The Emergence of the Griqua People', in R. Elphick and H. B. Giliomee, eds, *The Shaping of South African Society, 1652–1820*, Cape Town, 1979, 258.

81. *BPP*, Papers Relative to the Condition . . ., Report by Melvill to the Colonial Secretary, Dec. 1824, 214.

82. See, for example, Cobbing's evidences for the impact of the Taung by this period. As yet, they do not provide strong support. Cobbing, 'The Mfecane as Alibi', 497–8. See also Richner, 'The Withering Away of the "Lifaqane"', 5–6.

83. *BPP*, Papers Relative to the Condition . . ., Report by Melvill to the Colonial Secretary, Dec. 1824, 214–15; Legassick, 'The Griqua, the Sotho–Tswana and the Missionaries', 302–3.

84. Legassick, 'The Griqua, the Sotho–Tswana and the Missionaries', 347–8. By 1824 'Bushmanland' which had separated colonial society from the Griqua had been penetrated and the possibilities of illegal trading were more certain. Evidence of Bergenaar and Kora selling captives clandestinely dates, to a large extent, from this period. See *BPP*, Papers Relative to the Condition . . ., Lord C. H. Somerset to the Commissioners of Inquiry, 227, and Melvill to Colonial Secretary, Dec. 1824, 217; Legassick, 'The Griqua, the Sotho–Tswana and the Missionaries', 353–5; Ellenberger, *History of the Basuto*, 214; Arbousset and Daumas, *Narrative*, 228; Philip, *Researches in South Africa*, vol. 2, 81–91.

they have failed to show continuity between this later raiding, and Bergenaar-Kora attacks prior to 1823. Certainly these pressures must have played some role in the initial conflicts. It is not the intention of this essay to undermine the necessity for further research in this area. Detailed case studies of each raiding community are urgently needed and will no doubt establish a more prominent place for the Bergenaars and Kora. However, to suggest that they singly constituted the motors of violence in the trans-Orange region, is an over-ambitious claim, and lacks sufficient support. Such a thesis contravenes the existing evidence and requires stronger backing before it can be accepted.

It therefore becomes necessary to reconsider the traditional interpretations which attest that the initial devastations originated in the east. Largely on the basis of oral reports, it has traditionally been argued that the arrival of the Nguni-speaking invaders across the Drakensberg began a great cataclysmic event amongst the Sotho, sending the Tlokwa, Phuthing, Hlakwana and others into careers of violence. The first European travellers into the Vaal-Caledon region gave uniform reports, on the basis of their African informants, that it was Matiwane's Ngwane and Mpangazi-tha's Hlubi who began a desperate time of turmoil. Lye has collated this evidence from a range of European and African sources in his article, 'The Difaqane: The Mfecane in the Southern Sotho Area, 1822–24', and regarded it as 'tentatively substantiated' yet clear with respect to the identity of those involved. Lye was careful to corroborate the oral traditions with other oral and documentary evidence, and when traditions conflicted noted the differences.[85]

There is no disagreement pertaining to the arrival by the early 1820s of the Ngwane and Hlubi in the Vaal-Caledon region. However, both Cobbing and Richner assert that the scale of the violence between these groups and the established residents of the Vaal-Caledon has been grossly exaggerated. By 1824–5 the Tlokwa, Hlubi and Ngwane were living relatively close together and had sought out flat-topped mountains for defence, and Cobbing and Richner argue that this fact suggests that they were not mortal enemies, but, rather, had made local accommodations in response to exterior menaces common to them all. These exterior menaces are identified as Griqua-Bergenaar-Kora raiders.[86]

The revisionists deal briefly with the traditionally alleged severity of the conflicts between Nguni/Sotho-speakers around 1822–4. They notice correctly that the evidences for the activities of these groups are derived primarily from oral traditions. Few literate reporters had penetrated this region by 1823. It was only later that the oral histories were documented. Cobbing and Richner believe these traditions, when recorded years later, have been fundamentally tainted, and cannot be relied upon for determining original reality. Richner, for example, argues:

> Informants and interpreters sometimes consciously misinformed the recipient. Owing to their 'settler mentality', Europeans often took information purely

85. Lye, 'The Difaqane', 131.
86. Cobbing, 'The Mfecane as Alibi', 507–8; Richner, 'The Withering Away of the "Lifaqane"', 10.

literally. Their ignorance of the 'rules of the game' made it difficult to interpret such information and this led to misinterpretations. There was also ignorance of the language and the incompetence of interpreters. All this made the decoding of reality hazardous.[87]

For this reason, the revisionists tend to dismiss wholly African versions of the past. Oral traditions described as being overly generalised, dramatised and exaggerated, are almost totally neglected.

Certainly a highly critical reassessment of African responses, which have too often in the past been accepted at face value, is urgently needed. The decoding of these oral traditions offers no easy task, requiring a whole reconstruction of their own histories. But the approach of the revisionists which dismisses African sources is both unhelpful and unwarranted. By rejecting these sources, the revisionists are arguing the monolithic case that whites completely controlled the production of history, independent of the historical consciousness of the Africans concerned. It is difficult to suggest that nothing of African intellectual history from this period has reached the present.

Before serious revision of African responses is pursued, the following points related to the findings on Dithakong suggest, in the meantime, at least the partial authentication of these oral traditions. The fact the 'Mantatee' prisoners related that they had been driven from their countries in the east by the 'Matabele' gives these sources strong credibility. From the descriptions given, it was believed by Moffat and others that the 'Matabele' either referred to southern or northern Nguni-speakers.[88] This agrees with Ellenberger who, on oral evidence, noted the following about the derivation of the word:

> It was during this period [the Lifaqane] that the designation Matabele was given to the Kaffirs of Natal by the Basuto. It is a derivative of the verb *ho tebele*, 'to drive away', and means 'the destroyers' . . . the Basuto designated all those to the east of it [the Drakensberg] by the term Matabele, which includes the Zulus, Swazis, Mahlubi, Amangwane, and many others.[89]

The nature of the uprooted 'Mantatee' communities at Dithakong – numerous, destitute and desperate – reflects something of the heightened scale of violence in the Vaal-Caledon region originating in the east, and the corresponding destructive character of the fleeing communities forced into careers of violence. The very reference to 'Mantatee', which those at Dithakong themselves denied and insisted applied to numerous other powerful groups invading the interior, suggests that a number of peoples in the Vaal-Caledon suffered similar fates. Considering that the

---

87. Richner, 'The Withering Away of the "Lifaquane"', 3.
88. Moffat and Moffat, *Apprenticeship*, R. Moffat, journal, 31 May 1823, 85, 21 July 1823, 101. See also Hodgson, *Journals*, 182.
89. Ellenberger, *History of the Basuto*, 120. See also Arbousset and Daumas, *Narrative*, 134.

word specifically applied to 'MaNthatisi's Tlokwa and became the epithet by which other invading groups were known, indicates that the Tlokwa were engaged in a series of attacks in the Vaal-Caledon region. Having been displaced by forces from the east similar to the Phuthing and Hlakwana, these attacks appear to have been as devastating in this region as those of the Phuthing and Hlakwana beyond the Vaal.

It would appear that the African oral reports need to be taken more seriously and cannot be dismissed lightly. The dislocation of whole communities from east to west in a period of intensive deprivation and formidable strife, stemming from Nguni-speaking forces in the east and sustained by continued intra-Sotho/Tswana attacks, particularly around 1822–3, cannot easily be disregarded.

The Battle of Dithakong and 'Mfecane' Theory

It might be questioned at this point whether this study serves to ratify the traditional 'mfecane' model? To be sure, the study affirms in a limited way certain elements within 'mfecane' theory, but the concept of the 'mfecane' has become too broad and complex over the decades to preserve in the present any continued analytical usefulness. Today, the 'mfecane' can refer in its broadest sense to the Zulucentric diaspora, which affected vast regions of south-central Africa as far away as Lake Victoria, encompassing an era of history from the end of the eighteenth century to the end of the nineteenth century. Cobbing has pointed to the many myths that constitute this macro-theory, revealing errors of fact, problems of periodisation and the theory's pervading Afrocentricism.[90] The challenge has become to deconstruct the development of the 'mfecane' as macro-myth.

A review of the earlier 'mfecane' writers shows that they did not mean the word in this macro-sense.[91] In fact, the first writers, who used the term 'lifaqane' or 'difaqane', referred the word primarily to the trans-Orange disruptions amongst the Sotho west of the Drakensberg, in the relatively short period 1820–8. They emphasised little the self-generated internal revolution of Shaka and focused upon the displacements of chiefdoms west of the Drakensberg.[92] For this reason, the chains of violence west of the Drakensberg have been referred more strictly as the 'lifaqane' or 'difaqane', as opposed to the later, broader less tenable Zulucentric

---

90. See in particular, Cobbing, 'The Case Against the Mfecane'.
91. See for example: Ellenberger, *History of the Basuto*, 137–236; J.C MacGregor, *Basuto Traditions*, Cape Town, 1905; G.E. Cory, *The Rise of South Africa*, Cape Town, 1965, (originally publ. 1910–30), vol. 2, 230–9; Stow, *The Native Races of South Africa*, 460–87; Theal, *History of South Africa*, 428–56 (although Theal, Stow and Cory do not use the term 'mfecane', their view of the upheavals is similar to those who later referred to the concept); W.M. Macmillan, *Bantu, Boer, and Briton: The Making of the South African Native Problem*, London, 1929, 14–18; E.A. Walker, *A History of South Africa*, 3rd ed., London, 1964, 175–6. This is also true for recent writers such as W. Lye and C. Murray in *Transformations on the Highveld: The Tswana and Southern Sotho*, Cape Town, 1980, 28–39. It was only through Omer-Cooper in *The Zulu Aftermath* of the 1960s that the term assumed its broader meaning.
92. See Ellenberger, *History of the Basuto*, 137–236; MacGregor, *Basuto Traditions*.

'mfecane' theory. Once again, however, these writers over-elaborated the Afrocentric nature of the turmoil. Cobbing and Richner have rightly reassessed the extent of Bergenaar-Kora raiding after 1823–4. Although 'difaqane' writers included these forces in the 'difaqane' wars, they failed to address their nature and impact in a cohesive and analytical way.[93] Cobbing and Richner have begun this process. Indeed, the magnitude of their impact on the communities of the highveld has yet to be fully realised. These raids were especially destructive given the raiders' ready access to arms and ammunition. Both Sotho/Tswana and Nguni-speaking groupings suffered greatly. Mzilikazi's Ndebele faced many frontal assaults, just as it appears Griqua-Bergenaar attacks played an important part in driving the Ngwane southwards from the Caledon Valley.[94]

However, by attempting to explain the upheavals west of the Drakensberg primarily in terms of Bergenaar-Kora raids within the wider supposition of European expansion for labour, Cobbing and Richner make the very same mistake for which they criticise 'mfecane' theorists. Their error is to shift the pendulum to the other extreme by only emphasising the Eurocentric nature of the upheavals. They leave no effective place for African agency. Intent on demolishing virtually every aspect of 'mfecane' theory, they have inextricably linked their re-examination with their counter-paradigm of 'European' penetration as basis. Their view of the creation of the 'mfecane' myth, then, becomes as Eurocentric as 'mfecane' theory is Afrocentric.

Clearly, though, if there exists any truth within the concept of the 'mfecane', it must surely relate to the 'difaqane' and the initial chains of violence around 1822–3 west/north-west of the Drakensberg that appear, in essence, African. If the 'mfecane' ultimately refers to the 'coming of the Nguni', then surely its truth lies in the initial devastations they caused in the Vaal-Caledon region, devastations that were largely over by 1823–4. They set certain chains of violence in motion that over time involved many less well illuminated forces.

It appears the word 'mfecane' derived from the term 'fetcane', used in the eastern Cape to refer to northern Nguni-speakers, a word which itself derived from the Sotho 'lifaqane'. The Sotho west of the Drakensberg were the first to use the term, by alluding to northern Nguni-speakers as the 'Bakoni' or 'Lifakoni, that is to say, those who hew down, or cut their enemies in pieces with the chake, their formidable battle axe'.[95] Over time, the word appears to have gained a broader meaning amongst

---

93. See Ellenberger, *History of the Basuto*, 212–16; Lye and Murray, *Transformations on the Highveld*, 39–44; Cory, *The Rise of South Africa*, 230; Stow, *The Native Races of South Africa*, 485; Macmillan, *Bantu, Boer, and Briton*, 15.

94. See Richner, 'The Withering Away of the "Lifaqane"', chs 5 and 6; Cobbing, 'The Mfecane as Alibi', 508.

95. Arbousset and Daumas, *Narrative*, 134. This relates to Lye's translation of 'difaqane' as hammering which is rendered in Sotho orthography: Lye, 'The Difaqane', 107. Notice Mabille and Dieterlen in their *Southern Sotho English Dictionary*, Morija, 1961, refer 'kone (Mokone, Bakone, Dikone)' to a member of the Nguni-speaking groups. It does not appear tenable that the word 'fetcane' had its ultimate origins in the eastern Cape as Cobbing proposes in 'The Case Against the Mfecane', 14.

Sotho-speakers, signifying a period of wars 'waged by nomadic tribes accompanied on the warpath by their women, children and property, as distinct from the ordinary kind of war between settled tribes where only the fighting men go out'.[96] Its initial rendering, however, seems to relate to the coming of the Nguni-speakers who brought with them a distinctive time of trouble in the Vaal-Caledon region.

Certainly the precise functioning of the socio-economic and political processes behind the initial African motors of violence and subsequent chain reactions remains unresolved. To what extent were eastern European forces involved behind the coming of the Nguni-speakers? What part did economic and environmental factors together with their effects upon the internal dynamics within African polities play? These are questions that lie beyond the boundaries of this study. The essay does, however, attempt to provide a more adequate framework for approaching these questions. It has been suggested that Cobbing's Eurocentric theory of the chains of violence west of the Drakensberg is built upon an inadequate foundation. Instead, a synthetic approach has been proposed: the conflicts in the west need to be viewed as a complex interplay of European and African forces. They were essentially African in character in the years 1822–3, stemming from the arrival of northern Nguni-speakers west/north-west of the Drakensberg, with 'European' forces from the west increasingly coming to play after 1823–4. What is needed is the recognition of two macro-myths – one Eurocentric and the other Afrocentric – both of which require dismantling. They have both in their own ways created a barrier with respect to the history of the period.

In conclusion, the battle of Dithakong has shown itself to be crucial to the very heart of the latest debates on early nineteenth-century history of the southern African interior. Discussion of events at Dithakong has revealed both the poverty of the revisionists' singular Eurocentric theory of violence in the west and their methodology, posing questions for other areas of their work. To be sure, Dithakong remains more than just an historical battle site of the 1820s: it is a critical location for the very future of nineteenth-century southern African historiography of the interior.

Acknowledgement

The financial assistance of the Centre for Science Development towards this research is hereby acknowledged. Opinions expressed in this essay, or conclusions arrived at, are those of the author and are not necessarily to be attributed to the Centre for Science Development.

96. MacGregor, *Basuto Traditions*, 8. See also Ellenberger, *History of the Basuto*, 117.

16

Untapped Sources
Slave Exports from Southern and Central Namibia up to c.1850

JAN-BART GEWALD

This essay was written as a reaction to the attempts to prescribe the 'Mfecane' as a historiographical panacea for Namibian history. Until the mid-1980s Namibia's unique historiography – the idea that Namibian history did not exist prior to the German and South African occupations – served to shield it from mfecane mythology. However as historians have sought to develop an 'authentic African' Namibian history, they have begun taking nips of this addictive brew. Of late historians have had Kololo or other 'Zulu-ised' hordes zigzagging out of the southern African highveld and attacking Herero settlements in western Botswana and eastern Namibia.[1]

At present I do not dispute that these attacks took place for there is no question that central and southern Namibia were shaken up in the early nineteenth century. I do, however, dispute the idea of the mfecane as the cause of all these disturbances. The perspectives robs Namibia of its history, and might, as was the case with South African history, spawn decades of informationless history, obscuring details of Namibia's past. In no way do I wish to argue that Namibian history was formed within a unique area encapsulating present-day Namibia, untouched by events in surrounding areas. Jonker Afrikaner did not suddenly materialise out of nowhere. Namibian history is inextricably linked with that of the rest of southern Africa and the world; the same historical processes operating in the rest of Africa operated in Namibia. It would, however, be wrong to sully Namibian history with the myths of the mfecane. Instead this essay falls within the stream of thought which argues that the expulsion of the Oorlam into present-day Namibia and the raiding for cattle, goods and slaves for the Cape and Atlantic trade were the prime causes for the instability in central and southern Namibia in the early nineteenth century.

It is a generally accepted historical thesis that no slaving for the transatlantic or

---

1. Namibian National Archives (hereafter NNA): Accession 415, A transcription of the interview with Mr Kaputu on 17 May 1984, unpaginated; T. Tlou, *A History of Ngamiland 1750 to 1906: The Formation of an African State*, Gaborone 1985, 43.

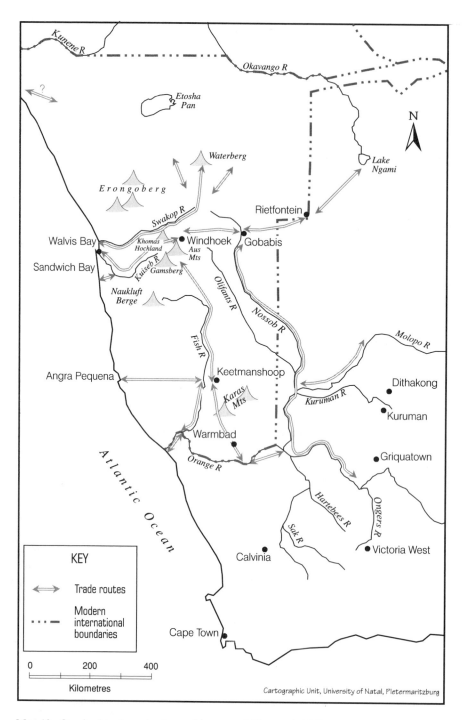

Map 13. Overland trade routes in south-western Africa up to 1840

Cape colonial trade ever occurred in precolonial central and southern Namibia.[2] Between 1800 and 1835 the partly intermeshing Cape colonial, Mozambican and Angolan slave systems were ensuring slave imports and exports throughout much of southern Africa. By 1825 the Cape colonial system had expanded into the areas of trans-Orange and trans-Vaal. Here it linked up with the Mozambican slave system which, further north, extended far into Africa along the Zambezi where it connected with the south-western fringes of the Angolan slave system. Thus in a swathe that extended from Cape Town to Delagoa Bay and beyond slaves were imported and exported from south-eastern Africa. Similarly, north of the Kunene River through to the Bight of Biafra and beyond, slaves were imported and exported from west central Africa; and within the confines of present-day South Africa Griqua and associated raiders operated along the Vaal, Orange, Molopo and Limpopo River systems supplying cattle and slaves to the frontier farmers of the Cape colony.[3]

When these systems are transcribed on to a topographical map of southern Africa one finds a *terra incognita*, as far as slavery is concerned, that extends from the north-western boundary of the Cape colony through to the Kunene and Okavango Rivers in the north and the Makgadigadi pans in the east. The expanse described contains most of what is now Namibia and a very large section of present-day Botswana.

Given that central and southern Namibia were surrounded on all sides by the Angolan, Mozambican and Cape colonial slave systems, the question that naturally arises is whether one can continue to believe that the territory of central and southern Namibia was indeed a vacuum within which no slaving for the transatlantic and Cape colonial trades took place. This essay argues that Namibia did not proceed through history unaffected by the demands of these slave trades. It provides evidence which substantiates this refutation and suggests further avenues of investigation.

Europe's First Recorded Contacts with Namibia

Europe's first contact with Namibia was characterised by slavery, indeed Namibia's first ocean-borne immigrants were slaves. When in 1486 Dias attempted to round the southern tip of Africa he had on board four women slaves taken from the coast of

---

2. W.G. Clarence-Smith, ed., *Economics of the Indian Ocean Slave-trade in the Nineteenth Century*, London, 1989; and J.C. Miller, *Way of Death: Merchant Capitalism and the Angolan Slave Trade, 1730–1830*, London, 1988, have detailed the overlap and the Angolan slave trade into northern Namibia.

3. See J.C. Miller, *Way of Death*; J. Cobbing, 'The Mfecane as Alibi: Thoughts on Dithakong and Mbolompo', in *Journal of African History*, 29 (1988), 487–519; 'Grasping the Nettle: The Slave Trade and the Early Zulu', in D.R. Edgecombe, J.P.C. Laband and P.S. Thompson, comps, *The Debate on Zulu Origins: A Selection of Papers on the Zulu Kingdom and Early Colonial Natal*, Pietermaritzburg, 1992.

Guinea. Two of the women were consigned to an almost certain death when they were put ashore at Angra Pequena and at Angra das Voltas, near the mouth of the Orange River, . . . 'to make discoveries and report to the next white man they should see'.[4]

The Dutch East India Company's (VOC) permanent settlement at the Cape of Good Hope, was dependant on slave labour and the settlement's appeals for slaves were frequent. Slaving expeditions, which sought to appease this demand, were regularly sent out. In 1669 the directors of the VOC expressly ordered an expedition up along the west coast from Table Bay. Captain Gerrit Ridder Muys, commander of the yacht *De Grundel*, was directed to sail:

> . . . along the coast and as much as seamanship allows until about the tropic, at the same time putting into all the bays, inlets and rivers which you are able to enter, . . . and as it is certain that along this coast you will meet no 'Hottentoosen' but a nation named 'caffres' you will have to deal with them carefully, . . . , Furthermore you are advised to (if it is possible) negotiate or trade for some of this nation as slaves.[5]

In May of 1670 a heavily armed landing party from *De Grundel* was repulsed by people living at Walvis Bay. Though the landing party had attempted to use their muskets, the damp mists so characteristic of Namibia's coastline had ensured that 'the powder in the pan refused to spark'.[6] A few years later, in 1677, a similar VOC expedition also ended in bloodshed following a dispute regarding cattle.[7]

The Northern Cape Frontier and its Movement into Southern Namibia

Slavery overland from southern and central Namibia appears to have been the by-product of the cattle trade: pastoralists deprived of their cattle became either captives or free San.[8] Within ten years of the founding of the VOC settlement the company, in an effort to feed its insatiable appetite for beef, began sending expeditions north to the 'cattle rich' Namaqua. The Namaqua, 'once they became aware of what contact with the Colony entailed', seldom ventured south beyond the Kamies Berg.[9] Khoi captain Hannibal, asked about to the paucity of his flocks, illustrated what colonial contact implied when he replied:

4. G. M. Theal, *History of Africa South of the Zambesi*, vol. 2, Cape Town, 1964, 29.
5. Author's translation of E. C. Godee Molsbergen, *Reizen in Zuid Afrika in de Hollandse Tijd*, Den Haag, 1916, tweede deel, 129, quoting from *Kol. Arch. No. 3982 f. 542–4*. 'Instructie voor den Schipper Gerrit Ridder Muys gaende met 't Hoeckertje de Grundel van hier noortwaerts dese Residentie, omme aldaer 't volgende ten dienste van d'E. Compe. te verrigten,' 12 Maart a'. 1670.
6. Molsbergen, *Reizen in Zuid Afrika*, 132.
7. Molsbergen, *Reizen in Zuid Afrika*, 132–3.
8. I use the term San as a prefix or suffix denoting dispossessed, as in San-Dama and Khoi-san. The Herero suffix -Tjimba denotes the same.
9. N. G. Penn, 'The Frontier in the Western Cape, 1700–1740', in J. Parkington and M. Hall, eds, *Papers in the Prehistory of the Western Cape*, Oxford, 1987, 464–5.

> A couple of years before a certain freeman, commonly known as Drunken Gerrit, accompanied by others, had arrived at his kraal, and without saying anything, opened fire from all sides, thereby chasing away the 'Hottentots', they had set all their houses alight, and took all the cattle with them, without them knowing what the reason was, as they had never insulted the Hollanders.[10]

Within the first twenty-five years of the eighteenth century the cattle raiders passed beyond the little Namaqua '. . . to the big "Amaquas" [Namaqua] and "Briquas" [Damara] who lay beyond the river . . . to take cattle from the above named nations'.[11] It has been estimated that the VOC consumed over 100 million kilograms of meat per year in the 1720s and that in the early 1720s the Company experienced an acute shortage of meat.[12] The shortage of meat led to an ever-expanding raiding frontier and the gravest excesses being committed by Company meat contractors.[13] In 1722 Company meat contractor, Jacobus Van der Heyden, armed and equipped a commando of no less than seventy men, which raided cattle and sheep nearly one thousand kilometres from Cape Town.[14]

By the third decade of the eighteenth century it had become the norm for the survivors of commando raids to be enslaved. The first recorded instance of this occurred in February 1731 when a commando attacked a Khoisan grouping known as the 'ten sons of Grebnan'. Six of the Khoi were killed, and a woman and three children were taken captive to be distributed amongst colonists over the mountains.[15]

By the late 1730s major expeditions were being sent into southern Namibia for hunting, trading and raiding purposes.[16] In one such instance ten colonists, some of whom had taken part in the 'ten sons' commando, accompanied by a number of Khoi servants, crossed the Orange River to the establishment of the Namaqua chief Gal. Here they spent a month. However,

> When the time came for their departure . . . the colonists slipped secretly away and instructed their servants [having supplied them with firearms] to return to the kraal, attack the Great Namaqua and carry off their cattle.[17]

An indication as to the profitability of these raids is given by the fact that in this instance no less than a thousand cattle and an unspecified number of captives were acquired.[18]

10. Molsbergen, *Reizen in Zuid Afrika*, 5.
11. C.F. Brink and J.T. Rhenius, *The Journals of Brink and Rhenius*, Cape Town, 1947, 144.
12. R. Ross, *The Economy of the Cape Colony in the Eighteenth Century*, Leiden, 1987.
13. Penn, 'The Frontier in the Western Cape', 471.
14. Penn, 'The Frontier in the Western Cape', 471. 'Commando' is used in this instance as referring to the groups of mounted gunmen used for raiding, slaving, hunting, defensive and offensive purposes characteristic of the South African frontier.
15. Penn, 'The Frontier in the Western Cape', 475–6.
16. Brink and Rhenius, *The Journals*, 94.
17. Penn, 'The Frontier in the Western Cape', 477.
18. Penn, 'The Frontier in the Western Cape', 478.

Given the incessant raids, instability and general insecurity of living close to the expanding frontier, it is hardly surprising that Khoi moved away. In 1760 Jacobus Coetsé's party encountered communities which had fled across the Orange River twenty years previously, now living a full five days' travel north of the Orange.[19] The people, whom Coetsé met living at present-day Warmbad, were the !Khami nun or Bondelswarts. An indication as to the extent of the flight of the !Khami nun is provided by the journals of Olof Bergh, who met the 'Caminge' in the neighbour-hood of Garies 240 kilometres to the south in 1682; and Simon van der Stel who encountered the 'Kamizons' on his trip to Namaqualand in 1685. Suggestive of the Namaqua distrust and fear of people from the colony is the fact that 'they did not hesitate to tell him [Coetsé] frankly that his arrival there pleased them little'.[20] This did not however prevent Coetsé from proceding further and returning to Cape Town with one of their number.[21]

One of the largest parties organised was the massive Hop expedition, which entered Namibia in September 1761, and which consisted of no less than 17 Europeans, 68 Basters, 15 wagons, 400 kilograms of powder and other goods.[22] The journals record the manner in which the Namaqua (!Khami nun) reacted to the appearance of the expedition and are instructive as to Namaqua perceptions of the colony and its representatives:

> . . . we arrived today at one of the 'Great Namaqua' kraals, of which the inhabitants, although they had been told of our approach, when they saw some of our company approaching on horseback, all fled, so that in the huts we could only find old wives and men, both of whom were very shy . . .[23]

By the early 1760s people associated with the colony – those people with firearms and horses – were actively sought after and involved in inter-community conflicts in southern Namibia. The Hop expedition was invited to take part in attacks and in March 1762 Baster wagon drivers reported that burghers Jacobus Coetsé and Josua Joubert were active in southern Namibia.[24]

Ross has estimated that in the fifty years prior to the 1770s the meat requirements of the VOC had risen by 150 per cent.[25] This spectacular increase was reflected in conditions along the Orange. The testimony of VOC runaway Wikar, who had been

---

19. H.J. Wikar, J.C.J. Jansz and W. van Reenen, *The Journal of Hendrik Jakob Wikar (1779) with an English Translation by A.W. van der Horst,* and *The Journals of Jacobus Coetse Jansz (1760) and Willem van Reenen (1791) with an English Translation by Dr E.E. Mossop,* ed., with an introduction and footnotes by E.E. Mossop, Cape Town, 1935, 281.
20. Wikar, Jansz and Van Reenen, *Journal,* 281.
21. Wikar, Jansz and Van Reenen, *Journal,* 288.
22. E.C. Tabler, *Pioneers of South West Africa and Ngamiland,* Cape Town, 1973, 58–9.
23. Author's translation of Brink and Rhenius, *The Journals,* 30.
24. Brink and Rhenius, *The Journals,* 65.
25. Cited in N. Penn, 'Pastoralists and Pastoralism in the Northern Cape Frontier Zone during the Eighteenth Century', *South African Archaeological Society, Goodwin Series,* 5 (1986), 63.

allowed to accompany a trading party, as he had a horse and a gun, indicates the tumultuous nature of the Orange River communities at the time.[26] Khoi cattle-owning communities which had impressed travellers with their wealth ten years previously were 'now scattered after one of Cupido Roggevelt's raids'.[27] Even the very well protected inhabitants of Paarden Eylandt in the Orange River – 'you have to walk for half an hour or a little longer through four streams of water and a dense thicket of trees before you get to their kraal' – hid their cattle at the approach of strangers as 'they thought we would treat them as Cupido Roggvelt had done, the terror of which had not yet left them'.[28]

Whilst Wikar was with the party they traded with Namaqua who lived in Namibia. These Namaqua were engaged in raiding to the north and supplying the colonial market to the south with cattle and slaves. Wikar provides first-hand evidence of Damara captives living amongst the Namaqua:

> I have seen four persons of this tribe among the Kamingou [!Khami nun]. They have not long hair as has been written of them.
>   . . . two men with two women and children of the Damrocqua tribe, who were as black as the natives of Terra de Natal . . .[29]

In 1774 the colony had grown to such an extent that the slaving massacre known as the 'general commando' of 1774 could take place. A total of 503 Khoi were killed and 241 captured. The captured were used to alleviate the labour shortage of the growing colony and were 'placed with the inhabitants'.[30] By the late 1770s the settlement frontier entered Namibia when farms were granted to colonists along the Orange River.[31] It was through these farms that VOC meat contractors, such as the Van Reenens, were actively engaged in channelling the herds tapped from the Namibian interior south to the slaughter houses and farms of the colony.[32]

The economic boom experienced by the Cape colony in the 1780s is reflected in the dramatic increase in slaves during the same period.[33] Though there was undoubtedly a definite labour shortage throughout the colony by the late 1700s, it was not until 1791 that the VOC permitted the free trade in slaves.[34] It is therefore no coincidence that in the same year Willem van Reenen, one of the affluent land-owning VOC meat contractor Van Reenen clan, returned from an expedition to

26. Penn, 'Pastoralists and Pastoralism', 63 n.6.
27. Brink and Rhenius, *The Journals*, 65; Wikar, Jansz and Van Reenen, *Journal*, 47.
28. Wikar, Jansz and Van Reenen, *Journal*, 121 and 125.
29. Wikar, Jansz and Van Reenen, *Journal*, 25 and n.12.
30. N. Penn, 'Anarchy and Authority in the Koue Bokkeveld, 1739–1779: The Banishing of Carel Buitendag', in *Kleio*, 17 (1985), 32 n.46.
31. Wikar, Jansz and Van Reenen, *Journal*, 34 and 197.
32. Tabler, *Pioneers*, 86, 112.
33. James C. Armstrong, 'The Slaves, 1652–1795', in R. Elphick and H.B. Giliomee, eds, *The Shaping of South African Society: 1652–1820*, Cape Town, 1979, 91.
34. Armstrong, 'The Slaves', 82.

central Namibia with eight Damara.[35] Interestingly, in the early 1860s, one of Willem's descendants, Johannes van Reenen petitioned the Governor of the Cape 'Recommending Introduction of Negroes from Damaraland' and 'Proposing to be Government Agent at settlement of Kaffirs in Damaraland'.[36]

With the colony's ever increasing pressure in the south the original inhabitants of central Namibia were forced into an accommodation with or retreat from the expanding Namaqua; whose acquisition of cattle was a very direct event:

> The Damraas, and even the Numaquas themselves, gave us to understand that if the Numaquas wish to obtain cattle they go to the Commaka Dammerassen and barter or steal as many as they want or can manage to take away.[37]

The increasing introduction of firearms into the Namibian interior during the second half of the eighteenth century had resulted in the Herero/Damara inhabitants between present-day Kalkrand and Windhoek being relieved of their stock and forced to withdraw north and into the mountains.

Between 1800 and 1840 the Namaqua inhabitants of Namibia were overtaken and subsumed in their northern expansion by the wave of people from the colonial frontier collectively known as the Oorlam. In the late eighteenth century Oorlam communities had emerged along the north-western Cape colonial frontier around the institution of the commando. They consisted of an amalgam of Khoi community remnants, runaway slaves, Basters, Cape outlaws and others. A contemporary succinctly sketched the development of an Oorlam community when he stated that Klaas Afrikaner

> . . . collected a band of his people of his own race, runaway slaves and other desperadoes, and having by some means procured firearms, commenced a regular system of depredation upon the defenceless Namaquas and Korannas, plundering them of great numbers of their cattle which he exchanged again with some unprincipled colonists for further supplies of arms and ammunition.[38]

35. Wikar, Jansz and Van Renen, *Journal*, 317. Van Renen, accompanied by a number of hunters, had been provided with oxen and servants by Guilliam Visagie who had fled the colony in 1784 after having assisted Josua Joubert, an accomplice of Coetsé and Hop, in the murder of his Khoi slaves. Visagie lived at Modderfontein, present-day Keetmanshoop in southern Namibia, where he built up a raiding/ trading dynasty based on the exchange of cattle and slaves for guns, powder and lead. In the 1820s Visagie's son was accompanying the !Khami nun on raids on the Herero.
36. Cape Archives Depot (hereafter CA): Source CO 4127, Memorial J.H. van Renen, Recommending Introduction of Negroes from Damaraland, 1862; Source CO 4117, Memorial J.H. van Renen, Proposing to be Government Agent at settlement of Kaffirs in Damaraland, 1860.
37. Wikar, Jansz and Van Renen, *Journal*, 317.
38. G. Thompson, *Travels and Adventures in Southern Africa*, Cape Town, 1967–68, 291.

The Development of the Atlantic Frontier and its Penetration of Namibia

By the 1790s whaling, sealing and cattle trading had become significant economic activities along the Namibian coastline.[39] In later years the American captain Benjamin Morrell, who claimed to have exported more than 50 000 cattle from the Namibian coast, wrote:

> For the lucrative jerking beef there is not a more eligible situation on the whole surface of the globe, as any number of bullocks, in finest order, may be purchased at 50 cents each, delivered at the beach; . . . thousands of fine cattle may be purchased for as many toys and the bargains consumated under the guns of your vessel.[40]

Not only cattle, oil, ivory, skins, and dried fish were exported from Angra Pequena, Sandwich Harbour and Walvis Bay, but also captives were sold to the passing ships.

A fine example of this combination of cattle and captive export is provided by the two journals, (which abound with reports of whalers and sealers), of the VOC slaving frigate *Meermin* under the command of slaving captain Renier Duminy.[41] In early 1793 the VOC ordered Duminy, to take possession, in the name of the United Provinces of the Netherlands and the VOC, of all the harbours between Cape Town and Walvis Bay, and to report on the position of mines, accessibility of wood, water and food, and whether the inhabitants could be used as 'werkvolk' (labourers). Furthermore the *Meermin* was to convey a party, financed by the meat contractors Van Reenen, to Walvis Bay where it would attempt to link up with a wagon party, sent up overland from the Cape via the outlaw Visagie's settlement at Modderfontein.[42]

En route the *Meermin* put in to Angra Pequena where Namaqua inhabitants refused to trust themselves on board as one of their number had previously been abducted by an English crew.[43] Upon arriving at Walvis Bay, a trading tent, with goods, was set up and a mounted commando of nine riflemen was landed.[44] The commando pursued Namaqua cattle, recaptured a runaway slave and captured two

39. J.L.M. Franken, *Duminy Dagboeke: Duminy Diaries*, Cape Town, 1938, 202–3.
40. E. Rosenthal, 'Early Americans in South West Africa', in *SWA Annual*, Windhoek, 1972, 25.
41. Nine years earlier, in 1784, the VOC had ordered Duminy, whose fame as a slaver off the East African and Madagascan coasts in the service of the French was well known, to captain the *Meermin* on a slaving trip off the Madagascan coast. Duminy was told to acquire 250–300 slaves, of whom two-thirds were to be adults and one-third adolescent men, named Capors by the French, and a number of women of either kind (my translation). In 1787 the *Meermin* and Duminy, being very experienced in the trade (my translation), were again sent to Madagascar. In 1791–92 Duminy captained the slaver *Meermin* to Delagoa Bay and Mauritius. Franken, *Duminy*, 14–15, 404–31.
42. Franken, *Duminy*, 202–3, and see note 35.
43. Franken, *Duminy*, 306.
44. The commando was led by the notorious *veld-kornet* and Gariep raider Petrus Pienaar, Franken, *Duminy*, 281–4.

Damara children.[45] The crew of the *Meermin* were also offered captives for sale.[46]

The captured survivors of the cattle raids that supplied the limitless demand for cattle were undoubtedly the main supply of people offered for barter. That it was not uncommon for the numerous ships that put into Walvis Bay to take on slaves is demonstrated by the inhabitants' offer to supply this demand. However as the testimony of Charles Medgett Goodridge, on board HMS *Princess of Wales*, clearly indicates, this demand for slaves was not always met with an enthusiastic welcome. Arriving in Walvis Bay in 1828 Goodridge reported that:

> The natives presented a very formidable appearance, to the number of nearly 500, all naked, but armed with spears. The hostile appearance we were led to believe, was from their fear that we were come to entrap and carry them away for slaves, as had been practised by other vessels on this coast.[47]

It is probable that Indian ocean slavers, who had sold part of their cargoes at Cape Town, sought to replenish their stocks lost to trade and mortality, as they sailed north-west along the Namibian coast upon the Benguela current. Slaves often reached the Cape 'semi-illegally as the "cargo" of sailors and officials on VOC ships'.[48] Writing in 1772, Thunberg clearly noted the manner in which VOC 'plakkaaten' (notices) prohibiting the clandestine import of slaves into the colony were ignored and the manner in which slaves were landed at Cape Town without the official knowledge of the Company:

> The company brings the greatest part of its slaves from Madagascar, whereas private persons buy their's [*sic*] of the officers belonging to the ships, as well Dutch as French, that are on their return home from the East Indies, seldom of the English and never of the Swedish.[49]

Apart from returning Company ships slaves were increasingly bought from French and English interlopers who put in for refreshment at the Cape prior to trading through to Barbados and later Virginia and Buenos Aires. In the late 1700s more than half the ships that put into Cape Town were not Dutch.[50] Boom conditions at the Cape in 1780s made it a profitable market for the slavers, who by this time were mainly French and Portuguese.[51]

Miller has noted that due to the currents and winds of the south Atlantic the barren coasts south of Benguela could not be reached directly from the principal Portuguese

45. Franken, *Duminy*, 294.
46. 'They proposed to Mr van der Roest to exchange a little blackie for tobacco and beads', Franken, *Duminy*, 289.
47. Reference provided by Dag Henrichsen. M. Goodridge, *Narrative of a Voyage to the South Seas, with the Shipwreck of the Princess of Wales Cutter . . . With an Account of Two Years Residence on an Uninhabited Island*, London, 1839, 33.
48. R. Ross, *Cape of Torments: Slavery and Resistance in South Africa*, London, 1983, 13.
49. Armstrong, 'The Slaves', 80.
50. Ross, *Cape of Torments*, 74.
51. Armstrong, 'The Slaves', 81.

ports in Angola. As the coasts remained permanently beyond the control of the Portuguese garrisons,

> they became havens for foreign slave buyers, particularly French slavers from the Indian Ocean on their way north down the coast laden with Asian textiles.[52]

In the 1780s Ovambo traders, responding to the growing demand for slaves in much the same way as the Walvis Bay traders, were engaged in selling slaves to French ships calling at the mouth of the Kunene.[53] The Finnish missionary Rautanen recorded reports of the Ongandjera, living to the south of the Kunene River, who built 'kraals' on the beach, 'where the slaves were locked in until the ship arrived'.[54] Recent archeological work in the area has provided material evidence to back Galton's claims of 1852 that the Herero had trade routes, with temporary settlements, from the hinterland to the coast, where they traded with the Portuguese and Ongandjera.[55] The missionary Hahn reported on his trip to northern Namibia in 1857 that Herero prisoners had been traded by the Ndonga to the Portuguese.[56]

The Namibian Interior

The arid climate of the Namibian interior ensured that the river systems that drain the central Namibian highlands became the main routes of trade and transhumance. The rivers that make up these systems only flow following heavy rains and years are apt to go by before this happens.

The Oorlam movement of conquest into the central Namibian highlands of the early 1800s was along the Fish River. The Oorlam communities received supplies through trade overland with the Cape colony or through trade with ships calling at Angra Pequena and later Walvis Bay. By the mid-1820s Jonker Afrikaner was established just south of the Auas mountains and raiding northward and eastward for Herero cattle. These cattle were driven to the coast along the Kuiseb River and traded at Walvis Bay where American whalers had been active since the late 1700s. The German missionary Schmelen, referring to these activities, wrote in 1828:

> The Afrikaners and most of my people treat the natives in an abominable manner, not only by depriving them of everything, but also by using the women and children as whores and by treating them worse than slaves. If we cannot close off the coast on this side, so that the whale fisherman cease selling gunpowder there then I believe that little good will be done here in future.[57]

---

52. Miller, *Way of Death*, 320.
53. Miller, *Way of Death*, 222.
54. Reference provided by Dag Henrichsen; author's translation, Martti Rautanen Kokoelma, HP XXVIII: 2, 1888 – 93 (microfiche 568 – 77), Finnish Missionary Archives, Helsinki.
55. Reference provided by Dag Henrichsen. Noli/Avery, Stone circles in the Cape Fria Area, *Archeological Bulletin*, 42 (1987), 59–63.
56. B. Lau, ed., *Carl Hugo Hahn Tagebucher 1837–1860 Diaries*, Part IV 1856–1860, A missionary in Nama- and Damaraland, Windhoek, 1985, 1051–2.
57. Schmelen quoted in B. Lau, *Namibia in Jonker Afrikaner's Time*, Windhoek, 1987, 28.

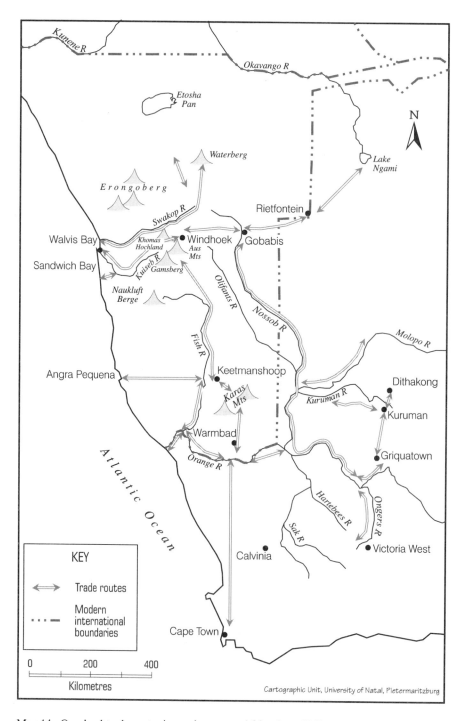

Map 14. Overland trade routes in south-western Africa from 1850

By the early 1830s Jonker Afrikaner had forced the Herero and Dama-speaking groups to the north of the Kuiseb River into the Khomas Hochland and beyond. At the same time the Mbanderu along the Nossob River had been driven north by the commandos of Amraal, away from their seasonal grazing grounds in the south-western Kalahari.[58] By the mid-1830s Jonker Afrikaner had partly created, and gained control over, the trade system that firmly linked and drained central-southern Namibia and western Botswana into the south Atlantic and the Cape colonial trade systems. The importance of river systems as routes of commerce and the extent of Afrikaner's dealings is reflected in his words:

> I have been to Latakoo [Dithakong] myself, but to reach it from the banks of the Fish river I was obliged to travel first South, towards the Orange, I next went up it, and then by Griquatown, I reached the Bechuanas.[59]

With the possibilities of cattle trade for the Atlantic shipping trade and the refreshment station at St. Helena in mind, Captain (later Sir) James Alexander was commissioned, in 1836, to explore the Namibian interior in order to 'promote trade [and] . . . to become acquainted with the Damaras [Ovaherero]'.[60] Apart from rambling on about the virtues of olives, Alexander's journals make for excellent reading and shed valuable light on a rather murky situation.

The journals describe the incredible violence in the societies affected by the Cape colony; a colony whose settlers thought it only natural that the original inhabitants be driven off the land.[61] Roaming Khoi groups armed with muskets preferred to trade the spoils of their Herero plunder with whalers at Angra Pequena rather than trading south and being robbed as 'verdoemde Hottentots' by Boer settlers.[62]

The journals indicate that raids were conducted by Oorlam commandos in Namibia not only on Herero but also on rival Namaqua/Oorlam groups.[63] As Van Reenen had reported forty years earlier, so too, Alexander noted that the Herero were,

> . . . a great nation, and their country is full of cattle – 'which,' say the Namaquas, 'they get from a cave as they require them; so there is no great harm in our taking a few from them now and then, as they can easily make up the loss.[64]

It is hardly surprising that travelling through Namaqua homesteads Alexander could note that:

58. E. Wilmsen, *Land Filled with Flies: A Political Economy of the Kalahari*, Chicago, 1989, 91.
59. J.E. Alexander, *Expedition of Discovery into the Interior of Africa*, 2 vols, Cape Town, 1967 (1st publ. in 1838), vol. 2. 159–61.
60. Alexander, *Expedition*, vol. 1, vi.
61. Alexander, *Expedition*, vol. 1, 94.
62. Alexander, *Expedition*, vol. 1, 96–102.
63. Alexander, *Expedition*, vol. 1, 188. Raid by Hendrik on Choubib in which women are raped, abducted and killed, and 30 oxen, 40 sheep and 2 guns taken.
64. Alexander, *Expedition*, vol. 2, 164.

Some of the cattle had the Damara mark upon them, vis., a deep cut in the dewlap.[65]

The Namaqua did not, however, raid solely for Herero cattle. Alexander reported Herero captives at Nama encampments in the vicinity of the Karas mountains.[66] After observing '2 or 3 fine Damara boys, carried off by Namaquas in northern forays', Alexander bought one of these captives, a boy of about nine years old, for two cloth handkerchiefs and two strings of glass beads.[67]

Even at the best of times the Namibian shoreline is plagued by cold winds, thick mists and a lack of fresh water; it is a harsh inhospitable place. Walvis Bay stinks and this is especially so during low tide when the tidal flats of the bay exude the cloying sulphuric smells of rotting seaweed and fish. To Alexander however, having barely survived the Namib, the bay, with its skeletons of murdered sailors, was a welcome sight. The bay meant direct contact with the wider world in the form of American whalers who landed there, shortly after Alexander's arrival, to trade muskets and powder for oxen and small stock.[68]

As noted earlier American whalers and others were active at the various bays of Namibia prior to 1793. Here the seaborne traders and raiders interacted and transacted with the inhabitants of Namibia; here Namaqua women were prostituted 'for cotton handkerchiefs, or brandy'; charcoal was traded as gunpowder and palm oil as brandy; Herero cattle for western goods and Herero captives as slaves.[69] By the 1830s trade with the interior of Namibia was extensive, an American captain 'expected to purchase cheaply two or three thousand cattle from the Nama in the interior and to return to the United States with a shipload of hides'.[70]

Cobbing has noted elsewhere that a number of United States slavers were converted or disguised whalers; it is possible that a number of these whaler slavers traded for slaves at Walvis Bay.[71] Alexander's conversations with Jonker Afrikaner demonstrate that slavers were indeed active among the Herero. Afrikaner claimed that it would be impossible for Alexander to approach the Herero from the south, as they were 'so exasperated against us [Afrikaners] for turning them out of this country', that

65. Alexander, *Expedition*, vol. 1, 203. Still the case in parts of Namibia described as Herero 'communal areas'.
66. Alexander, *Expedition*, vol. 1, 219–25; in this regard see earlier references in this essay to Wikar's reports fifty years previously regarding Herero captives among the Bondelswarts and Veldskoen-draers.
67. Alexander, *Expedition*, vol. 1, 221–3.
68. Alexander was told to, '. . . speak to the Niggers here, . . . a musket for two or three bullocks', Alexander, *Expedition*, vol. 1, 90–6.
69. Alexander, *Expedition* vol. 1, charcoal as gunpowder, 177; Prostitution, 196. Whilst at Hendrick Booi's kraal Alexander obtains sexual services for a handkerchief, 265–8.
70. A. Kienitz, 'The Key Role of the Oorlam Migrations in the Early Europeanisation of South West Africa', *International Journal of African Historical Studies*, 10 (1977), 556.
71. J. Cobbing, 'Grasping the Nettle'.

they can only be seen by going by sea to the coast, and from thence communicating with them, *though even then they might be suspicious of being carried off for slaves.*[72]

In driving the Herero off their lands the Oorlam had themselves carried off a number of them for slaves. Alexander, who went to the extent of checking their teeth, observed and described these captives with the eye of a stockman:

> . . . there were several Kamaka Damaras, of both sexes, prisoners of war . . . The young men were square built, and the finest specimens of bone and muscle I had almost ever seen whilst their skins shone like polished ebony. The young women were tall and graceful . . .[73]

> . . . a fine Damara slave boy of Choubib's, Appolon by name, appeared among my people, he had run away from his master, . . . Choubib sent two men after him, who carried him off by force . . . they flogged the poor fellow unmercifully with thorn bushes.[74]

That farmers from the colony made grateful use of this supply of slaves is shown by the fact that people along the Orange believed that Alexander's expedition was one sent to procure slaves.[75]

Subsequent to Alexander's reports, traders Dixon and Morris, who actively prevented others from penetrating the interior, established themselves at Walvis Bay to supply the Atlantic trade routes systematically with cattle from the interior.[76] In 1843 the guano rush along the Namibian coast started. Hundreds of ships thronged the Namibian islands. Ichaboe Island, with guano deposits up to four metres thick, was cleared of its guano within five years. At times up to three hundred ships visited Ichaboe Island, tensions ran high and rival guano collectors did not refrain from shooting at one another.[77] Rhenish missionary Heinrich Scheppmann reported that during his stay at Walvis Bay between January and March 1845, 'exceptionally many ships have come here, six to nine at once; they come from Ichaboe and purchase oxen here'. On his way to Walvis Bay Scheppman claimed that he saw three hundred and fifty ships with some six thousand crewmen at Ichaboe. These men were fed the beef of Herero cattle taken from the Herero in the interior of Namibia.[78]

The incredible demand for beef and labour engendered by the guano rush had direct and profound effects upon the Namibian interior. In March 1846 Jonker Afrikaner, already in debt to Morris to the tune of 800 head of cattle, successfully

72. Emphasis added, Alexander, *Expedition*, vol. 2, 157; note how this ties in with earlier references to Rautanen's reports of Ongandjeru slave pens.
73. Alexander, *Expedition*, vol. 2, 163.
74. Alexander, *Expedition*, vol. 2, 218.
75. Alexander, *Expedition*, vol. 2, 251.
76. Tabler, *Pioneers*, 29, 78, 93.
77. J. H. Esterhuyse, *South West Africa: 1880–1894*, Cape Town, 1968, 9.
78. This paragraph is based primarily on Wilmsen's study, *Land Filled with Flies*, 89.

raided eastwards among the Mbanderu. To the east of Afrikaner, Amraal Lambert
had moved up the Nossob River into the area around Naosanabis (Leonardville) and
Gobabis and now straddled the trade route eastwards into Ngamiland and
southwards to the Cape along the Nossob. It is important to note that by the
occupation of Gobabis and Eikhams the Oorlam had effectively cut off Herero
control over the trade routes east to Ngamiland, south to the Cape, and west to
Walvis Bay. This situation forced the Herero to rely solely on the produce of their
cattle without the ability to control or tax the trade in their own cattle. With the
supply of cattle through Walvis Bay being consumed by the guano industry Amraal
sought to supply the cattle demands of the Cape colony. Amraal was highly
successful in this and his resident missionary, Tindall, reported that between 1846
and 1851 Amraal was conducting annual raids on the Mbanderu.

What happened to the uncaptured survivors of the Oorlam raiding is well
illustrated by Chapman who wrote of the Ghanzi area in 1856:

> . . . here we met a party of Damaras [Ovaherero], poor emaciated and scabby
> creatures, equalling in poverty the most wretched Bushmen I had yet seen.
> They were once the possessors of immense flocks and herds, and owners of the
> soil where they now grubbed for roots.[79]

A reading of the contemporary trader reports in Namibia shows that the Herero were
extremely hard hit by the drain of cattle from their possession. Reports indicate a
preponderance of women in Herero society, women who were forced to sell their
bridal jewellery – the very last resource for pastoralist peoples – indicating that
they were either the widows of those who died attempting to defend their cattle, or
the wives left behind by the commandos that enslaved their husbands. Galton, who
travelled with Andersson through Namibia in 1850, accompanied one of the
quarterly Herero trading expeditions to the Owambo and reported that the caravan
consisted of

> . . . 86 Damara [Ovaherero] women, nearly half of whom had yelling babies
> on their backs, and 10 Damara men . . . the 86 women went on various
> speculations – some to get work in Ovamboland, some to try and get
> husbands, others merely to sell their ostrich-shell corsets.[80]

A number of Herero who survived the cattle raids as the captives of their aggressors
were exported along the trade routes draining central Namibia. In the late 1850s
H. Enslin, an inhabitant of the district of Victoria West, complained to the Governor
of the Cape colony regarding the manner in which his resident magistrate had

79. J. Chapman, *Travels in the Interior of South Africa Comprising 15 Years Hunting and Trading*,
    London, 1868, vol. 1, 166.
80. F. Galton, *The Narrative of an Explorer in Tropical South Africa*, London, 1971, 198–9; see also
    C. J. Andersson, *Lake Ngami; or, Explanations and Discoveries During Four Years' Wanderings in
    the Wilds of South Western Africa*, London, 1856, 180.

disposed of Damara children obtained from 'certain Bastards'.[81] However, the majority of Herero captives were enslaved by the Oorlam. Mbanderu traditions record that in the latter half of the nineteenth century, when Nama/Oorlam hegemony was declining, the Mbanderu leader Kanangati Hoveka travelled to southern Namibia and the northern Cape to collect and take these 'Oorlam Damara' back into central Namibia.[82] In the 1850s traders made numerous mention of these unfortunates. Two of these captives, 'Onesimus, who was a Damara by birth, but had been captured as a child . . . [and] Phillipus . . . also a Damara by birth', were presented to Andersson by William Zwartbooi in 1850.[83] Andersson's own perceptions with regard to Herero in his employ is to some extent demonstrated by his journal in which he recorded:

> I had intended to send two or three Damaras with Hans to Australia;[84]

The export of people to the east, and south to the newly established Boer republics, continued until at least 1870. Thomas Baines, commissioned by Andersson in the early 1860s, noted the following in his diaries:

> [1870] Saturday, September 17th. We were talking of traders in Damara-land . . . Wood told me that Martinus Swartz and others had made a good thing of going right across the country, having obtained 3 lb of best white feathers in Damaraland alone. I asked 'And how much black wool?' The answer was, '70 samples, most of whom walked along the road, while a few who were likely to run away were caged in the waggon by wooden bars lashed upright so as to close the fore and aft ends of the tent.' It must have been a curious sight, this *cafila* of boys and girls thus marched across from western Africa to east. . . . I made a sketch of the waggon from Mr Wood's description. It had a large wattled affair like a hen-coop and was probably set apart for the carriage of the weak and seckly, or those likely to run . . . there were about fourteen waggons.[85]

Conclusion

The introduction to this essay warned that if we are not careful the cause, answer and effect ascribed to all events in nineteenth-century Namibian history will be the 'Mfecane'. History did not stop at the 'boerewors line' of the Orange, Molopo and Limpopo Rivers. Namibia was involved in the same historical processes that

81. CA: Source CO 4108, Memorial H. Enslin, Complaining about the Resident Magistrate of Victoria West and Mr Horak regarding the disposal of Damara Children, 1859.
82. Interview conducted with Mr. E. Ndjoze, 'Ondangeri' of the Ovambanderu, on 4 January 1992 at Talismanus, Namibia.
83. Andersson, Lake Ngami, 134–5.
84. Andersson, Lake Ngami, 349.
85. T. Baines, The Northern Goldfields Diaries of Thomas Baines, ed. by J.P.R. Wallis, 3 vols, London, 1946, vol. 2, 486–8. Special thanks to Julian Cobbing for this reference.

affected the rest of southern Africa in the early nineteenth century. However, Namibia was not ravaged by 'Zulu-ised' hordes. Instead this essay supports the idea that the expulsion of the Oorlam into present-day Namibia and the raiding for cattle, goods and slaves for the Cape and Atlantic trade were the prime causes for the instability in central and southern Namibia in the early nineteenth century. The essay focuses on one specific aspect of these events, that of slavery.

The generally accepted historical thesis – that no slaving for the transatlantic or Cape colonial trade ever occurred in precolonial central and southern Namibia – is in need of review. It is unacceptable for us to continue believing that central and southern Namibia proceded through history unaffected by the demands of the Cape colonial and transatlantic slave trades.

Throughout this essay the overriding importance of Namibia's unique climate and river system has been made evident. Namibia's harsh shoreline and arid interior served to shield it from early white settlement but not from the effects of colonial depredations. From the early 1700s through to the late 1800s commandos, 'entirely dependent on the Cape-Colony [and later the Atlantic traders] for their supplies of arms and ammunition, clothing, and other commodities', were raiding into the Namibian interior.[86] It is clear that the southward trade with the colony dominated, though at times the trade with the Atlantic traders may have overshadowed the colonial trade. Defined and enforced by the aridity of the Namibian climate the routes of trade and transhumance were along the river systems of the territory. Merchandise was exported and imported from the Cape colony and the Atlantic traders along the river systems of the Kuiseb, Fish and Nossob/Molopo.

From the early 1700s onwards the enslavement of commando captives became standard policy. At all stages the acquisition of cattle appears to have been the prime motive for Atlantic traders and commando raiders alike. The commando raids to supply the trade ensured an increase in the number of free impoverished and dispossessed people, and ever-growing number of enslaved captives. At the same time the unceasing demand for cattle led to the advance of the raiding frontier ever further north. In the late 1700s ships calling at Walvis Bay could expect to be offered cattle, ivory, and hides as well as captives. In the early 1800s in southern and central Namibia travellers such as Alexander could be mistaken for slavers and could purchase captives.

A number of captives, the survivors of the commando raids that had robbed them of their cattle, were exported south along the trade routes to the colony during periods of labour shortage in the Cape. This illicit trade continued well into the second half of the 1800s, with Boer commandos raiding in the western Kalahari for slaves.

The conclusion of this essay must be a conditional one: slaves were indeed exported from south-central Namibia to supply the Cape colonial and transatlantic

---

86. Andersson, *Lake Ngami*, 287.

slave trades. It would, however, appear that at no time did the slave trade dominate the trade coming out of southern central Namibia. At all stages the slaves exported appear to have been the by-product of raided cattle.

Further research regarding the export of slaves from Namibia ought to concentrate on and attempt to analyse trade networks in south-central Namibia and southern Africa as a whole prior to 1850, the ships, particularly the New England whalers, that called at Namibia's harbours up to the 1850s, the slave and apprentice registers in the Cape colony, and the various missionary archives dealing with Namibia, the north-western Cape and Botswana.

It would be fortunate if further linguistic research into sources such as Koelle's *Polyglotta Africana* (which has Mbundu wordlists), was to provide linguistic evidence regarding the export of people from south-central Namibia.[87] However, it is unlikely that research regarding exported Namibian slaves centred on the countries of destination will provide much more than physical descriptions of people alleged to be Khoi and thus southern African.[88]

It is extremely frustrating to attempt to argue that slave exports from south-central Namibia did in fact take place when most of the evidence available is circumstantial. It is, however, clear that amongst historians dealing with Namibian history the evidence dictates the necessity of a broader awareness which encompasses the possibility of slave exports from south-central Namibia and western Botswana; an awareness that does not accept the mfecane as the be all and end all of early eighteenth-century southern African history.

Acknowledgements

With thanks to G. Janssen, D. Henrichsen, R. Ross, W. Hillebrecht, J. Cobbing and B. Lau, however unconvinced they were, for comments, criticisms and helpful hints. The financial assistance of the Netherlands Organization for Scientific Research (NWO) is gratefully acknowledged.

---

87. S.W. Koelle, *Polyglotta Africana: Or a Comparative Vocabulary of Nearly Three Hundred Words and Phrases in More Than One Hundred Distinct African Languages*, London, 1854; Koelle collected wordlists, ranging from Tuareg to Umbundu, from slaves landed by the British anti-slavery squadron in Sierra Leone.
88. Cobbing, 'Grasping the Nettle', 13.

Glossary

Burghers	Citizens
iButho (pl. *amaButho*)	Age group of men or women; 'regiment'
Bogadi	Bridewealth: cattle or goods handed over in marriage transactions by the man's family to the father or guardian of the woman
inDuna	Appointed official
baFaladi	Alien minority
Hopo	Pit trap
iLobolo	Bridewealth: cattle or goods handed over in marriage transactions by the man's family to the father or guardian of the woman
Kgamelo	System of vassal sub-chiefdoms
Kgotla	Court of a chief or headman
Landdrost	Paid district official with magisterial functions
iMpi (pl. *iziMpi*)	Military unit, force; army
Trekboers	Nomadic pastoralist farmers, mainly of Dutch extraction, particularly those on the move in the century before the Great Trek
Veldkornet	Elected local district official
Veldkos	Veld foods
Volk	A people
Volksraad	People's council; a parliament
Voortrekkers/Trekkers	Farmers, mostly of Dutch extraction who moved out of the Cape in organised parties from 1833 onwards as part of the Great Trek

Abbreviations

AC	Archives of the Council of Advice, 1825–1834.
AHU	Arquivo Historico Ultramarine. [Lisbon Overseas Archives].
AM	Albany Museum, Grahamstown.
AY	Archives of the Drostdy and Magistrate, Albany (Grahamstown).
BNA	Botswana National Archives and Records Services, Gaborone.
CA	Cape Archives Depot, Cape Town.
CL	Cory Library for Historical Research, Rhodes University, Grahamstown.
CO	Colonial Office.
CU	Robert Moffat Collection, University of Cape Town.
CWM	Council for World Missions Archives.
GH	Government House Archives.
KCAL	Killie Campbell Africana Library, Durban.
LCA	Clerk of the Legislative Council.
LMS	London Missionary Society Archives.
LNA	Lesotho National Archives, National University of Lesotho, Roma.
MMS	Methodist Missionary Society Archives, South Africa.
NA	Natal Archives Depot, Pietermaritzburg.
NAZ	National Archives of Zimbabwe, Harare.
NCD	Notarial Protocols, Cape Districts.
NNA	Namibian National Archives, Windhoek.
PRO	Public Record Office, London.
SAL	South African Library, Cape Town.
SAM	South African Museum, Cape Town.
SOAS	School of Oriental and African Studies, London.
SP	James Stuart Papers.
UCT	University of Cape Town.
UIT	Archives of the Magistrate, Uitenhage.
WITS	University of the Witwatersrand Library, Department of Historical Papers.
WMMS	Wesleyan Missionary Society Archives (incorporated in 1932 into Methodist Missionary Society Archives).
WP	Willoughby, W.C. Papers.
ZP	Zululand Province.

Bibliographer's Note

YVONNE GARSON

The Colloquium on the Mfecane Aftermath, held at the University of the Witwatersrand, Johannesburg, in 1991, stimulated a new interest in precolonial southern African studies. Up to now there has been no synthesised bibliographical aid in this field and it is clear that a bibliography of sources used by the authors of the published colloquium essays will provide scholars and students with a valuable resource for further research.

In order to create a workable list of items relevant to the study of precolonial southern Africa, each essay was carefully scanned for references, which were then put together to form a consolidated bibliography. Works which have appeared since the essays were completed have also been added and other works cited appear in a separate section at the end of the bibliography.

Each entry includes essential bibliographical details. Authors' names have been standardised so that all are entered in the form Smith, J.A. even though certain publications have appeared under other forms of the name. As the nature of debate around sources is so detailed in each contributor's field of study, entries seek where possible to distinguish between compilers, translators and editors of texts. Series statements are included, where relevant, in round brackets at the end of the entry. Information provided in square brackets indicates that it has been obtained from sources outside the item itself. Titles of nineteenth-century works, such as those by John Barrow and other contemporary observers of the southern African scene, have been given in full; they are informative in themselves. It is encouraging to note that extensive use has been made by researchers of classical works of Africana. Librarians who have gained intimate knowledge of these books and journals have long been aware of their potential as valuable sources of information covering a wide variety of fields. The focus on historiography in this debate has brought close attention to bear on these early published texts, many of which were formerly seen as conventional secondary sources.

Later (or earlier) editions of some of the older printed texts cited, have been included where it seemed practical to do so. Full information on the bibliographical history of these and other relevant early writings can be found in the *South African Bibliography*, 1979, and its *Supplement*, 1992, compiled at the South African Library, Cape Town. The *Bibliography* is referred to in the body of the list as *SABIB*. Standard bibliographical practice has been followed in listing titles within entries alphabetically rather than by date.

The research required for the checking of references, establishing accurate names, dates, titles and other bibliographical details was greatly facilitated by the admirable resources of the John G. Gubbins Library of Africana, University of the Witwatersrand, Johannesburg, as well as the Periodicals, Government Publications and Historical Papers Departments of that institution's Library. The willing assistance of the staff of these departments is gratefully acknowledged. The help of the staff of the African Studies Library of the Johannesburg Public Library, the Cory Library for Historical Research, Rhodes University, Grahamstown, as well as the knowledgeable advice of Carolyn Hamilton, the editor of this volume, has been invaluable. Thanks for information and advice are also due to Betsy Eldredge, Simon Hall, Neil Parsons, Jeff Peires, Christopher Saunders and John Wright.

Works of Reference consulted in the Compilation of the Bibliography

Dictionary of South African Biography. Edited by W.J. de Kock. Cape Town. Published for the National Council for Social Reearch, Department of Higher Education by Nasionale Boekhandel, Bpk., 1968 –. 5v. [Proceeding]

Skota, T.P.M., ed. *African Yearly Register. Being an Illustrated National Biographical Dictionary (Who's Who) of Black Folks in Africa . . .* Johannesburg, R.L. Esson & Co. The Orange Press, 1931.
2nd edition. 1932.
3rd edition with amended title: *The African Who's Who. An Illustrated Classified Register and National Biographical Dictionary of the Africans in the Transvaal.* Johannesburg, Central News Agency [1966].

South African Library, Cape Town. *South African Bibliography to the Year 1925.* Edited at the South African Library, Cape Town. London, Mansell, 1979. 4v. *Supplement.* v.5. Compiled by F. Rossouw. Cape Town, South African Library, 1991.

State Library, Pretoria. *A List of South African Newspapers 1800–1982.* With library holdings. Pretoria, State Library, 1983.

Switzer, L. and Switzer, J.D., eds. *The Black Press in South Africa and Lesotho: A Descriptive Bibliographical Guide to African, Coloured and Indian Newspapers, Newsletters and Magazines 1836–1976.* Boston, G.K. Hall, 1979. (Bibliographies and Guides in African Studies).

Webb, C. de B. *A Guide to the Official Records of the Colony of Natal.* Pietermaritzburg, University of Natal Press, 1965.
2nd, revised edition. 1968.

Webb's Guide to the Official Records of Natal. Expanded and revised edition. Compiled by J. Verbeek, M. Nathanson and E. Peel. Pietermaritzburg, University of Natal Press, 1984.

Bibliography

This bibliography is arranged under the following headings:

Bibliographies and Dictionaries
Unpublished Archival Sources
Published Compilations of Documents
Official Publications
Newspapers
Books and Journal Articles
Theses and Seminar Papers
Other Works Cited

Bibliographies and Dictionaries

Haliburton, G., comp. *Historical Dictionary of Lesotho*. Metuchen, N.J., Scarecrow Press, 1977. (African Historical Dictionaries 10).

Liebenberg, B.J., Smith, K.W. and Spies, B., eds. *A Bibliography of South African History 1978–1989*. Pretoria, University of South Africa, 1992.

Long, U., ed. *An Index to Authors of Unofficial, Privately-owned Manuscripts Relating to the History of South Africa 1812–1920*. With copies, summaries and extracts of documents, biographical notes on the authors, a chronological table and an appendix of documents originating outside Africa . . . London, Lund, Humphris, 1947.

Morton, B., comp. *The Botswana Society Bibliography. Part 2: Pre-colonial History to 1885*. Gaborone, The Botswana Society. [In press]

Morton, F., Murray, A. and Ramsay, J., eds. *Historical Dictionary of Botswana*. Metuchen, N.J., Scarecrow Press, 1992. (African Historical Dictionaries 44). [Revised edition of Stevens, R.P. *Historical Dictionary of Botswana*. Metuchen, N.J., Scarecrow Press, 1975]

Muller, C.J.F., Van Jaarsveld, F.A., Van Wijk, T. and Boucher, M., eds. *South African History and Historians: A Bibliography*. Pretoria, University of South Africa, 1979.

Parsons, N. and Hitchcock, R.K., comps. *Index to Publications 1969–1989*. Gaborone, Botswana Society, 1991.

Rasmussen, R.K., comp. *Historical Dictionary of Rhodesia/Zimbabwe*. Metuchen, N.J., Scarecrow Press, 1979. (African Historical Dictionaries 18).

Saunders, C., comp. *Historical Dictionary of South Africa*. Metuchen, N.J., Scarecrow Press, 1983. (African Historical Dictionaries 37).

Shillington, K. and Crowder, M. *Essays on the History of Botswana: A Bibliography of the History Research Essays Presented in Part Fulfilment of the B.A. Degree of the University of Botswana 1976–1984*. Gaborone, University of Botswana, Department of History, 1984.

South African Library. *South African Bibliography to the Year 1925*. Edited at the South African Library, Cape Town. London, Mansell, 1979. 4v.
Supplement. V.5. Compiled by F. Rossouw. Cape Town, South African Library, 1991.

Stevens, R.P. *Historical Dictionary of the Republic of Botswana*. Metuchen, N.J., Scarecrow Press, 1975.

Webb, C. de B. *A Guide to the Official Records of the Colony of Natal*. Pietermaritzburg, University of
   Natal Press, 1965.
   2nd edition, revised. 1968.
Webb's Guide to the Official Records of Natal. Expanded and revised edition. Compiled by J. Verbeek,
   M. Nathanson, and E. Peel. Pietermaritzburg, University of Natal Press, 1984.

Unpublished Archival Sources

The list of major collections within particular archives is by no means exhaustive, but should provide a
guide to the main sources used by the contributors to this volume. The repositories are listed
alphabetically and the collections, official and private, are then set out. Detailed citations are provided
where contributors consider them most necessary, or especially useful.

Albany Museum, Grahamstown. [AM]
   Bowker, J.M. Journal and Letter Book, 1835–1839.
Arquivo Historico Ultramarine. [Lisbon Overseas Archives]. [AHU]
Botswana National Archives and Records Services, Gaborone. [BNA]
   Histories of Kgabo-Kwena [as in S.3/1] and Mmanana-Kgatla. BP 33/1016.
   Histories of Kgabo-Kwena [as in BP 33/1016], Mbukushu, 'Ghanzi Tribes', and Ngwaketse. S.3/1.
   Histories of Ngwato and Kalanga. BP 34/N.3.
   Schapera, I. Papers.
   Sebina, P.M. Makalaka. 1931. BP 33/748–1.
Cape Archives Depot, Cape Town. [CA]
   Archives of the Council of Advice, 1825–1834. [AC]
   Archives of the Drostdy and Magistrate, Albany (Grahamstown). 1806– . 1/AY. [AY] *See esp.*:
      8/79 – Papers Received: Miscellaneous Private Individuals and Bodies 1828.
   Archives of the Magistrate, Uitenhage. [UIT] 1805– . 1/UIT. *See especially*:
      15/9 – Letters Despatched: Landdrost 1824–1825.
      15/12 – Letters Despatched: Civil Commissioner 1828. Ayliff, J. Papers. A.80.
      D'Urban, B. Papers. A.519.
   Government House Archives. [GH] *See especially*:
      1/15 – Papers Received: General Despatches Oct. 1814 – June 1815.
      1/39 – Papers Received: General Despatches June – Oct. 1824.
      19/3 – Specified Subjects: Miscellaneous Sept. 20, 1827 – Mar. 11, 1829.
      23/7 – Papers Despatched: General Despatches Dec. 13, 1821 – Dec. 16, 1826.
      23/8 – Papers Despatched: General Despatches Mar. 7, 1826 – Sept. 2, 1828.
      23/9 – Papers Despatched: General Despatches Sept. 11, 1828 – Jan. 31, 1832.
   Clerk of the Legislative Council. [LCA]
   Colonial Office. [CO]
   Minutes of the Cape Council of Advice 2. [AC]
   Notarial Protocols, Cape Districts. [NCD]
   Zululand Province 1/1/33, 1/1/36. [ZP]
Cory Library for Historical Research, Rhodes University, Grahamstown. [CL]
   Ayliff, J. Notebook, *c.*1851. PR 3826.
   Godlonton Papers.
   Sketch of Fingo History. MS 15, 543.
Killie Campbell Africana Library, Durban. [KCAL]
   Colenso, J.W. Papers.
   Stuart, J. Papers. [SP]
Lesotho National Archives, National University of Lesotho, Roma. [LNA]
   Theal, G.M. *Basutoland Records*, v.4–6, unpublished.
Namibian National Archives, Windhoek. [NNA]
   Accessions 415: Transcription of oral research into the history of the Herero, May 1984, done with
      Mr Kaputu.

Anderson, C.F. Papers.

Galton, F. Africa Diaries 1850–1851.

Lemmer, C.J.C. Collection of Books 1838–1946.

Van Warmelo, N.J. Papers.

Vedder, H. Papers.

Microform of the London (1797–1914), Wesleyan (1822–1967), and Finnish (1860–1956), Missionary Societies.

Natal Archives Depot, Pietermaritzburg. [NA]

Colenso, J.W. Papers.

Fynn, H.F. Papers.

Garden, R. Papers.

Shepstone, T. Papers.

National Archives of Zimbabwe, Harare. [NAZ]

Ellenberger, V.E. Papers. EL 2/1/1.

Hall, R.N. Papers. Notes on Native Tribes of Southern Africa. HA 7/1/1.

Moffat, R. Collection. Also available on microfilm at the University of Cape Town. [CU]

Posselt, F.W.T. Papers. Notes on Ndebele History 1913–1914. PO 9.

Public Record Office, London. [PRO]

Archives of the Colonial Office. [CO]

CO 48: Cape of Good Hope (Cape Colony). Original Correspondence 1807 to 1910.

CO 13:	1812 Jan. 23 – May 21	Despatches
CO 62:	1824 Jan. – Sept.	Despatches
CO 124:	1828 Jan. – June	Despatches
CO 133:	1829	Individuals
CO 211:	1841 Jan. – April	Despatches
CO 219:	1842 May – June	Despatches
CO 230:	1843 June – July	Despatches
CO 233:	1843 June – July	Despatches
CO 234:	1843 Jan. – June	Despatches (Natal)
CO 235:	1847 July – Nov.	Despatches
CO 243:	1844 July	Despatches
CO (Maitland) 270:	1846	Individuals
CO (L–Z) 287:	1848 Aug. – Oct.	Despatches
CO (Smith) 293:	1848	Individuals
CO 357:	1854 Aug. 25 – Sept. 19	Despatches (Darling)
CO 359:	1854 Oct. 27 – Nov. 4	Despatches (Darling)

Rhodes House Library, Oxford.

Mss. Afr.S.1198 (2): J. Ellenberger Papers, including 'A Few Notes Relative to Sebetwane' Wanderings from the Time He Reached Shoshong . . . Compiled from Native Sources, 1908; Notes on Chief Gaborone d. 1931 aged 106?, Ramontotwane d. 1935 aged 130?, Senau Ditsala d. 1938 aged 130?

School of Oriental and African Studies, London. [SOAS]

Council for World Missions Archives. [CWM]

London Missionary Society Archives (included in the above). [LMS]

Methodist Missionary Society Archives. South Africa. In-Letters. Boxes 1–32, 1797–1862. [MMS]

Moshoeshoe [Moshesh], Nehemia Sekonyana. Sesotho ms. sent to J.M. Orpen, 4 Dec. 1905.

Plaatje, S.T. Papers.

Société des Missions Evangéliques de Paris [Lesotho Evangelical Church].

Ellenberger, D.F. Histoire Ancienne et Moderne des Basotho, 31éme Periode.

Unpublished ms.

—— Papers.

Unpublished letters of T. Arbousset, Dr Casalis, R. Daumas, N. S. Moshoeshoe, J. M. Orpen, Azariel M.Sekese, G. M.Theal.

Wesleyan Missionary Society Archives (incorporated in 1932 into Methodist Missionary Society Archives). [WMMS]

Selly Oak Colleges Library, Birmingham.

Willoughby, W.C. Papers [WP]: Files 715 Kgalagadi, 730 Rolong (D. F. Ellenberger), 734 Kalanga, Shona, Tswapong, 739 Kgabo-Kwena, 740 Ngwaketse, 763 Tlhaping, 794 Ramochana on the Becwana, 795 Ngwato, includes The First White Man in Khama's Country, 796 Tawana (J. Ellenberger), 800 Historical Notes on the Becwana and Matabele (A.J. Wookey).

South African Library, Cape Town. [SAL]

Campbell, J. Diary.

Hodgson, T. L. Papers. [MMS]

Methodist Missionary Society. [MMS] Papers. A selection of these papers is deposited in SAL. Stow, G. Papers.

South African Museum, Cape Town. [SAM]

Smith, A. Papers.

University of Cape Town. [UCT]

Lestrade Papers. BC255, AC, folder 9.

University of the Witwatersrand, Johannesburg. Library, Department of Historical Papers. [WITS]

Molema, S. T. and Plaatje, S. T. Papers.

Published Compilations of Documents

Bird, J., comp. *The Annals of Natal: 1495–1845*. By the late Mr John Bird, of the Natal Civil Service. Pietermaritzburg, P. Davis and Sons, 1888. 2v.
Cape Town, Maskew Miller, [192?].
Pietermaritzburg, L.Bayly, [192?].
Facsimile of Maskew Miller edition. Cape Town, Struik, 1965.

British Parliamentary Papers. Edited by Ford, P. and Ford, G. Shannon, Irish University Press, 1970. Colonies. Africa. v. 1–70.
Index to the series.

Moodie, D., comp., transl. and ed. *The Record, or, A Series of Official Papers Relative to the Condition and Treatment of the Native Tribes of South Africa*. Cape Town, A. S. Robertson, 1838–[1841]. 3v. in 1.

Theal, G.M., comp. *Basutoland Records. Copies of Official Documents of Various Kinds, Accounts of Travellers, etc.* . . . Cape Town, W. A. Richards, Govt. Printers, 1883. 3v.
Reprint edition. Cape Town, Struik, 1964. 4v.

——— comp. *Documents Relating to The Kaffir War of 1835* . . . London, William Clowes and Sons, Printed for the Government of the Union of South Africa, 1912.

——— comp. *Records of the Cape Colony. Copied for the Cape Government from the Manuscript Documents in the Public Record Office, London*. London, Printed by William Clowes for the Government of the Cape Colony, 1897–1905. 36v.

——— comp. *Records of South–Eastern Africa; Collected in Various Libraries and Archive Departments in Europe*. London, Clowes, Printers for the Government of the Cape Colony, 1898–1903. 9v. Facsimile reprint. Cape Town, Struik, 1964. 9v.

Webb, C. de B. and Wright, J. B., eds. and transls. *The James Stuart Archive of Recorded Oral Evidence Relating to the History of the Zulu and Neighbouring Peoples*. Pietermaritzburg, University of Natal Press; Durban, Killie Campbell Africana Library, 1976– . 4v. [Proceeding]

——— eds. *A Zulu King Speaks: Statements Made by Cetshwayo kaMpande on the History and Customs of His People*. Pietermaritzburg, University of Natal Press, 1987.

Willoughby, W.C. 'Notes and Records on the Bakalanga', translated by M. Magojane and C. van Waarden. In Van Waarden, C. ed. *Kalanga Retrospect and Prospect*. Gaborone, Botswana Society; Francistown, Supa-Ngwao Museum, 1991.

Official Publications

Bloemhof Arbitration Court. *Evidence Taken Before the Commission Appointed to Investigate the Claims of the South African Republic, Captain N. Waterboer, Chief of West Griqualand, and Certain Other Native Chiefs, to Portions of the Territory on the Vaal River Now Known as the Diamond Fields.* Cape Town, Saul Solomon, 1871.

Board of Relief for the Destitute, Grahamstown. *Abstract of the Proceedings of the Board of Relief for the Destitute, Appointed in Graham's Town by His Excellency Sir Benjamin D'Urban . . . with a View to Mitigate the Sufferings of the Frontier Inhabitants Occasioned by the Irruption of the Cafir Tribes into the Eastern Province of the Colony During the Years 1834–5 . . .* [Chairman: J. Heavyside]. Cape Town, J. Pike, 1836.

Leverton, B. J. T., ed. *Records of Natal, Volume One 1823–August 1828.* Pretoria, Government Printer, 1984.

—— ed. *Records of Natal, Volume Two September 1828–July 1835.* Pretoria, Government Printer, 1989.

—— ed. *Records of Natal, Volume Three August 1835–June 1838.* Pretoria, Government Printer, 1990.

—— ed. *Records of Natal, Volume Four July 1838–September 1839.* Pretoria, Government Printer, 1992. [Continuing]

Rhodesia. Department of Native Affairs. 'The Origin of Some of the Tribes of the Belingwe Reserve.' By H. von Sicard. Salisbury, *Native Affairs Department Annual.* 25(1948):93–104.

South Africa (Republic). Department of Co-operation and Development. Jackson, A. O., ed. *The Ndebele of Langa.* Pretoria, Government Printer, [1983?]. (Ethnological Publications 54)

South Africa. (Union). Department of Agriculture. Division of Entomology. Fuller, C. *Tsetse in the Transvaal and Surrounding Territories.* Pretoria, Government Printer, 1923. (Entomology Memoirs 1)

South Africa. (Union). Department of Native Affairs. Breutz, P-L., ed. *Tribes of Mafeking District.* Pretoria, Government Printer, 1955–56. (Ethnological Publications 32).

—— Breutz, P-L., ed. *The Tribes of Marico District.* Pretoria, Government Printer, 1953–4. (Ethnological Publications 30)

—— Breutz, P-L., ed. *Tribes of Rustenburg and Pilansberg Districts.* Pretoria, Government Printer, 1953. (Ethnological Publications 28)

—— Van Warmelo, N. J., ed. *The Bahwaduba.* Pretoria, Government Printer, 1944. (Ethnological Publications 19)

—— ed. *The Copper Miners of Musina and the Early History of the Zoutpansberg.* Vernacular Accounts by S. M. Dzivhani, M. F. Mamadi, M. M. Motenda, E. Modau. Pretoria, Government Printer, 1940. (Ethnological Publications 8)

—— ed. *History of Matiwane and the amaNgwane Tribe as told by Msebenzi to His Kinsman Albert Hlongwane.* Pretoria, Government Printer, 1938. (Ethnological Publications 7)

—— ed. *The Ndebele of J. Kekana.* Pretoria, Government Printer, 1944. (Ethnological Publications 18)

—— ed. *A Preliminary Survey of the Bantu Tribes of South Africa.* Pretoria, Government Printer, 1935. (Ethnological Publications 5)

—— *Die Tlokwa en Birwa van Noord Transvaal.* Pretoria, Government Printer, 1953. (Ethnological Publications 29)

—— ed. *Transvaal Ndebele Texts.* Pretoria, Government Printer, 1930. (Ethnological Publications 1)

South West Africa/Namibia. Department of National Education. *Carl Hugo Hahn Tagebücher 1837–1860 Diaries. A Missionary in Nama– and Damaraland.* Edited by B. Lau. Windhoek, The Department, 1984–1985. (SWA/Namibia Archival Services Division)

Transvaal (Colony). Native Affairs Department. *Short History of the Native Tribes of the Transvaal* [Multiple compilers]. Pretoria, Government Printing and Stationery Office, 1905.

Newspapers

Holdings of the newspapers listed here can be found in *Periodicals in South African Libraries* [PISAL], available on microfiche, and *A List of South African Newspapers 1800–1982*. 2nd edition. Pretoria, State Library, 1986. Also useful is the bibliography by Switzer, L. and Switzer, J.D., eds. *The Black Press in South Africa and Lesotho: A Descriptive Bibliographical Guide to African, Coloured and Indian Newspapers, Newsletters and Magazines 1836–1976*. Boston, Hall, 1979. (Bibliographies and Guides in African Studies).

This list of newspapers is incomplete. It reflects and expands marginally the citations given in the essays in this volume.

Cape Town Gazette. Cape of Good Hope Government Gazette. August, 1800–May, 1910. From August, 1800–June, 1826 as *Cape Town Gazette and African Advertiser*. From 1803–1806 as *Kaapsche Courant: Offisieële Orgaan van de Bataafsche Regering*.
Colonist. December 1850–April 1859.
Grahamstown Journal. December, 1831–April, 1920. Full run. Absorbed by *Grocott's Daily Mail*.
Leselinyane la Lesotho (The Little Light of Basutoland). November 1863– . Issued irregularly; varies between weekly, fortnightly and monthly appearances.
Marico Chronicle. [Run not established]
South African Commercial Advertiser and Mail. Jan. 1824–Sept. 1869.

Books and Journal Articles

Agar-Hamilton, J. *The Native Policy of the Voortrekkers*. Cape Town, Maskew Miller, 1928.
'Aged Fingo, An' *see* Mhlanga, P.
Ahmed el Amin. 'Masunga, village of the man-made drought.' *Kutlwano*. 29,12(1991):14–15.
Alexander, J.E. *Expedition of Discovery into the Interior of Africa, through the Hitherto Undescribed Countries of the Great Namaquas, Boschmans, and Hill Damaras. Performed Under the Auspices of Her Majesty's Government, and the Royal Geographical Society*. London, Henry Colburn; Philadelphia, E.L. Carey and A. Hart, 1838. 2v.
    Facsimile reprint of Henry Colburn edition. Cape Town, Struik, 1967. (Africana Collectanea 22, 23)
—— *Narrative of a Voyage of Observation among the Colonies of Western Africa, in the Flagship Thalia; and of a Campaign in Kaffir-land* . . . London, Henry Colburn, 1837. 2v.
Allan, W. *The African Husbandman*. Edinburgh, Oliver & Boyd; New York, Barnes & Noble, 1967.
Almanaka ea Basotho, Selemo sa 1894. Khatiso ea A. Mabille. Morija, 1894.
Alpers, E.A. *Ivory and Slaves in East Central Africa: Changing Patterns of International Trade to the Later Nineteenth Century*. London [etc.], Heinemann, 1975.
—— 'State, merchant capital and gender relations in southern Mozambique to the end of the nineteenth century: Some tentative hypotheses.' *African Economic History*. 13 (1984):22– 55.
Ambrose, D. and Brutsch, A., eds. *Missionary Excursion: Thomas Arbousset*. Morija, Morija Archives, 1991.
Anderson, A.A. *Twenty-five Years in a Waggon*. London, Chapman and Hall, 1888.
Andersson, C.J. *Lake Ngami; or, Explanations and Discoveries During Four Years' Wanderings in the Wilds of South Western Africa*. London, Hurst & Blackett, 1856.
Arbousset, T. and Daumas, F. *Narrative of an Exploratory Tour to the North-East of the Colony of the Cape of Good Hope*. Translated from the French of the Rev. T. Arbousset by John Crumbie Brown. Cape Town, A.S. Robertson; Saul Solomon & Co., 1846.
    Repr. London, John C. Bishop; Aberdeen, George & Robert King, 1852.
    Facsimile reprint of the 1846 publication. Cape Town, Struik, 1968. (Africana Collectanea 27)
—— *Relation d'un Voyage d'Exploration au Nord-est de la Colonie du Cape de Bonne Espérance* . . . Paris, Arthus Bertrand, 1842.
Argyle, J. 'Dingiswayo Discovered: An Interpretation of His Legendary Origins'. In Argyle, J., Krige, E. and Preston-Whyte, E., eds. *Social System and Tradition in Southern Africa*, 1978, 1–18.

Argyle, J. 'Who were Dingiswayo and Shaka? Individual origins and political transformations.' In *Collected Seminar Papers on the Societies of Southern Africa in the 19th and 20th Centuries.* Institute of Commonwealth Studies, University of London. (1975–1976):8–18.

Argyle, J., Krige, E. and Preston-Whyte, E., eds. *Social System and Tradition in Southern Africa.* Cape Town, Oxford University Press, 1978.

Armstrong, J.C. and Worden, N. 'The Slaves, 1652–1795.' In Elphick, R. and Giliomee, H., eds. *The Shaping of South African Society: 1652–1820,* 1979, 109–83.

Ayliff, J. and Whiteside, J. *History of the Abambo, Generally Known as Fingo.* Butterworth, Gazette Printers, 1912.

Bain, A.G. 'Extracts from the journal of Mr. Andrew Geddes Bain.' *South African Quarterly Journal.* 1, 4(1830): 415–28.

―――― *The Journals of Andrew Geddes Bain; Trader, Explorer, Soldier, Road Engineer and Geologist.* Edited with biographical sketch and footnotes by Margaret Lister. Cape Town, Van Riebeeck Society, 1949. (V.R.S.30)

Baines, T. *The Gold Regions of South Eastern Africa.* London, Edward Stanford, 1877.

―――― *The Northern Goldfields Diaries of Thomas Baines.* Edited by J.P.R. Wallis. London, Chatto & Windus, 1946. 3v. (Oppenheimer Series 3)

Ballard, C. 'Drought and economic distress: South Africa in the 1800's.' *Journal of Interdisciplinary History.* 17,2(1986):359–78.

―――― *The House of Shaka.* Durban, Emoyeni Books, 1988.

Bannister, S. *Humane Policy; or, Justice to the Aborigines of the New Settlements.* London, Thomas & George Underwood, 1830.
Repr. London, Dawsons of Pall Mall, 1968.

Barrow, J. *An Account of Travels into the Interior of Southern Africa, in the Years 1797 and 1798: Including Cursory Observations of the Geology and Geography of the Southern Part of that Continent; the Natural History of such Objects as Occurred in the Animal, Vegetable, amd Mineral Kingdoms; and Sketches of the Physical and Moral Characters of of the Various Tribes of Inhabitants Surrounding the Settlement of the Cape of Good Hope. To which is Annexed, a Description of the Present State, Population, and Produce of that Extensive Colony; with a Map Constructed from Actual Observations Made in the Course of the Travels.* London, Printed by A. Strahan for T. Cadell jun. and W. Davies, 1801–1804. 2v.

―――― *Travels into the Interior of Southern Africa. In which are Described the Character and Condition of the Dutch Colonists of the Cape of Good Hope, and the Several Tribes of Natives Beyond the Limits: The Natural History of Such Subjects as Occurred in the Animal, Mineral and Vegetable Kingdoms; and the Geography of the Southern Extremity of Africa. Comprehending also a Topographical and Statistical Sketch of Cape Colony: With an Inquiry into its Importance as a Naval and Military Station, as a Commercial Emporium; and as a Territorial Possession.* The second edition, with additions and alterations . . . London, T. Cadell and W. Davies, 1806. 2v.

―――― *Voyage to Cochinchina in the Years 1792 and 1793 . . . To Which is Annexed an Account of a Journey Made in the Year 1801 and 1802 . . . To the Residence of the Chief of the Booshuana Nation, Being the Remotest Point of Southern Africa to which Europeans have Hitherto Penetrated. The Facts and Description Taken from a Manuscript Journal, with a Chart of the Route.* London, Printed for T. Cadell and W. Davies, 1806. [The full title of the annexed item, *An Account of a Journey to Leetakoo, the Residence of the Chief of the Booshuana Nation* . . . appears on the half-title page preceding the text, which is on pp. 361–437 of the volume. The account of the journey was written by Barrow from manuscript material supplied by William Somerville, P.J. Truter and P.B. Borcherds. For bibliographical background to the account see the introduction to Somerville, W. *William Somerville's Narrative of His Journeys* . . .]
Facsimile reprint. With an introduction by Milton Osborne. Kuala Lumpur, Oxford University Press, 1975. (Oxford in Asia. Historical Reprints)

Beach, D.N. 'Ndebele raiders and Shona power.' *Journal of African History.* 15(1974):633–51.

―――― *The Shona and Zimbabwe 900–1850: An Outline of Shona History.* Gweru, Mambo Press; London, Heinemann Educational, 1980.

Beach, D.N. *Zimbabwe before 1900.* Gweru, Mambo Press, 1984.

—— 'The Zimbabwe Plateau and its Peoples.' In Birmingham, D. and Martin, P.M., eds. *History of Central Africa,* 1983, v. 1, 245–77.

Beachey, R. *The Slave Trade of Eastern Africa.* London, Rex Collings, 1976.

Beaumont, P.B. 'On the origins of Hottentot culture in Southern Africa.' *South African Archaeological Society Newsletter.* 3,1(1980):2–3.

—— 'An ochre-mine near Postmasburg.' *South African Archaeological Society Newsletter.* 4,1 (1981):1–2.

Beaumont, P.B., Thackeray, F. and Thackeray, A. 'Dithakong.' *South African Archaeological Society Newsletter.* 6,2(1983):1.

Beaumont, P.B. and Vogel, J.C. 'Spatial Patterning of the Ceramic Later Stone Age in the Northern Cape Province, South Africa.' In Hall, M. *et. al.,* eds. *Frontiers: Southern African Archaeology Today,* 1984, pp.80–95.

Becker, P. *Path of Blood.* Harmondsworth, Penguin Books, 1962.

Beinart, W. *The Political Economy of Pondoland 1860–1930.* Cambridge [etc.], Cambridge University Press, 1982. (African Studies Series 33)

Benedict, B. 'Slavery and Indenture in Mauritius and Seychelles.' In Watson, J., ed. *Asian and African Systems of Slavery,* 1980, 135–68.

Biesele, M. *Women Like Meat: The Folk-lore and Foraging Ideology of the Kalahari Ju/'hoan.* Johannesburg, Witwatersrand University Press, 1993.

Biesele, M., Gordon, R. and Lee, R., eds. *Past and Future of !Kung Ethnography: Critical Reflections and Symbolic Perspectives.* Hamburg, Helmut Buske Verlag, 1986.

Birmingham, D. and Martin, P.M., eds. *History of Central Africa.* London, Longman, 1983.

Bleek, D.F. 'Beliefs and customs of the /Xam Bushmen.' Part 7, entitled 'Sorcerers.' *Bantu Studies.* 9(1935):1–47.

Bleek, W.H.I. 'Remarks on Orpen's "Mythology of the Maluti Bushman".' *Cape Monthly Magazine. New Series.* 9,49(1874):10–13.

—— *Brief Account of Bushman Folklore and Other Texts.* Cape Town, Government Printer, 1875.

Boeyens, J. '"Zwart Ivoor": Inboekelinge in Zoutpansberg, 1848–1869.' *South African Historical Journal.* 24 (1991):31–66. .

Bonner, P. 'The Dynamics of Late 18th-Century Northern Nguni Society: Some Hypotheses.' In Peires, J., ed. *Before and after Shaka: Papers in Nguni History,* 1981, 74–81.

—— *Kings, Commoners and Concessionaires: The Evolution and Dissolution of the Nineteenth-Century Swazi State.* Cambridge, Cambridge University Press; Johannesburg, Ravan Press, 1983.

Borcherds, P.B. *An Auto-biographical Memoir of Petrus Borchardus Borcherds, Esq.* . . . Cape Town, A.S.Robertson, 1861.

—— *See also* Barrow, J. *Voyage to Cochinchina* . . .

Boteler, T. *Narrative of a Voyage of Discovery to Africa and Arabia, Performed in His Majesty's Ships Leven and Barracouta from 1821 to 1826, Under the Command of Capt. F. W. Owen, R.N.* London, Richard Bentley, 1835. 2v.

Botelho, S.J.X. *Memoria Estatistica sobre os Dominios Portuguezes na Africa Oriental.* Lisbon, José Baptista Morando, 1835.

—— Second part of *Memoria Estatistica sobre os Dominios Portuguezes na Africa Oriental.* Lisbon, A.J.C. da Cruz, 1837.

Botha, H.C. *John Fairbairn in South Africa.* Cape Town, Historical Publications Society, 1984.

Breutz, P-L., A. *A History of the Batswana and the Origin of Bophutatswana: A Handbook of a Survey of the Tribes of the Batswana, S. Ndebele, Qwaqwa and Botswana.* Ramsgate, Natal, The Author, 1989.

—— *See also under* South Africa. (Union). Department of Native Affairs. In *Official Publications* section.

Brink, C.F. and Rhenius, J.T. *The Journals of Brink and Rhenius. Being the Journal of Carel Frederik Brink of the Journey into Great Namaqualand (1761–2) Made by Captain Hendrik Hop, and the Journal of Ensign Johannes Tobias Rhenius (1724).* Transcribed, translated and edited with an introduction, brief lives and footnotes by E.E. Mossop. Cape Town, Van Riebeeck Society, 1947. (V.R.S. 28)

Brinton, W. *History of the British Regiments in South Africa.* Cape Town, Department of Extra-mural Studies. University of Cape Town [1977].

'British Official, A', *pseud.* 'In Khama's country.' *Monthly Review.* 7(1902):115–16.

British Parliamentary Papers. In *Published Compilations of Documents.*

Broadbent, S. *A Narrative of the First Introduction of Christianity Amongst the Barolong Tribe of Bechuanas, South Africa: With a Brief Summary of the Subsequent History of the Wesleyan Mission to the Same People.* London, Wesleyan Missionary House, 1865.

Brookes, E. H. *Apartheid: A Documentary Study of Modern South Africa.* London, Routledge & Kegan Paul, 1968.

Brookes, E. H. and Webb, C. de B. *A History of Natal.* Pietermaritzburg, University of Natal Press, 1965.

2nd (paperback) edition with a considerably expanded bibliography. Pietermaritzburg, University of Natal Press, 1987.

Brown, J. T. *Among the Bantu Nomads; A Record of Forty Years Spent Among the Bechuana . . . With the First Full Description of their Ancient Customs, Manners and Beliefs.* London, Seeley, Service & Co., 1926.

—— *Secwana Dictionary.* Tiger Kloof, London Missionary Society, 1939.

Brownlee, C. P. 'The old peach tree stump: A reminiscence of the war of 1835.' *Cape Monthly Magazine.* New Series. 7,39(1873):129–43.

—— *Reminiscences of Kaffir Life and History and Other Papers . . .* With a memoir by Mrs Brownlee. Lovedale, Lovedale Mission Press, 1896.

Facsimile reprint. Edited by C. Saunders. Pietermaritzburg, Natal University Press, 1977. (Killie Campbell Africana Library Reprint Series)

Bryant, A. T. *A History of the Zulu and Neighbouring Tribes.* Cape Town, Struik, 1964. Reprint of articles which appeared in the Zulu paper *Izindaba Zabantu* from 1 Oct. 1910 to 15 March 1913.

—— *Olden Times in Zululand and Natal, Containing Earlier Political History of the Eastern-Nguni Clans.* London, Longmans, Green, and Co., 1929.

—— *A Zulu-English Dictionary with Notes on Pronunciation, a Revised Orthography and Derivations and Cognate Words from Many Languages; Including Also a Vocabulary of Hlonipa Words, Tribal–names, etc., Synopsis of Zulu grammar and Concise History of the Zulu People from the Most Ancient Times.* Maritzburg, Durban, P. Davis & Sons; Capetown, J.C. Juta; Pinetown, The Mariannhill Mission Press, 1905.

The following entries indicate imprints taken from labels on the title-pages of each volume. The original imprint is given in the initial entry.

London, Kegan Paul, Trench, Trübner & Co., [pref. 1905].

Durban, Maritzburg, Adams & Co., [pref. 1905].

Bulpin, T. V. *Shaka's Country: A Book of Zululand.* Cape Town, Timmins, 1952.

Burchell, J. *Travels in the Interior of Southern Africa.* With an entirely new map, and numerous engravings. London, Printed for Longman, Hurst, Rees, Orme, and Brown, 1822–24. 2v.

Facsimile reprint. Cape Town, Struik, 1965.

Cambridge History of Africa. General editors: J. D. Fage and Roland Oliver. Cambridge, Cambridge University Press, 1975–76. 8v. V.5 *c. 1790–c. 1870.* Edited by John E. Flint.

Cambridge History of the British Empire. Edited by A. P. Newton and E. A. Benians. Advisor in South Africa E. A. Walker. Cambridge, Cambridge University Press, 1936. v.8. *South Africa, Rhodesia and the Protectorates.*

2nd edition. 1963. Edited by Eric A. Walker. Cambridge, Cambridge University Press, 1963, v.8. *South Africa, Rhodesia and the High Commission Territories.*

Cameron, T. and Spies, S. B., eds. *Illustrated History of South Africa.* Johannesburg, Jonathan Ball, 1986.

Campbell, C. 'Images of war: A problem in San rock art research.' *World Archaeology.* 18 (1986): 255–68.

Campbell, G. 'Madagascar and Mozambique in the Slave Trade of the Western Indian Ocean 1800–1861.' In Clarence-Smith, W.G., ed. *The Economics of the Indian Ocean Slave–trade in the Nineteenth Century.* London, 1989, 166–93.

Campbell, J. *Travels in South Africa Undertaken at the Request of the Missionary Society.* London, J. Campbell, 1815.

2nd edition, corrected. London, Printed for Black, Parry & Co. and T. Hamilton, 1815.

3rd edition corrected. London, Printed for Black, Parry and Co. and T. Hamilton, 1816; Andover, Flagg and Gould, 1816.

Facsimile reprint of 3rd edition, corrected. Cape Town, Struik, 1974.

—— *Travels in South Africa Undertaken at the Request of the London Missionary Society; Being the Narrative of a Second Journey in the Interior of that Country.* London, Westley, 1822. 2v.

Facsimile reprint. New York, Johnson Reprint Corporation, 1967. 2v in 1. (Landmarks in Anthropology)

Capela, J. and Medeiros, E. *O Trafico de Escravos de Moçambique para as Ilhas do Indico 1720–1902.* Maputo, [n.p.], 1987.

Carlean, K. 'Myths of the *Mfecane* and South African Educational Texts.' In Edgecombe, D. R., Laband, J. P. C. and Thompson, P. S., comps. *The Debate on Zulu Origins: A Selection of Papers on the Zulu Kingdom and Early Colonial Natal,* 1992, 33p. [Pagination irregular]

Carter, M. and Gerbeau, H. 'Covert Slaves and Coveted Coolies in the Early 19th Century Mascareignes.' In Clarence–Smith, W. G., ed. *Economics of the Indian Ocean Slave-trade in the Nineteenth Century,* 1989, 194–208.

Casalis, E. *Les Bassoutos; ou Vingt-trois Années de Séjour et d'Observations au Sud de l'Afrique.* Paris, Librairie de Ch. Meyrueis et Cie, 1859.

Repr. 1860. (Nouvelle Bibliothèque des Familles).

—— *The Basutos, or, Twenty-three Years in South Africa.* London, James Nisbet, 1861. [Translation of the original French edition of 1859]

Chapman, J. *Travels in the Interior of South Africa Comprising Fifteen Years Hunting and Trading; With Journeys Across the Continent from Natal to Walfisch Bay, and Visits to Lake Ngami and the Victoria Falls.* London, Bell & Daldy; Edward Stanford, 1868. 2v.

—— *Travels in the Interior of South Africa* . . . Edited by E. C. Tabler from the original manuscripts. Cape Town, Balkema, 1971.

Chase, J. C. *The Cape of Good Hope and the Eastern Province of Algoa Bay* . . . London, Pelham Richardson, 1843.

—— 'Substance of the journal of two trading travellers, and of the communications of a missionary, regarding their recent visits to the countries in the rear of the Portuguese settlement at De la Goa Bay.' *South African Quarterly Journal.* 1,4(1830):404–7.

Clarence-Smith, W. G., ed. *Economics of the Indian Ocean Slave–trade in the Nineteenth Century.* London, Cass, 1989.

Cobbing, J. 'The absent priesthood: Another look at the Rhodesian risings of 1896–1897.' *Journal of African History.* 18,1(1977):61–84.

—— 'The evolution of Ndebele *Amabutho*'. *Journal of African History.* 15,4(1974):607–31.

—— 'Grasping the Nettle: The Slave Trade and the Early Zulu.' In Edgecombe, D. R., Laband, J. P. C. and Thompson, P. S., comps. *The Debate on Zulu Origins,* 1992 [Pagination irregular].

—— 'The mfecane as alibi: Thoughts on Dithakong and Mbolompo.' *Journal of African History.* 29,3(1988):487–519.

—— 'The Ndebele State.' In Peires, J. B., ed. *Before and After Shaka,* 1981, 160–7.

—— 'A tainted well: The objectives, historical fantasies, and working methods of James Stuart, with counter-argument.' *Journal of Natal and Zulu History.* 11(1988):115–54.

Coetzee, C. G. 'Die Kompanjie se Besetting van Delagoa-baai.' *Archives Yearbook for South African History.* 9th Year. Pretoria, Government Printer, 1948.

Cole, D. T. 'Old Tswana and new Latin.' *Botswana Notes and Records.* 23(1991):175–91. [Revised version of an article originally published in the *South African Journal of African Languages.* 10,4(1990):345–53.]

Colenso, J. W. *Ten Weeks in Natal. A Journal of a First Tour of Visitation Among the Colonists and Zulu Kafirs of Natal.* Cambridge, Macmillan & Co., 1855.

Comaroff, J. *Body of Power, Spirit of Resistance: The Culture and History of a South African People.* Chicago, Chicago University Press, 1985.

Comaroff, J. *Of Revelation and Revolution: Christianity, Colonialism and Consciousness in South Africa*. v.1. Chicago and London, University of Chicago Press, 1991. [v.2 in progress]

Cope, R. L. 'The Rise of the Zulu Kingdom, the Mfecane, and Colonial Expansion.' In Cope, R. L. *The Years of Conquest: Land and Labour in Nineteenth Century South Africa*, 1995, 23–40.

—— *The Years of Conquest: Land and Labour in Nineteenth Century South Africa*. Johannesburg, Sached Books and Heinemann Centaur, 1995.

Cornevin, M. *Apartheid, Power and Historical Falsification*. Paris, Unesco, 1980.

Cory, G. *The Rise of South Africa*. 5.v. London, Longmans, Green, 1910–30.

Facsimile reprint. Cape Town, Struik, 1965. 5v.

Crais, C. C. *The Making of the Colonial Order: White Supremacy and Black Resistance in the Eastern Cape, 1770–1865*. Johannesburg, Witwatersrand University Press, 1992.

—— 'Representation and the politics of identity in South Africa: An Eastern Cape example.' *International Journal of African Historical Studies*. 25(1992):99–126.

—— 'Slavery and freedom along a frontier: The Eastern Cape, South Africa: 1770–1838.' *Slavery and Abolition: A Journal of Comparative Studies*. 11,2(1990):190–216.

—— *White Supremacy and Black Resistance in Pre-industrial South Africa*. Cambridge, Cambridge University Press, 1992. Published in the same year by the Witwatersrand University Press, Johannesburg, under a different title. *See* Crais, C. C. *The Making of the Colonial Order . . .*

Dalby, D., ed. *Language and History in Africa: A Volume of Collected Papers Presented to the London Seminar on Lanuage and History in Africa*. Held at the School of Oriental and African Studies, 1967–69. London, Cass; New York, Africana Publishing Company, 1970.

Daniel, J. B. M. 'A geographical study of pre-Shakan Zululand.' *South African Geographical Journal*. 15(1973):23–31.

Daniell, S. *African Scenery and Animals*. London, The Artist, 1804–5.

Reprint edition. London, R. Havell, 1831.

Facsimile reprint. Cape Town, Balkema, 1976.

—— *Sketches Representing the Native Tribes, Animals and Scenery of Southern Africa from Drawings Made by the Late Mr Samuel Daniell, Engraved by William Daniell*. London, William Daniell and William Wood, 1820.

Darlow, D. J. *Tshaka: King of the Amazulu*. Lovedale, Lovedale Press, 1937. (African Heroes)

Davenport, T. R. H. *South Africa: A Modern History*. Toronto, University of Toronto Press; London, Macmillan, 1977.

2nd edition. 1978.

3rd edition, updated and extensively revised. Johannesburg and Basingstoke, Macmillan; Bergvlei, Southern Books, 1987.

4th edition, updated and extensively revised. Basingstoke, Macmillan, 1991.

Deacon, J. '"My place is the Bitterpits": The home territory of Bleek and Lloyd's /Xam San informants.' *African Studies*. 45(1986):135–55.

—— 'The power of a place in understanding southern San rock engravings.' *World Archaeology*. 20(1988):129–40.

[Defoe, D.] *The Adventures of Robert Drury during Fifteen Years of Captivity on the Island of Madagascar . . .* London, Printed by W. Meadows, 1743.

Repr. London, Hull, Stodart & Craggs, 1807.

—— *Madagascar: or, Robert Drury's Journal, during Fifteen Years Captivity on the Island . . . The Whole is a Faithful Narrative of Matters of Fact, Interspers'd with Variety of Surprising Incidents, and Illustrated with a Sheet Map of Madagascar, and Cuts. Written by Himself, Digested into Order and Now Publish'd at the Request of His Friends*. London, Printed, and sold by W. Meadows . . . J. Marshall . . . T. Worrall . . . and by the Author . . ., 1729.

2nd edition. London, Printed, and sold by J. Brotherton . . . T. Worrall . . . J. Jackson . . ., 1731.

—— *Madagascar; or, Robert Drury's Journal, during Fifteen Years Captivity on that Island; and a Further Description of Madagascar, by the Abbé Alexis Rochon*; edited with an introduction and notes by Capt. Pasfield Oliver . . . Illustrated. London, T. Fisher Unwin, 1890. (Adventure Series 2) The introduction by S. Pasfield Oliver contains notes on the authorship and identity of Robert Drury.

Repr. 1897.

Reprint of the 1897 version. New York, Negro Universities Press [1969]. For variant editions of the adventures of Robert Drury *see SABIB*.

De Kiewiet, C.W. *A History of South Africa: Social and Economic*. London, Oxford University Press, 1941.

Repr. London, London University Press, 1942.

Repr. Oxford, Oxford University Press 1942, 1943, 1946, 1950, 1957, 1960.

—— 'Social and Economic Developments in Native Tribal Life.' In *Cambridge History of the British Empire*, v. 8, 1963, 808–9.

Delegorgue, A. *Travels in Southern Africa*. Translated by Fleur Webb. Introduced and indexed by Stephanie J. Alexander and Colin de B. Webb. Durban, Killie Campbell Africana Library; Pietermaritzburg, University of Natal Press, 1990. 2v. [v.2 in progress]

Delius, P. *The Land Belongs to Us: The Pedi Polity, the Boers and the British in the Nineteenth-Century Transvaal*. Johannesburg, Ravan Press, 1983.

Denbow, J.R. 'A new look at the later pre-history of the Kalahari.' *Journal of African History*. 27(1986):3–28.

—— 'The Toutswe Tradition: A Study in Socio-economic Change.' In Hitchcock, R.R. and Smith, M.R., eds. *Proceedings of the Symposium on Settlement in Botswana. The Development of a Human Landscape*, 1972, 87–91.

Denbow, J.R., Kiyaga-Mulindwa, D. and Parsons, N. 'Historical and Archaeological Research in Botswana.' In Hitchcock, R., Parsons, N. and Taylor, J., eds. *Research for Development in Botswana*, 1987, 244–64.

Denoon, D. and Nyeko, B. *Southern Africa Since 1800*. London, Longman, 1972.

2nd edition 1984.

De Villiers, M. *White Tribe Dreaming*. New York, Viking, 1987.

Dicke, B.H. 'The tsetse fly's influence on South African history.' *South African Journal of Science*. 29 (1932):792–96.

Döhne, J.L. *A Zulu-Kafir Dictionary Etymologically Explained, with Copious Illustrations and Examples; Preceded by an Introduction on the Zulu-Kafir Language*. Cape Town, Printed at G.J. Pike's Machine Printing Office, 1857.

Dominy, G. 'Myths, Manipulation and Nettles: Historians and the Shaping of the Mfecane Controversy: A Critical Introduction.' In Edgecombe, D.R., Laband, J.P.C. and Thompson, P.S., comps. *The Debate on Zulu Origins: A Selection of Papers on the Zulu Kingdom and Early Colonial Natal*, 1992, 10p. [Pagination irregular]

Dowson, T.A. 'Revelations of religious reality: The individual in San art.' *World Archaeology*. 20 (1988):116–28.

—— *Rock Engravings of Southern Africa*. Johannesburg, Witwatersrand University Press, 1992.

Dowson, T.A., Blundell, G. and Hall, S. 'Finger paintings in the Harts River Valley, northern Cape Province, South Africa.' *South African Field Archaeology*. 1(1992):27–32.

Du Bruyn, J. 'The "Forgotten Factor" sixteen years later: Some trends in historical writing on precolonial South Africa.' *Kleio*. 16(1984):34–45.

—— 'Ousting both the Mfecane and the anti-Mfecane.' *South African Historical Journal*. 25(1991):166–70.

Du Buisson, L. *The White Man Cometh*. Johannesburg, Jonathan Ball, 1987.

Duly, L.C. *British Land Policy at the Cape, 1792–1844: A Study of Administrative Procedures in the Empire*. Durham, North Carolina, Duke University Press, 1972.

Duminy, A.H. and Guest, B. [W.R.], eds. *Natal and Zululand from Earliest Times to 1910: A New History*. Pietermaritzburg, University of Natal Press; Shuter and Shooter, 1989.

Du Toit, A. 'No chosen people: The myth of the Calvinist origins of Afrikaner nationalism and racial ideology.' *American Historical Review*. 88(1983):920–52.

Du Toit, A. and Giliomee, H.B. *Afrikaner Political Thought: Analysis and Documents*. Cape Town, David Philip, 1983. 2v. Berkeley, University of California Press, 1983.

Dzivhani, S. M. *See under* South Africa. (Union). Department of Native Affairs. Van Warmelo, N. J., ed. *The Copper Miners of Musina* . . . In *Official Publications* section.

Eden, C. H. *An Inherited Task; or, Early Mission Life in Southern Africa.* London, Oxford, [n.p., 1871?].

London, Society for Promoting Christian Knowledge, 1874.

London, Society for Promoting Christian Knowledge; New York, Pott, Young, & Co., [187?].

Edgecombe, D. R., Laband, J. P. C. and Thompson, P. S., comps. *The Debate on Zulu Origins: A Selection of Papers on the Zulu Kingdom and Early Colonial Natal.* Pietermaritzburg, University of Natal, Department of Historical Studies, 1992. [Pagination irregular]

Eldredge, E. A. 'Delagoa Bay and the Hinterland in the Early Nineteenth Century: Politics, Trade, Slaves and Slave-raiding.' In Eldredge, E. A. and Morton, F., eds. *Slavery in South Africa: Captive Labour on the Dutch Frontier*, 1994, 127–65.

—— 'Drought, famine and disease in nineteenth-century Lesotho.' *African Economic History.* 16(1987):61–93.

—— 'Land, politics and censorship: The historiography of nineteenth-century Lesotho.' *History in Africa.* 15(1988):191–209.

—— 'Sources of conflict in Southern Africa, *c.*1800–30. The 'Mfecane' considered. *Journal of African History.* 33,1(1992):1–35.

—— *A South African Kingdom: The Pursuit of Security in Nineteenth–century Lesotho.* Cambridge, Cambridge University Press; Johannesburg, Witwatersrand University Press, 1993. (Cambridge African Studies Series 78)

Eldredge, E. A. and Morton, F., eds. *Slavery in South Africa: Captive Labor on the Dutch Frontier.* Boulder, Westview Press; Pietermaritzburg, University of Natal Press, 1994.

Ellenberger, D. F. *History of the Basuto: Ancient and Modern*, compiled by D. Fred Ellenberger, V.D.M. and written in English by J. C. Macgregor . . . under the auspices of the Basutoland Government. London, Caxton Publishing Co., 1912.

Reprint of 1912 edition. New York, Negro Universities Press, [1969].

—— 'Mobokoboko, ou une page d'histoire'. *Journal des Missions Evangéliques.* 59(1884):420–26.

Ellenberger, V. 'History of the Ba-ga-Malete of Ramoutsa (Bechuanaland Protectorate).' *Transactions of the Royal Society of South Africa.* 25,1 (1937–38): 1–72.

Elphick, R. and Giliomee, H. B., eds. *The Shaping of South African Society, 1652–1820.* Cape Town, Maskew Miller Longman, 1979.

2nd edition with amended title: *The Shaping of South African Society, 1652–1840.* Cape Town, Maskew Miller Longman, 1989.

Elphick, R. and Malherbe, V. C. 'The Khoisan to 1828.' In Elphick, R. and Giliomee, H. *The Shaping of South African Society*, 1989, 3–65.

Epprecht, M. 'The Mfecane as Teaching Aid: History, Politics and Pedagogy in Southern Africa.' *Journal of Historical Sociology.* 7, 2(1994):113–30

'Ergates'. 'Bushmen's stock raids in Natal.' *Natal Agricultural Journal.* 8(1905):113–23.

Esterhuyse, J. H. *South West Africa: 1880–1894.* Cape Town, Struik, 1968.

Etherington, N. 'The aftermath of the aftermath.' *South African Historical Journal.* 25(1991): 154–62.

—— 'The Great Trek in relation to the *Mfecane*: A reassessment.' *South African Historical Journal.* 25(1991):12–13.

—— Review article of: Peires, J. B., ed. *Before and After Shaka: Papers in Nguni History.* Grahamstown, Institute of Social and Economic Research, 1981. *Journal of Southern African Studies.* 11,1 (1984):157–61.

—— 'Shrinking the Zulu.' *Southern African Review of Books.* September/October, 1992, 12.

Evers, T. M. 'Iron Age trade in the eastern Transvaal, South Africa.' *South African Archaeological Bulletin.* 29,113–14(1974):33–37.

—— 'Sotho-Tswana and Moloko Settlement Patterns and the Bantu Cattle Pattern.' In Hall, M. *et al.*, eds. *Frontiers: Southern African Archaeology Today*, 1984, 236–47.

Evers, T. M. and Hammond-Tooke, W. D. 'The emergence of South African chiefdoms: An archaeological perspective.' *African Studies.* 45(1986):37–41.

Evers, T.M. and Van der Merwe, N.J. 'Iron Age ceramics from Phalaborwa.' *South African Archaeological Bulletin*. 42 (1987):87–106.

Filliot, J.M. *La Traite des Esclaves vers les Mascareignes au XVIIIe Siècle*. Paris, Orstom, 1974.

Ford, J. *The Role of the Trypanosomiases in African Ecology*. Oxford, Clarendon Press, 1971.

Forsyth, P. 'The past in service of the present: The political use of history by Chief A.N.M. Buthelezi, 1951–1991.' *South African Historical Journal*. 26(1992):74–92.

Fortes, M. and Evans-Pritchard, E.E., eds. *African Political Systems*. London, New York, Toronto, Oxford University Press for the International African Institute, 1940.

Franken, J.L.M. *Duminy Dagboeke: Duminy Diaries*. Cape Town, Van Riebeeck Society, 1938. (V.R.S.19)

Friede, H.M. 'Notes on the composition of pre-European copper and copper-alloy artefacts from the Transvaal.' *South African Institute of Mining and Metallurgy*. 75,7(1975):185–91.

Friede, H.M. and Steel, R.H. 'Notes on Iron Age copper smelting technology in the Transvaal.' *South African Institute of Mining and Metallurgy*. 76,4(1975):221–31.

—— 'Tin mining and smelting in the Transvaal during the Iron Age.' *South African Institute of Mining and Metallurgy*. 76, 12(1976):461–70.

Fuller, C. *See under* South Africa. (Union). Department of Agriculture. In *Official Publications* section.

Fuze, M.M. *The Black People and Whence They Came*. Translated by H.C. Lugg. Edited by A.T. Cope. Pietermaritzburg, University of Natal Press; Durban, Killie Campbell Africana Library, 1979.

Fynn, H.F. *The Diary of Henry Francis Fynn*. Compiled from original sources and edited by James Stuart and D. McK. Malcolm. Pietermaritzburg, Shuter and Shooter, 1950.
2nd edition 1969.

Galton, F. *The Narrative of an Explorer in Tropical South Africa*. London, Murray, 1853.
2nd edition, London, Ward Lock, 1889.
3rd edition 1890.
4th edition 1891.
Facsimile reprint, New York, Johnson, 1971.

Gardiner, A.F. *Narrative of a Journey to the Zoolu Country in South Africa, Undertaken in 1835*. London, William Crofts; New York, Thomas George, 1836.
Facsimile reprint of William Crofts edition. Cape Town, Struik, 1966.

Garlake, P.S. *The Painted Caves: An Introduction to the Prehistoric Rock Art of Zimbabwe*. Harare, Modus, 1987.

—— 'Themes in prehistoric art of Zimbabwe.' *World Archaeology*. 19(1987):178–93.

—— 'Symbols of potency in the paintings of Zimbabwe.' *South African Archaeological Bulletin*. 45(1990):17–27.

General History of Africa. UNESCO International Scientific Committee for the Drafting of a General History of Africa. Paris, UNESCO; London, Heinemann International; Berkeley, University of California Press, 1981–85. 7v. v.4, 1984: *Africa from the Twelfth to the Sixteenth Centuries*. Edited by D.T. Niane; v.6, 1989: *Africa in the Nineteenth Century until the 1880s*. Edited by F.J. Ajayi. [F. Jacob Ade].

Germond, R.C., ed. *Chronicles of Basutoland: A Running Commentary on the Events of the Years 1830–1902 by the French Protestant Missionaries in South Africa*. Morija, Morija Sesotho Book Depot, 1967.

Gluckman, M. 'The rise of a Zulu empire.' *Scientific American*. 202,4(1963):159–69.

—— *Rituals of Rebellion in South-East Africa*. Manchester, Manchester University Press, 1954.

Godeé Molsbergen, E.C. *Reizen in Zuid Afrika in de Hollandse Tijd*. s'Gravenhage, M. Nijhoff, 1916.
4v. (Werken Uitgegeven door de Linschoten-Vereeniging, 11, 12, 20, 36)

Godlonton, R. *A Narrative of the Irruption of the Kafir Hordes into the Eastern Province of the Cape of Good Hope, 1834–35. Compiled from Official Documents and Other Authentic Sources, by the Editor of the 'Graham's Town Journal'*. Graham's Town, Meurant and Godlonton, 1836.
Facsimile reprint. Cape Town, Struik, 1965. (Africana Collectanea 11)

Golan, D. 'Inkatha and its use of the Zulu past.' *History in Africa*. 18(1991):113–26.

—— *Inventing Shaka: Using History in the Construction of Zulu Nationalism*. Boulder and London, Lynne Rienner, 1994.

Goldswain, J. *The Chronicle of Jeremiah Goldswain, Albany Settler of 1820*. Edited by Una Long (Mrs Colin Gill). Cape Town, Van Riebeeck Society, 1946. 2v. (V.R.S. 27, 29)

Goodridge, C. M. *Narrative of a Voyage to the South Seas, with the Shipwreck of the Princess of Wales Cutter . . . with an Account of Two Years Residence on an Uninhabited Island.* London, [Exeter printed], 1839.

Gray, R. and Birmingham, D., eds. *Pre-colonial African Trade: Essays on Trade in Central and Eastern Africa before 1900*. London, Oxford University Press, 1970.

Gray, S. *The Assassination of Shaka . . . see* Skotnes, C.

—— 'South African fiction and a case history revised: An account of research into retellings of the John Ross story of early Natal.' *Researches in African Literature.* 19,4(1988):473–47.

—— *See also* MacLean, C.R. *The Natal Papers of 'John Ross'* . . .

Grout, L. *Zulu-land; or, Life among the Zulu-Kafirs of Natal and Zulu-land, South Africa*. London, Trubner & Co., 1862.

Grundlingh, A. M. 'Politics, principles and problems of a profession: Afrikaner historians and their discipline, c. 1920–1965.' *Perspectives in Education.* 12(1990):1–19.

—— *Die 'Hensoppers' en 'Joiners': Die Rasionaal en Verskynsel van Verraad*. Cape Town and Pretoria, HAUM, 1979.

Grundlingh, A. M. and Sapire, H. 'From feverish festival to repetitive ritual? The changing fortunes of Great Trek mythology in an industrializing South Africa, 1938–1988.' *South African Historical Journal.* 21 (1989):19–37.

Gump, J. O. 'Ecological change and pre-Shakan state formation.' *African Economic History.* 18 (1989):57–71.

—— *The Formation of the Zulu Kingdom in South Africa, 1750–1840*. San Francisco, Mellen Research University Press, 1990.

—— 'Origins of the Zulu Kingdom.' *Historian.* 50,4(1988):521–34.

Guy, J. J. 'Analysing pre-capitalist societies in southern Africa.' *Journal of Southern African Studies.* 14,1 (1987):18–37.

—— *The Destruction of the Zulu Kingdom: The Civil War in Zululand, 1879–1884*. London, Longman, 1979.

Repr. Johannesburg, Ravan Press, 1982.

Repr. Pietermaritzburg, University of Natal Press, 1994.

—— 'Ecological Factors in the Rise of Shaka and the Zulu Kingdom.' In Marks, S, and Atmore, A. *Economy and Society in Pre-industrial South Africa*, 1980, 102–119.

—— 'Gender Oppression in Southern Africa's Precapitalist Societies.' In Walker, C., ed. *Women and Gender in Southern Africa to 1945*, 1990, 33–47.

—— 'The Political Structure of the Zulu Kingdom During the Reign of Cetshwayo kaMpande.' In Peires, J.B, ed. *Before and After Shaka: Papers in Nguni History*, 1983, 49–73.

—— 'Production and exchange in the Zulu kingdom.' *Mohlomi.* 2(1978):96–106.

Haarhoff, D. *The Wild South-West: Frontier Myths and Metaphors in Literature set in Namibia, 1760–1988*. Johannesburg, Witwatersrand University Press, 1991.

Haggard H.R. *King Solomon's Mines*. London, Cassell, 1885.

Between 1885 and 1914, numerous versions were printed by different publishers. For further bibliographic details *see SABIB*.

—— *Nada the Lily*. London, Longmans Green, 1892.

New edition. 1895. New impressions. 1898, 1901, 1904.

Repr. London, Hodder & Stoughton, 1914.

Haight, M. V. Jackson *see* Jackson, M. V. [later Jackson Haight, M.V.].

Hall, L. B. *Shaka: Warrior King of the Zulu*. Cape Town, Struik, 1987.

Hall, M. 'Archaeology and modes of production in pre-colonial southern Africa.' *Journal of Southern African Studies.* 14,1(1987):1–17.

—— *The Changing Past: Farmers, Kings and Traders in Southern Africa, 200–1860*. Cape Town, David Philip, 1987.

—— 'Dendroclimatology, rainfall and human adaptation in the Later Iron Age of Natal and Zululand.' *Annals of the Natal Museum.* 22(1976):693–703.

Hall, M., Avery, G., Avery, D.M., Wilson, M.L. and Humphreys, A.J.B., eds. *Frontiers: Southern African Archaeology Today*. Oxford, British Archaeological Reports, 1984. (Cambridge Monographs in African Archaeology, 10; BAR International Series, 207)

Hall, M. and Mack, K. 'The outline of an eighteenth century economic system in South-east Africa.' *Annals of the South African Museum*. 91,2(1983):163–94.

Hall, M. and Vogel, J.C. 'Some recent radio-carbon dates from southern Africa.' *Journal of African History*. 21,4(1980):431–55.

Hall, M. and Wright, J., eds. *Production and Reproduction in the Zulu Kingdom: Workshop Papers*. Pietermaritzburg, University of Natal, Department of History and Political Studies, 1977.

Hall, S.L. 'Excavations at Rooikrans and Rhenosterkloof: Late Iron Age sites in the Rooiberg area of the Transvaal.' *Annals of the Cape Provincial Museums*. 1,5(1985):131–210.

—— 'Pastoral adaptations and forager reactions in the eastern Cape.' *South African Archaeological Society Goodwin Series*. 5(1986):42–49.

Hallett, R. *Africa to 1875*. Ann Arbor, Michigan University Press, 1970.

Hamilton, C.A. '"An appetite for the past": The re-creation of Shaka and the crisis in popular historical consciousness.' *South African Historical Journal*. 22(1990):141–57.

—— '"Character and objects of Chaka." A reconsideration of the making of Shaka as Mfecane motor.' *Journal of African History*. 33,1(19 92):37–63. [Reprinted in this volume]

—— 'Ideology and oral traditions: Listening to the "voices from below".' *History in Africa*. 14 (1987):67–86.

Hamilton, C.A. and Wright, J.B. 'The making of the amaLala: Ethnicity, ideology and relations of subordination in a precolonial context.' *South African Historical Journal*. 22(1990):3–23.

Hammond, D. and Jablow, A. *The Africa That Never Was: Four Centuries of British Writing about Africa*. New York, Twayne, 1970.

Hammond-Tooke, W.D., ed. *The Bantu-speaking Peoples of Southern Africa*. London, Routledge & Kegan Paul, 1974. This is the 2nd edition of Schapera, I. *The Bantu-speaking Tribes of South Africa, 1937*.

—— 'Descent groups, chiefdoms and South African historiography.' *Journal of Southern African Studies*. 11(1985):305–19.

—— 'Kinship Authority and Political Authority in Pre-colonial South Africa.' In Spiegel, A.D. and McAllister, P.A., eds. *Tradition and Transition in Southern Africa*, 1991, 185–99.

—— *The Roots of Black South Africa*. Johannesburg, Jonathan Ball, 1993.

Harinck, G. 'Interaction between Xhosa and Khoi: Emphasis on the Period 1620–1750.' In Thompson, L.M., ed. *African Societies in Southern Africa: Historical Studies, 1969*, 145–69.

Harington, A.L. *Sir Harry Smith: Bungling Hero*. Cape Town, Tafelberg, 1980.

Harries, P. 'Slavery, social incorporation and surplus extraction: The nature of free and unfree labour in South-East Africa.' *Journal of African History*. 22,2(1981):309–30.

Harris, W.C. *Narrative of an Expedition into Southern Africa, during the Years 1836, and 1837, from the Cape of Good Hope through the Territories of the Chief Moselekate, to the Tropic of Capricorn, with a Sketch of the Recent Emigration of the Border Colonists, and a Zoological Appendix* . . . Bombay, Printed at the American Mission Press, 1833.
The second edition (1839) and later ones, were published under the title *The Wild Sports of Southern Africa*.

Haughton, E.J. Wells, L.H. 'Underground structures in caves of the southern Transvaal.' *South African Journal of Science*. 38 (1942):319–33.

Hawkins, E.B. *The Story of Harrismith: 1849–1920*. Ladysmith, Westcott, 1982.

Heymans, D. *The Voortrekker Monument, Pretoria*. Pretoria, Board of Control of the Voortrekker Monument, 1986.

Hindess, B. and Hirst, P.Q. *Pre-Capitalist Modes of Production*. London, Routledge and Kegan Paul, 1975.

Hitchcock, R.R. and Smith, M.R., eds. *Proceedings of the Symposium on Settlement in Botswana: The Historical Development of a Human Landscape*. Gaborone, Heinemann Educational Books for the Botswana Society, 1982.

Hitchcock, R., Parsons, N. and Taylor, J., eds. *Research for Development in Botswana*. Proceedings of a Symposium held by the Botswana Society . . . August 19–21, 1985. Gaborone, Botswana Society, 1987.

Hlongwane, A. *See under* South Africa. (Union). Department of Native Affairs. Van Warmelo, N. J., ed. . . . In *Official Publications* section.

Hodgson, A. *Memoirs of Mrs. Anne Hodgson; Compiled from Materials Recieved from her Husband, the Rev. T. L. Hodgson by William Shaw*. London, J. Mason, 1836.

Hodgson, T.L. *The Journals of the Reverend T.L. Hodgson. Missionary to the Seleka-Rolong and the Griquas 1821–1831*. Edited by R.L. Cope. Johannesburg, Witwatersrand University Press, 1977.

Hofmeyr, I. 'Jonah and the swallowing monster: Orality and literacy on a Berlin mission station in the Transvaal.' [Kekana-Ndebele oMokopane]. *Journal of Southern African Studies*. 17,4(1991): 633–53.

—— 'No chief, no exchange, no story.' *African Studies*. 48,2(1989):131–55.

Holden, W.C. *The Past and Future of the Kaffir Races. In Three Parts. 1. Their History. 2. Their Manners and Customs. 3. The Means Needful for Their Preservation and Improvement . . .* London, Published for the Author, 1866.

Holonga, N.M. 'Overview of the History of the Bakalanga of Botswana.' In van Waarden, C., ed. *Kalanga Retrospect and Prospect . . .* 1991, 35–37.

How, M. 'An Alibi for Mantatisi.' *African Studies*. 13(1954):65–76.

Huffman, T.N. 'Archaeological evidence and conventional explanations of southern Bantu settlement patterns.' *Africa*. 56,3 (1986):280–98.

—— 'Archaeology and ethnohistory of the African Iron Age.' *Annual Review of Anthropology*. 11(1982):133–50.

—— 'Broederstroom and the origins of cattle-keeping in southern Africa.' *African Studies*. 49,2(1990):1–12.

—— 'Ceramics, settlements and Late Iron Age migrations.' *African Archaeological Review*. 7(1989):155–82.

—— 'Cognitive studies of the Iron Age in southern Africa.' *World Archaeology*. 18(1986):84–95.

—— 'Iron Age settlement patterns and the origins of class distinction in Southern Africa.' *Advances in World Archaeology*. 5(1986):291–338.

—— 'The origins of Leopard's Kopje: An 11th-century *difaqane*.' *Arnoldia Rhodesiana*. 8,23(1978):1–24.

—— 'The trance hypothesis and the rock art of Zimbabwe.' *South African Archaeological Society Goodwin Series*. 4(1983):49–53.

—— 'The Waterberg research of Jan Aukema.' *South African Archaeological Bulletin*. 45 (1990): 117–19.

Huffman, T.N. and Hanisch, E.O.M. 'Settlement hierarchies in the northern Transvaal: Zimbabwe ruins and Venda history.' *African Studies*. 46,1(1987):79–116.

Hunt, D. 'An account of the Bapedi.' *Bantu Studies*. 5(1931):287–89.

Ingold, T., Riches, D. and Woodburn, J., eds. *Papers from the 4th International Conference on Hunting and Gathering Societies Held at the London School of Economics and Political Science, 1986*. Oxford, Berg, 1988. 2v. (Explorations in Anthropology). v. 1: *History, Evolution and Social Change*; v. 2: *Hunters and Gatherers: Property, Power and Ideology*.

Isaacs, N. Travels and Adventures in Eastern Africa, Descriptive of the Zoolus, their Manners, Customs, etc. etc., with a Sketch of Natal. London, Edward Churton, 1836. 2v.

  Repr. edited with footnotes and a biographical sketch by Louis Herrman. Cape Town, Van Riebeeck Society, 1936–1937. 2v. (V.R.S. 16, 17).

  Newly revised and edited in 1 v. with a biography of the author, notes and appendices by Louis Herrman and Percival R. Kirby. Cape Town, Struik, 1970.

Jackson, A.O., ed. *See under* South Africa. Department of Co-operation and Development. In *Official Publications* section.

Jackson, M. V. [later Jackson Haight]. *European Powers and South-east Africa: A study of International Relations on the South-east Coast of Africa, 1796–1856.* London [etc.], Longmans Green & Co., 1942.
Revised edition under the name Jackson Haight, M. V. London, Routledge & Kegan Paul, 1967.
Jackson Haight, M. V. *see* Jackson, M. V.
Jaffe, H. *A History of Africa.* London, Zed, 1985.
—— *See also* 'Mnguni'.
James, W. G. and Simons, M., eds. *The Angry Divide.* Cape Town, David Philip, 1989.
Jensen, F. H. W. 'Note on the Bahurutshe.' *African Studies.* 6(1949):41.
Jones, D. H. 'Problems of African chronology.' *Journal of African History.* 11,2 (1970):161–76.
Jordao, L. M. *visconde* de Paiva Manso. *Memoria sobre Lourenço Marques (Delagoa Bay).* Lisboa, Imprensa Naçional, 1870.
Kawa, R. T. *Imbali lama Mfengu . . . Lihlelwe ngu D.D.T. Jabavu.* Lovedale, Lovedale Press [pref. 1929].
Kay, S. *Travels and Researches in Caffraria: Describing the Character, Customs and Moral Condition of the Tribes Inhabiting that Portion of Southern Africa: With Historical and Topographical Remarks Illustrative of the State and Prospects of the British Settlement in its Borders, the Introduction of Christianity, and the Progress of Civilization.* London, John Mason, 1833.
Repr. New York, Harper & Bros, 1834.
Keegan, T. 'The making of the Orange Free State, 1846–54: Sub-imperialism, primitive accumulation and state formation.' *Journal of Imperial and Commonwealth History.* 17,1(1988):26–54.
Keen, K. *Two Decades of Basotho Development 1830–1850: Studies in Early Afro-European Contacts in Southern Africa.* Gothenburg: Universty of Gothenburg, 1975. (Bulletin of the Department of History, University of Gothenburg.)
Khama III. 'Khama's own account of himself.' Edited by Q. N. Parsons. *Botswana Notes and Records.* 4(1972):137–46.
Kienitz, A. 'The key role of the Oorlam migrations in the early Europeanisation of South West Africa.' *International Journal of African Historical Studies.* 10(1977):553–72.
Kinahan, J. *Pastoral Nomads of the Central Namib Desert: The People History Forgot.* Windhoek, Namibian Archaeological Trust, 1991.
King, H. *Richard Bourke.* Melbourne, Oxford University Press, 1971.
King, J. S. 'Some Account of Mr Farewell's Settlement at Port Natal, and of a Visit to Chaka, King of the Zoolas . . .' In Thompson, G. *Travels and Adventures in South Africa, 1827,* v. 2, p. 251.
Kinsman, M. 'Beasts of burden: The subordination of Southern Tswana women, *c.*1800–1840.' *Journal of Southern African Studies.* 10,1(1983):39–54.
—— 'Notes on the Southern Tswana Social Formation.' In University of Cape Town. Centre for African Studies. African Seminar. Collected Papers. Edited by K. Gottschalk and C. Saunders. Cape Town, University of Cape Town, 1981. v. 2, 167–94.
—— 'Populists and Patriarchs: The Transformation of the Captaincy at Griqua Town, 1804–1822.' In Mabin, A., ed. *Organisation and Economic Change.* Johannesburg, Ravan Press, 1989, 1–20.
Kirk, T. 'Progress and Decline in the Kat River Settlement, 1829–1854.' *Journal of African History.* 14,3(1973):411–23.
Kjekhus, H. *Ecology Control and Economic Development in East Africa: The Case of Tanganyika 1850–1950.* London, Heinemann Educational, 1977.
Klein, R. G., ed. *Southern African Prehistory and Paleoenvironments.* Rotterdam, Balkema, 1984.
Knobel, L. 'The history of Sechele.' *Botswana Notes and Records.* 1(1968):51–63.
Koelle, S. W. *Polyglotta Africana: Or a Comparative Vocabulary of Nearly Three Hundred Words and Phrases in More than One Hundred Distinct African Languages.* London, Church Missionary House, 1854.
Repr. Graz, Akademische, 1963.
Kotze, D. J., ed. *Letters of the American Missionaries, 1835–1838.* Cape Town, Van Riebeeck Society, 1950. (V.R.S.31)
Krige, E. J. *The Social System of the Zulus.* Pietermaritzburg, Shuter & Shooter, 1950.

Krige, J. D. 'Traditional origins and tribal relationships of the Sotho of the northern Transvaal.' *Bantu Studies.* 11(1937):321–56.

Kropf, A. *A Kaffir-English Dictionary.* [Lovedale], Lovedale Mission Press, 1899. 2nd edition. Edited by Rev. Robert Godfrey. (Lovedale), Lovedale Mission Press, 1915.

Kuper, A. 'The "house" and Zulu political structure in the nineteenth century.' *Journal of African History.* 34,3(1993):469–87.

—— 'A note on ruling generations and historical time in Botswana.' *Botswana Notes and Records.* 3(1971): 111–30.

—— *Wives for Cattle: Bridewealth and Marriage in Southern Africa.* London, Routledge, 1982.

Laidler, P. W. 'The archaeology of certain prehistoric settlements in the Heilbron area.' *Transactions of the Royal Society of South Africa.* 23(1935):23–70.

—— 'South African native ceramics: Their characteristics and classification.' *Transactions of the Royal Society of South Africa.* 26(1938):93–172.

Lancaster, J. C. S. 'A Reappraisal of the Governorship of Sir Benjamin D'Urban at the Cape of Good Hope, 1834–1835.' Master's dissertation, Rhodes University, 1980. In *Archives Yearbook for South African History.* 54th Year, v. 2. Pretoria, Government Printer, 1991.

Lau, B. *Namibia in Jonker Afrikaner's Time.* Windhoek, National Archives, Department of National Education, 1987. (Windhoek Archives Publication Series No. 8)

—— '"Thank God the Germans Came": Vedder and Namibian Historiography.' In University of Cape Town. Centre for African Studies. African Seminar. Collected Papers. Edited by K. Gottschalk and C. Saunders. Cape Town, University of Cape Town, 1981, v. 2, 24–53.

—— *See also* South West Africa/Namibia. Department of National Education. In *Official Publications* section.

Laydevant, H. 'La Misère au Basutoland.' *Les Missions Catholiques.* (1934):333–37.

Legassick, M. 'The Frontier Tradition in South African Historiography.' *The Collected Seminar Papers on the Societies of Southern Africa in the 19th and 20th Centuries.* Institute of Commonwealth Studies, University of London. 2(1971):1–33.

—— 'The Northern Frontier to 1820: The emergence of the Griqua people.' In Elphick, R. and Giliomee, H., eds. *The Shaping of South African Society, 1652–1820,* 1979, 358–420.

—— 'The Northern Frontier to c. 1840: The Rise and Decline of the Griqua People.' In Elphick, R. and Giliomee, H., eds. *The Shaping of South African Society, 1652–1840,* 1989, 358–420.

—— 'The Sotho-Tswana peoples before 1800.' In Thompson, L., ed. *African Societies in Southern Africa: Historical Studies,* 1969, 86–125.

Lestrade, G. P. 'Some notes on the political organisation of the Bechuana.' *South African Journal of Science.* 35(1928):427–32.

Lewis-Williams, J. D. *Believing and Seeing: Symbolic Meanings in Southern San Rock Paintings.* London, Academic Press, 1981.

—— 'The economic and social context of southern San rock art.' *Current Anthropology.* 23(1982):429–49.

—— 'Introductory essay: Science and rock art.' *South African Archaeological Society, Goodwin Series.* 4(1983):3–13.

—— 'Ideological Continuities in Prehistoric Southern Africa: The Evidence of Rock Art.' In Schrire, C., ed. *Past and Present in Hunter-Gatherer Studies,* 1984, 225–52.

—— 'Paintings of Power: Ethnography and Rock Art in Southern Africa.' In Biesele, M., Gordon, R. and Lee, R., eds. *Past and Future of !Kung Ethnography,* 1986, 231–73.

—— '"People of the Eland": An Archaeo-linguistic Crux.' In Ingold, T., Riches, D. and Woodburn, J., eds. *Papers from the 4th International Conference on Hunting and Gathering Societies Held at the London School of Economics and Political Science, 1986 . . .* 1988, v. 2: *Hunters and Gatherers: Property, Power and Ideology,* 203–11.

—— 'Southern Africa's place in the archaeology of human understanding.' *South African Journal of Science.* 85 (1989):47–52.

—— *Discovering Southern African Rock Art.* Cape Town, David Philip, 1990.

—— 'Ethnographic evidence relating to 'trancing' and 'shamans' among northern Bushmen.' *South African Archaeological Bulletin.* 47(1992):56–60.

Lewis-Williams, J.D. and Biesele, M. 'Eland hunting rituals among northern and southern San groups: Striking similarities.' *Africa.* 48(1978):117–34.

Lewis-Williams, J.D. and Dowson, T.A. *Images of Power: Understanding Bushman Rock Art.* Johannesburg, Southern Books, 1989.

Lichtenstein, M.H.K. *Travels in Southern Africa, in the Years 1803, 1804, 1805, and 1806.* Translated from the original German by Anne Plumptre. London, Henry Colburn, 1812–15. 2v. Repr. Cape Town. Van Riebeeck Society, 1928–30. 2v.(V.R.S.10,11).

Liesegang, G. 'A First Look at the Import and Export Trade of Mozambique, 1800–1914.' In Liesegang, G., Pasch, H. and Jones, A., eds. *Figuring African Trade . . .* 1986, 451–523.

—— 'Notes on the Internal Structure of the Gaza Kingdom of Southern Mozambique, 1840–1895.' In Peires, J.B., ed. *Before and After Shaka: Papers in Nguni History,* 1981, 178–209.

—— 'Nguni migrations between Delagoa Bay and the Zambezi, 1821–1839.' *African Historical Studies.* 3(1970):317–23.

Liesegang, G., Pasch, H. and Jones, A., eds. *Figuring African Trade. Proceedings of a Symposium on the Quantification and Structure of the Import and Export and Long Distance Trade in Africa 1800–1913.* Berlin, D. Reimer Verlag, 1986.

Litaba tsa Lilemo. Morija, Sesuto Book Depot, 1931.

Livingstone, D. *David Livingstone Family Letters 1841–1856.* Edited by I. Schapera. London, Chatto & Windus, 1959.

—— *David Livingstone: Letters and Documents 1841–1872: The Zambian Collection at the Livingstone Museum, Containing a Wealth of Restored, Previously Unknown or Unpublished Texts.* Edited by T. Holmes. London, Currey; Livingstone, Livingstone Museum; Bloomington, Indiana University Press, 1990.

—— *Missionary Correspondence 1851–1856.* Edited by I. Schapera. London, Chatto & Windus, 1961.

—— *Missionary Travels and Researches in South Africa; including a Sketch of Sixteen Years' Residence in the Interior of Africa, and a Journey from the Cape of Good Hope to Loanda on the West Coast, thence across the Continent, down the River Zambezi, to the Eastern Ocean.* With a map by Arrowsmith; and numerous illustrations. London, John Murray, 1857. For details of later re-issues of this work *see SABIB.*

Lobato, A. *Historia de Presidio de Lourenço Marques.* v.1: 1782–1786. Lisboa, [n.p.], 1949.

Loubser, J.H.N. 'Buffelshoek: An ethnoarchaeological consideration of a Late Iron Age settlement in the southern Transvaal.' *South African Archaeological Bulletin.* 40,142(1985): 81–87.

Louw, J. 'Hills hide secrets of unhappy past.' *Saturday Star,* 30 July 1993.

Lovejoy, P.E., ed. *Africans in Bondage: Studies in Slavery and the Slave Trade.* Madison, African Studies Program, University of Wisconsin, Madison, 1986.

Lye, W.F. 'The *Difaqane*: The *Mfecane* in the Southern Sotho Area, 1822–24.' *Journal of African History.* 8,1(1967):107–31.

—— 'The Distribution of the Sotho Peoples After the Difaqane.' In Thompson, L.M., ed., *African Societies in Southern Africa: Historical Studies,* 1969, pp.190–206.

—— 'The Ndebele Kingdom south of the Limpopo River.' *Journal of African History,* 10,1(1969): 87–104.

Lye, W.F. and Murray, C. *Transformations on the Highveld: The Tswana and Southern Sotho.* Cape Town, David Philip, 1980. Paperback edition 1985.

Mabin, A., ed. *Organization and Economic Change.* Johannesburg, Ravan Press, 1989. (Southern African Studies 5)

MacGregor, J.C. *Basuto Traditions: Being a Record of the Traditional History of the More Important of the Tribes which form the Basuto Nation of To-day up to the Time of Their Being Absorbed. Compiled from Native Sources . . .* Cape Town, Argus Printing and Publishing Co., [pref. 1905].

Machobane, L.B.J. 'Mohlomi: doctor, traveller and sage.' *Journal of Southern African Historical Studies.* 2(1976):5–27.

MacKenzie, J. *Ten Years North of the Orange River: A Story of Everyday Life and Work Among the South African Tribes from 1859 to 1869.* . . . Edinburgh, Edmonston & Douglas, 1871.

MacLean, C.R. *The Natal Papers of 'John Ross': The Loss of the Brig Mary at Natal with Early Recollections of that Settlement and Among the Caffres.* Edited by Stephen Gray. Durban, Killie Campbell Africana Library; Pietermaritzburg, University of Natal Press, 1992. (Killie Campbell Africana Library Publications)

MacLennan, B. *A Proper Degree of Terror: John Graham and the Cape's Eastern Frontier.* Johannesburg, Ravan Press, 1986.

Macmillan, W.M. *Bantu, Boer, and Briton: The Making of the South African Native Problem.* London, Faber & Gwyer, 1929.

—— *The Cape Colour Question.* London, Faber & Gwyer, 1927. Repr. Cape Town, Balkema, 1968.

—— 'The Frontier and the Kaffir Wars 1792–1836.' In *Cambridge History of the British Empire*, 2nd edition, 1963, v.8, 301–23.

—— *My South African Years: An Autobiography.* Cape Town, David Philip, 1975.

Maggs, T.M.O'C. *Iron Age Communities of the Southern Highveld.* Pietermaritzburg, Natal Museum, 1976. (Natal Museum Occasional Publications 2)

—— 'The Iron Age sequence south of the Vaal and Pongola Rivers: Some historical implications.' *Journal of African History.* 21,1 (1980):1–15.

—— 'Iron Age Settlement and Subsistence Patterns in the Tugela River Basin, Natal.' In Hall, M, *et al. Frontiers: Southern African Archaeology Today*, 1984, 194–206.

—— 'The Iron Age South of the Zambezi.' In Klein, R.G., ed. *Southern African Prehistory and Paleoenvironments*, 1984, 329–60.

—— 'Mabhija: Pre-colonial industrial development in the Tugela Basin.' *Annals of the Natal Museum.* 25(1982):123–41.

—— 'Mgoduyanuka: Terminal Iron Age settlement in the Natal grasslands.' *Annals of the Natal Museum.* 25,1(1982):83–113.

—— 'Msuluzi Confluence: A seventh-century Early Iron Age site on the Tugela River.' *Annals of the Natal Museum.* 24(1980):111–45.

Maggs, T.M.O'C., Oswald, D., Hall, M. and Ruther, H. 'Spatial parameters of Late Iron Age settlements in the Upper Thukela Valley.' *Annals of the Natal Museum.* 27(1986):455–79.

Maggs, T.M.O'C. and Sealy, J. 'Elephants in boxes.' *South African Archaeological Society Goodwin Series.* 4(1983):44–48.

Maggs, T.M.O'C and Whitelaw, G. 'A review of recent archaeological research on food-producing communities in Southern Africa.' *Journal of African History.* 32(1991):3–24.

Magubane, B. *The Politics of History in South Africa.* New York, United Centre Against Apartheid, 1982.

Majeke, N., *pseud* of Dora Taylor. *The Role of the Missionaries in Conquest.* Johannesburg, Society of Young Africa, 1952.

Makaula, D.Z. *UMadzikane, Okanye Imbali yamaBhaca.* Cape Town, Oxford University Press, 1966.

Maloka, T. 'Lifaquane fallout.' *South African Review of Books.* Jan./Feb. 1995.

Mamadi, M.F. *See under* South Africa. (Union). Department of Native Affairs. Van Warmelo, N.J., ed. *The Copper Mines of Musina* . . . In *Official Publications* section.

Manhire, A.H., Parkington, J.E., Mazel, A.D. and Maggs, T.M.O'C. 'Cattle, sheep and horses: A review of domestic animals in the rock art of southern Africa.' *South African Archaeological Society, Goodwin Series.* 5(1986):22–30.

Marker, M.E. and Evers, T.M. 'Iron Age settlement and soil erosion in the eastern Transvaal, South Africa.' *South African Archaeological Bulletin.* 31,123–24(1976):153–65.

Marks, S.'Khoisan resistance to the Dutch in the seventeenth and eighteenth centuries.' *Journal of African History.* 13,1(1972):55–80.

—— 'The Nguni, the Natalians, and their history.' *Journal of African History.* 8,3(1967):529–40.

—— *Reluctant Rebellion: The 1906–8 Disturbances in Natal.* Oxford, Clarendon Press, 1971.

Marks, S. 'The Rise of the Zulu Kingdom.' In Oliver, R., ed. *The Middle Age of African History*, 1967, 85–91.

—— 'South Africa: The myth of the empty land.' *History Today*. Jan. (1980):8–12.

—— 'Towards a People's History of South Africa? Recent Developments in the Historiography of South Africa.' In Samuel, R., ed. *People's History and Social Theory*, 1981, 297–308.

—— 'The Traditions of the Natal "Nguni".' In Thompson, L.M., ed. *African Societies in Southern Africa: Historical Studies*, 1969, 126–44.

Marks, S. and Atmore, A., eds. *Economy and Society in Pre-Industrial South Africa*. London, Longman, 1980.

—— 'The Problem of the Nguni: An Examination of the Ethnic and Linguistic Situation in South Africa Before the Mfecane.' In Dalby, D., ed. *Language and History in Africa: A Volume of Collected Papers Presented to the London Seminar on Language and History in Africa*. (Held at the School of Oriental and African Studies, 1967–69), 1970, 120–32.

Marks, S. and Gray, R. 'Southern Africa and Madagascar.' In *Cambridge History of Africa*, 1975, v. 4, 384–468.

Mason, R. *Origins of Black People of Johannesburg and the Southern Central Western Transvaal* AD *350–1880*. Johannesburg, Archaeological Research Unit, University of the Witwatersrand, 1986.

—— *Origins of the African People of the Johannesburg Area*. Johannesburg, Skotaville, 1987.

—— 'Transvaal and Natal Iron Age settlement revealed by aerial photography and excavation.' *African Studies*. 27, 4(1968):167–94.

Maylam, P.R. 'The death of the Mfecane?' *South African Historical Journal*. 25(1991):163–66.

—— *A History of the African People of South Africa: From the Early Iron Age to the 1970s*. London, Croom Helm; Cape Town and Johannesburg, David Philip, 1986.

Mazamisa, J. 'Izizwe za-Mamfengu.' *Indaba*. 1,11(1863):170–71.

Mazel, A.D. 'People making history: The last ten thousand years of hunter-gatherer communities in the Thukela Basin.' *Natal Museum Journal of Humanities*. 1(1989):1–168.

McMenemy, N. *Assegai!* London, Macmillan, 1973.

Mears, W.G.A. *Wesleyan Barolong Mission in TransOrangia, 1821–84*. Cape Town, The Author, 1968.

Meintjes, S. 'The *Mfecane* Colloquium: Impressions.' *South African Historical Journal*. 25(1991): 173–76.

Melvill, J. 'Missionary tour through the country of the Bashutoos.' *Transactions of the London Missionary Society*. 52(1829):123–28.

Methuen, H.H. *Life in the Wilderness, or, Wanderings in South Africa*. London, Richard Bentley, 1846.

2nd edition 1848.

Mettas J. *Repertoire des Expéditions Négrières Français au XVIIIe Siècle*. Ed. S. Daget et M. Daget. Paris, Societé Françaises d'histoire d'outre-mer, 1978, 1984, 2v.

Meyer, A. 'A Profile of the Iron Age in the Kruger National Park, South Africa.' In Hall, M., *et al. Frontiers: Southern African Archaeology Today*, 1984, 215–27.

Mhlanga, P. 'A story of Native wars by "An Aged Fingo".' *Cape Monthly Magazine*. New Series. 14,84(1877):248–52.

Michener, J. *The Covenant*. New York, Random House, 1980.

Miller, C.L. *Blank Darkness: Africanist Discourse in French*. Chicago, University of Chicago Press, 1985.

—— *Theories of Africans: Francophone Literature and Anthropology in Africa*. Chicago, Chicago University Press, 1990.

—— 'Theories of Africans: The Question of Literary Anthropology.' In Gates, H.L., ed. *Race, Writing and Difference*, 1986.

Miller, J.C. 'Slave Prices in the Portuguese Southern Atlantic.' In Lovejoy, P.E., ed. *Africans in Bondage: Studies in Slavery and the Slave Trade*, 1986, 43–77.

—— *Way of Death: Merchant Capitalism and the Angolan Slave Trade 1730–1830*. London, J. Currey; Madison, University of Wisconsin Press, 1988.

Millin, S.G. *The King of the Bastards*. London, Heinemann, 1950.

M'Intosh, D. *South Africa: Notes of Travel. First Gold Exploring Expedition into the Matabele Country, North of the Tatin River*. Glasgow, Bell & Bain, Printers for Author, 1876.

Mitford, B. *John Ames, Native Commissioner: A Romance of the Matabele Rising . . .* London, F.V. White & Co., 1900.

Mitford-Barberton, I., ed. *Comdt. Holden Bowker: An 1820 Settler Book Including Unpublished Records of the Frontier Wars*. Cape Town, Human and Rousseau, 1970.

'Mnguni', *pseud.* of Hosea Jaffe. *Three Hundred Years: A History of South Africa*. Cape Town, New Era Fellowship, 1952. 3v.

Modau, E. *See under* South Africa. (Union). Department of Native Affairs. Van Warmelo, N.J., ed. *The Copper Mines of Musina . . .* In *Official Publications* section.

Moffat, J.S. *The Lives of Robert & Mary Moffat, by Their Son, John S. Moffat . . .* London, T. Fisher Unwin, 1885.

For details of later editions and re-issues of this work *see SABIB*.

Moffat, M. and Moffat, R. *Apprenticeship at Kuruman. Being the Journals and Letters of Robert and Mary Moffat*. Edited by I. Schapera. London, Chatto & Windus, 1951. (Oppenheimer Series 5)

Moffat, R. *The Matabele Journals of Robert Moffat 1829–1860*. Edited by J.P.R. Wallis. 2v. London, Chatto & Windus, 1945. (Oppenheimer Series 1)

Repr. Salisbury, National Archives, 1976.

—— *Missionary Labours and Scenes in Southern Africa*. With engravings by G. Baxter. London, John Snow, 1842. For details of later editions and re-issues of this work *see SABIB*.

Molema, S.M. *Montshiwa 1815–1896: Barolong Chief and Patriot*. Cape Town, Struik, 1966.

Moloja. 'The Story of the "*Fetcani* Horde" by One of Themselves – Moloja, of Jozani's village, at Masite, near Morija, Basutoland.' *Cape Quarterly Review*. 1,2(1882):267–75.

Molsbergen, E.C. Godeé *see* Godeé Molsbergen, E.C.

Moodie, D.C.F. *The History of the Battles and Adventures of the British, the Boers, and the Zulus in Southern Africa, from 1495–1879, Including Every Particular of the Zulu War of 1879*. With a chronology. Adelaide, George Robertson, 1879.

—— *The History of the Battles and Adventures of the British, The Boers, and the Zulus & etc. from the Time of the Pharaoh Necto, to 1880*. With copious chronology. Cape Town, Murray & St Leger, 1888. 2v.

Morris, D. *The Washing of the Spears*. London, Sphere, 1967.

Moshoeshoe, N. 'A Little Light from Basutoland.' *Cape Monthly Magazine*. New Series. 2,10–11(1880):221–233; 280–292.

Mostert, N. *Frontiers: The Epic of South Africa's Creation and the Tragedy of the Xhosa People*. London, Pimlico, 1993.

Motenda, M.M. *See under* South Africa. (Union). Department of Native Affairs. Van Warmelo, N.J., ed. *The Copper Mines of Musina . . .* In *Official Publications* section.

Mpotokwane, J. 'A short history of the Bahurutshe of King Motebele, senior son of King Mohurutshe.' *Botswana Notes and Records*. 6(1974):37–45.

Msebenzi. *See under* South Africa. (Union). Department of Native Affairs. Van Warmelo, N.J., ed. *The Copper Mines of Musina . . .* In *Official Publications* section.

Mudenge, S.I.G. *A Political History of Munhumutapa c. 1400–1902*. Harare, Zimbabwe Publishing House, 1988.

Muller, C.F.J. *Die Oorsprong van die Groot Trek*. Cape Town, Tafelberg, 1974.

Ndamase, V.P. *AmaMpondo: Ibali ne-Ntlalo*. Lovedale, Lovedale Mission Press, [19?].

Neumark, S.D. *Economic Influences on the South African Frontier*. Stanford, Stanford University Press, 1957.

Newitt, M.D.D. 'Drought in Mozambique 1823–1831.' *Journal of Southern African Studies*. 15(1988):14–35.

Newton-King, S. 'The Labour Market of the Cape Colony, 1807–1828.' In Marks, S. and Atmore, A. *Economy and Society in Pre-industrial South Africa*, 1980, 171–207.

Ngcongco, L. with the collaboration of J. Vansina. 'In Africa from the Twelfth to the the Sixteenth Century.' In *General History of Africa* v. 4, *Africa from the Twelfth to the Sixteenth Centuries*. Edited by D. T. Niane. 1984, 578–96.

—— 'The Mfecane and the Rise of New African States.' In *General History of Africa*. v. 6: *Africa in the Nineteenth Century until the 1880s*. Edited by Ajayi, F. J. [F. Jacob Ade], 1989, 90–123.

Niven, C. R. *Nine Great Africans*. London, Bell, 1964.

—— 'Southern Africa: Its Peoples and Social Structures.' In *General History of Africa*. v. 4: *Africa from the Twelfth to the Sixteenth Centuries*. Edited by D. T. Niane, 1984, 578–96.

Noli, D. and Avery, G. 'Stone circles in the Cape Fria area, northern Namibia.' *South African Archaeological Bulletin*. 42(1987):59–63.

Okihiro, G. Y. 'Precolonial economic change among the Tlhaping.' *International Journal of African Historical Studies*. 17,1(1984):59–79.

Oliver, R., ed. *The Middle Age of African History*. London, Oxford University Press, 1967.

O'Meara, D. *Volkskapitalisme: Class, Capital and Ideology in the Development of Afrikaner Nationalism 1934–1948*. Johannesburg, Ravan Press, 1983.

Omer-Cooper, J. D. 'Aspects of Political Change in the Nineteenth–century *Mfecane*.' In Thompson, L. M., ed. *African Societies in Southern Africa*, 1969, 207–29.

—— 'Colonial South Africa.' In *Cambridge History of Africa*, v. 5, 1976, 353–92.

—— 'Has the Mfecane a future? A response to the Cobbing critique.' *Journal of Southern African Studies*. 19,2(1993):272–94.

—— *A History of Southern Africa*. London, James Currey, 1987.

—— 'The Mfecane defended.' *Southern African Review of Books*. July/October, 1991, 12–16.

—— 'The Nguni Outburst.' In *Cambridge History of Africa*, v. 5, 1976, 319–52.

—— *The Zulu Aftermath: A Nineteenth-century Revolution in Bantu Africa*. London & Ibadan, Longman, 1966.

2nd edition 1969.

'One of Themselves' *see* Moloja.

Orpen, J. M. 'A glimpse into the mythology of the Maluti Bushmen.' *Cape Monthly Magazine*. New Series. 9,49(1874):1–13.

—— *History of the Basutus of South Africa*: By the Special Commissioner of the Cape Argus. (Reprinted from that paper). Cape Town, Cape Argus Office; Saul Solomon & Co.; London, Alger & Street, 1857.

Repr. Mazenod, Mazenod Book Centre, 1979.

Owen, W. F. W. *Narrative of Voyages to Explore the Shores of Africa, Arabia and Madagascar; performed in H.M. Ships Leven and Barracouta, under the direction of Captain W. F. W. Owen*. . . . Edited by H. B. Robinson. London, Richard Bentley, 1833. 2v.

Oxford History of South Africa see Wilson, M. and Thompson, L. M., eds.

Palmer, R and Parsons, N., eds. *The Roots of Rural Poverty in Central and Southern Africa*. Berkeley, California University Press, 1977.

Repr. London, James Currey, 1988.

Pampallis, J. *Foundations of the New South Africa*. Cape Town, Maskew Miller Longman, 1991.

Parkington, J. 'Changing Views of the Late Stone Age of South Africa.' In Wendorf, F. and Close, A. E., eds. *Advances in World Archaeology* 3. New York, Academic Press, 1984.

—— 'Interpreting paintings without a commentary.' *Antiquity*. 63(1989):13–26.

Parkington, J. and Hall, M., eds. *Papers in the Prehistory of the Western Cape*. Oxford, British Archaeological Reports, 1987. (BAR International Series, 332).

Parsons, N. 'The Boer Trek, or Afrikaner Difaqane.' In Parsons, N., ed. *A New History of Southern Africa*, 1993, 93–108.

—— 'The Economic History of Khama's Country in Botswana, 1844–1930.' In Palmer, R, and Parsons, N., eds. *The Roots of Rural Poverty in Central and Southern Africa*, 1990, 119–20.

—— 'The economic history of Khama's country in Southern Africa.' *African Social Research*. 18 (1974):643–75.

—— *Focus on History. Book One: A Lower Secondary Course for Zimbabwe*. Harare, College Press, 1985.

Parsons, N. *Focus on History. Book Three: A Secondary Course for Zimbabwe.* Harare, College Press, 1991.

—— *A New History of Southern Africa.* London, Macmillan, 1982.

2nd edition. London, Basingstoke, Macmillan, 1993.

—— 'On the origins of the bamaNgwato.' *Botswana Notes and Records.* 5(1973):82–103.

Paver, F.R. 'Trade and mining in the pre-European Transvaal.' *South African Journal of Science.* 30(1933):603–11.

Peires, J.B. ed. *Before and After Shaka: Papers in Nguni History.* Grahamstown, Institute of Social and Economic Research, 1981.

—— 'The British and the Cape.' In Elphick, R. and Giliomee, H. *The Shaping of South African Society, 1652–1840,* 1989, 472–518.

—— 'The Emergence of Black Political Communities.' In Cameron, T. and Spies, S.B., eds. *An Illustrated History of South Africa,* 1986, 44–51.

—— *The House of Phalo: A History of the Xhosa People in the Days of their Independence.* Johannesburg, Ravan Press, 1981.

—— 'Paradigm deleted: The materialist interpretation of the Mfecane.' *Journal of Southern African Studies.* 19(1993):295–313.

Penn, N. 'Anarchy and authority in the Koue Bokkeveld, 1739–1779: The banishing of Carel Buitendak.' *Kleio.* XVII(1985):24–43.

—— 'The Frontier in the Western Cape, 1700–1740.' In Parkington, J. and Hall, M., eds. *Papers in the Prehistory of the Western Cape, South Africa,* 1987, 462–503.

—— 'Labour, Land and Livestock in the Western Cape during the Eighteenth Century: The Khoisan and the Colonists.' In James, W.G. and Simons, M., eds. *The Angry Divide,* 1989, 2–19.

—— 'Pastoralists and pastoralism in the northern Cape frontier zone during the eighteenth century.' *South African Archaeological Society Goodwin Series.* 5(1986):62–68.

Philip, J. *Researches in South Africa; Illustrating the Civil, Moral, and Religious Condition of the Native Tribes: Including Journals of the Author's Travels in the Interior; Together with Detailed Accounts of the Progress of the Christian Missions, Exhibiting the Influence of Christianity in Promoting Civilization.* London, James Duncan, 1828.

Repr. New York, Negro Universities Press, 1969.

Philipps, T. *Philipps, 1820 Settler; His Letters.* Edited by A. Keppel-Jones. Pietermaritzburg, Shuter and Shooter, 1960.

Plaatje, S. *Mhudi: An Epic of South African Native Life a Hundred Years Ago.* Lovedale, Lovedale Press, 1930.

Paperback reprint. Lovedale, Lovedale Press, 1957.

—— *Mhudi: An Epic of South African Native Life a Hundred Years Ago.* Introduction: Tim Couzens. Woodcuts: Cecil Skotnes. Johannesburg, Quagga Press, 1975. (African Fiction Library)

—— *Mhudi.* A new edition. Edited by Stephen Gray. Introduction by Tim Couzens. Woodcuts by Cecil Skotnes. London, Heinemann, 1978. [New edition based on original typescript of 1930 edition with corrections made by S.T. Plaatje.]

—— *Mhudi: An Epic of South African Native Life a Hundred Years Ago.* Edited by A.E. Voss. Johannesburg, Donker, 1989.

Plug, I. 'Aspects of Life in the Kruger National Park during the Early Iron Age.' *South African Archaeological Society Goodwin Series,* 6(1989):62–68.

Posselt, F.W.T. *Fact and Fiction: A Short Account of the Natives of Southern Rhodesia.* Bulawayo, Printed by the Rhodesian Printing and Publishing Co., 1935.

Facsimile reprint. Bulawayo, Books of Rhodesia, 1978. (Rhodesiana Reprint Library – Silver Series 19)

Pridmore, J. 'The Production of H.F. Fynn c.1830–1930.' In Edgecombe, D.R., Laband, J.P.C. and Thompson, P.S., comps. *The Debate on Zulu Origins: A Selection of Papers on the Zulu Kingdom and Early Colonial Natal,* 1992, 27p. [Pagination irregular]

Pringle, T. *African Sketches.* London, Edward Moxon, 1834. *Contents:* Part 1: *Poems Illustrative of South Africa.* – Part 2: *Narrative of a Residence in South Africa.* The *Narrative* was reproduced and re-edited in various forms. For bibliographical details *see SABIB.*

Pringle, T. *Narrative of a Residence in South Africa. See African Sketches . . .*

Ralushai, N.M.N. and Gray, J.R. 'Ruins and traditions of the Ngona and Mbedzi among the Venda of the northern Transvaal.' *Rhodesian History.* 8(1977):1–11.

Ramokate, Chief. 'Notes on the Khurutshe.' *Botswana Notes and Records.* 2(1970):14.

Randles, W.G.L. *The Empire of Monomotapa.* Gweru, Mambo Press, 1979.

Ranger, T.O., ed. *Aspects of Central African History.* London, Heinemann Educational, 1968.

Ransford, O. *The Great Trek.* London, John Murray, 1972.

Rasmussen, R.K. *Migrant Kingdom: Mzilikazi's Ndebele in South Africa.* London, Rex Collings with David Philip, Cape Town, 1978.

Ratidladi, L.D. *Motswasele II: Historical Drama in Tswana.* Revised and edited by D.T. Cole. Johannesburg, Witwatersrand University Press, 1970.

Raum, J. 'Historical concepts and the evolutionary interpretation of the emergence of states: The case of the Zulu reconsidered yet again.' *Zeitschrift für Ethnologie.* 114 (1989):125–38.

Rayner, M. 'Slaves, Slave Owners and the British State: The Cape Colony 1806–1834,' *The Collected Seminar Papers on the Societies of Southern Africa in the 19th and 20th Centuries.* Institute of Commonwealth Studies, University of London. 12(1981):15–32.

Reader's Digest. *Illustrated History of South Africa: The Real Story.* Edited by Dougie Oakes. Cape Town, The Reader's Digest, 1988.
   2nd edition with amendments. 1989.

Ridgway, V. *Stories from Zulu History. Izindaba zakwaZulu.* Pietermaritzburg, Shuter & Shooter, 1946.

Ritter, E.A. *Shaka Zulu.* London, Longmans, 1955.
   Repr. London, Panther, 1971.
   Facsimile reprint title: *Shaka Zulu: The Rise of the Zulu Empire.* London, Greenhill Books; California, Presidio Press, 1990.

Roberts, B. *The Zulu Kings.* London, Hamilton, 1974.

Roberts, E. *The Black Spear.* London, William Earl, 1950.

Rose, C. *Four Years in Southern Africa.* London, Henry Colburn and Richard Bentley, 1829.

Rosenthal, E. 'Early Americans in South West Africa.' *SWA Annual.* Windhoek, S.W.A. Administration, 1972.

Ross, R. *Adam Kok's Griqua.* Cambridge, Cambridge University Press, 1976.

—— *Cape of Torments: Slavery and Resistance in South Africa.* London, Routledge & Kegan Paul, 1983.

Sanders, P.B. *Moshoeshoe, Chief of the Sotho.* London, Heinemann, 1975.

—— 'Sekonyela and Mosheshwe: Failure and success in the aftermath of the Difaqane.' *Journal of African History.* 10,3(1969):439–55.

Sansom, B. 'Traditional Economic Systems.' In Hammond-Tooke, W.D., ed. *The Bantu-speaking Peoples of Southern Africa,* 1974, pp.135–76.

Satir, V.E. 'The *Difaqane*: Fact vs Fiction'. *Education Journal.* (1983):10.

Saunders, C. *C.W. de Kiewiet: Historian of South Africa.* Cape Town, Centre for African Studies, University of Cape Town, 1986. (Communications 10)

—— 'Conference report: Mfecane afterthoughts.' *Social Dynamics* 17,2(1991):171–77.

—— 'Early knowledge of the Sotho: Seventeenth and eighteenth century accounts of the Tswana.' *Quarterly Bulletin of the South African Library.* 20,2(1965):60–70.

—— *The Making of the South African Past: Major Historians on Race and Class.* Cape Town, David Philip, 1988.

—— 'Our past as literature: Notes on style in South African history in English.' *Kleio.* 8(1986): 46–55.

Schapera, I. *The Bantu-speaking Tribes of South Africa. An Ethnographical Survey.* London, Routledge, 1937.
   2nd edition: *see* Hammond-Tooke, W.D. *The Bantu-speaking Peoples of Southern Africa . . .*

—— ed. *Ditirafalo tsa Merafe ya Batswana ba Lefatshe le Tshireletso.* (Traditional Histories of the Native Tribes of Bechuanaland Protectorate). Alice, Lovedale Press, 1954.

—— 'The early history of the Khurutshe.' *Botswana Notes and Records.* 2(1970):1–5.

Schapera, I. *Ethnic Composition of Tswana Tribes*. London, London School of Economics & Political Science, 1952.

—— 'Ethnographic texts in the Boloongwe dialect of Sekgala gadi.' *Bantu Studies*. 12,3(19 38): 159–87. Repr. Cape Town, University of Cape Town, Communications from the School of African Studies, No. 4, [n.d.]

—— *A Handbook of Tswana Law and Custom*. London, Oxford University Press for The International Institute of African Languages and Cultures, 1938. 2nd edition. London, Cass, 1955.

—— *Notes on Some Herero Genealogies*. Cape Town, University of Cape Town, Communications from the School of African Studies, No. 14, 1945.

—— ed. *Praise-poems of Tswana Chiefs*. Oxford, Clarendon Press, 1965.

—— *A Short History of the BaKgatla bagaKgafela of the Bechuanaland Protectorate*. Cape Town, University of Cape Town, Communications from the School of African Studies, No. 3, 1942.

—— *Bogwera: Kgatla Initiation*. Mochudi, Phitadikobo Museum, 1978.

—— 'A short history of the Bangwaketse.' *African Studies* 1(1942):1–26.

—— *Tribal Innovators: Tswana Chiefs and Social Change 1795–1940*. London, University of London. The Athlone Press; New York, Humanities Press, 1970. (London School of Economics Monographs on Social Anthropology 43) Revised version of his *Tribal Legislation . . . see* following entry.

—— *Tribal Legislation among the Tswana of the Bechuanaland Protectorate: A Study in the Mechanics of Cultural Change*. London, Published for the London School of Economics and Political Science by Percy Lund, Humphries, 1943. (Monographs on Social Anthropology 9)

Schapera, I. and Van der Merwe, D. F. *Notes on the Tribal Groupings, History and Customs of the Bakgalagadi*. Cape Town, University of Cape Town, Communications from the School of African Studies, No. 13, 1945.

Schoeman, P. J. *Pamphatha: The Beloved of King Shaka*. Cape Town, Howard Timmins, 1983.

Schrire, C. 'An enquiry into the evolutionary status and apparent identity of San hunter-gatherers.' *Human Ecology*. 8(1980):9–32.

—— ed. *Past and Present in Hunter-gatherer Studies*. Orlando, Academic Press, 1984.

Scully, W. C. 'Fragments of native history.' *The State*. (1909):90–95, 194–204, 284–292, 435–41, 595–603.

Secord, A. W. *Robert Drury's Journal and Other Studies*. Urbana, University of Illinois Press, 1961.

Seddon, J. D. 'Kurrichane: A Late Iron Age site in the western Transvaal.' *African Studies*. 25(1966):227–31.

Shaw, W. *The Journal of William Shaw*. Edited by W. D. Hammond-Tooke. Cape Town, Published for Rhodes University, Grahamstown by A. A. Balkema, 1972. (The Graham's Town Series 2)

—— *see also* Hodgson, A.

Shillington, K. *History of Southern Africa*. Harlow, Essex; London, Longman, 1987.

Shrewsbury, J. V. B. *Memorials of the Reverend William J. Shrewsbury*. By his son, John V. B. Shrewsbury. London, Hamilton Adams, 1867. 2nd edition. 1868 (incl. portrait). 3rd edition. 1869. 4th edition. 1869.

Sillery, A. *The Bechuanaland Protectorate*. Cape Town, Oxford University Press, 1952.

Skotnes, C. and Gray, S. *The Assassination of Shaka by Mhlangane Dingane and Mbopa on 22 September 1828 at Dukuza by which Act the Zulu Nation First Lost Its Empire*. 43 Woodcuts by Cecil Skotnes. Text by Stephen Gray. Johannesburg, McGraw-Hill, 1974.

Smith, A. *Andrew Smith and Natal. Documents Relating to the Early History of that Province*. Selected, edited and annotated by Percival R. Kirby. Cape Town, Van Riebeeck Society, 1955. (V.R.S. 36)

—— *Andrew Smith's Journal of his Expedition into the Interior of South Africa, 1834–1836*. Introduction and notes by W. F. Lye. With contemporary illustrations by Charles Davidson Bell. Cape Town, Published for the South African Museum by A. A. Balkema, 1975.

Smith, A. *The Diary of Dr. Andrew Smith, Director of the 'Expedition for Exploring Central Africa',* *1834–6.* Edited with an introduction, footnotes, map and indexes by P.R. Kirby. Cape Town, Van Riebeeck Society, 1939–40. 2v. (V.R.S.20, 21)

—— 'Report of the expedition for exploring central Africa.' *Journal of the Royal Geographical Society.* 6(1836):394–413.

Smith, A.B. 'Competition, conflict and clientship: Khoi and San relationships in the western Cape.' *South African Archaeological Society Goodwin Series.* 5(1986):36–41.

—— *Pastoralism in Africa: Origins and Development Ecology.* London, Hurst, 1992.

Smith, A.K. 'Delagoa Bay and the Trade of South-east Africa.' In Gray, R. and Birmingham, D., eds. *Pre-colonial African Trade: Essays on Trade in Central and Eastern Africa Before 1900,* 1970, 265–89.

—— 'The Indian Ocean Zone.' In Birmingham, D. and Martin, P.M., eds. *History of Central Africa.* 2v. London, 1983, v.1, 233–36.

—— 'The peoples of southern Mozambique: An historical survey.' *Journal of African History.* 14,4(1983):568–80.

—— 'The Trade of Delagoa Bay as a Factor in Nguni Politics, 1750–1835.' In Thompson, L.M., ed. *African Societies in Southern Africa: Historical Studies,* 1969, 171–89.

Smith, E.W. *Great Lion of Bechuanaland: The Life And Times of Roger Price, Missionary.* London, Published for the London Missionary Society by Independent Press, [1957].

—— 'Sebetwane and the Makololo.' *African Studies.* 15,2(19 56):49–74.

Smith, K. *The Changing Past: Trends in South African Historical Writing.* Johannesburg, Southern Book Publishers, 1988.

Athens, Ohio, Ohio University Press, 1989.

Soga, J.H. *The South-Eastern Bantu.* Johannesburg, Witwatersrand University Press, 1930.

Somerville, W. *William Somerville's Narrative of His Journeys to the Eastern Cape Frontier and to Lattakoe 1799–1802.* With a bibliographical introduction and map and a historical introduction and notes by Edna and Frank Bradlow. Cape Town, Van Riebeeck Society, 1979. (V.R.S. New Series 10)

—— *See also* Barrow, J. *Voyage to Cochinchina . . .*

Spiegel, A.D. and McAllister, P.A., eds. *Tradition and Transition in Southern Africa.* Johannesburg, Witwatersrand University Press, 1991. (*African Studies* 50th Anniversary Volume. Vol.50, Nos.1 and 2)

Stanford, W.E. 'Statement of Silayi, with reference to his life among the Bushmen.' *Transactions of the Royal Society of South Africa.* 1(1910):435–40.

Steel, R.H. 'Ingot casting and wire drawing in Iron Age South Africa.' *South African Institute of Mining and Metallurgy.* 7,4(1975):232–37.

Stirke, D.W. *Barotseland: Eight Years among the Barotse.* London, John Bale & Danielsson, 1922.

Stockenström, Sir A. *The Autobiography of the late Sir Andries Stockenström, Bart.* Edited by C.W. Hutton. Cape Town, Juta, 1887. 2v.

Stow, G.W. *The Native Races of South Africa.* London, Swan, Sonnenschein, 1905.

Stow, G.W. and Bleek, D.F. *Rock Paintings in South Africa.* London, Methuen, 1930.

Streak, M. *The Afrikaner as Viewed by the English 1795–1854.* Cape Town, Struik, 1974.

Stretch, C.L. *The Journal of Charles Lennox Stretch.* Edited by B.A. Le Cordeur. Cape Town, Maskew Miller Longman, 1988. (The Graham's Town Series 8)

Stuart, J. *uBaxoxele.* London, Longmans, Green, 1924.

—— *uHlangakula.* London, Longmans, Green, 1924.

—— *uKulumetule.* London, Longmans, Green, 1925.

—— *uTulasizwe.* London, Longmans, Green, 1923.

—— *uVusezakiti.* London, Longmans, Green, 1926.

Switzer, L. *Power and Resistance in an African Society: The Ciskei Xhosa and the Making of South Africa.* Pietermaritzburg, University of Natal Press, 1993.

Tabler, E.C. *The Far Interior.* Cape Town, Balkema, 1955.

—— *Pioneers of South West Africa and Ngamiland.* Cape Town, Balkema, 1973.

Taylor, D. *see* Majeke, N.

Taylor, S. 'Zulu history rewritten and rerun.' *Times Higher Education Supplement.* 1 November 1991.

Teichler, G.H.J. 'Some historical notes on Derdepoort/Sikwane.' *Botswana Notes and Records.* 5(1973):125–30.

Theal, G.M. *Compendium of South African History and Geography.* Lovedale, Institution Press, 1873–74. 2v in 1.

2nd edition. 1876.

3rd edition. 1877.

—— *History and Ethnography of Africa South of the Zambesi from the Settlement of the Port at Sofala in September 1505 to the Conquest of the Cape Colony by the British in September 1795.* London, Swan, Sonnenschein, 1907–1910. 3v.

3rd edition entitled: *History of Africa South of the Zambesi from the Settlement of the Port at Sofala* . . . Carefully revised and enlarged. London, George Allen & Unwin, 1916–1922.

—— *History of South Africa [1486–1872].* London, Swan Sonnenschein, 1888–1893. 5v.

—— *History of South Africa . . . 1652–1860.* London, Swan Sonnenschein, 1897–1904. 5v.

—— *History of South Africa since September 1795 . . .* London, Swan Sonnenschein, 1908. 5v.

—— *History of South Africa from 1795–1872 . . .* 3rd edition carefully revised and enlarged. London, George Allen & Unwin, 1916–1920.

—— *History of South Africa from 1873 to 1884: Twelve Eventful Years. With Continuation of the History of Galekaland, Tembuland, Pondoland and Betshuanaland until the Annexation of those Territories to the Cape Colony, and of Zululand until its Annexation to Natal.* London, George Allen & Unwin, 1919. 2v.

—— *History of South Africa.* London, George Allen & Unwin, (1916–1922). 11v. ('Star' edition). In v. 1, adjacent to the title-page, the publisher has supplied a synopsis of the titles and editions of the volumes which have been included in the set.

Facsimile reproduction. Cape Town, Struik, 1964.

—— comp. *Records of South-Eastern Africa; Collected in Various Libraries and Archive Deposits in Europe.* (London, Clowes, Printers) for the Government of the Cape Colony, 1895–1903. 9v.

—— *The Republic of Natal. The Origin of the Present Pondo Tribe, Imperial Treaties with Panda, and Establishment of the Colony of Natal . . .* Cape Town, Saul Solomon & Co., 1886.

Repr. Cape Town, University of Cape Town Library. South African Library, 1961. (Willem Hiddingh Reprint Library)

—— *South Africa (the Cape Colony, Natal, Orange Free State, South African Republic, and All Other Territories South of the Zambesi).* London, T. Fisher Unwin, 1894.

2nd edition. 1894.

3rd edition. 1896.

4th edition. 1897.

5th edition. 1899.

6th edition. 1901.

7th edition with a new supplementary chapter. London, T. Fisher Unwin, 1910.

8th edition. 1925.

—— For further information on the works of G.M. Theal *see SABIB.*

Thompson, G. *Travels and Adventures in Southern Africa. By George Thompson, Esq., Eight Years Resident at the Cape. Comprising a View of the Present State of the Cape Colony, with Observations on the Progress and Prospects of the British Emigrants.* London, Henry Colburn, 1827. 2v.

Facsimile reprint. Edited by Vernon S. Forbes. Cape Town, Africana Connoisseurs Press, 1962.

Repr. Cape Town, Van Riebeeck Society, 1967–68. 2v. (V.R.S. 48, 49)

Thompson, L.M., ed. *African Societies in Southern Africa: Historical Studies.* London, Heinemann, 1969.

—— *A History of South Africa.* New Haven, Yale University Press; Sandton, Radix, 1990.

—— *The Political Mythology of Apartheid.* New Haven, Yale University Press, 1985.

—— *Survival in Two Worlds: Moshoeshoe of Lesotho 1786–1870.* Oxford, Clarendon Press, 1975.

Tindall, H. *Two Lectures on Great Namaqualand and its Inhabitants,* Delivered Before the Mechanics' Institute, Cape Town. Cape Town, Printed at G.J. Pike's Machine Printing Office, 1856.

Tlou, T. and Campbell, A. *History of Botswana.* Gaborone, Macmillan, 1984.
—— *A History of Ngamiland 1750–1906: The Formation of an African State.* Gaborone, Macmillan, 1985.
Tracey, H. *Zulu Paradox.* Johannesburg, Silver Leaf, 1948.
    Facsimile reprint. Cape Town, State Library, 1968. (Reprints 24)
Truter, P. J. *See* Barrow, J. *Voyage to Cochinchina* . . .
Vail, L. 'Ecology and history: the example of eastern Zambia.' *Journal of Southern African Studies.* 3,2(1977):129–55.
Van Aswegen, H. J. *History of South Africa to 1854.* Pretoria, Academica, 1990.
Van der Merwe, P. J. *Die Noordwaartse Beweging van die Boere voor die Groot Trek (1770–1842).* Den Haag, Van Stockum & Zoon, [1937].
Van Duin, P. and Ross, R. J. *The Economy of the Cape Colony in the Eighteenth Century.* Leiden, Centre for the History of European Expansion, 1987.
Van Jaarsveld, F. *From Van Riebeeck to Vorster 1652–1974: An Introduction to the History of the Republic of South Africa.* Johannesburg, Perskor, 1975.
—— *Van van Riebeeck tot Verwoerd 1652–1966.* Johannesburg, Voortrekkerpers, 1971.
Van Waarden, C. 'Archaeological investigation of Leeukop: A functional approach.' *Botswana Notes and Records.* 12(1980):151–64.
—— ed. *Kalanga Retrospect and Prospect.* Gaborone, Botswana Society; Francistown, Supa-Ngwao Museum, 1991.
—— *The Oral History of the Bakalanga.* Gaborone, Botswana Society, 1988. (Occasional Paper 2)
Van Warmelo, N. J., ed. *see under* South Africa. Department of Native Affairs. In *Official Publications* section.
Van Zyl, M. E. 'The quest for cattle, the firearm frontier and the *difaqane.' Acta Academica.* 24,4(1992):58–73.
Vedder, H. *South West Africa in Early Times; Being the The Story of South West Africa up to the Date of Maharero's Death in 1890.* Translated and edited by Cyril G. Hall. London, Oxford University Press, Humphrey Milford, 1938.
Vinnicombe, P. *People of the Eland: Rock Paintings of the Drakensberg Bushmen as a Reflection of their Life and Thought.* Pietermaritzburg, University of Natal Press, 1976.
Von Sicard, H. *see under* Rhodesia. Department of Native Affairs. In *Official Publications* section.
Voss, A. E. 'Die Bushie is dood: Long live the Bushie. Black South African writers on the San.' *African Studies.* 49(1990):59–69.
—— 'The image of the Bushman in South African English writing of the nineteenth and twentieth centuries.' *English in Africa.* 14,1(1987):21–40.
—— 'Thomas Pringle and the image of the "Bushmen".' *English in Africa.* 9,1(1982):15–28.
Wagner, R. 'Coenraad de Buys in Transorangia.' *Collected Seminar Papers on the Societies of Southern Africa in the 19th and 20th Centuries.* Institute of Commonwealth Studies, University of London. 4(1972–73):1–8.
—— Zoutpansberg: The Dynamics of a Hunting Frontier. In Marks, S. and Atmore, A., eds. *Economy and Society in Pre–Industrial South Africa,* 1980, 342–3.
Walker, C., ed. *Women and Gender in Southern Africa to 1945.* Cape Town, David Philip, 1990.
Walker, E. A. *The Great Trek.* London, A. & C. Black, 1934.
    2nd edition. 1938.
    3rd edition. 1948.
    4th edition. 1960.
—— A History of South Africa. London, New York, Longmans, Green, 1928.
    Reissue with extensive additions. 1935.
    2nd edition. 1940.
    New impression. London, New York, Longmans, Green and Co., 1941.
    Reissue with minor corrections. 1947.
    [3rd edition]. *A History of Southern Africa.* London, New York, Longmans Green, 1957.
Walker, N. 'Game traps: their importance in southern Africa.' *Botswana Notes and Records.* 23(1991):235–42.

Walter, E. V. *Terror and Resistance*. New York. Oxford University Press, 1969.

Walton, J. 'Early Bafokeng settlement in South Africa.' *African Studies*. 15(1956):37–43.

Watson, J., ed. *Asian and African Systems of Slavery*. Oxford, Blackwell, 1980.

Watson, R. L. *The Slave Question: Liberty and Property in South Africa*. Johannesburg, Witwatersrand University Press, 1991.

Watt, E. P. *Febana*. London, Peter Davies, 1962.

Webb, A. C. M. 'The immediate consequences of the Sixth Frontier War on the farming community of Albany.' *South African Historical Journal*. 10(1978):38–48.

Webster, A. 'The Mfecane paradigm overthrown.' *South African Historical Journal*. 25(1991):170–72.

Wentzel, P. J. *Nau Dzabakalanga: A History of the Kalanga*. Pretoria, University of South Africa, 1983. 3v.

Wetherall, I. 'The Mfecane: Fact or fantasy?' *Vrye Weekblad*. 25–31 October 1991.

Wiessner, P. 'Is There a Unity to Style?' In Conkey, M. and Hastorf, C., eds. *The Uses of Style in Archaeology*, 1990, 105–12.

—— 'Reconsidering the behavioural basis for style: A case study among the Kalahari San.' *Journal of Anthropological Archaeology*. 3(1984):190–234.

Wikar, H. J. and Jansz, J. C. J. and Van Reenen, W. *The Journal of Hendrik Jakob Wikar (1779) with an English Translation by A. W. van der Horst, and the Journals of Jacobus Coetse Jansz (1760) and Willem van Reenen (1791) with an English translation by Dr. E. E. Mossop*. Edited, with an introduction and footnotes, by E. E. Mossop. Cape Town, Van Riebeeck Society, 1935. (V.R.S.15)

Wilmsen, E. N. *Land Filled with Flies: A Political Economy of the Kalahari*. Chicago and London, University of Chicago Press, 1989.

Wilmsen, E. N. and Denbow, J. R. 'Paradigmatic history of San-speaking peoples and current attempts at revision.' With *CA* comment. *Current Anthropology*. 31(1990):489–524.

Wilson, M. 'The Sotho, Venda, and Tsonga.' In Wilson, M. and Thompson, L. M., eds. *The Oxford History of South Africa*, 1969–1971 v. 1: *South Africa to 1870*, 131–82.

Wilson, M. and Thompson, L. M., eds. *A History of South Africa to 1870*. Cape Town & Johannesburg, David Philip, 1982. This volume is a re-publication of the greater part of *The Oxford History of South Africa*, v. 1, with some additional material.

—— *The Oxford History of South Africa*. Oxford, Clarendon Press, 1969–1971. 2v. v. 1: *South Africa to 1870*; v. 2: *South Africa, 1870–1966*.

Wookey. A. J., ed. *Dinwao leha a le Dipolelo kaga Dico tsa Secwana*. (History of the Bechuana). Vryburg, Published by the South African District Committee of the London Missionary Society at the Book Room, Tiger Kloof Native Institution, 1913. Repr. 1929.

Wörger, W. 'Clothing dry bones: The myth of Shaka.' *Journal of African Studies*. 6,3(1979):144–58.

Wright, J. B. 'A.T. Bryant and "the Wars of Shaka".' *History in Africa*. 18(1991):409–25.

—— *Bushman Raiders of the Drakensberg 1840–1870*. Pietermaritzburg, University of Natal Press, 1971.

—— 'Political mythology and the making of Natal's *mfecane*.' *Canadian Journal of African Studies*. 23,2(1989):272–91.

—— 'Politics, Ideology and the Invention of the Nguni.' In Lodge, T., ed. *Resistance and Ideology in Settler Societies*, 4. Johannesburg, Ravan Press, 1986, 96–118.

—— 'Pre-Shakan age-group formation among the Northern Nguni.' *Natalia*. 8(1978):23–29.

Wright, J. B. and Hamilton, C. A. 'Traditions and Transformations: The Phongolo–Mzimkhulu Region in the Late Eighteenth and Early Nineteenth Centuries.' In Duminy, A. H. and Guest, B. [W.R]., eds. *Natal and Zululand from Earliest Times to 1910*, 1989, 49–82.

Wright, J. B. and Manson, A. *The Hlubi Chiefdom in Zululand-Natal: A History*. Ladysmith, Ladysmith Historical Society, 1983.

Wylie, D. 'Autobiography as alibi: History and projection in Nathaniel Isaacs's *Travels and Adventures in Eastern Africa (1836)*.' *Current Writing*. 3,1(1991):71–90.

Wylie, D. 'A Dangerous Admiration: E. A. Ritter's *Shaka Zulu*.' *South African Historical Journal.* 28(1993):98–118.
—— 'Textual Incest: Nathaniel Isaacs and the Development of the Shaka Myth.' *History in Africa.* 19(1992):411–33.
—— 'Utilising Isaacs: One Thread in the Development of the Shaka Myth.' In Edgecombe, D. T., Laband, J. P. C. and Thompson, P. S., comps. *The Debate on Zulu Origins: A Selection of Papers on the Zulu Kingdom and early Colonial Natal*, 1992, 19p. [Pagination irregular]
Yates, R., Golson, J. and Hall, M. 'Trance performance: The rock art of Boontjieskloof and Sevilla.' *South African Archaeological Bulletin.* 40(1985):70–80.
Yates, R., Parkington, J. and Manhire, T. *Pictures from the Past: A History of the Interpretation of Rock Paintings and Engravings of Southern Africa.* Pietermaritzburg, Centaur Publications, 1990.

Theses and Seminar Papers

Argyle, J. 'An Evaluation of Portuguese Shipwreck Narratives as Sources for Nguni Ethnology.' Unpublished paper, University of Natal, 1990.
Beach, D. N. 'Generational Cross-dating for Shona Dynasties.' Seminar paper presented to the Henderson Seminar, University of Rhodesia, *c.* 1974.
Beinart, W. 'Labour and Technology: Penetration into Pondoland. 1830–1930.' Paper presented to the Workshop on Pre-capitalist Social Formations and Colonial Penetration in Southern Africa, National University of Lesotho, Roma, 1976.
—— 'Production, Labour Migrancy and the Chieftaincy: Aspects of the Political Economy of Pondoland, 1860–1830.' Ph.D. thesis, University of London, 1979.
Bonner, P. 'Early State Formation Among the Nguni: The Relevance of the Swazi Case.' Paper presented to the Institute of Commonwealth Studies, African History Seminar, University of London, 1978.
—— 'The Rise, Consolidation and Disintegration of Dhlamini Power in Swaziland between 1820–1899.' Ph.D. thesis, University of London, 1977.
—— 'The Swazi Kingdom.' Paper presented to a workshop on Pre-Capitalist Social Formations and Colonial Penetration in Southern Africa, National University of Lesotho, Roma, 1976.
Campbell, C. 'Contact Period Rock Art of the South-eastern Mountains.' M.A. dissertation, University of the Witwatersrand, 1987.
Clarence-Smith, W. G. 'Capitalist Penetration among the Nyaneka of Southern Angola, 1840–1918.' Paper presented to the Workshop on Pre-capitalist Social Formations and Colonial Penetration in Southern Africa, National University of Lesotho, Roma, 1976.
Cobbing, J. 'The Case Against the Mfecane.' Seminar paper presented to the Centre for African Studies, University of Cape Town, 1983. Revised version, with the same title, given at the African Studies Institute, University of the Witwatersrand, 1984.
—— 'Grasping the Nettle: The Slave Trade and the Early Zulu.' Paper presented to the Workshop on Natal and Zululand in the Colonial and Precolonial Periods, University of Natal, Pietermaritzburg, 1990. (Reproduced in bound selected workshop papers. *See* Edgecombe, D. R., Laband, J. P. C. and Thompson, P. S., comps. *The Debate on Zulu Origins* . . . in *Books and Journal Articles* section.)
—— 'Jettisoning the Mfecane (with *Perestroika*).' Seminar paper presented to the African Studies Institute, University of the Witwatersrand, 1988. (Paper presented together with J. B. Wright's 'Political Mythology and the Making of Natal's Mfecane' in a joint seminar entitled 'The Mfecane: Beginning the Inquest.' The joint seminar was also presented to the Centre for African Studies, University of Cape Town, 1988.)
—— 'The Myth of the Mfecane.' Seminar paper presented to the Department of History, University of Durban-Westville, 1987.
—— 'The Ndebele Under the Khumalos 1820–1896.' Ph.D. thesis, University of Lancaster, 1976.
—— 'Overturning 'The Mfecane': A Reply to Elizabeth Eldredge.' Paper presented to the Colloquium on the Mfecane Aftermath, University of the Witwatersrand, 1991.
—— 'Rethinking the Roots of Violence in Southern Africa, *c.*1790–1840.' Paper presented to the Colloquium on the Mfecane Aftermath, University of the Witwatersrand, 1991.

Crais, C.C. 'Beasts of Prey: Capitalism and Resistance in the Eastern Cape.' Paper presented to the Centre for African Studies, University of Cape Town, 1989.
—— 'Some Thoughts on Slavery and Emancipation in the Eastern Cape, South Africa, 1770–1838.' Paper presented to the Conference on Slavery, University of Cape Town, 1989.
Delius, P. 'The Pedi Polity under Sekwati and Sekhukune, 1828–1880.' Ph.D. thesis, University of London, 1980.
—— 'The Structure of the Pedi State.' Paper presented to the Workshop on Pre-capitalist Social Formations and Colonial Penetration in Southern Africa, National University of Lesotho, Roma, 1976.
Denbow, J.R. 'Iron Age Economics: Herding, Wealth and Politics along the Fringes of the Kalahari Desert during the Early Iron Age.' Ph.D.thesis, Indiana University, 1983.
Donaldson, M.E. 'The Council of Advice at the Cape of Good Hope.' Ph.D. thesis, Rhodes University, 1975.
Dowson, T.A. 'Hunter-gatherers, Traders and Slaves: The 'Mfecane' Impact on Bushmen, Their Ritual and Their Art.' Paper presented to the Colloquium on the Mfecane Aftermath, University of the Witwatersrand, 1991.
—— 'Pictorial Pasts: Bushman Rock Art and Changing Perceptions of Southern Africa's History.' Ph.D thesis, University of the Witwatersrand. [In preparation]
Erwin, A. 'The Concept of the Mode of Production.' Paper presented to the Workshop on Pre-capitalist Social Formations and Colonial Penetration in Southern Africa, National University of Lesotho, Roma, 1976.
Evers, M. and Taylor, M. 'The Archaeologist and the Investigation of the Economic Base.' Paper presented to the Workshop on Pre-capitalist Social Formations and Colonial Penetration in Southern Africa, National University of Lesotho, Roma, 1976.
Gamede, V.W. 'The Oral Traditions of the Bhaca of Umzimkhulu.' M.A. dissertation, University of the Transkei, 1993.
Gewald, J-B. '"Mountaineers" as Mantatees: A Critical Reassessment of Events Leading up to the Battle of Dithakong.' M.A. dissertation, University of Leiden, 1989.
Golan, D. 'Construction and Reconstruction in Zulu History.' Ph.D. thesis, Hebrew University, Jerusalem, 1988.
Gump, J.O. *Revitalisation Through Expansion in Southern Africa* c. *1750–1848; A Reappraisal of the Mfecane.* Ann Arbor, University Microfilms International, 1984. [Facsimile reprint of a Ph.D. thesis, University of Nebraska, 1980].
Guy, J.J. 'Production and Exchange in the Zulu Kingdom.' Paper presented to the Workshop on Pre-capitalist Social Formations and Colonial Penetration in Southern Africa, National University of Lesotho, Roma, 1976.
Hall, M. 'The Ecology of the Late Iron Age in Zululand.' Ph.D. thesis, University of Cambridge, 1980.
Hall, S.L. 'Hunter-gatherer-fishers of the Fish River Basin: A Contribution to the Holocene Prehistory of the Eastern Cape.' Ph.D. thesis, University of Stellenbosch, 1990.
—— 'Iron Age Sequence and Settlement in the Rooiberg Thabazimbi Area.' M.A. thesis, University of the Witwatersrand, Johannesburg, 1981.
Hamilton, C.A. 'Authoring Shaka: Models, Metaphors and Historiography.' Ph.D. thesis, Johns Hopkins University, Baltimore, 1993.
—— '"The Character and Objects of Chaka" and their many representations in the 1820s: The Cobbing Thesis Reconsidered.' Paper presented to the Centre for African Studies, University of Cape Town, 1991.
—— 'Ideology, Oral Traditions and the Struggle for Power in the Early Zulu kingdom.' M.A. dissertation, University of the Witwatersrand, 1986.
—— 'The Production of Shaka and "the Weighing of Evidence Only Procurable in Prejudiced Channels".' Paper presented to the Conference on Enlightenment and Emancipation, University of Natal, Durban, 1989.
Harries, P. 'Labour Migration from Mozambique to South Africa; with Special Reference to the Delagoa Bay Hinterland, c. 1862 to 1897.' Ph.D thesis, University of London, 1983.

Hartley, G. F. 'Dithakong and the "Mfecane": A Historiographical and Methodological Analysis.' M.A. dissertation, University of Cape Town, 1992.

Hedges, D. W. 'Trade and Politics in Southern Mozambique and Zululand in the Eighteenth and Early Nineteenth Centuries.' Ph.D.thesis, University of London, 1978.

Keenan, J. 'On the Concept of the Mode of Production in Pre-capitalist Social Formations: An Anthropological View.' Paper presented to the Workshop on Pre-capitalist Social Formations and Colonial Penetration in Southern Africa, National University of Lesotho, Roma, 1976.

Kimble, J. 'The Economic History of Lesotho in the Nineteenth Century.' Paper presented to the Workshop on Pre-capitalist Social Formations and Colonial Penetration in Southern Africa, National University of Lesotho, Roma, 1976.

Kinahan, J. 'Pastoral Nomads of the Central Namib Desert.' Ph.D. thesis, University of the Witwatersrand, Johannesburg, 1989.

Kinsman, M. 'Between Two Stones'. Paper presented to the African Studies Seminar, University of Cape Town, 1982.

—— 'The Social Formation of the Southern Tswana.' Paper presented to the African Studies Seminar, University of Cape Town, 1980.

Lambourne, B. 'A Chip off the Old Block: Early Ghoya History and the Emergence of Moletsane's Taung.' Paper presented to the Colloquium on the Mfecane Aftermath, University of the Witwatersrand, 1991.

Le Cordeur, B.A. 'Robert Godlonton as Architect of Frontier Opinion.' M.A. dissertation, Rhodes University, 1956.

Legassick, M. 'The Missionaries, the Griqua and the Sotho-Tswana: The Politics of a Frontier Zone.' Ph.D. thesis, University of California, Los Angeles, 1969.

Lewis-Williams, J.D. 'Social Theory in Southern African Archaeology.' Paper presented at the South African Association of Archaeologists Conference, Grahamstown, 1985.

Liesegang, G. 'Beiträge zur Geschichte des Reiches der Gaza Nguni im Südlichen Moçambique, 1820–1895.' Ph.D. thesis. Cologne, 1967.

Loubser, J.H.N. 'Archaeological Contributions to Venda Ethnohistory.' Ph.D. thesis, University of the Witwatersrand, 1988.

—— 'Ndebele Archaeology of the Pietersburg Area.' M.A. dissertation, University of the Witwatersrand, Johannesburg, 1981.

Lye, W.F. 'The *Difaqane*: The Sotho Wars in the Interior of South Africa, 1822–1837.' Ph.D. thesis, University of California, Los Angeles, 1969.

Mael, R. 'The Problems of Political Integration in the Zulu Empire.' Ph.D. thesis, University of California, Los Angeles, 1974.

Makaula, A.M. 'A Political History of the Bhaca from Earliest Times to 1910.' Master's dissertation, Rhodes University, 1988.

Malaba, M.Z. 'Shaka as Literary Theme.' Ph.D. thesis, York University, 1986.

Manson, A.H. 'The Hurutshe in the Marico District of the Transvaal, 1848–1914.' Ph.D. thesis, University of Cape Town, 1990.

—— 'The Hurutshe, the Difaqane and the Formation of the Transvaal State 1820–1875.' Paper presented to the Colloquium on the Mfecane Aftermath, University of the Witwatersrand, 1991.

Martin, R.J. 'British Images of the Zulu c.1820–1879.' Ph.D thesis, University of Cambridge, 1982.

Moyer, R.A. 'A History of the Mfengu of the Eastern Cape 1815–1865.' Ph.D. thesis, London University, 1976.

Newton-King, S. 'The Enemy Within'. Paper presented to the Slavery Conference, University of Cape Town, 1989.

Ngoncgo, L.D. 'Aspects of the History of Bangwaketse to 1910.' Ph.D. thesis, University of Dalhousie, 1977.

Okihiro, G.Y. 'Hunters, Herders, Cultivators and Traders: Interaction and Change in the Kgalagadi, Nineteenth Century.' Ph.D. thesis, University of California, Los Angeles, 1976.

Omer-Cooper, J.D. 'The South African Frontier Revisited.' Paper presented at a Conference of the African Studies Association of Australasia and the Pacific, La Trobe University, Melbourne, 1985.

Peires, J.B. 'Economic History of the Xhosa up to 1835.' Paper presented to the Workshop on Pre-capitalist Social Formations and Colonial Penetration in Southern Africa, National University of Lesotho, Roma, 1976.

—— 'A History of the Xhosa, *c.* 1700–1835.' M.A. dissertation, Rhodes University, 1976.

Phimister, I. 'Colonial Goldmining in Southern Zambesia: A Reassessment.' Paper presented to a work shop on Pre-Capitalist Social Formations and Colonial Penetration in Southern Africa, National University of Lesotho, Roma, 1976.

Plug, I. 'The Faunal Remains from Rooikrans and Rhenosterkloof: Two Iron Age Sites from the Central Transvaal.' M.A. dissertation, University of the Witwatersrand, 1981.

Rainer, M. 'Madikane's Last Stand.' Unpublished manuscript, 1982.

Richner, J. 'Eastern Frontier Slaving and its Extension into the Transorangia and Natal.' Paper presented to the Colloquium on the Mfecane Aftermath, University of the Witwatersrand, Johannesburg, 1991.

—— 'The Withering Away of the *"Lifaqane"*: Or a Change of Paradigm.' B.A. Hons. essay, Rhodes University, 1988.

Scott, J.B. 'The British Soldier on the Eastern Cape Frontier, 1800–1850.' Ph.D. thesis, University of Port Elizabeth, 1973.

Shaw, B.P. 'State Formation, Nation Building, and the Tswana of Southern Africa.' M.A. dissertation, Duquesne University, Pittsburg, 1975.

Shell, R. 'Adumbrations of Cape Slavery: Other Forms of Labour.' Paper presented to a seminar, Rhodes University, 1989.

Slater, H. 'Transitions in the Political Economy of South-East Africa before 1840.' D.Phil. thesis, University of Sussex, 1976.

Slee, A.T.C. 'Some Aspects of Wesleyan Methodism in the Albany District Between 1830 and 1844.' M.A. dissertation, Rhodes University, 1946.

Smith, A.K. 'The Struggle for the Control of Southern Mozambique 1720–1835.' Ph.D thesis, University of California, Los Angeles, 1970.

Stewart, D. 'Trade and Politics in Transorangia 1800–1823: A Critical Examination of the "Cobbing Hypothesis"'. Paper presented to the Institute of Commonwealth Studies, University of London, 1991.

Taylor, M.O.V. 'Late Iron Age Settlements on the Northern Edge of the Vredefort Dome.' M.A. dissertation, University of the Witwatersrand, Johannesburg, 1980.

Wagenaar, E. 'A History of the Thembu and their Relationship with the Cape, 1850–1900.' Ph.D. thesis, Rhodes University, 1988.

Wagner, R. 'Coenraad de Buys and the Eastern Cape Frontier.' Paper presented to the African History Seminar, School of Oriental and African Studies, University of London, 1972.

Webb, A.C.M. 'The Agricultural Development of the 1820 Settlement down to 1846.' M.A. dissertation, Rhodes University, 1975.

Webb, C. de B. 'Of Orthodoxy, Heresy and the Difaqane.' Paper presented to the Teacher Conference on African History, University of the Witwatersrand, 1974.

Webster, A.C. 'Ayliff, Whiteside, and the Fingo "Emancipation" of 1835: A Reappraisal.' B.A. Hons. essay, Rhodes University, 1988.

—— 'Examination of the "Fingo Emancipation" of 1835.' Paper presented to the African Studies Seminar, University of Cape Town, 1990.

—— 'Land Expropriation and Labour Extraction Under Cape Colonial Rule: The War of 1835 and the "Emancipation of the Fingo".' M.A. dissertation, Rhodes University, 1991.

Wright, J.B. 'Beyond the Mfecane: What Do We Put in its Place?' Paper presented to the History Teachers' Conference held by the History Workshop, University of the Witwatersrand, 1990.

—— 'The Dynamics of Power and Conflict in the Thukela-Mzimkhulu Region in the late Eighteenth and Early Nineteenth Centuries: A Critical Reconstruction.' Ph.D thesis, University of the Witwatersrand, 1990.

—— '"If We Can't Call It the Mfecane, Then What Can We Call It?" Moving the Debate Forward.' Seminar paper presented to the Institute for Advanced Social Research, [Formerly African Studies Institute], University of the Witwatersrand, 1994.

Wright, J.B. 'Political Mythology and the Making of Natal's Mfecane.' Seminar paper presented to the African Studies Institute, University of the Witwatersrand, 1988. (Paper presented together with J. Cobbing's 'Jettisoning the Mfecane (with *Perestroika*)' in a joint seminar entitled 'The Mfecane: Beginning the Inquest.') Published *Canadian Journal of African Studies*. 23.2(1989):272–91.
—— 'Political Transformations in the Thukela–Mzimkhulu Region of Natal in the Late Eighteenth and Early Nineteenth Centuries.' Seminar paper, University of Antananarivo, 1991.
Zimmerman, M. 'The French Slave Trade at Moçambique, 1770–1794.' M.A. dissertation, University of Wisconsin, 1967.

Other Works Cited

The following works do not deal directly with the subjectof this book and are therefore not included in the main bibliography.

Atkinson, P. *The Ethnographic Imagination: Textual Construction of Reality*. London, Routledge, 1990.
Barthes, R. *Writing Degree Zero, and Elements of Semiology*. Translated from the French by Annette Lavers and Colin Smith. London, Jonathan Cape, 1967. (Cape Editions 3)
New York, Hill and Wang, [1968]
Boston, Beacon Press, [1970]
Buckhout, R. 'Eyewitness testimony.' *Scientific American*. 231(1974):31–32.
Caplan, J. 'Postmodernism, poststructuralism, and deconstruction: Notes for historians.' *Central European History*. 22(1989):272–73.
Carr, E.H. *What is History?*. London, Macmillan; New York, St Martin's Press, 1961.
New York, Knopf, 1962.
Harmondsworth, Penguin, 1965. (Pelican Books).
Chalk, F. and Jonassohn, K., eds. *The History and Sociology of Genocide: Analyses and Case Studies*. New Haven, Yale University Press, 1990.
Clifford, J. and Marcus, G.E., eds. *Writing Culture: The Poetics and Politics of Ethnography*. Berkeley, University of California Press, 1986. (School of American Research Advanced Seminar Series)
Cock, J. *Maids and Madams: A Study in the Politics of Exploitation*. Johannesburg, Ravan Press, 1980.
Coetzee J.M. *Age of Iron*. New York, Random House, 1990.
—— *White Writing: On the Culture of Letters in South Africa*. New Haven, Yale University Press, 1988.
Cohen, D.W. *The Combing of History*. Chicago, University of Chicago Press, 1994.
Comaroff, J. and Comaroff, J. *Ethnography and the Historical Imagination*. Boulder, San Francisco, Oxford, Westview Press, 1992. (Studies in Ethnographic Imagination)
Conkey, M. and Hastorf, C., eds. *The Uses of Style in Archaeology*. Cambridge, Cambridge University Press, 1990.
Deagan, K. 'Avenues of inquiry in historical archaeology.' *Advances in Archaeological Method and Theory*. 5(1982):151–77.
Dippie, B.W. *The Vanishing American: White Attitudes and US Indian Policy*. Middletown, Wesleyan University Press, 1982.
Eltis, D. *Economic Growth and the Ending of the Transatlantic Slave Trade*. Oxford and New York, Oxford University Press, 1987.
Fabian, J. *Time and the Other: How Anthropology Makes its Object*. New York, Columbia University Press, 1983.
Fairchild, H.N. *The Noble Savage: A Study in Romantic Naturalism*. New York, Russell, 1961.
Gates, H.L., ed. *'Race', Writing and Difference*. Chicago, University of Chicago Press, 1986. Originally published in two special issues of *Critical Inquiry*. 12,1(1985); 13,1(1986).
Gilson, C.J.L. *In the Power of the Pygmies*. London, Humphrey Milford, 1919.
JanMohamed, A.R. 'The Economy of Manichean Allegory: the Function of Racial Differences in Colonialist Literature.' in Gates, H.L., ed. *'Race', Writing and Difference*, 1986, 78–106.

Lakoff, G. and Johnson, M. *Metaphors We Live By*. Chicago University Press, 1980.

Lukacs, G. *The Historical Novel*. London, Merlin Press, 1962.

Mallory, J.K. 'Abnormal waves on the south-east coast of South Africa.' *International Hydrographic Review*. 51,2(1974):99–129.

Rosenau, P.M. *Postmodernism and the Social Sciences: Insights, Inroads and Intrusions*. Princeton, Princeton University Press, 1992.

Said, E.W. *Orientalism*. New York, Pantheon, 1978.
Harmondsworth, Penguin, 1978.

Samuel, R., ed. *People's History and Social Theory*. London, Routledge and Kegan Paul, 1981.

Schuyler, R. 'The spoken word, the written word, observed behaviour and preserved behaviour: The contexts available to the archaeologist.' *Conference on Historic Sites Archaeology Papers*. 10(1977):99–120.

Sen, A. *Poverty and Famines: An Essay on Entitlement and Deprivation*. Oxford, Clarendon Press, 1982.

Vansina, J. *Oral Tradition: A Study in Historical Methodology*. London, J. Currey, 1985.

White, P. *Voss*. London, Longmans, 1957.
Repr. 1965.

Woodman, A.J. *Rhetoric in Classical Historiography: Four Studies*. London, Croom Helm; Portland, Ore., Areopagitica Press, 1988.

Papers Presented or Tabled at the 1991 Colloquium

Julian Cobbing. Overturning the Mfecane: A Reply to Elizabeth Eldredge.

Thomas Dowson. Hunter-Gatherers, Traders and Slavers: The 'Mfecane' Impact on Bushman Ritual and Art

Elizabeth Eldredge. Sources of Conflict in Southern Africa, c. 1800–1830: 'Mfecane' Reconsidered.

Norman Etherington. Reassessing the Great Trek: Historiographical Twin Brother of the Mfecane

Jan-Bart Gewald. Slave Exports from Southern and Central Namibia up to the Mid-Nineteenth Century.

Cathy Gorham. Port Natal: A 'Blind' Darkness: Speculation, Trade, the Creation of a Vortex of Violence and the 'Mfecane'.

Stephen Gray. Report on the John Ross Project

James Gump. Origins of the Mfecane: An Ecological Perspective.

Simon Hall. 'Difaqane' Caverns: A Preliminary Assessment of Age, Content and Structure

Carolyn Hamilton. 'The Character and Objects of Chaka': A Reconsideration of the Making of Shaka as 'Mfecane' Motor.

Guy Hartley. The Battle of Dithakong and 'Mfecane' Theory.

Margaret Kinsman. Resketching the 'Mfecane': The Impact of Violence on Rolong Life, 1823–36.

Brigid Lambourne. A Chip off the Old Block: Moletsane's Taung and the False History of the Early Nineteenth-century 'Interior'.

Mbongeni Malaba. Reconstruction of History: The Case of Shaka

Andrew Manson. Conflict on the Western Highveld/Southern Kalahari, c. 1750–1820.

Andrew Manson. The Hurutshe, the Difaqane and the Formation of the Transvaal State, 1820–1875.

John Omer-Cooper. Has the Mfecane a Future?

Neil Parsons. Pre-Difaqane Wars in the West.

Jeff Peires. Matiwane's Road to Mbholompo: A Reprieve for the Mfecane?

Jürg Richner. Eastern Frontier Slaving and its Extension into Transorangia and Natal, 1770–1843.

Christopher Saunders. Cobbing, the Mfecane and (some) Historians

Alan Webster. Unmasking the Fingo: The War of 1835 Revisited.

John Wright. Political Transformations in the Thukela–Mzimkhulu Region of Natal in the Late Eighteenth and Early Nineteenth Centuries.

Dan Wylie. Language and Assassination: Some Aspects of White Writers' Portrayal of Shaka and the Zulu.

Index

Notes

Where information is to be found in a footnote and not in the text the reference is in the form 81n. The numbers of relevant footnotes are given where there is more than one note on the page, for example, 36n 18.

The entries *Difaqane* and *Lifaqane* refer to discussions of these *words*. All material relating to the *concept* is entered under **Mfecane**.

The terms '**pre-***difaqane*' and '**proto-***difaqane*' have been coined by Neil Parsons as convenient labels for the periods *c*.1600 to *c*.1750 and *c*.1750 to *c*.1822. They are used here in quotation marks as they are not in general use among historians.